★ MOVIES ON TELEVISION ★

THE SUNDAY TIMES GUIDE TO

MOVIES ON TELEVISION

by ANGELA and ELKAN ALLAN

Foreword by Dilys Powell

Times Newspapers Limited

First published in Great Britain in 1973
by Times Newspapers Limited,
Printing House Square, London EC4P 4DE

Copyright © Angela and Elkan Allan 1973

ISBN 0 7230 0104 9

Designed by Edwin Taylor

Line illustrations by Richard Yeend

Printed and bound in Great Britain
by Cox & Wyman Limited,
London, Reading and Fakenham

Inclusion of a film in this book does not guarantee
that it has been or will be sold for showing
on British television

All good films coming on British television that are
not in this book will be listed in
The Sunday Times Critical Viewers' Guide

Films reviewed here which have been distributed under
different titles in the UK and the USA will be found
in the Index of Alternative Titles on page 393

Dedicated to
**The Managers of the Queen's, Cricklewood,
and the Embassy, Chesham,
where we first got the taste**

Acknowledgements

Among the many people we would like to thank for their help, encouragement and inspiration are the staff of the British Film Institute Library, who have checked every fact in the book (their advice has been followed about everything except the dates of some films, which vary between the year of production, American release and British release); Harold Evans, Oscar Turnill, Edwin Taylor, Vincent Page of *The Sunday Times*; Derek Jewell, Barry Winkleman, Candida Geddes, Liz Bland of the TNL Publishing Division; Leslie Halliwell, the ITV film buyer; Alan Howden of the BBC film purchasing department; Fred Zentner of the Cinema Bookshop.

We are also grateful to the following for permission to reproduce illustrative material in this book: ANGLO EMI FILM DISTRIBUTORS LTD: *The Hasty Heart, Billy Liar, King and Country*; CINEMA INTERNATIONAL CORPORATION (UK): *Sunset Boulevard, The Rose Tattoo, Breakfast at Tiffany's, Summer and Smoke, Becket, The Spy Who Came In from the Cold, Alfie*; CINERAMA RELEASING (UK) LTD: *They Shoot Horses, Don't They?*; CINE CENTRE FILM DISTRIBUTORS LTD: *Repulsion*; HEMDALE FILM DISTRIBUTORS LIMITED: *The African Queen, Richard III, The Servant, The Entertainer*; METRO-GOLDWYN-MAYER: *The Search, King Solomon's Mines, Quo Vadis?, Ivanhoe, Singin' in the Rain, Seven Brides for Seven Brothers, Lust for Life, Gigi, Cat on a Hot Tin Roof, The Brothers Karamazov, Ben Hur, Butterfield 8, The VIPs, The Dirty Dozen, Goodbye Mr Chips*; ROMULUS FILMS: *Room at the Top*; UNITED ARTISTS CORPORATION LTD: *Johnny Belinda, Treasure of Sierra Madre, High Noon, Moulin Rouge, Around the World in 80 Days, Twelve Angry Men, The Big Country, Some Like It Hot, The Apartment, The Alamo, Elmer Gantry, Never on Sunday, Exodus, West Side Story, Judgement at Nuremberg, The Miracle Worker, Tom Jones, Irma La Douce, Lilies of the Field, The Russians are Coming, The Russians are Coming, In The Heat of the Night, The Graduate, The Happy Ending, Midnight Cowboy*; WARNER BROS: *A Star is Born, Auntie Mame, The Old Man and The Sea, The Nun's Story, The Sundowners, What Ever Happened to Baby Jane?, Who's Afraid of Virginia Woolf?, Bonnie and Clyde, Rachel, Rachel*; and to the BBC for kindly supplying photographs for: *Johnny Belinda, Treasure of Sierra Madre, The Search, A Star is Born, Lust for Life, The Old Man and The Sea, Some Like It Hot, Lilies of the Field*.

XXX
VVV
VV

What the ratings mean

√√√	**Cancel all other arrangements**
√√	**Catch it if you can**
√	**If you've nothing better to do**
×	**Find something better to do**
××	**Don't waste your time**
×××	**Ring up and complain**

(c)	**Film in colour**
(b/w)	**Film in black and white**

FOREWORD

Perhaps you think it is easy. A few lines about a film, a brief verdict – I am reminded of the wry fable told by a film critic, a friend and colleague of mine: whenever he went on holiday, he used to say, his Editor would receive half a dozen letters from candidates who claimed that they could do the job twice as well for half the money. Other people's work always looks easy.

I doubt whether any single human being could have watched all the films included in this collection. I have seen a great many of them; some have escaped me. The Allans, too, are only human. But they have seen an enormous number, and they will explain how they have coped with the escapers.

Elkan Allan's job is difficult. It is précis-writing of a high order, and précis-writing allied with knowledge, sensitivity to the climate of opinion on the subject, and – something rare in précis-writing – readability. Every Sunday Mr Allan writes about the films revived on the television screen – about Sunday's films, about a selection of the pieces to be shown during the week. Often he says what he has to say in fewer than forty words. Occasionally he runs to sixty; sometimes fewer than twenty. Try it yourself. You are writing, remember, for some people who saw *Love Me Yesterday*, or *The Putrefying Corpse*, or *Torrents of Sex*, or whatever the title may be, when it was shown years ago on the cinema screen; they want just a reminder. However, most of those who are going to read or at any rate glance at what you say know nothing about the film. Shall they make a note to switch on – or perhaps to switch off?

I used to have a friendly correspondent who, on looking at my review of some film or other, would post off a letter to say that I had explained too much. All that was needed, he would insist, was for me to write Go! or Don't Go! But the newspaper critic can't take such an attitude of divine rightness. His readers are all creatures of prejudice. They like, or don't like, Westerns, musicals, thrillers, science fiction.

They will or won't sit through anything with Spencer Gable or Bette Crawford. The Allans have to make clear what kind of film is being shown and what players you can expect to see.

Possibly you want to be sure how recent it is; they will let you know when it was made and by whom. You may like a hint about the esteem in which it was held in its day; if it won any Oscars they will tell you. Look at even the shortest among their verdicts and you will usually find that they offer you a great deal more – and all in that handful of words. Believe me, it isn't easy.

What I find especially noteworthy is the element of personal feeling which in the restricted space available repeatedly comes through. Sometimes it is a social-cum-moral feeling; a long running jump, for instance, at the social politics of a film which I admit I didn't myself dislike (in fact at the time I liked it, though I haven't seen it since: *The Angry Silence*). Sometimes an admirably humane comment is slipped in; have you, a note asks angrily, ever wondered how they get bucking bronchos to buck? The book likes (don't we all?) Marilyn Monroe. It admires the late and, as it says, much-mourned Judy Holliday. There is recognition for the charm of David Niven, the greatness of Spencer Tracy and the splendid absurdity of Bette Davis. Joan Crawford is 'marvellous, of course'; agreed, now that one can look back with a kind of ironic nostalgia.

But these are views one might expect. More interesting, perhaps, are the unexpectedly adverse comments. This book has not much use for Kirk Douglas and less for Ingrid Bergman (though *Casablanca* is described as 'one of the greats'), one reads in a rage of disagreement which is positively enjoyable. An example of Robert Aldrich's direction is 'attitudinising'. Elizabeth Taylor has long been hailed a star, but not always as the beautiful actress she is capable of being; her exceptional gifts are here apprehended, and her performance in *Who's Afraid of Virginia Woolf?* is called 'stunning'. And an actor who has never quite won the recognition he deserves is singled out for praise – the excellent Lee J. Cobb.

Now and then there is some bludgeoning – and who is to complain? *Soldier Blue* is 'infamous'. I leave in obscurity the titles of the films summarised as 'a quite awful nonsense' and 'a monument of inefficient movie-making', but I feel less soft-hearted about *Desert Song*, put down as 'extremely boring'. After that one can join in the appreciation of the genuine American musical, or at any rate of its music; happily reminiscent, one comes on a list of songs by Cole Porter, or Irving Berlin, or Rodgers and Hart, or Rodgers and Hammerstein, or finds *Singin' in the Rain* hailed as 'one of the great musicals of all times'. Occasionally enthusiasm breaks out of its space-limits and as it were stretches itself. I find it a mark of balance in the book that while it glances in twelve words over some routine action stuff, for *Citizen Kane* it lets rip in over two hundred. And that, as you would find if you tried, isn't much for all it manages to say about a masterpiece.

A book – well, a handbook which does much more than inform, though it certainly does that; did you know, for instance, who supplied the singing voices for most of the leading players in *Carmen Jones* or who sang for Deborah Kerr in *The King and I*? You will find films which have been neglected or half-forgotten discovered afresh here; read the note on Elia Kazan and *Baby Doll* or the appreciation of *Hot Millions*. You will be reminded of talents you had perhaps begun to undervalue; 'David Lean could do no wrong in 1945,' says a warm and, goodness knows, deserved eulogy of *Blithe Spirit*. Reverence is never without the caution of common sense. Many of us are all for John Huston, but what about *Beat the Devil*? 'It's amusing' (perhaps the brush-off is a bit overdone) 'if you enjoy other people's home movies'.

There is assessment – I like the summing-up of Visconti's *The Damned* which calls the film a magnificent failure; and there is the valuable reminder – I had quite forgotten, though at the time I drew attention to it, the superb sequence of Henry Fonda's flight through the changing light of the day in John Ford's *Drums Along the Mohawk*.

All kinds of cinema are dealt with, from the experimental (*Shadows* was experimental in its time) to such audacities as Joseph Strick's version of *Ulysses*. The classics – for already films less than half a century old are held to be classics – are here; lovely Garbo in *Camille*, Hitchcock's *Blackmail*, Lang's *Fury* ('a bit disappointing now'), marvellous Katharine Hepburn and Cary Grant in *Bringing Up Baby*. The names which echo in the ears of the devotees are here, from Arthur Penn to the incomparable Billy Wilder, from Don Siegel to the controversial Joseph Losey and the variable Vincente Minnelli. And now, turning over pages crammed with the record of plots half-remembered and titles wholly forgotten, I wonder how I ever got on without such a handbook. My own files, my own scrapbook don't tell me the quarter of it. Nothing else covers quite the same ground.

Thank goodness for the Allans.

Dilys Powell

INTRODUCTION

THE MGM lion . . . the Columbia lady . . . the man with the gong . . . the pleasure begins there for the real film fan. Then the swelling music, the opening credits, and we are swept into the magic world of the movie. Film as art, film as sociology, film as politics – all are superseded, at least while the movie lasts, by film as fun.

But which of the fifty or so films that every viewer is offered each month on TV is worth watching? You may recognise a few of the names; the rest is speculation. We hope that this book will make the choice easier by giving the facts about most of the movies that compete with each other and the rest of the programmes for your time. We have also given a critical opinion on each one – you may not agree with it, but at least it will give you some guide, if only to watch the film because we hate it.

These opinions and the tick-and-cross ratings are the fruit of many years of film-watching. When we haven't seen a film – or can't remember what we thought of it – we have fallen back on a critical consensus of never fewer than five contemporary reviews.

Over the next two years, even without the fourth channel coming into operation, about one thousand films will be shown on British television, taking into account the variations and duplications of the fifteen ITV programme areas. Most of them are summarised and criticised in this book, but inevitably there will be some we haven't covered – either because they were not known to be available, or considered, for TV showing, or simply because they slipped through our net. There are more than 20,000 movies theoretically available, and we have cut out all foreign language films, made-for-TV efforts and such products as Walt Disney's which are unlikely to be sold to TV.

Conversely, we must have included a large number that will not get a showing in the lifetime of this edition. Some have not yet been sold to television; others may not be available for many years, until their cinema box-office potential has been completely exhausted. Others may have been bought, but not yet scheduled in your area.

Any good films that are coming on which are not in the book will be listed in the weekly *Sunday Times* Critical Viewers' Guide to Television, from which this book sprang. Incidentally, all summaries that have appeared in the paper have been rewritten and, in most cases, expanded for this book.

The viewer might be forgiven for wondering why so many bad old films are shown on television. Why don't those in charge choose only the best ones out of the 20,000-plus available to them? The answer is that the distributors who own the rights of the films force the TV companies and the BBC to buy the rotten ones along with the good. They sell in blocks of twenty to thirty; a typical 'package' contains two or three outstanding movies, half a dozen very bad ones, and a majority of in-betweens. In order to get the winners, the companies have to buy the losers. The question then is what to do with the bad ones? The overwhelming temptation, having paid for them, is to show them. Can one really plead with programme controllers not to succumb? In difficult financial times, probably not; but when the revenue is rolling in, it's cheap-skate of them to put out films that they must know are pretty awful – usually at times when a large proportion of viewers is assured, as when the opposition is off the air or has scheduled something unappealing to the mass audience.

The art of scheduling is a complicated and expert one. While some programme controllers have been rumoured to sit down at the kitchen table with their friends and relatives and pick out the films that they personally would like to see again, the more painstaking station-heads will take the 'track record' of films on previous showings in other areas into account. Some ITV controllers rely on a forecasting system called TAPE that awards points to every available movie in terms of audience appeal – proven or speculative. For instance, Robert Mitchum rates 90 points, Henry Fonda 50, Judy Garland 10. A 'non-sadistic modern dress action' gets 70 points; but stories set in newspaper offices or the Deep South only 10, and so on. This is the creation of Mr Mike Firman who is an awfully nice chap personally, but an enemy of all film-lovers.

We decided against including the original lengths of films because the figures can be very misleading. Television shows film at the speed of 25 frames per second against the cinema's 24; thus all movies run just over 4 per cent faster. In addition, the calculation as to how many minutes a film will run on TV has to take into account the number and length of breaks that are inserted in it – for advertisements in the case of ITV, and for news bulletins in the case of longer films on BBC 2. We have indicated after every film whether it was originally made in colour (*c*) or black-and-white (*b/w*). But sometimes only a black-and-white print of a colour film is available for showing, so don't blame the TV people for that.

However, you can blame them for their reprehensible practice of cutting movies to fill a pre-ordained slot. Frank Capra, the veteran film director, speaking on Film Night in March 1973 expressed his feelings about this: 'I can't explain to you the horror of seeing a film mutilated ... It's like destroying any work of art, like putting a moustache on a Picasso painting.'

The ITV answers are that it is done discriminatingly and that they have to time their programmes to fit into fixed slots because of the networking system. Is this a valid excuse for cutting 21 minutes out of *The Ship That Died of Shame*, as Ulster Television did on 11 December 1972? Or for slashing whole crucial scenes out of *The Pumpkin Eater*, as London Weekend did? There may even be a case under the Trade Descriptions Act for insisting on the word 'Abridged' going in front of the title when the product is so substantially altered.

Introduction

You may find this a highly opinionated book. It certainly would have been much easier merely to have listed the facts about each film, but we are out to stimulate and entertain as well as to suggest what may be worth watching – and missing. We couldn't claim to be unprejudiced. What is there about Humphrey Bogart or Hitchcock to make one overlook their faults? And Ingrid Bergman or Otto Preminger to make one seek out their weaknesses? But perhaps it's the other way round for you. You are entitled to your prejudices too, and there are no absolute standards of critical opinion. Putting your prejudices against ours will, we hope, be part of the fun.

Enjoy yourselves.

Angela and Elkan Allan
April 1973

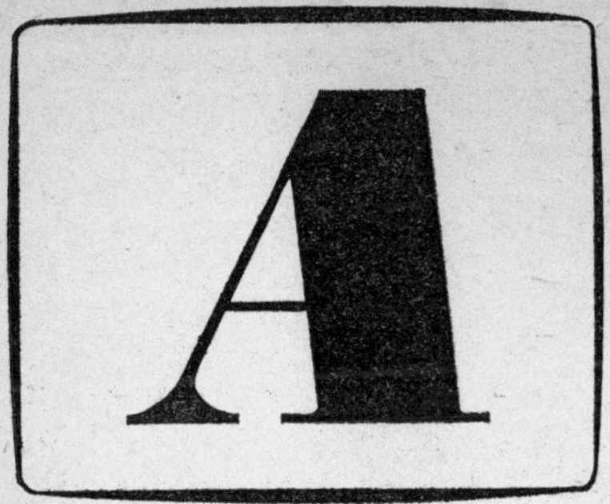

Aaron Slick From Punkin Crick × ×
Dinah Shore trilling her way through
creaky old stage comedy served up with
a few weak songs; Robert Merrill is city
lad trying to con her. Claude Binyon;
1952. (*c*)

Abandon Ship √
Suspiciously like Hitchcock's 1944 *Lifeboat*, only here there are 27 passengers
overcrowding the craft; Tyrone Power
has to choose which go, which stay.
You may want to push prissy Mai
Zetterling in immediately but writer-
director has paid good money for her
services; other floaters: Lloyd Nolan,
James Hayter, Stephen Boyd. Richard
Sale; 1957. (*b/w*)

Abbott and Costello ... Meet the killer,
directed by Charles T. Barton (1950),
**Meet the Invisible Man (1951), Meet Dr
Jekyll and Mr Hyde (1953), Meet the
Mummy (1954), in the Foreign Legion**
(1950) all directed by Charles Lamont,
in Hollywood, directed by S. Sylvan
Simon (1945) ×
Strictly for those with debased tastes or
nostalgia addicts; the slapstick is crude,
the gags ancient, the fun less furious than
the discriminating viewer. (*b/w*)

Abbott and Costello Meet Frankenstein √
Remarkably successful blend of horror
and comedy, with Dracula and the
Wolfman thrown in for value. Lon

Jack Lemmon in *The Apartment*

Chaney and Bela Lugosi repeat their roles, but not Boris Karloff. Charles Barton; 1948. (*b/w*)

The ABC Murders ✕ ✕
Agatha Christie wrote a clever murder story; Frank Tashlin made a dreary, absurd film. Just imagine All-American funny guy Tony Randall made up as Hercule Poirot and you'll see the starting-point of the general ghastli-ness; 1966. (*b/w*)

The Abductors √
Andrew McLaglen directing his father Victor in based-on-real-life story of man robbing the grave of Abraham Lincoln; Fay Spain looks on helplessly; 1957. (*b/w*)

Abilene Town √
Sturdy Marshal Randolph Scott going from cattlemen to homesteaders (remember that battle from Shane?) and from dance hall girl Ann Dvorak to grocer's daughter Rhonda Fleming; Edward L. Marin made this above-average Western in 1946. (*b/w*)

The Abominable Snowman √
Made in the dizzy heights of an English studio, this comes out quite well, thanks to Peter Cushing and Richard Wattis camping it up at the base camp. Val Guest seems to have enjoyed directing it in 1957. (*b/w*)

About Face ✕ ✕
Tiresome All-American triple romance; Gordon MacRae and Eddie Bracken toothily warble. Directed by Roy del Ruth, from play, Brother Rat; 1952. (*b/w*)

About Mrs Leslie ✕
Come back, little Sheba, all is forgiven. This is Shirley Booth and director Daniel Mann trying to recapture the dubious charms of their earlier hit; but this 1954 sudser about her happy holidays with Robert Ryan before she found out he was married, never catches fire. (*b/w*)

Above and Beyond √
Robert Taylor as husband chosen to drop first A-bomb and Eleanor Parker as his racked wife; Mel Frank and Norman Panama manage some interesting technical footage about preparations, however. More a whimper than a bang; 1952. (*b/w*)

Above Us the Waves √
John Mills, John Gregson, Donald Sinden prominent among the well-spoken young (it was shot in 1956, about wartime naval hunt) as the upper classes save Britain again. Sub crew stalks German warships; Ralph Thomas keeps up the excitement. (*b/w*)

The Absent-Minded Professor √ √
Fred MacMurray defying gravity and giving great pleasure all round; Robert Stevenson; 1961. (*c*)

Accident √ √
If you didn't see this Joseph Losey–Dirk Bogarde–Harold Pinter piece of cleverness in 1967 don't miss it now; if you did, you may be disappointed on second viewing at the dramatic flaws, the inadaquacy of Jacqueline Sassard, and the ultimate emptiness. (*c*)

Accidental Death ✕
Routine Edgar Wallace whodunit about mutually set death traps, with John Carson, Richard Vernon; BBC producer Derrick Sherwin turns up in his acting days (1963). Geoffrey Nethercott directed fitfully. (*b/w*)

The Accursed ✕ ✕
Murder mystery solved at regimental reunion; Donald Wolfit hams it up and who can blame him? Anton Diffring does his sinister foreigner bit. Michael McCarthy; 1958. (*b/w*)

The Accused √
One of those maddening plots in which if the panicked hero (or, in this case heroine–Loretta Young) had only told the police the full story (she was being attacked by rape-minded student) there needn't be any film–or not this one, at any rate. Having said that, William Dieterle made a smashing job of on-the-run suspensing in this 1948 thriller; Wendell Corey is tec, Robert Cummings, Sam Jaffe, Sara Allgood support (*b/w*).

Accused of Murder ✕
Vera Ralston is, but surely she didn't do it? Have faith, along with policeman. Joe Kane produced-directed from a W. R. Burnett story; 1956. (*b/w*)

Ace in the Hole √√
Stunning Billy Wilder attack on yellow journalism, through reporter Kirk Douglas's deliberate delaying of rescue so that story of trapped man makes him bigger and bigger headlines and meal-ticket. No less relevant today than when made in 1951. Jan Sterling, Porter Hall support; Billy Wilder directs with strong sense of purpose. (*b/w*)

Across the Bridge √
Ken Annakin directed this in 1957 from a Graham Greene story. Rod Steiger defaults with a wanted man's stolen identity. (*b/w*)

Across the Pacific √
Humphrey Bogart, Mary Astor, Sydney Greenstreet together again; John Huston didn't quite manage to make a Maltese Falcon out of this second world war thriller in 1942, but its pot boils merrily enough. (*b/w*)

Across the Wide Missouri √
Under veteran William Wellman's seasoned direction, Clark Gable turned in routinely attractive performance as Flint Mitchell who led pioneers into Blackfoot territory in 1829. This 1951 effort has some fine photography and J. Carrol Naish. Unfortunately, it also has a yawnful script and John Hodiak, Adolphe Menjou. (*c*)

Action in the North Atlantic √
Made in 1943 by Lloyd Bacon as contribution to keeping up morale, this actioner tells how brave merchant seamen are. And they were. Humphrey Bogart, Raymond Massey, Alan Hale, Sam Levene score; Dane Clark takes too many chances. (*b/w*)

Action of the Tiger ✕
Terence Young directing Sean Connery, but years before James Bond–1957, in fact. Dogged Van Johnson is the star and the story is something about escaping from Albania and those Un-American Reds; Herbert Lom, Martine Carrol keep it dragging. (*c*)

Act of Love √
Irwin Shaw turned this Albert Hayes novel of GI and near-tart in wartime Paris into an acceptable script in 1954, Anatole Litvak did his directorial best. Unfortunately the front office cast rugged Kirk Douglas as the man, Dany Robin as the girl, and chickened out on the *denouement*. (*b/w*)

Act of Murder √
Tentative 1965 attempt of TV director Alan Bridges to make a big-screen movie remained just too tethered to the more intimate medium but should play well on television. John Carson is man Justine Lord once had affair with, but now she's married to Anthony Bate. (*b/w*)

An Act of Murder √
Heavy, portentous drama about Fredric March as a judge euthanasing his wife. Director Michael Gordon indulged himself in appallingly ubiquitous music, which considerably detracts from the tension. Florence Eldridge, Geraldine

Brooks do their best to compete with soundtrack; 1948. (*b/w*)

Act of Violence √√
Exciting thriller about Van Heflin being chased by old army anti-chum Robert Ryan; Mary Astor is friendly tart; Janet Leigh love interest. Fred Zinnemann (*The Men, High Noon*) could certainly pack a punch in 1949. (*b/w*)

Act One ✕✕
Disastrous 1963 attempt by Dore Schary to convey the flavour of playwright Moss Hart's Broadway autobiography. Jason Robards' impersonation of George S. Kaufman isn't absolutely embarrassing, which George Hamilton's essay at M. Hart is. Stalwarts Jack Klugman, Eli Wallach, Sam Levene clomp unhappily around. (*b/w*)

The Actress √
Touching period piece set in the Twenties about author Ruth Gordon's own fight to get out of a small town and into Broadway. Jean Simmons does fine as the girl, while Anthony Perkins made his debut (it's 1953) as her beau. But Spencer Tracy dominates the film, as he did everything he was in, as her disapproving Dad. George Cukor obviously enjoyed himself directing, so did the cast. So will you. (*b/w*)

Ada ✕✕
Unfortunate attempt to make Dean Martin into an actor founders less on his inadequacies than on director Daniel Mann's desperate effort to make an incredible story of Southern political manipulation stand up. Susan Hayward is cute where she should have been dangerous, Wilfrid Hyde White monumentally miscast; only Martin Balsam survives this 1961 disaster. (*c*)

Adam and Evelyn ✕✕
Sub-sub-Coward about gambler Stewart Granger and dead friend's daughter,

Jean Simmons; 1949 Harold French production–direction all gloss and no substance. (*b/w*)

Adam Had Four Sons √
Take cover when you see Gregory Ratoff's name as director–it means that a film's going over the top emotionally. Susan Hayward, Warner Baxter, Fay Wray oblige in this one about brave Ingrid Bergman as governess looking after widowed Baxter's sons. Maybe you could get servants like her in 1941– thought it's doubtful. (*b/w*)

Adam's Rib √√
In his book *Tracy and Hepburn*, Garson Kanin tells how Katharine Hepburn made him build up litigious wife's part so that Judy Holliday would want to play it. Hepburn even refused to do a reaction shot in Holliday's introductory scene lest it distracted. But Judy Holliday almost refused part because she was called Fatso in the script. Altogether a delightful Tracy–Hepburn team job, playing husband-wife lawyers on opposing sides of wife *v.* husband case. Judy Holliday, Tom Ewell are warring spouses. Directed by George Cukor; 1949. (*b/w*)

The Admirable Crichton √
Kenneth More as the perfect butler who becomes natural leader when family is shipwrecked; Barrie play adequately filmed by Lewis Gilbert in 1957 has Diane Cilento, Cecil Parker, Gerald Harper, Jack Watling, Martita Hunt, Sally Ann Howes. (*c*)

Advance to the Rear ✕✕
The Civil War wasn't funny and nor is this 1964 attempt by George Marshall to make it so; Glenn Ford, Melvyn Douglas and Joan Blondell are lost in there somewhere. (*c*)

Adventure ✕
Clark Gable's first film after air force service was this 1945 would-be comedy

of torpedoed bo'sun who meets meek librarian, marries her, divorces her, and –well, you know the old story, Boy Meets Girl, Boy Loses Girl, Boy Gets Girl–the only plot in the movies, according to Joan Blondell in *Stand In*. Oddly enough, she's in this one, too, along with Thomas Mitchell; so it can't be all bad, despite Victor Fleming's tired direction. (*b/w*)

Adventures of a Young Man × ×
If you've read the Ernest Hemingway short stories on which this 1962 hotch-potch directed by Martin Ritt is based, don't bother with the movie; don't bother with it anyway, unless you are a Paul Newman fan. Arthur Kennedy, Susan Strasberg do their limited best. In the main role, Richard Beymer does his worst–and that's pretty bad. (*c*)

Adventures of Don Juan √
This 1949 effort marked Errol Flynn's last swashbuckle; he strides a little slowly through Spanish court drama, fighting baddie Robert Douglas on a staircase watched by Queen Viveca Lindfors. Vincent Sherman makes it as easy for him as possible, and keeps the excitement going with Alan Hale, Raymond Burr–who actually walked quite springily in those days. (*c*)

Adventures of Gallant Bess ×
Should Cameron Mitchell choose the nag or the nagger? OK for kids who like watching horses. Lew Landers churned this one out in 1948. (*c*)

(1) Adventures of Huckleberry Finn √
The old (1938) Mickey Rooney version; nice for the kids, and it sticks to the story. Richard Thorpe. (*b/w*)

(2) The Adventures of Huckleberry Finn ×
Don't expect more than a pretty picture-book illustration of Mark Twain's story from this 1960 attempt of Michael Curtiz; it's desperately short of real actors and even Tony Randall drowns in this insippippi. (*c*)

Adventures of Mark Twain √ √
Probably the best of all its period's epics (1944), with Fredric Marsh impersonating the grand old man with fire and devotion. Watch for the moment on his global tour when the camera pulls away to show the vast crowd listening to him at Allahabad. Irving Rapper never got the credit he deserved for this super-production; solid old Alan Hale, C. Aubrey Smith, Donald Crisp back up splendidly. (*b/w*)

The Adventures of Quentin Durward ×
Robert Taylor in drag wooing Kay Kendall under Richard Thorpe's direction; the general vulgarity is only slightly lightened by the presence of Robert Morley, Alec Clunes, Wilfrid Hyde White, Marius Goring, Ernest Thesiger; 1955. (*c*)

The Adventures of Robin Hood √
Despite all those Richard Todd repeats, this is the definitive version–with Errol Flynn, Olivia de Havilland, Basil Rathbone, Claude Rains, Eugene Pal-lette's Friar Tuck, Alan Hale's Little John. Belongs to a purer (1938) age when Michael Curtiz was left alone to tell a good yarn. (*c*)

Adventures of Sadie × × ×
Weak British attempt by Noel Langley to bring Norman Lindsay's naughty-naughty novel about three men and a girl castaway to life. Doubtless Joan Collins, Kenneth More, George Cole, Hattie Jacques will blush in excruciating agony when it comes chattering out of the television set at them, reminding them of the things they did for money in 1953. (*c*)

The Adventures of Sherlock Holmes √ √
Basil Rathbone and Nigel Bruce made

such a hit with *The Hound of the Baskervilles* that they were quickly hurried into this remake of William Gillette's stage play *Sherlock Holmes* the same year, 1939. It has to do with Moriarty's attempt to steal the Crown jewels and is splendid. Director, Albert Werker. (*b/w*)

The Adventures of Tartu ✕✕
Robert Donat helping Czech resistance destroy chemical plant during second world war. Predictably far-fetched, with Glynis Johns, Valerie Hobson, Walter Rilla acting cluelessly under Harold Bucquet's bottom-of-the-bucket direction; 1943. (*b/w*)

Advise and Consent √√
Lovely piece of hokum should have you fooled as to what Washington DC is like. Henry Fonda, Don Murray, Franchot Tone as the President and, above all, Charles Laughton as conniving Southern senator, are great. Otto Preminger served up a steamy brew of scandal in 1962, and it still smells rancid. (*b/w*)

Affair in Havana ✕
John Cassavetes, Raymond Burr, Sara Shane are triangle involving songwriter, crippled man, revenge and murder; Laslo Benedek makes it all rather heavy weather, but there are always Cuban backgrounds to look at, fortunately; 1957. (*b/w*)

Affair in Monte Carlo ✕✕
It isn't worth trying to work up too much interest in this silly yarn of Merle Oberon, Richard Todd, Leo Genn in Monte Carlo; can the gambler give it up? Can you fail to? Victor Saville must have dozed in the Riviera sunshine–or did he just stay at home? 1952 (*c*).

Affair in Reno ✕
Do they really have lady bodyguards in Arizona and Nevada? If they do, you can bet they don't look like Doris Singleton, who gets involved with her assignment, John Lund, R. G. Sprinsteen; 1957. (*c*)

Affair in Trinidad ✕
Rita Hayworth's tawdry glamour can't quite save this post-Casablanca spy excitement from utter disbelief. Glenn Ford sleepwalks through, suggesting that director Vincent Sherman couldn't rouse enough enthusiasm in him to wake up; 1952. (*b/w*)

An Affair to Remember ✕✕
Much-flawed attempt to recreate the Boyer-Dunne Love Affair with Cary Grant and Deborah Kerr, made by Leo McCarey in 1957. Starts well, tails off. (*c*)

Affair With a Stranger √
Jean Simmons, Victor Mature plan divorce but adopt child; Jane Darwell does her usual service in making mush seem plausible; Roy Rowland; 1953. (*b/w*)

The African Queen √√√
Won 1951 Oscar for Bogart as tough riverboat captain and nomination for Katharine Hepburn as forbidding spinster. Her humour wasn't in C. S. Forester's novel nor screenplay by James Agee, John Collier and director John Huston; in fact the whole project was going stickily until Huston suggested that Hepburn play Rosie 'as Eleanor Roosevelt'. Then it really took off, and this journey down river to escape in 1915 has become a classic. Topped *Sunday Times* poll for movie most wanted to be seen on TV. (*c*)

Africa Screams ✕
1950 Abbott and Costello puts them in the jungle with Clyde Beatty and Frank Buck, famous white hunters of the period (1950) or, to tell the truth, a bit before. Even the lions are long in the tooth and

claw. Somehow Max and Buddy Baer, slapsy heavyweight boxers, are involved, too. Pity director Charles Barton. (*b/w*)

After the Ball × ×
If you like *The Good Old Days*, you'll love this prettied-up picture of Vesta Tilley's life and times; Pat Kirkwood's rendering is spirited if nothing else (and it's nothing else); Laurence Harvey, Clive Morton, Leonard Sachs, Eric Chitty pop in and out as stage door johnnies, lovable Cockneys and the like; 1957. (*c*)

After the Fox ×
Peter Sellers has clearly ignored director Vittorio de Sica and decided to play it for the broadest laughs possible. Alas, they don't come in this silly story of jailbird pretending to be film director to cover gold caper in Italy. A mystery is the provenance of this 1966 effort—a Neil Simon script. (*c*)

After the Thin Man √√
Neat 1936 follow-up to smash success of sophisticated detective hit, *The Thin Man*, with same stars Myrna Loy, William Powell, dog Asta, plus James Stewart, Elissa Landi. W. S. van Dyke II directed tale of several murders in San Francisco, with classic ending where all seven suspects are gathered for *denouement*. (*b/w*)

Against All Flags ×
If you like pirates, Errol Flynn, Anthony Quinn, Maureen O'Hara don't be put off by the sound of our yawns. George Sherman; 1952. (*c*)

Against the Wind ×
1948 wartime adventure about training Belgian saboteurs in England and parachuting them back home. Sticky beginning leads to rip-roaring chase near the end, with director Charles Chrichton pulling all the stops out. Benefits from presence of Simone Signoret. Stiff upper lips include those of Gordon Jackson, Jack Warner. (*b/w*)

Agent for H.A.R.M. × ×
For H.A.R.M. read U.N.C.L.E. with Mark Richman in the Robert Vaughn role and Wendell Cory as overseer. The one about saving a scientist from the Reds; Gerd Oswald, 1966. (*c*)

The Agony and the Ecstasy × ×
Much more of the former than the latter in this ill-conceived chunk of marble about Michelangelo and Pope Julius II. Carol Reed seems to have suffered a mental lapse in 1965 and considered that a documentary on the artist followed by bits of his life would so overawe us we wouldn't notice we weren't being entertained. On the contrary, we're overbored. Charlton Heston, Rex Harrison, Diane Cilento go along. (*c*)

Ain't Misbehavin' ×
Reginald Gardiner and Jack Carson do their experienced best to save this rich boy (Rory Calhoun) who loves chorus girl (Piper Laurie) yarn, but writer-director Edward Buzzell makes it tough going for the veterans; 1955. (*c*)

Air Force √
Exciting story of a bomber crew made in 1943 by Howard Hawks; William Faulkner helped write it, and John Garfield, Gig Young, Arthur Kennedy, Harry Carey are outstanding. (*b/w*)

The Alamo √
John Wayne directed-produced-starred in this tribute to the 185 Americans who held off 7,000 Mexicans. He's Davy Crockett, Richard Widmark's Jim Bowie (of the knife). It's very long, very loud, and great entertainment, if you like super-Westerns; 1961. (*c*)

Alaska Seas ×
Why Jan Sterling is supposed to prefer

Brian Keith to Robert Ryan is as obscure as the rest of this fishy yarn is obvious. Documentary montage of salmon trawlers is splendid, though. Jerry Hopper; 1954. (_b/w_)

Albert RN √
PoW escape yarn about building a dummy to fool the Boche. Anthony Steel, Jack Warner, Robert Beatty show upper-class upper-lip under Lewis Gilbert; 1953. (_b/w_)

Al Capone √√
Remarkable and underrated tour de force on the part of Rod Steiger as king of the underworld and Richard Wilson as director of the underworld. Made when gangster movies were out of fashion – in 1959–it ranks with the earlier _Scarface_ and later _Godfather_ as convincing picture of the seamy side. Nehemiah Persoff is outstanding in strong supporting cast. (_b/w_)

Alexander's Ragtime Band ×
Slickly made (by Henry King in 1938) but extremely boring account of show biz from 1911–38 with 26 overrated Irving Berlin songs – pretty tunes but insipid lyrics, if you can bear to listen intently enough. All the Fox stable including Ty Power, Don Ameche, Alice Faye, Jack Haley. (_b/w_)

Alexander the Great √√
Or at least greater than the usual run of epics. This actually has a convincing script by director Robert Rossen and real acting by Richard Burton, Fredric March, Harry Andrews. They more than make up for Claire Bloom, Danielle Darrieux, Stanley Baker, Peter Cushing. The battle scenes are exciting; 1955. (_c_)

Alfie √√
Michael Caine as Bill Naughton's Cockney Don Juan convinces remark-
ably; Shelley Winters, Millie Martin, Julia Foster, Jane Asher, Vivian Merchant, as some of his conquests, equally outstanding. Lewis Gilbert did a fine and, let's admit it, unexpected job in 1966. (_c_)

Alfred the Great ×
Well, not very. At least in this movie, which ends before his mature 'greatness', if he ever was. And nor could the string of banal cliches that issue from the mouths of a distinguished but not very happy supporting cast be called great; Clive Donner makes some marvellous pictures and occasionally makes you feel what it must have been like in the ninth century, but in come the words again to wash all reality away. Nor is David Hemmings' playing of the cakeburner anything to savour; 1969. (_c_)

Alias John Preston ××
What are the strange dreams that bother this young man on his way to success? They may be yours, as you doze in your armchair. Alexander Knox portentous, Christopher Lee puzzled. David MacDonald; 1955. (_b/w_)

Alias Nick Beal √√
Ray Milland was never better than in this 1949 reworking of the Faust legend, with Thomas Mitchell as his politician-prey and Audrey Totter as his winsome accomplice. John Farrow (Mia's father) directed with distinction and understatement. (_b/w_)

Ali Baba and the Forty Thieves √
Jon Hall, hopefully being built up as Universal's answer to Errol Flynn in 1943, played Robin Hood in curved sandals, with Maria Montez and Andy Devine; much of the lavish production was so spectacular that you'll see the same footage appearing in lots of later pix. Arthur Lubin. (_c_)

Alive and Kicking √
Kathleen Harrison and Sybil Thorndike

abscond from old people's home; quite a jolly geriatric romp. Cyril Frankel; 1958. (*b/w*)

All About Eve √√
Highly literate Bette Davis vehicle, written and directed by Joseph L. Mankiewicz in 1950; she's marvellous as ageing stage star fighting to stay at the top, while newcomer (brilliant Anne Baxter) tries to claw her down. Neat ending. Applause, applause! (*b/w*)

The All-American ×
Tony Curtis in his younger days (1953) as football star–what could those rules be?–romancing Lori Nelson. Another later TV package star, Stuart Whitman hovers. Director Jesse Hibbs. (*b/w*)

All Ashore √
Lively musical about three sailors on shore leave (yes, again) which Richard Quine–so promising, so ultimately unfulfilled–directed in 1953. Mickey Rooney is lead, Dick Haymes croons along. (*c*)

All Fall Down √
Sincere attempt to reflect the problems of growing up which fails, admits director John Frankenheimer, because it wasn't all told from the boy's (Warren Beatty's) point of view, as was original James Leo Herlihy novel that William Inge wrote script from. Splendid performances from Karl Malden as potty father, Brandon de Wilde as kid brother, Angela Lansbury as over-mothering mother, Eva Marie Saint as loving suicide; 1962. (*b/w*)

All For Mary ××
One of those dreadful genteel comedies Nigel Patrick specialised in. This time it's Kathleen Harrison making young couple happy in Switzerland. Wendy Toye; 1956. (*c*)

All Hands on Deck ××
Mild fun and games aboard a docked Navy boat; strictly for lovers of Buddy Hackett and crooner Pat Boone, if any. Norman Taurog; 1961. (*c*)

All I Desire ×
Barbara Stanwyck goes the way of all flesh to return from a wicked career on the stage to see her daughter graduate. It was ludicrous enough in 1953–what on earth will we make of it now? Douglas Sirk directed King of the Soapsuds, Ross Hunter's production. (*b/w*)

An Alligator Named Daisy ××
There's this suitcase taken in mistake. And there's a real alligator in it. J. Lee Thompson propels archetypal 1955 cast of British cameo players–Diana Dors, Donald Sinden, Stanley Holloway, Roland Culver, Margaret Rutherford Stephen Boyd–through subsequent complications. (*c*)

All in a Night's Work √
Shirley MacLaine is seen coming out of dead tycoon's room clad only in a towel; she manages to make the ensuing 90 minutes amusing enough, with help from Dean Martin, Cliff Robertson, Charles Ruggles, Jerome Cowan, under Joseph Anthony's touch; 1960. (*c*)

All Mine to Give √
Our own Glynis Johns turns up as pioneer lady with Cameron Mitchell in this hard slog of life on the frontier, sparely directed by Allen Reisner with considerable respect for the hardships of early Wisconsin; 1957. (*c*)

All My Sons √
Edward G. Robinson ruggedly plays profiteer father in Irving Reis' version of Arthur Miller award-winning play. Burt Lancaster, looking skinny in 1948, is son who finds out that Pop's defective aircraft part killed brother. (*b/w*)

All Night Long ×
Michael Relph and Basil Dearden did their double act of producing and

directing this in 1961; a jazzed up version of Othello, it misses Shakespeare badly. Patrick McGoohan, Betsy Blair do their best; among those present who later made it big are Richard Harris, Keith Michell, Bernard Braden. (*b/w*)

All Quiet on the Western Front　√√
One of the greats. Although 1930 dialogue from Maxwell Anderson is winceable and the sound primitive, its story of German schoolboys joining up and being slaughtered is as powerful pacifist argument as ever. Lew Ayres was starred by director Lewis Milestone but Louis Wolheim steals the picture. Final minutes among most famous movie moments. (*b/w*)

All That Heaven Allows　×
Jane Wyman lowers herself to love a gardener; Rock Hudson elevates himself to love trees; whether you'll love either depends on how indulgent you're feeling; Agnes Moorehead wasted, as usual. Douglas Sirk; 1956. (*c*)

All the Brothers were Valiant　×
... if not particularly convincing. It's all to do with pearl-fishing, but you'll be lucky to find much to thrill you in this high-spirited, action-packed yarn, with MGM's second eleven–Robert Taylor Stewart Granger, Keenan Wynn–slugging it out. Richard Thorpe; 1953. (*c*)

All the Fine Young Cannibals　×
One of those small-town Texan dramas that they used to force poor Natalie Wood through in 1960. Here she's involved with Robert Wagner and George Hamilton, and very boring it is, with Michael Anderson's nerveless direction. Even Pearl Bailey singing doesn't help. (*c*)

All the King's Men　√√
Triple Academy Award winner (Best Film of 1949, Best Actor, Broderick Crawford, Best Supporting Actress,

Mercedes McCambridge). Story of Willie Stark, idealist turned corrupt politician, based on the career of Huey Long, the Louisiana Kingfish. Robert Rossen directed. (*b/w*)

All the Way Home　×
James Agee's very personal novel, *A Death in the Family*, can't be entirely brought down by Alex Segal's version of the Tad Mosel play based on it, but it's so poorly cast and minimally acted (Robert Preston, Jean Simmons, Michael Kearney are way out of their depth) that it fails to deliver; 1963. (*b/w*)

All the Young Men　××
Cheap attempt to cash in on liberal feelings towards 'negroes' in this 1960 Korea war-drama just embarrasses. Sydney Poitier is put in charge of platoon, amid resentment from Alan Ladd. Luckily Mort Sahl is around, but even he has to mouth writer–producer–director Hall Bartlett's lines. (*b/w*)

All This and Heaven Too　×
Escape to 19th-century France with Charles Boyer in front of a roaring fire mouthing sentimental nuggets to eye-fluttering Bette Davis; Anatole Litvak was the chap to bring you something to look at and forget the reality of 1940 while doing it. It might perform the same function for you now, but your worries hadn't better be too pressing–it has lost a certain magic with the years. (*b/w*)

All This and Money Too　√
All this being sexy millionairess Hope Lange. It's supposed to be a comedy, with Charles Boyer being sneaky, Ricardo Montalban being boring, Glenn Ford being noble and Telly Savalas the brightest spot. A 1963 American-eye view of the Riviera directed by David Swift. (*b/w*)

All Through the Night √
Humphrey Bogart lifts this otherwise routine (but nonetheless exciting) second world war counter-spy sleuthing in New York to a film worth an effort; Vincent Sherman packed it with other fine actors in 1942–Conrad Veidt, Jane Darwell, Frank McHugh, Jackie Gleason, Phil Silvers and, above all, Peter Lorre.
(*b/w*)

Alvarez Kelly √
North *v* South, William Holden *v* Richard Widmark, fightin' and feudin' over a vast herd of steers. Expertly directed by Edward Dmytryk in 1966, it's a prime cut above most Westerns–and most Civil War movies, come to that.
(*c*)

Aloma of the South Seas × ×
Jon Hall puts on clothes to leave Dorothy Lamour and his South Sea island to get some education in the US; but he comes back to thwart the baddies. Alfred Santell; 1941. (*c*)

Along Came Jones √
Incomparable Gary Cooper in case of mistaken identity–cowboy for killer. Only film he ever produced himself–in 1945. Director Stuart Heisler gets fine performance from Gary's old partner, Loretta Young. (*b/w*)

Along the Great Divide √
Kirk Douglas's first Western (1951) and it's a wonder that his career survived all the clichés as well as the mechanical hazards the script provides, as he struggles to deliver prisoner to jail; Walter Brennan, Virginia Mayo play standard types; Raoul Walsh directed the traffic. (*b/w*)

Always a Bride × ×
Ronald Squire as man from the Treasury who gets caught with con-men via Peggy Cummins; Terence Morgan and James Hayter drag it down, and Ralph Smart's direction isn't very; 1954. (*b/w*)

The Amazing Mrs Holliday × ×
Or the Inn of the Eighth Sadness as Deanna Durbin struggles with plot and lines to look after Chinese orphans; she sings dully, too. Barry Fitzgerald and Arthur Treacher are put through their usual paces by Bruce Manning; 1943.
(*b/w*)

Ambassador's Daughter ×
Norman Krasna tried for pre-war sparkle in 1956 in tale of soldier picking up title-lady Olivia de Havilland but it doesn't quite come off, despite presence of Adolphe Menjou and Myrna Loy.
(*c*)

Ambush ×
Wooden Robert Taylor as scout in Indian territory juts his pretty jaw into various bits of mild trouble; director Sam Wood obviously treated as strictly routine for the 1950 MGM factory. (*b/w*)

Ambush at Tomahawk Gap √
Four released convicts looking for the fortune they stashed away in the Wild West. The Indians get three of them— who will be left alive? John Hodiak who was being paid most for his name above the title, at a guess. Fred F. Sears directed; 1953.
(*c*)

Ambush Bay ×
1966 was a bit late to churn out a drama about war behind the Japanese lines, but then Mickey Rooney, Hugh O'Brian are old enough to remember it well. Director Ron Winston does his very best with creaky patrol story, but he can't do anything about James Mitchum as young soldier who learns the hard way.
(*c*)

The Ambushers × ×
Childish and rather boring Matt Helm adventure, made extremely glossily by Henry Levin, but empty as a prop revolver. Janice Rule tries hard, but Dean Martin and Senta Berger shrug

their way through a poor script, never even convincing themselves, let alone us. As for the man-killing bra, see *The Tenth Victim*; 1968. (*c*)

Ambush in Leopard Street × ×
Norman Rodway is only bright thing in this dull British story of diamond robbery directed by J. Henry Piperno; 1961. (*b/w*)

American Guerilla in the Philippines ×
Fritz Lang's name as director should have meant better film than this one (1950) about brave Ty Power doing his bit; Tom Ewell uncomfortable in non-comedy role. (*c*)

An American in Paris √√
Gershwin music (Our Love Is Here To Stay, I Got Rhythm); Gene Kelly, Leslie Caron; wry Oscar Levant; 17-minute climactic ballet; Alan Jay Lerner script; Vincente Minnelli direction (he knocked off another film, *Father's Little Dividend*, in the four weeks it took to rehearse the ballet), made this the outstanding musical of 1951 and an all-time favourite. (*c*)

The Americanization of Emily √√
What's a nice girl like Julie Andrews doing in a sharp, cynical movie like this one about American brass pushing James Garner around? Answer: rather well. This 1964 Paddy Chayevsky-scripted bitter comedy never got the response it deserved. Arthur Hiller. (*b/w*)

The Americano ×
Standard Western that happens to take place in the Matto Grosso. A Southern, in fact. Otherwise, its the same old rustling and hustling, with Glenn Ford doing his pint-sized toughie bit and Cesar Romero adding local colour. William Castle; 1955. (*c*)

The Amorous Adventures of Moll Flanders × ×
Instead of some good honest Defoe-type

pornography all Terence Young can serve up is titillations that don't tickle. In the part of Moll, Kim Novak is laughable, and 'supports' Richard Johnson, Angela Lansbury, Lilli Palmer, George Sanders, Leo McKern, Vittorio de Sica and Daniel Massey provide a gallery of failure. Mrs Tom Jones, it isn't; 1965. (*c*)

The Amorous Prawn ×
Super people—Dennis Price, Ian Carmichael, Cecil Parker, Joan Greenwood—manage to make this trifle about salmon-fishing money-making scheme mildly amusing; Anthony Kimmins; 1962. (*b/w*)

Anastasia √√
Helen Hayes as the dowager empress who questions whether Ingrid Bergman is real royal or pretend princess is outstanding; everyone else is just a little hammy—but then what else do you expect from La Bergman (*pace* her Oscar for it), Akim Tamiroff, Yul Brynner? Anatole Litvak keeps the guessworks going merrily enough, however, and it's a nice hour or two's look; 1956. (*c*)

The Anatolian Smile √
Elia Kazan's biography/autobiography of Greek immigrant not quite making it; he has put so much of his own emotions in that it's beastly to remain unmoved; 1963. (*b/w*)

The Anatomist √
Alastair Sim and George Cole in a rather grim account of Burke-and-Harey grave-robbings; Jill Bennett suitably frightened; Leonard William; 1961. (*b/w*)

Anatomy of a Murder √√
Otto Preminger's 1959 detailed murder trial with James Stewart splendid as defence lawyer, Lee Remick as equivocal rapee, Ben Gazzara as client. (*b/w*)

Anchors Aweigh √√
Delightful musical about shore leave (in Hollywood, not On the Town in New York) with Frank Sinatra and Gene Kelly bouncing happily along with Kathryn Grayson, who never had it so good. George Sidney gave Sinatra his first hit movie–and vice versa–in this 1945 smash. (*c*)

And Baby Makes Three ×
The bride faints at the altar. She's pregnant! If that sounds like the start of a wicked Preston Sturges comedy, you'll be disappointed. This is Harry Levin and she was safely married to first husband when conceiving. She's Barbara Hale and wants to stay married to Robert Young; lucky Robert Hutton; 1950. (*b/w*)

And Now Miguel √
Slow but seductive open-air adventure of young shepherd attempting to prove himself; Guy Stockwell does well. James Clark directed; 1966. (*c*)

And Now Tomorrow ×
Little Alan Ladd climbs on a chair to cure Loretta Young of deafness and then–of course–falls in lurve with her; Irving Pichel made this one for the dying handkerchief trade in 1944. (*b/w*)

Androcles and the Lion × ×
Photographed theatre by the man who screwed up so many GBS plays in the cinema, Gabriel Pascal. He somehow talked the old man into letting him have near-monopoly, and the result – as in this artificial, unconvincing case–is fatty ham. Dreadful casting shows the level of his taste: Alan Young, Victor Mature, Robert Newton, Maurice Evans. Pity poor Jean Simmons who must have thought this was going to give her career a boost in 1953. Charles Erskine. (*b/w*)

And the Same to You × ×
British boxing comedy with Brian Rix, William Hartnell, Tommy Cooper, Sid James, Shirley Ann Field; director George Pollock; 1959. (*b/w*)

And Women Shall Weep × × ×
Embarrassing 1960 piffle about Ruth Dunning handing over her son to face murder charge. Pull the other one, John Lemont. (*b/w*)

Angela × ×
Dennis O'Keefe falling in love with Mara Lane and over the body of her employer. He directed it, too; Rossano Brazzi and lots of Italians are there, because that's where it was made in 1955. (*b/w*)

Angel and the Badman √
Don't be put off by the title, this is an unusual Western with Gail Russell playing a Quaker girl who gradually turns John Wayne away from his wicked path; Harry Carey, Bruce Cabot support strongly, and James Edward Grant fords problems derivatively. (*b/w*)

Angel Baby √
A pity that George Hamilton was cast as post-Elmer Gantry character. Salome Jens as deaf-mute he may have cured, Mercedes McCambridge, Joan Blondell, Burt Reynolds all act him off the screen despite Paul Wendkos's best efforts; 1963. (*b/w*)

Angel Face ×
Otto Preminger going all pretentious about psychology in 1953, but ending up with as phoney a movie as he ever turned out (even more so than usual, in fact). Robert Mitchum does his moody bit as chauffeur, but looks as though he's as baffled as we are by what homicidal murderer Jean Simmons, Daddy Herbert Marshall, wicked stepmother Barbara O'Neil are up to. (*b/w*)

Angels One Five √
Jack Hawkins makes this personal fight to fly again during Battle of Britain

memorable, despite familiar plane shots and heroics from Michael Denison, John Gregson. George O'Ferrall is good on detail; 1954. (*b/w*)

The Angel Who Pawned Her Harp   ✕
A rather similar East End excursion to *A Kid for Two Farthings*, which was made in the same year, 1954. Alan Bromly and Sidney Cole had Diane Cilento, Felix Aylmer and Robert Eddison trying to suggest something of what the place was really like. (*b/w*)

The Angel With The Trumpet   ✕ ✕
Could you care about the lives of an Austrian family of piano-makers from 1888 to the day the second world war ends and they decide to start all over again? If so, Anthony Bushell is the director for you—he leaves nothing out and plods deliberately through it all. To help, he has Eileen Herlie growing old, plus Maria Schell, Andrew Cruickshank, Wilfrid Hyde White, Norman Woland, Basil Sydney; 1950. (*b/w*)

Angels with Dirty Faces   √
James Cagney and Pat O'Brien as two East Side kids who grow up as gangster and priest, but bound together by friendship. Cagney is idol of the Dead End Kids who spun off into series of own films; Humphrey Bogart is double-crossing racketeer, Ann Sheridan girlfriend. Sadly, this 1938 blockbuster survives largely as museum-piece, mainly due to a risible sentimental ending and heavenly choir. Michael Curtiz delivered the product Warner Bros wanted. (*b/w*)

The Angel Wore Red   √
Fascinating cop-out attempt to tell the story of a whore and a priest in love during Spanish Civil War. Dirk Bogarde and Ava Gardner make excellent attempts at authenticity, but Nunnally Johnson made too many concessions to 1960 Hollywood. Strong supports include Joseph Cotten, Vittorio de Sica, Finlay Currie. (*b/w*)

The Angry Hills   ✕
Stanley Baker, Theodore Bikel, lovely Gia Scala and authentic Greek scenery are plusses; Robert Mitchum as American involved with guerrillas, Raymond Stross's typically tasteless production, Robert Aldrich's attitudinising direction are minuses; 1959. (*b/w*)

The Angry Red Planet   ✕ ✕
It's Mars as imagined by a poor comic-strip artist, realised on the cheap by American International Pictures, with unknowns (Jack Kruschen is only little name around) playing comic and serious explorers with a girl along. Lauritz Melchior's son, Ib, takes the blame—and the profit; 1959. (*c*)

The Angry Silence   √
A rather nasty film about Richard Attenborough refusing to join an unofficial strike and being persecuted by his fellow-workers; it pretends to stand up for individualism, but is in fact a sneaky way of knocking men with grievances who have been forced to turn to their ultimate weapon, the right to withhold their labour; Guy Green should be Sir Guy if the Tories looked after their own properly. Bernard Lee created the archetype shop steward (still, since this was made in 1960, the popular caricature of the man who gives his spare time to his mates) and Alfred Burke must be a bit ashamed of the on-the-phone-to-Moscow organiser he played so well. (*b/w*)

Animal Crackers   √ √
Marx Brothers' second film, made in 1930. It's hooray for Captain Spaulding, the big-game hunter, who wrecks Margaret Dumont's party. Director, Victor Heerman. (*b/w*)

Animal Farm   ✕
This 1954 effort is one of the few full-length cartoons made in England; it should have been great, given the possi-

bilities of Orwell's savage novel, but Halas and Batchelor gooed it all up and it stands as neither satirical nor even entertaining for children. (*c*)

Anna and the King of Siam √√
1946 original of later musical *The King and I*, with Rex Harrison as the King, Irene Dunne the governess, plus Linda Darnell, Lee J. Cobb. John Cromwell did sumptuous job of direction. (*b/w*)

Anna Karenina ×
None of the 13 filmings begin to measure up to the magnificence of the novel; in 1935 Basil Rathbone was merely sinister as the husband in Garbo's; Ralph Richardson merely Ralph Richardson in Vivien Leigh's (1947). We await a good version. (*b/w*)

Anna Lucasta × ×
It's a toss-up who is more embarassingly awful, Eartha Kitt as the whore with a good heart or Sammy Davis Jr as a brash, money-spending sailor. Arnold Laven doesn't do much to help his black cast; 1949. (*b/w*)

Annie of the Indies ×
Suspend your disbelief, if you can, and accept Jean Peters as pirate captain; starting from this pantomimic premise you won't be surprised when she spares Louis Jourdan. Debra Paget, Herbert Marshall and bluff, boring James Robertson Justice muck in. Jacques Tourneur; 1951. (*c*)

Annie Get Your Gun √
Betty Hutton bulldozes her way into the spirit of her action as gun-slinging Annie Oakley, eventually making it with a Howard Keel who hates bossy women. Based on the Irving Berlin Broadway hit, directed by George Sidney, the production numbers still seem stage-starched, but the songs are fine (Anything You Can Do, Doin' What Comes Naturally) and the pathos tender; 1950. (*c*)

The Anniversary ×
Black comedy from Bill MacIlwraith's play about highly possessive mother gives Bette Davis in an eye-patch a field day; Sheila Hancock as daughter-in-law and James Cossins as transvestite son outstanding; rest of the cast a bit weak, and Roy Baker's direction decidedly so; 1968. (*c*)

Another Man's Poison ×
Val Guest must take the blame for dreadful script about lady doing in her husband, sussed out by a vet. Director Irving Rapper doesn't help, but Bette Davis and Emlyn Williams almost made this 1952 British pic worth watching, (*b/w*)

Another Part of the Forest ×
About the Hubbard family who appear in Lillian Hellman's other film, *The Little Foxes*, only set twenty years earlier; Frederic March, Edmond O' Brien, Florence Eldridge, Betsy Blair shine; Michael Gordon doesn't quite make it much more than photographed stage play; 1949. (*b/w*)

Another Thin Man √√
William Powell and Myrna Loy sort out the threats to life of C. Aubrey Smith, particularly from Sheldon Leonard (who later–this was 1939–himself produced *I Spy, My World and Welcome to It*, etc.). Otto Kruger, Ruth Hussey, Nat Pendleton, Marjorie Main add to the pleasures. W. S. Van Dyke directed as usual. (*b/w*)

Another Time, Another Place ×
Another woman, and just another movie. Cast of second-line stars (Lana Turner, Glynis Johns, Sean Connery, Barry Sullivan, Sid James) can't do much with this 1957 weepie about a man in love with two women, nor can director Lewis Allen. (*b/w*)

Any Number Can Play ×
You don't have to be ashamed of your

father just because he's a big-time gambler. That's the stirring message of this 1949 'woman's picture', as they used to call 'em. Clark Gable is Dad, Alexis Smith Mum, Darryl Hickman his little lad. Luckily, Mervyn Le Roy has Wendell Corey, Frank Morgan, Mary Astor, Marjorie Rambeau and the rest of the MGM stock company along to keep you awake. (*b/w*)

Anything Goes √
Bing Crosby made this twice; in 1936 and this 1956 version (with Donald O'Connor, director Robert Lewis). Only the Cole Porter songs are memorable, but they are superb: I Get a Kick Out of You; You're the Tops; It's De-lovely. (*c*)

Any Wednesday ✕
Called *Bachelor Girl Apartment* when first released here in 1967, this sophisticated comedy has Jason Robards as businessman who puts Jane Fonda down on his expenses; his wife gets suspicious, and it's all quite good fun, not exactly clean, but not actually dirty; directed by Robert Ellis Miller. (*c*)

Apache Rifles ✕
If you think you've seen this one about Audie Murphy rounding up naughty braves before, you may be right; it uses chunks of other Westerns liberally. What a swizz! Stand in the corner, William Witney; 1964. (*c*)

Apache Territory ✕
Rory Calhoun defeating the entire tribe all alone. Pull the other one, Ray Nazarro; 1958. (*c*)

Apache Uprising ✕
1966 Cowboys *v.* Injuns has array of earlier stars–Rory Calhoun, Corinne Calvet, Lon Chaney Jr, Richard Arlen, Jean Parker, and same old story too. R. G. Springsteen. (*c*)

Apache Warrior ✕
Made 1957, before Hollywood dis-

covered the virtues of the Red Indians; here they are the baddies, as they always used to be, a starless cast routinely directed by Elmo Williams. (*c*)

Apache War Smoke ✕
Gilbert Roland as heavy redeeming himself when the Indians attack; others in lonely frontier fort are Glenda Farrell, Robert Horton, Gene Lockhart, Henry Morgan, Douglass Dumbrille. Directed by Harold F. Kress; 1953. (*b/w*)

Apache Woman √
Lloyd Bridges proving that the Red Indians aren't the villains; other baddies want to get the old wars going again. Lively Western directed by Roger Corman; 1955. (*c*)

The Apartment √√√
The great Billy Wilder comedy from his own and I.A.L. Diamond script about the office schnook who lends his flat to his bosses in return for advancement. Shirley MacLaine just right as the girl who gets left behind. It's funny, tender, sharply-observed and unbeatable entertainment. 1960 Oscar-winner. (*b/w*)

Apartment for Peggy ✕
William Holden's a returned GI, Jeanne Crain's preggers, and this is a simple story of their solvable problems; but Edmund Gwenn and Gene Lockhart lift the film away from them with a small smile of experience; writer-director George Seaton just gives up and lets them; 1949. (*c*)

Appointment in Honduras ✕
Suffers from jungle fever as Ann Sheridan oomphs her way (Glenn Ford staggers manfully alongside) through a steamy bit of the RKO lot, supposedly in the middle of a South American revolution. Zachary Scott and a handful of convicts glumly join in. Jacques Tourneur; 1953. (*c*)

Appointment in London √
Dirk Bogarde, Ian Hunter make this routine bomber yarn (set 1943, made 1952), culminating in raid, rather more meaningful than it deserves. Philip Leacock. (*b/w*)

Appointment With a Shadow ×
Hard-drinking reporter is marked as murder victim; not much to write home about (or in his paper either). George Nader, Virginia Field; Joseph Pevney churned it out; 1956. (*b/w*)

Appointment With Venus × ×
Coy, heavy-handed war pic about rescuing a cow. Ralph Thomas lumbered it along in 1951; David Niven, Kenneth More, Glynis Johns perk it up. (*b/w*)

April in Paris √
Doris Day, as always, makes this a watchable experience, although the story (she's a chorus girl invited to Paris by mistake–it should have been Ethel Barrymore at the cultural conference) is dismal and everyone (even British revue veteran Herbert Farjeon) except Ray Bolger, who can dance, pretty awful. Even the songs are substandard Sammy Cahn. But David Butler makes a silly script zing and you'll forgive it all for Miss Day; 1952. (*c*)

April Love × ×
Dull little effort about Kentucky and a horse that's ill; Henry Levin works hard to put some life into it, but is defeated by pleasant but weak Pat Boone, Shirley Jones; 1957. (*c*)

April Showers √
Minor backstage musical with the peppy team of Jack Carson and Ann Sothern rowing and Cuddles Sakall picking up the pieces; James M. (not Jerome) Kern directed; 1948. (*b/w*)

Arabesque √ √
Delightful concoction of nonsense in-volving Gregory Peck as linguistics expert forced to do some deciphering with the help of Sophia Loren, doing what she does nicely. Alan Badel makes a splendid heavy and Stanley Donen makes it all move, particularly the final chase; 1966. (*c*)

Arabian Nights ×
Whatever happened to the great desert cycle? Here it is at its height (1942) with Jon Hall leading revolt against caliph, Maria Montez urging him on in harem bra like they never wore and Billy Gilbert milking laughs from being fat and camp; John Rawlins directed. (*c*)

Arena √
Rodeo yarn that throws you more with its plot clichés than bucking broncos. Have you ever wondered how they get them to buck? This film won't tell you but it's pretty disgusting. This is all about Gig Young's rotten marriage with Polly Bergen, extra fun and games with Barbara Lawrence. Robert Fleischer; 1953. (*c*)

Are You With It? ×
Not really, we're afraid. Donald O'Connor tries too hard as maths whizz-kid who joins the carnival and sings, too. But Jack Hively didn't have much else going for this picture in 1948. (*b/w*)

Arise My Love √
Charles Brackett and Billy Wilder wrote this one about reporter Claudette Colbert in love with flyer Ray Milland in civil war Spain, but you wouldn't know it. 1940 was a hack year for them, and Mitchell Leisen, Paramount's top comedy director, did a neat, self-effacing job on their scripts. (*b/w*)

Arizona Mission ×
James Arness, Harry Carey and the girl who was later to prove herself an actress (but not here) Angie Dickinson in revenge-for-being-left-to-die plot. Andrew McLaglen shot from the hip. 1956. (*b/w*)

Armored Attack √
The changing political allegiances of America towards Russia made this account of USSR being defended against the nazis change script in mid-1943. The result is a mess, but an interesting one, with Erich von Stroheim *v* Walter Huston and wife Ann Harding being tortured; Jane Withers, Anne Baxter strongly supporting. But it's all too much for Lewis Milestone. (*b/w*)

Armored Car Robbery √
One of those familiar movies (since *Rififi*) of a caper that goes wrong; here a policeman is killed. But Richard Fleischer did superior job in 1950 with virtual unknowns to add authenticity. (*b/w*)

Armored Command ✕
Tedious, improbable wartime stuff about Tina Louise being exposed as spy by Howard Keel, having already exposed herself (but not too much–this was made in pre-permissive 1961) for the troops. Byron Haskin is the man to blame–or pity for having to direct such a script. (*b/w*)

Around the World in 80 Days √√
Lightly based on Jules Verne novel, with lovely aerial shots and a galaxy of stars making cameo appearances around David Niven as globe-encircling Phileas Fogg. One point each for spotting Robert Newton, Shirley MacLaine, Charles Boyer, Ronald Colman, Noel Coward, Marlene Dietrich, Trevor Howard, Buster Keaton, Peter Lorre, Victor McLaglen, John Mills, Robert Morley, Jack Oakie, George Raft, 1956. Michael Anderson directed. (*c*)

Around the World Under the Sea ✕✕
Sorry little attempt to do a major sci-fi undersea spectacular on a shoestring and a diving bootlace; non-stars Lloyd Bridges, David McCallum, Shirley Eaton squabble in a sub. Andrew Marton directs-produces-boobs; 1966. (*c*)

Arrowhead ✕
Goody cavalry (Charlton Heston) *v* nasty Indians (Jack Palance), with moody Katy Jurado in the middle. Strictly simplistic and before (it's 1953) enlightened Westerns came on the scene. Director Charles Marquis Warren is the real heavy. (*c*)

Arrow in the Dust ✕
American Civil War deserter takes on commander's identity and finds himself having to lead wagon train defence against Indians; Sterling Hayden may be sterling but he's also dull; Lesley Selander's brisk direction helps; 1954. (*c*)

Arsenic and Old Lace √
Frantic 1944 version of hit play about two old ladies who see nothing wrong in poisoning their guests' elderberry wine. Frank Capra directed this wholesome black comedy so that Cary Grant appears pottier than the old girls. (*b/w*)

Artists and Models ✕
One of those Dean Martin–Jerry Lewis not-nearly-so-funny-as-they-ought-to-be's with Shirley MacLaine, Dorothy Malone as the luscious neighbours; it's even got a 1955 model parade to make you laugh at the corny fashions. Frank Tashlin directed-co-wrote. (*b/w*)

The Art of Love ✕
Comedy based on the unfunny premise that only dead artists sell well, so Americans in Paris James Garner, Dick van Dyke fake a suicide. A Norman Jewison flop, 1965. (*c*)

Ask Any Girl √
Delightful David Niven trying to pair dependable Gig Young off with Shirley

MacLaine, for some reason, like that's what it says in the script. Of course, she fancies Niven. Charles Walters wisely lets the male stars keep the fun going; 1959. (*c*)

As Long as They're Happy × ×
A grisly Jack Buchanan comedy (director J. Lee Thompson) made in 1955 about a Johnnie Ray-type singer invited to a nice English home with Jeanette Scott, Diana Dors. (*c*)

The Asphalt Jungle √√
One of the great thrillers; an unpretentious masterpiece by John Huston in 1950. Sam Jaffe is brains behind jewel caper, but accomplices Sterling Hayden and Louis Calhern could screw him up. Also noteworthy for brilliant brief debut by the unique Marilyn Monroe. Sam Jaffe's final scene makes you want to stand up and cheer. (*b/w*)

The Assassin ×
The scenery is Venice and real; the actors are English and phoney. It really was a nerve to cast such weakies as Richard Todd, Eva Bartok, John Gregson in roles that cry out for real acting. Ralph Thomas's tension isn't very tense, either; 1953. (*b/w*)

The Assassination Bureau × ×
Strained and tedious Man-Who-Was-Thursday type plot about head of international Murder Inc organisation (Oliver Reed) who accepts assignment to kill himself; Diana Rigg as reporter who falls in love with him, Kenneth Griffith, Clive Revill are to be pitied for having to go through this nonsense with a smile on their lips; Basil Dearden directs energetically; 1969. (*c*)

Assault on a Queen √
Despite the regally-rapist come-on of the title, it's about Frank Sinatra leading band of adventurers to invade bank vaults of the good ship Queen Mary. Directed by Jack Donohue; 1966. (*c*)

Assignment K × ×
Rubbishy spy story with absurdly over-complicated plot but some nice skiing locations; what Michael Redgrave, Leo McKern, Jeremy Kemp were doing in it must be as big a mystery to them as it will be to you, even after it's over (if you wait that long). Val Guest directs somnambulistically; 1968. (*c*)

Assignment Paris ×
Dana Andrews is reporter saving the West from the Reds, with George Sanders as spy chief; French location shooting lifts it a little above usual run and Robert Parrish does conscientious job of direction. Marta Hari–sorry, Toren–is Delilahesque; 1952. (*b/w*)

The Astonished Heart × ×
Noel Coward wrote (it was one of the 'Tonight at 8.30 plays') and even acts in this disappointing version of psychiatrist who can't solve his own problem–wife, Celia Johnson, or her friend, Margaret Leighton? Terence Fisher and Antony Darnborough somehow shared the direction–perhaps by telephone from the Bahamas? 1949. (*b/w*)

As Young As You Feel √√
Monty Woolley proving that a retiring age of 65 is all wrong, trying to get his old job back by impersonating company president; Marilyn Monroe delightful, as always, as his secretary; strong aid from Thelma Ritter, Constance Bennett, Allyn Joslyn. Harmon Jones made this one of the pleasant trifles of 1951. (*b/w*)

At Gunpoint √
Look here, mister, I'm a peaceful citizen and don't want no gunplay, but if you and your band of hooligans speak to this lady like that I'm going to be forced to do something about it. That's Fred

MacMurray's line in this well-made (by Alfred L. Werker), 1955 Western. Dorothy Malone is the lady, Walter Brennan does his ornery old cowpoke act. (*c*)

Athena ×
Crazy family comedy about lawyer and singer falling for two granddaughters of weight-lifting nut crank and star-gazing wife. Richard Thorpe has to work hard to keep the fun going, but has some yeomen helpers in Jane Powell, Debbie Reynolds, Louis Calhern; as suitors, Edmund Purdom and Vic Damone are so-so; 1954. (*c*)

Atomic City ×
Kidnap at Los Alamos to influence nuclear scientist; Gene Barry puckers his brow, otherwise it's capably acted and directed, by Jerry Hopper; 1952. (*b/w*)

At Sword's Point ×
Three-Musketeer-type swordplay at the French court; Maureen O'Hara queens it, Cornel Wilde leads goodies; Lewis Allen should have known better by 1952. (*c*)

Attack! √
Robert Aldrich's taut 1956 war film about a cowardly officer's actions causing the death of his troops was un-American enough to cause a US ambassador to walk out of the Venice Film Festival. Well cast with Jack Palance, Eddie Albert, Lee Marvin. (*b/w*)

Attack of the Crab Monsters √
Roger Corman yarn about scientists eaten by 25-ft crustaceans, who assume their personalities! Nobody you ever heard of is in it; 1957. (*b/w*)

Attack on the Iron Coast √
Neat, economical war film about a suicide mission which characterises German defenders particularly well.

Paul Wendkos gets almost believable portraits from Lloyd Bridges and Sue Lloyd, which is pretty clever; 1968. (*c*)

At the Circus √
The Marx Brothers save a travelling circus from bankruptcy, and if you like 'em, you'll love 'em. Margaret Dumont, Nat Pendleton add to the fun; Kenny Baker detracts from it. Edward Buzzell; 1939. (*b/w*)

At the Stroke of Nine × ×
Stephen Murray and Patricia Dainton in low-budgeter about kidnapping of girl reporter by revengeful pianist; Lance Comfort; 1957. (*b/w*)
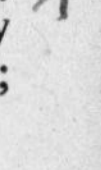

At War With the Army ×
Strictly for fans of Dean Martin and mugging Jerry Lewis, this 1951 assembly-line job had Hal Walker as director, but both their characters are so tedious that you'll hate 'em unless you love 'em. (*b/w*)

Aunt Clara √
Margaret Rutherford inherits pub, greyhounds, fairground sideshow and brothel (a bit vague this last one, as you can imagine in a 1954 family comedy) and gradually and amusingly cleans them up. Anthony Kimmins has marvellous cast to help him: Ronald Shiner, A. E. Matthews, Fay Compton, Nigel Stock, Jill Bennett, Sid James. (*b/w*)

Auntie Mame √
Rosalind Russell in high-spirited camp comedy based on novel and play about wacky lady and nephew who appeals to her hidden sentimental side; Morton DaCosta lets her get away with anything she wants; 1958. (*c*)

Autumn Leaves √
If you can suspend your disbelief and imagine Joan Crawford making her disturbed husband (Cliff Robertson) well

again by exposing roots of his mental trouble. (Vera Miles, first wife; Lorne Greene, father), you'll enjoy this 1956 weepie directed by Robert Aldrich. She's marvellous, of course. (*b/w*)

Away All Boats   ✕
Turn the sound down if walls are thin as guns blast away incessantly in this dreadfully heroic action 1956 naval war movie. Lex Barker (ex-Tarzan) swims, Jeff Chandler fights, Japanese kami-kazes commit hari-kari, Joseph Peveny directs. (*c*)

The Awful Truth   ✓✓
Classic comedy with Irene Dunne and Cary Grant divorcing-making up, was written–directed–produced by Leo McCarey and it won him 1937 Oscar. Ray Milland and Jane Wyman remade it as *Let's Do It Again*. (*b/w*)

Babes in Arms   ✓✓
First Mickey Rooney–Judy Garland partnership musical under the great choreographer and here director Busby Berkeley; Rooney dominates even the old-timers like Charles Winninger and Guy Kibbee, but ultimately the success is due to Rodgers & Hart's and others' Lady Is a Tramp, Where or When, You Are My Lucky Star, I Cried for You, I'm Just Wild About Harry, etc., etc.; 1939. (*b/w*)

Vanessa Redgrave in *Blow-up*

Baby Doll √√
It's a bit sad that all that's passed into the mythology about this smashing evocation of poor-white South are Carroll Baker's nightdress and thumb-sucking; there's much else to admire, not least Tennessee Williams' cunning script and Elia Kazan's steamy direction; Eli Wallach as fast-talking stranger seducing Baby Doll is every city slicker, and Karl Malden was never better; 1956. (*b/w*)

Baby, The Rain Must Fall √√
Steve McQueen as a man just released from prison with all the uncertainties of the future … Lee Remick as his wife, coming to him with the daughter he has never seen … Don Murray as the solid deputy he grew up with … the flat, desolate landscape of Texas. A beautiful start for a distinguished film by Robert Mulligan, produced by him and Alan J. Pakula in 1965. Perhaps we could see the full version? It was shortened by 12 minutes for British distribution. (*b/w*)

The Baby and the Battleship √
Happy cast of jolly tars enjoy themselves in this harmless comedy about a child smuggled aboard; John Mills, Richard Attenborough, Bryan Forbes, Lionel Jeffries, Gordon Jackson, Michael Hordern, Kenneth Griffith sent up conventional naval heroics under Jay Lewis; 1956. (*b/w*)

Baby Face Nelson √√
Mickey Rooney remarkably convincing under Don Siegel's direction as Public Enemy No 1. Exciting stuff, using some authentic facts; 1957. (*b/w*)

Bachelor Flat ×customize×
Sure is. Flat. Terry-Thomas finds that grinning and grimacing isn't enough to get him by in Hollywood; Celeste Holm as fiancée and Tuesday Weld as her daughter waltz rings round him as visiting archaeologist in southern Cali-fornia. Frank Tashlin directed and co-wrote in his usual slap-happy way; 1962. (*c*)

Bachelor in Paradise ×
Bob Hope as writer living out a kind of Peyton Place existence to provide him with copy. Lana Turner decorative; Paula Prentiss, Janis Paige, Agnes Moorehead among married ladies on hand. Jack Arnold directed; 1961. (*c*)

Bachelor Mother √√
Ginger Rogers finds a baby, and employer Charles Coburn gives her back her sacked job in sympathy, thinking she's the Mum. From then on, complications proliferate as David Niven falls for her. This 1939 riot, directed by Garson Kanin, was later remade, less successfully, as Bundle of Joy. (*b/w*)

Bachelor of Hearts ××
Wolf Willa's mild May Ball goings-on with Sylvia Syms and Hardy Kruger; 1958. (*c*)

Bachelor Party √√
In the wake of *Marty*'s success, Hollywood thought that every Paddy Chayevsky teleplay would be a goldmine if opened out on the big screen. Alas, this 1957 version, also directed by Marty's Delbert Mann, didn't deliver at the box office, but was still a superior fiction, with Don Murray accepting marriage in the course of his stag party. Carolyn Jones turned in a fine performance as a philosophising whore. The British censor cut scene showing men's reactions to stag movie—maybe TV could put it back, please? (*b/w*)

Back Door to Hell ×
Supposedly about conflicts among three American soldiers and between them and Philippino guerrilla leader during second world war, it may also by implication be about conflicts in Viet Nam; directed by Monte Hellman on tiny budget; 1965. (*b/w*)

Back from Eternity ✕
Plane crash in jungle picture with Robert Ryan, Rod Steiger, Anita Ekberg, Gene Barry, Fred Clark among quarrelling, loving stranded; John Farrow; 1956. *(b/w)*

Backlash ✕
Richard Widmark hunting his father's murderer in Western which gets superior John Sturges treatment, but is let down by Donna Reed as widow he tangles with; 1956 *(c)*

Back Street ✕
Fannie Hurst's archetypal soap-opera story about the 'other woman' has been filmed three times: (1) 1932, with John Boles and Irene Dunne, director John M. Stahl; (2) 1941, with Charles Boyer and Margaret Sullavan, director Robert Stevenson; (3) 1961, with John Gavin and Susan Hayward, director David Miller. Pity the only one that's likely to bathe your small screen in tears is No 3. *(c)*

Back To Bataan ✕
John Wayne winning the war again, this time in the Pacific, leading the guerrilla band he forms to help the Yanks; Anthony Quinn adds his clumsy two-centsworth; Edward Dmytryk proving his patriotism in 1945. *(b/w)*

Back to God's Country ✕
Steve Cochran trying to murder Rock Hudson for his wife Marcia Henderson and cargo of furs; can brave dog Wapi stop him? Joseph Pevney churned this out in 1953. *(b/w)*

The Bad and the Beautiful √
One of those movies that pretend to take the lid off the movie-world but really keep it tightly on. Kirk Douglas is supposed to be director who's a shit, and Vincente Minnelli has surrounded him with a splendid cast of haters: Lana Turner, Walter Pidgeon, Dick Powell, Gloria Grahame. But, despite Charles Schnee's acerbic script it just doesn't gel. It won a lot of Oscars in 1952 (best support–Grahame; script; photography art direction; costumes) but if it had been truer to life, would Hollywood have voted for it? *(b/w)*

Bad Day at Black Rock √√
Why the hostility when Spencer Tracy gets off the train at this God-forsaken Western town to deliver a medal? The answer is chilling, exciting, suspenseful; besides the superb Tracy, John Sturges' 1954 cast included Ernest Borgnine, Lee Marvin, Robert Ryan, Walter Brennan. *(c)*

Bad for Each Other ✕
In what must have been very strange 1953 partnership Irving (*Carpetbaggers*) Wallace and Horace (*They Shoot Horses, Don't They?*) McCoy came up with this light exposé of the risks run by society doctors when they forget their Hippo oaths. Unfortunately, neither Charlton Heston as the hero nor Lizabeth Scott as society gal, can do more than look pretty; only Ray Collins gives it the real acid and director Irving Rapper lets it fall through his fingers. *(b/w)*

The Badlanders ✕
Alan Ladd and Ernest Borgnine get their own back on horrid rancher Kent Smith by robbing him of his gold and his girl, Claire Kelly; Delmer Davies directed from W. R. Burnett novel, the moral of which seems to be that old Hollywood morality–it's OK to steal if your victim is a baddie; 1958. *(c)*

Bad Lord Byron ✕✕
They said it–sure is, bad. The poet on his death bed remembers his life well, what David Macdonald insists it was, anyway. The biographies tell it differently. Dennis Price miscast, Joan Greenwood camps her way through it, Mai Zetterling limps along with old clubfoot; 1949. *(b/w)*

Badman's Territory ✕
Randolph Scott forcing law and order on tough town; Tim Whelan; 1946. (*b/w*)

The Bad Seed ✕
Enough to send all environmental-influence believers wailing into the night, this shocker's thesis is that some kids (this one especially) are Born Bad. Such unscientific rubbish enables director-producer Mervyn LeRoy to have apparently sweet little Patty McCormack wreak havoc all round her. You won't believe the ending, but if you've got any sense you won't believe the beginning, either; 1956. (*b/w*)

The Baited Trap ✓
Richard Widmark agonisingly bringing his father's murderers to justice; Norman Panama had Lee J. Cobb and unusual setting of lonely desert town going for him; 1958. (*b/w*)

The Balcony ✓✓
Very X-y version of the Genet play, set in brothel during a revolution. Fantastic is a literal description for once. Shelley Winters is the Madame, Peter Falk the Police Chief, Leonard Nimoy leader of the revolutionaries. Directed by Joseph Strick; 1962. (*b/w*)

Ballad in Blue ✕
Not content with a blind star, Ray Charles, Paul Henreid has a blind boy (Piers Bishop, only acting), to make it difficult for you to turn a blind eye. Mary Peach and Tom Bell play parents who are brought together again by Ray Charles' friendship with their son. It's all a bit tearful, but the songs are good; 1965. (*b/w*)

Ball of Fire ✓✓
If this lark about dancer Barbara Stanwyck moving in with eight professors, including Gary Cooper, reminds you of Snow White, the resemblance isn't coincidental. Excuse is, he's studying slang. Howard Hawks at his zingiest; 1941. (*b/w*)

Bandido ✓
Robert Mitchum in Butch Cassidy country, trying to make a bit on the side out of the 1916 Mexican revolution; Richard Fleischer directs with a sense of fun; 1956 (*c*)

The Bandit of Zhobe ✕✕
Victor Mature as an unlikely Indian tribal chief is duped into fighting the British—or nearly; Anthony Newley, Walter Gotell, Norman Wooland go through the motions under John Gilling's automatic direction; 1959. (*c*)

Band of Angels ✕
Comic-strip values make this attempt at showing life during the Civil War into a strictly two-dimensional flop, despite presence of Clark Gable. Yvonne de Carlo as once-rich high yaller gal is sold into slavery. Raoul Walsh permits all kind of excesses except the interesting ones, and Sidney Poitier's educated slave is just embarrassing. A long way from the Robert Penn Warren novel; 1957. (*c*)

Bandolero! ✓
Superior Western with James Stewart beginning by impersonating the official hangman in order to free his brother (Dean Martin) and gang; George Kennedy is sheriff, Raquel Welch decorative but dispiriting love interest; Andrew McLagen and several of the others who worked on the earlier Shenandoah were reunited for this 1968 show. (*c*)

The Band Wagon ✓
Made in 1953 by Vincente Minnelli at his most energetic, this teaming of Fred Astaire and Jack Buchanan in a backstage musical was a critics' delight, but never got off the ground at the box-

office. Hard to see why, as it also had Cyd Charisse, whose legs dazzle. (*c*)

Bang! You're Dead √
Little boy with passion for guns mistakenly kills; crime blamed on another man. Jack Warner, Gordon Harker in surprisingly sensitive period piece (1953), directed by Lance Comfort. (*b/w*)

Bang, Bang, You're Dead × ×
Basically British spy movie shot partly in Morocco with American Tony Randall to make it palatable to Stateside audiences, but it would take more than even his charming talents. Producer Harry Alan Towers collected a cast of well-known if inferior talents (Senta Berger, Herbert Lom, Terry-Thomas) but director Don Sharp couldn't make Peter Yeldham's frantic chase script work; 1966. (*c*)

The Bank Dick √ √
Often cited as W. C. Fields' best movie, it's the one where he is made a guard after capturing a bank robber accidentally. In the opening, he tears the American family myth apart, and there's a splendid chase up a mountain. Made in 1941 by Eddie Cline; four years later, he was dead. (*b/w*)

Banning ×
This eponymously-titled drama has the unusual setting of a golf course as Robert Wagner tries to win the tournament and pick the right girl among those smuggling themselves into his golf-bag. Jill St John naturally loses to the less obvious Anjanette Comer; Ron Winston directs James Lee's neat script neatly; 1967. (*c*)

Barabbas × ×
Long, heavy, ultimately off-putting speculation as to what might have been the life of the thief saved from the cross when Jesus was crucified. In the end, he's crucified anyway. Anthony Quinn seems to be enjoying all the flagellation under the moans and groans, and Silvano Mangano, Arthur Kennedy, Jack Palance, Ernest Borgnine appear to be under delusion they are partaking in an Important Picture. Alas, despite the deeply-buried respectable origins (Pär Lagerkvist's novel) director Richard Fleischer drowns in a load of tomato-ketchup gore; 1962. (*c*)

Barbarella √
Sexy comic strip heroine provocatively brought to life by Jane Fonda under Roger Vadim's hand; great fun; 1968. (*c*)

The Barbarian and the Geisha ×
If you tried really hard you couldn't find an actor less fitted to play the man who opened up Japan to the rest of the world, the first American consul, Townsend Harris, than—you'll never guess—John Wayne. Quite why John Huston allowed his otherwise beautiful picture to be made ludicruous by this casting probably lies buried in one of Hollywood's skeleton-cupboards; 1958. (*c*)

The Barefoot Contessa √
Flashbacking biography of beautiful (if you like the type) movie star played by Ava Gardner, cynically promoted by producer Humphrey Bogart and press agent Edmond O'Brien (he won an Oscar for this), but still remaining the simple, barefoot girl they found dancing in Spain (oh yeah?). 1953 location shooting had another star around, who wasn't in the picture but was in love with Ava—Frank Sinatra. Joseph L. Makiewicz turned in pro job, but there's no real heart there. (*c*)

Barefoot in the Park √
Some very funny moments, linked together with a thin story line about newlyweds in walk-up apartment, from Neil Simon play. Robert Redford, Jane Fonda, Mildred Natwick are all treats;

Gene Saks hasn't directed the funniest film ever, but it's good enough for a few laughs, so don't complain; 1966. (*c*)

The Barkleys of Broadway ✗
Fred Astaire and Ginger Rogers teamed up again in 1949 after ten years apart to make this mild behind-the-scenes musical with a relatively undistinguished Henry Warren score; they play double-act that splits up only to find that . . . well, you know. Oscar Levant, Billie Burke hover around. Charles Walters unobtrusively directed. (*c*)

Barnacle Bill √
Called *All at Sea* in America. Neat little 1957 time-filler for Alec Guinness as seasick sailor who buys a pier; T. E. B. Clarke script and Charles Frend direction are impeccable if slightly old-fashioned. Maurice Denham among strong supports. (*b/w*)

The Baron of Arizona √
Vincent Price as land-grabbing heavy in slightly out-of-the-rut Western directed by latter-day cult figure Samuel Fuller; Beulah Bondi; 1950. (*b/w*)

The Barretts of Wimpole Street √
(1) 1934 version starred Charles Laughton as father, Norma Shearer as Elizabeth, Fredric March as Robert Browning, directed by Sidney Franklin, was a wild success. (*b/w*)

The Barretts of Wimpole Street ✗✗
(2) 1957 version with John Gielgud, Jennifer Jones, Bill Travers was dismal flop (unsurprising, seeing who was playing the young lovers), although Sidney Franklin was still in there pitching. (*c*)

The Bat ✗
Agnes Moorehead, least appreciated great actress of the American screen, goes all-too-competently through the motions as lady terrified by masked prowler. Could it be Vincent Price? Gavin Gordon? John Sutton? Richard Nixon? Crane Wilbur directed; 1959. (*b/w*)

Bataan ✗
Routine 1943 war story with Robert Taylor and the American army bravely running away; Senator George Murphy, millionaire Desi Arnez among them. Tay Garnett manfully directed. (*b/w*)

Bathing Beauty ✗✗
Awful musical about Esther Williams pursued by jilted husband enrolling at her girls' school. Pity Basil Rathbone. George Sidney shows his embarrassment in directing it fluffily; 1944. (*c*)

Batman √
Caped crusader Adam West and his little buddy Robin from the TV series in full-length feature, introducing all the favourite villains – Catwoman Lee Meriweather, Joker Cesar Romero, Penguin Burgess Meredith, Riddler Frank Gorshin; director, Leslie H. Martinson; 1965. (*c*)

Battle Circus ✗
Humphrey Bogart fought many a tough scrap in his screen life, but none more taxing than this one with dreadful script and a downright embarrassing performance by cutie June Allyson as his nurse girlfriend. It's all about a medical unit in Korea; Richard Brooks directed his own wordy script reverently but it's hollow stuff; 1953. (*b/w*)

Battle Cry ✗
The cry concerned being 'tell it to the Marines!' That tough, hard-drinking, hard-swearing outfit of professionals must laugh when they see sentimental cliché versions of their lives like this one by Raoul Walsh, from Leon (*Exodus*) Uris' script. It purports to follow careers from rookies to battle-hardened veterans, with interludes with

girlfriends Dorothy Malone (Tab Hunter's) and Nancy Olson (Aldo Ray's), 1955. (*c*)

The Battle for Anzio   ✕
Just another war picture, tricked out with the pretence that it's about Robert Mitchum's search for why men risk death for their country; Edward Dmytryk was, perhaps, kidding himself. He won't kid you; 1968. (*c*)

Battleground   ✕
Somebody must like war pictures–if you're among them this is for you: Van Johnson and John Hodiak fighting their way through France, set in 1944, made five years later; director William Wellman. (*b/w*)

Battle Hell   ✕
Richard Todd keeping his upper lip stiff in naval drama done documentary style. Michael Anderson; 1956. (*b/w*)

Battle Hymn   ✕✕
Flying Parson Colonel Dean Hess is made the object of a panegyric positively Victorian in its sentimental prettifying. He certainly did great work for Korean orphans in between making them orphans, but director Douglas Sirk and stalwart Rock Hudson combine to turn him into improbable perfection; 1957. (*c*)

Battle of Britain   ✕
Considering the resources and the cast (Olivier, Michael Caine, Trevor Howard, Redgrave, Richardson, Robert Shaw *et al.*), Guy Hamilton came up with the stinker of 1969. Blame partly the feeble script, partly lack of imagination in the air sequences. (*c*)

Battle of Rogue River   ✕
Action-starved Western about Oregon seeking statehood in 1850 but needing Indian truce first; only George Montgomery really wants sincere peace. William Castle; 1954. (*c*)

Battle of the Bulge   ✕
Or rather, one small incident in it, involving Henry Fonda, Robert Shaw, Robert Ryan, Dana Andrews. Ken Annakin makes it all very old-fashioned for 1965, and any deeper message has been allowed to remain buried. (*c*)

Battle of the Coral Sea   ✕
Cliff Robertson as submarine commander caught by the Japs escaping with enough info to help the freedom-lovers to win the eponymous battle; Paul Wendkos: 1959. (*b/w*)

Battle of the River Plate   ✓
Navally fine, personally wanting, account of early British victory in second world war; John Gregson, Anthony Quayle, Peter Finch, Patrick MacNee, Christopher Lee presented more as types than people by Michael Powell and Emeric Pressburger; 1956. (*c*)

Battle of the Sexes   ✓
Perhaps Peter Sellers' best film; he had Charles Crichton directing him in this 1960 story of American business efficiency expert, Constance Cummings, invading the tweed firm where he works, driving him to thoughts of murder. Plus Robert Morley, Ernest Thesiger, Donald Pleasence, William Mervyn. (*b/w*)

Battle of the V1   ✕✕✕
Nasty novelettish 1958 reconstruction of Polish underground wink-tipping to England that Germans are making flying bombs there. Pretends it's factual, but isn't. Vernon Sewell directs Michael Rennie, Patricia Medina. (*b/w*)

The Battle of the Villa Fiorita   ✕✕
One of those sickly dramas about children of divorcing couple screwing up the proceedings. Delmer Daves directed Maureen O'Hara, Rossano Brazzi, Richard Todd, Phyllis Calvert in 1965. (*c*)

Battle on the Beach ✕
Japanese attack on the Philippines seems important mainly because it makes up the mind of Dolores Michaels whether she prefers her American husband or local guerrilla leader; Audie Murphy, Gary Crosby pick their way through the battle lines and script lines, both equally fatal; Herbert Coleman; 1961. (*c*)

The Beachcomber √
(1) 1938 version was notable for superb performance by Charles Laughton as lotus-eater and his wife Elsa Lanchester as missionary; Erich Pommer directed. (*b/w*)

The Beachcomber ✕✕
(2) 1955 saw ham-fisted attempt by Sydney and Muriel Box to improve on the original, with swaying Robert Newton in the Laughton part and Glynis Johns the plum-and-prune reformer; Donald Pleasence, who played small part, would have been better lead. (*c*)

Beachhead ✕
Tony Curtis and Frank Lovejoy as two American soldiers outwitting Japanese in wartime Hawaii to get vital info to HQ. Unfortunately for the action they get mixed up with Mary Murphy as French planter's daughter and her 'lovable character' of a father. Stuart Heisler should have known better; 1954 (*c*)

The Beast from 20,000 Fathoms √
1953 classic of science-fiction film-making, allegedly based on Ray Bradbury's story, *The Foghorn,* but the poignant idea of foghorn and sea monster communicating has gone and only King-Kongruous 'Loch Lomond Monster' (*sic*) remains. Super effects from director Eugene Lourie on skimped budget. (*b/w*)

Beast With Five Fingers √
The idea of a hand, unjoined to human body, with a life of its own is pretty horrifying, and Robert Florey's 1947 invention packs a powerful charge. Peter Lorre watches it play Bach, wriggle across the floor, disarrange a bookshelf. In the climax, he vainly attempts to nail it to a table, then the most awful thing of all happens ... Florey had intended to show it was all in Lorre's imagination, but Jack Warner cut all the 'flim-flam' out. (*b/w*)

Beat the Devil √
Thoroughly indulgent spoof of con-men after uranium; the joke is supposed to be that nobody – not even scriptwriter Truman Capote and director John Huston – knows what's going on. Throwing all attempt at coherence to the winds, Humphrey Bogart, Robert Morley, Peter Lorre, Gina Lollobrigida enjoy themselves. Jennifer Jones seems to have wandered in from a more dramatic picture. But somehow it's amusing, if you enjoy other people's clever home movies; 1954. (*b/w*)

Beau Brummell ✕✕
Highly embarrassing for all concerned – Stewart Granger as Beau, Elizabeth Taylor as his belle, Peter Ustinov as fat Prinny, Robert Morley, Rosemary Harris. Director Curtis Bernhardt presumably wasn't upset; after all, it's his baby, although Karl Tunberg must take the blame for the dreadful script; 1954. (*c*)

Beau Geste √
(1) 1939 remake of Ronald Colman classic has Gary Cooper, Ray Milland, Robert Preston as Foreign Legion brothers up against tough sergeant Brian Donlevy and desert hordes. (*b/w*)

Beau Geste ✕
(2) 1965 director-writer Douglas Heyes has ignored the possibilities in original P. C. Wren book of asking when should a man rebel and settled for a routine

adventure; unfortunately, he hasn't even managed that very well, and the result is a bit of a bore with Telly Savalas, Guy Stockwell and others playing a caricature Foreign Legion yarn that hasn't even got the virtue of satire. (*c*)

Beau James ✕
Poor attempt to retell New York mayor Jimmy Walker's story with Bob Hope, Paul Douglas, Alexis Smith, directed by Mel Shavelson; 1957. (*c*)

The Beautiful Blonde from Bashful Bend ✕
Preston Sturges disappointment, meant to be satire on Western musicals but let down by flabby Betty Grable as Annie Oakley-type character. Cesar Romero, Rudy Vallee; 1949. (*c*)

Beautiful Stranger ✕
Ginger Rogers upsetting Stanley Baker on the Riviera by falling in love with Jacques Bergerac (real-life husband); David Miller doesn't really rise to his star and the occasion; 1953. (*b/w*)

Because of You ✕
Loretta Young conceals her (not very terrible) past from husband Jeff Chandler, who reels around as though she's admitted to being Eva Braun, escaped from Hitler's bunker. Joseph Pevney directs with a desperate pretence that it all makes sense; 1952. (*b/w*)

Becket √
Don't expect to see the epic spectacular the posters (and perhaps the trailers TV may still run ahead of it) promised, although with Peter O'Toole and Richard Burton starring you might expect it. This is an extended chat between weak Henry II and Burton's correct Archbishop of Canterbury, often witty, set prettily by Peter Glenville who rather lets the stars get on with their own ideas. From Jean Anouilh's play, not the historical records; 1964. (*c*)

Bedevilled ✕
Paris locations lift this out of its deep rut of silly plot about night club singer (Anne Baxter) fleeing scene of murder helped by postulant (Steve Forrest), but not far enough. Mitchell Leisen, subject of some cult worship, directs; 1955.

The Bedford Incident √
Magazine reporter Sidney Poitier nearly screws up wartime mission in which destroyer commander Richard Widmark hunts German sub with Ahab-like determination. Apart from plot extravagances, this is well-directed by producer James B. Harris with claustrophobic strength; Martin Balsam turns in particularly unlikeable but convincing portrayal of ship's doctor: 1955. (*b/w*)

Bedtime Story √
Tasteless but funny con-men comedy with Marlon Brando and David Niven out-smarting each other on the Riviera; Ralph Levy; 1964. (*c*)

Before Winter Comes ✕
Padded story of multilingual would-be defector (Topol) in 1945 Displaced Persons' camp; with David Niven and John Hurt as British representatives and Anna Karina as dragged-in love interest. J. Lee Thompson fails to make it matter; 1969. (*c*)

The Beggar's Opera ✕
Olivier is Macheath in Peter Brook's first major film, 1953. Lacks the confidence of his later work, and Stanley Holloway, Dorothy Tutin, George Devine can't turn it into more than tuppenny opera. (*b/w*)

Behind the Mask ✕
Surgeon's, that is; Michael Redgrave and Niall McGinnis as opposing surgeons, Tony Britton as honest young doctor; Vanessa Redgrave in small

part (it was made in 1958); director Brian Desmond Hurst is more fascinated by the details of a heart operation than all viewers will be. (*c*)

Behemoth The Sea Monster   ✕
If only a bit more trouble and expense had been taken over the model of the 'monster' this sci-fi of London threatened by Thames-cruising bit of prehistory might have been really exciting. As it is, Gene Evans and André Morell seem to be excited over a largely imaginary fear; directors Douglas Hickox and E. Lourie; 1959. (*b/w*)

Behold A Pale Horse   √
Gregory Peck as former Spanish Republican fighter and Anthony Quinn as civil guard captain for Franco are well-matched in this Basquerade; unfortunately, Fred Zinnemann has let the milky ideological chit-chat get in the way of the action; 1964. (*b/w*)

Bell, Book and Candle   √
James Stewart, Jack Lemmon, Ernie Kovacs, Elsa Lanchester, Hermione Gingold carry miscast Kim Novak as modern witch in a funny 1958 version of John van Druten play. Richard Quine does his best as director. (*c*)

The Bellboy   ✕
Jerry Lewis is writer-producer-director-star of this collection of short sketches about Miami's ghastly Fountain Blue (they spell it Fontainebleau) Hotel. Despite occasional sniggers, he misses the chance to satirise the awfulness of the place; 1960. (*b/w*)

The Belle of New York   ✕
The old operetta about life in the nineties doesn't make a very inspiring vehicle for Fred Astaire (already 53 in 1952) and Vera-Ellen, who had to have her songs dubbed by Anita Ellis. He's playboy, she's Salvation Army-type, you're yawning. Charles Walters does

his very best to put some zing in it, but he's defeated by the material of most of the cast. (*c*)

The Belles of St Trinian's   √
Alastair Sim in double role of headmistress and bookie; George Cole, Joyce Grenfell plus younger versions of Beryl Reid, Joan Sims, Hermione Baddeley (it was made in 1954) as Searle's schoolteachers. Director, part writer-producer, Frank Launder. (*b/w*)

Belles on Their Toes   √
Sequel to *Cheaper by the Dozen* lacks Clifton Webb; instead, Myrna Loy is working widow bringing up the brood, coping with love-affairs and sundry domestic dramas, but not stepping outside the never-never land of the studio re-creation of turn of the century middle America. Jeanne Crain, Debra Paget are insipid Belles; Edward Arnold is surrogate father figure. Director Henry Levin; 1952. (*c*)

A Bell for Adano   ✕
Sentimental stuff about nice kind Americans finding church bell for war-torn Italian village; William Bendix. Directed by Henry King, 1945, when it was much praised. (*b/w*)

The Bells are Ringing   √
Judy Holliday carries this slight musical comedy about a girl who runs a telephone answering service and organises the lives of her clients, especially Dean Martin (terrible in his part). Saved by Vincente Minnelli's briskness as director, two songs (Just in Time, The Party's Over) and the incomparable, much-mourned Judy, whose final film (1960, five years before her death), this was. (*c*)

The Bells of St Mary's   ✕
Sickly affair with Ingrid Bergman as chirpy nun out-cloying even Bing Crosby's priest in their joint efforts to raise money for school. Even (particu-

larly?) Irish catholics will find it too much. Leo McCarey produced and directed, doubtless laughing all the way to church; 1945. (*b/w*)

Beloved Infidel × ×
Sheilah Graham's side of the last years of Scott Fitzgerald, mawkishly screened in 1959 by a running-scared (of the facts, the screenplay and Cinema-Scope) Henry King, and starring a self-conscious Gregory Peck and Deborah Kerr. It starts on note of high comedy with the Marquis of Donegal, 'her fiancé', waving sadly goodbye on the dock, but soon stumbles. Oh, if only Scott could write his version. (*c*)

Be My Guest ×
1965 pop scene comedies tend to be as depressing as yesterday's mashed potatoes, but this one, directed-produced by Lance Comfort with David Hemming as newspaper - reporter - cum - musician, might just stand up. (*b/w*)

Bend of the River √
James Stewart and Arthur Kennedy make splendid sparring partners in this superior Western about the battles between miners and farmers. ITV film editors looking for cuts, please excise the intrusive, degrading scenes where Stepin' Fetchit libels his own race. Otherwise, Anthony Mann makes an impeccable, exciting job: 1952. (*c*)

Beneath the Twelve-mile Reef × ×
Sponge-fishermen fight between themselves off Florida, and it's hard to get involved. Pallid romance between boy (Robert Wagner) of one and girl (Terry Moore) of other, doesn't help. Only J. Carrol Naish and underwater filming flicks the interest in otherwise poor show by Robert D. Webb; 1953. (*c*)

Bengal Rifles ×
Rock Hudson in Lancer (Bengal division) territory, fighting both rotten officers and the Rajah; Laslo Benedek; 1953. (*c*)

The Benny Goodman Story ×
Boring biopic of bandleader, sketchily impersonated by Steve Allen. The music's good to listen to, if that's your era. Writer-director Valentine Davies settles for shots and lines he and (and we) have seen too often before; 1956. (*c*)

Best Foot Forward √
June Allyson's 1943 debut as high school kid, also Nancy Walker's as the ugly girl, when Lucille Ball as film star accepts boy's invitation to graduation dance; Edward Buzzell made it buzz. (*c*)

The Best House in London × ×
A really dreadful attempt to squeeze some humorous mileage out of the idea that the whores of the 19th century weren't driven to it by unspeakable social conditions but because they were really nymphomaniacs. One David Hemmings in this sort of nonsense is bad enough, but he plays a double role, which is much too much. Philip Saville has cast badly all through (except Joanna Pettet, in a thankless role), and there is no point in listing the rather inferior players who turn in decidedly inferior performances. Denis Norden is credited with the script, which is surprising; 1969. (*c*)

The Best Man √ √
Gripping battle between Henry Fonda and Cliff Robertson for presidential nomination makes gorgeous 'in' movie from Gore Vidal's play. Franklin Schaffner's cast is impressive–Edie Adams, Margaret Leighton, Shelley Berman, Lee Tracy, Ann Sothern, Gene Raymond, Richard Arlen, Mahalia Jackson–and proved, in 1964, that the old-timers could more than hold their own. (*b/w*)

The Best of Enemies √
Underrated anti-war movie using comic battle between British commander David Niven and Italian opposite number Alberto Sordi to point out ironies. Harry Andrews strong support in Guy Hamilton's slightly soft direction of Jack Pulman's script; 1962. (*b/w*)

Best of the Badmen ✗
Ex-Union officer becomes outlaw: Robert Ryan in grimly strong performance matched by Claire Trevor, Walter Brennan in William Russell's 1951 actioner. (*c*)

The Best Things in Life Are Free √
Biopic of songwriters Buddy De Sylva, Lew Brown and Ray Henderson (never heard of them? they wrote Sonny Boy, Button Up Your Overcoat, Sunny Side Up, If I had a Talking Picture of Yoo-oo; all here) played decorously by Ernest Borgnine, Dan Dailey, Gordon MacRae; director Michael Curtiz makes it pleasing entertainment, but the John O'Hara original story seems to have been softened up somewhat; 1956. (*c*)

Betrayed ✗
Can you care whether Lana Turner as improbable Dutch resistance worker was a two-timer? Clark Gable has to, in this dull plot, and looks suitably fed up with having to go through the motions. It suits Victor Mature's solid style of unimaginative acting much better. He's American liberator—rah, rah, rah. Gottfried Reinhardt provides some nice locations in Holland to look at; 1954. (*c*)

Between Heaven and Hell ✗
War film about sergeant under neurotic officer, Robert Wagner, Broderick Crawford, Frank Gorshin; director Richard Fleischer at least makes the battle scenes fairly exciting; 1956. (*c*)

Beyond a Reasonable Doubt √
Dana Andrews as newspaperman making the mistake of setting himself up as innocent victim of miscarriage of justice so that he can prove inefficiency of the system; instead, as you can guess, it's his alibi that goes wrong; Fritz Lang makes it almost credible and very exciting, with help from Joan Fontaine, Sidney Blackmer; 1956. (*b/w*)

Beyond the Curtain ✗ ✗
Eva Bartok unconvincingly searching for brother in East Germany; Richard Greene, Marius Goring, Andree Melly uncomfortably involved. Compton Bennett; 1961. (*b/w*)

Beyond the Forest √
Bette Davis in apotheosis of a part as small-town wife of worthy Joseph Cotten who kicks over the traces and follows a discouraging David Brian to Chicago, where terrible fates await her. She is marvellous, far larger than life but lighting up the whole screen with her erotic vitality. King Vidor was content to give her the chances, knowing that she'd take them—and how; 1949. (*b/w*)

Beyond this Place ✗ ✗
Van Johnson in England trying to prove father's innocence; Vera Miles, Emlyn Williams, Bernard Lee; directed by former top cameraman Jack Cardiff; 1958. (*b/w*)

Bhowani Junction √
Stewart Granger as British colonel loves unsuitable Ava Gardner as the riots explode in British withdrawal from India—filmed in Pakistan; George Cukor uncomfortably emphasises more questionable aspects of John Masters novel; 1956. (*c*)

The Bible . . . In the Beginning ✗
John Huston only managed to get to the 23rd chapter of Genesis before quitting, and that took him 174 minutes in the cinema. You may not wait so long. It has all the faults of the epic: portentous,

picture-book script by Christopher Fry; fancy-dress performances from Richard Harris, Stephen Boyd, George C. Scott, Peter O'Toole and Huston himself. The original's better and quicker; 1965. (*c*)

The Bigamist √
Ida Lupino directs/acts in this serious soaper as bigamous wife of Edmond O'Brien, trapped into marrying her out of compassion because she's pregnant; Joan Fontaine real wife; 1953. (*b/w*)

The Big Bankroll × ×
One of Diana Dors' ghastly Hollywood films – gangsters and politicians in the twenties, directed by Joseph Newman, with Jack Carson and David Janssen; 1961. (*b/w*)

The Big Caper √
Starts well, with Rory Calhoun and Mary Costa posing as man and wife while casing small town for dynamiting and pay-or-else threat, but goes to pieces when the friendliness of the townspeople softens their hearts and they want to switch. Robert Stevens fails to lift it directorially; 1957. (*b/w*)

The Big Circus ×
Five-ringed circus extravaganza with real acts stealing the show from frowsty old plot about bankruptcy and lions turned loose by rival. Climax of wire-walk attempt over Niagara Falls is well-directed by Joseph M. Newman, however. But Victor Mature, Red Buttons are weak, Vincent Price, Gilbert Roland adequate; 1959. (*c*)

The Big Clock √ √
When Charles Laughton as the head of a huge publishing empire murders his mistress, he is forced to track down the only witness, a man glimpsed on a stairway. But Ray Milland, picked for the job of tracking the witness down, is himself his prey. Wonderfully conceived, imaginatively shot by John Farrow, and full of the ironies of power, this makes

an unusual, almost expressionist film to come out of America; 1948. (*b/w*)

The Big Combo ×
For some reason, police lootenant Cornel Wilde and gangster Richard Conte are both potty about the limpid Jean Wallace; director Joseph Lewis does his best to make it exciting, but you get the feeling that all concerned know it's just fatty ham; 1955. (*b/w*)

The Big Country √ √
'There are better Westerns, but it is difficult to think of many which have been more enjoyable', say Michael Parkinson and Clyde Jeavons in their *Pictorial History of Westerns*. Burl Ives won 1958 Oscar for his performance as cattle baron; Gregory Peck, Carroll Baker, Charlton Heston, Jean Simmons blossomed under William Wyler's direction. (*c*)

Big Deal at Dodge City √ √
Poker movie in the style of *The Cincinnati Kid*, this time with Henry Fonda as compulsive gambler disregarding his little kid's plea not to risk all his money in a compulsive (for us) game with Paul Ford, Jason Robards, Charles Bickford, Kevin McCarthy *et al.* Joanne Woodward, Burgess Meredith, Chester Conklin, contribute to the excitement, and director-producer Fielder Cook has pulled off what should be even better on TV than the big screen; 1965. (*c*)

The Big Gamble ×
Three would-be but never-were stars, Stephen Boyd, Juliette Greco, David Wayne, in a routine man-against-the-jungle epic which Richard Fleischer does his best to make exciting. But you feel that this was just one more excuse in 1961 for producer Darryl F. Zanuck to take La Greco on safari. (*c*)

Bigger than Life √
Unwarranted attack on cortisone, taken

from *New Yorker* article; James Mason needs it to keep going and he takes too much of it, thus upsetting his body and his family. Nicholas Ray has since (it was made in 1956) admitted that he made a big mistake in naming the drug; he had meant to make the point that people accept 'miracle cures' too easily. (*c*)

The Biggest Bundle of Them All ✕
Edward G. Robinson, Robert Wagner, Godfrey Cambridge wasted in Ken Annakin's failure to put some zip into a story of three capers; Vittorio de Sica and Raquel Welch are about right weight (very light) for this rather self-indulgent comedy-thriller which fast editing fails to save; 1968. (*c*)

The Big Gundown √
Superior European-made Western about Lee Van Cleef chasing the wrong suspect to a rape and murder. Sergio Sollima makes this consistently worth watching; 1969. (*c*)

The Big Heat √
Corruption in police force, Glenn Ford exposing with Gloria Grahame's aid. Lee Marvin as sadist is encouraged by director Fritz Lang into all sorts of gratuitous violence, including throwing scalding coffee in girl's face. Made in 1953, as old Hollywood codes started breaking down. (*b/w*)

Big House, USA √
Ralph Meeker demands ransom for missing boy, is caught, jailed, pursued by Broderick Crawford and bloodthirsty convicts; Howard W. Koch made two pictures here in effect, neither specially impressive; 1955. (*b/w*)

Big Jim McLain ✕ ✕
John Wayne on his Save-America kick in 1952, prefaces this spy-ring stuff in Hawaii with a solemn dedication to the Un-American Activities Committee who are 'undaunted by the slander against them'. God should have preserved them from their friends, like Wayne and his director Edward Ludwig. (*b/w*)

The Big Job √
Less suggestive than the Carry-Ons, this is a jolly romp about some crooks (Sid James, Dick Emery) trying to get at some loot they have stashed in a tree – now in the police station garden, they find when they get out of jail. Joan Sims is a grasping landlady, Deryck Guyler a police sgt. Gerald Thomas directed; 1965. (*b/w*)

The Big Knife √
Jack Palance is only inadequate player in very low-down on Hollywood drama written by Clifford Odets, who was there and should have known. Rest of the cast: wife Ida Lupino, studio boss Rod Steiger, cover-up publicist Wendell Corey, Jean Hagen, Shelley Winters, Everett Sloane, Ilka Chase all super. But Robert Aldrich never makes it really convincing; 1955. (*b/w*)

The Big Land ✕
Texas cattle raisers want the railroad nearer them and fight for it. What could have been gorgeous epic is shoelaced into routine melo and director Gordon Douglas has to do what he can with cut-price location footage and cut-price acting talent like Alan Ladd and Virginia Mayo. Edmond O'Brien, always better as a heavy, is a goodie here; 1957. (*c*)

The Big Lift ✕
Misguided attempt to salute American flyers who airlifted supplies to Berlin during blockade, has miscast Montgomery Clift falling for German girl Cornell Borchers; Paul Douglas just hates Germans. Writer-director George Seaton can't quite pull it off; 1950. (*b/w*)

Big Money ✕
Ian Carmichael as fumbling scion of a

crooked family; quite good fun, with Robert Helpman, Kathleen Harrison; directed by John Paddy Carstairs; 1957. (*c*)

The Big Operator ✕
Union drama with Mickey Rooney trying to take it over and honest Steve Cochran trying to stop him; Charles Haas must be kidding; 1959. (*b/w*)

The Big Show ✕
Cliff Robertson goes to prison for father Nehemiah Persoff's negligence, emerges to find brother Robert Vaughn conniving to oust him from circus heritage. It should have been taut, exciting, but somehow even the acts seem dull; James B. Clark must accept the blame, 1961.

The Big Sky √
Fur-trappers go up the Missouri in a keel-boat, scrapping along the way. Producer-director Howard Hawks does usual superior job, and has A. B. Guthrie's fine novel, *The Big Star*, as basis. Arthur Hunnicutt out-acts Kirk Douglas (not difficult); 1952. (*b/w*)

The Big Sleep √√
'Neither the author (Raymond Chandler), the writer (William Faulkner), nor myself (Howard Hawks) knew who had  killed whom,' admitted the director of this muddled but otherwise marvellously atmospheric 1946 thriller of society girls (Lauren Bacall, Martha Vickers), drug addict, nymphomaniac (Dorothy Malone, when brunette) and, above all, detective (Humphrey Bogart). (*b/w*)

The Big Store √
Margaret Dumont: I'm afraid after we've been married a while a beautiful young girl will come along and you'll forget all about me. Groucho: Don't be silly—I'll write you twice a week. ... The greatest detective since Sherlock Holmes and his assistants foil a plan to murder the heir to the store ... Charles Riesner; 1941. (*b/w*)

The Big Trees √
Kirk Douglas only slightly less wooden than the Californian redwoods he's so keen to grab for himself in turn-of-the-century California. Felix Feist provides some spectacular shots of the trees, but the rest is strictly splinters; 1952. (*c*)

Billy Liar √√
More than just a marvellous comedy of frustrated adolescence; an all-too-true picture of urban society being sold down the river of false hopes. Only the size of TV screens and the shopping precincts have improved since 1963. John Schlesinger got cracking performances from Mona Washbourne, Helen Fraser, Leonard Rossiter, Wilfred Pickles—and, of course, Tom Courtenay in the title role. Julie Christie as understanding heroine is just too twee, perhaps the fault of Schlesinger who retreated into toothpaste commercials whenever she appeared. (*b/w*)

Billie √
Nearly a good film, as Patty Duke who won a minor award for this best juvenile performance of 1965, embarrasses male supremecist politican father by beating all the high school boys athletically; Jim Backus an asset as Pop; producer-director Don Weiss does highly competent job. (*c*)

Billion-Dollar Brain √
Disappointing Harry Palmer (Michael Caine), ex-Len Deighton, thriller, set in Finland and Texas, with the bespectacled owl agent taking on Karl Malden and Ed Begley. Ken Russell self-indulgently used it as chance to show off some over-bloated effects; 1967. (*c*)

Billy Budd √√
Outstanding sea drama based on Melville's novel of slow-wit sailor (Terence Stamp, with blonde rinse, in his best-

ever part) v. evil master-at-arms (Robert Ryan), with Peter Ustinov taking on just a little too much as director-producer as well as actor–it's his part as captain that suffers, badly needing either another director to sharpen him up or another actor for him to look at more objectively; 1962. (*b/w*)

Birdman of Alcatraz   √ √
Compelling, often touching, 1962 study from John Frankenheimer of Robert Stroud, who became world-famous birdlife authority while serving time for murder. One of Burt Lancaster's best as extraordinary Stroud. (*b/w*)

The Birds   √ √ √
If you think the idea of the bird population turning on us humans is far fetched, know that Daphne du Maurier based her fantasy on a real-life story. A real director's film, with the acting (Tippi Hedren, Rod Taylor) adequate, but all the tricks of angles, editing, perspective, soundtrack, and above all the *trompe l'œil* that the birds really are attacking. Hitchcock at his best; 1963. (*c*)

The Birds and the Bees   √
Mitzi Gaynor as con girl, plus David Niven as her father, make a set at George Gobel (TV funnyman, although you wouldn't know it); if this sounds familiar, it's because you've seen it not only in dozens of other movies but specifically in *The Lady Eve* (1941) when Barbara Stanwyck, Charles Coburn, Henry Fonda played the parts. This 1956 Norman Taurog version just isn't in the same class. (*c*)

Birthday Present   √
Tony Britton makes the mistake of trying a little bit of smuggling for wifey Sylvia Syms in this pleasant low-budgeter directed by Pat Jackson; 1957. (*b/w*)

Birth of the Blues   √
Slight plot of younger (1941) Bing Crosby trying to form Dixieland band in early New Orleans is good enough vehicle for St Louis Blues, St James Infirmary, Melancholy Baby; with Mary Martin and high note from Jack Teagarden. Victor Schertzinger directs. (*b/w*)

The Bishop's Wife   √
Cary Grant as angel sent to help bishop David Niven (odd casting) and especially his wife, Loretta Young; strong supports: Gladys Cooper, James Gleason, Monty Woolley, Elsa Lanchester; Henry Koster; 1947. (*b/w*)

Bitter Harvest   ×
Janet Munro longs for the Big City, but there's tragedy waiting; John Stride, Alan Badel are waiting, too. Peter Graham Scott; 1963. (*c*)

Bitter Sweet   √
Doubtless this will be remade, and better than this sweeter rather than bitter version of Noel Coward operetta with the arch Jeanette MacDonald trilling and Nelson Eddy hohumming; Ian Hunter, George Sanders looking grave but gay, weak but strong, paradoxical but obvious. You'll see it again, never fear. And it won't take much to improve on Woody van Dyke's 1941 version. (*c*)

Bitter Victory   √
Stiff Curt Jurgens awarded medal he didn't earn in raid on Rommel's HQ; Richard Burton had affair with his wife, Ruth Roman. Nicholas Ray's direction (set in 1942, made 1957) disappoints, perhaps because it was made in French and dubbed. But surely Burton & Co spoke English originally? Confusing, like the plot. (*b/w*)

Blackbeard, The Pirate   ×
Hammy Robert Newton captures, pallid Richard Egan frees, simpering Linda Darnell in Raoul Walsh's 1952 swasher. (*c*)

The Blackboard Jungle √
A shocker in its day, this exposure of violent conditions in New York schools now looks as dated as its theme-music, Rock Around the Clock. Richard Brooks got sincere performances from Glenn Ford, Anne Francis in 1955; an absurd sub-sub-Brando one from Vic Morrow. (*b/w*)

The Black Castle √
Not very horror movie with Boris Karloff and Lon Chaney the reasons for Richard Greene's pals going missing on hunting trip. So he goes on the next one. Nathan Juran directed fitfully, 1952.
(*b/w*)

The Black Dakotas ✕
Gary Merrill getting his nasty hands on gold sent by Abe Lincoln to Indians as peace offering; Ray Nazzaro helmed routine Western; 1954. (*c*)

Black Devils of Kali ✕✕
Lex Barker in 1955 hokum about human sacrifices in India; Ralph Murphy did his best; 1955. (*b/w*)

Black Gold ✕✕
Sickening story of brave Indian Anthony Quinn adopting Chinese boy, and his faithful horse that he loves; Phil Karlson; 1947. (*b/w*)

Black Horse Canyon √
Joel McCrea hunting big black stallion and Mari Blanchard; Jesse Hibbs made it move; 1953. (*c*)

Blackjack Ketchum, Desperado ✕
Victor Jory's familiar heavy is only compensation in this yarn of badman trying to become goodman but having to fight one last battle first; Earl Bellamy; 1956. (*c*)

The Black Knight ✕
Alan Ladd's only a common smithy like you and me, but in this Camelot he disguises himself as a knight to protect King Arthur from the baddies. If you can't guess the ending, go to the bottom of the class. Tay Garnett keeps it moving and happily makes us overlook the awful script (Bryan Forbes, Dennis O'Keefe, Alec Coppel) and the performances of Peter Cushing, Harry Andrews, Patricia Medina; 1954. (*c*)

Black Magic √
Orson Welles turns this heavy-handed Italian spectacle into watchable melo with his usual larger-than-life performance, here as Cagliostro. But what a waste this Gregory Ratoff-directed 1947 hokum was of his talents.(*b/w*)

Blackmail √√
(1) 1929 Hitchcock, first talking picture made in England, still marvellously exciting, particularly in classic bread-knife scene with Anny Ondra.

Blackmail √
(2) 1939 Edward G. Robinson melo about escapee blackmailed by Gene Lockhart; directed H. C. Potter.

Blackmail ✕✕
(3) 1947 Ricardo Cortez B-pic about tycoon and blackmailing girlfriend.
(*all b/w*)

Black Narcissus √
If you can take nuns building mission school in the Himalayas, this is your film. Deborah Kerr, Jean Simmons head finely-handled (by directors Michael Powell and Emeric Pressburger) cast, and it was way ahead of its time (in 1947) by admitting that some nuns went off their rockers due to sex repression. Won Oscars for photography and art direction; Miss Kerr won New York Critics' best actress award. (*c*)

The Black Orchid ✕
Poorly developed soaper about two threatened marriages: Papa Anthony

Quinn's to gangster's widow Sophia Loren; daughter Ina Balin's determination that he shouldn't and subsequent up-screwing of her own engagement. Director Martin Ritt seems to have accepted Sophia's spouse Carlo Ponti's production values–a grim mistake; 1959. (*b/w*)

Blackout ✕
(1) Maxwell Reed as blind ex-serviceman solving murder when eyesight restored. 1950. Robert S. Baker and Monty Berman; (*b/w*)

Blackout ✕
(2) Dane Clark, broke, accepts job that leads him to murder, with Belinda Lee, Betty Ann Davies, director Terence Fisher; 1954. (*b/w*)

Black Patch ✕ ✕
Poor Western about sheriff trying to clear name; George Montgomery falsely accused of murder and hiding loot, stands rightly accused of appearing in rotten picture. Allen H. Miner; 1957. (*b/w*)

The Black Rose √
Henry Hathaway's 1950 romp set in mediaeval Orient. Orson Welles' enthusiastic hamming nearly overbalances Tyrone Power's handsome underplaying as Saxon hero. Not to be taken seriously, but the action scenes are special. (*c*)

The Black Shield of Falworth ✕
Costume nonsense about rightful earls and trials by combat, with Tony Curtis appearing only slightly more out of place than Janet Leigh. Rudolph Maté's direction looks as though he once read Walter Scott at school a very long time ago; 1954. (*c*)

The Black Swan √
Tyrone Power *v* George Sanders in 17th-century Jamaica, with Laird Cregar camping it up as the Governor; finely designed and bawdily written by Ben

Hecht and Seton I. Miller, it received less than its due from director Henry King, who seemed bored with the whole thing; 1942. (*c*)

The Black Tent ✕ ✕
The love of a simple Arab girl for Eighth Army officer Anthony Steel makes for a dull actioner; Brian Desmond Hurst; 1957. (*c*)

The Black Torment ✕
Heather Sears, Ann Lynn in chiller about conspirators trying to scare widower by Robert Hartford-Davis; 1965. (*c*)

Black Tuesday √
If you like to watch Edward G. Robinson as king of the gangsters, escaped from prison and tracked to warehouse, this is the picture for you. Surprise is it was made as late as 1955, by Hugo Fregonese. (*b/w*)

Black Widow √
Who kills the nasty little Peggy Ann Garner? Well, she's so infuriating that anyone might, but the list of suspects is down to five: Van Heflin as Broadway producer, Ginger Rogers, Gene Tierney, George Raft or Reginald Gardiner. Writer-producer-director Nunnally Johnson cooks a steamy brew; 1954. (*c*)

Black Zoo ✕ ✕
Lovely people (Michael Gough, Jerome Cowan, Elisha Cook) in lousy film about killer loose in zoo; Robert Gordon; 1963. (*b/w*)

Blaze of Noon √
The men who fly and the women who wait for them to crash in the setting of early air mail planes. William Holden, Howard de Silva outstanding; Anne Baxter among wives; also William Bendix, Sonny Tufts (Sonny Tufts?). John Farrow; 1947. (*b/w*)

The Blazing Forest ✕
John Payne, Agnes Moorehead, William

Demarest, Richard Arlen in old-timers' benefit-night logging yarn with heart and brain of wood. Edward Ludwig; 1952. (*c*)

Blindfold × ×
Rock Hudson is unbelievable psychologist in this even more incredible yarn about two governments in tug-o'-war for scientist's mind; Claudia Cardinale is scientist's draggy sister. Philip Dunne wrote-directed; 1966. (*c*)

The Bliss of Mrs Blossom × ×
Desperately embarrassing attempt to make inflatable dreams of bra-maker's wife funny; Shirley MacLaine, Richard Attenborough, James Booth play a triangle that seems to be a contest for tastelessness. Joe McGrath, director, must take a large part of the blame; 1968. (*c*)

Blithe Spirit √ √
Absolutely delicious Noel Coward comedy; Margaret Rutherford making Madame Acarti the happiest medium, Rex Harrison as harassed husband Constance Cummings and Kay Hammond as real and ghostly wives are absolutely divine. David Lean could do no wrong in 1945. (*b/w*)

The Blob √
In 1958, before he made it big, Steve McQueen was involved in ridding mankind of fungus from falling star. Irwin S. Yeaworth made it highly watchable, even without seeing the youthful Steve doing his bit. (*c*)

Blood Alley ×
John Wayne saving the world from communism again, this time one whole Chinese village and Lauren Bacall as doctor's orphan daughter. William Wellman makes it all moderately exciting if you can bear 'The Duke' and his mission; 1955. (*c*)

Blood and Sand √ √
Superb colour and careful, loving direction by Rouben Mamoulian lifted this bullfight story out of the sensational into a higher bracket. Despite inadequate casting, he made even Tyrone Power, Linda Darnell, Rita Hayworth and Anthony Quinn seem impressive, and the bullfighting shots are delicately yet excitingly filmed; 1941. (*c*)

Blood of the Vampire × ×
Donald Wolfit forcing doctor to get the bad blood out of his veins, yet. Director Henry Cass doesn't seem to believe it either; 1958. (*b/w*)

Blood on the Arrow ×
Dale Robertson, lone survivor of Indian massacre, helps Wendell Cory and Martha Hyer get back their child, held captive by redskins; Sidney Salkow; 1964. (*c*)

Blood on the Moon √
Roberts Mitchum and Preston fall out over underhanded scheme to rob old Walter Brennan and Barbara Bel Geddes; Robert Wise; 1945. (*b/w*)

Blood on the Sun √
James Cagney sniffs out Japan's plans for world conquest in 1928 (made 1945). Frank Lloyd directs. (*b/w*)

Blossoms in the Dust ×
A lovely cry, ever since 1940. Greer Garson founds a home for illegitimate children. The shamelessly sentimental script is, astonishingly, by Anita Loos, who wrote *Gentlemen Prefer Blondes*. Director: Mervyn LeRoy. (*c*)

Blowing Wild √
You've seen it all before–rough-tough oil-man (Gary Cooper), his tough-rough pal (Anthony Quinn), the heart-of-gold wife (Barbara Stanwyck), the gushers, the explosions, the fires, the disappointments, the triumphs, the

bandits. Don't let us stop you if you want to see it again – Hugo Fregonese makes it all very watchable; 1953. (*b/w*)

Blow Up
Antonioni's British picture, 1967, had David Hemmings earnestly letting down an otherwise sparkling overlay of Italian conjecture on the swinging London scene. Condemnation of a photographer's un-involvement with his subjects is brilliantly implied; the episodes each dazzle indivi-dually, even if the totality is disappointing. (*c*)

Blue √
Terence Stamp in a pretentious cowboy movie that manages to carry its preten-sions about being existentialist and sig-nificant remarkably well. Director Silvio Narizzano tells the story of the ruthless orphan who ends up leading the goodies against his pals in too moody a way and without sufficient technical care; but Karl Malden and Ricardo Montalban are encouraged to give fine performances. Stamp just looks menacing and doesn't even speak for the first forty minutes; 1968. (*c*)

The Blue Angel √
(1) Famous 1930 Germany melo about professor (Emil Jannings) squandering All for night-club singer (Marlene Dietrich) was made in both German and English, and the song Falling In Love Again established Dietrich inter-nationally. Trickily directed by Joseph von Sternberg. (*b/w*).

The Blue Angel × ×
(2) The awful 1959 remake by Edward Dmytryk with Curt Jurgens and May Britt even had a happy ending. (*c*)

Bluebeard × ×
John Carradine murdering every girl who poses for him in Paris; Edward Ulmer; 1945. (*b/w*)

Bluebeard's Ten Honeymoons × ×
Same plot as Chaplin's *Monsieur Verdoux* – both are based on the career of bride-murderer Landru. But here it's George Sanders, playing it for real, or as near-real as lightweight director W. Lee Wilder can get. Parade of British lady has-beens (only one can act, but you won't get us naming her) provide the victims; 1960. (*b/w*)

The Blue Dahlia √ √
Who killed Alan Ladd's unfaithful wife? Was it the little chap himself? His pal, William Bendix, with blank periods due to war wound? Smoothie Howard de Silva? George Marshall keeps the sus-pense going; 1946. (*b/w*)

The Blue Gardenia √
Anne Baxter arrested on say-so of smart reporter Richard Conte, who then de-cides she's innocent; as heavy Raymond Burr (later reformed as Ironside) is around, maybe there's a clue there? However, Fritz Lang's direction lifts above the banal; 1953. (*b/w*)

Blue Hawaii × ×
Fourteen Elvis Presley songs and a travel-poster Honolulu will either turn you on or put you off, so that's all you need to know. Norman Taurog's homage to Presley happened also to be the top-grossing motion picture in the us; 1962. (*c*)

The Blue Lagoon ×
Soppy, slow-moving but ultimately pleasant idyll on desert isle as kids grow up into lovers; Jean Simmons, Donald Houston; directed earnestly by Frank Launder; 1949. (*c*)

The Blue Lamp ×
Have a glance at it to see just how soft, sentimental and indulgent we were in 1950. Ted Willis' script and Basil Dear-den's direction will embarrass anyone who watches *Softly, Softly* or even *Z Cars*. Dirk Bogarde is the nasty who kills PC Dixon, only to rise again, the Messiah of Dock Green. (*b/w*)

The Blue Max √
Spectacularly shot and directed (John Guillermin) re-creation of a German fighter squadron in first world war, with flyers George Peppard, Jeremy Kemp (marvellous) vying for honour of shooting down 20 planes and thus winning title medal; James Mason cynical co. Unfortunately, the ground action is severely tethered to *terra firma*; 1965. (*c*)

Blue Murder at St Trinian's √
Made in 1958, it has Sabrina among the girls; Terry-Thomas, George Cole, Joyce Grenfell, Alastair Sim, Lionel Jeffries make absurd story of crook hiding out there and army called in more than watchable, actually enjoyable. (*b/w*)

The Blue Peter × × ×
Not the great success of BBC children's television, but wooden Kieron Moore rediscovering himself as instructor to Outward Bounders. John Pudney helped script. Wolf Rilla directed; 1954. (*c*)

A Blueprint for Murder √
Is Jean Peters planning to murder Joseph Cotten's nephew, having already done in brother and niece? Good suspenser, written and directed by Andrew Stone; 1953. (*b/w*)

Blue Skies ×
Fred Astaire in a little nothing of a musical with familiar but dull Irving Berlin songs; Bing Crosby, Billy de Wolfe come out best. Stuart Heisler; 1946. (*c*)

Bobbikins × × ×
Shirley Jones, Billie Whitelaw in tepid comedy about 14-month-old who talks like adult and gives stock exchange tips. For some reason, Robert Day cast Max Bygraves in it; 1960. (*c*)

Body and Soul √ √
The classic boxing picture, directed in 1947 by Robert Rossen, with Robert Aldrich as first assistant, James Wong Howe, cameraman. John Garfield was golden boy, Lilli Palmer romantic interest. (*b/w*)

The Body Snatcher √
Boris Karloff and producer Val Lewton got together for the first time in this 1945 version of the Burke and Hare saga. Robert Wise directed darkly, and Bela Lugosi's haunting of the Edinburgh streets for young girls under Karloff and Henry Daniell's direction is masterly. The end is guaranteed to chill. (*b/w*)

The Body Stealers × ×
Cheaply-made, weak sci-fi about parachuters disappearing. Nobody around seems to believe in what they are doing, including George Sanders, Hilary Dwyer or director Gerry Levy; 1969. (*c*)

Boeing-Boeing ×
Silly, embarrassing 'comedy' about swinger Tony Curtis keeping three airhostess girlfriends on the go while Jerry Lewis drools. John Rich seemed under the impression that if everybody walked even faster and talked louder than stage version, they would be funnier, too; 1965. (*c*)

The Bofors Gun √ √
Tight, prim David Warner and wild Irish gunner Nicol Williamson play out a lethal game on guard duty in Germany, with Ian Holm and John Thaw drawn in. Jack Gold makes this a vivid and unnerving piece of theatre, and almost an outstanding film; 1968. (*c*)

Bond Street × ×
Individual performances pop up like rockets in this episodic and on the whole dreadful film directed by Gordon Parry. Cripple girl and twister husband– Patricia Plunkett and Kenneth Griffith– steal the show; 1947. (*b/w*)

Bonjour Tristesse ×
Miscasting (Jean Seberg, Deborah Kerr, David Niven, Juliette Greco) sinks this adaptation of Sagan novel about father and daughter relationship on the Riviera; Otto Preminger hokes it up, to no avail; 1957. (*c*)

Bonnie and Clyde √√√
Warren Beatty and Faye Dunaway in influential blockbuster, which may not seem as gratuitously violent as it did in 1967–a lot of blood has run under the bridge since then. Michael J. Pollard, Gene Hackman, Estelle Parsons, Gene Wilder all superb; in case you didn't know, the eponymous couple are bank-robbers in it for kicks as well as money and there's a gruesome shoot-up at the end; Arthur Penn. (*c*)

The Bonnie Parker Story √
Made nine years before Bonnie and Clyde–in 1958–this tells the lady's fall from waitress to gangster rather more conventionally. Dorothy Provine essays her under William Witney's unambitious direction. (*b/w*)

Bonnie Scotland √√
Classic 1935 Laurel and Hardy rib-tickler (as they used to say). Director Jimmy Horne managed to keep some sort of story about Stan being dis-appointed over a Scottish legacy going, but all that matters is interplay between the divine couple in India. (*b/w*)

Boom! ×
How could Elizabeth Taylor, Richard Burton, Noel Coward acting a Tennesse Williams script for Joseph Losey, photo-graphed by Douglas Slocombe, come up with an almighty flop? If it doesn't seem possible, here is the evidence–self-indulgence and (one suspects) the sin of hubris all round. Of course, there are marvellous bits in this tale of the poet and the 'older woman', but watching is a disheartening experience; 1969. (*c*)

Boomerang √√
First of the socially-conscious thrillers that blossomed in 1947 Hollywood, only to be killed soon after by McCarthy era; Elia Kazan directed Dana Andrews as politically-motivated DA. Exciting, brilliantly-made, true-life story. (*b/w*)

Boom Town √
Clark Gable and Spencer Tracy as oil wildcatters. Need to know more? How about Claudette Colbert as Tracy's wife, Hedy Lamarr as Gable's girlfriend. Plus gushers, fires and the rest of the oil movie excitements. Jack Conway; 1940. (*b/w*)

Borderlines √
Joan Crawford (harsh) *v* Robert Stack (gentle) battle out approaches to the mentally sick; Polly Bergen cracks up, Janis Page is a whore. It once had a postscript by President Kennedy; also gone are two scenes with Miss Bergen–one where she's nearly raped by the men's ward and one showing her shock treatment. Hal Bartlett produced-directed; 1963. (*b/w*)

Border River ×
Confed Joel McCrea gets arms and a girlfriend Yvonne de Carlo from Pedro Armendariz; George Sherman; 1953. (*b/w*)

The Borgia Stick √
Excitingly filmed entirely on location in New York, this 1967 actioner by David Lowell Rich shows how the Mafia is going into legit business. Don Murray and Inger Stevens take them on. (*c*)

Born to be Bad ×
Or not very good, anyway. Joan Fontaine is tough girl on the make–she makes rich man Zachary Scott, writer Robert Ryan, artist Mel Ferrer, but is shown up to be what she is–and no better. Nicho-las Ray doesn't even try to make this hokum believable; 1950. (*b/w*)

Born Yesterday √√
Outstanding comedy that won 1950 Oscar for Judy Holliday, as dumbest blonde, after she desperately slimmed for film of her Broadway success. William Holden as her Professor Higgins and Paul Douglas fine supports. George Cukor directed from script covertly supplied by play's writer, Garson Kanin. (*b/w*)

The Boss √
Corruption in St Louis after first world war exposed by John Payne; rather good of its kind, thanks to Byron Haskin's meticulous direction; 1956. (*b/w*)

The Boston Strangler √√
Exciting and, on the whole, well-made (by Richard Fleischer) partisan account of the deeds and apprehension of real-life murderer. Tony Curtis, as the strangler, and Henry Fonda, interrogator, are solidly backed by George Kennedy, Jeff Corey, Sally Kellerman; 1969. (*c*)

Botany Bay √
Formula follow-up to *Mutiny on the Bounty* by same authors, has James Mason as Blighted captain, Alan Ladd as convict hero; would you believe Patricia Medina as a ladylike lady prisoner being transported, too? John Farrow turned in pro job; 1953. (*c*)

Bottom of the Bottle √
Or of the barrel. Successful lawyer pretends alchoholic brother is just a friend. Van Johnson and Joseph Cotten act like mad, but Henry Hathaway hasn't attempted any of the subtlety of the Simenon book it's taken from; 1956. (*c*)

Bottoms Up ××
If, by some personal aberration, you happen to think Jimmy Edwards in his Will Hay-type schoolmaster role is funny, don't let us stop you from chortling over this nonsense about rebellion at his school; others, keep away; 1960. (*b/w*)

The Boy Cried Murder ×
The boy who cried 'Wolf' sees a murder, nobody believes him; filmed in Yugoslavia by George Breakston with Veronica Hurst; 1966. (*c*)

Boy, Did I Get a Wrong Number ×
Well, yes he did, except that it's No. 312 on Variety's list of all-time US box-office grossers, which can't be bad. Otherwise, it's strictly for Bob Hope fans, as their lad involves himself with Elke Sommer as disillusioned film star, his wife Marjorie Lord and maid Phyllis Diller misunderstanding him. George Marshall; 1966. (*c*)

Boy on a Dolphin √
Sophia Loren in and out of the water discovering sunken statue and trying to make a dishonest buck (or, rather, seeing it's Greece, drachma) selling its whereabouts to Clifton Webb. Unfortunately, tepid Alan Ladd plays an archaeologist and foils her; Jean Negulesco made it all very easy to look at, if not to think about; 1957. (*c*)

The Boys ×
Nothing looks more outdated than films about Youth and this 1962 effort with Robert Morley, Felix Aylmer, Wilfred Brambell, Richard Todd suffers more than most. Yet Sidney J. Furie's inventive direction and ensemble playing of (then) teenagers makes this effort at understanding worth trying to watch. (*b/w*)

The Boys from Syracuse √
Beguiling screen transfer in 1940 of Rodgers and Hart reworking of *The Comedy of Errors*. Includes This Can't Be Love, Sing For Your Supper; plus Martha Raye, Alan Mowbray, Eric Blore. Notable direction from Edward Sutherland. (*b/w*)

Boys' Night Out √
Tony Randall does his usual job of saving wobbly movie, as one of four men who decide to share a girl and an apartment. Snags are that the girl is (a) a sociology student studying them and (b) she's Kim Novak, the worst actress ever to become a household name. Director Michael Gordon makes it all move merrily enough along; 1962. (*c*)

Boys Town ×

This *schmaltz* won every award in sight in 1938, but it comes over as awfully gooey now, despite Spencer Tracey's sincere attempts at being sincere. Mickey Rooney is toughie transformed. Incidentally, as the result of this movie, the Boys Town charity has become one of the wealthiest in the world, living on its interest. Norman Taurog pulled out all the stops. (*b/w*)

The Boy With Green Hair √
Early (1948) message pic about discrimination, worth seeing for Dean Stockwell's kid, veterans Pat O'Brien and Robert Ryan and Joseph Losey's first mannered essay in directing. (*c*)

The Brain ×
Phoney sci-fi horror flick that has scientist discovering who was the murderer by probing dead man's brain; Anne Heywood, Cecil Parker. Gerard Oury; 1965. (*b/w*)

Brainstorm ×
Jeff Hunter, Anne Francis, Dana Andrews are triangle in so-so thriller about attempted suicide and murder. William Conrad directed unimaginatively; 1965. (*b/w*)

The Bramble Bush ×
Richard Burton sits uneasily in soap-opera part of doctor returning to Cape Cod to perform op on dying friend and falling for his wife, Barbara Rush. Holds the superficial interest well enough, and

Daniel Petrie has strong supports in Jack Carson, Angie Dickinson; 1960. (*c*)

Branded ×
Anastasiac Western, with diminutive Alan Ladd pretending to be Charles Bickford's long-lost son; snag is he falls in love with Mona Freeman for some reason, like the script—so has to produce the real son before it can all end happily ever after. Rudolph Maté directs ably enough; 1950. (*c*)

The Brass Bottle ×
The old F. Anstey novel, disastrously updated to contemporary New York with Tony Randall as the man who buys Aladdin-type curio and conjures up a particularly pompous demon in Burl Ives. The smashing Barbara Eden is the lady he nearly gets parted from in ensuing shenanigans. Harry Keller could surely have done better with these ingredients; 1964. (*c*)

The Brass Legend √
Raymond Burr makes a splendid villain in this Western about an 11-year-old boy in jeopardy; Gerd Oswald; 1956. (*b/w*)

The Bravados √
Superior adult Western in which Gregory Peck realises that tracking down killers of his first wife with such single-minded thirst for vengeance has drained him of love and mercy. He tries to make amends with Joan Collins, doing her best (which isn't that good). Henry King makes it exciting, sustained viewing; 1958. (*c*)

The Brave Bulls √
Despite the double disadvantage of casting Mel Ferrer as matador and Anthony Quinn as his manager, producer-director Robert Rossen manages to translate Tom Leas' novel about the Mexican bullring into a more than competent film; at least Ferrer's doleful countenance makes his wracked inde-

cision believable. Don't worry, soft-hearts, the moments of truth are offscreen. 1951. (*b/w*)

The Brave One   √
Sad story of little Mexican boy who loves a bull only to see it matched against matador; Irving Rapper's direction will pull at your heartstrings; 1957. (*c*)

The Brazen Bell   √
Western about timid teacher realising that A Man Has to Be a Man, but strong casting (George C. Scott, James Drury Lee J. Cobb) helps puts some realisation into director James Sheldon that A Film Has to Be a Film; 1962. (*b/w*)

Breakaway   × ×
1957 suspenser-that-isn't about racketeers and others' attempts to obtain secret formula for overcoming fatigue in flight. Better to have looked for one to overcome fatigue caused by watching such bosh. Tom Conway, Honor Blackman, Bruce Seton. (*b/w*)

Breakfast At Tiffany's   √ √
Whacky New York playgirl Audrey Hepburn shocks, charms small-town George Peppard in cleverly-bowdlerised (by George Axelrod) version of Truman Capote novella. Confidently directed by Blake Edwards; 1961. (*c*)

The Breaking Point   √
Hemingway's *To Have and Have Not* was filmed under its own name (Bogart, 1944), once as *The Gun Runners* (Audie Murphy, 1958) and here, 1950, with John Garfield as the fishing boat skipper who rents boat to baddies then shoots it out with them. Patricia Neal and Patricia Thaxter have been written in as tramp and wife. Otherwise, Michael Curtiz did competent job, and got the most out of Juano Hernandez's death scene. (*b/w*)

Breaking the Sound Barrier   √
Ralph Richardson won the New York critics award as best actor for this 1952 drama of inventor who costs son-in-law's life; there was an Oscar, too, for sound recording. Alas, it all looks terribly dated and slow nowadays; David Lean. (*b/w*)

Break in the Circle   × ×
If you can believe Eva Bartok is a Scotland Yard agent you can take the rest of this routine smuggling-scientist-out-of-Red-infested-Germany 'thriller'; Forrest Tucker is boat-owner; Val Guest knocked it off in 1955. (*b/w*)

Breakout   √
(1) 1959: conventional PoW escape drama, set in Italian camp with nazi commander; Richard Todd, Richard Attenborough, Michael Wilding. Don Chaffey directed competently enough. (*b/w*)

Breakout   ×
(2) 1960: Lee Patterson, Hazel Court, Billie Whitelaw in quickie about jailbreak. Peter Graham Scott. (*b/w*)

Breakout   ×
(3) 1967: James Drury, Red Buttons in mountain escape thwarted by little boy lost situation. Richard Irving. (*c*)

A Breath of Scandal   × ×
The scandal is to have made this awful picture at all, let alone spend goodness knows how much on re-creating Austria of the Habsburgs and their nasty minds. Michael Curtiz hurries it along embarrassedly, Sophia Loren is angry as compromised princess (and doubtless that's not all she's angry about), John Gavin is plain inadequate, Maurice Chevalier forced to parade all his schmaltzy charm; 1960. (*c*)

The Bridal Path   × × ×
Really awful comedy about rough-hewn Scot, Bill Travers, on mainland in search of a wife; Frank Launder should have known better; 1959. (*c*)

The Bride of Frankenstein √√
Generally agreed to be about the best horror film ever, flowering of James Whale's directorial talents, Boris Karloff's likeable monster and, above all, Elsa Lanchester's incredible bride, with stunning help from make-up. Made in 1935, when they really cared. (*b/w*)

Brides of Dracula √
1960 Hammer horror: Martita Hunt keeps her bloodsucking son under lock and key but he cons a girl to let him out; it's lucky Peter Cushing is around to catch him, or he might have sucked director Terence Fisher's blood instead of vice versa; 1960. (*c*)

The Bridge at Remagen ×
One of those war pix that pretend to philosophise about war while milking it of all the excitement it can provide. This one is particularly nasty because of director John Guillermin's penchant for blood and brutality; George Segal, Ben Gazzara, E. G. Marshall are among the Americans; Robert Vaughn, Peter van Eyck among the Germans who meet on the bridge. It's got a particularly noisy soundtrack; 1969. (*c*)

Bridge to the Sun ×
Carroll Baker as American girl married to Japanese diplomat and her life during the second world war filmed in situ, Tokyo. It's all a bit naive and propagandoid for Japanese-US relations, but Etienne Perier makes you almost believe in it; 1961. (*b/w*)

The Bridges at Toko-Ri √
Personally, we can't see why anyone wants to watch war pictures, but obviously plenty of people do–this was the top moneymaker of its year–and you can't do any better than this if you're among them. William Holden, Fredric March, Mickey Rooney, Grace Kelly in detailed account of Navy carrier-based jet pilots and helicopter rescue teams during Korean War. Won Oscar 1955 for its special effects. Mark Robson handled the whole naval structure, cosmic battles and personal dramas within them with a firm, strong hand. (*c*)

Brief Encounter √
David Lean's direction of Noel Coward's script about Celia Johnson and Trevor Howard's furtive meetings to Rachmaninov's second piano concerto moved the whole forties generation to tears; 1945. (*b/w*)

Brigadoon ×
Disappointing version of stage musical about Scottish village coming to life on only one day every 100 years; Gene Kelly, Van Johnson, Cyd Charisse out of their element and director Vincente Minnelli clearly ill at ease; 1955. (*c*)

Brighton Rock √√
More than adequate 1947 version by the Boulting brothers of Graham Greene novel with Richard Attenborough outstanding as Pinkie, Alan Wheatley as gang boss he murders, Carol Marsh as 16-year-old he marries to keep quiet. (*b/w*)

Bright Victory √
Arthur Kennedy won New York critics' poll as best actor of 1952 for his part as blinded GI who learns to readjust and find love; Mark Robson directed delicately, avoiding maudlin dangers. (*b/w*)

Bringing up Baby √√
Delicious Cary Grant-Katharine Hepburn comedy made when they knew how (1938) by a man who knew how (Howard Hawks.) Later plagiarised (it's called 'homage') for *What's Up, Doc?* Wild leopard mistaken for pet provides hilarious sequences. (*b/w*)

Brink of Hell ×
William Holden trying to win back

superiors' confidence in his flying during Korean War; Mervyn LeRoy does best in the air; 1956. (*b/w*)

Broadway √
Amusing curiosity from 1942 with Pat O'Brien and George Raft playing rival Prohibition gangsters, and Raft playing (and dancing) autobiographical part. Broderick Crawford, S. Z. Sakall giving strong support. William A. Seiter directed. (*b/w*)

The Broken Horseshoe × ×
Deliberate hit and run involves Elizabeth Sellars and Robert Beatty in drug ring. Martyn C. Webster; 1953. (*b/w*)

Broken Journey ×
One of those how-each-reacts-in-airplane-crash movies; Phyllis Calvert, James Donald, Francis L. Sullivan were in this 1948 version. Ken Annakin. (*b/w*)

Broken Lance √ √
This 1954 vehicle for Spencer Tracy provoked bitchy comment from Clark Gable: 'Spence *is* the part. The old rancher is mean, unreasonable and vain. All he has to do is show up and be photographed.' Result was pretty spectacular with Spence as patriarch failing to unify family of Robert Wagner, Richard Widmark, Hugh O'Brian, tautly directed by Edward Dmytryk. (*c*)

Bronco Buster √
Rodeo star John Lund teaches Scott Brady the ropes, but soon they are rivals for Joyce Holden; made with Budd Boetticher's usual economical directorial skill in 1952. (*c*)

The Brotherhood ×
The movie that proves that it wasn't the subject that made *The Godfather* such a compelling film, and the reason Paramount took so much persuading to give the ultimately No. 1 box office grosser ever the financial backing it needed. This

1968 attempt at the same sort of Mafia plot, even down to the Sicilian scenes, was ruined by Kirk Douglas' insensitive performance and director Martin Ritt's nerveless grasp. Luther Adler makes it live for the moments he is on the screen, but that isn't enough. (*c*)

Brother Orchid √ √
Funny 1940 gangster movie with boss Edward G. Robinson hiding in monastery gradually becoming converted to the simple life. Humphrey Bogart is rival gang-leader, Ann Sothern girlfriend, Ralph Bellamy square rancher. Lloyd Bacon provides neat directorial touches. (*b/w*)

Brothers-in-Law √
Boulting Brothers' pretty successful attempt to do a *Doctor in the House* about the bar; Richard Attenborough, Ian Carmichael, Terry-Thomas, Irene Handl, John Schlesinger (John Schlesinger?), George Rose enjoy themselves; 1956. (*b/w*)

The Brothers Karamazov ×
The story's the same—or nearly—but this Pandro S. Berman production has about as much to do with Dostoyevsky as Peyton Place has with real life. Richard Brooks, writer-director, has turned it into a yarn of murder, false trial and escape, period. Casting is awful with Maria Schell, Yul Brynner, Lee J. Cobb, Claire Bloom, Richard Basehart either incompetent or unconvincing. 1958. (*c*)

The Brothers Rico √
Richard Conte gets involved with gangsters threatening his family; briskly and tautly directed by Phil Karlson in 1957. (*b/w*)

Broth of a Boy ×
Barry Fitzgerald holding out for more money as TV readies for celebration of his birthday; he's world's oldest man (or is he?) Hugh Leonard's play makes pleasant vehicle for Fitzgerald, and director

George Pollock lets him get on with it; 1959. (*b/w*)

The Browning Version   √
Michael Redgrave makes the most of schoolteacher-in-crisis part in Anthony Asquith's rather literal translation of Terence Rattigan play; 1951. (*b/w*)

The Buccaneer   ✗
The blind leading the blind when Anthony Quinn tries his hand at directing Yul Brynner, Claire Bloom, Charlton Heston Charles Boyer in remake of 1938 success (Fredric March) about pirate Jean Lafitte helping US in war of 1812. Very stiff and spotty; 1958. (*c*)

Buchanan Rides Alone   √
Better-than-average Western with Randolph Scott in danger of hanging for befriending Mexican who killed to avenge sister; Budd Boetticher; 1958. (*c*)

Buck Privates   ✗ ✗
Abbott and Costello in the army, 1941, Arthur Lubin (*b/w*). Sequel, *Buck Privates Come Home*, is about smuggling little French boy into America – stupid stuff; Charles T. Barton; 1947. (*b/w*)

Buffalo Bill   √
(1) 1944 William Wellman biog of legendary cowboy with Joel McCrea. (*c*)

Buffalo Bill   ✗
(2) 1965 oater with Gordon Scott taming ambitious young Sioux. (*c*)

Bugles in the Afternoon   ✗
Ray Milland, stripped of rank for assaulting cavalry officer, rejoins as private. You can guess the rest; Roy Rowland churned out usual actioner in 1952. (*c*)

A Bullet for Joey   √
George Raft gets a fit of unlikely conscience when kidnapping atomic scientist on behalf of a foreign power; Edward G. Robinson hams along under Lewis Allen's direction; 1955. (*b/w*)

A Bullet is Waiting   √
Sheriff Stephen McNally force-lands with prisoner Rory Calhoun on Jean Simmons' ranch on way to murder trial; Jean falls for Rory; John Farrow turned out this competent, incredible melo in 1954. (*c*)

Bullitt   √ √ √
Stunning duel between detective Steve McQueen and DA Robert Vaughn for possession of key witness; brilliantly shot in San Francisco and the second-best chase ever put on film (first is in same producer's *The French Connection*). Peter Yates; 1968. (*c*)

Bundle of Joy   ✗
Once upon a time, 1939 to be exact, Ginger Rogers made a lovely picture called *Bachelor Mother*. Casting around for a vehicle to show off the minuscule combined talents of the newly-married Eddie Fisher and Debbie Reynolds in 1956, the eyes of some bright Hollywood lads fell upon the old movie and they decided it would be a good idea to remake this story of shopgirl picking up baby from steps of orphanage and thus getting her job back from sympathy. They gave it to Norman Taurog to direct, and they were wrong. It was a rotten idea and this is a rotten film. (*c*)

Bunny Lake is Missing   √
Laurence Olivier makes a believable policeman, Carol Lynley makes an almost believable mother whose child disappears, Keir Dullea makes an unbelievable brother, while Noël Coward doesn't even try to make his sinister neighbour believable. But, then, credibility never was Otto Preminger's strongest point; it's entertaining, all right; 1965. (*b/w*)

Buona Sera, Mrs Campbell   √
For the first nine reels this is a smart, amusing comedy about three ex-GIS, returning to Italy with their formidable

wives (Shelley Winters outstanding) who all believe they are father to Gina Lollobrigida's child; Phil Silvers, Peter Lawford, Telly Savalas competent 'fathers'. But Melvin Frank's invention (he directs, produces, co-writes with Denis Norden) flags at the end, and it lacks that extra twist that would have made it memorable; 1969. (*c*)

Bushfire ✗
Commies holding Americans prisoner in SE Asia, made in 1962 before war became too shameful a subject to make features about; John Ireland and Everett Sloane; directed and produced by young Jack Warner. (*b/w*)

Bus Riley's Back in Town √
Ann-Margret wants Michael Parks back when he is demobbed from the Navy; moodily shot by Harvey Hart, it does build a sentimental but convincing picture of small-town life; 1965. (*c*)

Bus Stop √√
In 1956, back from 18 months at Lee Strasberg's actors' studio, Marilyn Monroe really gave a performance here – even if director Josh Logan had to retake scenes 20 times because she kept forgetting her lines. Her part as night-club floozie picked up by cowboy (Don Murray) fitted her beautifully. George Axelrod adapted from William Inge play. (*c*)

The Buster Keaton Story ✗
Keaton himself supervised the making of this biopic but, perhaps because of that, it doesn't really work. Donald O'Connor gives a faithful enough imitation and Peter Lorre is at hand as film director, but real director and co-writer Sidney Sheldon lets it all get very vacuous; 1957. (*b/w*)

But Not For Me √√
Clark Gable acts his age (58 in 1959) as Broadway producer chased by his secretary, Carroll Baker. Lilli Palmer stands there laughing as his ex-wife, while Lee J. Cobb provides a, for him unusually light rendering of anxious playwright. Altogether fun, and Walter Lang has done a neat job, recalling something of Noel Coward's *The Scoundrel*. (*b/w*)

Butterfield 8 √
Elizabeth Taylor as the nympho can't help it in a rather milky adaptation of John O'Hara novel; Daniel Mann hasn't got much of a cast apart from her – Laurence Harvey, Eddie Fisher, Jeffrey Lynn, it reads like a list of the weaker available leading men in 1960. (*c*)

By Love Possessed ✗
Too many plots spoil the book when it comes to making this movie. James Gould Cozzens's bestseller had some insight – but John Sturges has ironed all that out. Mind you, what could any director do with such poor leads as Lana Turner, George Hamilton, Effram Zimbalist Jr? Next layer – Jason Robards, Barbara Bel Geddes, Tom Mitchell, Everett Sloane – can't save the wreck; 1961. (*c*)

Bye Bye Birdie √
Put on a happy face and forgive this 1953 stage adaptation about a rock-'n'-roll singer called up for the Army for Paul Lynde's splendid father and recently-rediscovered Ann-Margret. George Sidney. (*c*)

By the Light of the Silvery Moon √
Wholesome Doris Day and clean-limbed Gordon MacRae awash in sentiment as he returns from war to 1918 America. Directed 1953 by David Butler. (*c*)

Cabin in the Sky ✓
All-Negro retelling of Faust legend reflects 1943 attitudes, but Ethel Waters, Lena Horne's singing and Louis Armstrong's playing transcend 'simple souls' attitude of white director Vincente Minnelli. (*b/w*)

The Cabinet of Dr Caligari ××
Disappointing 1962 remake of silent classic horror with Dan O'Herlihy, Glynis Johns, directed and produced by the over-ambitious Roger Kay. (*b/w*)

The Caddy ×
Jerry Lewis outshines partner Dean Martin to score with several amusing solos, but the whole thing, only nominally directed by Norman Taurog (he seems to have let them get away with whatever came into their heads) is pale stuff vaguely about golf; 1953. (*c*)

Caesar and Cleopatra ✓
Gabriel Pascal's best attempt at a Shaw play but still pretty grotty; he supplied the lavish dressing, GBS the clever chat, and luckily Vivien Leigh and Claude Rains managed to play it as though they were being well-directed; 1946. (*c*)

Caged ✓
Eleanor Parker goes to prison a framed innocent and emerges a hardened criminal, of course. John Cromwell enjoys harrowing us with the details, and Agnes

Orson Welles in *Citizen Kane*

Moorehead turns in her usual fine performance as the warden; 1950. (*b/w*)

The Caine Mutiny √√
Taken, unfortunately, more from the novel than from the stage-play, this 'opened out' the court-martial drama which was the whole play, thus rather pre-empting the ultimate trial. Heavy plusses, though, are Humphrey Bogart's sadistic, framed, crumbling Queeg, Fred MacMurray's shifty officer and Van Johnson's simple mutineer. Edward Dmytryk used special effects excellently, and worked loyally to Stanley Kramer the producer; 1954. (*c*)

Cairo ✕
George Sanders leads caper to steal Tutankhamun jewels which comes unstuck partly through his weakness for belly dancers; Richard Johnson; directed by Wolf Rilla; 1962. (*b/w*)

Calamity Jane √
'Doris Get Your Gun' would have been better title as Miss Day chases success of Annie Oakley; she's a spirited gal, but Howard Keel's Wild Bill Hickock is a booming bore and the songs are poor; David Butler did his best, but that just weren't good enough, pard, in 1953. (*c*)

California √
Routine Western with Barbara Stanwyck gambling for love and money and Ray Milland as wagon-master with a past. 1946, directed by John Farrow. (*c*)

California Holiday ✕✕
Weak Elvis Presley beach-surfer which does him no good, nor us either; Norman Taurog; 1966. (*c*)

Calling Bulldog Drummond √
Oh-so-dated, but still fascinating Victor Saville view (1951) of what the pre-war fictional legend was all about. Walter Pidgeon is a pleasant Bulldog, with the teeth of his Sapper-sadism drawn; Margaret Leighton co-starred. (*b/w*)

Call Me Bwana ✕✕
All Bob Hope's frantic wisecracking can't bring to life this silly story of him as phoney author competing with Red agent Anita Ekberg for missile head lost in Africa; all you can do is ignore the mechanics and look for peripheral laughs from Lionel Jeffries. Gordon Douglas directed in what looks more like deepest Burbank than the Dark Continent; 1963. (*c*)

Call Me Madam √
If you can stand noisy Ethel Merman bounding about singing some inferior Irving Berlin tunes, you'll quite enjoy this snappy story based on the real hostess-with-the-mostest, Pearl Mesta, in Liechtenstein. But Walter Lang is so indulgent that he doesn't seem to have controlled George Sanders and 'young lovers' cocky Donald O'Connor and Vera-Ellen, who doesn't even sing her own songs either. Billy de Wolfe is momentarily amusing but the whole thing drowns in its own Broadway Babycham; 1953. (*c*)

Call Me Mister ✕✕
Rather boring backstage musical about Betty Grable staging a troop show in Japan after that little unpleasantness at Hiroshima and Nagasaki. A thousand laughs–all falling flat; Lloyd Bacon fails to bring it home; 1951. (*c*)

Camelot √
The music's fine, although there isn't a hit in the whole Lerner-Loewe score. But everything else about this attempt to make a popera out of Mallory and T. H. White is heavy going; Richard Harris outdoes David Hemmings in the winceability ratings; Vanessa Redgrave outdoes them both; no wonder none of them has appeared in a major musical since 1967. Josh Logan directs with too

much regard for his stage piece; it needed more of a film director to make a film – all it gets is opulent photography. *(c)*

Camille √
Garbo's finest performance was needed by this kitsch old tearjerker, and she came up with it. She makes you believe in the dying classy fallen woman, battling against Robert Taylor's wooden acting, Lionel Barrymore's self-indulgence and MGM's vulgarity. Only Henry Daniell as her current Baron helps with a fine performance. George Cukor did all he could but Metro in 1937 was only concerned with a vehicle for Garbo, Cukor was just the chauffeur. *(b/w)*

Campbell's Kingdom √
Rugged attempt to make a British Western set in the Rockies, but not filmed there. Dirk Bogarde's long-suffering look fits his part of claimant to mining valley but may also have come from having to act out a limpid script; about the performances of Stanley Baker, Michael Craig and Barbara Murray there is nothing to be said except that they are better than their counter-parts in *Hopalong Cassidy*. Ralph Thomas; 1957. *(c)*

Canadian Pacific ✕
Randolph Scott pushes the railroad through, with help and hindrance from Jane Wyatt, J. Carroll Naish, Victor Jory and director Edward L. Marin; 1950. *(c)*

The Canadians √
After Custer's Last Stand, the whole Sioux nation crossed into Canada; this Western-with-a-difference shows what happened to them. Robert Ryan; director Burt Kennedy; 1960. *(c)*

Can-Can ✕
Ignore the rest and enjoy Frank Sinatra strolling unconcernedly through the frenzied attempts to make the greatest musical ever and finishing up among the – well, not quite the worst, but the lower end of the league. Juliet Prowse dances better than Shirley MacLaine but can't deliver lines as well. Maurice Chevalier outdoes Louis Jourdan in acting stage Frenchmen. Cole Porter's songs are divine (It's Alright with Me, You Do Something to Me, Let's Do It, Just One of Those Things, I Love Paris, *et al*), but not always well delivered. If this one goes down in history it will be because it upset Mr Khrushchev who was visiting Hollywood when it was being made in 1960. It won't do much for you, either. *(c)*

Can Hieronymus Merkin Ever Forget Mercy Humppe and Find True Happiness? ✕ ✕
Can Anthony Newley ever remember that he is just a pleasant light comedian and settle down to earn an unpretentious living? Pity Joan Collins, Milton Berle, Stubby Kaye, Patricia Hayes, Judy Cornwell, Joyce Blair for being mixed up in this actor – director – writer – producer's ego trip; 1969. *(c)*

Canon City √
On December 30, 1947, twelve desperate men broke out of Colorado State Prison; this film is dramatic documentary of their escape to limited freedom, with some of the people playing real-life parts; actors include Scott Brady, Jeff Corey; director Crane Wilbur; 1949. *(b/w)*

Canyon Crossroads ✕
Man against helicopter in uranium search; mildly exciting stuff with Phyllis Kirk and Richard Basehart; Alfred L. Werker; 1955. *(b/w)*

Canyon Pass ✕
Patricia Neal only reason for watching this dim 1951 oater directed by Edwin L. Marin. She's girl on the make, marrying ranch-owner Dennis Morgan. *(b/w)*

Canyon River　　　　　　×
George Montgomery first makes deal with rustlers, then fights them. Harmon Jones; 1956. (*c*)

Cape Fear　　　　　　√ √
Super thriller with Robert Mitchum perfectly cast for once as ex-con out to terrorise the man who sent him down, Gregory Peck, and his family, climaxing in a haunting section on and around a moored houseboat. J. Lee Thompson twists the thumbscrews tighter and tighter. Weak-hearts, don't watch it alone in a lonely spot; strong supporting cast includes Polly Bergen, Martin Balsam, Telly Savalas, Jack Kruschen; 1962. (*b/w*)

Caprice　　　　　　√
Doris Day meets Richard Harris in comic spy plot with help of writer-director Frank Tashlin; glossy rubbish but good fun; 1967. (*c*)

Captain Boycott　　　　　　√
Robert Donat makes brief appearance as Parnell in Frank Launder's satisfactorily souped-up slice of Oirish history, with Cecil Parker as horrid, eponymous Boycott; young (it's 1947) Stewart Granger as stubborn hero; Abbey-full of character actors. (*b/w*)

Captain from Castille　　　　　　×
Tyrone Power displays his startling good looks and lack of personality in this expensive costume drama about Spaniard in the New World. Competently directed by Henry King in 1947. (*c*)

Captain Horatio Hornblower, RN　　√
Gregory Peck duelling his way to the greater glory of Nelson's England; the supports are a bit weak (director Raoul Walsh must have asked the casting department for three ha'porth of British he-men and to hell with whether they can act) and Virginia Mayo's wayo out

of place. Nevertheless, it moves so fast and furious that a good time is had by all; 1951. (*c*)

Captain Lightfoot　　　　　　×
W. R. Burnett wrote this yarn about nineteenth-century Irish rebellion against the British, Rock Hudson leads the rebels. Douglas Sirk directed; 1955. (*c*)

Captain Nemo and the Underwater City √
Attempt by James Hill to provide a sequel to Jules Verne story, full of neat effects. Robert Ryan, Chuck Connors, Kenneth Connor; 1969. (*c*)

Captain Newman M.D.　　　　　　√
Gregory Peck plays officer-psychiatrist at war with Army; strong cast includes Angie Dickinson as admiring nurse, Tony Curtis as unorthodox orderly and Bobby Darin in strong role as guilt-ridden flier. David Miller failed to make this a premature M*A*S*H but directed it all competently enough; 1963. (*c*)

Captains Courageous　　　　　　√ √
1937 sea epic in which Victor Fleming achieved exciting action on the fishing boats. It is also Kipling's story of Spencer Tracy with a Portuguese accent teaching the spoiled brat Freddie Bartholomew (perfectly suited for the part) what it means to be a Man. Tracy won an Oscar; Lionel Barrymore, Melvyn Douglas, and in a small part, Mickey Rooney, pitched in well. (*b/w*)

The Captain's Paradise　　　　　　√
Neatly-made comedy of bigamist Alec Guinness with wives Yvonne de Carlo and Celia Johnson at either side of the Straits of Gibraltar that comes unstuck when they both change character; Anthony Kimmins produced–directed; 1952. (*b/w*)

The Captain's Table　　　× × ×
Stilted nonsense about John Gregson's vicissitudes as captain of luxury liner; 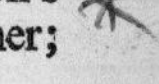

Peggy Cummins, Maurice Denham, Richard Wattis go through the motions. Jack Lee; 1958. (*c*)

The Captive City √
It's Athens in 1944 (the movie was made in 1963) and there is considerable confusion who's a goodie and who's a baddie because the Reds have risen after fighting with our lads against the nazis. In the midst of this, David Niven has to guard some armaments, and Joseph Anthony's direction ensures a tight hour or so with the help of Ben Gazzara and Michael Craig. (*b/w*)

The Captive Heart ×
PoW's, womenfolk at home, readjustment; Michael Redgrave, Mervyn Johns, Basil Radford. Basil Dearden; 1946. (*b/w*)

Carbine Williams ×
James Stewart in biopic of the carbine gun's inventor who was jailed for shooting revenue man. The casting and direction (by Richard Thorpe) tends to make him sympathetic, although he behaves most unpleasantly. Wendell Corey backs up doggedly; 1952. (*b/w*)

The Card √
Alec Guinness delightful in Ronald Neame's careful transition of Arnold Bennett's book about loan shark who becomes mayor. Glynis Johns, Michael Hordern stand out of rather old-fashioned cast; 1951. (*b/w*)

The Cardinal ×
Otto Preminger's colourful picturisation of Henry Morton Robinson's novel about priest's rise from Boston to Rome, filled with strong cameos, including John Huston's older cardinal, Burgess Meredith, Dorothy Gish. Unfortunately, main player Tom Tryon was one of Preminger's try-ons that didn't work; 1963. (*c*)

Career × ×
Why anyone should be presumed to care about the career of the nasty young actor played here by Tony Franciosa is beyond comprehension; neither his performance, Dean Martin's as a director or Carolyn Jones' as an agent move or intrigue. Shirley MacLaine is given a few moments by director Joseph Anthony, but it's all familiar stuff; 1959. (*b/w*)

Carefree √
These old Ginger Rogers–Fred Astaire musicals might not quite stand up today (this one was made in 1938) but it's a pleasure to hear the songs (Change Partners, I Used to be Colour Blind) and see them dance. Mark Sandrich. (*b/w*)

The Caretaker √√
For those who have not yet dreamed of picking up their papers in Sidcup, a magical experience awaits. For the rest of us, a chance to re-enter the closed mocking world of Davies (if that is his name), Aston and Mick–Donald Pleasence, Robert Shaw, Alan Bates–Pinter's archetypes, respectfully filmed by Clive Donner in 1963. (*b/w*)

Caribbean ×
Harmless costume yarn (1952) with heroic John Payne and plastic Arlene Dahl tackling pirates and slave traders; might keep the kids quiet. Director, Edward Ludwig. (*c*)

The Cariboo Trail ×
Routine settlers *v.* cattlemen and Randolph Scott *v.* Victor Jory. Edwin L. Marin; 1950. (*c*)

Carlton-Browne of the F.O. √√
Lovely satire on diplomacy by the Boulting Brothers with Terry-Thomas as forgotten ambassador; plus Peter Sellers, Ian Bannen, Miles Malleson, Irene Handl; 1958. (*b/w*)

Carmen Jones √ √
Otto Preminger's dazzling switch of Bizet's opera to black army camp. Embarrassingly, neither Dorothy Dandridge, Harry Belafonte nor Joe Adams actually sang in the picture; their voices were supplied by Marilyn Horne, Le Vern Hutcherson, Marvin Hayes; Pearl Bailey's for real; 1954. (*c*)

Carnival × ×
(1) 1935–Lee Tracy must marry or welfare will take his baby away from him and the circus. Herbert Wilcox. (*b/w*)

Carnival × ×
(2) 1946–draggy British ballet film with Sally Gray and Michael Wilding. Stanley Haynes. (*b/w*)

Carnival × ×
(3) 1956–Sydney Chaplin as carnival barker who elopes with mayor's daughter. (*b/w*)

Carnival of Souls √
Very low-budget but extremely well-made supernatural thriller about a girl who may have been drowned but may equally well be hypnotised; Herk Harvey directs and also plays The Man, the mysterious stranger who seems to control Candace Hiligloss; 1962. (*b/w*)

Carnival of Thieves ×
Caper in Pamplona; Russell Rouse has motley, many-accented and largely uninspired lot of actors, including Stephen Boyd, Yvette Mimieux, Giovanna Ralli; 1967. (*c*)

Carnival Story ×
Anne Baxter plays a trapeze lady whose partner is killed by a jealous barker. Will her new boyfriend, a photographer, finish up the same way? Kurt Neumann knows that you know the answer and hasn't the heart to direct the picture with any conviction, although he was co-writer, too; 1954. (*c*)

Carousel √ √
If I loved you . . . June is busting out all over . . . You'll never walk alone . . . Mister Snow . . . Shirley Jones, Gordon Macrae . . . Rodgers and Hammerstein . . . Henry King. Top money-maker of 1956. (*c*)

The Carpetbaggers × ×
Irving Wallace's novel (not about Howard Hughes?) was given the lusty, audience-teasing treatment you'd expect in 1964, just before films got permissive. Edward Dmytryk was lumbered with a mostly inferior lot of actors by producer Joe Levine; George Peppard as the aviation-movie tycoon, Alan Ladd, Robert Cummings, Carroll Baker *et al* come out as petty and unsympathetic characters. (*c*)

Carrie √
William Wyler's 1952 movie of farm girl who runs off with married man, becomes famous actress, and discards those who helped her. Laurence Olivier does the carrying, Jennifer Jones is carried. (*b/w*)

Carrington V.C. √
David Niven takes battery office funds in protest at not getting back pay; Margaret Leighton, Clive Morton, Mark Dignam and cast of solid British character-players make this a satisfying exercise; Anthony Asquith from Dorothy and Campbell Christie play; 1955. (*b/w*)

Carry On Admiral ×
Not one of the regular *Carry-Ons* but a stage farce *Off the Record*; director Val Guest. David Tomlinson, Peggy Cummins, A. E. Matthews, Joan Sims, Ronald Shiner, Alfie Bass; 1957. (*b/w*)

Carry On Cabby √
The 1963 vintage wasn't a bad year, with Sid James and Hattie Jacques as rival husband and wife taxi-owners, plus such joys as Kenneth Connor, Charles Hawtrey, Jim Dale, Liz Fraser. Gerald Thomas directed. (*b/w*)

Carry On Camping √
Nudist nuttery with Barbara Windsor, Terry Scott, and regulars. Gerald Thomas; 1969. (*c*)

Carry On Cleo √
Kenneth Williams plays Caesar, Sid James Mark Antony, Amanda Barrie Cleopatra—and if you think that's funny you'll love it. Gerald Thomas; 1965. (*c*)

Carry On Constable √
Eric Barker welcome guest in this 1960 farce about Sid James, Kenneth Connor, Leslie Phillips being sent to police station where they make Dock Green look like serious drama; Joan Sims winsome WPC. (*b/w*)

Carry On Cowboy √
Sid James as The Rumpo Kid; plus the usuals and Angela Douglas; Gerald Thomas; 1966. (*b/w*)

Carry On Cruising √
Captain finds that on the eve of his departure for the Med he has a Fred Karno crew of Kenneth Connor, Kenneth Williams and the rest of the carriers-on. Wilfrid Hyde White a guest in this 1962 lark. Gerald Thomas. (*c*)

Carry On–Don't Lose Your Head √
1967 lark with Sid James, Jim Dale, Kenneth Williams, Charles Hawtrey involved in the French Revolution. Gerald Thomas. (*c*)

Carry On Jack √
Juliet Mills and hard-trying Donald Huston guest in Jolly Roger-land on the rolling Spanish Main when Nelson

expected every man to pay his duty; Gerald Thomas, 1964. (*b/w*)

Carry On, Nurse √
One of the best Carry-Ons, with Kenneth Connor as boxer with broken wrist, Kenneth Williams as nuclear student, Wilfrid Hyde White as race-loving patient, Charles Hawtrey, Hattie Jacques, Irene Handl; Gerald Thomas; 1959. (*b/w*)

Carry On Regardless √
The one about the Labour Exchange and the extremely odd job men; Sid James, Kenneth Connor, Liz Fraser, Joan Sims; directed, as always, by Gerald Thomas, his fifth; 1961. (*b/w*)

Carry On Screaming ✗
Poor example of the type with Harry H. Corbett and Fenella Fielding looking unhappy; Gerald Thomas; 1966. (*c*)

Carry On Sergeant √
William Hartnell turning Bob Monkhouse, Kenneth Connor, Charles Hawtrey, Kenneth Williams into soldiers. This 1959 effort was one of the very best Carry Ons, directed of course by Gerald Thomas. (*b/w*)

Carry On Spying ✗
Owing to a fatal shortage of spies, Kenneth Williams is sent to recover a stolen formula, with the help of Barbara Windsor, Bernard Cribbins, Charles Hawtrey; Gerald Thomas; 1964. (*b/w*)

Carry On Teacher √
Fair (1963) and funny, with Leslie Phillips and Ted Ray as additions to regulars Kenneth Connor, Kenneth Williams, Joan Sims. Gerald Thomas. (*b/w*)

Carry On . . . Up the Khyber √
Perhaps the best, certainly the most lavish, of the series, sending up the Bengal Lancers—and you know where. Additions to Gerald Thomas's regulars

include Roy Castle, Angela Douglas. Great fun; 1969. (*c*)

Carve Her Name with Pride ✕
Virginia McKenna giving a not very convincing portrayal of real-life heroine parachuted into France twice, caught and dying a heroine's death; Lewis Gilbert does what he can with Jack Warner, Sydney Tafler, Bill Owen; gets fine performances from Paul Scofield, Billie Whitelaw, Harold Lang; 1957. (*b/w*)

Casablanca √ √ √
Play it again, Sam – and again and again. Somehow the hokum has such durable powers that when Bogie sends Bergman packing (literally) you really believe he would. It won three Oscars in 1943 (Best Picture, director, Michael Curtiz, screenplay), and among the nominees were Humphrey Bogart and Claude Rains; even Ingrid Bergman–an overrated actress if there ever was one– manages to score, as do Sydney Greenstreet and Peter Lorre. One of the greats. (*b/w*)

Casanova Brown √
Gary Cooper chose this light comedy about a divorced wife who finds she's pregnant for his first movie free from Paramount in 1944. Couldn't go wrong with Teresa Wright, Frank Morgan, Anita Louise helping and Sam Wood directing. (*b/w*)

Casbah ✕ ✕
Peter Lorre is only saving grace of this otherwise execrable musical version of Pepé Le Moko, jewel thief of Algiers. Tony Martin, would you believe, plays the Charles Boyer–Jean Gabin part; John Berry directed nervily; 1948. (*b/w*)

Cash McCall √
Nearest Hollywood has got to the machinations of The Power Game, has James Garner as unconvincing plastics businessman making deals and Natalie

Wood. E. G. Marshall outstanding among colleagues and rivals; Joseph Pevney; 1960. (*c*)

Casino Royale ✕
A mish-mash cish-cashing in on James Bond novel's success; somehow the producers of the Sean Connery opi didn't have the rights to this one, so the lads who did tricked it up with every star who could spend a few days, half a dozen directors and a simply awful script that rattles along on three flat tyres. David Niven, Orson Welles, Ursula Andress manage to get some mileage out of it; Woody Allen, Daliah Lavi, Peter Sellers, Deborah Kerr do not; 1967. (*c*)

Cass Timberlane √
Spencer Tracy married to Lana Turner; will she have it away with friend Zachary Scott? Actually, George Sidney's transfer of novel is less crude than this, doing its best within the 1947 conventions to be honest. Mary Astor, Albert Dekker strong back-ups. (*b/w*)

Cast a Dark Shadow √
Strong drama of retribution with Dirk Bogarde as wife-murderer, Margaret Lockwood earmarked as his next victim; Lewis Gilbert; 1955. (*b/w*)

Cast a Giant Shadow ✕ ✕
Kirk Douglas as Jewish hero, formerly with US forces in second world war, then Palestinian freedom fighter. Melville Shavelson wrote, produced and directed it in 1966 with more stodgy reverence than professional ruthlessness. It also co-starred Yul Brynner, Topol, Frank Sinatra and John Wayne. See it only if you intend to read Shavelson's wisecracker account of the troubles it took to make in *How To Make A Jewish Movie* (W. H. Allen); *that* he should film. (*c*)

Cast a Long Shadow ✕
Audie Murphy in Western adult enough

to cast him as bastard son who returns prodigally to ranch and makes it a going concern instead of cashing it in, thanks to luvverly Terry Moore; Thomas Carr; 1959. (*b/w*)

Castle of Evil × ×
The most evil thing about this tired old plot (about the mad scientist who invites the five people he hates most to the lair where he has created an electronic robot in his own image) is the *chutzpah* needed to make it all over again. Virginia Mayo reminds us what a pretty girl she used to be (this is 1967 and it may be bounderish to say she was 45 but she was) and Francis D. Lyon directed it without much imagination. (*c*)

Castle of the Living Dead ×
Count counted out by own petrifying liquid; Christopher Lee, Donald Sutherland a long way from M*A*S*H; 1964. (*b/w*)

Cat! × ×
Wildcat saves boy when rustler attacks him; not as exciting as it sounds. Peggy Ann Garner is only near-name around. Director, Ellis Kadison; 1966. (*c*)

Catacombs × × ×
Awful little British pic with Gary Merrill as wife-murderer who's afraid she's still alive; Gordon Hessler seems to be directing from a script he made up from pages found on a tour of Wardour Street dustbins; 1965. (*b/w*)

Cat Ballou √ √
Spoof Western that made stars out of Lee Marvin (in double role of drunken gunfighter and arch-enemy with silver nose held in place by elastic band) and Jane Fonda, the eponymous schoolteacher whose Pa is due to be hanged at the start of the movie. The music palls, but otherwise director Elliott Silverstein did a great comedy job; 1965. (*c*)

Cat on a Hot Tin Roof √ √
Tennessee Williams lifts the lid from rich Southern family to reveal impotence, alcoholism and Big-Daddy-domination simmering away. Elizabeth Taylor marvellous as love-yearning girl married into family via tormented Paul Newman; Burl Ives perversely patriarchal. Richard Brooks directed, 1958, with lush atmospherics. (*c*) 

The Cat People √ √
Classic horror picture so superior to most of the genre that it mustn't be missed by anyone who likes to be scared; Simone Simon is convinced that when her passions are aroused she turns into a large dangerous cat. When clawings begin is it she–or what? Jacques Tourneur made it in 1942. (*b/w*)

Cattle Drive √
Kid, Dean Stockwell, learns what life is really all about (perhaps) during big drive from veteran Joel McCrea; Kurt Neumann; 1951. (*c*)

Cattle Empire √
Joel McCrea on cattle drive again (see previous entry), this time in 1958, with revenge of those who once jailed him, in mind; Charles Marquis Warren. (*c*)

Caught √
Barbara Bel Geddes discovers she is married to nutter–James Mason–and worse. Max Ophuls gave it some distinction; 1949. (*b/w*)

Cause for Alarm √
Loretta Young being set up for murder rap by husband Barry Sullivan; Tay Garnett; 1951. (*b/w*)

Cavalry Command ×
Richard Arlen helps to restore law and order in Philippine village during Spanish–American war; a bit unconvincing, but then so was the war; 1965. (*c*)

Cave of Outlaws √
Among those present are Macdonald Carey, Alexis Smith, Edgar Buchanan, Victor Jory—all searching for gold hidden after Wells Fargo hold-up; William Castle; 1952. (*c*)

The Ceremony ✕✕
Limp crime and sex (don't expect much actual—it was made in 1963) yarn about springing master criminal from Tangier jail; both Laurence Harvey (also directing, a mistake) and Robert Walker fancying Sarah Miles. (*b/w*)

A Certain Smile ✕✕
Practically all of Françoise Sagan's bittersweet charm has been evaporated by clumsy script; instead, the cloying obviousness that is director Jean Negulesco's trademark takes its place, seen at its worst in the indulgence he permits to Rosanno Brazzi's really sickening playing of his 'older man' part. French actress Christine Carère, who went to Hollywood to play heroine, made only one other major picture, and no wonder; 1958. (*c*)

Chain Lightning ✕
Mainly airborne pic, from war bombers to testing jets, with Humphrey Bogart sacrificing scruples and honour but winning all back in climax; Raymond Massey, Eleanor Parker are around; 1950. (*b/w*)

The Chalk Garden √
Hayley Mills being set on right path by governess Deborah Kerr under gaze of Edith Evans. Sob-stuff, but it works. Ronald Neame directed, 1964, from Enid Bagnold play. (*c*)

A Challenge for Robin Hood ✕✕✕
Pathetic British picture, 1968 vintage, sketching the familiar Robin Hood stuff but never making it fresh or even interesting; Barrie Ingham an inadequate Robin against Errol Flynn or even

Richard Todd; James Hayter and Alfie Bass can't save it; much of the blame must be allocated to director C. M. Pennington Richards. (*c*)

Chamber of Horrors ✕✕
Afraid it is; this rip-off from House of Wax desperately needs that old camp magic of Vincent Price; all it has is Wilfrid Hyde White ambling through as if he can smell the staleness of the plot; Hy Averback; 1967. (*o*)

Champagne for Caesar √
Ronald Colman's last starring picture gave an enjoyable opportunity to score as professor who won't stop doubling his money in radio quiz show. Celeste Holm is one hazard planted by the panicky radio company that he overcomes. Vincent Price camps it up as sponsor. Richard Whorf can't really keep it going, but it's fair enough fun; 1950. (*b/w*)

The Champagne Murders √
Superficially a whodunit, this Chabrol-directed, Derek Prouse-co-written drama is really study of French bourgeoisie under pressure. Anthony Perkins, Yvonne Furneaux; 1968. (*c*)

Champion √√
Strong prizefight drama based on Ring Lardner's book about a heel who becomes champ. Kirk Douglas was dead right and should have stuck to playing unsympathetic parts after this breakthrough in 1949. It made the reputations of director Mark Robson and producer Stanley Kramer, as well; 1949. (*b/w*)

The Chapman Report ✕
Inexplicitly sexy (1962 was too early for orgiastic couplings) it's a four-stranded hokum about Kinseyish researchers adding to the statistics. Jane Fonda and Shelley Winters stand out and lie down under George Cukor's direction. (*c*)

Charade √√
Absolutely delightful Hitchcockian thriller given rather more comedy than the Master would have permitted, by director-producer Stanley Donen. Cary Grant and Audrey Hepburn fit perfectly, Walter Matthau, James Coburn solid support, Henry Mancini's hummable theme tune will stick in your mind; 1963. (*c*)

Charge at Feather River ××
3D Western rather tame in 2D; Guy Madison rescuing Vera Miles from Indians, Gordon Douglas directing; 1953. (*c*)

The Charge is Murder √
Richard Chamberlain defends man accused of murder; Claude Rains makes director Boris Sagal's job easier; 1964. (*b/w*)

Charge of the Lancers ××
Paulette Goddard as gypsy is only flicker of interest in this hokum supposedly set in Crimean War; William Castle; 1954. (*c*)

The Charge of the Light Brigade √
(1) 1936 bit of excitement taking place mainly in India but switching to Crimea for Errol Flynn, Olivia de Havilland to live and love under the shadow of the great self-sacrifice. (*b/w*)

The Charge of the Light Brigade ×
(2) 1968 version by Tony Richardson is nearer historical truth but inferior in almost every other way. Trevor Howard, John Gielgud, Vanessa Redgrave are encouraged to go off on their own wavelengths, while David Hemmings is just blush-making. The animated political cartoons by Richard Williams that interrupt the action may have sounded a good idea, but they don't really work, either. (*c*)

Charley's (Big-Hearted) Aunt ××
A reworking of the Brandon Thomas play to accommodate Arthur Askey, Richard Murdoch and various other British comedy stars (using the phrase pejoratively). Walter Forde; 1940. (*b/w*)

Charlie Bubbles √
This is the 1968 drama, about a successful man revisiting his Northern background, that couldn't get a proper distribution even though it was directed by Albert Finney and starred himself and Liza Minnelli. It's constantly held up by some critics as an example of the wrong-headedness of the commercial cinema system, but the industry chieftains may have shown better critical faculties than the critics in this case. Really, it wasn't much of a film, and Finney is all too obviously worrying about how the shots look to concentrate on his acting; Billie Whitelaw (wife) and Colin Blakely (mate) turn in their usual solid performances but they aren't enough to save a pretentious picture. As for Minelli (mistress), she is desperate. (*c*)

Charlie Chan √
These movies vary considerably, but the best are the early (1931–37) ones with Warner Oland; the Sydney Toler ones (1938–46) are less good but more polished; the final ones with Roland Winters are worse. They all feature wise Oriental detective biting off wise Oriental sayings while snubbing No. 1 and No. 2 sons while solving murder mysteries. On the whole, great fun.

Charly √
Flashy director Ralph Nelson has come up with a different kind of love story here. He (Cliff Robertson) is feeble-minded, briefly supernormal. She (Claire Bloom) is a therapist who falls in love with him. Sadly, it ends up as sickeningly coy; 1968. (*c*)

The Chase √√
Enormously interesting failure to say something profound about the nature of

evil and the American South. The making (in 1965) was marred by moody fights between star Marlon Brando, writer Lillian Hellman ('decision by democratic vote is a fine form of government, but it's a stinking way to create', she said afterwards), director Arthur Penn and producer Sam Spiegel. Yet the movie itself, with Robert Redford as victim, Brando as *High Noon*-type sheriff, Jane Fonda, Angie Dickinson, is marvellous in places, and if you share any of Brando's masochism, very exciting. (*c*)

Chase a Crooked Shadow   ✕
Is Richard Todd really Anne Baxter's brother or only pretending to be? Various British minor players pretend to care under Michael Anderson's routine direction; 1958. (*b/w*)

Che!   ✕✕✕
Strong candidate for worst movie of 1969, with Omar Sharif's Guevara only worsened by Jack Palance's Castro. Maybe it's all a deep plot by director Richard Fleischer to goad Cuba into disastrous war with America. (*c*)

Cheaper by the Dozen   √
Charming turn of the century story of the 12 real Gilbreth children, their organising father Clifton Webb and patient mother Myrna Loy. Walter Lang's 1950 box office runaway escaped sentiment by dry, humorous playing of its stars. (*c*)

Cheyenne Autumn   √√
Outstanding John Ford account of the deceit practised on tribe of Cheyenne Indians who were fooled out of their land and pushed on to arid territory 1,500 miles away. In 1878 they really did attempt to march back to their own place, touching the whole American nation. Fine cast carries this epic story along: James Stewart, Edward G. Robinson, Karl Malden, Dolores Del Rio, Richard Widmark, Carroll Baker, Sal Mineo; 1964. (*c*)

Chicago Confidential   ✕✕
State attorney breaks up crime syndicate; Brian Keith *v.* Beverly Garland; Sidney Salkow; 1957. (*b/w*)

Chicago Syndicate   √
Rather a nifty little thriller about an accountant being planted on the racketeers by the police. Dennis O'Keefe can't convince in the main part and he's happier being chased with the evidence than adding up the figures; but Paul Stewart's a great heavy and director Fred F. Sears keeps it moving; 1955. (*b/w*)

Chicken Every Sunday   √
Heart-warming, if your heart warms to *schmaltz*, boarding-house owner Celeste Holm and her lovable no-goodnik of a husband Dan Dailey. Set at turn of the century and belonging there, not even to 1948, when it was made. George Seaton. (*b/w*)

Chief Crazy Horse   ✕
Director George Sherman couldn't make up his mind whether this 1955 Western was supposed to be a sensitive biography of the greatest of the Sioux (improbably played by Victor Mature, better known as The Hunk) or an excuse for as many screeching Red Indian attacks as he could work in. Final stool-falling denouement simply doesn't work; 1955. (*c*)

A Child in the House   ✕✕
Mandy Miller bringing happiness to Eric Portman, Stanley Baker, and Phyllis Calvert in Charles de Latour's sudsy 1956 drama. (*b/w*)

A Child is Waiting   √
Burt Lancaster and Judy Garland fight over retarded children's treatment. John Cassavetes directed with honesty; 1963. (*b/w*)

Children of the Damned   √
Six other-worldly children defy the

military; sequel to *Village of the Damned* has Ian Hendry and Barbara Ferris involved; Anton Leader doesn't add much directorwise; 1964. (*b/w*)

Child's Play × ×
Super quiz-kids beat security to play with atomic apparatus; most unlikely; Mona Washbourne is biggest star it can boast; 1954. (*b/w*)

Chimes at Midnight √
Long-in-the-making Orson Welles attempt to put Falstaff in the centre of *Henry IV*, parts one and two; John Gielgud, Jeanne Moreau, Keith Baxter seem ill-at-ease, while Welles appears to be wondering where the next injection of finance is coming from. However, the good bits are very good indeed; 1967. (*b/w*)

China Seas √ √
Piracy, romance on the high seas in this great pre-war (1935) actioner with smashing cast of Clark Gable, Jean Harlow, Wallace Beery, Rosalind Russell, Robert Benchley, C. Aubrey Smith; directed by Tay Garnett. (*b/w*)

China Venture √
Edmond O'Brien capturing Jap general given some distinction by Don Siegel's sharp direction; 1953. (*b/w*)

Chitty Chitty Bang Bang √ √
Ian Fleming's magic car takes wings under Ken Hughes' cheerful direction and Dick Van Dyke's driving. Jolly cast includes Sally Ann Howes, Lionel Jeffries; 1969. (*c*)

A Christmas Carol √
1951 version with Alastair Sim a highly satisfactory Scrooge and the emphasis on ghosts. (*b/w*)

Christopher Columbus ×
Yawnful 1949 attempt to make organisation of expedition to discover America into drama. Fredric March and English cast struggle but David MacDonald's direction and talky script bogs them down. (*c*)

Chubasco ×
Poor little youth movie, made in 1968, about the regeneration of Christopher Jones as tuna-fisherman, with help from old-timers Ann Sothern, Richard Egan; Susan Strasberg; Allen H. Miner wrote-directed. (*c*)

Chuka √
Made in 1967 when Westerns were at last growing up, this attacked-fort drama was rather more real than others before it, with John Mills commanding a batch of drunks, Rod Taylor speaking up for the starving Injuns, Ernest Borgnine lumbering around; the hard-trying director was Gordon Douglas. (*c*)

Cimarron ×
Dreary 1960 remake of 1931 super-Western with Richard Dix and Irene Dunne. Glenn Ford and Maria Schell are totally inadequate substitutes, and Anthony Mann can't match the sweep and vigour of the earlier Wesley Ruggles. (*c*)

The Cincinnati Kid √ √
The Hustler in spades, poker replacing pool as the showdown game. A hard, brainy Steve McQueen confronts the seasoned and civilised Edward G. Robinson. Norman Jewison; 1965. (*c*)

Cinderfeila × ×
Jerry Lewis produced this floperoo for the sole benefit of Jerry Lewis, who is in front of the camera and twice as big as anyone else around–which is a shame, when some of the others are Ed Wynn, Judith Anderson and Count Basie. Frank Tashlin served his guv'nor well–much too well, the concept of a male Cinderella, complete with wicked step-brothers and all, doesn't gel; 1960. (*c*)

Circle of Danger √
Ray Milland returns to England to find out who killed brother and discovers that two governments are involved; shot by Jacques Tourneur in Britain; 1951. (*b/w*)

Circle of Deception ✕
Can you believe that Bradford Dillman is set up to be captured by the nazis, having been filled with false information, in the expectation that he will reveal all he knows and thus trick them? If you can't, forget this rather nasty thriller directed in 1961 by Jack Lee from a Nigel Balchin script. Suzy Parker inadequately fills the American quota, while British backbones Harry Andrews, Paul Rogers, Robert Stephens look as if they are on the side of those who can't believe it. (*b/w*)

Circus of Horrors √
Compelling little British chiller about plastic surgeon Anton Diffring taking over a circus to escape from vengeance of bungled patients and staffing it with ladies he has put together again; when he has to get rid of them all the accidents you fear in real circuses actually occur— like the trapezist falling, the knife-thrower not missing; Donald Pleasence; director Sydney Hayers; 1960. (*c*)

The Citadel ✕
Pre-war best-seller made into competent 1938 movie by King Vidor pretends to be realistic but really plays on worst instincts. Of course, nobody can fault the selfless Robert Donat as he spurns Harley Street to practise in Welsh valley but his solution for solving typhoid problem is melodramatic and dangerous; Ralph Richardson abets him; Rex Harrison, Emlyn Williams in their younger days, are around. (*b/w*)

Citizen Kane √√√
A poll of international critics voted this the best film of all time in 1972, 21 years after it was made, and their verdict stands unchallenged today. The direction and acting of Orson Welles, Herman J. Mankiewicz's script (modelled on megalomaniac publisher William Randolph Hearst), Gregg Toland's camera, Bernard Herrmann's music are all best of their kind, and the performances of Joseph Cotten (Kane's friend), Everett Sloane (his manager), Agnes Moorehead (his mother), George Colouris (his guardian), Ray Collins (his political opponent), Paul Stewart (his butler), Dorothy Comingore (his second wife) launched most on giddy careers. Above all towers Orson Welles, as actor —playing the many ages of the crusading newspaperman who does the dirt on everyone but somehow retains our sympathy to the end—and as producer-director—opening new vistas for the art of film with every dazzling scene, from the pastiche of the March of Time to the endless crane shot of his lifetime's possessions. True film-lovers will be hunched in front of the screen, chanting the lines with the players; and if by any chance you've never seen it, look forward to a stunning experience. It's a bit sad to see Orson Welles and Joseph Cotton made up to be the ages they now are, but fascinating to compare the make-up man's guesses with the reality. (*b/w*)

City Beneath the Sea ✕
Robert Ryan and Anthony Quinn diving for gold bullion off Jamaica; directed by Budd Boetticher; 1953. (*c*)

The City Jungle √
Paul Newman defends army chum Robert Vaughn, hoping to win Barbara Rush en route. Otto Kruger is rival lawyer, Alexis Smith his frustrated wife. Vincent Sherman directed; 1959. (*b/w*)

City of Bad Men √
Unusual Western caper in that it re-creates big prizefight between Bob

Fitzsimmons and Jim Corbett; Dale Robertson, Richard Boone are involved in attempt to rob the gate money; Harmon Jones; 1953. (*c*)

City of Fear ×
That stolen canister contains dangerous radioactive cobalt, not money for once; Vince Edwards; directed by Irving Lerner in 1959. (*b/w*)

City That Never Sleeps ×
Gig Young in the days before he developed into leading light comedian (1953) as cop who nearly throws away his good name (ha-ha); John H. Auer; 1953. (*b/w*)

City Under The Sea ×
Appalling script defeats veteran director Jacques Tourneur's attempt to make British horror movie with Vincent Price as ruler of subterranean world, and Tab Hunter discovering it woodenly. David Tomlinson does what he can with silly-ass; and the underwater fighting goes on and on; 1965. (*c*)

Clambake × ×
Elvis Presley as rich boy (at 33 in 1968 he ought to know better – if he didn't, a glance at the size of his waistband might have helped) changing places with water-ski instructor to see if any girl will love him for himself. Oh, dear. Arthur H. Nadel must have been well-paid or desperate director. (*c*)

Clash By Night √
Strong stuff with strong cast (Barbara Stanwyck marrying Paul Douglas, liaisoning with Robert Ryan; Marilyn Monroe, J. Carroll Naish supporting), strongly directed by Fritz Lang from strong script by Alfred Hayes from tough Clifford Odets play. Could even have done with a little weakening; 1962. (*b/w*)

Claudelle Inglish × ×
Phoney Erskine Caldwell novel makes phoney Gordon Douglas film about jilted Diane McBain Burning the Candle at Both Ends; 1961. (*b/w*)

Claudia ×
Dorothy McGuire growing up; strictly soap-opera. Edmund Goulding; 1943. (*b/w*)

Claudia and David ×
Dorothy McGuire's married life; even soapier; Walter Lang; 1956. (*b/w*)

Cleopatra √
(1) 1934: considering the date this is a very sexy item, what with its seductions, slave-girls, near-nudity and (in the famous barge set-piece), whipping and suggested animalism. Director Cecil B. de Mille knew what he was doing, but did the Hays Office? Claudette Colbert looks right as Cleo; Warren Williams, Henry Wilcoxon are rather wooden Caesar, Antony. (*b/w*)

Cleopatra ×
(2) 'Who do you sleep with to get out of this picture?' was just one of the jokes that went the rounds when the 1962 version was made by writer-director Joseph L. Mankiewicz, the most expensive (over $30,000,000) fiasco in the history of pictures. Liz Taylor and Richard Burton were being extra-marital while filming. The result was awful. It managed to pick up minor Oscars for photography, sets, costume and special effects, but the critics gave it the booby prize otherwise. (*c*)

The Climbers × ×
Social, that is, Andrea Parisy brings destruction to marriage in clawing way up ladder; who cares? Edmond O'Brien, Richard Basehart have to make like they do; 1964. (*c*)

Clive of India √
All-starring (Ronald Colman, Loretta

Young, C. Aubrey Smith, Cesar Romero) all-talking, all-action epic of 1935. About empire-building, made when we still were. Director Richard Boleslawski. (*b/w*)

Cloak and Dagger √
Fritz Lang spy thriller set in second world war with Gary Cooper probing nazi atomic progress; 1947. (*b/w*)

The Clouded Yellow √
Jean Simmons trying to prove she didn't do murder in loony haze, with help of ex-MI5's Trevor Howard; Ralph Thomas's direction is notable for some splendid location shots all over England, including Lake District; 1951. (*b/w*)

The Clown ×
Those old enough to remember the Jackie Coogan–Wallace Beery weepie, *The Champ*, will recognise this as a 1953 updating of the same sob-story by Frances Marion. Only here, the champ is a clown, the come-back is on television, the old wino is Red Skelton (not a patch on beery Beery) and the little chap who takes good care of him (ugh!) is a competent little dwarf (no, that's unfair, he is a child) named Tim Considine; Robert Z. Leonard does his best to open your tear-ducts. (*b/w*)

Coast of Skeletons × ×
A bit of a rip-off from *Sanders of the River* which will probably cause all concerned (director Robert Lynn, actors Richard Todd, Derek Nimmo, Dale Robertson) to cover their faces with shame when it comes on the TV screen; it's that old hokum about how the lust for gold ruins all who are touched by it; 1965. (*c*)

The Cobweb ×
Inside a mental institution played strictly for soap-opera, and it's a bit unnerving the way the picture keeps stopping and starting as though reaching the end of one thrilling, cliff-hanging episode before lurching on to the next. Lauren Bacall and Richard Widmark are young lovers (that shows how long ago it was made–1955), and supporting inmates include Oscar Levant, Charles Boyer, Gloria Grahame, Susan Strasberg. Vincente Minnelli. (*c*)

The Cockleshell Heroes ×
José Ferrer kindly did us the favour of coming to Britain to direct and star in this 1956 account of a British raid in five small boats on occupied Bordeaux; no wonder Trevor Howard fights with him the whole time. Too much of the picture is taken up with training, and it only fares briefly into life for the actual raid; Anthony Newley among the heroes, which is pretty depressing news. (*c*) 

The Colditz Story √
Straightforward, well-made can-this-prison-hold-our-brave-PoWs story with John Mills, Eric Portman, Lionel Jeffries, Bryan Forbes, Ian Carmichael, Richard Wattis, directed by Guy Hamilton; 1955. (*b/w*)

A Cold Wind in August √ √
Example of how a low-budget sexploitation sleeper (*le mot juste*) can outstrip (ditto) fancier films by knowing what it's doing. Lola Albright's seduction of 17-year-old is honest as well as erotic, and no one must have been more surprised than director Alexander Singer when his 1961 effort got taken up as OK intellectuals' movie. (*b/w*)

The Collector √
William Wyler tried to realise the significance in John Fowles' novel, only to discover that there wasn't any. Result is a rather tame, rather silly thriller about a nutter (competently played by Terence Stamp) who kidnaps a girl (Samantha Eggar) because he fancies it and her; 1965. (*c*) 

Colorado Territory √
Moody, fatalistic Western from Raoul Walsh (1949) with Joel McCrea escaping law. (*b/w*)

The Colossus of New York ✕
Mad scientist puts dead son's brain into robot; Eugene Lourié achieves some great effects; 1958. (*b/w*)

Colt .45 ✕
Scotts wha' hae: Randolph chases Zachary in this tame 1950 'tribute to the great six-shooting gun'; Edward L. Marin just treats it as one more Western. (*c*)

Column South ✕
Mediocre Western with a touch of concern for the Navajo Indians, as Union officer Audie Murphy fights for their protection; credibility bites the dust early in this story directed by Frederick de Cordova; 1953. (*c*)

Comanche ✕
Dana Andrews' job is to try to make the Indians see that it's more sense to make peace not war; director George Sherman's job is to make you stay watching. He tries hard but might not be able to manage it; 1955. (*c*)

Comanche Station √
One of the best Budd Boetticher–Randolph Scott small-scale Westerns, with the tall leathery hero escorting Nancy Gates through hostile territory; marred by undue violence (a wounded man dragged along by the stirrup) but always exciting; 1959. (*c*)

The Comancheros √
Everyone seems to have enjoyed making this lark of a Western, with John Wayne and Stuart Whitman playing hard-drinking goodies, lined up against baddies Lee Marvin, Nehemiah Pershoff, Edgar Buchanan. Michael Curtiz strays convincingly into John Ford territory; 1961. (*c*)

Come Back, Little Sheba √
1952 adaptation of William Inge Broadway play, which won Shirley Booth, as sluttish housewife, an Oscar and Burt Lancaster, as alcoholic husband, undeserved upstaging by that award; he was extraordinarily subtle – for him. Daniel Mann directed, but never quite opened up the idea from inhibiting stage structure. (*b/w*)

Come Blow Your Horn √
Sinatra as expert on swinging life finds he doesn't know everything. Bud Yorkin's first film, 1963, takes Neil Simon's Broadway winner and makes it rattle along in a series of frantic jokes. Lee J. Cobb is father. (*c*)

The Comedians √
Graham Greene's novel of Papa Doc's Haiti transferred moodily to the screen by Peter Glenville, with a rather theatrical cast of Burton–Taylor, Peter Ustinov, Paul Ford, Lillian Gish; but Alec Guinness walks away with it – possibly he is well suited and sympathetic to Greene's tortured Catholic world; 1967. (*c*)

The Comedy Man ✕
Unusual showbiz backstage story with Kenneth More as actor who finally makes it in commercials; Billie Whitelaw, Dennis Price do their very best but are let down by Alvin Rakoff's spotty direction; 1964. (*b/w*)

The Comedy of Terrors √
Macabre slapstick about two undertakers who improve business by creating a few corpses, it has a gorgeous cast – Vincent Price, Peter Lorre, Boris Karloff, Basil Rathbone – and Jacques Tourneur making his first (1963) comedy. Great fun and quite thrilly at times. (*c*)

Come Fill the Cup √
James Cagney is ex-drunk who now guides newspaper proprietor's son on to the straight and narrow. It's all a bit

simple and silly, but Cagney's charisma counts for a lot, and the supports are strong: Raymond Massey, Gig Young, Jimmy Gleason. Gordon Douglas; 1951. (b/w)

Come Fly With Me ✕
Three airline hostesses get involved with romance on a trip to Paris and Vienna; strictly for the wide blue yonder, though Karl Malden almost saves the picture with his skilful warmth; Henry Levin keeps it flying; 1963. (c)

Come Next Spring √
Rather a touching little picture with Ann Sheridan and Steve Cochran, usually in flashier, worse pictures than this 1956 idyll by R. G. Springsteen, determined to make their Arkansas farm work. . . . come next spring. (c)

The Come-On ✕
Anne Baxter is crook's partner involved with honest boat-owner; Russell Birdwell spins murder story with help of Sterling Hayden; 1956. (b/w)

Come September √
Early (1961) Robert Mulligan-directed comedy about the annual holiday Rock Hudson and Gina Lollobrigida take in his villa overlooking Positano, only to find, arriving early, that Walter Slezak uses it as an hotel; mildly funny and glossy but beware, Bobby Darin sings 'Multiplication'. A big box-office hit. (c)

The Command √
Unpretentious little Western directed by David Butler that falls down only in its principal players—Guy Madison, James Whitmore, Joan Weldon; civil war soldier *v* the Indians; 1954. (c)

Command Decision ✕
Clark Gable wants to send bombing planes deeper into Germany in this 1948 actioner, made when bombing was not a dirty word; John Hodiak, Walter Pidgeon, Edward Arnold involved in heart-searching under veteran director Sam Wood. (b/w)

The Committee ✕
So breathtakingly pretentious is this parable that it almost gets away with breaking all the rules. Paul Jones kills the driver of a car he has hitched a lift in by cutting off his head, then he sews it back on and the chap drives on. And that's only the start. The rest is Kafkaesque stuff about being summoned before an all-powerful, all-mysterious Body. You've got to hand it to Peter Sykes and Max Steuer for actually making it and not just talking about it; 1968. (b/w)

Companions in Nightmare ✕
Which nutter is killing the others at therapy institute? Melvyn Douglas, Anne Baxter, Dana Wynter, Gig Young all getting on a bit in 1967. (c)

Compulsion √√
Richard Fleischer's strong adaptation of Meyer Levin's book about Leopold and Loeb 'thrill-killers', earlier inspirers of Hitchcock's *Rope*. A bit too much courtroom, with Orson Welles delivering Clarence Darrow speeches. Set 1920s, shot 1959. (b/w)

The Condemned of Altona √
The Hamburg ship barons, as seen by Jean-Paul Sartre, made over by Abby Mann in 1963; with Fredric March as chief capitalist, Maximillian Schell as lingering nazi officer son, Sophia Loren. (b/w)

Confessions of an Opium Eater ✕✕
Not your de Quincy, but your Vincent Price hamming it up among San Francisco slave-girls; Albert Zugsmith didn't believe it, either; 1962. (b/w)

Confidential Agent ✕
Disappointing attempt by stage director

Herman Shumlin (never to make another picture, understandably) to bring the Graham Greene novel about fascist business dealings to life. Despite super cast (Charles Boyer, Peter Lorre, Katina Paxinou, Miles Mander, Lauren Bacall) he never convinces for a moment. Read the book instead; 1945. (*b/w*)

Confidential Report √
The butchered remains of an Orson Welles masterpiece, this tells of the shady past of an eccentric and mysterious financier. Unfortunately, control passed out of Welles' hands, and what should have been a meaningful and exciting thriller with deeper undertones became a confusing release in 1955, with Welles, Michael Redgrave, Akim Tamiroff, Mischa Auer involved in impenetrable goings-on. Still, enough remained of Welles the director–writer to make it fascinating for those who worship at his shrine. (*b/w*)

Conflict √
Humphrey Bogart as wife-killer versus Sydney Greenstreet, psychiatrist; Curtis Bernhardt directed with high competence; 1945. (*b/w*)

The Connection √√
Remarkable mock *ciné-vérité* of junkies waiting for a fix; Shirley Clarke magically managed to involve the audience, which was much easier in the theatre; 1961. (*b/w*)

Conquest of Cochise ✕
Routine William Castle movie with Robert Stack trying to subdue blacked-up John Hodiak's braves; 1953. (*c*)

Conspiracy of Hearts √
Nuns shelter Jewish children in wartime Italy and get away with it because Ronald Lewis as Italian commander turns a blind eye. But then German officer Albert Lieven takes charge and it's all very tricky, exciting and sentimental for Lilli Palmer, Sylvia Syms, Yvonne Mitchell; set in 1943, made 1959, directed by Ralph Thomas. (*b/w*)

Conspirator ✕
Taylors, Elizabeth and Robert, in a silly little Gaslit story about a husband ordered by the Reds to whom he is in thrall (for some unexplained reason) to kill his wife; Victor Saville did uninspired directorial stint in 1949. (*b/w*)

The Constant Husband √
Rex Harrison's stylish performance almost saves silly comedy of multi-married amnesiac, with Kay Kendall, Margaret Leighton. Launder-Gilliatt; 1955. (*c*)

Convict 99 √
Lovely old (1938) Will Hay–Graham Moffat–Moore Marriott comedy of mistaken identities, with Googie Withers, Basil Radford, Kathleen Harrison in and out of jail. (*b/w*)

Convicts Four ✕
True story of John Resko (Ben Gazzara) who was freed after serving large part of 17-year stretch because of understanding warden's (Stuart Whitman) interest in his paintings. Great back-up cast include Ray Walston, Vincent Price, Rod Steiger, Brod Crawford, Jack Kruschen. Alas, director Millard Kaufman couldn't put any zip into dull script because he wrote it; 1962. (*b/w*)

Coogan's Bluff √√
Sleeper of its year, 1968–that is to say, the surprise success–thanks mainly to veteran director Don Siegel's way with a thriller. Given an A-picture budget for a change Siegel made this yarn of a small-town cop (the wooden Clint Eastwood, his unacting ability well-used in this steely part) tracking down his man in wild New York, exciting and involving.

Lee J. Cobb turned in one of his always-great performances as the Manhattan tough-cop driven wild by the hick. (*c*)

Cool Hand Luke √ √
Haunting drama of chain-gang prisoner Paul Newman with strong undercurrent of comedy as he sasses his bosses; stunning camerawork by Conrad Hall makes Stuart Rosenberg's direction look even better than it is. Jo van Fleet contributes marvellous cameo as his mother, while George Kennedy and Dennis Hopper stand out in brilliantly marshalled cast; 1967. (*c*)

Cornered √
Good, tough little thriller with Dick Powell searching Europe and Argentina for nazi killers of his wife; before its time in 1946; Edward Dmytryk. (*b/w*)

The Corn is Green √
Bette Davis woefully miscast but battling on like a good trouper in Emlyn Williams' famous yarn about schoolmistress who puts star pupil through university. Disguised propaganda for private (school) enterprise, this version, directed by Irving Rapper, manages to catch the Welsh ambience; 1946. (*b/w*)

Corridors of Blood √
Although Boris Karloff is in it and despite title, this is reasonably sincere account of introduction of anaesthetics to relieve suffering. Goes over the top when he goes mad because of overdose turning him addict; Robert Day; 1958. (*b/w*)

Corruption × × ×
Crazy Peter Cushing mutilating ladies so that girlfriend's vanished beauty can be restored. Horribly done, in every sense of the word. Robert Hartford-Davis has some pretty sick ideas, and obviously hopes that you share them; 1968. (*c*)

Cosa Nostra – Arch-enemy of the FBI ×
This clumsy title comes from the fact that this was originally two episodes of *The FBI* TV series put together; it's a pre-*Godfather* (1967) view of the Mafia as simple gangsters, beefed up with a few over-the-hill stars – Walter Pidgeon, Celeste Holm, Telly Savalas, Susan Strasberg. Don Medford directed. (*c*)

The Counterfeit Traitor √
Spy thriller with William Holden as Swedish businessman forced by Allies to snoop on nazis; Lilli Palmer, Hugh Griffith. Supposedly it all really happened. George Seaton; 1962. (*c*)

Counterpoint ×
Rather awful adaptation of Alan Sillitoe's novel *The General* further vitiated by Ralph Nelson's insensitive direction. Maximilian Schell is nazi officer who captures symphony orchestra led by Charlton Heston, whose spirited performance is the only bright spot in a dull landscape; 1968. (*c*)

A Countess from Hong Kong × ×
Charles (to give him the pompous Christian name he insisted on when directing) Chaplin's howling failure to make a thirties-type comedy out of State Department official Marlon Brando finding stowaway Russian countess Sophia Loren in his cross-Pacific cabin. Should have been thrown overboard but will doubtless hang around as monument to an old man's hubris; 1967. (*c*)

The Count of Monte Cristo √
First glimpsed on television in 1938 (at Radiolympia) this swashbuckler was directed four years earlier by Rowland Lee. Robert Donat was the wrongly imprisoned Count, Louis Calhern chief heavy. Elissa Landi was heroine. (*b/w*)

The Country Girl √
Oscar-winning performance from Grace

Kelly, holding up drunken Bing Crosby with encouragement from William Holden. Strong stuff and competently directed by George Seaton; 1954. (*b/w*)

Count the Hours √
Macdonald Carey takes blame for pregnant wife Teresa Wright when employers are murdered; Don Siegel made it tight and trim in 1953. (*b/w*)

Count Three and Pray ✗
Raymond Burr, one of the great Hollywood heavies in both senses of the word, tangling with Van Heflin, rogue turned pastor. Joanne Woodward is romantic interest in this 1955 Western. George Sherman. (*c*)

Count Your Blessings ✗ ✗
Deadly comedy with some of the deadliest stars in the business: Deborah Kerr, Maurice Chevalier, Rossano Brazzi, directed by the deadly Jean Negulesco. How a che-ild brings parents together again; 1959. (*c*)

Courage of Lassie ✗
Elizabeth Taylor reforms Lassie, used in war as killer. Directed by Fred Wilcox; 1946. (*c*)

The Court Jester √
Made by Panama-and-Frank while Danny Kaye was still as funny (in 1956) as he later thought he was, this is a romp through the Middle Ages with Basil Rathbone and Cecil Parker backing up nicely (and rather nastily, but that's only the plot). Henry Hathaway. (*c*)

The Courtship of Eddie's Father ✗ ✗
Quite horrible comedy with Glenn Ford as widower giving up the girl he wants to marry (fashion consultant Stella Stevens) for the nurse who lives next door (Shirley Jones), at the grinding insistence of his ghastly six-year-old son (the precocious Ronny Howard). Vincente Minnelli, who should have known

better, perpetrated this cute concoction in 1963. (*c*)

Cowboy √
The imaginative idea of filming Frank (*Life and Loves*) Harris's adventures as a nineteenth-century cow-poke (and that's nearly the right word) grinds to a disappointing movie as Delmer Davis makes compromise after compromise with convention, ending up as just another Western with Glenn Ford and Jack Lemmon trading chitchat, and Brian Donlevy doing his usual bit. 1957. (*c*)

Crack in the Mirror √
Laudable attempt to try something different; Orson Welles, Juliette Greco, Bradford Dillman each play two parts in parallel love stories set in Paris. Richard Fleischer; 1960. (*c*)

Crack in the World √
Superior 1965 sci-fi about Dana Andrews trying to harness earth's energy but only succeeding in causing vast earthquakes. Janette Scott screams convincingly but real star is director Andrew Marton's special effects. (*c*)

Creature from the Black Lagoon √
Allegorical and beautifully filmed sci-fi, directed by Jack Arnold, 1954. A Gill-Man lives in the depths of the Amazon, menacing our moral world in general and Julie Adams in particular. If you don't like the genre, it's easy to laugh at this low-budget example; but if you will allow yourself to enter into its premises you may find it haunting and unsettling. Achieved added fame when Marilyn Monroe went to see it in *The Seven Year Itch* and sympathised with the Creature. (*b/w*)

Creature from the Haunted Sea ✗
Villain plans to blame mythical monster for crime; then—how did you guess?—real one appears; 1961. Roger Corman. (*b/w*)

Crest of the Wave × ×
Dull little Boulting Brothers effort to accommodate Gene Kelly as American torpedo expert; 1954. (*b/w*)

Crime and Punishment, USA √
Dostoievsky's much-filmed drama of death and retribution transferred to Santa Monica and the 1959 beat set; George Hamilton is adequate as the law-student, but the attempt of brothers Terry and Denis Sanders founders on trying to do too many things (tell the story, bring out the meanings, transfer the locale) all at once. (*b/w*)

Crime in the Streets √
Don Siegel's rather sentimental yarn about juvenile delinquents on the East Side: John Cassavetes, Sal Mineo, Mark Rydell; 1957. (*b/w*)

Crime of Passion √
Sad little story of love and the police; Barbara Stanwyck's ambition for her husband leads her to commit adultery and murder; Sterling Hayden, Fay Wray, Raymond Burr; Gerd Oswald kept his ambition low and achieved it; 1957. (*b/w*)

The Criminal √ √
Exciting if overly symbolic (is freedom outside jail or inside yourself?) yarn with sharp Alun Owen script and closely-observed performances from Stanley Baker, Sam Wanamaker, Patrick Magee. Despite later acclaim, Joseph Losey has never done better than this 1960 thriller.
(*b/w*)

The Crimson Kimono √
San Francisco detectives fall out over art student Victoria Shaw while investigating murder of a stripper; Samuel Fuller gave this B-pic his special touch in 1959. (*b/w*)

The Crimson Pirate √
Burt Lancaster playing the buccaneer in what might have been intended as a spoof but ends up another swashbuckler under Robert Siodmak's direction; 1952. (*c*)

Cripple Creek ×
George Montgomery on the trail of gold bandits poses as member of the gang; this 1952, Ray Nazarro-directed Western should not be confused with *Cripple Creek Bar-Room*, made in 1898 and the first Western ever made, although you might have preferred seeing the latter. (*c*)

Crisis √
Cary Grant as American doctor forced to treat South American dictator; Richard Brooks did it competently in 1950. (*b/w*)

Criss Cross √
Burt Lancaster in tough gangster yarn directed by Robert Siodmak that grips the interest, partly because it isn't too obvious; only snags are Yvonne de Carlo as his wife and rest of weak cast except for Dan Duryea; 1949. (*b/w*)

Critic's Choice ×
Presenting the flimsiest ethical problem of 1963: should Bob Hope review wife Lucille Ball's play? Don Weis contrives to make it as appealing as possible, which isn't very. (*c*)

The Crooked Road ×
Robert Ryan in British-made, Don Chaffey-directed Balkan thriller about a dictator and a newspaperman; not very convincing; 1965. (*b/w*)

Crooks and Coronets × × ×
Dreadful failure involving Dame Edith Evans as unendearingly eccentric old lady that the self-consciously funny-peculiar Telly Savalas hopes to rob; Cesar Romero and Harry H. Corbett try throwing in echoes of some of their other, more successful roles, but it doesn't help. Jim O'Connolly wrote and directed, so he must take the main share of the blame; 1969. (*c*)

Crooks Anonymous √
Harmless little British comedy about villains trying not to be. Ken Annakin had a better cast than thin script deserved: Leslie Phillips, Stanley Baxter, Wilfrid Hyde White, Julie Christie, Robertson Hare, Harry Fowler, John Bennett, Dick Emery, Dandy Nichols, Alfred Burke, Norman Rossington; 1962. (*b/w*)

Crossfire √√
Strong thriller about anti-semitic killer (Robert Ryan) who tries to pin the rap on soldier-buddy. Robert Young makes a fine detective who states the theme—that persecution is sickness and Jew-hating is evil. Edward Dmytryk made this 1947 Doré Schary production taut and exciting all the way. (*b/w*)

Crossplot × ×
Indistinguishable from a routine *Saint* churn-out, this 1969 effort has Roger Moore preventing the assassination of a visiting statesman; Alvin Rakoff skims through it with the help of a batch of familiar TV faces. (*c*)

Crosswinds ×
Dashing John Payne, after cargo of gold from a plane that crashed in New Guinea, inevitably meets head-hunters and Rhonda Fleming. Directed 1951 by Lewis R. Foster. (*b/w*)

Crowded Paradise √
Tight little drama about how badly Puerto Rican immigrants are treated in New York, with Hume Cronyn; 1956. (*b/w*)

The Crowded Sky ×
One of those who-will-be-saved air disaster yarns with Anne Francis, Efrem Zimbalist Jr, Dana Andrews, Keenan Wynn among possibly-doomed; Joseph Pevney; 1960. (*b/w*)

The Cruel Sea √
Rugged account of corvette in battle of the Atlantic convinces and sobers; in a huge distinguished cast Jack Hawkins, Donald Sinden, Denholm Elliott, Alec McCowen stand out. Charles Frend directed, from Eric Ambler's script from Nicholas Monsarrat's novel; 1953. (*b/w*)

Cry Danger √
Creditable product of tough Hollywood school with Dick Powell as convict paroled under say-so of ambiguous pillar of the community. William Conrad among those threateningly present. Nice tight job from Robert Parrish; 1951. (*b/w*)

Cry for Happy × ×
Dull little comedy about expectations of American sailors Donald O'Connor, Glenn Ford over services performed by geisha girls in Japan; George Marshall makes the best (which isn't very good) of it; 1961. (*c*)

A Cry from the Streets ×
Max Bygraves, Barbara Murray, Kathleen Harrison, sundry children in modest 1958 yarn about homeless kids and social workers; Lewis Gilbert's sympathetic direction helps. (*b/w*)

Cry Havoc ×
Nurses on wartime Philippines include Margaret Sullavan, Ann Sothern, Fay Bainter, Ella Raines; director Richard Thorpe; 1943. (*b/w*)

A Cry in the Night √
Peeping Tom kidnaps girl, and the chase that follows. Plenty of incident and tension served up by Frank Tuttle with the help of Natalie Wood, Raymond Burr, Edmond O'Brien, Brian Donlevy; 1956. (*b/w*)

Cry of Battle ×
Contrasting Americans Van Heflin and James MacArthur (later to settle down in his rightful place as minor support in *Hawaii Five-O*) caught in the Philippines

at outbreak of war; tame direction from Irving Lerner doesn't help; 1963. (*c*)

Cry of the City ✗
Childhood mates grow up to opposite sides of the law; kid brother could go either way; Richard Conte, Victor Mature, Shelley Winters. Robert Siodmak made it all so predictable; 1948. (*b/w*)

Cry of the Hunted ✗
Louisiana marsh locations give this routine chase a touch of distinction; otherwise, some tiresome philosophising interrupts the action. Polly Bergen, Barry Sullivan; director Joseph H. Lewis; 1953. (*b/w*)

Cry Terror! ✓
One of those family-held-hostage movies, this time with Rod Steiger as chief heavy and James Mason as father of beleaguered family; Andrew Stone plays it for thrills and should succeed in holding your attention, at least; 1958. (*b/w*)

Cry, the Beloved Country ✓
This 1952 version of Alan Paton's novel about apartheid undoubtedly has its heart in the right place but so much has changed in twenty years. It couldn't be shot in South Africa now; and the moral that men of goodwill of all colours must work together seems pathetic. Sidney Poitier and Canada Lee acted with dignity; Zoltan Korda directed. (*b/w*)

Cul-de-Sac ✓✓
Gorgeously conceived and carried out black comedy-thriller with the superb Lionel Stander forcing himself on Donald Pleasence and Françoise Dorléac on Holy Island. Roman Polanski made this one unforgettable; 1966. (*b/w*)

The Cure for Love ✗
Robert Donat having to get rid of fiancée Dora Bryan (27 when this was made in 1949) to marry Cockney Renée Asherson; he also directed and produced it, nine years before his death. (*b/w*)

The Curse of Frankenstein ✓
Hammer horror with Peter Cushing, Christopher Lee, going through the usual antics; it's a flashback of how the Baron comes to be awaiting death sentence. Terence Fisher directed competently; 1956. (*c*)

The Curse of the Cat People ✓✓
Although she's in it, this isn't really a sequel to Simone Simon's earlier *Cat People* (q.v.). This title was forced on director Robert Wise and producer Lew Lewton by the studio. Instead, it's a sensitive and haunting story of the impression a visit to a cranky old lady has on the mind of a seven-year-old, caught in a world of terror while the grown-ups squabble and disregard her; beautifully done; 1944. (*b/w*)

Curse of the Mummy's Tomb ✗
Uninspired remake of the old mummy plot by Hammer's Michael Carreras in 1964; stiff Terence Morgan stars in this one which does at least have a surprise twist of sorts in that the heavy isn't the one you first think. (*c*)

Curse of the Undead ✗
The only horror Western? Gunman who turns out to be a vampire; E. Dein crashing between stools in 1959. (*b/w*)

Curse of the Voodoo ✗✗
Native chief curses safari hunter; could have been exciting, but like so many British horror-attempts it tails off to boredom. Dennis Price gamely soldiers on, Lisa Daniely screams; director Lindsay Shonteff; 1965. (*b/w*)

Curse of the Werewolf ✗
Oliver Reed was bewitched in this rather ordinary horror pic directed by Terence Fisher; 1960. (*b/w*)

Custer of the West ✓
Robert Shaw, Mary Ure, Robert Ryan in attempt to marry epic Western (originally made in Cinerama) and political tract with dubious origins; Robert Siodmak; 1967. (*c*)

Cyrano de Bergerac ✗
Disappointing version of Rostand's play, founders less on the size of José Ferrer's nose than the inadequacy of his performance; Michael Gordon directs faithfully from a rather desperate Carl Foreman script; 1950. (*b/w*)

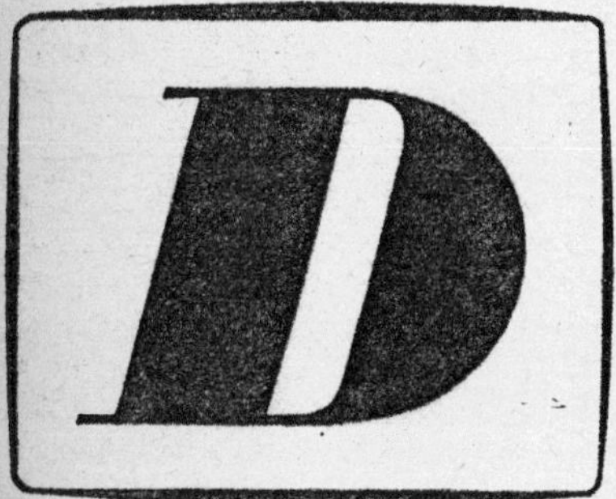

Daddy Long Legs ✓
1955 musical remake of 1919 Mary Pickford and 1930 Janet Gaynor vehicles, with Leslie Caron as the orphan who loves her benefactor, this time Fred Astaire. Johnny Mercer supplied some pretty tunes (including Something's Gotta Give) and Jean Negulesco's schmaltzy directorial style is well-suited to this load of sentiment. (*c*)

Daddy's Gone A-Hunting ✓
Carol White being chased round San Francisco by a photographer all set on killing her little baby; all very far-fetched and only moderately chilling; Mark Robson; 1969. (*c*)

Bela Lugosi in *Dracula*

Daisy Kenyon ✕
Joan Crawford in 1947 Otto Preminger epic he'd rather forget; should she marry Dana Andrews now he's divorced or stay with nice Henry Fonda? You guessed. *(b/w)*

Dakota Incident √
Linda Darnell's in the stage-coach, the Indians are outside attacking; Lewis R. Foster; 1956. *(c)*

Daleks' Invasion Earth 2150 A.D. √
It may be 2150 in the title but it looks strictly 1966 from here. Quite an amusing comic strip, with Bernard Cribbins scoring as special constable from the sixties caught up in the future. Peter Cushing plays Dr Who; unfortunately he was ill during the filming which is the real reason he is absent through so many of the adventures; director Gordon Flemyng. *(c)*

Dallas √
Gary Cooper's the goodie, Raymond Massey and Steve Cochran the baddies in standard Western, directed by Stuart Heisler in 1950. *(c)*

The Dam Busters √
Michael Redgrave as Dr Barnes Wallis, the man who made the bouncing bomb to destroy Möhne and Eder dams. Michael Anderson directed this one with a straight bat in 1954 and got absolutely decent performances from Richard Todd as Wing-Commander Gibson, Basil Sydney, Nigel Stock, Robert Shaw; but it's Redgrave's film. *(c)*

The Damned √
On the level of sci-fi thriller this 1962 Joseph Losey parable works fine; only when it starts taking itself seriously does it stumble. A bunch of cold-blooded (literally) kids are kept in a cave to repopulate the world after the holocaust –and at anything but the lowest level it gets pretentious and confusing. Poorly cast with Macdonald Carey, Shirley Ann Field, Alexander Knox, Oliver Reed each adding their contribution to the general unbelievability. *(b/w)*

The Damned √ √
Visconti's history of the nazis' rise to power, made in 1969, is a heavy, sombre catalogue of one family's selling-out that glowers with burnished tones, but ultimately lacks the moral standpoint necessary to put the evil into perspective. Dirk Bogarde never seems happy in the central role, and none of the other main players rises to any heights of realism or insight. A magnificent failure. *(c)*

Damn Yankees √ √
Irresistible-sounding idea of an ageing baseball fan being Fausted into great player, becomes slightly more resistible amid all that alien home-running; somehow the opening-out of the stage play hasn't helped. But Ray Walston's Devil and Gwen Verdon as his tempting helper are fine. Her Whatever Lola Wants stops the show. Stanley Donen gave it polish; 1958. *(c)*

The Dance of Death √ √
National Theatre's production of Strindberg drama about a chained marriage photographed by director David Giles with only a desultory minute's opening-out for filming. Olivier incredibly powerful, Geraldine McEwan adequate, Robert Lang plodding; 1969.*(c)*

Dance of the Vampires √
This heavy-handed satire on horror movies has taken on a totally different and macabre aspect since its star Sharon Tate, wife of its director Roman Polanski, was so tragically involved in manifestations of occult madness. Polanski appears himself with Jack MacGowran as vampire hunters. Sad that it wasn't a better memorial; 1968. *(c)*

A Dandy in Aspic ✗
Russian-British double-agent Laurence Harvey is told to kill the spy we know to be himself; he manages to make it all languorous and tiresome, abetted in his general stupefaction by Mia Farrow. Tom Courtenay, Peter Cook, all of whom shuffle around as if waiting for the funny lines director Anthony Mann promised them. Only Lionel Stander ignored the general apathy and hams it up as Russian spymaster; 1968. (*c*)

Danger Grows Wild ✗
Has laudable aim of reminding us of necessities of international co-operation and the dangers of narcotics. But a better aim would have been to supply some good entertainment. As it is, one's interest is held mostly by spotting the guest stars (among those to look for: Yul Brynner, Rita Hayworth, Marcello Mastroianni, Hugh Griffith, Jack Hawkins, Omar Sharif, Eli Wallach), while Trevor Howard and E. G. Marshall play agents and Angie Dickinson a mystery woman. Terence Young does what he can to accommodate all those kindly working for honoraria, but the end result is a mess; 1966. (*c*)

The Dangerous Days of Kiowa Jones √
Robert Horton is the awkwardly-named hero in this superior Western, taking two captured murderers to jail, meeting up with Diane Baker, surprisingly driving a covered wagon around at the time. As the baddies, Nehemiah Persoff and Sal Mineo turn in strong performances, and the whole effort is a restrained and distinguished first film for director Alex March; 1966. (*c*)

Dangerous Mission √
The Glacier National Park is the real star of this otherwise heavy-going drama with Victor Mature and William Bendix on the side of Good; Vincent Price representing Evil; Louis King seems happier with the scenery than the automatons he is directing. Piper Laurie saw a murder and fled there; 1954. (*c*)

Dangerous Moonlight ✗
Brian Desmond Hurst's 1941 romantic tear-jerker that launched the Warsaw Concerto upon us. Famous Polish pianist Anton Walbrook meets American journalist Sally Gray in shattered Warsaw, escapes to join a bomber squadron to avenge his country. (*b/w*)

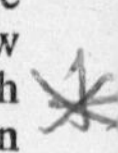

Danger Route ✗ ✗
Hard to care about this cold-spy melo. Richard Johnson fails to inject spy with any charm and director Seth Holt to discipline a wayward and gnomic story; 1967. (*c*)

The Daring Game ✗
Lloyd Bridges in his Sea Hunt kit doing his underwater bit, combined this time with parachuting, to save American scientist and daughter trapped in South America; unconvincing story is just about saved by the special effects; veteran director Laslo Benedek has tried hard; 1968. (*c*)

The Dark at the Top of the Stairs √ √
If William Inge play was more profound in the theatre, this version of family-and-neighbours small-town drama, with Eve Arden, Angela Lansbury, Dorothy McGuire, Robert Preston, escapes banality. Delbert Mann; 1960. (*c*)

Dark of the Sun √
Thriller set in troubled Congo well-directed by ex-cameraman Jack Cardiff in 1968. Rod Taylor and Jim Brown are mercenaries, hardly heroic figures, one would have thought. (*c*)

Dark Passage √ √
Humphrey Bogart escapes from prison to prove he isn't wife-killer; helper is Lauren Bacall; Agnes Moorhead among splendid cast; tautly and excitingly directed by Delmer Daves; 1948. (*b/w*)

The Dark Past √
How a psychiatrist tries to talk his way out of being held hostage by potty killer; William Holden, Lee J. Cobb; director Rudolph Maté; 1948. (*b/w*)

Dark Purpose × ×
Hammy old Rosanno Brazzi is the heavy, conning lightweight Shirley Jones to come to Amalfi to catalogue his paintings; but who has he hidden upstairs, Rochester-style? It's terribly hard to care and veteran director George Marshall can't make you; 1964. (*c*)

Darling √ √
Overrated triple Oscar-winning (the 1965 doorstops for female actress, Julie Christie; story, Frederic Raphael; costumes, Julie Harris) purports to show that upward drift of mod model—including abortions, orgies, conversion, a prince for a husband—only brings unhappiness. John Schlesinger's skill only partly conceals emptiness of the film, Dirk Bogarde among saving graces. (*b/w*)

David and Bathsheba √
Slightly better than the usual Hollywooden Biblical epic in that it has Gregory Peck giving the appearance of integrity as only he knows how. For the rest, it's stilted dialogue, a doll-like Susan Hayward as Bathie, and competent direction by Henry King, particularly of the battle scenes. The supporting cast doesn't much; 1951. (*c*)

David and Lisa √ √
Outstanding Frank and Eleanor Perry movie underrated by the industry in 1962 (never properly released) but hailed by critics and gaining Academy Award nomination. Keir Dullea, Janet Margolin as inmates of school for disturbed adolescents who reach out for mutual help. (*b/w*)

David Copperfield √ √
(1) 1934: David Selznick proved two important lessons: don't tamper with a classic; don't worry about a picture's length, as long as it is good. Reminded that Dickens made no mention of Micawber's juggling, W. C. Fields (who played him) replied: 'He probably forgot it.' Freddie Bartholomew, Basil Rathbone, Roland Young; George Cukor directed. (*b/w*)

David Copperfield √
(2) 1969: inferior in every way except casting (Micawber: Ralph Richardson rather more faithful to the original; Mr Creakle: marvellously horrid Olivier; Ron Moody's slimy Uriah Heep; Wendy Hiller, Michael Redgrave, Susan Hampshire, Edith Evans) this slow and oddly time-structured version, directed by Delbert Mann, doesn't satisfy either Dickensians or non-Dickensians. (*c*)

Dawn at Socorro √
Standard Western about gambler who intends to reform (Rory Calhoun) and Piper Laurie as the girl who prays for him in the shoot-out; George Sherman; 1954. (*c*)

A Day at the Races √ √
'Marry me and I'll never look at another horse,' says Groucho to Margaret Dumont; and Marxists won't need reminding of Harpo's ice-cream vendor-cum-racing-tipster or the scene where Groucho comes to believe his own false tip. Sam Wood; 1937. (*b/w*)

Day of the Badman √
Fred MacMurray in standard Western (1958) about judge determined to hang despite condemned man's brothers trying to free him; Harry Keller. (*c*)

Day of the Outlaw √
Two days of terror in a cattle town changes a lot of lives, including those of Robert Ryan (as herd-owner), Tina Louise (another man's wife he fancies), Burl Ives (leader of the hell-raisers); strong direction by André de Toth

makes this 1959 Western a cut above most. (*b/w*)

The Day of the Triffids   ✕
Disappointing version of John Wyndham's scary novel about the veg. that blinds the Earth's inhabitants, preparatory to taking over, has at least one superior sequence–just before the blind turn on the blind in frustrated anger. And Janette Scott gives a better performance as scientist fighting the menace than director Steve Sekeley has managed to get from the rest of his somewhat inadequate cast, led by Howard Keel(!); 1963. (*c*)

The Day the Earth Caught Fire   ✓✓
One of the best sci-fi movies ever made in Britain, this is the one about the earth's axis having been tilted by atomic explosion so that we get too dangerously near the sun. Set mostly in the *Daily Express* offices, it starred Edward (whatever-happened-to) Judd and Janet Munro, both excellent, and a whole gallery of believable performers. Val Guest co-wrote with Wolf Mankowitz, produced, directed and never did better; 1962. (*b/w*)

The Day the Fish Came Out   ✕ ✕
Pretentious Michael Cacoyannis rubbish about seeking planeload of atomic material on Greek isle; the second-eleven cast (Tom Courtenay, Sam Wanamaker, Colin Blakeley, Candice Bergen) don't help; 1969. (*c*)

The Day the Earth Stood Still   ✓✓
Superior sci-fi about convincingly wooden Michael Rennie visiting from another planet. Pat Neal, Sam Jaffe play supports to flying saucer; Robert Wise made it most watchable; 1951. (*b/w*)

The Day the World Ended   ✓
Roger Corman sci-fi about small group that survived atomic radiation; Richard Denning, Lori Nelson, Adele Jergens; 1956. (*b/w*)

The Day they Gave Babies Away   ✓
Glynis Johns in calculated heart-warmer about immigrant family who raise six kids in Wisconsin; Allen Reisner turns on the water-taps a bit too readily but catches the historical flavour well; 1956. (*c*)

The Day They Robbed the Bank of England   ✕
Only Peter O'Toole (restrained and wry in 1960, before he started believing his own publicity) makes this standard caper movie worth looking at. Nominal star Aldo Ray is a bit of a pill; supports Elizabeth Sellars, Hugh Griffith, Kieron Moore likewise. John Guillerman. (*c*)

Days of Wine and Roses   ✓✓
Jack Lemmon's an alcoholic, marries Lee Remick and gets her on the bottle, too. Daddy Charles Bickford's appalled; AA member Jack Klugman tries to help them kick it. It's all a bit pat, but Blake Edwards does tight (sorry) directorial job that falls just short of slickness; 1962. (*b/w*)

Dayton's Devils   ✕ ✕
Rather wearisome caper about stealing $1\frac{1}{2}$ million from US Army base; Jack Shea hasn't got the tautness in his direction that's needed for a good robbery movie, and cast of Leslie Nielsen, Rory Calhoun and unknowns haven't the charisma; 1968. (*c*)

D-Day The Sixth of June   ✕ ✕
Weak little effort with Robert Taylor unconvincing as American soldier about to invade Germany, which he eventually does most unconvincingly. Only Edmond O'Brien turns in anything like a performance as a blustering GI under Henry Koster's flaccid direction; 1956. (*c*)

Deadfall   ✓
Bryan Forbes out of his depth trying to make a plushy Riviera caper into a

significant character study. He's not helped by the performances of Michael Caine, Giovanna Ralli, Eric Portman and Mrs Bryan Forbes; 1968. (*c*)

Dead Heat on a Merry-go-Round √√
Cheerful caper about robbing an airport when it's all taken up with the arrival of VIP; James Coburn carries it disarmingly, and writer-director Bernard Girard provides some nifty touches; 1965. (*c*)

Dead of Night √√
Classic 1945 chiller in which Cavalcanti, Basil Dearden, Robert Hamer each directed episodes, dreams within a dream, most haunting of which is Michael Redgrave's ventriloquist controlled by his doll. (*b/w*)

Dead Reckoning √√
Humphrey Bogart, unofficially investigating death of paratrooper pal, finds that Lizabeth Scott (the poor man's Lauren Bacall) is at the centre of the web; John Cromwell; 1946. (*b/w*)

Dead Ringer √
Bette Davis playing murderous twins, planning to do herself in and then pretend to be herself; of course it's all absurd hokum, but as *Time* said in 1964: 'Two Bette Davises are better than one ... exuberantly uncorseted, her torso looks like a gunnysack full of galoshes ... her face like a U2 photograph of Utah. And her acting, as always, isn't really acting; it's shameless showing-off. But just try to look away'. Paul Henried. (*b/w*)

Deadlier Than the Male ××
Exceptionally boring and tedious Miss J. Bond thriller with the gimmick that it's the ladies (Elke Sommer, Sylvia Koscina –groan!) who do the killing. Nigel Green employs them, Richard Johnson as Bulldog Drummond exposes them. A waste of all their time–don't add yours; Ralph Thomas; 1967. (*c*)

The Deadly Affair √
Sidney Lumet must have hoped that this would get under the tape before sordid-spy cycle ended, but 1967 was too late for this *In From the Cold*-type thriller, even though it was from John le Carré's *Call for the Dead*. James Mason and Simone Signoret do their best, but it has got the chilly breath of failure about it all–of course, it's meant to have, but not this deep. (*c*)

Deadline √√
Strong newspaper stuff from Richard Brooks, directing a particularly well-cast Humphrey Bogart as Front Page-type managing editor fighting to save a dying daily with crime scoop in last issue. Solid support from Ethel Barrymore, Ed Begley, Kim Hunter, Paul Stewart, Martin Gabel; 1952. (*b/w*)

The Deadly Bees ××
Deadly is the word; this low-budget whodunit-with-bee-stings flops in all departments; Freddie Francis must have churned it out and Frank Finlay, displaying his usual lack of charisma, can't carry it; 1967. (*c*)

The Deadly Companions √√
A remarkable first film by Sam Peckinpah in 1962, foreshadowing many of the themes and excitements that later established him (*The Wild Bunch, Straw Dogs*) as an original if abrasive talent. The escorting of a coffin over Indian territory becomes a violent and riveting parable; Maureen O'Hara, Brian Keith, Steve Cochran. (*c*)

The Deadly Mantis √
New York is threatened by giant insect from the Arctic; can Craig Stevens save the city? Director Nathan Juran; 1957. (*b/w*)

Dear Brigitte ××
Why a star of the stature of James

Stewart permits himself to be embroiled in this kind of farrago is beyond comprehension. He's the father of an eight-year-old boy who's a whizz at picking winners but won't do so until he has met Brigitte Bardot. So–would you credit it? –Jimmy schlepps him all the way to France and BB does us all a favour with a guest appearance. Positively embarrassing all round, and Henry Koster (producer as well as director) should blush; 1965. (*c*)

Dear Heart ✗
Glycerine magazine story about spinster Geraldine Page meeting lonely Glenn Ford and getting together; Delbert Mann's poor taste runs right down to the weak casting which includes Angela Lansbury and Michael Anderson jr; 1965. (*b/w*)

Death Curse of Tartu ✗ ✗ ✗
Dreadful nonsense about reincarnations of a witch doctor protecting graves from desecration – and the plot's the best thing about it; William Grefe is the name of the director; 1968. (*c*)

Death is a Woman ✗ ✗ ✗
A really awful attempt to make like Patsy Ann Noble is an actress–and one capable of playing a triple murderess. And the worst thing about it is that she's the best thing in the picture. Desperately padded and badly made in all departments, this stands as a monument of inefficient moviemaking. Director Frederic Goode must take most of the blame, although anyone who accepted any assignment having read Wally Bosco's script obviously needed the money; 1967. (*c*)

Death of a Gunfighter √
Old-style Marshal Richard Widmark won't resign, so he has to be bumped off out of office is theme of this unconvincing Western. But Richard Widmark, Lena Horne, John Saxon, Carroll O'Connor

get some mileage out of the improbabilities, thanks to direction by 'Allan Smithee', a pseudonym for Don Siegel and Robert Totlen; 1969. (*c*)

Death of a Salesman √ √
More important for its influence than its profundity, this filming of Arthur Miller's stage success about failure hopped effortlessly about in time and space, as it traced Frederic March's reasons for not wanting his son to follow his saga in search of the fast buck. Competently directed by Laslo Benedek, 1951, it did rather romanticise the stage-play's meaner salesman. (*b/w*)

Decision at Sundown √
Superior Budd Boetticher Western has Randolph Scott arriving to kill John Carroll thinking he was responsible for his wife's death during the Civil War; 1957. (*c*)

The Decks Ran Red √
Broderick Crawford's murderous plan is to kill off the crew of a rusty old tub for the salvage money; James Mason, the cap'n, is out to thwart him; made by the Andrew and Virginia Stone reliable team of thrill-raisers in 1958. (*c*)

Decline and Fall ✗
By avoiding doing Waugh's novel in its only possible setting, the twenties, John Krish has thrown away most of the chance to make this progress towards enlightenment work. What's left is a rather ordinary tale, not more than competently acted by Robin Phillips and Genevieve Page, and allowing too much indulgence to Donald Wolfit and Leo McKern; 1968. (*c*)

The Deep Blue Sea √
Vivien Leigh as tragic heroine, with Kenneth More as her RAF lover. Eric Portman and Emlyn Williams are fine in slow, stagey version (1955) of Terence Rattigan's play. (*c*)

Deep In My Heart × ×
Pretty awful musical biography of one of the weaker popular composers – Sigmund Romberg – soggily cast (José Ferrer, Merle Oberon, Helen Traubel, Walter Pidgeon, Paul Henried) and directed by Stanley Donen; 1954. (*c*)

The Deep Six × ×
Rather nasty and embarrassing second world war actioner that features Alan Ladd, ashamed of his previous pacifism, leading a dangerous naval attack; Rudolph Maté; 1958. (*c*)

The Deerslayer × ×
Lex Barker, Forrest Tucker, Rita Moreno in disappointing adaptation of James Fenimore Cooper's novel about white boy brought up by Indians; Kurt Neumann; 1957. (*c*)

The Defector √
Unusual espionage thriller in that it is 1966 Franco-German co-production, with Montgomery Clift in last role, Hardy Kruger as communist agent and Jean-Luc Godard *acting*. Raoul Lévy directing. (*b/w*)

The Defiant Ones √ √
Stanley Kramer's still powerful 1958 racial drama of two Southern chain-gang convicts on the run. Superb performances from Sidney Poitier and Tony Curtis. (*b/w*)

Demetrius and the Gladiators √
The 1954 follow-up to the previous year's epic, *The Robe*, stars Victor Mature, not the most sensitive of actors, and features Anne Bancroft before Hollywood realised she was Academy Award potential. (*c*)

The Desert Fox √ √
Exciting and cool account of Field-Marshal Rommel, the North African war and his part in anti-Hitler plot. James Mason, Luther Adler, Everett Sloane; directed by Henry Hathaway; 1951. (*b/w*)

Desert Legion ×
With Alan Ladd in the Foreign Legion; utterly predictable; director Joseph Peveney; 1953. (*c*)

The Desert Rats √ √
Second world war suspenser about the siege of Tobruk saved by Richard Burton's tough officer slowly winning respect of troops. James Mason does his splendid Rommel (as in *The Desert Fox*) and there's a standout performance from Robert Newton as professor turned soldier. Robert Wise's 1953 direction is action-packed. (*b/w*)

The Desert Song × ×
Extremely boring version of the old Sigmund Romberg operetta; Gordon Macrae, Kathryn Grayson. Only Raymond Massey gives it flicker of life; H. Bruce Humberstone; 1953. (*c*)

Designing Woman √
Stylish 1957 comedy directed by Vincente Minnelli with Gregory Peck as sports-writer who marries Lauren Bacall after whirlwind courtship and finds that she's top fashion designer. Nub is conflict between their worlds. Dolores Gray, Sam Levene give strong support. (*c*)

Desirée × ×
A quite awful rendering of the Napoleon story with Marlon Brando ludicrous as Bonaparte and Jean Simmons not much better as the lady of the title. Daniel Taradash's script is balderdash, and the luckless Henry Koster stumbles directorially about letting the chat go on and on, and vainly trying to marshal the rest of his weak cast to little effect; 1954. (*c*)

Desire in the Dust ×
Ex-con Ken Scott gets mixed up with

Raymond Burr's family, and the blood-hounds come out in an overcooked ending; William F. Claxton; 1960. (*b/w*)

Desire Under the Elms √
This is the poorly-cast (Sophia Loren, Burl Ives, Anthony Perkins), poorly-set (you can smell the studio arc lamps burning, not the farmyard dung), poorly-directed (Delbert Mann) 1958 version of Eugene O'Neill's long, passionate drama. A pity because it's basically splendid. (*b/w*)

The Desk Set √√
Katherine Hepburn heads a research team threatened by new office broom Spencer Tracy; also in the cast are Gig Young and Joan Blondell. Do you need to know any more except that Walter Lang let them enjoy themselves hugely in 1957? (*c*)

The Desperados ×
Parson Jack Palance rides into town with his sons ready to avenge his dead wife; son Vince Edwards rebels, but Pop goes after him, too. It all ends badly. As a matter of fact, it starts and goes on badly, too. Unfortunately, director Henry Levin makes it all seem loose and lacking in tension; Palance does well enough but everyone else in sight seems uncertain. 1969. (*c*)

The Desperate Hours √√
High tension nail-biter as three escaped convicts hide out in a suburban home, terrorising a family. With Humphrey Bogart at his meanest. Directed 1955 by William Wyler. (*b/w*)

Destination Inner Space ×
Undersea sci-fi drama about monster terrorising marine research station; looks like director Francis D. Lyon was told to economise on the special effects and the result isn't as scary as it should be; Sheree North loons around; 1966. (*c*)

Destination Moon ×
This was huge success in 1950, thanks to George Pal's meticulously-assembled special effects team, but underneath the scientific blah it's a hollow vessel with poor story and acting, largely overlooked by director Irving Pichel as he struggled with his other priorities. Today, it looks pretty ludicrous all round. However, any serious student of sci-fi must have it logged. (*c*)

The Destructors × ×
Despite some lively moments and the occasional imaginative touch from director Francis D. Lyon, this is essentially just another Chinese communist - spy - foiled - by - American-counter - intelligence plot that rarely wholly grips. Richard Egan's physical flabbiness (it was made in 1967 when he was 46) is excused by some lines of dialogue suggesting that he's afraid of middle age, but he has got a flabby film to go with him. (*c*)

Destry √
This is *Destry Rides Again*, remade in 1954 without the satire. Now it's just Audie Murphy as sheriff who keeps law'n' order without using the guns he's shy of; George Marshall, same director as classic version, seems only too aware of the stars he lacks. (*c*)

Destry Rides Again √√
A landmark both as a Western and in Hollywood comedy was this 1939 slam-banger with James Stewart as pacifist marshal, Marlene Dietrich singing See What the Boys in the Back Room Will Have, Una Merkel fighting with her in classic unladylike brawl, and Brian Donlevy as the heavy. George Marshall put it all together with wit while retaining respect for the conventions of the oater. (*b/w*)

The Detective √√
If only this had been directed by some-

one with flair instead of Gordon Douglas it might have reached real heights; as it is, it's still an exciting, unusual murder thriller with a domestically-troubled cop, believably played by Frank Sinatra, arresting a man he suspects isn't guilty of the murder. Original references to homosexuality and other real-life events may result in a few cuts; hopefully it won't be butchered too much; 1968. (*c*)

Detective Story √ √
One day in New York precinct station, with burglars, shoplifters and sundry crooks dealt with by contrasting detectives, concentrating on bent Kirk Douglas. Made in 1951 by William Wyler. (*b/w*)

The Devil at Four O'Clock √
Frank Sinatra and Spencer Tracy are two of a quartet who volunteer to bring out patients and staff of volcanic island's leper colony when the eruption occurs. Mervyn LeRoy could be trusted to wring every ounce of action and sentiment out of this basically phoney yarn; 1961. (*b/w*)

Devil Doll √
Modest but genuinely creepy little thriller using the ventriloquist idea from *Dead of Night* to transfer 'soul' into dummy; William Sylvester fine; director Lindsay Shonteff, 1964; not to be confused with **The Devil Doll**, a 1936 Lionel Barrymore horror movie about escapee from Devil's Island using the tricks he learnt there about shrinking humans, for revenge; Tod Browning. (both *b/w*)

The Devil Never Sleeps × ×
Rather unpleasant drama set in China that caricatures the communists, glorifies the priests, and does its best to cash in on the prejudices of the American public in 1962. Leo McCarey stirs the brew meretriciously. William Holden,

Clifton Webb, France Nuyen go along cheerfully enough; 1962. (*c*)

The Devil Rides Out ×
Surely a better version of Dennis Wheatley's yarn about black magic could have been contrived than this stilted, silly effort? Director Terence Fisher must take a large part of the blame, though script and production values are equally null. Christopher Lee and Charles Gray just flounder; 1968. (*c*)

The Devil's Agent × × ×
Scandalously bad and mutilated in the cutting room. It's supposed to be one of those double-agent dramas, but if you or anyone else (including Peter van Eyck, Macdonald Carey, Christopher Lee or Marius Goring) can work out what's happening or, at the end, what happened, you are gifted with second sight. Director John Paddy Carstairs obviously gave up early; 1964. (*b/w*)

The Devil's Brigade ×
Another attempt at *The Dirty Dozen's* box-office bonanza doesn't come off under Andrew McLaglen's so-so direction. The battle scenes aren't as good as they should be, and William Holden can't hold it together. He looks awfully tired, poor chap, and no wonder; 1968. (*c*)

Devil's Canyon √
Marshal, jailed for self-defence shoot-out, becomes involved in prison riot; Dale Robertson, Virginia Mayo; director Alfred L. Werker was a worker; 1953. (*c*)

The Devil's Disciple √
Olivier is best thing about rather uninspired adaptation of Shaw's War of Independence drama directed by Guy Hamilton in 1959, in a different class from Burt Lancaster, Kirk Douglas; but Harry Andrews supports strongly. (*b/w*)

The Devil's 8 ✕ ✕
Federal agent breaks up 'moonshine' liquor gang, using it to gain power in the south; Christopher George just isn't up to this sort of part and such weak casting as Fabian doesn't help Burt Topper's efforts at authenticity; 1969. (c)

The Devil-Ship Pirates √
Rather a good Hammer movie, which says something about the nature of collaborators as a Spanish privateer puts into a Cornish port in 1588 and cons the local squire and villagers into thinking that Spain has won the war and they are part of occupying force. Christopher Lee is unbending as the captain of the ship although Natasha Pyne makes a weak heroine; conscientiously and occasionally imaginatively directed by Don Sharp; 1964. (c)

Devils of Darkness √
Some efforts have been made to produce as authentic a picture about vampires as possible and the care pays off; set in the West Country and Chelsea, it has Hubert Noel as a 400-year-old Frenchman who needs the blood of an occasional virgin to keep going; directed by Lance Comfort; 1965. (c)

The Devil's Own (more likely to turn up as **The Witches**, so see under this title.).

Dial M for Murder √ √
It took Hitchcock only thirty-six days to theatre and direct this theatre classic in 1954. Tennis player Ray Milland is worried about rich wife Grace Kelly's friendship with novelist Robert Cummings. Princess Grace loses her cool but will she lose her life? Tension runs high. (c)

Diamond Head ✕
Charlton Heston playing the heavy brother in Hawaii when sister Yvette Mimieux, not one of the greatest actresses of our time, wants to marry 'beneath her'. As cobbled by Guy Green in 1963, it's strictly for the pineapples
(c)

Diamond Horseshoe ✕
Poorly-cast musical with Betty Grable renouncing all for medical student Dick Haymes; set in gaudy real-life nightclub. Only real moment of pleasure – song The More I See You muted by singing; George Seaton; 1945. (c)

Diamonds for Breakfast ✕ ✕
Weak comedy about diamond caper (the Soviet government handily keeping the Russian Crown Jewels in English country house!) with Marcello Mastroianni utterly unbelievable as thief so irresistible to the ladies that seven of them act as his accomplices. Directed by Christopher Morahan, who has made only one other movie (the untidy *All Neat in Black Stockings*) but has had rather more luck with television, having finished up as Head of BBC plays; 1968.
(c)

Diane ✕
The only interesting fact about this costumer is that it was written by Christopher Isherwood, though you wouldn't notice by the time David Miller has finished directing the inadequate cast of Lana Turner, Pedro Amendariz, Roger Moore. It's supposed to be about the relationship of France's Francis I and Diane de Poitiers, but isn't; 1956. (c)

Diary of a Bachelor ✕ ✕
Mild little comedy of engaged fella who reforms only to find that his wife isn't as pure as he'd thought; director Sandy Howard's cast were unknowns and have stayed that way; 1964. (b/w)

The Diary of a Chambermaid √ √
(1) Paulette Goddard in the 1946 Jean Renoir American production managed remarkably well with the nuances of Mirabeau's novel of sexual deviation, mad neighbours and villainous valets.
(b/w)

The Diary of a Chambermaid
(2) Jeanne Moreau was, by comparison, disappointing–especially as one hoped much more from her–in Bunuel's 1964 French version. (both *b/w*)

Diary of a Madman ✕
De Maupassant story of magistrate who thinks evil spirit in man whom he condemned has entered into him, hokumised by Vincent Price and director Reginald Le Borg; 1963. (*c*)

The Diary of Anne Frank ✓✓
True story of nazi occupation of Amsterdam seen through eyes of 13-year-old couldn't fail; although George Stevens' 1959 casting of Millie Perkins in main part nearly makes it founder. It's saved by supporting performances from Shelley Winters (it won her an Oscar), Ed Wynn, Joseph Schildkraut.
(*b/w*)

Did You Hear the One About the Travelling Saleslady? ✕✕
If you happen to be a fan of Phyllis Diller you'll enjoy this mishmash about a crazy inventor in the American backwoods. Otherwise, not. Director Don Weis clearly doesn't know how to handle her talents; 1967. (*c*)

Dillinger ✓✓
Exciting account of Public Enemy No 1, tautly played by Lawrence Tierney, with Elisha Cook Jr and Edmund Lowe shooting along; Max Nosseck; 1945.
(*b/w*)

Dimension Four ✕✕✕
Phoney little Red Menace (they're going to blow up Los Angeles with an atom bomb for some reason) yarn made even less interesting by a sci-fi gimmick in which the hero can go forward or backward in time by pressing a button; hardly surprising that the Reds are foiled, is it? Jeffrey Hunter and France

Nuyen are trapped in this nonsense; directed by Franklin Adreon; 1967. (*c*)

Dingaka ✕✕✕
South African drama, in line with racist government's policy to show how primitive and backward native tribesmen are; Stanley Baker is tough lawyer, Juliet Prowse his wife; Jamie Uys directed; 1964. (*c*)

The Dirty Dozen ✓✓
Lee Marvin, Ernest Borgnine, Charles Bronson, John Cassavetes, Jim Brown, George Kennedy, Trini Lopez and half a dozen other dirties are released from jail to form suicide squad against the nazis; brilliantly made by Robert Aldrich, it's a huge box-office money-spinner and won't be shown on TV until it can't take another penny. But when it does appear, see it–again or for the first time–and whatever you may think of its morals, violence or subject, you'll be gripped; 1967. (*c*)

The Disorderly Orderly ✓
If you happen to like both Jerry Lewis and movies set in hospitals you'll adore this 1964 Frank Tashlin writer-director effort. Otherwise, you'll be turned off by the usual mugging and posturing and a total effect of sentimental grossness. (*c*)

Distant Drums ✓
Straightforward Western about hero falling in love with Indian maid after attacking fort held by gun-runners, given distinction by the fact that it's Gary Cooper in the main part. Raoul Walsh did routine job of direction; 1951.
(*c*)

A Distant Trumpet ✕✕
Not so much distant, as out of sight. If Westerns can ever be boring, this is the one. And if Troy Donahue, Suzanne Pleshette are capable of being anything other than wooden, Raoul Walsh isn't

the man to enliven them, not with John Twist's script about the army fighting Indians, anyway; 1964. (*c*)

Dive Bomber √
Pre-war (1941) aviation story about overcoming pilot blackout made for an exciting movie, with Michael Curtiz getting the best out of Fred MacMurray, Ralph Bellamy, Errol Flynn and some good effects. (*c*)

The Divided Heart √
Based on true-life story about boy torn between two mothers in wartime. Charles Crichton coaxes best performances Yvonne Mitchell, Theodore Bikel, Alexander Knox are capable of; 1954. (*b/w*)

Divorce American Style ✗
From the man who later adapted *Steptoe and Son* and *Till Death Us Do Part* for American television, Norman Lear, comes title rip-off of *Divorce–Italian Style*, a funnier, earlier, foreign-language pic. This one, directed for producer Lear by Bud Yorkin, has Dick Van Dyke and Debbie Reynolds at its soft centre; Jason Robards and Jean Simmons as veterans of the divorce hassle, put them to shame; 1967. (*c*)

The Dock Brief √
Opening-out of John Mortimer's television play about a lawyer and his client by James Hill stretches it a bit too far, and Peter Sellers and Richard Attenborough know it and try to overcompensate; 1962. (*b/w*)

Doctor … In the House √
Dirk Bogarde, 1954, very funny; … **At Sea,** Dirk Bogarde, 1956, quite funny but spoiled by extravagances of the pompous James Robertson Justice, who has continued to dominate the series with his smugness ever since; … **At Large,** Dirk Bogarde, 1957, still amusing but beginning to run out of steam; … **In**

Love, Michael Craig, 1960, without Bogarde it flags; … **In Distress,** Dirk Bogarde, 1963, it is rather–in distress; … **In Clover,** 1966 Leslie Phillips, reduced to *Carry On* proportions without that marvellous Crazy Gang; … **In Trouble,** Leslie Philips, 1970; at 46, Phillips is getting just a bit old for being the bright young doctor. All Ralph Thomas. (all *c*)

Doctor Blood's Coffin ✗ ✗
Notable only for Sidney J. Furie, later to become successful Hollywood director, cutting his teeth in this gruesome 1960 yarn about mad son of a Cornish doctor. Unfortunately, the casting of Keiron Moore in the main part ensured that Furie had no real chance. (*c*)

The Doctor's Dilemma √
Over-talky Shaw play treated reverently by Anthony Asquith in 1958. Dirk Bogarde tries to humanise the young patient, but Robert Morley, Alastair Sim, John Robinson and Felix Aylmer walk off with the honours as the Harley Street harlots. Leslie Caron is miscast and inadequate, 1958. (*c*)

Doctor, You've Got to be Kidding ✗ ✗
Director (Peter Tewksbury), you've got to be kidding! You can't really mean that this is supposed to be funny, frothy, worth watching? All that rubbish about cute Sandra Dee getting into trouble. George Hamilton as an executive? Mort Sahl and Celeste Holm certainly try to give the appearance of kidding, but it defeats them. Watch it? You've got to be kidding! 1967. (*c*)

Dodge City √
Errol Flyn puts down Bruce Cabot and the other baddies to make the town a place for decent folks (until the next Western). Olivia de Havilland is nice girl, Ann Sheridan bad (but golden-hearted). Michael Curtiz directed this archetypal Western in 1939. (*c*)

A Dog of Flanders √
What chance have even Donald Crisp and Theodore Bikel against appealing dog and kid in this happy tear-jerker for children? James B. Clark laid it on thick, 1959. (*c*)

Do Not Disturb ×
After this disastrous British effort in 1965, Doris Day (then pushing 42) decided to give up being a giggly kid and has since made some grown-up movies. But this nadir, an embarrassing echo of her previous delightful frothy comedies, still has her as a young married (to Rod Taylor) who loses her husband, then gets him back in a giddy whirl. Part of the blame is director Ralph Levy's, who seems to have gone along blindly with the whole confection. (*c*)

Donovan's Brain √
Rather better than routine sci-fi with Lew Ayres as scientist who seeks to control kept-alive brain but is himself taken over by it; writer-director Felix Feist; 1953. (*b/w*)

Donovan's Reef √
John Ford enjoying himself in Hawaii in 1963 with John Wayne and Lee Marvin as ex-Navy men scrapping and drinking and wenching (with Elizabeth Allen, Dorothy Lamour). All good tough fun. (*c*)

Don't Bother to Knock √
Devotees of Marilyn Monroe will squirm with delight at the sight of her first dramatic part–a loony babysitter– in 1952. The rest of you can enjoy Richard Widmark, the debut of Anne Bancroft, Roy Baker's not too certain direction. (*b/w*)

Don't Bother to Knock × ×
Unremarkable farce with Edinburgh travel agent Richard Todd, in love with good girl June Thorburn, handing out his flat keys to Elke Sommer and others. Directed (1960) by Cyril Frankel. (*b/w*)

Don't Go Near the Water ×
Dull little comedy with Glenn Ford romancing Gia Scala on Pacific isle during naval occupation. Only Fred Clark scrapes by, doing his usual bluff bit; Charles Walters; 1957. (*c*)

Don't Just Stand There × × ×
Remarkably unfunny comedy about Mary Tyler Moore and Robert Wagner trying to smuggle girl out of Paris brothel; Glynis Johns lurks around as man-hungry novelist. Clearly director Ron Winston is not much of a dab at judging how to make people laugh; 1969. (*c*)

Don't Make Waves ×
Tony Curtis as swimming pool salesman with the arch Claudia Cardinale lurking around; much falling-in – including a house into the sea; Robert Webber, Mort Sahl look dismayed, as well they might. Sad that Alexander Mackendrick, who made *The Ladykillers* and *Sweet Smell of Success*, should come to this in 1967. (*c*)

Don't Raise the Bridge, Lower the River × ×
Jerry Lewis' British picture couldn't be called a success by any standards. Despite efforts from all concerned, the mixture–like the bridge–failed to rise; Jerry Paris from a Max Wilk script about turning an estranged wife's home into a Chinese restaurant; 1968. (*c*)

Doppelgänger ×
Gerry and Sylvia Anderson show that although you can treat puppets as people (they make Thunderbirds, etc.), it doesn't work the other way round; Ian Hendry, Patrick Wymark, Herbert Lom and others discover new planet which is mirror-image of ours. Strictly for the puppets. Director Robert Parrish; 1969. (*c*)

Double Bunk ×
Could have been called 'Carry On Down

the River' as Ian Carmichael and Janette Scott sail the Thames in an old houseboat, helped and hindered by Sid James, Liz Fraser, Dennis Price, Irene Handl, Terry Scott, Gerald Campion, Graham Stark; directed by C. M. Pennington-Richards; 1960. (*b/w*)

Double Indemnity √√√
Sharp, sour, stunning *tour de force* about wife (Barbara Stanwyck) who seduces insurance salesman (Fred MacMurray) to kill husband and collect huge insurance. Billy Wilder, who directed, wrote the script with novelist James M. Cain and it's a masterpiece of driving economy; Edward G. Robinson, Porter Hall perfect too; 1944 (*b/w*)

A Double Life √√
Ronald Colman won 1948 Oscar for performance as actor whose work so affects his life that he becomes schizophrenic and murderous; George Cukor made what is basically hokum into convincing melodrama; Edmond O'Brien, Shelley Winters, Ray Collins helped considerably. (*c*)

The Double Man ××
Yul Brynner in two-part spy bore along with Britt Ekland and the CIA in the Austrian Alps. Franklin Schaffner; 1967. (*c*)

Dracula √√
(1) Bela Lugosi was original in 1931 Tod Browning classic (*b/w*);

Dracula √
(2) Peter Cushing and Christopher Lee were in Terence Fisher's excellent version in 1957, which used the trapping of heart-stakes and neck-fangs with good effect. (*b/w*)

Dracula ×
(3) But Fisher's own 1966 rip-off, *Dracula–Prince of Darkness*, like most

of the later attempts to cash in on the brand-name, didn't equal the original. (*c*)

Dracula Has Risen From the Grave √
Best of the three sequels Hammer produced from its own *Dracula*; Freddie Francus took over as director of this 1968 effort and improved it colourwise, sexwise and subtlewise. However, a certain gusto is missing, although Christopher Lee is his usual menacing self. Rupert Davies weighs in with a priest-cum-avenger. (*c*)

Dracula's Daughter √√
1936 sequel to first *Dracula*, this was scrupulous and convincing, achieving a near-Lesbian quality between biter (Gloria Holden) and bitten; Lambert Hillyer. (*b/w*)

Dragnet ×
Spin-off of the once-successful Jack Webb TV series has the solemn-faced actor-director going through the routine of bringing in suspect and pinning gang-murder on him; 1954. (*c*)

Dragonwyck √
High drama, romance, terror, murder in a big mysterious old mansion; Gene Tierney is the girl, Walter Huston, Vincent Price are part of the creaking furniture; Ernst Lubitsch produced, Joseph L. Makiewicz directed; 1945. (*c*)

Dr Crippen ×
Who didn't murder his wife, according to this unconvincing version by Leigh Vance, directed with even less *élan* by Robert Lynn–it was all an accident, like the movie. Only Donald Pleasence as the archetypal worm-that-turned is worth switching on for; but neither Coral Browne as Belle, nor Samantha Eggar as Ethel, convinces; 1964. (*b/w*)

Dreamboat √√
Great fun: Ginger Rogers and Clifton Webb in 1952 spoof about his old movies being shown on television. Lovely old 'clips' from silents; Anne

Francis and Elsa Lanchester add to the enjoyment under Claude Binyon's direction. (*b/w*)

Dream of Kings   ✕
Anthony Quinn overacting all over the screen as Chicago Greek trying to raise the money to send ill son to Greece; unfortunately, he's so unsympathetic that none of Director Daniel Mann's schmaltzy tricks can make us care; Irene Papas enjoys herself as long-suffering wife ; Sam Levene is almost only non-Greek in rest of large cast; 1969. (*c*)

Dream Wife   ✕
Weak little snippet about man who believes men are superior and wives should be subservient. When Eastern princess turns up as his bride for State Dept. reasons he demonstrates his theories to fiancée. Most amazing fact is that Cary Grant plays the chap; Deborah Kerr his girl–they must have been mad to take the parts; Sidney Sheldon; 1953. (*b/w*)

Dr No   √√
Don't expect to see this first James Bond winner on the little screen until it has realised all its cinema box-office potential, but when it is on, watch and see how it was the best of the cycle it spawned. Sean Connery *v.* Joseph Wiseman in Jamaica, with Ursula Andress in bathing suits, were slick and exciting; Terence Young directed; 1963. (*c*)

Drop Dead Darling   ✕
Solid cast (Tony Curtis, Lionel Jeffries, Nancy Kwan, Fenella Fielding) wasted in rubbishy stuff about con-man marrying and murdering for money. Ken Hughes; 1967. (*c*)

Dr Strangelove or How I Learned to Stop Worrying and Love the Bomb √√√
Stanley Kubrick's brilliant, if chilling, 1963 comedy which sought pre-release Presidential approval. (Kennedy okayed it–would Nixon?) Peter Sellers is at his best in a triple performance. What happens when the Button is pressed and Doomsday arrives . . . (*b/w*)

Dr Terror's House of Horror   √
Peter Cushing reads grim tarot cards for five future victims of supernatural death and we dutifully follow their dead-of-night fates; unfortunately, this is one of Milton Subotsky's quick-buck British churn-outs and Freddie Francis's best efforts can't overcome a painfully derivative script and low budget; a good cast (Christopher Lee, Donald Sutherland, Harold Lang included) try hard; music by Elisabeth Lutyens and Tubby Hayes; 1965. (*c*)

Drum Beat   √
Alan Ladd warring, peace-parleying with Indians; tautly directed by Delmer Daves in 1954. (*c*)

Drums Across the River   √
Considering it's only an Audie Murphy vehicle, this 1954 Western is really rather good. Gold-seekers push Indians off their lands, with Hugh O'Brian and Walter Brennan in the serviceable cast; Nathan Juran. (*c*)

Drums Along the Mohawk   √√
Classic 1939 actioner with Claudette Colbert, Henry Fonda, Edna May (scene-stealing) Oliver, John (varmint) Carradine fighting against and with the Indians isn't a Western, more an Eastern. The drums are those of Iriquois paid by the British to fight Fonda, Colbert and fellow Americans during the revolution; John Ford's first colour film used the new medium superbly, particularly in silhouette sequence of hero's flight. (*c*)

Dr Who and the Daleks   ✕✕
Vulgarised version of an already vulgar television series, far removed from the wit and nuances of good science fiction. This is comic-book stuff, and bad comics at that. Peter Cushing takes the main part but without even the depth of

character the TV Doctors Who have had; the story is about his meeting with the Da-a-a-aleks for the first time; 1965. (*c*)

Dry Rot ✗
Long-running stage farce about switching horses makes rather too broad a film without audience laughter; Ronald Shiner, Brian Rix, Sid James, Joan Sims; directed by an indulgent Maurice Elvey; 1956. (*b/w*)

Duck Soup √√
The (four) Marx brothers, Margaret Dumont, Louis Calhern, Edgar Kennedy in classic 1933 spoof of banana republics. Groucho says it's their craziest. Banned by Mussolini. Director, poor chap: Leo McCary. (*b/w*)

Duel at Diablo √√
More than a Western, a bloodbath. Ralph Nelson, who was later to direct the infamous *Soldier Blue*, warmed up for it with this Indian ambush with the blood spilling like a hot-dog bathed in tomato ketchup–which is probably what is here, too. But he does get the best out of James Garner, Sidney Poitier, Bibi Andersson; 1966. (*c*)

Duel in the Jungle ✗ ✗
Is between sterling insurance detective Dana Andrews and horrible David Farrar, swindler and jungle-dweller; set in pre-UDI Rhodesia, in 1954. George Marshall fails to excite. (*c*)

Duel in the Sun √√
Gone With the High Noon?–five directors (mainly King Vidor, but William Dieterle shot Tilly Losch dance opening), eight stars (Jennifer Jones, Joseph Cotten, Gregory Peck, Lionel Barrymore Lillian Gish, Herbert Marshall, Walter Huston, Charles Bickford), orchestrated by David Selznick in the big-spending days of 1946. (*c*)

Duffy ✗
One of those near-spoof capers with the increasingly tiresome James Coburn putting himself about in a prententious, over-dressed, over-produced thriller about stealing a million from a liner. Some good English players – James Mason, James Fox, Susannah York, John Alderton – are pushed around by him and director Robert Parrish; 1968. (*c*)

Dunkirk √√
Leslie Norman's ambitious 1958 account of historic event succeeds partly because he avoids unnecessary false heroism, partly because of graphic, almost documentary, approach. Top performances from stalwarts John Mills, Richard Attenborough, Bernard Lee, Robert Urquhart. (*b/w*)

Dutchman √√
Gripping little film of the LeRoi Jones one-acter tightly directed by Anthony Harvey with Al Freeman Jr as black passenger and Shirley Knight (Hopkins) as flaunting white passenger in New York subway, recreated in London studio; 1967. (*b/w*)

The Eagle and the Hawk ✗
Dennis O'Keefe and John Payne thwarting plots in Texas when it was still part of Mexico; Lewis R. Foster never manages to hold the interest; 1950. (*c*)

The Early Bird ✕✕✕
Dreadful British comedy with Norman Wisdom as milkman who loves his horse and somehow saves his boss from a takeover bid. Hard to care about milkman, boss, or horse. Director Robert Asher; 1965. (*c*)

Easter Parade ✓✓
Judy Garland, Fred Astaire, a couple of swells; Fred's trying to forget ex-partner Ann Miller; plus sixteen other Irving Berlins. Charles Walters; 1948. (*c*)

East of Eden ✓✓
Elia Kazan's successful interpretation of (part of) Steinbeck's novel about Cal (James Dean's great performance) rebelling against father (Raymond Massey). Julie Harris his equal as strange local girl; and Jo Van Fleet won Oscar for her Kate. Set in 1917, made in 1955. (*c*)

East of Sumatra ✓
Budd Boetticher gives some distinction to this routine adventure about mining engineer in Far East, with Jeff Chandler and Anthony Quinn; 1952. (*c*)

Easy Come, Easy Go ✕
Elvis Presley was so taken up with a (sadly false) vision of himself as an actor that he sang only three songs in this 1967 stuff about a frogman. Maybe the frog was in his throat? John Rich indulged him. (*c*)

Easy Rider ✓✓
The movie that caused a revolution in picture-making in 1969. Until then, nobody had quite realised that the young provided such a huge untapped market, but for this low-budget odyssey of producer-directors Peter Fonda and Dennis Hopper travelling across the southern states by motor-bicycle chopper, they turned out in their millions all over the world. Jack Nicholson, as a drunken lawyer who joins them for a while, walks

David Niven in *Eye of the Devil*

away with the acting honours. While much of the action and dialogue is banal, it does have guts, however; and the end is genuinely horrific. (*c*)

Easy to Love   ✕
Esther Williams in water-spectacle, falling for boorish boss Van Johnson; Charles Walters managed to make water-skiing quite lavish; 1953. (*c*)

The Eddie Cantor Story   ✕ ✕
The comedian's own voice emerges, spiritwise, out of the mouth of the just-competent Keefe Brasselle (actor who later unhappily turned TV executive). If you happen to adore Mr Cantor you might find this not too distasteful; otherwise, it's just creepy; Alfred E. Green; 1952. (*c*)

The Eddy Duchin Story   ✕
George Sidney directed this 1956 biopic about Thirties pianist. Tyrone Power gave it more than it deserved, Kim Novak about as good as she got. (*c*)

Edge of Eternity   √
Don Siegel actioner in, around and over the Grand Canyon; unfortunately, actors Cornel Wilde, Mickey Shaughnessy can't match it in any particular; 1960. (*c*)

Edward My Son   √
Compelling performance from Spencer Tracy as the father who not quite honestly builds a fortune for his son, and discovers that he and his wife, Deborah Kerr, and their precarious marriage drove the boy to suicide. George Cukor's 1949 direction is a touch gimmicky, but Ian Hunter, Mervyn Johns and Felix Aylmer lend strong support. (*b/w*)

The Egg and I   √
Chicken farmer Fred MacMurray marries city slicker Claudette Colbert, who learns how to survive on a farm. Supposedly true story introduces Ma and

Pa Kettle who were spun off to make long successful series of their own. Chester Erskine; 1947. (*b/w*)

The Egyptian   ✕
Darryl F. Zanuck's 1954 biblical epic owes most to set and costume designers. Edmund Purdom, Jean Simmons, Peter Ustinov, Victor Mature, Michael Wilding and 5,000 extras are lavished on indifferent story. But director Michael Curtiz loads on the spectacle. (*c*)

Eight on the Run   ✕ ✕
Dire attempt at humour about bank clerk on the lam as suspected embezzler. Bob Hope is cute enough, but here is out-joked by a veritable galaxy of unfunnies including Phyllis Diller, Jonathan Winters, seven children and a big dog. Shirley Eaton must have thought she was going to make it big after being cast in this 1968 'comedy' but it turned out to be a killer for her career; George Marshall. (*c*)

80,000 Suspects   √
Disease is the villain of this 1963 suspenser set in Bath in the middle of smallpox and flu epidemics; Val Guest does usual uninspired professional job with the help of Claire Bloom, Cyril Cusack. (*b/w*)

El Cid   √
It's a long time between highlights (a single-handed combat near the beginning and the final battle) during which Charlton Heston slowly unites the Moors and Christians of Spain under one king. You'll have plenty of time to study director Anthony Mann's deliberate compositions; 1962. (*c*)

El Dorado   √
In 1959 Howard Hawks made Rio Bravo; in 1967 he made this, and it's pretty hard to tell them apart, particularly as John Wayne's in both of them. Robert Mitchum's along for the ride this time, and

the old master knows how to rope your attention. (*c*)

Elephant Walk √
Elizabeth Taylor, Peter Finch, Dana Andrews, and herd of rampaging elephants in Rebecca-type story in Ceylon; William Dieterle; 1953 (*c*)

El Greco ✕
Worthy, well-photographed but boring account of the painter from Crete who lived in Toledo. Mel Ferrer produced it as a vehicle for himself. Maybe director Luciano Salce would have preferred a better actor but didn't quite like to say so? 1967. (*c*)

Elmer Gantry √√
Well-cast Burt Lancaster as charlatan evangelist exploiting Jean Simmons' touring pulpit in 1920s mid-west. Arthur Kennedy is journalist out to expose him, Shirley Jones discarded girlfriend-turned-prostitute. Neatly directed (1960) by Richard Brooks from Sinclair Lewis' novel. (*c*)

The Emperor Waltz √
Quite what Billy Wilder was doing in a studio like this except earning his living in 1948 isn't altogether clear, but he manages to put a few nice touches into Viennese yarn about travelling salesman Bing Crosby meeting Austrian princess Joan Fontaine circa 1901. Should have been called 'The Emperor Schmaltz'. (*c*)

The Enchanted Cottage √
Pirandello play desperately whimsied up by director John Cromwell but still retaining enough of its depends-who-you-are origins to take story of ugly girl (Dorothy Maguire) and broken flyer (Robert Young) interestingly out of the rut; Herbert Marshall, Spring Byington giving their stock performances don't help; 1945. (*b/w*)

Enchanted Island ✕
If you can guess the origin of this tritely produced 1963 tale of two sailors jumping ship and living idyllic South Sea island life, you must be psychic; particularly with casting of Dana Andrews and Jane Powell, and Allan Dwan's lighthearted direction. It's a Herman Melville novel. (*c*)

End as a Man √√
Sadism and perversion in a Southern military academy brilliantly realised by director Jack Garfein from Calder Willingham's question-begging but burning script. Ben Gazzara stunning as chief sadist; 1957. (*b/w*)

The Endless Summer √
Paean of praise for the joys of surfing, directed, produced, edited and narrated by Bruce Brown. Sometimes very beautiful, interesting for a time, absorbing only if you are an addict; 1966. (*c*)

The End of the Affair ✕
Adaptation of the Grahame Greene novel about finding God after infidelity. It's too American in influence, with Van Johnson as the lover and Edward Dmytryk the director. Deborah Kerr and Peter Cushing as the other sides of the triangle are adequate, and the rest of the cast is old-school English; 1955. (*b/w*)

The Enemy Below √
Duel between Robert Mitchum's destroyer and Curt Jurgens' U-boat is unlikely but moderately successful pacifist plea; Dick Powell turned out to be more than competent director in 1957. (*c*)

The Enforcer √
Assistant DA Humphrey Bogart *v.* crime boss Everett Sloane in no-nonsense toughie, with Zero Mostel; director Bretaigne Windust; 1951. (*b/w*)

Ensign Pulver √
Drama? Comedy? Comedy-drama? It isn't clear with this story of a very junior

member of the Navy taking on the hated captain of his boat, and that's typical of the way the whole film falls (or rather, plunges, being mostly at sea) between stools. But Burl Ives pulls off the feat of making the martinet sympathetic, and Walter Matthau is the ship's doctor. Unfortunately, Robert Walker can't reach the demands of the main part, though the blame (and the praise – it's not that bad) must go to Joshua Logan, who produced and directed from a play by Josh Logan that he wrote with someone else, having rewritten it for the screen with another partner; 1965. (*c*)

Enter Laughing √
Carl Reiner, comedy writer turned director, obviously thought he was going to deliver a mighty laugh in this thin but basically autobiogaphical tale of a boy's first Broadway chance, but he mucked it up by casting Reni Santoni as the lad and José Ferrer as an ageing actor. Only Elaine May, as his daughter, really works well. Pity. 1967. (*c*)

The Entertainer √ √ √
Stunning performance by Laurence Olivier as music hall comedian who tries heartbreakingly hard to kid himself that he's going to make it. John Osborne's play translates smoothly to the screen, and Brenda de Banzie, Joan Plowright, Roger Livesey, Albert Finney, Thora Hird provide matching contributions. Tony Richardson's direction doesn't intrude on star or script; 1960. (*b/w*)

Escape from East Berlin × ×
Actuality-based account of how 28 East Germans tunnelled through to the West under the Wall. Don Murray and Christine Kaufmann starred in this 1962 casualty of cold war hysteria. Director Robert Siodmak held the patient's hand to no avail; it expired from over-earnestness. (*b/w*)

Escape From Fort Bravo √
North *v*. South *v*. Red Indians. William

Holden, Polly Bergen, Eleanor Parker, William Demarest in well-directed (John Sturges) Western; 1953. (*b/w*)

Escort West ×
Victor Mature beating the Red Indians and winning his daughter's affection, at the end of Civil War; Faith Domergue; director F. D. Lyon; 1958. (*c*)

Esther and the King ×
Failed attempt at epic by Raoul Walsh, with dull battles and even duller performances by Joan Collins and Richard Egan; 1960. (*c*)

Eve ×
Forty minutes shorter than Joseph Losey originally intended, this impenetrable fable of loquacious Welsh writer being destroyed by a *femme fatale* never takes a grip, and the Venice-in-winter backgrounds take on the importance that scenery only does when the foreground action is boring or inconsequential. Jeanne Moreau does what she can with the inexplicable and unexplained Woman of the World; Stanley Baker can't do anything with the writer who fancies himself too much. As empty and pretentious as an issue of 1963 *Vogue*, and as dated. (*b/w*)

Everybody Does It √
'It' being singing, not what you were thinking. Linda Darnell thinks she has a voice, but hasn't; Paul Douglas, husband, doesn't think he has, but has; Nunnally Johnson's story is neat as usual, Edmund Goulding's direction unassuming; 1950. (*b/w*)

Everything I Have is Yours √
Dancers Marge and Gower Champion in routine backstager about couple coming together, splitting, reuniting. Director Robert Z. Leonard has brought out some nice sly observations on marriage, however; 1953. (*c*)

The Evil of Frankenstein   ✕
Peter Cushing busily reviving the monster he thought dead but was, luckily for Hammer, only ice-bound; Freddie Francis is the director in this 1963 extension of a profitable but clapped-out series. (*c*)

Excuse My Dust   √
Worth staying during the faintly tedious, good-old-summertime stuff for climax of early buggy race; lead Red Skelton's a bit wearing, though; director Roy Rowland; 1951. (*c*)

Executive Suite   √
Power game in the American furniture-making world, circa 1954, with William Holden, Fredric March, Paul Douglas, Walter Pidgeon among the strugglers; Barbara Stanwyck, Shelley Winters, Nina Foch soften it, and Robert Wise directed with jumpy cutting. (*b/w*)

Exodus   ✕
Mort Sahl is said to have stood up at the preview of this long, apparently endless chronicle of the birth of Israel after three hours and shouted to producer-director Otto Preminger 'Let my people go!' Luckily you can always turn off, although Paul Newman, Ralph Richardson, Lee J. Cobb should delay bottom-ache; 1960. (*c*)

The Eye of the Cat   √ √
Highly satisfactory and well-made low-budgeter about the way cats take over as murder agents when the family of Eleanor Parker, Gayle Hunnicutt and Michael Sarrazin get to murdering each other. You'll find yourself glancing at your own mog in quite a new way as the pic unfolds; David Lowell Rich milks it well; 1969. (*c*)

Eye of the Devil   ✕ ✕
Dreadful attempt at suggesting how supernatural forces threaten a family

that, despite frenetic cutting, succeeds only in documenting a fight between the risible and the incredible, rather than the intended one between good and evil. David Niven looks thoroughly embarrassed, as well he might, as chatelaine, although David Hemmings and Deborah Kerr seem under the mad impression that they are taking part in a serious film. J. Lee Thompson is director of the farrago and seems to have settled for restlessness in the camerawork in an attempt to disguise the poor material he is stuck with; 1968. (*c*)

A Face in the Crowd   √ √
Superficially a protest movie about the manipulation of the public by a cynical entertainer, this is in fact a brilliant example of Elia Kazan's contempt for the public who'll believe anything as long as it looks as if it is on their side. Andy Griffiths and Patricia Neal are startlingly good; 1957. (*b/w*)

Face of a Fugitive   √
Fred MacMurray, on the run in a Western town, makes good and proves his innocence; Paul Wendkos; 1959. (*c*)

The Face of Fu Manchu   √ √
Rather fun – a carefully preserved relic from an earlier world where oriental super-villains lurk and the assistant commissioner of Scotland Yard takes on

Boris Karloff in *Frankenstein*

the Man Who Wants to Rule the World Single-handed. Full marks to director Don Sharp for not allowing it all to become campy spoof – that's really too easy; instead, he has given us a delicious re-creation of what people used to pass the time agreeably with before television arrived. Christopher Lee makes a splendid Fu Manchu; 1965. (*c*)

Faces   √
Pretentious, long-winded, action-starved account of middle-class American marriage whose ambience conned critics into thinking they were seeing something profound. John Cassavetes' direction is significant for its indulgence and he was lucky to have cameraman Al Ruban to save his excesses–he could have done with an equally tough editor. Cassavetes used friends and spouses who improvise adequately; 1968. (*b/w*)

The Facts of Life   √
Considering that Bob Hope and Lucille Ball play the main parts, this is a remarkably quiet and understated comedy of thwarted adultery; credit must go to director Melvin Frank. Still, it was a strange and rather weak choice for the Royal Film Performance of 1961. (*b/w*)

Fahrenheit 451   ×
Disappointing marriage of Ray Bradbury's horrific vision of the future where the firemen make fires of the books, and Francois Truffaut's pretentions, which are fine when they work, but not when they stumble as here. Possibly the fact that the director and star Oskar Werner weren't on speaking terms for most of the picture and basic inadequacy of female star Julie Christie were to blame; 1966. (*c*)

Fail Safe   √√
Relatively unnoticed in the fall-out from Dr Strangelove, this 1964 Sidney Lumet suspenser postulates B52 bombers being sent to Moscow by mistake, and not

even President Henry Fonda can stop them. Walter Matthau, Fritz Weaver add to masterly, all-too-convincing warning. *(b/w)*

Fair Wind to Java × ×
Pirate yarn with skipper Fred Mac-Murray and slave girl Vera Ralston searching for buried treasure; Joe Kane produced and directed; 1953. *(c)*

The Fake × ×
Dull British B-picture about theft of Leonardos with Denis O'Keefe guarding one at the Tate (an unlikely gallery to show it, to start with). Godfrey Grayson directed; 1953. *(b/w)*

Fallen Angel √ √
Good strong early (1946) Otto Preminger about Dana Andrews marrying nice girl Alice Faye only so that he can get her money to run off with bad girl Linda Darnell. But then there's a murder and the plan gets all fouled up; earthily done with strong supports Charles Bickford, Bruce Cabot, John Carradine. *(b/w)*

The Fallen Idol √ √
Absorbing tragedy of embassy butler and secretary as observed by protective but blundering small boy (Bobby Henrey); Ralph Richardson and Michèle Morgan marvellous in these parts, but the picture belongs to Carol Reed for bringing Graham Greene's screenplay from his short story so convincingly to life; 1949. *(b/w)*

The Fall of the House of Usher √
Roger Corman's first big success – in 1960 – is ponderous and poorly acted (Vincent Price *et al*), but is reasonably true to Poe's story. *(b/w)*

Fall of the Roman Empire × ×
Illustrates better the reasons for the Fall of the Hollywood Empire. Vast sets, chariot races and duels are no substitute for a strong script, and you can't get good acting just by hiring good actors. James Mason, Alec Guinness look embarrassed; Sophia Loren and Stephen Boyd let it all wash over them; Christopher Plummer apparently takes it seriously; Anthony Mann must be kidding; 1964. *(c)*

The Family Jewels × ×
Unbelievably unfunny Jerry Lewis script-direction-acting shows no signs of awareness of the dire results; it's supposed to be about a nine-year-old orphan heiress choosing one of her uncles as a new father. The most awful thing is that Jerry Lewis plays them all; 1965. *(c)*

The Family Way √ √
Remarkably successful adaptation of Bill Naughton's play *All in Good Time*, exploring two sets of working-class relationships. Parents are John Mills (never quite getting the earthiness of the character but making a splendid try) and Marjorie Rhodes (excellent). Son (Hwyel Bennett, well-cast) and Hayley Mills (outstandingly right in her bright little way) agonise through the reasons for the non-consummation of their marriage. Full of lovely touches and as good as anything John and Roy Boulting ever did; 1967. *(c)*

Fanatic √
For the first part a fine menace movie about crazy old lady – Tallulah Bankhead, dahlings – imprisoning son's fiancée Silvio Narizzano lets it get out of hand towards the end, but it was a lovely shiver in 1965 and still is. Strong TV names support: Peter Vaughan, Yootha Joyce, Maurice Kaufman. *(b/w)*

Fancy Pants √
Can you believe Bob Hope in Charles Laughton role? This is Ruggles of Red Cap musicalised by George Marshall in 1950, with Lucille Ball helping to make it amusing if not rollicking. *(c)*

Fanny ×
Sloppy sentimental broadening of the Marcel Pagnol trilogy brought to the American screen via the stage by Joshua Logan. Leslie Caron coos her way through the little waif bit, lumbered by clumsy Horst Bucholtz, but comforted by kindly, wrinkly-eyed old Maurice Chevalier in a Marseilles that never existed. Charles Boyer, Lionel Jeffries gamely play along; 1961. (*c*)

Fantastic Voyage √√
Exciting idea of miniaturised sub with scientists in, speeding through bloodstream of body to wipe out brain lesion, is somewhat let down by obviousness of story about rugged hero (Stephen Boyd), shapely cutie (Raquel Welch), naughty villain (Donald Pleasence) inside; but effects are marvellous. Richard Fleischer 1966. (*c*)

The Far Country √
James Stewart bringing law'n'order to the Wild West, pursued by Steve Brodie and other villains, Bad Girl Ruth Roman and Good Girl Corinne Calvert. Anthony Mann; 1953. (*c*)

Far From The Madding Crowd √
Rare evocation of the English countryside rather let down by bare attempt to convey the strength of Hardy's plot; John Schlesinger never really convinces with absurdly modern miss Julie Christie, Alan Bates looking wan in a part that one reviewer commented 'might have been written for a well-mannered Airedale'; Terence Stamp making his usual unsuccessful attempt to get by on his looks. Only Peter Finch manages to seem at all convincing, and even he is too samey; 1967. (*c*)

Farewell My Lovely √√
Dick Powell as Raymond Chandler's beaten-about private eye in classic thriller directed in 1945 by Edward Dmytryk; Claire Trevor, Otto Kruger stand out among supports. (*b/w*)

A Farewell To Arms ××
David O. Selznick's great floperoo. The remake of the famous Helen Hayes-Gary Cooper 1933 version in 1957 was meant to be a crowning achievement for him and his wife Jennifer Jones. But he wouldn't listen to advice, forced first director John Huston to resign, tried to cower replacement Charles Vidor and spent money in grand, hopeless gestures. Although Ernest Hemingway had long before signed away his rights on his First World War novel about a nurse and a soldier, Selznick cabled him that he was allocating £50,000 of the profits as ex gratia payment. Hemingway cabled back that the chances of a profit on any film by Selznick with the 38-year-old Mrs S playing his 24-year-old heroine were nil, but if a miracle did occur Selznick could go change the money into nickels and shove them up himself until they came out of his ears. (*c*)

Fargo √
Bought for Marlon Brando but held up by production difficulties until he had grown too old for the beatnik that the girl prefers to her foster-parents when the real father they find together rejects her; the part went to the over-earnest Michael Parks. Celia Kaye was engaging as the girl in this 1965 drama which paradoxically came out too soon to cash in on the hippy wave of the late sixties. Brian Hutton went on to direct *Where Eagles Dare*. (*b/w*)

The Far Horizons ××
Unbelievable to the point of subversiveness, this prettied-up account of Lewis and Clark's epic journey through the wilderness of early America is plain awful; Fred MacMurray and Charlton Heston are supposed to be feuding but really they are engaged in a sorry battle

over which is the worse actor. Astonishing that such an old reliable as Rudolph Maté let himself be roped in to direct such a dreadful script; 1955. (*c*)

The Fastest Gun Alive   √
Moral-studded Western about a storekeeper who has gun-slinging reputation foisted on to him, is then challenged by a real gunman. Russell Rouse directed, 1956, and Glenn Ford, Broderick Crawford, Jeanne Crain kept the idea and pace moving towards inevitable stand-up-and-fight climax. (*b/w*)

The Fast Lady   × ×
1962 British comedy with Stanley Baxter, Leslie Phillips and James Robertson Justice which could be called 'Carry On Vintage Driving' and is notable only for Julie Christie's debut; Ken Annakin.
(*b/w*)

Fate is the Hunter   √
Glenn Ford investigating why a plane crashed. Was it Rod Taylor's fault? Ralph (*Soldier Blue*) Nelson directed, 1964; supports include Dorothy Malone, Jane Russell, Nehemiah Persoff, Wally Cox. (*b/w*)

Father Brown   √
Alec Guinness in the 1954 – and only – English film of G. K. Chesterton's detective. Robert Hamer had dream cast to direct: Guinness plus Joan Greenwood, Peter Finch, Cecil Parker, Bernard Lee, Sid James. (*b/w*)

Father Goose   √
Featherweight comedy with Cary Grant as undercover agent obliged to act as shiftless South Seas beachcomber until along trips schoolmarm Leslie Caron and miniature St Trinian's. With Trevor Howard, Jack Good, directed by Ralph Nelson. It won the 1964 Oscar for writers, but looks a bit coy now. (*c*)

Father of the Bride   √
Elizabeth Taylor, then 17, marrying Don Taylor (no kin) means a hundred funny headaches for Dad Spencer Tracy. Joan Bennett plays his wife and mother of the groom is Billie Burke. Vincente Minnelli directed but it's all too coy; 1950. (*b/w*)

Father's Little Dividend   √
Same cast and director as *Father of the Bride*, takes story on a stage when Spencer Tracy is going to be a Grandpa. Has same faults as the original; 1951.
(*b/w*)

Fathom   √
Entertaining spoof of spy thriller with the minus of Raquel Welch as skydiver who plummets into middle of villainous Tony Franciosca, Ronald Fraser, Clive Revill, Tom Adams. Director Leslie Martinson makes it all good fun; 1967.
(*c*)

The FBI Story   √
Without James Stewart this would have been one more feds-and-hoods picaresque drama, but his patina and Mervyn LeRoy's 1959 direction lift it up by its shoulder-holster. (*c*)

Fear Strikes Out   √ √
Don't be put off by subject, which superficially is baseball. In fact, it's a gripping and sympathetic true story of father's obsessive driving of son to glory, and the boy's crack-up and treatment. Karl Malden, Anthony Perkins marvellous. Robert Mulligan-Alan Pakula's director-producer debut; 1957. (*b/w*)

Female on the Beach   √
Joan Crawford thinks Jeff Chandler is trying to murder her in this 1955 toughie. Is he? Joe Pevney directed with gusto. (*b/w*)

The Feminine Touch   √
(1) Author of treatise on jealousy (Don Ameche, miscast) succumbs to it when he thinks wife (Rosalind Russell) is carrying on with Van Heflin, while she

thinks he fancies Kay Francis; old-fashioned but has that 1941 Woody Van Dyke style. (*b/w*)

The Feminine Touch × ×
(2) Five girls train to be nurses; unfortunately, this was dated when it was first shown in 1956, and is desperately antique now. Pat Jackson assembled cast of nice competent second-raters but couldn't make it catch fire. (*c*)

Ferry to Hong Kong √
Curt Jurgens and Orson Welles ham it up as perpetual traveller unable to land either in Hong Kong or Macao, and boat's skipper; director Lewis Gilbert didn't seem to know whether it was meant to be comedy or melodrama; 1959. (*c*)

Fever Heat × × ×
Boring little film vaguely about dirty work in stock car racing, with Nick Adams and Jeannine Riley hopelessly inadequate; same goes for director Russell S. Doughton; 1968. (*c*)

A Fever in the Blood √
Three men all try to use a murder trial to further their political ambitions; an unusual and quite gripping melo with Efram Zimbalist Jr, Don Ameche, Herbert Marshall and Angie Dickinson as the girl in the middle; but director Vincent Sherman ran out of conviction in 1960. (*b/w*)

The Fiend Who Walked the West √
Western for grown-ups is about psychopathic killer in cowboy gear; Gordon Douglas made this one genuinely exciting in 1958; Hugh O'Brian. (*c*)

The Fiercest Heart × ×
White men pushing Red Indians out of their territory and made heroes for it in Western movies are bad enough, but Boers shoving Zulus out of their land in South Africa and having heroic films

made about them seem much worse somehow. Are Stuart Whitman, Juliet Prowse, Geraldine Fitzgerald, Raymond Massey happy about this 1961 adventure, looking back? George Sherman. (*c*)

55 Days At Peking √
The Boxer Rebellion and siege of the legations retold with some idea of its being allegorical plea for Uniting Nations; Charlton Heston and Ava Gardner strike attitudes among the fireworks; Nicholas Ray directs manfully; 1963. (*c*)

The Fighting Prince of Donegal ×
A chunk of Irish history that's a bit too heavily served to swallow easily; Peter McEnery attempts an Errol Flynn role with moderate success; Susan Hampshire, Gordon Jackson among other Elizabethan period furniture; Michael O'Herlihy; 1966. (*c*)

The File of the Golden Goose × ×
Only the smaller parts played by such dependables as Edward Woodward, Graham Crowden, Charles Gray, manage to make this picture worth a desultory look. Yul Brynner's arrogant walk-through as American undercover agent breaking up counterfeiting gang is his usual terse, boring performance; Sam Wanamaker's idea of direction is to whizz through as many London locations as possible; 1969. (*c*)

The Final Hour √
Western with the difference that the antagonism is between ranchers and Polish workers imported for the coalmines. Robert Douglas directs imaginatively and Lee J. Cobb lends distinction; 1963. (*c*)

The Final Test √
Terence Rattigan enjoying himself writing about cricket and the last game that a father is playing. He wants his son to watch him but the lad isn't interested. Anthony Asquith squeezes the last drop

of Englishness out of a very posh script, and Robert Morley stands out; 1954. (c)

A Fine Madness √
Berserk poet Sean Connery soon becomes tedious, despite Joanne Woodward's hard work as his wife; Jean Seberg and Patrick O'Neal don't help. Director Irving Kershner has done better with the New York locations than the people in this attempt at crazy comedy; 1966. (c)

Finian's Rainbow √
Made in 1968 before 'Godfather' Francis Ford Coppola became the golden boy of Hollywood, this rather pleasant and expensive version of the stage musical (*How Are Things in Glocca Morra?*) never made it with the public, but pleased discerning critics. An ageing Fred Astaire (69) still managed to appear sprightly, and it is perhaps unfair that Pet Clark and Tommy Steele haven't been asked to make a major movie since. (c)

Fireball 500 × ×
The stock cars in this racing low-budgeter are fine; Frankie Avalon and Fabian not so fine; William Asher; 1966. (c)

Firecreek × ×
Both Henry Fonda and James Stewart have proved in their choices of television series to be utterly incapable of selecting material worthy of their talents and charisma, and this 1968 Western seems to suggest that the rot set in at around their sixtieth birthdays (Fonda was born 1905, Stewart 1908). It's dull, slow-moving, poorly-scripted, inadequately-directed (by Vincent McEveety). Fonda's a villain, leader of a bunch of hired hands terrorising the community where Stewart is part-time sheriff. Not until the final shoot-out, when a crippled Stewart takes on the whole gang, does it rise even to the lowest heights. (c)

Fire Down Below ×
Robert Mitchum and Jack Lemmon fighting in a tramp steamer for tramp Rita Hayworth. Made in England for some reason (like blocked currency), it used a lugubrious lot of British actors as weak supports. Director Robert Parrish; 1957. (c)

First Men in the Moon √
Amiably-eccentric version of the H. G. Wells story, made in 1964, with gorgeous special effects by Ray Harryhausen and equally gorgeous performance by Lionel Jeffries as the first lunar-tic, claiming the moon for Queen Victoria. Director Nathan Juran. (c)

The First of the Few √
In 1942 Leslie Howard produced, directed and starred in real-life story of R. J. Mitchell, designer of the Spitfire, who died early, in 1937. It was Howard's last film: in 1943 he died in a shot-down aircraft. David Niven, Rosamund John, Roland Culver; Sir William Walton's famous score. (b/w)

The First Texan √
Joel McCrea as Sam Houston who led the fight for the state's freedom and became President; Byron Haskin; 1956. (c)

The First Travelling Saleslady ×
She's Ginger Rogers desperately trying to sell barbed wire to Texans, James Arness, Clint Eastwood among them; Arthur Lubin; 1956. (c)

Fitzwilly Strikes Back × × ×
Acute embarrassment is the only possible reaction to this outsized booboo with Dick Van Dyck as butler organising crime syndicate to keep distressed gentlewoman in the style to which she is accustomed. Dame Edith Evans must have been mad to accept the part of the eccentric dowager, and Delbert Mann's direction is so sentimental that it defies belief; 1968. (c)

Five ✓
The last quintet on Earth after an atomic explosion are all unknowns, but Arch Oboler, who directed and produced in 1951, is dab hand at the scientifically-fictitious. (*b/w*)

Five Against the House ✓
Reno casino caper–Guy Madison and Brian Keith stand out as college buddies in the gang; Kim Novak is their inside girl. Director Phil Karlson; 1955. (*b/w*)

Five Card Stud ✓
Late (1968) attempt by veteran Henry Hathaway to come up with something new in Westerns (Ten Little Indians in a game of poker, with each of the players getting shot in turn). However, he hasn't been able to make it sufficiently different from his routine work to distinguish it and the whodunit element is never exploited. Dean Martin, Robert Mitchum and Roddy McDowall turn in fairly obvious performances. (*c*)

Five Finger Exercise ✕
Disappointing version of Peter Schaffer play that was gripping in the theatre but has been coarsened in its screen translation directed by Daniel Mann. Nor are Rosalind Russell, Jack Hawkins convincing as parents of family disrupted by German student Maximilian Schell; 1962. (*b/w*)

Five Fingers ✓✓
Splendid performance from James Mason as the Operation Cicero spy rifling the safe of the British ambassador to Turkey. Joseph L. Mankiewicz; 1961. (*b/w*)

Five Miles to Midnight ✓
Sophia Loren well-cast for once as Italian wife of American living in France who plots to swindle insurance company after he survives air-crash; Gig Young, Jean-Pierre Aumont support. Anatole Litvak made it moderately gripping; 1962. (*b/w*)

The Five Pennies ✕
Supposed biopic of jazz musician Red Nichols in the Twenties, all so familiar you want to chant the next lines even if you haven't seen it before. To make things worse, Danny Kaye does usual hammy over-acting; Barbara Bel Geddes is given an awful hair-do and told not to steal the picture – that's left to Louis Armstrong; Mel Shavelson; 1959. (*c*)

Five Weeks in a Balloon ✓
Splendid spoof of Victorian exploration, with race across Africa to claim territory; Red Buttons, Barbara Eden, Cedric Hardwicke, Peter Lorre, Billy Gilbert, Herbert Marshall, Reginald Owen make up strong cast for Irwin Allen in 1962. (*c*)

The 5,000 Fingers of Dr T ✓
Imaginative nightmare of little boy who dreams of a 500-seater piano, lush apartments, dreary dungeons in Dr Terwilliker's Musical Academy, with Peter Lind Hayes. Director Roy Rowland; 1953. (*c*)

The Fixer ✓
A clash of opposites that never gel is the fault of this well-meaning, often moving, but never satisfactory account of one Jew's persecution in Czarist Russia. Dalton Trumbo's talky script fights with John Frankenheimer's natural flashy but suppressed style of direction. Symbolic importance of the theme fights with cliché lines ('Respect is what you have in order to get'; 'Where there is no fight for it, there is no freedom'; 'I'm not a hero, I'm an accident'). And the casting – with the exception of Alan Bates as the hero/accident, who surprisingly overcomes his physical wrongness for the part – is wrong: a whole string of British bit players doing their nuts (Georgia Brown, Ian Holm, David Warner, Carol White among the most out of place) and Dirk Bogarde indulges himself as a lawyer; 1969. (*c*)

The Flame and the Arrow √
Burt Lancaster as Italian Robin-Hood-type hero in the 12th century, Virginia Mayo the gal he wins; Jacques Tourneur lets everyone enjoy themselves, including you, if sufficiently uncritical; 1950. (*c*)

Flame and the Flesh × ×
This dreary soaper with Lana Turner as bad woman and Pier Angeli as good is fortunately dominated by some scenes of Naples; Richard Brooks understandably preferred it to the plot and the principals; 1954. (*c*)

Flame in the Streets ×
Dated yarn about racial prejudice in 1961 Britain with Sylvia Syms falling for black teacher and causing her parents' marriage (John Mills, Brenda de Banzie) to blow up; Earl Cameron, Johnny Sekka, Ann Lynn, Wilfred Brambell, do their best with a Ted Willis script; director Roy Baker. (*c*)

Flamingo Road ×
Joan Crawford, stranded carnival queen in small town, gets involved with politician Sydney Greenstreet, while losing heart to Zachary Scott. Michael Curtiz desperately tries to make sense out of twisting and often motiveless plot; 1949. (*b/w*)

Flaming Star √
What? a good movie with Elvis Presley in it? Well, not quite, but nearly. Possibly because as half-breed Indian, he has to share the lead with Steve Forrest and Dolores Del Rio, and Nunnally Johnson had a hand in the script. But most likely it's because the director was Don Siegel, since recognised (this was made in 1960) as one of Hollywood's major talents. (*c*)

A Flea in Her Ear × × ×
There have been few more disastrous attempts to cash in on the success of a stage play than this profoundly unamusing version of Feydeau's farce which was helplessly funny on the stage. Perhaps it was that the mechanics of opening the wrong doors at the right time and dressing up to get out of naughty situations needs the magic box of the theatre. Or it may be that Rex Harrison, Rosemary Harris, Louis Jourdan and Rachel Roberts are simply unsuited to high farce. Or that Jacques Charon is a rotten director; 1968. (*c*)

Flesh and Fury ×
The presence of Tony Curtis as a boxer might tempt you into watching this, but be warned, he's deaf and dumb, and is given his hearing back by magazine writer Mona Freeman; Joseph Pevney must have known it was hokum, but he bravely puts a good face on it; 1951. (*b/w*)

The Flesh and the Fiends ×
Film-makers are endlessly fascinated by the Burke and Hare grave-robbing mythology, and this is a 1950 version of the Edinburgh anatomist story with Peter Cushing, Donald Pleasence, Billie Whitelaw, directed by John Gilling. (*b/w*)

The Flesh is Weak × ×
Trite little melo about tarts and bully-boys in London; nifty direction by Don Chaffey is about all it's got; 1957. (*b/w*)

Flight From Ashiya ×
One of those back-flashing melos about characters caught in air-sea rescue, sunk before it starts by a banal script well matched by the luckless direction of Michael Anderson, never the man to add inspiration. Richard Widmark and Shirley Knight manage to rise a little above the general boredom; Yul Brynner and George Chakiris don't; 1964. (*c*)

Flight of the Phoenix √
Superior survivors-in-the-desert drama with stand-out performances from James Stewart as crashed plane's pilot, Richard

Attenborough as his navigator. Beautifully understated direction from Robert Aldrich overcomes tendency to stereotyping among the others. They gradually fight to rebuild the plane, and the climax is guaranteed to keep you on the edge of your seat; 1966. (*c*)

Flipper √
Pleasant little Florida adventure with, one suspects, a whole school of dolphins acting the part of Flipper. After all, we wouldn't know them apart, would we? Strictly boy-meets-dolphin, boy-loses-dolphin, boy-gets-dolphin despite hurricane. Director, James B. Clark; 1963. (*c*)

Flipper and the Pirates ×
Luke Halpin, Pamela Franklin and precocious dolphin in run-in (and swim-in) with ex-convicts. But there aren't any pirates. Leon Benson; 1964. (*c*)

Flower Drum Song ×
Endless musical about Chinese girl from Hong Kong who loves Chinese boy in San Francisco but he loves Chinese stripper; no great songs from Rodgers and Hammerstein and no great shakes from director Henry Koster; Nancy Kwan, James Shigeta, Juanita Hall; 1961. (*c*)

Fluffy × × ×
Boring and predictable yarn about a pet lion on the loose that wastes the talents of owner Tony Randall, Shirley Jones, Celia Kaye, Jim Backus; director is Earl Bellamy, who does his best with over-stretched material; 1964. (*c*)

The Fly √
A huge success in 1958, surprising its makers, who thought they had an average-to-good low budgeter (it cost £350,000; made £3 million in its first few weeks' release) but had reckoned without the morbid attraction of a man's head and arm being fixed by scientific mischance on to a fly – and vice versa.

Vincent Price admits he couldn't keep a straight face during filming, but although producer-director Kurt Neumann didn't exploit the possibilities, it remains genuinely chilling. (*c*)

Flying Leathernecks √
The standard army drama transferred to the flying corps with John Wayne as the tough commander and Robert Ryan, resenting him, finds he has to act the same way when he takes over. Nicholas Ray gives it great zing; 1951. (*c*)

Folies Bergère √
Maurice Chevalier plays double role in musical museum piece with vast chorine numbers, Ann Sothern, Merle Oberon; director Roy del Ruth; 1935. (*b/w*)

Follow That Dream √
The best Elvis Presley vehicle – though that's not saying much. He's a country hick moving to Florida in order to homestead and he beats the slickers at their own game; Director Gordon Douglas; 1962. (*c*)

Follow That Horse × ×
British comedy directed by Alan Bromly wastes a marvellous cast of good character actors in rubbish about horse swallowing microfilm; David Tomlinson Cecil Parker, Richard Wattis, Dora Bryan, George A. Cooper, Arthur Lowe; 1959. (*b/w*)

Follow That Man × ×
Sydney Chaplin, Dawn Addams in Jerry Epstein-directed tripe about a con man and a journalist; 1960. (*b/w*)

Follow the Boys ×
Low-spirited comedy of American gals who (nicely) traipse after the American fleet in the Med. Picture postcards of Cannes and Santa Margherita; pleasant legs in front of them belong to Paula Prentiss, Janis Paige. The rest is noise; Richard Thorpe; 1963. (*c*)

Follow the Sun ✕
Over-dramatised biopic of golfer Ben Hogan's fight against accident damage; Glenn Ford, Anne Baxter, Sam Snead. Sidney Lanfield; 1951. (*b/w*)

Folly to be Wise √
One of the funnier British comedies of the early fifties (1952 to be precise) has Alastair Sim organising and embarrassing 'brains trust'; Roland Culver, Martita Hunt, Miles Malleson helped Frank Launder come up with a smiler. (*b/w*)

Fools Rush In ✕ ✕
Weak British comedy of 1949 about on-off-on wedding directed by John Paddy Carstairs in rather limp style and with thoroughly undistinguished cast. (*b/w*)

Footsteps in the Fog √
Gas-lit melo with Stewart Granger as wife-murderer – is Jean Simmons next on the list? Arthur Lubin does his best to milk the suspense; 1955. (*b/w*)

For Better For Worse ✕
Dirk Bogarde gives this thin little domestic comedy about young couple facing early years of marriage what distinction it has with Cecil Parker backing him up solidly. Distaff side weaker, with Susan Stephen and Eileen Herlie less convincing; J. Lee Thompson; 1954. (*c*)

Forbidden Planet √ √
Raves John Baxter in *Science Fiction in the Cinema:* 'Was and still is the most remarkable of sf films, the ultimate recreation of the future'. Loosely based on *The Tempest*, it has Walter Pidgeon as survivor of AD 2000 expedition to Altair, with Anne Francis as his Miranda of a daughter; a robot is their Caliban. Done with more verve and imagination than scientific accuracy or plausibility, it is nevertheless a major achievement for director Fred. M. Wilcox and special effects expert Joshua Meador; 1956. (*c*)

Force of Arms √
Updating of Hemingway's *A Farewell to Arms* to Second World War but based on a short story by Richard William Tegaskis. William Holden is battle-weary soldier, Nancy Olson a WAC officer frightened to fall in love again; Michael Curtiz treats it as superior soap-opera, which is what it always was; 1951. (*b/w*)

Foreign Correspondent √ √
Classic 1940 Hitchcock with Joel McCrea caught up in web of international espionage, and Herbert Marshall, George Sanders, Laraine Day, Robert Benchley turning in their best work under his direction. Gary Cooper turned it down because it was a thriller, and Hitchcock has since criticised McCrea as being too easy-going. (*b/w*)

Foreign Intrigue ✕
Robert Mitchum uncovering neo-nazis, with Genevieve Page; Sheldon Reynolds directs-produces this competent, if ultimately disappointing thriller; 1956. (*c*)

Forever Amber ✕
Otto Preminger took over after John Stahl had already shot two million dollars worth of unusable film. He told Darryl Zanuck then he couldn't even finish reading the book, but he was under contract. Then they rowed about the star – he wanted Lana Turner but Zanuck insisted on Linda Darnell. 'The picture, in spite of all the whittling that was done, the censorship difficulties, the cuts that were made for the Catholic League of Decency, brought back its money and eventually made a profit. (Otto Preminger in Gerald Pratley's book). It shouldn't have – it just shows the power of the dirty word; 1948. (*c*)

Forever Female √
Satisfyingly bitchy glimpse into world of the theatre with Ginger Rogers as ageing

actress, husband-producer Paul Douglas, ambitious playwright William Holden; Irving Rapper; 1953. (*b/w*)

For Love of Ivy × ×
Appalling longueur on the part of Sidney Poitier (who devised and starred in it), Daniel Mann (who directed) and all aboard this so-called comedy about a racketeer who woos a housemaid for the despicable purpose of keeping her employed by white household. Offensive to anyone, black or white, who sees the need for radical change. Poitier, doing very nicely thank you out of the present situation, obviously isn't among them; 1967. (*c*)

For Love or Money ×
Widow Thelma Ritter hires lawyer Kirk Douglas to be matchmaker for her three daughters; the only question which might idly occupy your attention is which one he'll end up marrying himself. Bright little, dull little Mitzi Gaynor is closest to a star so she's the favourite; William Bendix and Gig Young can't save it from Michael Gordon's nerveless grasp; 1963. (*c*)

The Forsyte Saga ×
A bit of a laugh, when Errol Flynn is Soames, Robert Young the architect Bossiney, Greer Garson moderately well cast as Irene; pity poor Compton Bennett having to squash it all into a couple of hours. Can't be done; 1950. (*c*)

Fort Apache √
Classic John Ford 1948 super-Western, with Henry Fonda as embittered officer in charge of outpost, John Wayne as his disgusted aide. Shirley Temple makes an unexpected entry as Fonda's daughter – she was 20 at the time. (*b/w*)

Fort Defiance √
Coward deserts during Civil War, causing all but one man in his company

to be killed; the survivor pledges revenge Dane Clark and Ben Johnson do well in main parts; John Rawlins directs competently; 1951. (*c*)

For the First Time × ×
Mario Lanza fans can tune in for a weep-in as our stodgy star, playing of course a temperamental opera king, falls for a beautiful girl who is deaf – fortunately? With Johanna von Koczian, Zsa Zsa Gabor, directed (1958) by Rudy Mate. (*c*)

For Those Who Think Young × ×
Cheap little picture about the extra-curricular activities of girl at college, with James Darren and Nancy Sinatra; only occasionally amusing; Leslie H. Martinson; 1964. (*c*)

Fort Massacre ×
Joel MacCrea takes over command of survivors of Indian massacre, determined on vengeance; Forrest Tucker; director Joseph Newman; 1958. (*c*)

Fort Osage ×
The fort was the last safe stop for pioneers heading into the West; Rod Cameron fronts routine Western using it as background; Leslie Selander; 1952. (*c*

Fort Ti ×
3D effects are unfortunately missing from this otherwise standard Western, on TV. All that's left is George Montgomery riding to the rescue in French-Indian war of late 18th century; William Castle; 1953. (*c*)

Fort Worth ×
Randolph Scott has to pick up his guns again when his newspaper can't rid the town of scoundrels – a dubious message. Edwin L. Martin; 1951. (*c*)

Forty Guns √
A Samuel Fuller script-production-direction of Barry Sullivan coming up

against the forty-strong gang headed by Barbara Stanwyck; Gene Barry, Dean Jagger; 1957. (*c*)

Forty Pounds of Trouble √
A bit cute but often amusing comedy about gambling casino owner Tony Curtis having to cope with five-year-old girl left on his hands; Phil Silvers, Stubby Kaye score, and there's a lot of Disneyland. Norman Jewison brought some nice touches to what could have been insufferably whimsical; 1962. (*c*)

For Whom the Bell Tolls √
Sam Wood's war film with a convincing Gary Cooper and a less-so Ingrid Bergman carefully played down Hemingway's essential placing of it in the Spanish Civil War. Despite this, it probably educated a large number of hitherto isolated Americans about which side was which in the world conflict they had somehow become embroiled in (it was made in 1943). The tendency was towards cartoon in Katina Paxinou's and Akim Tamiroff's performances, but the whole effect was exciting and involving. (*b/w*)

The Fountainhead ×
Gary Cooper gravely miscast as hero of Ayn Rand's philosophical novel about modern architect battling with Establishment. 'I thought it should have been someone like Bogart, a more arrogant type of man,' said director King Vidor, looking back. 'But Pat Neal I thought marvellous, splendid.' 1949. (*b/w*)

Four for Texas √
Clanny romp through the Wild West with Frank Sinatra, Dean Martin, Anita Ekberg, Ursula Andress. Robert Aldrich gave it expert touch; 1963. (*c*)

Four Guns to the Border × ×
Rory Calhoun as bank-robber laid low by pretty Colleen Miller; director Richard Carlson makes it last from fight to clinch to fight somehow; 1954. (*c*)

The Four Horsemen of the Apocalypse × ×
Not, alas, the 1921 Valentino version but Vincente Minnelli's 1962 updating to second world war which only revealed story's novelettishness and Glenn Ford's inadequacies. Divided loyalties in Argentinian family in Paris. Those old horsemen come thundering through in visions. (*c*)

Four In the Morning √ √
Three sets of London stories intertwine to make an unusual and memorable film which gives the impression that director Anthony Simmons allowed his talented cast (Judi Dench, Norman Rodway, Joe Melia in outstanding episode; Ann Lynn, Brian Phelan in another) to improvise. Some nice moody of London, too; 1966. (*b/w*)

The Fourposter ×
Made in 1952, when Rex Harrison and Lilli Palmer were married, they are the only players in filming of dreary Jan de Hartog play about various stages of a married life with the title-bed as part of each scene's action. Sadly, it's neither very sexy nor edifying; Irving Reis; 1952. (*b/w*)

Fourteen Hours √
Will Richard Basehart throw himself off skyscraper edge? Can Paul Douglas or Barbara Bel Geddes save him? Can you spot Grace Kelly in a sub-plot? Henry Hathaway; 1951. (*b/w*)

The Fox √
In the dear dead pre-permissive days of 1968 this was a great sensation with implied lesbianism and a glimpse or two of bared breasts, but now it's just an unsatisfactory attempt to translate the D. H. Lawrence story to the screen, with awful overplaying by Keir Dullea, Anne

Heywood and Sandy Dennis. Director Mark Rydell must take part of the blame. (*c*)

The Foxes of Harrow ×
Lush mush with Rex Harrison, Maureen O'Hara, Victor McLaglen put through tiresome hoops by John M. Stahl in 1947 failure to recapture copied grandeur of *Gone With The Wind*. (*b/w*)

Foxfire × ×
A very ill-assorted pair (Jeff Chandler as Apache miner, Gail Russell as posh girl from the East) somehow meet and get married. Their problems and their search for a goldmine take up this drama routinely directed by Joseph Pevney; 1955. (*c*)

Francis ×
First of seven pretty grim comedies about a talking mule, with Donald O'Connor as his mate (1950); spawned **Francis Goes to the Races** (1951); **Francis Goes to West Point** (1952); **Francis Covers the Big Town** (1953); **Francis Joins the WACS** (1954); **Francis in the Navy** (1955), all munch of a munchness (and that's about the level of the jokes); when director Arthur Lubin went on to create Mr Ed, a talking horse (wonder where he got the idea?) on TV. Charles Lamont made a final film with Mickey Rooney replacing Donald O'Connor, **Francis in the Haunted House** (1956). (*all b/w*)

Francis of Assisi ×
No, not a follow-up to the above. This sixth film on the animal-loving saint is pictorially beautiful, being made on the actual locations in Italy, but a bit dull. Still, that's better than being sensational. Bradford Dillman plays St Francis carefully, and Dolores Hart, Finlay Currie, Athene Seyler don't give offence; Michael Curtiz probably achieves the effect he was seeking if not the success; (*c*. 1916)

Frankenstein √ √ √
A great, great movie, much more than just a horror picture, like so many of its imitators. Director James Whale wrung masterly performance from Boris Karloff in 1931; you feel sympathy and understanding for this almost-human and through him, for all life's abnormals.' (*b/w*)

Frankenstein Created Woman ×
And Terence Fisher created disappointment in this creaky 1967 attempt to project the myth further than it will stretch; Peter Cushing does his best. (*c*)

Frankenstein Must be Destroyed ×
But you can bet he won't as long as he goes on making money with such farragos as this 1969 one about the Doc transplanting brains; Peter Cushing and Freddie Jones, directed perfunctorily and bloodily by Terence Fisher.

(lots of *c*)

Frankenstein 1970 ×
Time has overtaken this lame attempt to squeeze one more chiller out of the old story; it wasn't made in 1970 but twelve years earlier and is about Boris Karloff being made in the basement while a TV crew films a programme about him upstairs. Strictly for collectors; Howard W. Koch. (*c*)

Frankie and Johnnie ×
As Elvis Presley vehicles go, this one from 1966 isn't too awful. Frederick de Cordova keeps it lively and Harry Morgan has some quite jolly comedy lines to say. Nancy Kovack makes a sweet Nellie Bly. (*c*)

Fraulein ×
Prettied-up version of novel which dwelt lovingly on all the degradations a German had to go through as the war collapsed. Here, Dana Wynter finds love with an American officer after a

certain amount of tough times but nothing to the book; Henry Koster; 1958. (*c*)

French Dressing × ×
Awful Ken Russell debut which at least doesn't have the pretentiousness of his later epics. Imagine casting a dull little Austrian actress, Marisa Mell, as a French starlet when there were so many French possibilities. From this beginning the half-hearted attempt to satirise the English seaside is just gloom-plunging, despite James Booth and Roy Kinnear doing their best; 1964. (*b/w*)

The French Line × × ×
Jane Russell has quite big breasts. When you've said that, you have exhausted all possible points of interest about that over-publicised lady. Certainly this dull comedy about heiress looking for man not after her money and going to Europe to find him has none. Lloyd Bacon slices it thin; 1954. (*c*)

Frenchie √
Strongly-cast–Joel McCrea, Shelley Winters, Elsa Lanchester–Western about a gambling lady; Louis King; 1950. (*c*)

Frenchman's Creek ×
Daphne du Maurier novel not all that well translated to the screen but making an undemanding swashbuckler with Arturo de Cordova as the pirate who's a perfect gent and Joan Fontaine as grand lady with romantic ideas; Basil Rathbone, Nigel Bruce were their 1945 best; Mitchell Leisen. (*c*)

Freud – The Secret Passion √
While avoiding the usual biopic pitfall of glamorising his subject, John Huston hasn't made Freud at all believable. He isn't helped by a monotonous, pop-eyed performance from Montgomery Clift; nor is the rest of this poorly chosen cast very convincing; it's sensational enough, in parts, and the Viennese locations are authentic. But there's a block somewhere. When did you first start having these dreams of being a significant film director, Mr Huston? 1962. (*b/w*)

Friendly Persuasion √ √
Delightful morality tale of Quaker family (Gary Cooper, Dorothy McGuire, Tony Perkins) whose pacifism is put to the test in Civil War. William Wyler; 1956. (*c*)

From Hell to Texas √ √
Superior Western with Don Murray on the run from a crime he hasn't committed. Dennis Hopper is among well-etched band of characters he runs into. Henry Hathaway can usually be relied on to bring the best out of an oater script and certainly did so here in 1958. (*c*)

From Here to Eternity √ √
Conflict between director Fred Zinneman and producer Harry Cohn over length (Cohn insisted on two big scenes being cut out so as to bring it under two hours) and casting of this drama of army life in Hawaii at start of Second World War; Joan Crawford was Cohn's choice for the part Deborah Kerr turned sexy in, and it was only when she walked out over a fight about the wardrobe that he gave in. And he accepted Frank Sinatra cheap (£1,000 a week) after the then-failed singer offered to pay to get into the picture; Sinatra was right–it marked the turning point in his career and won him one of its seven Academy Awards. See *The Godfather* for fictionalised version of how Sinatra got the role; Donna Reed also won Oscar for it; 1953. (*b/w*)

From Russia With Love √ √
The second James Bond film–the one about his being snaffled in Istanbul as he goes after Russian cipher machine; usual slick *mélange* of guns, athleticism and sex, presided over by Terence Young.

109

Sean Connery does his famous bit, aided by Robert Shaw, Lotte Lenya, Pedro Armendariz; 1963. (*c*)

From the Earth to the Moon ✕
Pretty ludicrous adaptation of Jules Verne sf about a millionaire who chooses to stay on the moon for love of a lady; somehow Joseph Cotten, George Sanders, Debra Paget got involved in 1964 version of 1868 yarn. Byron Haskin directed. (*c*)

From the Terrace √
Paul Newman as another of his early ruthless, ambitious working boys marrying (Joanne Woodward) social status, from John O'Hara chronicle. Myrna Loy is splendid as drunken mother; directed, 1960, by Mark Robson. (*c*)

The Fugitive √
Critics were upset in 1947 because John Ford softened Graham Greene's *The Power and the Glory* by not making Henry Fonda's priest alcoholic. But this produced a greater challenge in that he never has this excuse. It is now recognised as Ford's most personal work, celebrating the solace of religion, and Fonda's sincerity is matched by Dolores del Rio as his Mary Magdalene, J. Carrol Naish his Iscariot, Pedro Armendariz his Pilate. (*b/w*)

The Fugitive Kind √√
Marlon Brando as drifting Romeo ready to settle. As try-outs he gets involved with passionate Anna Magnani and powerful Joanne Woodward – who gives a great performance. Sidney Lumet's uneven 1959 direction doesn't quite do justice to Tennessee Williams' original *Orpheus Descending*, but it smoulders along satisfactorily. (*b/w*)

Full of Life √
The superb Judy Holliday as pregnant wife dependent on excitable father-in-law Salvatore Baccaloni; a good laugh.

Highly efficient direction by Richard Quine; 1956. (*b/w*)

Funeral in Berlin √
This is the Len Deighton about Colonel Stok (Oscar Homolka) purportedly defecting, with Michael Caine as bespectacled hero from *The Ipcress File*. Guy Hamilton didn't manage the coherence of the book; 1966. (*c*)

Fun in Acapulco ✕✕
Elvis Presley might have had some fun counting the money he was going to make from this rotten movie, but it doesn't extend to us. He's supposed to be a trapeze artist who regains lost nerve when high-diving in this fancy Mexican resort; Paul Lukas scores as temperamental chef; Ursula Andress wears bathing suits. Richard Thorpe; 1963. (*c*)

Funny Face √
Photographer Fred Astaire lures bookshop assistant (Audrey Hepburn) into becoming model girl; lots of pleasant dancing, singing and clothes; Stanley Donen; 1956. (*c*)

Funny Girl √√
Sometimes a performance is so legendary that audiences don't see the person – only the myth. This was the case with Barbra Streisand's film debut in the performance that had already conquered Broadway and the West End, in a show allegedly based on the life-story of Follies star Fanny Brice. The first half transferred well to the screen under veteran William Wyler's respectful direction, but after the interval it goes to pieces when her drama with her unsatisfactory husband (played with inappropriate self-satisfaction by Omar Sharif) has been opened out. The end is pure Streisand, singing a song that wasn't in the original show, My Man, in a manner quite unlike Miss Brice's. The rest of the cast are only back-drops to la Streisand; 1968. (*c*)

110

Walter Huston (centre) in John Huston's *The Treasure of the Sierra Madre* (Best Supporting Actor Oscar, 1948); Tim Holt (left) and Humphrey Bogart made up trio of gold-
seekers divided by Bogart's selfishness.

Jane Wyman (Best Actress Oscar, 1948) played raped deaf-mute in *Johnny Belinda*; for
authenticity, director Jean Negulesco blocked her ears. Lew Ayres (bareheaded), local
doctor, is her only friend. Charles Bickford in the hat.

Montgomery Clift as US soldier who cares for war-orphan Ivan Jandl in *The Search*, 1948.

Richard Todd (seated) in *The Hasty Heart* (nominated as Best Actor, 1949). Gov. Reagan offers a kilt to a dying man.

Gloria Swanson and Erick von Stroheim made a stunning double act as faded star and butler in *Sunset Boulevard*, both Oscar nominees, 1950. Swanson, then 52, had started in 1915; von Stroheim (1885–1957) in 1919.

Stewart Granger in *King Solomon's Mines*, 1950.

Humphrey Bogart (Oscar winner, 1951) and Katharine Hepburn (nomination) in *The African Queen*.

Peter Ustinov as Nero in *Quo Vadis?* (Oscar Support nomination, 1951). Director Mervyn LeRoy called for 'the Shredded Wheat set' during one of Ustinov's more extravagant scenes – 'If you're going to eat the scenery, we may as well make it edible.'

Finlay Currie has a good laugh in *Ivanhoe* (nominated for Best Picture, 1952) at the expense of George Sanders and Robert Douglas, while jester Emlyn Williams snoozes.

Donald O'Connor and Gene Kelly with 'Fit as a Fiddle' from the 1952 *Singin' in the Rain*.

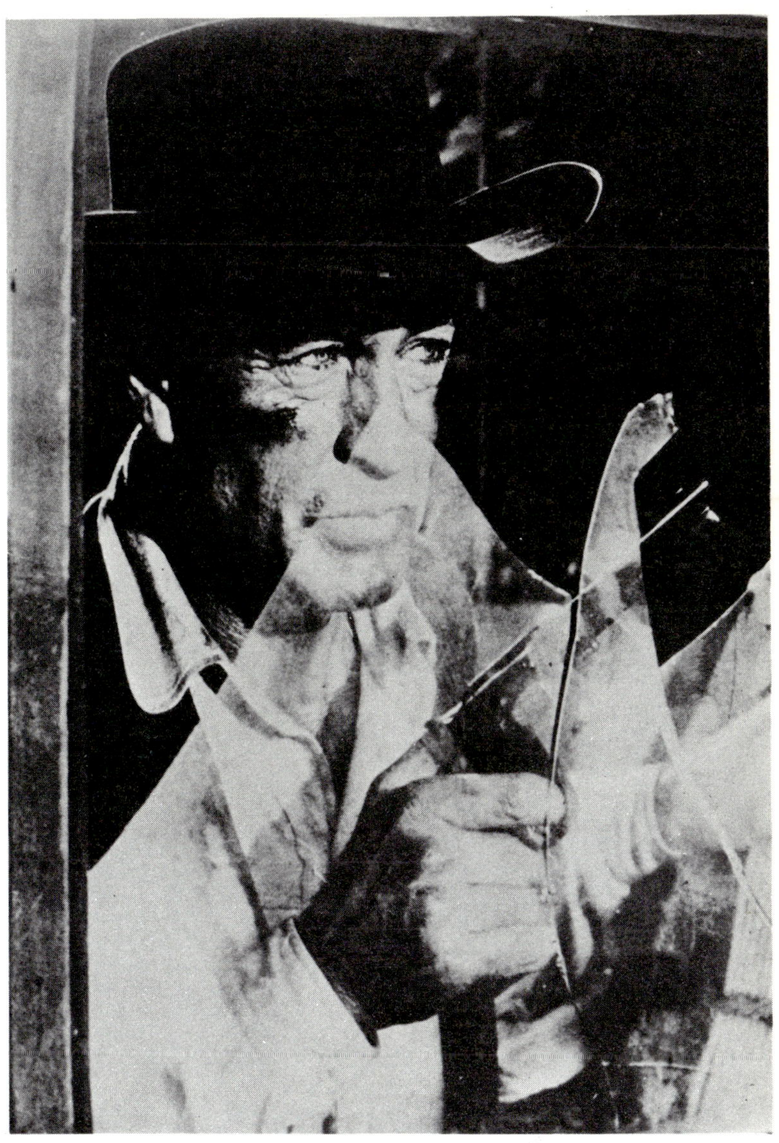

High Noon won Gary Cooper the Best Actor Oscar, 1952, was nominated as Best Picture, and won Music and Editing Oscars too.

José Ferrer in *Moulin Rouge* (nominated as 1952 Best Picture), with Colette Marchand.

Judy Garland, here in *A Star is Born* (1952), had that aching quality of giving too much.

Seven Brides for Seven Brothers (1954 Best Picture nomination) ties with *The Wizard of Oz* for best musical never shown on British TV. At least up to the time of going to press, MGM thought these both still had big cinema box office potential – they're probably right.

Anna Magnani lambasting truck-driver Burt Lancaster in *The Rose Tattoo* (Oscar for Best Actress, 1955), in which she played emerging widow. Despite acclaim, she never made another successful American movie, and went home.

Kirk Douglas as van Gogh in *Lust for Life* (Best Actor nomination, 1956) managed more credibility than usual biopic.

Around the World in 80 Days (five Oscars) wasn't nearly as good as Mike Todd's publicity. David Niven and Cantinflas in flight.

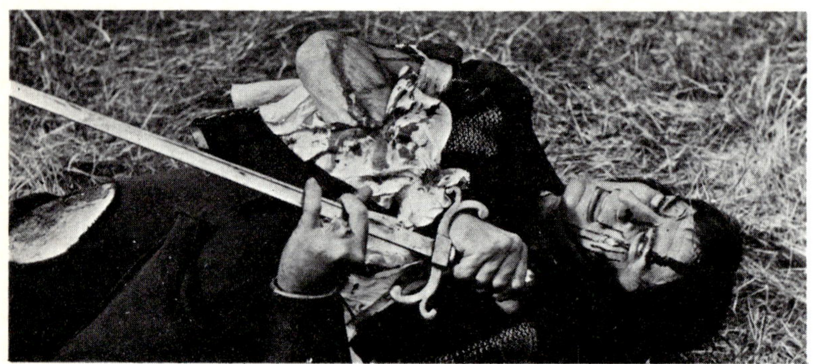

Laurence Olivier's Richard III was ludicrously pipped for Best Actor Oscar, 1956, by Yul Brynner's *The King and I*. Olivier's confiding villain-hero, so close to high camp, is deeper into Shakespeare's heart than his elderly Hamlet, or proud Henry V.

Henry Fonda's hold-out juror in *Twelve Angry Men* (Best Picture nomination, 1957) comes over as even more honest than Gary Cooper's Mr Deeds, James Stewart's Mr Smith, and is challenged only by his own Tom Joad. For rest of jury, see text.

Funnyman √
Low-budgeter which shows with some success, some over-pretentiousness, how young San Francisco revue actor searches for something to make his life meaningful. Altogether too pleased with itself; John Korty; 1968. (part *c* part *b/w*)

A Funny Thing Happened on the Way to the Forum √
But not nearly as funny as everyone involved seems to think. The original stage musical was a bit yawny, but the frantic opening-out by fey Dick Lester is even more so; ancient Rome must have been wittier than this lumbering attempt to weld Buster Keaton, Zero Mostel, Phil Silvers and Swinging Rome into any kind of satisfactory whole; 1966. (*c*)

The Furies √
Routine epic Western about cattle-baron feud, with Barbara Stanwyck as defiant Juliet (it was made in 1950 when she was only 43!) and Walter Huston her crusty old pop; Anthony Mann directed. (*b/w*)

Further up the Creek ✕
Frankie Howerd turns last voyage of Naval frigate into paying holiday cruise with David Tomlinson, Shirley Eaton, Thora Hird among passengers and crew. Provides a laugh or two. Director: Val Guest; 1958. (*b/w*)

Fury √
'MGM's picture *Fury* is a powerful and documented piece of fiction about a lynching for half its length, and for the remaining half a desperate attempt to make love, lynching and the Hays Office come out even' (*The Film Criticism of Otis Ferguson*). Spencer Tracy (36 in 1936) was chosen by Fritz Lang, making his American picture debut, as innocent victim who turns the tables; Alistair Cooke called it 'best film of this or maybe of any coming year' – but it's a bit disappointing now. (*b/w*)

The Gallant Hours √
Admiral Halsey biopic served better than might have been expected by fine performance from James Cagney and a low-key script. Robert Montgomery directed reverently (in 1960) and the movie is stopped from degenerating into usual string of naval battles by the fact that Halsey was mostly stuck at HQ. (*b/w*)

Gambit √ √
Michael Caine recruits Shirley MacLaine for a caper; Ronald Neame directed in 1966 with unsure hand, but the best bits are excellent. (*c*)

The Gambler From Natchez ✕ ✕
It's Dale Robertson in the usual mythical riverboat rubbish, directed this time by old reliable Henry Levin. Debra Paget is belle; only Kevin McCarthy's superior performance reminds one what a load of cold tea the rest is; 1954. (*c*)

Games √
If rich and beautiful young couple James Caan and Katherine Ross invited moneyless shopgirl Simone Signoret to stay with them because they fancied her, we might have had a superior sexpic. As it is, we've got an inferior whodunit. Pity. Curtis Harrington; 1967. (*c*)

Kenneth More in *Genevieve*

The Gang's All Here ✓
1944 boy-meets-loses-gets-girl musical with Alice Faye, Carmen Miranda; rapidly becoming collector's item since director Busby Berkeley was canonised. *(c)*

Gangster Story ✗ ✗
Walter Matthau wasn't being funny when he directed and starred in this straightforward cops-and-robber about nice girl mixed up with a guy like that. Pity he wasn't; 1960. *(b/w)*

Garden of Evil ✓
Fine old-fashioned big-league Western with Gary Cooper, Cameron Mitchell, Richard Widmark, hired by Susan Hayward to extricate her husband from goldmine; Apaches and greed thicken stew and Henry Hathaway keeps it boiling; 1954. *(c)*

The Garment Jungle ✓
Lee J. Cobb shines as dress manufacturer in this gangster-union drama set unusually in the Seventh Avenue enclave. Vincent Sherman got the credit but it was Robert Aldrich who directed most of it and kept it exciting; 1957. *(b/w)*

Gaslight ✓ ✓
Even if Ingrid Bergman didn't really deserve the 1944 Best Actress Oscar as Victorian wife being driven mad (preferred over Barbara Stanwyck's *Double Indemnity*), it's a powerful piece. Charles Boyer is sinister husband, Dame May Whitty, Angela Lansbury, Joseph Cotten support strongly. Décor won award, too, but not George Cukor's direction. *(b/w)*

A Gathering of Eagles ✗
Rock Hudson neglects his wife for his Strategic Air Command planes, so enter Rod Taylor eyeing Mary Peach;

director Delbert Mann takes wings in the air, crashes on the ground; 1963. (*c*)

Gay Purr-ee ✕
Warner Brothers tried to do a Disney in 1963 with this full-length cartoon about cats, but hadn't got the touch; despite Garland and Gingold on the sound-track and pastiches of Lautrec and van Gogh, it just didn't come off; Abe Levitow. (*c*)

The Gazebo ✕✕
Silly little attempt at a funny whodunit from a play by the artifice-prone Alec Coppel, which gets the poor performances it deserves from Glenn Ford, Debbie Reynolds. Director George Marshall does his best which isn't much help; 1960. (*b/w*)

The Geisha Boy ✕
Jerry Lewis in Japan. That's really all that needs to be said. Frank Tashlin; 1959. (*c*)

Genevieve √
One of the few authentic British movie classics. This race, between John Gregson's old crock, a 1904 Darracq (passenger Dinah Sheridan), and Kenneth More's 1904 Spyker (passenger Kay Kendall), has weathered the years since it was made by Henry Cornelius in 1953 to become a vintage film itself. (*c*)

Genghis Khan ✕
James Mason, Eli Wallach and Robert Morley cheerfully send up this pretentious costumer shot in Yugoslavia for some reason (like cheap extras) in 1964, but Omar Sharif, Stephen Boyd and Françoise Dorleac take it all more seriously with disastrous results. Old-timer Henry Levin must have known it was hokum, but maybe he thought it wiser not to tell them. (*c*)

Gentleman's Agreement √
Don't be fooled by the 1947 Oscars (best picture; best support, Celeste Holm; director, Elia Kazan), it was slick then, and it's out-of-date now. Gregory Peck's goody-goody journalist posing as Jew to experience anti-semitism seems stiff; only John Garfield's cameo as genuine Jew stands up. Still it's a fascinating period piece, especially for outraging Un-American Activities Committee. (*b/w*)

Gentlemen Prefer Blondes √
Howard Hawks cast Marilyn Monroe as the classic dumb blonde bombshell, an image she was never able to lose. But without her and Jane Russell, as two big little girls from Little Rock on the make in Paris, Hawks' 1953 film would have served Anita Loos' novel poorly. Great comedy support from Charles Coburn, but film – especially Diamonds are a Girl's Best Friend – is all Monroe's. (*c*)

The Gentle Rain ✕✕✕
Christopher George is Brazilian mute in this terrible little movie about the frigidity of Lynda Day; Burt Balaban is the director and the bossa-nova isn't all bad; 1965. (*c*)

Geordie ✕✕✕
Frank Launder's awful 1955 yarn about puny youth who takes bodybuilding course to stop the world kicking porridge in his face and heads for Olympics via Highland Games. Dull, depressing stuff. With Bill Travers, Alastair Sim. (*b/w*)

The George Raft Story ✕
It's supposed to be a true biopic, but don't you believe it. Ray Danton isn't bad at impersonating Raft, the gang groupie turned film star, but it might have made a more amusing pic if Joseph Newman had let Frank Gorshin – seen here in a smaller role – do his famous take-off of the coin-spinning star. Jayne Mansfield, Julie London provide less than competent distaff interest; 1961. (*b/w*)

Georgy Girl √
Lynn Redgrave only too well cast as plain girl who gets involved with Older Man James Mason and zany Alan Bates; London had stopped swinging by 1966, but Silvio Narizzano hadn't noticed. Now all those tricksy shots and cuts look fit for a museum. (*b/w*)

Geronimo √
Chuck Connors does well as legendary Indian chieftain of the Apaches and his struggles against injustice; Arnold Laven is producer-director; 1962. (*c*)

Gaby × ×
Waterloo Bridge updated to second world war, with Leslie Caron not a patch on Vivien Leigh and John Kerr a poor substitute for Robert Taylor; Curtis Bernhardt; 1956. (*c*)

Gentlemen Marry Brunettes ×
Hopeless attempt to repeat flavour and success of *Gentlemen Prefer Blondes* without the main ingredient, M. Monroe. Jane Russell couldn't sustain a suntan, let alone a major movie, and Jeanne Crain, as her friend, isn't much help. The Paris locations are pretty but Richard Sale seems to know he is fighting a losing battle; 1955. (*c*)

Get Off My Back ×
Inept attempt to show how ex-junkies are readied for normal life in Californian home, Synanon. Quite unbelievable, despite attempts by Edmond O'Brien as unit head, Chuck Connors and Alex Cord as inmates. Richard Quine produced-directed and had the ludicrous idea that Eartha Kitt could act; 1966. (*b/w*)

The Ghost Catchers √
Great fun in a haunted house with Olsen and Johnson. The ghost concerned is a soft-shoe dancing gentleman from the nineties and his manifestation is a treat; Leo Carrillo, Andy Devine add to fun; Edward Cline; 1944. (*b/w*)

The Ghost Goes West √ √
Delightful pre-war (1936) comedy of Eugene Pallette unknowingly purchasing Robert Donat's ancestor when he buys Highland castle to rebuild in America. Robert Sherwood co-wrote, René Clair lightly directed. (*b/w*)

Ghost in the Invisible Bikini × × ×
What on earth are Francis X. Bushman, Boris Karloff, Basil Rathbone doing in a mess like this? Even Nancy Sinatra is too good for this dreary mishmash of a teenage beach romp and the haunted house cliché–and that's really saying something; Don Weis is director; 1966. (*c*)

Ghost of Frankenstein √ √
If the Frankenstein saga was tiring in 1942, when Erle C. Kenton took over direction, Lon Chaney Jr gave a creditable impersonation of Boris Karloff and Bela Lugosi was still around to do his Ygor bit. (*b/w*)

Giant √ √
Cattle barons, oil tycoons and a tremendous cast make this one of the big ones. Of course, it's all bombast but is great stuff and George Stevens milks Edna Ferber's novel for all it can give. Among those present: Elizabeth Taylor (at her 1956 peak), Rock Hudson, James Dean, Carroll Baker, Jane Withers, Mercedes McCambidge. (*c*)

GI Blues ×
Cash-in on Elvis Presley's return from the army in 1960 has him as private who dates a night-club singer for a bet, in Germany. Good location shots let down by studio-bound rest and Norman Taurog's idea of how Germans look and sound. (*c*)

Gideon of Scotland Yard √
Surprisingly directed in England in 1959 by John Ford. Jack Hawkins as the detective taken over on TV by John Gregson. Shows one day in Gideon's life, Anna Massey supporting. (*b/w*)

Gidget ✗
1959 forerunner of endless series (e.g. *G. Goes Hawaiian*, 1961; *G. Goes to Rome*, 1963), in which Sandra Dee as Girl-Midget was involved with beach-boy Cliff Robertson; Paul Wendkos rendered it all harmless, and pretty funless. (*c*)

Gift Horse √
One of those second world war muted heroics British studios were so fond of around 1952, when Compton Bennett directed this one. Trevor Howard as captain of lease-lend destroyer ultimately winning his men's respect; with Richard Attenborough, and Sonny Tufts for US sales. (*b/w*)

The Gift of Love √
Tear-jerker with Lauren Bacall about how important little adopted girl becomes to Robert Stack after wife's death; suits Jean Negulesco's schmaltzy style; 1957. (*c*)

Gigi √√
Eight 1958 Oscars were won by this musical version of Colette story (best picture, screenplay, photography, art direction, costumes, editing, scoring, direction – Vincente Minnelli), although Leslie Caron won no honours for her wide-eyed rebel who prefers marriage to concubinage. Lerner-Loewe wrote the music, Beaton designed, as in *My Fair Lady*. Maurice Chevalier remembered it well, thanked heaven for little girls – the dirty old man. (*c*)

Gigot ✗✗
Should be watched on an empty stomach, otherwise you might make a nasty mess when you throw up over the excessive sickly saccharine that director Gene Kelly smears over this already sticky yarn about a deaf-mute (Jackie Gleason) who befriends animals and children. Yuch! 1962. (*c*)

Gilda √
Rita Hayworth in archetypal forties film (actually 1946) about South American café owner hiring American Glenn Ford, with complicated Gilda as wife; Charles Vidor. (*b/w*)

The Girl and the General ✗✗
Dull little squib about Rod Steiger as Austrian general captured by two Italian peasants who decide they love each other. So what? Virna Lisi can't convince as a peasant, and director Pasquale Festa Campanile doesn't seem to know what he's all about; 1969. (*c*)

The Girl Can't Help It √
Edmond O'Brien wants to buy his girl-friend Jayne Mansfield into movie stardom; Tom Ewell is broke so he helps. But then the complications set in. Occasionally funny moments from director Frank Tashlin; 1956. (*c*)

Girl in the Headlines ✗✗
Soppy little murder hunt whose cast (Ian Hendry, Ronald Fraser, Margaret Johnston, Jeremy Brett, Jane Asher, Zena Walker, James Villiers) might attract you into wasting your time watching it. Director Michael Truman really should have done us better; surely the obvious inconsistencies and thin-ice skating could have been avoided? 1963. (*b/w*)

The Girl in the Red Velvet Swing √
The real-life scandal of Stanford White-Evelyn Nesbit Thaw, architect-showgirl-millionaire triangle provided basis for adequate movie about life in New York, 1906. Joan Collins, trying hard; Ray Milland, Farley Granger, too; directed by Richard Fleischer; 1955. (*c*)

A Girl Named Tamiko ✗
Laurence Harvey well-cast for once as unpleasant half-Russian, half-Chinese photographer in Tokyo, choosing between the American passport marriage with Martha Hyer would bring and

True Happiness with France Nuyen; Michael Wilding lurks charmingly; John Sturges; 1963. (*c*)

Girl of the Night × ×
Proves that a call girl can go straight if she wants to. Apparently it takes psychiatry and goodness knows what, however. It's all rubbish, and director Joe [Cates' cursory way with the plot shows that he thought so, too. Anne Francis is the girl, Lloyd Nolan her therapist, John Kerr her leering pimp whom she loves for some deep reason not vouchsafed to the audience; 1961. (*b/w*)

Girl on a Motorcycle √
A rather unpleasant adaptation of André de Mandiargue's novel about the fantasies of a schoolmaster's wife, most of which involve riding a bike without anything under her fur-lined catsuit to see her love. Made real by the inadequate Marianne Faithfull and even more inadequate Alain Delon. Jack Cardiff's romantic style with a camera and director's chair seems both too explicit and yet to miss the point; 1968. (*c*)

Girl on Approval ×
Modest little 1963 effort all shot on location in a children's home about a teenage girl 'on approval' to foster parents, Rachel Roberts and James Maxwell. Annette Whiteley, as the girl, can't quite meet the demands of the script, but director Charles Frend did a competent, likeable job. (*b/w*)

The Girl Who Knew Too Much × ×
But not enough to stay out of this farrago about Red Chinese plot to take over the American rackets and thus weaken the great old USA. Nancy Kwan's the girl, Adam (Batman) West's the hero, Nehemiah Pershoff the chief heavy. Francis D. Lyon; 1969. (*c*)

Girl With Green Eyes √ √
Rita Tushingham had the critics cheering in 1964 with her young Edna O'Brien provincial let loose in Dublin, falling for Older Man Peter Finch. 'Embodies all that is naive and silly and noble and wonderful and heart-breaking and funny about being young,' wrote Judith Crist in *New York Herald Trib*. Desmond Davis directs. (*b/w*)

Girls at Sea × ×
Awful little 1958 remake of Ian Hay's *The Middle Watch*, with Ronald Shiner doing his best to put some fun in the proceedings. His best isn't good enough. Director Gilbert Gunn. (*c*)

Girls, Girls, Girls! ×
Elvis Presley sings a dozen songs, romances Stella Stevens and Laurel Goodwin in featherweight item about fishing boats; Norman Taurog slogs along, as usual; 1962. (*c*)

The Glass Bottom Boat √
Nice 1966 Doris Day diversion mixing spies and tourist high-jinks. Writer-director Frank Tashlin makes time pass pleasantly. (*c*)

The Glass Key √ √
1942 version of Dashiell Hammett thriller about political boss Brian Donlevy accused of murder. In *Magic and Myth of the Movies*, Parker Tyler comments: 'If ever there was a mannequin gangster, he was Alan Ladd in *The Glass Key*, and if he ever reached for the upper crust and took down a mannequin moll to load his mannequin gat for him, she was Veronica Lake.' (*b/w*)

The Glass Menagerie √
Inside the dream worlds of Tennessee Williams; a slow, fey but entrancing weepie with Gertrude Lawrence and Arthur Kennedy (right); Jane Wyman and Kirk Douglas (wrong). Irving Arnold; 1953. (*b/w*)

The Glass Web √
'Crime of the Week' is a TV show. One week it features a murder, just too similar to real-life one of girl blackmailer. Could murderer be show's authority, Edward G. Robinson? Jack Arnold; 1953. (*b/w*)

The Glenn Miller Story √
James Stewart plays the bandleader in 1954 biopic which includes all his biggest hits meticulously played; strong support from June Allyson, Frances Langford, Louis Armstrong, Gene Krupa; director Anthony Mann manages it all excellently; 1954. (*c*)

A Global Affair ✕
One of those effortful Bob Hope comedies, this time involving children. 1964 attempt has him a bachelor UN official having to look after baby, with Russians (in the person of an unlikely gynaecologist Lilo Pulver) stirring up international trouble; Jack Arnold does his best. (*b/w*)

The Glory Guys √
They're Andrew Duggan, who disobeys general's order to attack the Sioux on a certain date and brings his men into battle a day early to claim the victory for himself, and his men. Sam Peckinpah wrote the script but the direction is by Arnold Laven, who does well, considering the shadow he is working in; 1966. (*c*)

The Goddess √
Kim Stanley as Hollywood star who could never find lasting love gives fine methodical performance in script by Paddy Chayefsky, humbly directed by John Cromwell; 1958. (*b/w*)

God's Little Acre √
For once, a movie that is better than the original novel. Erskine Caldwell's novel was a steamy sexy yarn of lusts down on the farm; this 1958 version directed by Anthony Mann, prevented by censorship from being too randy, has developed a sense of humour instead. So, Robert Ryan's pitting of holes throughout his farm looking for gold (and continually moving the tract of the title) becomes amusing, and his crucial decision to stop looking for gold and get on with being a farmer the force of reality. (*b/w*)

Going My Way √
Famous sentimental throat-lumper (or sick-maker) about young, new-broom priest, Bing Crosby, winning over old, tetchy but lovable priest Barry Fitzgerald and gang of poor New York kids with a smile and a song. Director Leo McCarey carried off seven 1944 Academy Awards to the tune of Too-ra-Loo-ra-Loo-ra. (*b/w*)

The Golden Hawk ✕
Frank Yerby swashbuckler with Rhonda Fleming sailing the troubled Caribbean; Sidney Salkow made it all very actionful in 1952. (*c*)

The Golden Rabbit ✕ ✕
Silly little bit of rubbish about man who can make gold – it's *The Man in the White Suit* without any clothes on. Timothy Bateson, Maureen Beck; director David Macdonald; 1962. (*b/w*)

Golden Salamander √
Gentlemanly archaeologist Trevor Howard gets involved with delicious Tunisian beauty Anouk Aimée and gang of gun smugglers. Directed 1949 by Ronald Neame, with Herbert Lom, Wilfrid Hyde White, Miles Malleson. (*c*)

Goldfinger √ √
Bond-lovers will cheer when this finally reaches the little screen, but those who never worshipped at the shrine of vulgar art direction, nifty sadism and unsexy sex may wonder what all the fuss was about; Sean Connery judoes with Honor Blackman, saves Fort Knox, shows off the special Aston Martin. Shirley Eaton in gold make-up all-over is worth a

glimpse – which is about all we get. Guy Hamilton; 1964. (*c*)

Go Naked in the World √
An appealing idea – son Anthony Franciosa dates the town whore Gina Lollobrigida, not realising who she is, but Papa Ernest Borgnine knows only too well – thrown away in histrionics. Needs remaking in today's more honest atmosphere; 1961 was too early for implications to be explored properly, and director-writer Ranald MacDougall had to make too many compromises. (*c*)

Goodbye Again ×
Anatole Litvak's rotten title for *Aimez-Vous Brahms*, the Françoise Sagan novel. Anthony Perkins, coming between Ingrid Bergman and Yves Montand, manages to suggest that he feels more attraction for Montand than Bergman. It's all a bit world-weary and dull, however, despite the French locations; 1961. (*b/w*)

Goodbye Charlie ×
All the skills of author George Axelrod and comedian Walter Matthau can't make this one about a murdered man returning to Earth (with vengeance in mind) in the shape of Debbie Reynolds stand up. Tony Curtis looks as baffled as us; Vincente Minnelli; 1964. (*c*)

Goodbye Columbus √
Hello, *The Graduate;* but Richard Benjamin, lacking the charm of Dustin Hoffman, is matched only too well by the arch self-satisfaction of Ali McGraw. A disappointing translation of Philip Roth's novella about sex and money in the American Jewish country club set. Larry Peerce; 1969. (*c*)

Goodbye Mr Chips √√
(1) vintage 1939 Sam Wood version of schoolteacher weepie with Robert Donat winning Academy Award and Greer Garson winning hearts. Look out for the young John Mills. (*c*)

Goodbye Mr. Chips ××
(2) unfortunate 1969 musical remake with Peter O'Toole, manages to screw most of the charm out of the story, with awful Leslie Bricusse music and Michael Redgrave, Pet Clark looking lost. Partly blame director Herbert Ross. (*c*)

The Good Die Young √√
Strong caper, with Lewis Gilbert's firm 1955 touch bringing out the best in Richard Basehart, Gloria Grahame, Stanley Baker, Margaret Leighton and even Laurence Harvey. (*b/w*)

The Good Earth √√
Simple-minded but magnificent reconstruction of Chinese farm-life up to the revolution, made on a spectacular scale and winning Oscars for Luise Rainer's wife and Karl Freund's camera. Special effects like the locust plague are stunning, and Paul Muni's phlegmatic playing suits part of peasant visited by it as punishment for taking dancer Tilly Losch as second wife. Director Sidney Franklin deserves credit for keeping theme of the land, which ran through Pearl Buck's bestseller, always in forefront; 1937. (*b/w*)

The Good Guys and the Bad Guys √
Attempt to make a funny Western by Burt Kennedy is let down by self-conscious direction and performances by Robert Mitchum, George Kennedy, as good, bad, respectively, joining forces to fight progress. Morally, politically, artistically shaky; 1969. (*c*)

Good Morning, Boys √
Will Hay-Graham Moffatt-Charles Hawtrey classic, supposedly about prison-break but really an excuse for incomparable music-hall act. Marcel Varnel; 1936. (*b/w*)

Good Morning, Miss Dove ×
Gooey yarn of schoolteacher Jennifer Jones solving everyone's problems ex-

cept yours; should you turn off or will it get any better? Henry Koster; 1955. (*c*)

Good Neighbour Sam √
Jack Lemmon in tailor-made 1964 role as frustrated ad-man. David Swift (who co-wrote, too) spins it along from chuckle to snort, although Dorothy Provine and Romy Schneider drag it all up a bit. (*c*)

Good Sam ×
Disappointing 1948 Gary Cooper 'comedy' in which the lanky veteran is put through sentimental jog-trot about a fumbling good Samaritan; Leo McCarey just didn't have astringent enough touch. (*b/w*)

Gorgo √
She's a prehistoric monster whose offspring is captured by sailors William Sylvester and Bill Travers (whose acting is pretty monsterlike at the best of times). When the human race puts the babe on exhibition Gorgo rises from the sea and, Konglike, devastates London to rescue it. Director Eugene Lourié is great special effects whizz and pulls off a stunner here; 1960. (*c*)

The Gorgon √
Plenty of Hammer horrors here; though they didn't persist with the idea of a Medusa snake-haired lady after this promising 1964 start. Terence Fisher brought out the best in his talented cast (Peter Cushing, Richard Pasco, Barbara Shelley) although Christopher Lee's a bit unhappy as a goodie. (*c*)

Gorilla at Large √
Strong cast—Anne Bancroft, Lee J. Cobb, Raymond Burr, Lee Marvin, Cameron Mitchell—in circus whodunit. Gorilla is chief suspect. Harmon Jones; 1954. (*c*)

The Grace Moore Story × ×
Kathryn Grayson warbles her way through the 1953 story of the girl who was determined to make the New York Met and did. With Merv Griffin, Joan Weldon, Walter Abel, directed by Gordon Douglas. (*c*)

The Graduate √ √ √
Hilarious, wry, influential comedy of young Dustin Hoffman's affairs with married Anne Bancroft and her daughter, Katherine Ross. Mike Nichols rightly won 1967 Oscar as director; wonder is that *In the Heat of the Night* beat it for best picture and actor. (*c*)

Grand Hotel √ √
Don't expect to see very much of Garbo in this, her 19th film. She had to share equally with John and Lionel Barrymore, Wallace Beery, Joan Crawford in creaky multi-storied extravaganza based on Vicki Baum's bestseller. But as a tired ballet star who falls in love with a crook she completely dominated the others. See what the word 'glamour' really means. Director, Edmund Goulding; 1932. (*b/w*)

Grand Prix √ √
Lively blockbuster about Formula One motor racing that's marvellous on the track, but tends to break down off it. See it on as large a screen as possible because John Frankenheimer indulges himself in countless splitting into two, three and lots more simultaneous images. Yves Montand, James Garner drive; Eva Marie Saint waits; 1967. (*c*)

Grand Slam √ √
Bank caper with Edward G. Robinson and Janet Leigh, and Rio de Janeiro at carnival time; Giuliano Montaldo orchestrates international cast neatly and the plot is taut; 1968. (*c*)

The Grapes of Wrath √ √ √
This account of the Okies fleeing the Oklahoma dustbowl in piled-high jalopy and finding little to cheer them

in the golden hope of California, touched the conscience of the nation, as director John Ford intended. Although set in the Depression years, it seemed only too relevant to a nation that contained so many poor in 1940. All the performances were great, but Jane Darwell won an Oscar for her Mother, and Henry Fonda is unforgettable as the young Joad. (*b/w*)

The Grass is Greener   ✗
Too-too-old-fashioned stage drama that went down awfully well in Shaftesbury Avenue but bores in a sub-sub-*Private Lives* sort of way. Stanley Donen failed to make it catch fire in 1960 despite presence of Cary Grant. Rest of cast— Deborah Kerr, Jean Simmons, Robert Mitchum—just not up to it. (*c*)

The Great Caruso   ✗
The music, if you like the more obvious operatic arias and such corn as *The Last Rose of Summer*, is all right; but the plot (boy meets girl, boy pursues girl, boy gets girl, boy dies) is only matched in awfulness by the acting of Mario Lanza and Ann Blyth; Richard Thorpe does his best to make him seem like an actor, but can't win; 1951. (*c*)

Great Catherine   ✗ ✗
It must have sounded a good idea— Jeanne Moreau and Peter O'Toole in Shaw's playlet extended with some fooling from Zero Mostel. Under Gordon Flemyng's direction it was a disaster; Akim Tamiroff, Jack Hawkins swept along on a current of awfulness; 1968. (*c*)

The Great Dictator   ✓ ✓
Chaplin's burlesque of Hitler, like a brilliant marionette show. Unfortunately, final pompous speech lets it down; 1940. (*b/w*)

The Great Escape   ✓ ✓
Three hours of escaping prisoners-of-war with Americans Steve McQueen, Charles Bronson scoring over typecast James Donald, Richard Attenborough; John Sturges laid on the excitement; 1963. (*c*)

The Greatest Show on Earth   ✓ ✓
If you like circuses you'll like this celebration of the love affair that Cecil B. de Mille naturally had with them. If you love 'em, you may be frustrated when the documentary opening gives way to a rather ordinary series of lovely plots involving Betty Hutton, Cornel Wilde, James Stewart, Dorothy Lamour, Charlton Heston. If you hate 'em, forget it; 1952. (*c*)

The Greatest Story Ever Told   ✗
Jesus Christ! the book was better. All very tasteful, but Bergman rep. player Max von Sydow as New Testament lead only proves what a good director Ingmar is—unfortunately, it's George Stevens in charge here. The result, partly shot in Monument Valley, is a Monumental bore. Charlton Heston, Dorothy McGuire, David McCallum are among unlikely cast; 1965. (*c*)

Great Expectations   ✓ ✓
Best Dickens film ever, gripping from marvellous Finlay Currie in graveyard, through the young (it's 1947) Alec Guinness and John Mills, to Martita Hunt's Miss Havisham and Jean Simmons as young, Valerie Hobson as older Estella. Nice that Dickens altered the end to make it happy. David Lean's direction faultless. (*b/w*)

The Great Impostor   ✓ ✓
In real life, Ferdinand Demara really did get away with passing himself off as, variously, a Canadian naval surgeon, prison warden and Trappist monk, among other hoaxes, and Tony Curtis enjoys passing himself off as Ferdinand Demara. Robert Mulligan's direction helps us to enjoy it almost as much, too; 1961. (*c*)

The Great Jesse James Raid √
Rather superior Western about the old outlaw's last caper; Willard Parker, Tom Neal respond to Reginald Le Borg's 1953 direction. (*c*)

The Great Lie √
Definitive soaper with Bette Davis battling Mary Astor in 1941 after George Brent is in air crash; Astor won one fight–for the Oscar as best support of the year; Edmund Goulding served them faithfully. (*b/w*)

The Great McGinty √√
This 1940 Preston Sturges has become political comedy classic; chronicling Brian Donlevy's rise to fame and fortune. (*b/w*)

The Great Man √
José Ferrer does an Orson Welles on this one, but only proves that it takes more than sheer nerve to direct, co-write and play the main part. Indeed, with other people doing these various jobs Al Morgan's novel of the truth about a popular radio idol might have become a masterpiece of clay-feet exposure. As it is, the movie is just a minor piece of hokum, with Ed Wynn walking away with the honours under Ferrer's nose with a cameo about the man who started the idol off; 1957. (*b/w*)

The Great Missouri Raid ✗
Wendell Corey, Macdonald Carey in routine Western about Jesse James and brothers; Gordon Douglas couldn't make it live; 1950. (*c*)

The Great Race √√
Genevieve with lots of knobs on, including Tony Curtis in the nice John Gregson part, Jack Lemmon as demonised, moustachioed Kenneth More. This time it's New York to Paris and three long hours of it. Blake Edwards almost manages to keep it going, but you may finally conk out before it does; 1965. (*c*)

The Great St Trinian's Train Robbery ✗✗
Pathetic attempt to wring something out of more train robberies and St Trinian's–Launder and Gilliat didn't seem to care which in 1966–but which, alas, fails miserably on both counts. Neither Dora Bryan nor Frankie Howerd can do anything right and those girls seemed impossibly out of date even then. (*b/w*)

The Great Sioux Raid √
Joseph Cotten in superior account of Custer's Last Stand; Sidney Salkow; 1965. (*c*)

The Green Berets ✗✗
Whatever you may think about John Wayne as an actor, there's no doubt that morally and politically his heart is in the wrong place. By this 1968 effort, glorifying America troops in Vietnam, he may well have put more full-blooded patriots off the war there than all the platitudes of the peace lobby, so inept, so callous and so meretricious did it show itself through the Goodies-and-Baddies veneer. He directed it himself, with Ray Kellogg, and it is not without significance that 1968 was the year the opinion polls first showed that the majority of Americans were ashamed of what they were doing in south-east Asia, and wanted Out. (*c*)

Green Fire ✗✗
Rather more green than fire about this rather tame South American adventure yarn with Stewart Granger and Paul Douglas as mining engineers, Grace Kelly as coffee plantation owner. Andrew Marton settles for the easy thrills; 1954. (*c*)

The Greengage Summer √√
Susannah York incredibly good as the schoolgirl on holiday in France who

grows up as the result of a fascination with a rotter–Kenneth More, too nice to be able to convey the necessary rotten-ness. Danielle Darrieux a bit tight as proprietress of chateau hotel where they are staying. But director Lewis Gilbert never falls into the trap of sentimentality; 1961. (*c*)

Green Grow the Rushes　　　√
Richard Burton in 1951 union-financed attempt to break out of film industry grip which produced interesting if tame comedy about illegal whisky-brewing; Derek Twist. (*b/w*)

The Green Helmet　　　× × ×
Wretched little British effort using some exciting newsreels of motor racing to save shooting their own. Bill Travers his usual wooden self as driver, Ed Begley's only role is to give it some USAppeal. Sid James gets no chance to show any subtlety. The director was Michael Forlong; 1961. (*b/w*)

Green Mansions　　　× ×
Pretty disastrous attempt by actor-turned-director Mel Ferrer to steer his then (1959) wife Audrey Hepburn through a version of W. H. Hudson's novel. She plays Rima, 'spirit of the forest', a sort of refined lady Tarzan, with Anthony Perkins as gold-seeker whose life she saves. It's all very coy and embarrassing and not helped either by Villa-Lobos' music, Katherine Dun-ham's dancers or the location pix of Venezuela, Colombia and British Guiana. (*c*)

The Grip of Fear　　　√ √
Lee Remick has to steal $100,000 or she and her young sister will be done in; San Francisco has served as backdrop for many an excitement, and this is one of the most exciting, thanks to director-producer Blake Edwards; 1962. (*b/w*)

The Group　　　√
Disappointing attempt to translate Mary McCarthy's evocative, astringent novel of whatever-happened-to-the-girl-you-were-at-college-with by Sidney Lumet. For the reasons for failure see Pauline Kael's long, bitchy but engrossing account of how the film was made, in *Kiss Kiss Bang Bang*; Shirley Knight and Candice Bergen shine out best; 1966. (*c*)

Guadalcanal Diary　　　√
If you like war films, this is for you. Made in 1943, only a year after real-life first victory against Japan, Lewis Seiler was more concerned with glories of war than the horrors. Hard-sweating cast includes Preston Foster, Lloyd Nolan, William Bendix, Anthony Quinn, Lionel Stander. (*b/w*)

Guess Who's Coming to Dinner　　　√
Hailed at the time as 'a human document of great importance for the future of all free-thinking peoples' (one Roy Moseley, critic, in *Films & Filming*), this can now be seen as a cash-in on liberal sensibil-ities towards black people. Indeed, by 1968 anyone thinking free could see that this rich, charming, intelligent, healthy, handsome, successful young doctor would have been welcomed as a son-in-law by crusty old heart-in-the-right-place Spencer Tracy with wide-open arms even if he had been green, let alone black like Sidney Poitier. So what were he and Katharine Hepburn agonis-ing about? Someone should remake it with the prospective addition to the family as a dope-pushing, homosexual flashy pimp that the girl loves (or even a poor steelworker)–then we'd see where his liberal sensibilities really belonged. Stanley Kramer directed this slick slice of meretriciousness. (*c*)

A Guide for the Married Man　　　×
Even Walter Matthau's desperate and skilful attempts can't salvage this series

of black-out sketches in which cocky Bobby Morse teaches him how to cheat on his wife. Frank Tarloff writes, Gene Kelly directed and they are obviously going for the cheap laugh at every point. Only the episode with the man convincing his wife that she didn't see what she saw is genuinely comic–the rest just trip up. Basically, a nasty, dishonest film; 1967. (*c*)

Gulliver's Travels   √
Well, not all of them–just the first voyage, to Lilliput. Max Fleischer challenged the Disney monopoly with this full-length cartoon in 1939, and if it's got the crudity of his Popeye against the comparative subtlety of *Snow White*, it should keep the smaller children happy. (*c*)

Gunfight at Comanche Creek   ✕
Audie Murphy as undercover detective who thwarts particularly unpleasant gang of bankrobbers, forcing escaped prisoners to commit crimes so that the price on their heads will go higher and they can make a good profit handing them back. But it stays filmbound; you can never really believe in it, thank goodness. Frank McDonald; 1963. (*c*)

The Gunfight at Dodge City   √
Welcome change from standard Western is Joseph M. Newman's rather ironic yarn of Joel McCrea's clean-up of outlaw-plagued town; 1959. (*c*)

Gunfight at the OK Corral   √
John Sturges tries this time, but John Ford did it better in the classic *My Darling Clementine*. Burt Lancaster and Kirk Douglas are the legendary ex-friends who shoot it out. Leon (*Exodus*) Uris wrote the script but he doesn't make you really care; 1957. (*c*)

The Gunfighter   √
Superior Western with Gregory Peck as the man who has learned to dislike his own title as top gun of the West but who has to go on fighting against those who would take it off him or avenge the past. Director Henry King; 1950. (*b/w*)

Gunfight in Abilene   ✕
Will Bobby Darin recover his nerve in time to shoot it out with the outlaws? Well, if he doesn't, the title's a cheat. Director William Hale; 1967. (*c*)

Gun for a Coward   √ √
Fred MacMurray tries to keep the peace between his two younger brothers in a Western that for once puts a believable human conflict before cattle drives and suchlike. Abner Biberman does superior directing job; 1957. (*c*)

Gung Ho!   √ √
While on the surface this is just another second world war actioner of marines taking a Jap-held island, there is a far greater subtlety in Ray Enright's direction than one sees with half an eye. The way he holds Randolph Scott and crew captive in a submarine while they sweat out their days of waiting gives a dimension of understanding and horror that is notably lacking in many war pix; 1943. (*b/w*)

Gun Glory   ✕
Stewart Granger proving that he has reformed and is no longer a baddie; routine Western by Roy Rowland; 1957. (*c*)

The Gun Hawk   √
A Western weepie? Well, maybe that's unfair, but this 1963 departure of actually giving an oater a theme as well as a plot is an innovation to be cheered. Paternalism is the theme and is explored in real situations such as Rory Calhoun's relationship with his father, the town drunk; in the way he runs hotel for wanted men; and his particular attitude towards one young man he has befriended but cannot guide away from

Evil. If all this sounds suspiciously like a Bette Davis tearjerker in drag, there are similarities. But at least it's interesting, for a change. Director Edward Ludwig manages to ride both horses–conventional Western and emotional heartstringer–at the same time, and do it well. (*c*)

Gunman's Walk √
Tab Hunter and James Darren as fightin' sons of rancher Van Heflin. Rather better than most Westerns in having characters instead of ciphers; Phil Karlson did intelligent director's job; 1958. (*c*)

Gunn ✕
Just a bigger-budget long episode from the TV series with Craig Stevens, directed by Blake Edwards. There's a neat surprise ending but nothing much else to recommend it over any halfway-watchable American cops-and-robbers series chunk; 1968. (*c*)

Gunpoint ✕
An Audie Murphy Western with the doughty lad as sheriff hunting kidnapped Joan Stanley; a 1966 effort from Earl Bellamy. (*c*)

The Gun Runners ✕
Disappointing 1958 version of Hemingway's *To Have and Have Not* with Audie Murphy far inferior to Bogart and Garfield, who preceded him. Director Don Siegel must have had an off-month–it's below his best by a long chalk; Eddie Albert and Everett Sloane look ready to respond, but can't find what to. (*b/w*)

Guns at Batasi ✕
Congo-go-go skirmishes with frightfully British performances from Jack Hawkins, Richard Attenborough, Flora Robson; climax is Red Indian-style attack on the whites. Mia Farrow is love interest: John Guillermin; 1964. (*c*)

Guns for San Sebastian ✕
Cross between *The Power and the Glory* and *The Seven Samurai* doesn't come off, partly because Anthony Quinn hams it up as adventurer mistaken for priest, but mostly because of Henri Verneuil's uninspired direction; 1968. (*c*)

Guns in the Afternoon √√√
A really great Western–strictly for adults–by Sam Peckinpah, which since its unheralded debut in 1961 has taken its place as one of the cult movies of recent times. It tells of an ageing Joel McCrea's attempt to transport some gold in his care, but it's the astonishingly real-lifelike set pieces that stay in the memory–the saloon with its flabby Madame and raddled girls; the wedding celebration where all four of the bridegroom's brothers intend to have the bride; and the final insane shoot-out with Randolph Scott. (*c*)

The Gunslinger √
Roger Corman can be relied on to come up with something different and this yarn of Beverly Garland taking over as town marshal after her husband's ambush has a nicely equivocal undertone; 1956. (*c*)

Gunsmoke ✕
Nothing to do with the TV series but a 1953 Audie Murphy with him turning over a new leaf and marrying the ranch boss's daughter, Susan Cabot. Pleasantly directed by Nathan Juran. (*c*)

Guns of Darkness √
Literate–perhaps over-literate–script by John Mortimer gives this South American actioner, about David Niven and Leslie Caron helping wounded ex-president of banana republic to escape, a dimension usually missing in this kind of movie. Anthony Asquith directs unobtrusively; 1962. (*c*)

Guns of Diablo   ✕
Shortie (under an hour) with familiar plot about girl forced to marry a baddie when her lover disappears. Of course he comes back and of course there's a shoot-out. Charles Bronson's the hero; Boris Sagal's the director, and the art department's either on a reality kick or is short of funds–it's all bare walls and boards; 1964. (*b/w*)

The Guns of Fort Petticoat   ✕
Audie Murphy teaches Texas ladies how to ward off Indian attack; George Marshall makes it all fair fun; 1957. (*c*)

The Guns of Navarone   √ √
Massive second world war actioner about Gregory Peck and explosives expert David Niven destroying two big guns on Crete. At climax of shooting, Niven became seriously ill, which was inconvenient for writer-producer Carl Foreman. So, Niven recalls, he was 'pumped full of drugs, went back to work against doctors' orders ... and suffered a relapse that lasted seven weeks. The Big Brass never even sent me a grape.' Never mind, the movie made a lot of money. Director, J. Lee Thompson; 1961. (*c*)

Guns of the Magnificent Seven   ✕
Same old Seven stuff, this time in a 1969 version directed by Paul Wendkos who vainly hoped that his fine compositions and well-shot fights would make us forget the original; George Kennedy and James Whitmore come off best among the Seven Deadly Dwarfs but nobody manages very well. (*c*)

Guns of the Timberland   ✕
When it's Alan Ladd as leader of the loggers versus Jeanne Crain, leader of the ranchers whose land they invade, guess how it all ends. Frankie Avalon embarrasses everyone in sight by singing a couple of songs, but this was 1960, when the great rock boom was

under way and producers desperately tried to get into the act. As Ladd had some money in it–director is Robert Webb–he can't complain if the action is slowed while the lad warbles. (*c*)

Guns of Wyoming   √
This Western has Robert Taylor as successful rancher defending his land against hired gunmen and Robert Middleton. Towering old Tay Garnett gives this one guts; 1962. (*c*)

The Gun That Won the West   ✕
It's the Springfield rifle that's celebrated in William Castle's efficient oater; Dennis Morgan is chief shooter; 1955. (*c*)

The Guru   ✕
Director James Ivory, who has made some charming vignettes of the Indian scene, comes to grief when presented with the resources of 20th Century Fox to make a wide-screen, star-filled (Michael York, Rita Tushingham) study of the effect on Beatlesy musician who seeks enlightenment on the sub-continent; 1969. (*c*)

Guys and Dolls   √ √
Fun musical of Damon Runyon stories that has become almost vintage since it was made in 1955. Marlon Brando works pretty well as lead; Frank Sinatra was at his peak; but dolls Jean Simmons and Vivian Blaine manage to wrest the honours from under their famous noses. Writer Joseph L. Mankiewicz does adequate directorial job, and if the whole show's a bit stage-bound, that suits its theatrical essence. After all, it could hardly have been done realistically. (*c*)

Gypsy   √
Although this 1962 biopic of Gypsy Rose Lee suffers from unpleasant story of mother-driving domination, miscasting of Rosalind Russell as Ma and

Natalie Wood as daughter, Mervyn LeRoy does manage to catch tawdry fascination of dying vaudeville. Stephen Sondheim's lyrics flow happily out of the action – Let Me Entertain You, Everything's Coming Up Roses, included. (c)

The Gypsy and the Gentleman ✕
Joseph Losey's first credited picture in 1957, after Hollywood blacklisting, seems to have depressed him. Not that swashbuckling plot about Regency rake and girlfriend cheating sister out of inheritance gives much scope, but Melina Mercouri, Keith Michell and Patrick McGoohan might have responded to enthusiasm. (c)

The Gypsy Moths ✓
Disappointing John Frankenheimer epic about early air circus in a Kansas town, wonderful in the air, rather less so on the ground. Burt Lancaster, Deborah Kerr are supposed to be leads, but Gene Hackman and Sheree North take it away from them; 1969. (c)

Hail the Conquering Hero ✓✓
Great piece of satire from Preston Sturges; Eddie Bracken is returning soldier, mistakenly thought to be medal-winner. Ella Raines, Raymond Walburn, William Demarest, Franklin Pangborn outstanding; 1944. (b/w)

Gary Cooper in *High Noon*

Half Angel × ×
Feel sorry for Joseph Cotten and Loretta Young in this embarrassing comedy about a sleepwalking nurse; Richard Sale; 1951. (*c*)

Half a Sixpence ×
Director George Sidney lets over-lavish production swamp charm that H. G. Wells' original story and stars Tommy Steele, Julia Foster have in this musical version of Kipps; 1968. (*c*)

The Half-Breed √
One of the earliest Westerns (1952) that sided with the Red Indians against the white man. Robert Young is gambler who takes on white supremacists Barton MacLane, Porter Hall, Reed Hadley. Stuart Gilmore's heart was in the right place, even if his camera wasn't always. (*c*)

The Hallelujah Trail √ √
A fun send-up of the Western in which five groups of different predators all want to get their hands on forty wagon-loads of whisky; Burt Lancaster's fine (the title was changed from *The Hallelujah Train*, to avoid confusion with *The Train*), and Lee Remick, Donald Pleasence, Martin Landau all enjoy themselves. With John Sturges fully in command (if a bit over-indulgent), so should you; 1965. (*c*)

The Halliday Brand √
Joseph Cotten plays dominating rancher whose despotism leads to bloody revolt among his workers and family. Betsy Blair, Viveca Lindfors; directed by Joseph Lewis; 1957. (*b/w*)

The Halls of Montezuma √ √
Strong and mostly successful second world war drama, with Richard Widmark, Jack Palance, Robert Wagner, Richard Boone fightin' and dyin' for the flag on island like Okinawa; makes an honourable companion to director Lewis Milestone's *All Quiet on the Western Front* and *A Walk in the Sun;* 1950. (*c*)

Hamlet √ √ √
Olivier's five-Oscar-winning version in 1948 was a clear reading of the text, presented as a Portrait of a Man Who Could Not Make Up His Mind; his Oedipal attitude towards his mother was emphasised with the kiss smack on her lips; Jean Simmons and Eileen Herlie did best after his own towering performance. (*b/w*)

Hammerhead × ×
Depressing little thriller set mostly in Portugal with Peter Vaughan as erotically trendy spy foiled by American agent Vince Edwards. Judy Geeson, Diana Dors, Michael Bates, Beverly Adams swan around. Director David Miller tries desperately hard, but just can't make it; 1969. (*c*)

Hand in Hand × ×
Soppy little comedy-drama about two children who overcome religious differences between their Jewish and Catholic backgrounds; Philip Leacock manages OK with the kids, but the adult scenes are more embarrassing; 1960. (*b/w*)

The Hand of Night × × ×
A right mess of Egyptological pretensions with William Sylvester as guilt-ridden archaeologist; Frederic Goode; 1968. (*c*)

The Hands of Orlac × × ×
Poor little effort that couldn't even get distribution when it was made in 1958, about concert pianist, played by a pallid Mel Ferrer, who believes that a murderer's hands were grafted on to him after accident; Edmond T. Greville. But if 1934 version (Karl Freund) with Peter Lorre surfaces, don't miss. There's a 1924 Conrad Veidt silent one, too.
(all *b/w*)

The Hanged Man √
Remake in 1965 by Don Siegel of the 1947 Robert Montgomery thriller, *Ride the Pink Horse*. Nice touches like the climax at the New Orleans Mardi Gras, but Robert Culp can't carry the main part of small-time crook blackmailing trade union boss Edmund O'Brien. And there isn't any hanged man. (*b/w*)

Hang 'Em High ✕
Clint Eastwood survives a lynching and tracks down the nine men who strung him up; ritualised killing follows, but Ted Post has no redeeming point of view. It's brutality for its own sake – and that of the box office; 1968. (*c*)

The Hanging Tree √
Gold fever in the Old West mixes uncomfortably with justification for medicine as practised by Dr Gary Cooper in this 1959 drama. Karl Malden is lecherous half-wit. Delmer Daves falls between stools, but does have George C. Scott and Maria Schell in the cast to help out. (*c*)

The Hangman √
An adult Western for childlike minds. Robert Taylor can't just rescue Tina Louise – he has to talk about it and his inner problems, too; Michael Curtiz directed the action bits splendidly in this 1959 fashionable oater, but nobody could have made that script stand up. (*c*)

Hangmen Also Die ✕
Incredibly, this uneven 1943 second world war drama about assassinating nazi leader was written by Bertolt Brecht and directed by Fritz Lang; Gene Lockhart shines as framed man. (*b/w*)

Hangover Square √
The superb and lamented Laird Cregar in horror-emphasised 1945 version of Patrick Hamilton's novel; Edwardian composer becomes unconscious homicidal maniac. John Brahm let it all go over the top in the climax. (*b/w*)

Hannibal Brooks ✕
An elephant crossing the Alps with a British PoW (Oliver Reed) meeting up with American guerrilla (Michael Pollard) must have sounded irresistible as an idea. Unfortunately, under Michael Winner's direction (1968) it proves only too resistible. (*c*)

Hans Christian Andersen ✕
Sickly script purporting to tell life of great story-teller is made worse by Danny Kaye's nauseous performance in the title role; however, the dancing's fine and the music–Inchworm, Ugly Duckling–pleasant; Charles Vidor; 1952. (*c*)

The Happening √
Shame about that desperately 1967 title, which dates much more than the movie, a wry parable of kidnapped big-shot who can't find anyone–associates, wife, mother – who likes him enough to put up the ransom money. Then he–Anthony Quinn–and captors–Faye Dunaway, Michael Parks outstanding–join forces against those whom he feels have betrayed him; Elliot Silverstein makes all this almost credible. (*c*)

The Happiest Days of Your Life √
Margaret Rutherford in 1950 role of girls' headmistress billeted on boys in charge of Alastair Sim. Superior to subsequent St Trinian's saga. Frank Launder directed. (*b/w*)

Happy Anniversary ✕
Mild domestic spatting provides what comedy there is in this David Niven–Mitzi Gaynor effort which dates from the period (1959) when Hollywood regarded television as its arch enemy. Villain is the TV set they buy and which causes domestic divisions; David Miller does his best to make it work, but it's awfully uphill work. (*b/w*)

Happy Go Lovely ✕
Edinburgh Festival provides unlikely

background for musical about producer and chorus girl Vera-Ellen; David Niven, Cesar Romero. Bruce Humberstone directed; 1950. (*c*)

The Happy Thieves   √
Farce about three unlucky posh crooks in Madrid, marred by taking itself a bit too seriously; Rita Hayworth, Rex Harrison, directed by George Marshall; 1962. (*b/w*)

A Hard Day's Night   √ √
The first Beatles film, 1964, and it tells unpretentiously a day in their lives; stands up well as a museum piece, and Dick Lester's direction is always neat and apposite. (*b/w*)

The Harder They Fall   √
Humphrey Bogart's final film–1956 –was as nasty a boxing story as ever made the screen. From Budd Schulberg's novel about the exploitation of a South American giant; Rod Steiger, Jan Lane, Nehemiah Persoff come off well, and there are appearances by real-life fighters Max Baer and Jersey Joe Walcott; Mark Robson directs. (*b/w*)

Harem Holiday   × ×
Ten songs in a plodding 1966 Elvis Presley vehicle, about the lad as a sheiky film-star, kidnapped when visiting the Middle East for a première; cursory direction from Gene Nelson. (*c*)

Harlow   √
(1) Not quite as ghastly as it might have been, this pseudo-biography of early thirties sex symbol leaves out a couple of marriages and the all-important Christian Science of her mother. The rise to stardom is competently told, however, and the marriage to an impotent agent tactfully–too tactfully?– alluded to. What redeems it are the performances by Carroll Baker in the main part and Martin Balsam as a slimy studio boss; for the rest, director

Gordon Douglas can't wring convincing performances from Red Buttons, Peter Lawford or Angela Lansbury, but that might not be his fault; others have tried and failed, too; 1965. (*c*)

Harlow   ×
(2) At the same time, Alex Segal was shooting another version with Carol Lynley miscast as the sex symbol, which had the advantage of Ginger Rogers as her mother but little else; 1965. (*b/w*)

Harriet Craig   √
Joan Crawford as ruthless wife in 1950 remake of *Craig's Wife*; Rosalind Russell played the part in 1936. Crawford gave it more histrionic value but the script has withered with the years. Or maybe it was Vincent Sherman's direction. (*b/w*)

Harry Black and the Tiger   ×
Fearless tiger killer Stewart Granger is visited by old friends Barbara Rush and Anthony Steel in steaming Indian jungle. Disloyal love makes it even steamier, which must be how the plot got lost. Directed, if that's not too strong a word, by Hugo Fregonese in 1958. (*c*)

Harvey   √ √
James Stewart scores in famous role as drunk who is accompanied by six-foot rabbit; Josephine Hull won 1950 Oscar as his upset relation. Henry Koster faithfully translated stage play. (*b/w*)

The Harvey Girls   √
One of Judy Garland's best (made in 1946 before limelight burned her up). She's one of an invasion of classy waitresses trying to alter ways of Western town. Score and songs won an Oscar (e.g. Atcheson, Topeka and the Santa Fé) and deserved to. Director, George Sidney. (*c*)

Hatari!   ×
Howard Hawks clearly fell in love with

the hunting of wild beasts and wouldn't sacrifice any of the endlessly repetitive chases in this long, long film; as they are the best thing about this junglepic (apart, perhaps, from Henry Mancini's score), it's a hard slog to sit through–particularly as you have to put up with the incompetent Hardy Kruger, Elsa Martinelli, Red Buttons and a Fordless John Wayne; 1962. (*c*)

A Hatful of Rain √
Powerful, if specious, drug-addiction movie, 1957; Eve Marie Saint and Don Murray shone under Fred Zinnemann's direction. (*b/w*)

The Haunted and the Hunted √
This was knocked off by Roger Corman's callow young assistant, Francis Coppola (in the days–1963–before he put the Ford in the middle of his name and made *The Godfather*). Corman had a crew in Europe, and Coppola pointed out that for another $20,000 they could make a quickie in Ireland. 'I described a scene of some lady who goes into a pond and sees the corpse of a little child and gets axed to death–everything I knew Roger would like.' The censor did some hacking of his own, but the result is still exciting stuff, if hokum. The cast were all unknowns and have stayed that way. (*b/w*)

The Haunted Palace √√
A really enveloping horror movie that chills you deep into your spine; Roger Corman disciplines Vincent Price, for once, into ironing out his weakness for sending himself up, and manages to extract a double performance of virtuosity as both victim and evil-doer. Do those deformed children come from his experiments or from puritans' own repressed imaginations? Lon Chaney gives a superior performance, too, as a sinister butler; 1966. (*c*)

The Haunting √√
Creepy respectfully directed by Robert Wise in 1963 from Shirley Jackson story. Elegant and literate, it has Claire Bloom as lesbian assistant to scientist Richard Johnson, menacing Julie Harris. (*b/w*)

Hawaii × ×
The story of missionary Max von Sydow and his wife Julie Andrews (enamoured of sea captain Richard Harris), who go and destroy the happy sinful lives of the South Sea Islanders, bringing in return a grubby Christianity that corrupts them. Long (over three hours), frequently boring, plagued by inadequate casting, and without a truly sympathetic character, it still manages to impress with sheer weight of sincerity. And with George Roy Hill's painstaking direction; 1967. (*c*)

The Heart is a Lonely Hunter √
Weepie about deaf-mute who is shown to be so superior to the other characters as to be almost unbelievable, if it wasn't for Alan Arkin's fine interpretation; directed by Robert Ellis Miller from the Carson McCullers novel. Stacy Keach in a minor role; 1969. (*c*)

Heart of a Child ×
About little boy, his dog and nasty Daddy (Donald Pleasence), all predictable and stoically directed by Clive Donner in 1958. (*b/w*)

The Heart of the Matter √
Fair 1953 try by George More O'Ferrall at the Graham Greene novel about a police commissioner in Sierra Leone tortured over his sinful love–Trevor Howard for Maria Schell. But Greene's plots are less important than his words and ideas, and these lost out, as usual in the films from his books. (*b/w*)

Heaven Can Wait √√
Ernst Lubitsch told Don Ameche's story, as head of posh family, from

tenderest age until he is turned away from the gates of hell by perfectly-cast Laird Cregar; Gene Tierney made an appealing wife; 1943. (*c*)

Heaven Knows, Mr Allison √
Got the critical thumbs-down when shown in 1957, as being too obvious a reworking of *The African Queen*, also by John Huston, with Robert Mitchum and Deborah Kerr alone on an island instead of a boat and the Japs replacing the Germans. She was a nun this time. (*c*)

Heavens Above! √
The Boultings take on Christianity, and it's no surprise that they should come out the losers. However, there are compensations in Peter Sellers' beautifully-judged performance as the well-meaning vicar that even the dogs pee on. There are also some rather nasty cracks at 'skyvers' on the social services, some gipsies who cheerfully bite the hands that feed them, a long way after Bunuel's *Viridiana*. A gallery of splendid British comic actors keep it going happily— Cecil Parker, Eric Sykes, Ian Carmichael, Irene Handl, Miriam Karlin, Eric Barker, Roy Kinnear, Kenneth Griffith —but the total effect isn't all that pleasant; 1963. (*b/w*)

Heaven With a Gun √
Pastor Glenn Ford forces peace between the cowboys and the sheep-herders with frequent use of firearms; sadly, the implications of this on the Christian religion are not even considered and Lee H. Katzin directs as though it had no possibility of being more than a conventional Western; 1969. (*c*)

The Heiress √√
Shows the winsome way Olivia de Havilland won the Oscar in 1949 as daddy-dominated plain girl falling victim to fortune hunter Montgomery Clift. As a father even more Freudian than Mr Barrett, Ralph Richardson acted everyone else into mere appendices to his case-history. Adapted from Henry James' *Washington Square*. William Wyler directed with prosy elegance. And there's that lovely moment at the end that will appeal to all scorned women. (*b/w*)

Helen of Troy ✕✕
Although Brigitte Bardot is in the cast, she doesn't play the title role; this belonged to plump, pouting Rossana Podesta in 1955, and director Robert Wise must still be kicking himself round the cutting room for acquiescing in this monumental mistake. It wasn't the only one in this huge, expensive epic: the script was another howler. Stanley Baker, Cedric Hardwicke, Harry Andrews battle gamely on, but it's disaster all the way. (*c*)

The Helicopter Spies ✕✕
Tired and boring Man from UNCLE with Robert Vaughn and David McCallum saving the world yet again; sad to see such excellent supports as Lola Albright, John Carradine, Julie London reduced to capering about for cliché-director Boris Sagal in 1968. (*c*)

Hell and High Water ✕✕
This routine submarine rubbish may awake critical interest because it is the 1954 work of Samuel Fuller, one of the most respected American *auteurs*. But beware—even Fuller's hagiographer, Nicholas Garnham, in his book on his idol admits 'I find *Hell and High Water* almost unwatchable.' So what about the rest of us? Condolences to Richard Widmark, Cameron Mitchell, Bella Darvi. (*c*)

Hell Below Zero ✕✕
Whoever dreamed up the idea of a girl commanding a whaler while she hunted for her Daddy's killer must have been bemused; then whoever cast Joan Tetzel in the role must have been even

pottier. Plucky Alan Ladd does his best as her number two, but he's right out at sea, as are Stanley Baker and Basil Sydney. Director Mark Robson appears to have gone along with the whole thing; 1954. (*c*)

Heller in Pink Tights √√
Unusual Western with Sophia Loren in a blonde wig as star of travelling theatrical company saved by killer Steve Forrest; she's the 'heller' or hell-raiser concerned. George Cukor brings off some nice touches—Loren tied to a galloping horse; Indians dressing up in troupe's costumes after they raid them —and there's strong support from old-timers Margaret O'Brien, Ramon Navarro, Anthony Quinn, Edmund Lowe; 1960. (*c*)

The Hellfighters ×
The one about putting out oil fires that has been coming round ever since movies were made, this time with John Wayne and Jim Hutton among the fire-dampers; if the story is formula, so is Andrew McLaglen's direction; 1969. (*c*)

The Hellfire Club ×××
Really dreadful little costumer about aristocrat who becomes circus performer; Robert S. Baker and Monty Berman share the credits and the discredit of having produced one of the worst films ever to come out of a British studio—and that's saying something. Condolences to Keith Michell, Adrienne Corri, Peter Cushing, Andrew Faulds, Miles Malleson—all of whom have appeared in better movies; 1961. (*c*)

Hell in the Pacific √√√
A remarkable film in many ways, not least in taking a situation that lesser writers (Alex Jacobs and Eric Bercovici here) and directors (John Boorman) would have allowed to degenerate into the sort of boring war-pic that the poor title suggests, and creating a parable of

great power. American Lee Marvin and Japanese Toshiro Mifune find themselves in a Robinson Crusoe situation during the war. How they make their personal peace, only to find it shattered on return to 'civilisation' is brilliantly conveyed, particularly in the use of our expectations aroused by lesser, earlier films of the same genre. 'Personal contact', typified in the Christmas meeting across the trenches in the first war and so many sentimental movies since, is not, alas, the answer to international conflict and that's brought out here. The roots of that lie deep, deeper than the cinema usually permits itself to peer; 1969. (*c*)

The Hellions ××
A rotten 'Western' set in the Transvaal, with Richard Todd as the sheriff or whatever he's called there, and such great classical actors as Marty Wilde to marvel at; director was Ken Annakin; 1962. (*c*)

Hell is a City ×
Location crime thriller on the American model provides Stanley Baker, Donald Pleasence, Billie Whitelaw with some exciting moments in Manchester and Oldham, culminating in the inevitable roof-top fight; Val Guest copies faithfully, but his studio sequences between Inspector Baker and wife Maxine Audley come over as very artificial; 1960. (*b/w*)

Hell is for Heroes √
Technically brilliant war drama from Don Siegel, with Steve McQueen, Bobby Darin, Fess Parker attacking German pillbox in 1944 Belgium. But all it says is War is Hell all over again; 1962. (*b/w*)

Hello, Frisco, Hello ××
Dreary 1943 musical comedy with Alice Faye trying to make a break, plus John Payne, Jack Oakie and Oscar-winning song You'll Never Know. H. Bruce Humberstone directs. Goodbye, movie, goodbye. (*c*)

Hell on Frisco Bay √
The ex-con who's out to uncover how he got framed is a standard plot and Frank Tuttle's direction doesn't attempt to lift it above the hackney carriage. But the cast is so strong they have their own momentum: Edward G. Robinson, Alan Ladd, Paul Stewart, William Demarest, Joanne Dru, Fay Wray; 1955. (*c*)

Hell's Island × ×
John Payne in weak little murder mystery in the Caribbean, momentarily enlivened by Francis L. Sullivan; Phil Karlson; 1955. (*c*)

Hell to Eternity ×
1960 look back to trueish story of Japanese-American marine behind the enemy's lines–the Japanese, that is; he isn't too sure at first, either. Jeffrey Hunter acts to the limits of his ability, which aren't much; David Janssen, Vic Damone are buddies. Director Phil Karlson seems to have had a big budget. (*b/w*)

The Hell With Heroes √
Improbable, familiar smuggler in Algeria plot is redeemed by fast cutting and Joseph Sargent's slick direction; although neither Rod Taylor nor Claudia Cardinale are capable of more than perfunctory characterisation; 1969. (*c*)

Hellzapoppin √ √
If it isn't quite as funny and novel now as it was in 1941, that's because it has been copied a hundred times since. But this zany farce deserves a place in any celebration of the history of the movies for the way it liberated the screen. Olsen and Johnson, Mischa Auer, Martha Raye, Hugh Herbert all gorgeous, and director H. C. Potter did more than just translate the Broadway hit to film. (*c*)

Help! √
From the standpoint of history, which the Beatles now are, this second movie they made–in 1965–isn't a patch on their first, documentaryish effort, *A Hard Day's Night*, also directed by Dick Lester. The elaborate, nonsensical plot involving magic rings never fulfils its eastern promise, and there is far too much indulgent scampering around; Roy Kinnear and Victor Spinetti slow things up further in superfluous sub-plot. (*c*)

Henry V √ √ √
Hailed as 'one of the movies' rare great works of art' (*Time* magazine), the thirty-odd years since its first showing (1944) have unfairly eroded its reputation. Yet Olivier's production, direction and playing are consummate, the well-assimilated borrowings from the earlier films are triumphantly justified, the bold but honourable re-arrangements of Shakespeare's text never jar, the performances of Robert Newton (Pistol), Renée Asherson (the French princess), Leo Genn (Constable of France), rich and human. And Olivier's 'Gentlemen of England now abed' at Agincourt is still among the most rousing minutes of speech on film. (*c*)

He Ran All The Way √ √
One of John Garfield's last movies (1951) was this suspenser about criminal-on-the-run holding up Shelley Winters' nice American family. John Berry did more than adequate directing job. (*b/w*)

Here Comes Mr Jordan √ √
Much-copied 1941 comedy about Robert Montgomery, popping off before he was supposed to and given a new body by Heaven; Alexander Hall got the best from a cast that included Claude Rains, Edward Everett Horton. (*b/w*)

Here Comes the Groom ×
Frank Capra steers Bing Crosby, Jane Wyman, Franchot Tone, Anna Maria Albergetti through sticky newspaper comedy with Bing needing a Mum for the two orphans he impulsively adopts; 1951. (*b/w*)

Here Come the Girls   ✕
Dull little muscial with Bob Hope in his younger (well, a bit younger–he was 49 when this was made in 1953) days as chorus boy involved with star Arlene Dahl, threatening boyfriend, and his True Love Rosemary Clooney; Claude Binyon directed cheerfully. (*c*)

Here We Go Round the Mulberry Bush ✕
This was dated when it finally appeared in 1968 and is even more of a museum piece of the early sixties now. The out-of-dateness is further emphasised by the swinging way in which Clive Donner has shot and edited it all, looking like the television commercials he himself made at the time. Barry Evans is adequate as the virgin-obsessed main boy; Judy Geeson, Angela Scoular, Adrienne Posta are sufficiently different to provide acceptable contrasts; Denholm Elliott and Michael Bates as usual walk off with the honours. (*c*)

He Rides Tall   ✕ ✕
Routine Western. Dan Duryea being villainous is the only bright bit in prairie landscape; director R. G. Springsteen; 1965. (*b/w*)

The Heroes of Telemark   ✕
Three attempts to destroy nazi heavy water plant have to be made so that they won't get the atomic bomb first. Kirk Douglas and Richard Harris are chief destroyers and neither is particularly convincing. The script is more full of holes than the bombed factory, and such incidentals as Malcolm Arnold's music pretty awful. Anthony Mann is trapped into conventional war-stuff by inauthentic introduction of girl at saboteurs' camp; 1966. (*c*)

The Heroin Gang   ✕ ✕
David McCallum as a really nasty hero, Sol Madrid. Utterly ruthless, he even kills his best friend on the vague suspicion that he may be mixed up in the Mafia-drug biz being investigated in Mexico; the appearances of Telly Savalas, Ricardo Montalban, Rip Torn, Pat Hingle, Paul Lukas are welcome but not enough to save this Brian G. Hutton-directed damp squib; 1968. (*c*)

Hero's Island   ✓ ✓
Not quite a pirate pic, although James Mason does play the bearded captain of a pirate ship. Put ashore on a raft, he comes to the aid of the widowed Kate Manx and helps her claim the island that's rightfully hers. Leslie Stevens directs resourcefully and the whole unusual drama really comes off; 1961. (*c*)

Her Twelve Men   ✕ ✕
Repulsively coy comedy with Greer Garson smilin' her way thru' troubles at a boy's school where she teaches. A measure of the general ghastliness is that the men of the title are boys. Robert Ryan and Barry Sullivan shuffle noiselessly around; Robert Z. Leonard directed; 1964. (*c*)

He Who Rides a Tiger   ✕
1966 drama from veteran director Charles Crichton is about recidivist who gets involved with orphanage girl thinking she's rich; Tom Bell, Judi Dench. (*b/w*)

Hide and Seek   ✕ ✕
Comedy-thriller that is neither, alas; Ian Carmichael, Janet Munro, Curt Jurgens, lost in a rambling script, which director Cy Endfield does nothing to clear up; 1964. (*b/w*)

The High and the Mighty   ✕
One of those multi-storey dramas, 1954, of passengers on disabled aircraft each flashbacking to their reasons for living; Robert Stack, Laraine Day, John Wayne, Claire Trevor come off best under William Wellman's direction. (*c*)

The High Bright Sun × × ×
Embarrassing naive drama about the British in Cyprus that must surely make everybody concerned blush to the roots of their hair today. Made in 1965, when almost everyone except this film's makers, director Ralph Thomas and producer Betty Box, realised that British days in Cyprus were numbered—and rightly so—they chose to make a Union Jack-waving, wog-hating piece of propaganda. Dirk Bogarde plays the major who persuades American neutral Susan Strasberg to come out against the 'terrorists' (mainly sneaky George Chakiris). (*b/w*)

The High Cost of Loving ×
José Ferrer directing himself in tepid little tragedy of an over-the-hill employee who loses his job when his firm is taken over. The screenplay is by Rip van Ronkel—obvious jokes are hereby avoided; 1958. (*b/w*)

High Noon √ √ √
Oscar-laden classic about Marshal Gary Cooper searching for support against outlaws against the clock (time-span of film is from 10.40 a.m. to noon). Fred Zinnemann directed, Carl Foreman wrote, Grace Kelly, Thomas Mitchell, Otto Kruger, Lon Chaney acted. And do not forsake Dimitri Tiomkin's haunting music. 1952. (*b/w*)

High Sierra √
Convict Humphrey Bogart is sprung to stage hold-up. On the way he falls for Good Girl Joan Leslie and then gets mixed up with Bad Girl Ida Lupino; you can't believe a frame, but Raoul Walsh manages to make you suspend disbelief; 1941. (*b/w*)

High Society √ √
Cole Porter's music (Who Wants To Be A Millionaire, Well Did You Evah?); Sinatra and Crosby's singing and fooling; Grace Kelly's poise, Celeste Holm's bite, sadly can't combine to make you forget original *Philadelphia Story*. Charles Walters, 1956. (*c*)

High Time √
Pleasant trifle about middle-aged Bing Crosby enrolling in college and giving the young (Fabian, Tuesday Weld, Richard Beymer) a lesson in how to enjoy themselves. Blake Edwards skilfully avoids its being patronising. The songs aren't much cop, however; 1960. (*c*)

A High Wind in Jamaica √ √
A beautiful film of great integrity from Richard Hughes' novel. Director Sandy Mackendrick has brought off the feat of sailing between an ordinary (if exciting) pirate adventure and an earlier-set *Lord of the Flies*, in telling this tale of children captured by pirates and the way they are made to turn against them. If you're left with too much sympathy for the pirates, this is probably due to Anthony Quinn's ingratiating performance as their chief. But James Coburn and all the children are marvellous; 1965. (*c*)

Hilda Crane × ×
Embarrassing detergent opera about Finding Happiness, with Jean Simmons doing her plucky best. Philip Dunne; 1956. (*c*)

The Hill √ √
Brutality in a North African prison camp during the last war, imposed by Ian Hendry on Sean Connery, Jack Watson, Roy Kinnear and Ossie-Davis. Main punishment is running up the hill of the title. It's hard to see why such a stark, horrid drama was made; unlike *The Brig*, which it resembles, the punishment no longer applied in 1965. Perhaps director Sidney Lumet felt that he was

exposing military sadism of all kinds. Others present: Ian Bannen, Michael Redgrave, Harry Andrews, Alfred Lynch, Norman Bird. (*b/w*)

Hills of Home √
1948 follow-up to *Lassie Come Home* with Edmund Gwenn, Donald Crisp and the wonder dog stealing scenes from each other in story of doctors in the Highlands; Fred M. Wilcox. (*c*)

His Butler's Sister ✕
Title may sound like naughty-naughty Charing-X roader, but it's ever-so-pure Deanna Durbin falling in love with employer–Franchot Tone, Pat O'Brien. Director Frank Borzage; 1943. (*b/w*)

His Girl Friday √ √ √
Sparkling remake of *The Front Page* with sex of quitting reporter switched so that Rosalind Russell can score in part and Ralph Bellamy as her drippy fiancé. Cary Grant's the managing editor who connives to keep her working, and Gene Lockhart, Porter Hall, Frank Jenks, Billy Gilbert all shine under Howard Hawks' creative 1940 direction. (*b/w*)

The History of Mr Polly √
John Mills in tame version of H. G. Wells novel of lower middle-class shopkeeper's revolt. Directed by Anthony Pelissier; 1949. (*b/w*)

The Hitch-hiker √
Edmond O'Brien picks up nutter; premature woman's-libber Ida Lupino directed and co-wrote this one in 1953 and kept it pretty exciting. (*b/w*)

Hitler ✕ ✕
Inept, incompetent, inefficient, unconvincing attempt to whizz through the dictator's life. Richard Basehart was a ludicrous choice as Hitler and he's the best actor in it. Director Stuart Heisler couldn't really have tried; 1962. (*b/w*)

H. M. Pulham Esq √
Robert Young lets his stuffing out as he goes into middle-aged fling; from John P. Marquand novel; Hedy Lamarr was flingee in 1941. King Vidor the director. (*b/w*)

HMS Defiant √ √
Super-patriotism on Nelson's high seas, from the novel *Mutiny* by Frank Tilsley; Alec Guinness, Dirk Bogarde, Anthony Quayle all more than adequate under Lewis Gilbert's direction; 1962. (*c*)

Hobson's Choice √ √
Charles Laughton could have overweighted this custom-made comedy from Harold Brighouse's play, but he settles down comfortably to some fine ensemble playing with Brenda de Banzie and Daphne Anderson. John Mills is built up by one of his rebellious daughters as his rival in the Lancashire of the eighties. David Lean; 1954. (*b/w*)

Hold Back the Dawn √
Charles Boyer conning Olivia de Havilland into marriage so that he can get into the USA. Mitchell Leisen directed. The script, which may have had some heartfelt feeling as it was written by Billy Wilder and Charles Brackett in 1940, only a few years after Wilder, a refugee from Germany, married the daughter of a Californian attorney. (*b/w*)

Hold That Ghost √
Best Abbott and Costello farce has Joan Davis as girl whose job in life is to scream on the radio; Arthur Lubin's frantic direction makes it great fun; 1941. (*b/w*)

A Hole in the Head √ √
Delightful 1959 Frank Capra sentimental comedy about Frank Sinatra's money troubles, beset by an irascible brother (Edward G. Robinson), sister-in-law (Thelma Ritter), nasty old buddy-buddy (Keenan Wynn), and warring

ladies (Eleanor Parker, Carolyn Jones). All are at their best under Capra's relaxed and masterly direction. (*c*)

Holiday √√
Katharine Hepburn and Cary Grant in Philip (*Philadelphia Story*) Barry's play neatly adapted for the screen about rebel Grant clashing with society gal Hepburn. George Cukor got the best out of them in 1938 with Binnie Barnes, Edward Everett Horton, Henry Daniell fine supports. (*b/w*)

Holiday for Lovers ✕✕
Doubtful if the intention of this 1959 tour round South America was to show up how embarrassing and awful some American tourists are, but that's the result that Henry Levin achieves. Papa is Clifton Webb, Mom Jane Wyman, nubile daughters Jill St John and Carol Lynley. (*c*)

Hombre √√
Although Martin Ritt was obviously trying to move the Western on a pace or two by making his hero as much an anti-hero as the film is an anti-Western, the genre is so strongly fixed in our experience and imagination that it works only intermittently. Yet if the script is too talky, the performances–particularly Paul Newman in the main part–are outstanding; 1967. (*c*)

Home Before Dark √
Typical 1958 Warner Bros drama about a distraught Jean Simmons returning from a mental hospital. Veteran Mervyn LeRoy directed slickly. Dan O'Herlihy is heavy husband, Efrem Zimbalist reliable friend. (*b/w*)

Home from the Hill √
Solid 2½ hours-worth of southern drama with Robert Mitchum unhappily married to Eleanor Parker, and strong perform-ance from Everett Sloane; George Peppard and George Hamilton are

around; Vincente Minnelli directed in his florid 1960 style. (*c*)

Home is the Hero ✕
Sentimental drama about difficulty Walter Macken (who also wrote play on which it's based) has in readjusting after five-year prison term. Directed by J. Fielder Cook with cast of Abbey Theatre players; 1959. (*b/w*)

Home of the Brave √
Black soldier finds wartime discrimina-tion worse than the enemy; strong stuff for 1949; Douglas Dick, James Edwards; director Mark Robson makes it feel real. (*b/w*)

Hondo √√
Signs are that this 1953 Western with John Wayne working for John Farrow instead of John Ford, for once, set out to push the frontier of the genre on a bit but took fright before the final film was issued. Certainly the script is far more ambiguous and literate than usual, and the relationship between the scout and widder Geraldine Page more interesting. (*c*)

Honeymoon ✕✕✕
Boring trip round Spain with Anthony Steel, Ludmilla Tcherina, with ballet interludes; Michael Powell, 1958. (*c*)

Honeymoon Hotel √
An oh-so-familiar mix-up in a hotel reserved for honeymoon couples, with Robert Goulet, Robert Morse, Nancy Kwan, Jill St John–and Elsa Lanchester stealing it from under their noses as a comic chambermaid. The wonder is the lateness of the date–1964. You might have reasonably expected this sort of inconsequence to have passed away long before then. Henry Levin. (*c*)

The Honeymoon Machine √
Unremarkable comedy about two sailors with a scheme to beat the roulette wheel in Monte Carlo saved by Steve

McQueen, Jim Hutton, Paula Prentiss. Richard Thorpe directed; 1961. (*c*)

The Honey Pot √
Rex Harrison invites three old girl-friends back to his palazzo in Venice but Maggie Smith is there already; Susan Hayward and Cliff Robertson were strange choices of writer-director Joseph L. Mankiewicz, but it all keeps going cheerfully–and there's a murder; 1967. (*c*)

Hong Kong ×
Tedious tale of Ronald Reagan as GI tangling with improbable mission teacher Rhonda Fleming in bid to rob Chinese waif. Directed 1951 by Lewis R. Foster against plywood Hong Kong. (*c*).

The Hoodlum Priest ×
First hour is muddled record of priest's attempts to set up reform home for criminals. Last section shows young crook Keir Dullea judicially murdered in the gas chamber; Don Murray wrote (under a pseudonym), co-produced and played the priest; Irvin Kershner directed, in 1961. (*b/w*)

The Hook ×
Routine will-the-escaped-prisoner-blow-up-the-ship drama given a Korean War setting; Kirk Douglas, Nehemiah Persoff, Robert Walker give competent but uninspired performances under George Seaton's direction; 1962. (*b/w*)

Horizons West √
Budd Boetticher Western (which guarantees its superiority) with Rock Hudson, Robert Ryan as brothers on rival sides of the law; Julie Adams, Raymond Burr stirring it; 1952. (*c*)

The Horizontal Lieutenant ×
Awful example of the way a director can ruin a film: played fast fast fast, this comedy of accident-prone Jim Hutton capturing pilfering Japanese guerrilla

could have been quite funny; as it is, it's so slow that it droops away under Richard Thorpe's lacklustre touch; Paula Prentiss, Jack Carter look as wearied as us; 1962. (*c*)

The Horror of Dracula √
Once more round the blood-sucking vampire tale, this time with Peter Cushing, Christopher Lee, Michael Gough; directed by Terence Fisher; 1958. (*c*)

The Horrors of the Black Museum × ×
Michael Gough and less than stunning cast nervelessly handled by Arthur Crabtree and incredible hypnotised-murderer yarn; 1959. (*c*)

Horse Feathers √ √
The one about Groucho as college president fixing the football game in which Harpo zanily shines; Norman McLeod; 1932. (*b/w*)

The Horse's Mouth √
As well as acting the main part of Gully Jimson, the artist who can't stop painting murals on every empty wall he sees, Alec Guinness wrote the screenplay for this mild comedy from Joyce Cary's novel. Director Ronald Neame seemed overawed by the combination in 1959 and came up with a slightly disappointing movie. Great Artists are notoriously difficult to convey, particularly when their genius is the excuse for spoiled brat behaviour. Still, John Bratby painted some convincing pictures, and Guinness did win the acting award at the Venice Film Festival for his performance. (*c*)

The Horse Soldiers √ √
Big-budget Civil Warrer by John Ford with contemptuous John Wayne and William Holden; based on a true incident when the north raided deep into the south, defended only by its women and the children of a military academy; the

emphasis is even more action than usual in Ford movies, with the character clash between Colonel Wayne and Doctor Holden providing most of the character tension. Two notable bit players are both called Gibson–tennis star Althea and veteran cowboy actor Hoot; 1959. (*b/w*)

Hotel × ×
The star is the set, a remarkable mock-up of a grand hotel in New Orleans, the centre of a takeover bid; there are a number of sub-plots involving various guests, but it's never very gripping–due to feckless direction by Richard Quine and his weak ideas on casting (Rod Taylor, Catherine Spaak, Michael Rennie, Merle Oberon, Richard Conte). Melvyn Douglas has some moments as the place's proud owner and Karl Malden manages to lift the action slightly whenever he does his hotel thief bit. But you may want to check out early; 1967. (*c*)

Hotel Paradiso × ×
Disastrous transfer to film of Feydeau farce with Guinness, Lollobrigida, Robert Morley tripping over the gorgeous decor and failing to provide the fast and furious fun the genre demands. Blame rest squarely on director-producer-writer Peter Glenville; 1966. (*c*)

Hot Enough for June ×
Unfortunate attempt by Ralph Thomas to make spy spoof involves Robert Morley as M-type and Dirk Bogarde as 007-type; the city of Prague comes off best, as do the Czechs altogether; 1964. (*c*)

Hot Millions √
Ustinov versus the computer, with the human embezzler winning; pleasant and unassuming with the humour coming from character–Ustinov's own warmth supplemented by a peach of a performance from Maggie Smith as his helpmate; Karl Malden, Robert Morley contribute their strengths, too. If Eric Till didn't turn out to be the greatest new director of 1968, he at least didn't detract from the proceedings. Ustinov wrote himself in a scene where he conducts a symphony orchestra because he had never done it before. (*c*)

Hot Rods to Hell × ×
Nasty little drama of Dana Andrews and Jeanne Crain tormented by car freaks; unsympathetic to the young but hardly showing the middle-aged in a very kindly light; John Brahm directed; 1967. (*c*)

Hot Spell √
Anthony Quinn is sleeping around while Shirley Booth tries to hang on to drifting children; Daniel Mann directed tautly; 1958. (*b/w*)

Houdini × ×
Conventional show-biz biography of great escapologist, made 1953, illustrated with tricks. Tony Curtis (born Bernie Schwartz) plays Harry Houdini (born Henry Weiss). Janet Leigh, then married to Tony/Bernie, played his wife, very unlike the real Mrs H.; George Marshall. (*c*)

Hound Dog Man × ×
The only surprise about this routine 1960 teenage mush is the director–Don Siegel, king of the crime thrillers. Otherwise it's just Fabian and Stuart Whitman chatting up Carol Lynley and Dodie Stevens. (*c*)

The Hound of the Baskervilles √
(1) 1939 Sidney Lanfield version with Basil Rathbone as Sherlock Holmes, Nigel Bruce as Dr Watson, doesn't convince in its Englishness, but is full of excitement otherwise. (*b/w*)

The Hound of the Baskervilles ×
(2) 1959 version is oddly dull, plodding down the beaten track without benefit

of surprise, inspired direction (though Terence Fisher's is workmanlike enough) or distinguished acting (Peter Cushing and André Morell as Holmes and Watson; Christopher Lee as Sir Henry B.). Perfectly competent, nothing more. (*c*)

Hour of the Gun √
Ten years before this 1967 Western, director John Sturges ended *Gunfight at the OK Corral* with the famous shoot-out between the Earps and the Clantons. This is what happened next; if it isn't quite so exciting, it is at least authentic, with James Garner and Jason Robards looking, moustachewise, rather more like Earp and Doc Holliday than is usually shown in movies and TV. (*c*)

Houseboat √
Sophia Loren has said she learnt more from this, playing with Cary Grant as *au pair* hired by widower for his three kids, than from any other actor (guess what happens–and you're right!) Mel Shavelson directed; 1958. (*c*) ·

A House is Not a Home ×
No, and despite the title-song in this case it's a brothel. Doubtful if Miss Polly Adler (played by Shelley Winters) who wrote a book about her famous real-life cat-house, was anything like the bewildered innocent shown here. And despite 1964 freedoms, it's still an awfully respectable place. Robert Taylor plays her gangster-protector with an air of familiarity–he has seen the character in as many movies as we have; Russell Rouse. (*b/w*)

House of 1000 Dolls × ×
Dreadful plot and dialogue about white slave traffic in Tangiers is partly compensated for by Vincent Price's enjoyment as magician who literally makes girls disappear; but Jeremy Summers can't make it exciting or even interesting; 1968. (*c*)

House of Bamboo √ √
Tough little thriller about American gang in Tokyo led by Robert Ryan was filmed there in 1955. Director was Samuel Fuller, now a cult figure. (*c*)

House of Strangers √
Strong stuff from Joseph L. Mankiewicz with Edward G. Robinson as paterfamilias who uses his sons ruthlessly; Richard Conte is the eldest; Luther Adler, Susan Hayward support; 1949. (*b/w*)

House of the Damned √
Freaky, in more ways than two, is this thriller about a mysterious house with strange goings-on; it's all quite creepy in a mechanical sort of way, and at least the explanation is logical if far-fetched; Maury Dexter directs an unknown cast with competence; 1963. (*b/w*)

The House of the Seven Hawks ×
Robert Taylor seeking Nazi gold with aid of map he finds on murdered man on his charter ship. Richard Thorpe directed in 1959, using Dutch locations. Adapted from novel by Victor Canning called *The House of the Seven Flies*–but hawks do better at the box office. (*c*)

House of Wax √
This version of *The Mystery of the Wax Museum* was made for viewing through 3D glasses in 1952. André de Toth directed, Vincent Price starred. The old story still packs a thrill or two. (*c*)

House on Haunted Hill √
Veteran horror director William Castle had Vincent Price as his sinister host in this 1958 remake. Mind you, a spot of oil on the hinges and half the excitement would be gone. Stay with it for Elisha Cook Jr's famous last line. (*b/w*)

The House on 92nd Street √
The March of Time was never as strictly accurate as some cinemagoers imagined, using recreations quite calculatingly.

Similarly, this FBI *v.* the nazis semi-documentary by the same producer, Louis de Rochemont, may have aped authenticity but wasn't quite as scrupulous as it pretended. Lloyd Nolan, Gene Lockhart stood out in what was to start a cycle of true-to-life location-shot dramas; Henry Hathaway; 1945. (*b/w*)

House on Telegraph Hill √
Thrills despite unconvincing plot about assumed identities. Creaking doors and lines, but Robert Wise got better than expected performances from Richard Basehart, Valentina Cortesa in 1951. (*b/w*)

How Green Was My Valley √√
Winning 1941 Oscars as best picture, best support (Donald Crisp), best direction (John Ford), best photography (Arthur Miller) was a bit excessive in the year that also produced *Citizen Kane* and *The Maltese Falcon*; but the Welsh mining village story can still warm hearts and catch throats. (*b/w*)

How I Won the War ✕
Richard Lester's frantic, frenetic, flashbacking comedy-to-make-you-weep, sending up war movies more than war. John Lennon remarkably accomplished as bespectacled private, Michael Crawford a bit one-note as officer; Roy Kinnear, Michael Hordern doing their familiar acts. It's really *Carry on Sergeant* treated surrealistically, and Charles Wood's script soon folds under the attempt; 1967. (*c*)

How Sweet It Is ✕✕
Pretty dreadful updating of traditional Hollywood comedy, comes into line with 1968 teenage morals by showing how broadminded Pop James Garner and Mom Debbie Reynolds react to their son's holidaying in Europe with his girlfriend; Jerry Paris lets it all slip through his nerveless fingers. (*c*)

How the West Was Won √
Cinerama pageant that may well look very dwarfed on the little screen. Three major directors–John Ford, George Marshall, Henry Hathaway–directed a raft of stars (Carroll Baker, Lee J. Cobb, Henry Fonda, Karl Malden, Gregory Peck, Robert Preston, Debbie Reynolds, James Stewart, Eli Wallach, John Wayne, Richard Widmark) but as it's just a comic-strip of clichés, they don't accomplish much; 1961. (*c*)

How to be Very, Very Popular ✕
Features the Betty Grable of 1955, with that hair and those legs, as a chorus kid on the run with girl friend Sheree North. They hide out in a college fraternity house–but where else?–and meet Robert Cummings wearing his vacant face (the other one is earnest). The comedy is a bit frantic, but see North do a wild shake rattle and roll number that steals Grable's thunder. Nunnally Johnson. (*c*)

How to Marry a Millionaire √√
Marilyn Monroe, Betty Grable, Lauren Bacall, generously helped by William Powell, Fred Clark, witty Nunnally Johnson script, Jean Negulesco direction, in gold-digger of 1953. Marilyn is funny as well as gorgeous as near-sighted dope who won't wear glasses. (*c*)

How to Murder a Rich Uncle ✕✕
Dull 1957 Nigel Patrick-directed, Nigel Patrick-starring 'comedy thriller' (i.e. a film that is neither) in which he tries to do Charles Coburn in but knocks off others by mistake. Spot Michael Caine, Anthony Newley. (*b/w*)

How to Murder Your Wife ✕
What could have been another tart comment on contemporary life, written by George Axelrod and starring Jack Lemmon, becomes, in the hands of director Richard Quine, more than a bit gooey. It needed a Billy Wilder to

bring out the ironies of explaining to the world in a comic-strip just how he was going about doing in Virna Lisi; but it all ends 'happily', with American Woman very much American Mom, however shapely she looks in this version; 1964. (*c*)

How to Steal a Million √ √
Peter O'Toole and Audrey Hepburn in slick, enjoyable 1966 caper about Paris museum theft. William Wyler expertly juggles stars plus Charles Boyer, Eli Wallach, Hugh Griffith. (*c*)

How to Steal the World × ×
The Men from UNCLE saving the world yet again; ho-hum. David McCallum and Robert Vaughn walk through their parts as if zombied by the nerve gas which is this particular villain's secret weapon. Barry Sullivan and Eleanor Parker sort of pretend they aren't there; and director Sutton Roley doesn't seem to mind; 1968. (*c*)

How to Succeed in Business Without Really Trying √ √
One of the better and relevant musicals of the sixties (1967 to be precise), well-translated from the stage with Robert Morse, who played the part of the thrusting junior on Broadway, repeating his success without trying too hard. A pity that the astringent setting of I Believe in You, which he sang to himself in the washroom mirror on the stage, should have been turned into a conventional (and dully shot) twosome, though. Rudy Vallee also repeats his stage bumbler. David Swift produced, wrote, directed this version, and does well, while not realising all the possibilities. (*c*)

The Hucksters √
Sending up advertising doesn't seem so daring now as it was in 1946, when Jack Conway directed a fine bunch of players Gable, Gardner, Greenstreet, Deborah

Kerr—and some nice satires on commercials. (*b/w*)

Hud √ √ √
Portrait of a heel who, unlike so many horrid heroes on TV, is properly seen to be nasty, alienating everyone including the audience. Paul Newman superb; director Martin Ritt master of Western setting and complex characterisations; Oscars won by stunning Pat Neal, Melvyn Douglas; 1963. (*b/w*)

Hue and Cry √ √
Alastair Sim and Jack Warner plus bunch of kids in splendid chase after gang of thieves. Fine location direction by Charles Crichton in 1946, trendsetter of British comedy-realism. (*b/w*)

Humoresque √
They don't make movies like this any more—solid vehicles for confident stars, here Joan Crawford striding through her tears as the wealthy lover and patron of violinist John Garfield, fated to part despite their love. Jean Negulesco; 1946. (*b/w*)

The Hunchback of Notre Dame √ √
Grotesque masterpiece of German director William Dieterle, made in Hollywood, 1939, with Charles Laughton, at his imitable best as lonely dwarf, Maureen O'Hara his love-object, Edmond O'Brien explorer of Breughelish mediaeval underworld, Thomas Mitchell king of the beggars. Avoid 1956 remake with Anthony Quinn (director: Jean Delannoy). (*b/w*)

Hungry Hill × ×
Daphne du Maurier has expressed herself as disappointed with most of the adaptations of her books for the screen, including this one. She has cause for complaint as director Brian Desmond Hurst shoves competent cast (Jean Simmons, Dennis Price, Margaret Lockwood) through their paces in lacklustre way; 1947. (*b/w*)

The Hunters ✕
Drama among the Korea War air force, with Robert Mitchum romancing May Britt, wife of alcoholic Lee Phillips; it isn't much more gripping in the air, either; produced-directed by Dick Powell in 1958. (*c*)

The Hurricane ✓✓
Jon Hall and Dorothy Lamour make it heavy going for John Ford until he can unleash his massed wind machines on the biggest blow in motion pictures; Raymond Massey is nasty governor of island which numbers Mary Astor, Jerome Cowan, Tom Mitchell, John Carradine among its inhabitants; 1937. (*c*)

Hurry Sundown ✓✓
With its heart not only in the right place but on its sleeve, too, this Otto Preminger indictment of southern whites is marred by being, if you will excuse the expression, too black and white. The whites are all nasty in various ways; the blacks are all virtuous. The whites hate; the blacks suffer. It isn't that way in real life, but then real life has never been Preminger's main aim. As a cinematic exercise it's superior stuff, however, and Jane Fonda is given the opportunity to act, and Faye Dunaway, George Kennedy, Michael Caine do more than adequately, too. Set in 1946 (which gives the opportunity to show the differing welcomes the returning soldiers get), it was shot in 1966. (*c*)

Hush, Hush, Sweet Charlotte ✓✓
Gorgeous performances from Bette Davis, Olivia de Havilland, Agnes Moorehead, Mary Astor in this scary in the *Baby Jane* tradition; Robert Aldrich directed again with such a lack of subtlety that it's like watching a send-up of horror movies at times; at others, though, it's genuinely frightening; 1965. (*b/w*)

The Hustler ✓✓✓
Charismatic Paul Newman as cocky young billiard player out to beat Jackie Gleason as ageing legendary king Minnesota Fats in Robert Rossen's memorable 1961 film of dingy pool hall circuit—and youth *v.* age universally. George C. Scott as gambling manager is just right. (*b/w*)

I Accuse ✕
José Ferrer unexcitingly directs José Ferrer in disappointing 1958 retelling of Dreyfus case; plus Viveca Lindfors, Anton Walbrook. (*b/w*)

I Aim at the Stars ✕✕
Glorification of the German scientist Werner von Braun, whose V2 rocket-bombs caused so much damage in Britain, and who later led the dizzily costly American prestige effort into space. Curt Jurgens plays the man sympathetically, and J. Lee Thompson seems prepared to forgive and forget, even if many of his British audience won't; 1960. (*b/w*)

I am a Camera ✕✕
It started with Isherwood in Berlin; became a John van Druten play; turned into this weak little film with Julie Harris and Laurence Harvey both

Paul Muni in *I am a Fugitive From a Chain Gang*

miscast and showing it; then it became a Broadway show with music, *Cabaret*; and finished up as the Liza Minnelli movie. This 1955 stop along the way, directed by Henry Cornelius, was not exactly a highspot. (*b/w*)

I am a Fugitive from a Chain Gang √√
Harrowing tale of an innocent (which is a cop-out) prisoner subjected to barbaric punishment. *Films in America, 1929–1969* recalls: 'Director Mervyn LeRoy has contended that the picture was responsible for chain gangs being taken off the road in Georgia . . . Many feel this is Muni's top screen performance, far superior to Pasteur and Zola'; 1932. (*b/w*)

I Can Get It For You Wholesale √
Not much left of Jerome Weidman's novel about New York rag trade except the title. But director Michael Gordon got good performances from Susan Hayward, as ruthless designer who wants to get ahead and doesn't mind how, Dan Dailey, George Sanders in 1951. (*b/w*)

Ice Cold in Alex √
A *Wages of Fear* translated to the Libyan desert during the last war with nitro-glycerine as cargo, and nurses plus a spy to complicate the lives of drivers John Mills and Harry Andrews. You may not be too aware of the soggy script in J. Lee Thompson's taut directtion; 1958. (*b/w*)

Ice Palace √
Old-fashioned melodrama about ruthless Richard Burton sacrificing Robert Ryan and Carolyn Jones, among others, on his way to the top. Set in Alaska, with a bit of history of the place thrown in. Vincent Sherman made it the equivalent of a good old-fashioned read in 1960. (*c*)

Ice Station Zebra √
Unpretentious adventure yarn has Rock

Hudson, Ernest Borgnine, Jim Brown, Patrick McGoohan aboard submarine on a secret mission to the North Pole. John Sturges did an honest job of work in 1968, and it's great stuff for little boys of all ages. (*c*)

I Confess √
Hitchcock disappointed in 1953 with this slow-moving story of priest (Montgomery Clift) who refuses to reveal murderer's confession to police even when he finds his own freedom at stake; strong support from Anne Baxter, Karl Malden. Hitchcock confesses failure. (*b/w*)

I Could Go On Singing √
What was at the time (1962) dismissed as mawkish, now posthumously comes over as Judy Garland's own heartbreak: it's all there–public Palladiumising, private despairs. Director Ronald Neame and co-star Dirk Bogarde hold Judy up magnificently. (*c*)

An Ideal Husband ✕ ✕
Stiff and ultimately boring transfer of elegant theatre piece to the screen; failure's not Oscar Wilde's so it must be director Alexander Korda's. Certainly his casting of Paulette Goddard was off-key, and the rest of the cast is terribly British but terribly second-rate; 1948. (*c*)

I Died a Thousand Times √
1955 remake of Bogart's *High Sierra* with Jack Palance as gangster who loves dog and club-foot girl. Stuart Heisler hams up direction, but Shelley Winters and Lee Marvin make it viewable. (*c*)

Idiot's Delight √
Clark Gable as song-and-dance man stranded at hotel near Italian border, encountering Norma Shearer and assorted luminaries such as Edward Arnold, Joseph Schildkraut. Clarence Brown directed, 1939, but never quite achieved the passion of the Pulitzer

Prize pacifist play by Robert E. Sherwood upon which it's based. (*b/w*)

The Idol ✕ ✕
Pedestrian little number with Jennifer Jones uncomfortable in role of remarrying but seduceable divorcée, which she took over in 1966 at the last minute from the more suitable Kim Stanley. American director Daniel Petrie is equally far from home in that boring old Swinging London, and has cast the supports from type. They might accept this England in the Middle West–but you know better. (*b/w*)

I'd Rather be Rich ✕
1964 remake of Deanna Durbin's *It Started With Eve*, with Sandra Dee smudged carbon copy. Updated fairy story with Andy Williams, Maurice Chevalier, Charlie Ruggles. Jack Smight directed from earlier script. (*c*)

If √ √
Lindsay Anderson's masterly parable. Fantasies in public school–expressed and merely imagined–of masters and boys, Malcolm McDowell gives outstanding performance as intelligent rebel; 1969. (*c*)

If a Man Answers ✕ ✕
Newlyweds Sandra Dee and Bobby Darin think they have problems. With such weak stars and a silly plot director Henry Levin certainly did in 1962. Don't waste your time. (*c*)

If He Hollers, Let Him Go ✕
Absurd plot involving negro on the run being forced to murder Kevin McCarthy's wife but twists and double-twists screw everything up. Charles Martin, who wrote, directed, produced in 1969, can't escape the blame. Raymond St Jacques does well in the main part. (*c*)

If I Had a Million √ √
Series of episodes about reactions of

people handed a million dollars: classic 1932 omnibus had bevy of directors (among them Ernest Lubitsch, James Cruze), and Gary Cooper, George Raft, Mary Boland, Charles Laughton, W. C. Fields, Charlie Ruggles, Jack Oakie *et al.* (*b/w*)

I Know Where I'm Going √
Wendy Hiller outstanding as heiress who flees the rich life for true love in Scotland; Powell–Pressburger coaxed lovely performances, too, from Roger Livesey, Finlay Currie, and a 14-year-old Petula Clark; 1945. (*b/w*)

I'll Cry Tomorrow √√
Triumph for Susan Hayward as the real-life alcoholic star Lillian Roth, her mother (Jo Van Fleet), and husbands (Richard Conte, Eddie Albert, Don Taylor). Daniel Mann's relatively restrained direction made this stand out in 1955. (*b/w*)

Illegal √
Modest but exciting Edward G. Robinson thriller. He plays former DA who gets involved with baddies; Lewis Allen even got effective brief performance out of Jayne Mansfield, though Nina Foch was star; 1955. (*b/w*)

Ill Met by Moonlight √
Famous war movie made in 1957 about dashing Dirk Bogarde kidnapping German General Marius Goring in Crete. Powell and Pressburger keep it rattling along. (*b/w*)

I'll Never Forget You ✕✕
Poor 1951 remake of *Berkeley Square*. Tyrone Power time-slips back into 18th-century London and love with Ann Blyth. Roy Baker directed only too forgettably in 1951. (*c*)

I'll See You In My Dreams √
Formula musical biography treatment of songwriter Gus Kahn's life with 1951 vintage bubbly Doris Day, Danny Thomas; director Michael Curtiz. (*b/w*)

I'll Take Sweden ✕✕
If we tell you it's about father Bob Hope protecting daughter Tuesday Weld's virtue in 'sexy' Sweden, you could guess the rest. One would have thought they were more grown up in 1965. Frederick de Cordova directed. (*c*)

The Illustrated Man √
Ray Bradbury's knock-out book of sixteen short stories taking off from the tattoos on one man's (Rod Steiger's here) body has been reduced to three. While the prologue and epilogue, involving the tattooed gentleman, a wayfarer and an enigmatic spirit (Claire Bloom–Mrs Steiger at the time) are fine, none of the stories really work. Director Jack Smight uses his camera effectively enough, but the special effects are mouldy; 1969. (*c*)

I Love Melvin ✕
Pleasant enough time-passer if you happen to love Debbie Reynolds and Donald O'Connor. She's a chorus girl, he's a magazine photographer, but director Don Weis knew that was just an excuse for some lively but undistinguished song-and-dance routines; 1953. (*c*)

I Love You, Alice B. Toklas ✕
There is–anyway, there was in 1969– a marvellous film to be made about the comic clash of the two cultures of middle-class Jewish America and the world of the hippie, but this isn't it. Occasional flashes such as the conversations between straight Peter Sellers and sex-manual-obsessed Joyce Van Patten have a momentary brilliance; but the descent into slapstick when he embraces the creed of the flower-children just embarrasses. And why do directors like Hy Averback put up with unconvincing performances from non-Jewish actors pretending to be Jewish when there are so many good real ones around? Ditto hippies. The end is a cop-out. (*c*)

I'm All Right, Jack   √
Cynical, malicious comedy from the Boulting Brothers, concerned to satirise both sides in industrial relations but finishing up as a union-bashing exercise, partly due to Peter Sellers' brilliance in portraying archetypal (falsely archetypal, but enduringly so) shop steward and Irene Handl's knowing-her-place wife. Plenty of beautifully-composed cameo performances, but the whole film leaves a nasty taste in the mouth; 1959. (*b/w*)

I Married a Monster from Outer Space   √
Off-putting title hides well-made thriller about alien planet taking over human beings; ex-film editor Gene Fowler Jr made it good and taut in 1958. (*b/w*)

I Married a Witch   √ √
Beguiling René Clair-directed original of *Bewitched* has Veronica Lake peek-a-booing deliciously at Fredric March, descendant of Salem-burners and bumblingly endearing Robert Benchley; 1942. (*b/w*)

I Married a Woman   × ×
Overworked George Gobel married to oversexy Diana Dors; Hal Kanter didn't give it any sparkle in 1958. (*b/w*)

Imitation General   ×
That's Glenn Ford taking officer's place in George Marshall-directed second world war comedy with Red Buttons, Taina Elg; 1958. (*b/w*)

Imitation of Life   √
(1) Soppy but just credible version of Fannie Hurst book with Claudette Colbert making a million out of pancake recipe of ole black lady whose daughter passes for white; John M. Stahl; 1934. (*b/w*)

Imitation of Life   ×
(2) Over the top in 1959 remake with Lana Turner, and Susan Kohner as the white-passer; the death of the black mammy is sobbiest sickiest scene of the kind ever filmed; Douglas Sirk. (*c*)

The Importance of Being Earnest   √ √
Oscar Wilde's impeccably-mannered comedy splendidly cast with grave Michael Redgrave, Michael Denison, Dorothy Tutin and Joan Greenwood, and Edith Evans the definitive Lady Bracknell. Plus bonus of Margaret Rutherford, Miles Malleson and Richard Wattis and elegant direction by Anthony Asquith; 1952. (*c*)

The Impossible Years   × ×
David Niven, Lola Albright wasted as thoroughly modern parents worried about daughter Christina Ferrare's virtue. Hard to believe director Michael Gordon raised even a snigger in 1968. (*c*)

Inadmissible Evidence   √
Disappointing adaptation of John Osborne's riveting play about a totally unsatisfactory man, brilliantly realised by Nicol Williamson, here as on the stage; though Anthony Page and Osborne have fallen into the trap of 'opening it out' and inserted a comic-strip running gag about a court case. On film, it's more difficult to believe that he is tolerated in running the office and home where he somehow stays as boss. But film is always involving and unlike most surface-skimming movies; 1969. (*b/w*)

In a Lonely Place   √ √
Humphrey Bogart at top of his form in 1950 as Hollywood scriptwriter suspected of hat-check girl murder, shielded by neighbour Gloria Grahame. Nicholas Ray directed, with eye for detail and the sickly smell of corrupt Hollywood hangs over the whole film. (*b/w*)

Incendiary Blonde   × ×
Tiring Betty Hutton as equally fatiguing Texas Guinan, queen of the night-clubs in the twenties. True story has been

laundered by writers and director George Marshall, who also has unfortunate penchant for character-caricaturers like Charlie Ruggles, Barry Fitzgerald, Albert Dekker; 1945. (*c*)

The Incident √
Passengers on New York subway are held prisoner by vicious hoodlums; director Larry Peerce rather overdid it in 1967, with Tony Musante, Beau Bridges. (*b/w*)

Incident at Owl Creek √√√
Classic half-hour of the thoughts and memories of a hanging man (Roger Jacquet), superbly realised by Robert Enrico, from Ambrose Bierce's *An Occurrence at Owl Creek Bridge*; 1962. (*b/w*)

In Cold Blood √√
Richard Brooks' narrative pseudo-documentary, based on Truman Capote best-seller about two hold-up men who rob a farmer and make sure there are no witnesses left alive, and the judicial murder of them after a lengthy trial. Undeniably gripping, it is flawed by the device of jumping over the killing in the first part of the film so it can be shown near the end. There are no surprises and, since one knows the end, the only *raison d'être* is to condemn the death penalty. Or, of course, ghoulishness on the part of the makers and audience. Robert Blake and Scott Wilson, unknowns, play the killed killers; Jeff Corey, Paul Stewart, with their well-known faces, seem rather out of place; 1968. (*b/w*)

The Incredible Mr Limpet ×
Incredible plot, too, about a timid Don Knotts turning into a dolphin and helping US Navy during second world war. Kids may like it. Arthur Lubin; 1964. (*c*)

The Incredible Shrinking Man √√
'Arguably the peak of sf film,' writes John Baxter in *Science Fiction in the Cinema*. A man gets smaller and smaller until spider is monster menace; but it has a message, too: there's a place for everybody and everything in the universe, no matter what their size. Jack Arnold directed; 1957. (*b/w*)

The Indian Fighter √
Routine but lively Western with Kirk Douglas, Elsa Martinelli, Walter Matthau; director André de Toth keeps it moving; 1955. (*c*)

Indiscreet √√
Stylish comedy has Cary Grant and Ingrid Bergman in and out of love, (though not in and out of bed–after all it was only 1958); a sumptuous Mayfair background and some solid British support (Cecil Parker, Phyllis Calvert, Megs Jenkins, David Kossoff). Stanley Donen gave it plenty of gloss. (*c*)

Indiscretion of an American Wife ×
Will Jennifer Jones go back to her husband or stay with lover Montgomery Clift? She obviously cares, but will you? Director Vittorio de Sica tried to make you in 1954. (*b/w*)

In Enemy Country √
Neat and exciting double-espionage thriller, with Tony Franciosa framing his girlfriend so that she can marry German officer and betray his secrets. Reflects 1968 ethos in suggesting there was not much to choose between the two sides in the last war. Harry Keller. (*c*)

Inferno √
Lovers Rhonda Fleming, William Lundigan leave husband, Robert Ryan, to die in desert–they think. Director Roy Baker keeps us in suspense; 1953. (*c*)

The Informer √√
Victor McLaglen as shambling Gypo who plays Judas during the Irish Troubles, winning director John Ford

his first Oscar in 1935; successful on a variety of levels, this version of the Liam O'Flaherty's novel has never been bettered in its theatrical statements on men under pressure. (*b/w*)

The Informers √
Rather well-made (by Ken Annakin) police yarn about Nigel Patrick (beautifully polished and always better when not directing himself) as inspector getting framed for the killing when one of his snouts is killed; realistic support from Colin Blakely, Frank Finlay, Michael Coles, George Sewell; 1963. (*b/w*)

In Harm's Way ×
Otto Preminger had big-star cast of John Wayne, Kirk Douglas, Henry Fonda, Dana Andrews, Franchot Tone, Patricia Neal, Brandon de Wilde, Paula Prentiss, Burgess Meredith, making love and war after Japanese attack on Pearl Harbour. It was poorly received in 1965, but isn't quite that bad. (*b/w*)

Inherit the Wind √
Flawed retelling of real-life Dayton Monkey Trial, when schoolteacher was arrested for teaching evolution. Stanley Kramer directed Spencer Tracey as Clarence Darrow, Fredric March as Bryan in 1960, but departed from truth in having heart attack kill one of them, when it was really overeating, and tacking on false final twist. (*b/w*)

In Like Flint ×
James Coburn as carbon-copy James Bond manages to be both smug and boring in tedious comic strip about stealing the President and replacing him with living, breathing doll. As if there'd be any difference! Gordon Douglas probably thought he was directing slickly and amusingly, in 1967; he wasn't. (*c*)

In Love and War ×
Sentimental second world war melo about effects of war on lives and loves of three young marines–Robert Wagner, Bradford Dillman, Jeffrey Hunter. Philip Dunne directed; 1958. (*c*)

Inn for Trouble × × ×
Desperately unfunny translation of the never-very-funny TV Larkins family to the big screen in early (1960) attempt to cash in on what was later in the decade to become an industry in itself–the switching of British TV comedy to the cinema. All sorts of well-known faces (Peggy Mount, David Kossoff, Leslie Phillips among them) stumble about from one silly situation to the next; Pennington Richards. (*b/w*)

The Innocents √ √
Atmospheric rendering of Henry James' *Turn of the Screw* with emphasis on governess Deborah Kerr's fight against 'forces of evil' in children, which with our post-Freudian hindsight we might interpret less supernaturally. A good chill, though. Jack Clayton; 1961. (*b/w*)

Innocent Sinners ×
1958 adaptation of sickly Rumer Godden novel about two cockney kids, *An Episode of Sparrows*. Philip Leacock directs June Archer, Christopher Hey, Brian Hammond, Flora Robson, David Kossoff, Andrew Cruickshank with restraint. (*c*)

The Inn of the Sixth Happiness √
Successful tearjerker despite all its faults (Ingrid Bergman's ludicrous accent in a part that is supposed to be utterly English; the obviousness of the set pieces, the over-simplification of character), from Mark Robson. The story holds up even if it isn't very convincing; both Robert Donat and Athene Seyler stand out; Curt Jurgens gets by; 1959. (*c*)

Inside Daisy Clover √
The Mulligan working-over of Gavin Lambert's screenplay from his cliché-

ridden novel about the rise of a teenage film star was given some sharp teeth in 1966, but somehow fails to bite. Natalie Wood is never less than adequate as the girl concerned, but neither Robert Redford, Christopher Plummer, nor Roddy McDowall can quite bring off important contributory roles. Nor is the ending convincing. But, having knocked, one has to say that there are compensations like the vivid picture of thirties Hollywood and Ruth Gordon's mother; let's hope that TV restores the 20 minutes cut out by the British distributor. (*c*)

The Inspector × ×
Neither a thriller nor a melodrama nor a character-study, this is a nothing of a film about a girl saved from white slavery in 1946 (it was made 16 years later); depressing acting from Stephen Boyd, Leo McKern, Donald Pleasence, Robert Stephens, mostly the fault of director Philip Dunne. (*c*)

An Inspector Calls √ √
Alastair Sim at his enigmatic best in J. B. Priestley flash-backer on family responsibility; Guy Hamilton directed stolidly; 1954. (*b/w*)

Inspector Clouseau ×
Heavy-handed third in series has Alan Arkin replacing Peter Sellers, and yawns replacing jokes. Arkin, who mercifully dispenses with Sellers' irritating mannerisms in the part, doesn't replace them with anything worth watching, and director Bud Yorkin lacks both wit and style. The supports–Frank Finlay, Beryl Reid, Richard Pearson and a string of other familiar players–do not seem to be able to respond to anything comic in either the script or the direction; 1969. (*c*)

The Intelligence Men ×
Despite an appalling script, an attempt to turn them into characters different from their established personas, awful support acting and pathetic direction from Robert Asher, Eric Morecambe and Ernie Wise rise above it all to do their sublime act, only occasionally being dragged down by aforementioned disadvantages; 1965. (*c*)

Intent to Kill ×
Jack Cardiff's directional debut in 1958 had that old script idea about the South American dictator (here in a Montreal hospital) that Richard Todd and Alexander Knox are trying to save the life of, while Warren Stevens tries to do him in. Herbert Lom plays the dictator in his usual beetle-browed style. Quite exciting in a less than nailbiting way; (*b/w*)

Interlude √
That weepy old one about falling in love with a married man who can't get a divorce. In 1957 *she* was nice young American girl, June Allyson, *he* was European conductor Rossano Brazzi; director was Douglas Sirk. In 1968 *she* was nice young English girl Barbara Ferris, *he* was Oskar Werner and still a conductor; director was Kevin Billington. (both *c*)

The Interns ×
Soap opera about hospital life with Cliff Robertson, James MacArthur, Michael Callan, Suzy Parker. You've seen it all before in countless TV series and so had director David Swift in 1962. (*b/w*)

Interrupted Melody √
Moving story of Marjorie Lawrence, the real-life opera singer who survived polio. Director Curtis Bernhardt got fine performances from Eleanor Parker and Glenn Ford in 1955. (*c*)

In the Cool of the Day × ×
Jane Fonda, Peter Finch, Arthur Hill in Greece should have been glossy, fascinating. In fact, only Angela Lansbury

pleases, under Robert Stevens' 1963 direction. (*c*)

In the French Style ✗
Jean Seberg learning the hard way that sex and sophistication in Paris isn't as satisfying as life with a solid doctor in America. This message is so obviously packaged for Stateside consumption and the whirl of Paris reduced to a gentle wind so as not to offend (the date is 1963, too early for the sexual explicitness demanded by the theme) that Irwin Shaw's treatment of his stories becomes anodynical; Miss Seberg's own life, which–if one is to believe the newspaper interviews–is curiously similar to this heroine's, might make a much better movie some time; Robert Parrish. (*b/w*)

In the Good Old Summertime √
Made in the good old days of 1949 when Judy Garland and Van Johnson could fall in love by mail, and Cuddles Sakall and Spring Byington could cluck schmaltzily on the porch. Only Buster Keaton gives much life; Robert Z. Leonard. (*c*)

In the Heat of the Night √√√
1967 Oscars rightly went to Rod Steiger for his racist policeman who learns live-let-live, Stirling Silliphant for script. Norman Jewison's best film falls into usual trap of making Sidney Poitier too goody, but it's exciting and must have been educative in its setting, the deep south. (*c*)

In the Nick √
1960 British comedy about prison psychologist, Anthony Newley, trying to reform racketeer James Booth; with Harry Andrews, Bernie Winters, Anne Aubrey, Ian Hendry. Ken Hughes gave it some laughs. (*b/w*)

In This Our Life √√
Bette Davis as prize bitch in director John Huston's second movie (a year after his smashing *Maltese Falcon*),

ruining everybody's life including sister Olivia de Havilland's; 1942. (*b/w*)

Intruder in the Dust √
Faulkner's lynch-mob novel transfers well under Clarence Brown's direction, 1949; Claude Jarman Jr, Porter Hall do best. (*b/w*)

Invaders From Mars √
Flying saucer brings nasties from outer space who insert crystals into brains of Jimmy Hunt's parents; when he runs to police, chief has scar too. William Cameron Menzies makes it all belief-suspensible; shot in 1953. (*c*)

Invasion ✗✗
One of those slices of hokum about another world invading ours. Some respected TV names (director Alan Bridges, writer Roger Marshall, actors Edward Judd, Valerie Gearon, Tsai Chin, Barrie Ingham, Glyn Houston) fail to make it credible or even technically competent; 1966. (*b/w*)

Invasion of the Body Snatchers √√√
Silly title for powerful picture that Don Siegel thinks is his best. Framework is alien world taking over human beings, but Siegel uses this to criticise contemporary zombiedom (which hasn't improved since 1956). Dana Wynter, Carolyn Jones. (*b/w*)

Invasion Quartet ✗✗
Spike Milligan, John le Mesurier and Eric Sykes are almost the only excuses for looking at this pathetic 1961 effort at a wartime comedy, crassly directed by Jay Lewis, who clearly had no idea how to get the best from his cast or just how rotten a script he was trying to film; it's supposedly about a private invasion to spike (or milligan) a German gun. (*b/w*)

Invitation ✗✗
Glossy 1952 tearjerker has rich girl

(Dorothy McGuire) worrying that father (Louis Calhern) 'bought' husband (Van Johnson) to brighten up her last days. Gottfried Reinhardt didn't seem to worry too much, and nor should you.
(*b/w*)

Invitation to a Gunfighter ✕
Director Richard Wilson didn't deserve the good performances he got from Yul Brynner as hired gunman and George Segal as victim. Apart from Janice Rule, nothing else convinces; 1964. (*c*)

In Which We Serve √
Noel Coward's tribute to the Navy, 1942. No fool he, Coward got Anthony Havelock-Allan as his co-producer, David Lean as his co-director and Noel Coward as his scenarist. He also played Captain D. of HMS Torrin (based on Lord Louis Mountbatten's *HMS Kelly*). As her crew cling to a float, upper-lips stiff as ramrods, they remember their loved ones. Impossible to fault without appearing unpatriotic. (*b/w*)

I Passed for White ✕ ✕ ✕
Sick little story of black girl who wishes she wasn't; they *couldn't* make films like that anymore, thank goodness and Black Power. Fred M. Wilcox directed James Franciscus and Sonya Wilde; 1960. (*b/w*)

The Ipcress File √ √
Spy stuff adapted from Len Deighton book with Michael Caine as bespectacled Callan precursor. Nigel Green makes perfect dept. boss; Sidney J. Furie; 1965.
(*c*)

I Remember Mama √
Extremely sentimental, about plucky Irene Dunne raisin' her brood in San Francisco; George Stevens piled on the goo but those who like a good cry will love it. Barbara Bel Geddes does well among daughters; 1948. (*b/w*)

Irish Eyes Are Smiling ✕
1944 Irish-American blarney about songwriter's troubles with inevitably fiery-tempered colleen, has little plot, familiar tunes, Dick Haymes, June Haver, Anthony Quinn, director Gregory Ratoff. (*c*)

Irma la Douce ✕ ✕
One of Billy Wilder's few failures was this attempt to stretch already thin musical play without its sixteen numbers. It makes a silly comedy about a ponce who's so jealous that he disguises himself to be his girl's only client; Jack Lemmon flounders in the part Keith Michell was able to gloss over by song in the stage version, Shirley MacLaine just doesn't have the presence to make the golden-hearted tart anything but fitfully interesting; 1964. (*c*)

The Iron Maiden ✕ ✕
Made by *Carry On* producer Peter Rogers and director Gerald Thomas, this appallingly dreary comedy is only significant in showing how important those comedians are in the *Carry Ons*. Without them (and with Michael Craig, Noel Purcell and Cecil Parker) the script and direction reveal a terrible sense of flop, and the story of traction engines and British aircraft is equally dull; 1963.
(*c*)

The Iron Petticoat ✕ ✕
Katharine Hepburn and even Bob Hope wasted in embarrassing 1957 Ralph Thomas-directed comedy about cold Russian Air Force captain (Hepburn) melting under charm of American pilot (Hope). (*c*)

Isadora √ √
Intermittently brilliant, this biopic of the modern dancer and free soul is marred by remembrances of movies past, as though Karel Reisz couldn't or didn't want to get away from the MGM screen biographies of the thirties. However, Vanessa Redgrave makes a persuasive Isadora and her expressionistic love-

scenes are as good as anything filmed of this kind. James Fox as Gordon Craig does better than Jason Robards as her husband. And that end, which we all know is waiting for us, when the scarf catches in the wheel of the car, does work; 1969. (*c*)

I Saw What You Did   √
They didn't really; it was just two silly girls (Andi Garrett, Sarah Lane) playing a practical joke over the telephone. But how was their 'victim' (John Ireland) to know? And how were they to know they'd picked on a dangerous psycho-path? Thrills begin as they start to find out, but director William Castle could have done a more chilling job. Joan Crawford disappears early on; 1965.
(*b/w*)

I Shot Jesse James   √
Actually, Samuel Fuller did, in 1948, the first that the writer also directed, and the forerunner of a distinguished series of Westerns that made him King of the Respected Oaters; John Ireland begins a dishonourable tradition for Fuller by shooting his best friend in the back. Preston Foster is lead; (*b/w*)

Island Escape   × ×
Tawdry, unconvincing reconstruction of the one American left alive on the island of Guam after over two years of Japanese occupation; Jeffrey (*I Was a Teenage Jesus*) Hunter weak; only the newsreels convince. John Monks, who wrote, produced and directed all the bits between the authentic clips, doesn't either; 1962. (*c*)

Island in the Sky   ×
Best thing about this William Wellman air rescue drama is the marvellous photography; John Wayne, Lloyd Nolan, James Arness aren't nearly as impressive; 1953. (*b/w*)

Island in the Sun   ×
Old-fashioned (1957) view of black *v.*

white struggle in Jamaica, poorly adapted from Alec Waugh novel. Robert Rossen directs strong cast of James Mason, Joan Fontaine, Dorothy Dandridge, Joan Collins, Stephen Boyd, Harry Belafonte, who must at least have got a nice holiday out of it all. (*c*)

Island of Love   √
Robert Preston as con-man, Walter Matthau as gangster he conned, Tony Randall and beautiful Greek locations should have added up to something more; maybe it was director Morton DaCosta's fault; 1963. (*c*)

The Island of the Blue Dolphins   √
Taken from an account of a female Robinson Crusoe who lived off California from 1835 to 1853, this modest children-oriented adventure, directed by James B. Clark, is beguiling enough; Celia Kaye plays the main, monologuey part; 1965. (*c*)

Island of Terror   ×
Poor example of the *Creatures from the Sea* genre directed by Terence Fisher in 1966; Peter Cushing manages his usual competent job. It's kinder to their hard-working agents who miraculously got them parts in this one, not to name the rest of the cast. (*c*)

Is Paris Burning?   ×
Only from embarrassment at such a poor film being made of its liberation and confused nazi orders as to its fate; René Clément just couldn't control his cast from going off in all directions—Charles Boyer, Leslie Caron, Alain Delon, Kirk Douglas, Glenn Ford, Gert Fröbe, Simone Signoret, Claude Dauphin—the list reads like a party-game of overrated actors; what was Orson Welles doing mixed up with this lot? 1966. (*b/w*)

Istanbul   × ×
Tired Joseph Pevney-directed hokum, about stolen jewels and lost love

Cornell Borchers suffering from amnesia, is strictly for Errol Flynn fans; 1957. (*c*)

Istanbul Express　　　　　　　　×
A made-in-Hollywood 1969 mock-up of the Orient Express provides the luxurious setting for a predictable but pleasant spy adventure, whose premise is no sillier than most Saintly TV episodes. Strictly second-eleven 'stars' fill the main stereotypes–Gene Barry, Senta Berger, John Saxon–but Richard Irving knows he's only providing entertainment and more or less manages to. (*c*)

It Always Rains on Sunday　　　　√
One day in the East End from Arthur La Bern's novel, directed by Robert Hamer in 1947 with the minimum of genteel falsification and a melancholic charm. Googie Withers, Jack Warner, Alfie Bass responded. Perhaps someone will remake it as it was originally written–sexy and gritty. (*b/w*)

It Came From Outer Space　　　　√
Clever trick photography is best thing about this routine sci-fi with Richard Carlson, Barbara Rush, Charles Drake. Jack Arnold directed; 1953. (*c*)

I Thank a Fool　　　　　　　× × ×
Speak for yourself. This must be one of the worst scripts (Karl Tunberg wrote it) that ever got put on film, and the sheer waste of Susan Hayward, Peter Finch, Diane Cilento, and some fine supports from the British 1962 stable is staggering. Director Robert Stevens does his best but the stupid plot (QC engages woman he got convicted as nurse to his potty wife) is matched by pretentious dialogue, non-motivation and soggy development. (*c*)

It Happened at the World's Fair　×
If it didn't have Elvis Presley in it, this could be dismissed as a lousy film that desperately uses the 1962 World's Fairground in Seattle in an effort to inject some novelty. With Elvis, it's a lousy film with ten musical numbers that desperately uses the 1962 World's Fairground in Seattle in an effort to inject some novelty; Norman Taurog must be the most faithful, if not the most inspired director ever in Hollywood. (*c*)

It Happened Here　　　　　　√ √
Remarkable imaginary reconstruction of what would have happened if the nazis occupied Britain; ten years in the financing and making by Kevin Brownlow and Andrew Mollo, it was publicly shown in 1966; Sebastian Shaw is only well-known full-time actor in the cast. (*b/w*)

It Happened in Athens　　　× × ×
Really awful 'comedy' about the earliest Olympic games, with Jayne Mansfield kindly offering herself (in marriage) to winner of the marathon; Andrew Marton, director, must be kidding–but if so, why aren't we laughing? 1962. (*c*)

It Happened One Night　　　　√ √
Frank Capra's classic holds up well despite its age–it was made in 1934–and its famous set-pieces–hitching a lift with a glimpse of stocking, hanging the blanket between their sleeping arrangements–still work; Clark Gable, Claudette Colbert enchant as reporter and heiress. (*b/w*)

It Happened to Jane　　　　　√
Comedy has Doris Day and Jack Lemmon selling lobsters, and a villainous Ernie Kovaks; Richard Quine made it quite a lot of fun in 1959. (*c*)

It Happened Tomorrow　　　　　√
Nice René Clair 1944 fantasy (set at turn of century) about newspaper reporter getting tomorrow's news today; Dick Powell, Jack Oakie, Edgar Kennedy, Sig Ruman play their familiar parts energetically; a young (21-year-old) Linda Darnell enchants. (*b/w*)

It's a Great Feeling √
Musical excuse (by I. A. L. Diamond, director David Butler, 1949) for cameo performances by Gary Cooper, Joan Crawford, Errol Flynn, Sydney Greenstreet, Edward G. Robinson *et al*, in story of Jack Carson trying to direct a movie with himself and Doris Day. (*c*)

It's Always Fair Weather √
Reunion of three ex-army pals (Gene Kelly, Michael Kidd, Dan Dailey) is excuse for a musical sending up TV; co-directors Kelly and Stanley Donen gave it zing in 1955. (*c*)

It's a Mad, Mad, Mad, Mad World √ √
Over, over, over, overlong comedy chase after money, money, money, money, which wearies at least an hour before the end of its 192 (cinema) minutes, involving six greedy people chasing after loot that Jimmy Durante, before pegging out, confides he has buried. Stanley Kramer has endless cast of comedians (among them: Phil Silvers, Terry-Thomas, Milton Berle, Jonathan Winters, Jim Backus, Edward Everett Horton, Buster Keaton, the Three Stooges, Andy Devine, Zasu Pitts, Buddy Hackett, Sid Caesar, plus Spencer Tracy) pulling every gag in the Joe Miller gag book. Best bits are the car crashes, but you hate yourself for enjoying their wanton destructiveness— but, then, all the film is rather unpleasant, if you think about it; 1963. (*c*)

It's a Wonderful Life ×
Dated bit of whimsy lifted by James Stewart as dejected, hard-working citizen suddenly shown good things of life by obliging angel. Donna Reed, Lionel Barrymore. Directed (1946) by Frank Capra. (*b/w*)

It Should Happen To You √ √
Treat from George Cukor in 1954 has out-of-work model (delicious Judy Holliday) renting advertising space for herself on New York billboard; Jack Lemmon, Peter Lawford help keep up the fun. (*b/w*)

It's Only Money ×
Down the drain, as far as we're concerned. Jerry Lewis fans will probably love him, though, as TV repair man in Frank Tashlin-directed slapstick with Zachary Scott, Joan O'Brien; 1962. (*b/w*)

It Started in Naples × ×
And finishes in a yawn. Clark Gable, Sophia Loren, Vittorio de Sica go through some cumbersome motions in what is supposed to be a Mel Shavelson comedy about custody of a rather repulsive little waif; the scenery comes off best, though there's rather too much even of that; Gable is an American lawyer, Loren a hard-up Italian auntie, battling for the kid, so if you have ever seen a film before you'll be able to guess the ending; 1960. (*c*)

It Started in Tokyo × ×
Butchered to get down to length in England, this moderate thriller directed by Joseph M. Newman played as a second feature in 1962. Agnes Moorehead and William Demarest were cut completely out, and the plot, about a murder and missing heiress, has been rendered meaningless. David Janssen and Jeanne Crain are still there, but it's all a muddle, so don't watch unless it's at least 85 minutes long when it reaches your screen. (*b/w*)

It Started with a Kiss ×
Painless comedy about Debbie Reynolds newly-married to GI Glenn Ford has some striking Spanish backgrounds; also Eva Gabor, Fred Clark and easy direction from George Marshall in 1959. (*c*)

It's That Man Again × ×
Made in 1943 to cash in on Tommy Handley & Co's immense popularity; nostalgic wallow for the over-40s, and

an explanation to those younger why Dad and Mum think such phrases as 'TTFN' and 'This is Funf speaking' are funny. Director, Walter Forde. (*b/w*)

Ivanhoe √
If you can overlook the American accents you'll enjoy star-studded (Elizabeth Taylor, Robert Taylor, Joan Fontaine) 1952 Richard Thorpe version done with joust the right panache. (*c*)

I Walked with a Zombie √√
And very terrifying it is, as Frances Dee takes catatonic Christine Gordon through the dark cane fields to meet voodoo priest in Haiti; Jacques Tourneur and producer Val Lewton turned this into one of the most frightening films on the screen; 1943. (*b/w*)

I Want To Live! √√
Susan Hayward won Oscar for her histrionics in this Robert Wise-directed 1958 attack on capital punishment. She plays real-life drug-addicted whore, unfairly (it says) convicted for part in brutal attack on old woman. (*b/w*)

I Want You ××
Effect of Korean War on typical American family—or rather how director Mark Robson imagined it in 1951. Phoney and embarrassing, and poor cast of Dana Andrews, Farley Granger, Dorothy McGuire doesn't help. (*b/w*)

I Was Happy Here √
Desmond Davis' rather muted version of an Edna O'Brien short story, with Sarah Miles. Moving and sensitive, if never completely absorbing; 1966. (*b/w*)

I Was Monty's Double ×
To fool the Germans, British Intelligence sent M. E. Clifton-James off to North Africa dressed as General Montgomery; he did it all over again in 1958 for this mild but amusing actioner, with John Mills and Cecil Parker; John Guillermin directed competently enough. (*b/w*)

I Wonder Who's Kissing Her Now ×
June Haver, Reginald Gardiner in very ordinary eighties musical, pleasantly directed by Lloyd Bacon; 1947. (*c*)

Jack of Diamonds √
Routine caper with the weak George Hamilton playing jewel thief in league with Maurice Evans, Joseph Cotten planning to lift diamond and ruby necklace from Munich bank. Momentarily enlivened by two 'famous film stars' playing themselves as his victims—it's a measure of Don Taylor's minuscule budget that the best they could afford were Carroll Baker and Zsa Zsa Gabor; 1967. (*c*)

The Jackpot √
James Stewart wins it and how it changes his life. Unfortunately, it's all terribly dated, being made in 1950—even the quiz game he wins is on radio and not TV; Walter Lang directs adequately. (*b/w*)

Jailhouse Rock √
Despite the lamentable title, this isn't at all a bad Elvis Presley vehicle, with the lad as convict who can play the guitar and sing; having Richard Thorpe direct, in 1957, helped; they don't go in for class directors much in Presley movies. (*b/w*)

Jane Eyre ✓✓
The most pornographic novel in the English language, D. H. Lawrence called it, and Robert Stevenson, nominally the director, conveyed its heavy eroticism splendidly in this 1944 version. But it more strongly bears the imprint of Orson Welles, playing Rochester and casting long shadows (actual as well as metaphorical) with his Mercury mates, actress Agnes Moorehead, co-writer (with Aldous Huxley) John Houseman, composer Bernard Herrmann, designer William Pereira. If Joan Fontaine is just too one-note as Jane, the rest of the cast (including the young Elizabeth Taylor and a malicious Henry Daniell) make up for her. (*b/w*)

Jason and the Argonauts ✗
Cut-price special effects spoil this little attempt to inject some grandeur into the Argo's voyage to find the Golden Fleece; the cast comes from the less expensive pages of *Spotlight*, too. Don Chaffey directs, hopefully; 1963. (*c*)

The Jayhawkers ✗✗
Talky 'psychological' Western about unbelievable character played by Jeff Chandler who intends to take over Kansas with his outlaws. The fact that he lives in a book-lined cave, drinking wine and entertaining ladies, doesn't add to the rapidly-evaporating feeling of authenticity; Melvin Frank, better-known as a comedy writer and producer, unintentionally added another farce to his long list in 1960. (*c*)

Jazz on a Summer's Day ✓✓
Best jazz film ever made, with Anita O'Day, Chico Hamilton, Gerry Mulligan, Louis Armstrong, Mahalia Jackson beautifully shot and recorded against the background of the Newport Jazz Festival, 1958; a bit long, but nearly always a joy. Bert Stern. (*c*)

The Jazz Singer ✗
Danny Thomas takes over the Al Jolson

Bette Davis in *Jezebel*

role in a 1953 remake of the early talkie, as a cantor's son who makes it big in show biz; as corny as ever and drippy entertainment. Director Michael Curtiz. (*c*)

Jeanne Eagels　　　　√
The speed is too fast for Kim Novak in this story of real-life twenties star who drove herself to an early grave. Luckily Agnes Moorehead and Gene Lockhart are there to give it some distinction. George Sidney; 1957. (*b/w*)

Jesse James　　　　√
Ambitious Western that made a hero out of title villain in keeping with Tyrone Power's 1939 box-office standing. Henry Fonda plays brother and director Henry King's supports include reliable Randolph Scott and Brian Donlevy. (*c*)

Jessica　　　　× ×
Angie Dickinson as American nurse in Italian village; unconvincing direction by Jean Negulesco leaves Agnes Moorehead and Maurice Chevalier high and dry along with the ill-served Angie; 1962. (*c*)

Jet Over The Atlantic　　　　×
Neither director–Byron Haskin–nor cast–George Raft, Guy Madison, Virginia Mayo–can inject much excitement into this corny old one about will the, won't the, plane crash; 1960. (*b/w*)

Jet Pilot　　　　×
A five million dollar budget, and all they could come up with was John Wayne as airman falling for Russian spy Janet Leigh. Howard Hughes kindly let Josef von Sternberg direct in 1958. (*c*)

Jet Storm　　　　√
Richard Attenborough gives fine performance as father of murdered child who plans to blow up plane in revenge. On board: Stanley Baker, Diane Cilento, Virginia Maskell, Harry Secombe, Mai Zetterling and other

dependables. Cy Endfield keeps the tension driving, even if the sub-plots do get lost in the end; 1959. (*b/w*)

Jezebel　　　　√
1938 winner of Oscars for Southern Belle Bette Davis and aunt Fay Bainter. Henry Fonda and George Brent are duelling suitors. William Wyler's set pieces are so successful that you can almost forgive the famous red dress that scandalises polite society for not being in colour. (*b/w*)

Jigsaw　　　　× ×
Dull little British detective plodder with Jack Warner as a promoted PC 49 in plain clothes and Ronald Lewis as Sgt to his Insp. It's mostly just a series of long and boring interrogations and there are no characters, only cliché-cartoons; Val Guest's to blame–he wrote, produced and directed, as well as being married to one of the more decorative members of the cast; 1962. (*b/w*)

Jivaro　　　　×
Unconvincing jungle journey with Indian siege and triangle plot with Fernando Lamas, Rhonda Fleming, Brian Keith. Ho-hum direction by Edward Ludwig; 1954. (*c*)

Joanna　　　　× ×
Indulgent–to writer-director Michael Sarne's psyche and his vapid heroine's aimless life–and overlong. Tour round the Never-Never Land of Swinging London does have some nice performances, notably from Calvin Lockhart and Donald Sutherland. Eponymous Genevieve Waite is a dead loss. On the strength of this dubious exercise, Sarne was invited to Hollywood to make the disaster of all time, *Myra Breckinridge*. They should have got themselves a good director and asked *Joanna*'s cameraman Walter Lassally instead; perhaps they didn't realise where the credit for this well-photographed exercise should have gone; 1969. (*c*)

Joan of Arc ✗ ✗
Pretty dull adaptation of Maxwell Anderson's turgid play about the Maid, not helped by wooden casting of Ingrid Bergman in the part, supported by such so-so performers as José Ferrer, J. Carrol Naish, Ward Bond; director Victor Fleming went with the wind; 1948. (*c*)

Joe Macbeth ✗
Interesting idea of adapting Shakespeare's *Macbeth* to Soho quickly runs out of steam, partly due to poor casting (Paul Douglas, Ruth Roman, Sid James, Bonar Colleano) but mostly to direction of Ken Hughes; 1956. (*b/w*)

Joey Boy ✗ ✗ ✗
Hopelessly unfunny comedy of skyving soldiers, involving raft of good TV comics–Harry H. Corbett, Stanley Baxter, Bill Fraser, Reg Varney–that director Frank Launder simply doesn't know how to get going; 1965. (*b/w*)

John Goldfarb Please Come Home ✗ ✗
And stop this tiresome movie. Shirley MacLaine as forerunner to that ghastly *Shirley's World* reporter and Richard Crenna as football coach assigned to improve Middle East king Peter Ustinov's football team. This is J. Lee Thompson's first comedy, made in 1965, and he hasn't made one since–understandably. Notre Dame football team, parodied here, sued; 1964. (*c*)

Johnny Belinda √ √
Sentimental, slushy and successful. Jane Wyman won 1948 Oscar for her deaf-mute in Nova Scotia who, raped, has to fight to keep bastard with help of Dr Lew Ayres. Director Jean Negulesco had wax poured into her ears so that she really couldn't hear. Charles Bickford and Agnes Moorehead won supporting nominations. (*b/w*)

Johnny Concho ✗
Frank Sinatra is the coward who has to find courage; he set it up in 1956 and gave old pal Don McGuire first chance to direct. He also put his current flame Gloria Vanderbilt in star role, but as she was no actress they had a row and she left, to be replaced by Phyllis Kirk. Don't be fooled by his speed on the draw at the end–it's a trick spring holster. (*b/w*)

Johnny Cool ✗
Sixties (1964 to be precise) gangster melo with the characteristic amorality of this period; a Sicilian bandit takes on gangster's identity at his request to become instrument of his revenge. Far-fetched and calculatingly horrid it may be; it still has some nicely-judged moments from director William Asher and a host of old-time names (Elisha Cook, Jim Backus, Mort Sahl, Sammy Davis) backing up Telly Savalas and Henry Silva. (*b/w*)

Johnny Guitar √ √
Outstanding Western for the conflict between Joan Crawford as saloon owner and Mercedes McCambridge as gang-leader. Nicholas Ray picked sides among Hollywood's toughest hombres to make their teams, and the plots ride forcefully over the prairie alongside Dr Freud. McCambridge records that Crawford's hatred of her wasn't reserved for the screen–a group of technicians applauded after McCambridge finished a scene and that maddened Crawford– 'quite understandably' says the lesser star, magnanimously; 1954. (*c*)

Johnny Nobody ✗ ✗
One of that 1960 crop of movies shot over here for cheapness with American stars to sell it back home, and as botched as most of them. Nigel Patrick directed himself, Yvonne Mitchell and Abbey-full of Irish, in Dublin-based murder. Aldo Ray and William Bendix statutory Yanks. (*b/w*)

Johnny Reno ✗
Low-budget Western shows its penny-pinching when R. G. Springsteen uses fights scene and tracking shot of hero Dana Andrews on horseback twice over. He is lawman who alienates community as he tries to prove that murder rap is frame up. Jane Russell, alas, shows her years–she was 45 when this was made in 1966–and other old-timers like Lon Chaney, Tom Drake, Richard Arlen, John Agar don't all wear too well, either. (*c*)

Johnny Tiger ✗
When Robert Taylor arrives to Americanise the Seminole Indians in Florida there's bound to be trouble. Paul Wendkos makes the most of it, with Chad Everett well-cast as younger tribesman who wants to reject parents' values; Geraldine Brooks is doctor attracted to the teacher. All a bit pat, but quite pleasant; 1966. (*c*)

John Paul Jones ✗
Sprawling historical biopic of the founder of the American navy, back in the War of Independence. Doubtless the fervent patriotism went down well in the Middle West in 1959, but it's a bit cold-leaving now. John Farrow can't really control his vast cast, and Robert Stack is inadequate as John Paul (he added Jones later). If you're still watching after nearly two hours, you will be rewarded with a three-minute glimpse of Bette Davis. (*c*)

The Joker is Wild √
Frank Sinatra film fictionalising own myth: the cynical swinger. Charles Vidor directed this true story of Joe E. Lewis, singer forced to turn comedian when Al Capone's sidekick slashed his vocal cords. Good 1957 recreation of roaring twenties. Includes All The Way, Mitzi Gaynor. (*b/w*)

The Jokers √
Time-passing Michael Winner 1967 caper about Oliver Reed and Michael Crawford pinching the Crown Jewels; all a bit obvious, like the supporting cast (Harry Andrews, Michael Hordern, Frank Finlay, *et al*), but amusing enough. (*c*)

A Jolly Bad Fellow √
Leo McKern given his gargoyle's head in *Cruel Hearts and Coronets*-type of black comedy partly written by Robert Hamer just before his death in 1963 and directed by Don Chaffey. Oxford professor finds poison-without-trace and proceeds to dispose of rivals and others he dislikes; Dennis Price, Leonard Rossiter, Janet Munro help to make it wicked fun; 1964. (*b/w*)

The Journey ✗✗
Deborah Kerr, Robert Morley, E. G. Marshall, Jason Robards as travellers held up by Hungarian uprising with Yul Brynner hamming it as nasty Red. Anatole Litvak; 1959. (*c*)

Journey Into Fear √√
Spy melo that was started by Orson Welles in 1942, taken over by Norman Foster, but is still gripping for Welles' performance and that of Joseph Cotten. (*b/w*)

Journey to the Centre of the Earth √√
Boisterous adaptation of Jules Verne novel, directed by Henry Levin with at least one eye on the children, who should enjoy the ludicrous but delightful adventures as James Mason, Pat Boone, Arlene Dahl descend via Iceland and emerge in the Mediterranean; 1960. (*c*)

Journey to Shiloh √
Seven young men set out to fight in the Civil War. Only one remains alive. William Hale makes this more than a Western, if less than a major film; Michael Sarrazin, James Caan are among the seven; 1969. (*c*)

Joy in the Morning ✗
Richard Chamberlain and Yvette

Mimieux unbelievable as young marrieds at college; luckily, Arthur Kennedy's Pop learns to understand them. Alex Segal; 1965. (*c*)

Juarez √ √
Paul Muni as Mexican leader almost having the screen stolen from under his make-up by Brian Aherne as his opponent, the gentle, baffled Maximilian. Other inspired bits of William Dieterle's casting were John Garfield as Mexican gunman and Claude Rains as Napoleon III; 1939. (*b/w*)

Jubal √ √
Tough stuff on the ranch in this adult, gory Western, with Glenn Ford, Ernest Borgnine, Rod Steiger, Noah Beery Jr at each other's throats and women, Valerie French and Felicia Farr; directed moodily by Delmer Daves; 1956. (*c*)

Judgement at Nuremberg √
TV original has been expanded here to 190 minutes (cinema running time). This isn't the Nuremberg Trials of Goering and Co, but a dramatic affair of four judges pleading that all they were doing was obeying the law of their land. Unfortunately, what could have been a sharp political examination has been debased by Stanley Kramer into an entertaining series of histrionics, with Marlene Dietrich, Judy Garland, Montgomery Clift, Maximillian Schell (he won the 1961 Oscar for it), Burt Lancaster all doing their nuts, while Spencer Tracy presides. The critics divided sharply; Gavin Lambert called it an All-Star Concentration Camp Drama, with Special Guest Victim Appearances. Others responded to its pretensions to greatness with homilies as to the vital importance of going to see it 'if you have the slightest concern for the future of civilisation'. Bitingly, Pauline Kael called its dramatisation of large issues 'ludicrous'. Writer Abby Mann, she says, 'accepted his Academy Award, with excruciating humility, not only for himself, but for all intellectuals.' (*b/w*)

Judith × ×
Banal melodrama set in Israel in first days of independence, with ex-nazi planning Syrian attack. Oddly enough, his ex-wife is Jewess Sophia Loren and she obligingly shoots him. Peter Finch unconvincing as Jewish leader; and Daniel Mann directs with verve (and should it be nerve?) in the hope that somehow the literate paucities of the uncinematic Lawrence Durrell script will be concealed; ;1966. (*c*)

The Juggler ×
Kirk Douglas doing his Israeli bit again, this time in a chase after he has clonked a cop; lucky for him, Milly Vitale is waiting on a kibbutz. Edward Dmytryk; 1953. (*b/w*)

Julie × ×
Doris Day being terrorised in 1956 by crazy husband Louis Jourdan. Would you believe that Doris the stewardess could fly the plane herself? Director Andrew Stone seems to expect you to swallow it. (*b/w*)

Julius Caesar √ √
Only one of the many film versions likely to reach your TV screen at the moment is Joseph L. Mankiewicz's 1953 effort with Marlon Brando memorably spouting the Friends, Romans, Countrymen speech and Gielgud's serpentine plotting against (an ill-cast) Louis Calhern's Caesar. The ladies–Greer Garson, Deborah Kerr–are pretty awful, and James Mason has a tough slog as Brutus. (*b/w*)

Jumbo √
Called *Billy Rose's Jumbo* in America. Safe, dull, pretty two-circus picture (son of one spies on another, falls for daughter); Doris Day, frankly too old–

38 in 1962–for this kind of ingénue role; Martha Raye, Jimmy Durante along for the laughs. Charles Walters tries to recapture the innocence of the thirties, inevitably fails. (*c*)

Just For You √
Bing Crosby 1952 musical about his relations with his kids–Natalie Wood, Robert Arthur–and how Jane Wyman, without a touch of jealousy, shows him how to cope; Elliott Nugent directed this fairy-story. (*c*)

Just Like a Woman ×
Little programmer episodically showing what happens to Wendy Craig and Francis Matthews when they split up. She's always reliable, in any part, and makes the best of this rewarding one. Matthews fumbles most of his chances. Director Robert Fuest has managed lots of splendid little touches, but they don't add up to anything like a compulsive film; 1967. (*c*)

Kaleidoscope √√
1966 thriller about successful caper which results in playing cards marked only for Warren Beatty and Susannah York; credibility becomes strained when Clive Revill, as her father, turns out to

Dirk Bogarde in *King and Country*

be Scotland Yard detective who offers a deal. Jack Smight cast small parts splendidly: John Junkin, Yootha Joyce, Eric Porter, plus Jane Birkin, Murray Melvin. (*c*)

Kansas Raiders √
How Audie Murphy got leads like this when there were such fine actors as Brian Donlevy, Tony Curtis, Richard Arlen in it is one of the minor Hollywood mysteries, but here he was as Jesse James, joining up with well-known fellow-dodgers to wreak revenge on the Yankees after the Civil War; 1951 Ray Enright direction. (*c*)

Keeper of the Flame √ √
Katharine Hepburn–Spencer Tracy team job, 1942, has her as widow of distinguished hero, him as muck-raking reporter. Donald Ogden Stewart wrote, George Cukor directed. (*b/w*)

The Kentuckian √
In his ill-starred effort as a director (1955) Burt Lancaster couldn't decide whether he was making a farce, a drama or a movie of significance. Actually, it was just a Western with his own face in front of the camera most of the time. Walter Matthau, Una Merkel, John Carradine didn't get much of a look in.
(*c*)

The Key ×
Blown-up, over-long (134 minutes when in the cinema) wartime triangle drama in which Trevor Howard, inopportunely killed off halfway through, comes back as a ghost to haunt William Holden and Sophia Loren. Oddly enough, Carol Reed directed; 1958. (*c*)

Key Largo √ √
Humphrey Bogart dominates this transposed (by Richard Brooks with director John Huston) Maxwell Anderson play, as gangster taking over Florida hotel in storm; others in closed set include Edward G. Robinson, Lauren Bacall, Claire Trevor, Lionel Barrymore. It's all a bit predictable but never loses its grip; 1948. (*b/w*)

The Keys of the Kingdom √
Epic is the none-too-complimentary word for this big-deal adaptation of A. J. Cronin novel of missionaries in 19th-century China. Young (1944) Gregory Peck and Vincent Price are priests, Thomas Mitchell is crusty old unbeliever; and plot is mostly about bandits. John M. Stahl directed from Mankiewicz–Nunnally Johnson script.
(*b/w*)

Khartoum √ √
A good, solid reconstruction of the relationship and ultimate battle between General Gordon (Charlton Heston, not at all bad, considering he has evidently been cast more for his American box office appeal than proven acting ability) versus the Mahdi (a blacked-up Olivier, superb, as always). Meanwhile, back in London, Ralph Richardson's brilliant Gladstone plays devious political games. If the other parts are disappointingly cast and Basil Dearden's direction borders on the mundane, at least Robert Ardrey's script is literate and the camels look lovely; 1966. (*c*)

A Kid for Two Farthings × ×
Phoney, phoney, phoney East End types in phoney, phoney, phoney yarn about boy who thinks lamb is unicorn; even Carol Reed can't do much with schmaltzy Wolf Mankowitz script and some indulgent performances from Celia Johnson, Diana Dors, David Kossoff, and some sundry boxers; 1956. (*c*)

The Kid From Brooklyn √
Danny Kaye is no Harold Lloyd and it shows when he tries remaking *Milky Way*, the story of milkman who

accidentally becomes boxer; best in Norman Z. Macleod's cast are Lionel Stander, Fay Bainter, Steve Cochran; 1946. (*c*)

Kid Galahad √√
(1) 1937 Bette Davis–Edward G. Robinson boxing story, with Robinson as promoter building up Wayne Morris but losing his gal to him; Humphrey Bogart is rival manager, who also carries a gun. Michael Curtiz. (*b/w*)

Kid Galahad √
(2) 1963 remake had Elvis Presley in the boxer role, Gig Young and Lola Albright excellent pinch-hitters for Edward G. and Bette D., but somewhat soft-centred direction from Phil Karlson loses much of the punch of the original; mind you, what could the poor guy do when Elvis insisted on keeping his singing voice in training? (*c*)

The Kidnappers √
Get your furtive handkerchief ready for this 1953 sob-story about flint-hearted Nova Scotian Duncan Macrae who drives his grandchildren into stealing a baby because he won't let them have a pet. Philip Leacock's direction makes it almost believable. (*b/w*)

Kidnapped ✕
(1) 1938 version of R. L. Stevenson's Scottish adventure of the mid-18th century had the sickening little Freddie Bartholomew as the lad, plus Warner Baxter, C. Aubrey Smith, John Carradine, Nigel Bruce, all playing their usual type-cast roles. Alfred L. Werker directed. (*b/w*)

Kidnapped ✕
(2) 1948 attempt had the interesting Dan O'Herlihy, Jeff Corey but too low a budget to do it justice. William Beaudine. (*b/w*)

Kidnapped √
(3) Michael Caine has recently made a

bit of a fool of himself by doing a version for Delbert Mann; with an accent that comes and goes as the wind changes o'er the heather; 1971. (*c*)

The Killers √√
(1) Robert Siodmak shot this 1946 version of Hemingway's story with tense authority, with Burt Lancaster making his first big success as the ex-pug who won't run away; Edmond O'Brien, Albert Dekker, Sam Levene all outstanding, and Ava Gardner at her most effective. (*b/w*)

The Killers √√
(2) Don Siegel, commissioned to remake it for television in 1964, produced such 'a flippant view of violent death and nihilistic philosophy' that he horrified the sponsors, according to John Baxter's *Hollywood in the Sixties*. So he obtained a cinema release. 'Siegel and actor Lee Marvin crystallised the sixties gangster movie–flip, artificial, hinged on a poetic use of violence . . . To him, corruption and sudden death are so common and essential to modern life they cannot be wrong.' John Cassavetes plays the victim who won't run away–but not from courage. If you can bear the amorality, you will be gripped finding out why. Angie Dickinson excellent, as was Ronald Reagan in his last movie before becoming Governor of California. (*c*)

The Killing √√
Tough, tight, tantalising thriller about racetrack robbery that made 27-year-old Stanley Kubrick's reputation in 1956. Elisha Cook Jr and Sterling Hayden are convincing crooks. (*b/w*)

The Killing of Sister George √
Robert Aldrich, who has commercialised

and coarsened Frank Marcus' funny and fairly tender stage play (with the help of professional scriptwriter Lukas Heller) must be charged with exploiting lesbianism as a box office attraction. Where the original was frank but subtle, this 'opening out' is crude. Only the performances–Beryl Reid is splendid as the actress whose imminent demise in her daily serial makes life such hell for her and results in the slipping away of her girl-friend, marvellously played by Susannah York–lift the film above the level of vulgarity; 1969. (*c*)

Kim √
Kipling's Indian adventure made satisfactorily rousing 1950 actioner for Errol Flynn, subduing the restless natives and fighting the conniving Russians on behalf of the Queen; Dean Stockwell as the young courier; Paul Lukas, Thomas Gomez weigh in with strong portrayals; Victor Saville shot on the actual locations, and it paid off. (*c*)

Kind Hearts and Coronets √√√
Alec Guinness plays the eight victims of Dennis Price's insouciant murderer in Robert Hamer's 1948 stylish comedy. Beautifully achieved in all departments. (*b/w*)

A Kind of Loving √√
Tail-end of Angry Young Man movement now notable for John Schlesinger directorial debut in 1962. When Alan Bates 'has to' marry June Ritchie, can their marriage succeed? Waterhouse and Hall script still works and Thora Hird's mother-in-law is archetypal. (*b/w*)

King and Country √√
Joseph Losey's powerful 1965 piece about the private who walked away from the first world war (Tom Courtenay doing his hurt innocence bit) and the rather more interesting complexities of his defending officer (Dirk Bogarde

grasping the opportunity brilliantly). It's all a bit simplistic and overloaded but none the less moving for this. Losey insists that it isn't a war picture ('there are no scenes of battle, and the only scenes of death and desolation are stills or static'). For him, it's a restatement of his continuous theme, hypocrisy–about people who 'have to face the fact that they have to be rebels in society . . . with all the penalties this entails, or else they have to accept hypocrisy' (*Losey on Losey*, S&W; 1967). (*b/w*)

The King and Four Queens √
Ironic title, as by the time Clark Gable came to churn this one out in 1956 he was no longer King–and this was the sort of squandering of his talent that brought him down. It's supposed to be how he rides into town and charms four bandits' widows into telling him where their late husbands hid the swag. Utterly unbelievable, except for Jo Van Fleet's tough mother. Raoul Walsh. (*c*)

The King and I √√
Yul Brynner and Deborah Kerr are outstandingly good in Rodgers-and-Hammerstein's musical version of *Anna and the King of Siam*, and it transplants beautifully to the screen; Deborah Kerr provides the face for Marni Nixon's top notes. The songs endure: Getting to Know You, Shall We Dance?, Hello Young Lovers; and the movie stands up. Walter Lang; 1956. (*c*)

King Creole √√
Elvis Presley's third film (1958) was his best; he had a strong director, Michael Curtiz; a solid plot from a Harold Robbins novel about musician caught up among New Orlean gangsters; and outstanding actors like Walter Matthau, Paul Stewart, Carolyn Jones, Dolores Hart, to back him up. If he had taken this as the starting-point for a serious career he might really have achieved

something besides adoration and money, but presumably he didn't like to have to be just one of a team. (*b/w*)

King Kong √√√
The unsurpassed classic of 1933, with the lovable, pitiable, oversized gorilla, sexily (but not as much as intended–the censor's scissors were busy) grabbing Fay Wray, buzzed by biplanes on top of the Empire State building. Great stuff, and we're forever in the debt of director Merian C. Cooper. (*b/w*)

King of Kings ✕✕
Or *I Was a Teenage Jesus*. Directors can be miscast just as easily as actors and Nicholas Ray was simply the wrong man to attempt a meaningful, emotion-involving life of Christ. And his casting is ludicrous–Jeffrey Hunter as Jesus, Ron Randell as Lucius the Centurion, Robert Ryan as John the Baptist, Rip Torn as Judas . . . it's like a sick game to choose the least apt Hollywood hams for the divine parts. This 1961 effort had the same title as de Mille's 1924 epic, which was pretty grotesque but preferable to this mess. (*c*)

King of the Khyber Rifles ✕
Not a very entertaining *North-West Frontier* effort with Tyrone Power unconvincing as half-caste British officer (unlikely) who leads the Queen's troops to victory over the troublesome natives; veteran director Henry King had a weak cast to back up his star in 1953–Terry Moore, Michael Rennie, John Justin, Guy Rolfe. (*c*)

King Rat √√
This sets out to be realistic account of life in Changi PoW camp, but has three disadvantages. First is the melodrama that has to be introduced if it has any hope of a mass-market success; second is that emaciated actors are hard to come by (maybe they should have paid

them to starve for a couple of months before shooting?); and third is Bryan Forbes' fatal fascination with heroics. In its favour, however, are remarkable performances from John Mills, Tom Courtenay, Leonard Rossiter; and George Segal acquits himself well in the inevitable bit of casting for that hopeful American appeal; 1965. (*b/w*)

King Richard and the Crusades ✕✕✕
Settle down for a good laugh at this one– in all the wrong places. David Butler has managed to reduce Sir Walter Scott's *The Talisman* to a bad comic-book, and actors Rex Harrison and George Sanders to the level of travesty. Laurence Harvey and Virginia Mayo were there already. It isn't even strong on the fighting; 1954.
(*c*)

Kings Go Forth √
Glib, incredible war drama about Frank Sinatra falling in love with white-passing daughter of black millionaire (what?), who switches to psychotic Tony Curtis. Naturally, they are sent out on mission together. Naturally, it ends happily. The tragedy is that Sinatra was never easier to believe in, and Delmer Daves is such a dab hand that he almost makes it credible for as long as it's on the screen; 1958. (*b/w*)

Kings of the Sun ✕✕
Depressing trivialisation of noble theme –the Mayan civilisation's collapse– minimised by J. Lee Thompson's direction and Yul Brynner's performance into a rather poor Western in slightly changed costumes. A mess; 1964. (*c*)

King Solomon's Mines √√
This 1950 version didn't trust Rider Haggard's plot or its uninspired cast (Stewart Granger, Deborah Kerr, Richard Carlson) and went nap on African spectacle; the result is an eye-catching entertainment, directed jointly

by Compton Bennett and Andrew Marton in a manner old-fashioned even in 1950, but perfectly acceptable. (*c*)

The King's Pirate √
The one about the naval officer (Doug McClure, very UnBritish) who joins the pirates to expose them; a fun-film, with nothing intended to be taken seriously–certainly hope not, anyway–considering what a confused lot of historical hokum it is. Jill St John (oddly clothed), Torin Thatcher, Guy Stockwell enthusiastically respond to Don Weis' cheerful direction; 1967. (*c*)

King's Row √√
One of the big ones of 1941. Sam Wood's wide-sweep of small town at turn-of-the-century, with eager Ann Sheridan, Claude Rains as local doctor, Betty Field his loony daughter, young physician Robert Cummings, the future Governor of California Ronald Reagan in his best-ever part, superbly shot by James Wong Howe. (*b/w*)

The King's Thief ✕
David Niven, George Sanders, Alan Mowbray enjoy themselves in 17th-century hokum about the Cavaliers at the court of Charles II, and carry us and director Robert Z. Leonard along with them. The more wooden Roger Moore, Edmund Purdom, and Ann Blyth don't seem too sure of what's happening, but plunge gamely on; 1955. (*c*)

Kismet √
(1) Lush version of Arabian Nights romp (1944) directed by William Dieterle. Ronald Colman and Marlene Dietrich–she dances with that fabulous body painted gold. (*c*)

Kismet ✕
(2) Remade from the Broadway musical taken from first film, in 1955, it had two smashing songs–Baubles, Bangles and

Beads, Stranger in Paradise–ripped off from Borodin–but despite presence of Monty Woolley and Dolores Gray, precious little else. Vincente Minnelli simply couldn't make Howard Keel or Ann Blyth believable. (*c*)

A Kiss Before Dying ✕✕
Robert Wagner, Mary Astor, Joanne Woodward in dreadful will-he-get-caught directed by Gerd Oswald, from Ira Levin's slightly better book; 1956. (*c*)

Kisses For My President ✕✕✕
Only as recently as 1964 the idea of a woman president was so comic that Curtis Bernhardt could attract quite reasonable players like Polly Bergen (as Madame President), Fred MacMurray as her frustrated husband, and Eli Wallach to act in this comedy laughing at it. Woman's Lib will surely tear down the mast of any station that dares to put this one out again. (*b/w*)

Kissin' Cousins ✕
If one Elvis Presley turns you off (or on) prepare to be doubly repulsed (or excited) when he plays both a clever Air Force officer and a hillbilly determined not to let the Army use his land as testing site; the wrong Presley wins. Gene Nelson directs, sporadically; 1964. (*c*)

The Kissing Bandit ✕✕
1948 was a down year for Frank Sinatra and Laslo Benedek's directorial debut did nothing to halt the rot. He plays a tenderfoot son of Western bandit. Not even a decent song to relieve tedium. (*c*)

Kiss Me Deadly √
Mickey Spillane thriller suited Robert Aldrich's sadistic style and this broody gangster-private eye melo works with strong performances from Ralph

Meeker, Albert Dekker, Paul Stewart, Cloris Leachman; 1955. (*b/w*)

Kiss Me Kate √√
The Spewacks' bouncy version of *The Taming of the Shrew* translated happily to the screen in 1953. None of the leads (Howard Keel, Ann Miller, Kathryn Grayson, Keenan Wynn) has much charisma, although George Sidney manages to project a reasonable facsimile. The music is what counts, however, and all hail to Cole Porter's So in Love, I Hate Men, We Open in Venice, From This Moment On, Always True to You in My Fashion. (*c*)

Kiss Me, Stupid √√
'Tasteless' was the word that greeted this wild Wilder-Diamond collaboration in 1964, though 'gamey' would have been better gastronomic metaphor. Dean Martin sends himself up rotten; Kim Novak ('Why does your husband call you lamb chop?'–'Maybe because I wear paper panties'), Felicia Farr, Ray Walston splendid in satire on small-town America. (*b/w*)

Kiss of Death √
Hard, tight, exciting 1947 thriller about stool-pigeon (Victor Mature, convincing for once) pursued by killer he fingered (Richard Widmark). Solid script by Ben Hecht and Charles Lederer brought to real life by New York locations and Henry Hathaway's taut direction. (*b/w*)

Kiss of Fire ××
So what did you expect with a title like that, art? What you get is Jack Palance and Barbara Rush on the way up from Mexico in the 17th century; she renounces the Spanish throne, yet, to remain in the New World. Joseph M. Newman; 1955. (*c*)

Kiss of the Vampire √
Rather sprightly and entertaining Dracu-
loid thriller, neatly directed by Don Sharp in 1962, with bats playing The Birds and a solid battle between Good and Evil. Clifford Evans is the mysterious Professor Zimmer. (*c*)

Kiss The Blood Off My Hands ×
Despite the come-on in the title, this mish-mash of two accidental murders is never gripping, partly due to Robert Newton's eye-rolling performance, but mostly to Norman Foster's inadequate direction; Burt Lancaster, Joan Fontaine can't rise above it; 1948. (*b/w*)

Kiss Them For Me ×
What was Cary Grant doing backing and appearing in this soapsy 1957 wartime comedy about three naval officers on leave? Maybe Suzy Parker is the answer. Sadly, neither they nor Jayne Mansfield, Ray Walston nor director Stanley Donen could make it come alive. (*c*)

Kiss Tomorrow Goodbye ×
And tonight, too, if you waste your time watching this sub-standard gangster melo with James Cagney parodying himself in 1950 under Gordon Douglas' lacklustre direction; he's supposed to be escaped con who gets married but can't escape from himself; only Luther Adler as lawyer pleases. (*b/w*)

Kit Carson ×
Jon Hall plays title-role, Dana Andrews is cavalry officer, Lynn Bari femme. Made in 1940 by George Seitz when Westerns didn't have to be adult. (*b/w*)

The Kitchen ××
Cut-price attempt to translate Wesker's play to screen in 1961 failed lamentably. In the theatre, it had a vitality partly due to the conjuring-trick of miming all the actions in the restaurant kitchen. Made concrete here, it all sinks like a stone with Carl Mohner, Mary Yeoman. James Hill directed. (*b/w*)

Kitty Foyle √
Ginger Rogers as working-class girl loving rich boy won her 1940 Oscar but looks awfully faded today; from Christopher Morley's novel, directed by Sam Wood. Eduardo Ciannelli does well as waiter. (*b/w*)

The Knack √
Ray Brooks, with it; Michael Crawford, without it; Rita Tushingham, object of it in Dick Lester's much too jazzed-up 1965 version of Ann Jellicoe's play. (*b/w*)

Knights of the Round Table ✕
Only in the fights does Richard Thorpe manage to make this King Arthur stuff even begin to be acceptable; performances are awful, so raspberries for Robert Taylor, Ava Gardner, Mel Ferrer, Anne Crawford, Stanley Baker; 1954. (*c*)

Knock On Any Door √
Humphrey Bogart as defending attorney picks a loser in slum boy; a bit heavy with social significance. Nicholas Ray handles the court scenes well; 1949. (*b/w*)

Knock on Wood ✕
Those who happen to like Danny Kaye will find this 1954 indulgence by Panama and Frank hugely enjoyable; the rest of us will wonder where on earth he ever got his reputation. (*c*)

Konga ✕✕
Dreadful little rip-off from *King Kong*, with Michael Gough as a Dr Frankenstein who injects an ape with serum to make him bigger and bigger. Ends with the usual smashing down of London town by the monster; you've seen it all before, more convincing. Best moment is when the enlarged ape kills off Jess Conrad, who richly deserves it for the performance he has been giving. John Lemont; 1961. (*c*)

Lad: A Dog ✕✕
Soppy sub-Lassie tale, about a collie and a crippled child. Aram Avakian directs lamely; 1961. (*c*)

The Ladies' Man ✕✕
Jerry Lewis-directed comedy about Jerry Lewis working in girls' hostel soon fizzles out; 1961. (*c*)

Ladies Who Do √
Charladies that is. Peggy Mount, Dandy Nichols, Miriam Karlin pick up stock market tips from the waste-paper bins in the offices where they work. Robert Morley, Harry H. Corbett; C. M. Pennington-Richards directed in 1963. (*b/w*)

The Lady Eve √√
Preston Sturges' memorable 1941 comedy of millionaire's son falling for Barbara Stanwyck, daughter of a card-shark. Henry Fonda, Charles Coburn, Eugene Pallette. Poorly remade in 1956 as *The Birds and the Bees*. (*b/w*)

The Lady from Shanghai √√
Few films have had such sharply divided critical comment as this one: ever since Orson Welles directed it in 1948 (way over budget and in total confusion), some have hailed it as a thriller masterpiece, others have dismissed it as incomprehensible, murkily photographed,

Peter Sellers in *The Ladykillers*

badly sound-recorded. All agree, however, that the final scene in the mirror maze is fantastic. Welles cast himself as young, devil-may-care Irishman involved with wicked Rita Hayworth (they were about to divorce in real life) and old pal Everett Sloane. Do not adjust your set, only your ears. (*b/w*)

Lady Godiva of Coventry　　×　×
Considerably less than the bare truth about that famous ride through Coventry. Arthur Lubin's direction doesn't encourage anyone to be a Peeping Tom. Maureen O'Hara, Victor McLaglen; 1955. (*c*)

Lady in a Cage　　√ √
Genuinely frightening 1964 thriller about Olivia de Havilland caught in private lift and menaced by intruders. Director Walter Grauman's use of oppressive heat and the world outside's apathy is particularly effective; as is his working on audience's ambivalence towards helpless but nasty victim. (*b/w*)

Lady in Cement　　√
Frank Sinatra in the follow-up to *Tony Rome* looked a bit tired of it all in 1969, which goes well enough with the world-weary private detective but gives a slightly so-so look to the film. But Gordon Douglas has managed to get some cheerful balancing performances from most of the cast (not from Raquel Welch – nobody could desynthesise her); Martin Gabel, Dan Blocker, Richard Conte particularly. The bed scenes were pretty frank which may mean some cuts for TV. (*c*)

Lady in the Dark　　√
If you're going to make a movie out of a Moss Hart theatre piece, why leave out most of the songs? Particularly when they are by Kurt Weill. Maybe Ginger Rogers objected to their doubtless hidden communist undertones in 1944. The result is that Mitchell Leisen turned

out respectable (i.e. dull) film about dreams, with Ray Milland, Warner Baxter supporting Ginger. (*c*)

The Lady in the Lake   √
Robert Montgomery is director-star in this 1946 version of Raymond Chandler thriller. What makes it particularly interesting is use of camera as hero's eyes. (*b/w*)

The Lady is a Square   × × ×
Utterly appalling Herbert Wilcox–Anna Neagle farrago, with Frankie Vaughan as dude 'butler' with the mission to make her groovy. A 1958 disaster, directed by Herbert Wilcox. (*b/w*)

The Ladykillers   √ √
Funny 1955 charmer from Sandy Mackendrick about inept gang of bank robbers. Alec Guinness masterminds Peter Sellers, Cecil Parker, Herbert Lom, Danny Green. Plus Katie Johnson as dear old lady who thwarts them all. (*b/w*)

Lady L   × ×
$2 million had already been spent when Peter Ustinov arrived to take over script and direction. Sophia Loren married to both aristocrat David Niven and chauffeur Paul Newman simultaneously and happily is an engaging enough idea. But Ustinov admits 'there was no real story there. [It was] too ambitious [and] on the wrong scale'; 1965. (*c*)

The Lady Says No   × ×
So will you to silly story of Joan Caulfield as writer of best-selling anti-man book finding herself not quite so anti dishy magazine photographer David Niven. Frank Ross; 1952. (*b/w*)

The Lady Vanishes   √ √ √
The last great thriller Hitchcock directed in England before first going to Hollywood–made in 1938. Scripted by Launder and Gilliat (who were so furious the reviews didn't mention them that they immediately set up as director-producers on their own) from Ethel Lina White's novel *The Wheel Spins*. It's a version of the famous old fable about a young woman being convinced by a conspiracy that an older one didn't exist (a later version of the original was Terence Fisher's 1950 *So Long at the Fair*). It all takes place on a train with Margaret Lockwood as the girl, Dame May Whitty as the older woman, Michael Redgrave helping the lady in distress, Naunton Wayne and Basil Radford exchanging endearing banalities, Paul Lukas and Cecil Parker. (*b/w*)

The Lady with a Lamp   × ×
Anna Neagle painfully trying to recreate Florence Nightingale with the assistance of director-husband Herbert Wilcox; 1951. (*b/w*)

The Lamp in Assassin Mews   × ×
Mild little English comedy about a couple who are so against progress that they murder a trio of vacuum salesmen and almost do in a 'progressive' councillor. The part in question is played by Francis (Paul Temple) Matthews. As the gentle assassins, Amy Dalton and Ian Fleming have a certain charm, even if Godfrey Gayson's direction doesn't; 1962. (*b/w*)

Lancelot and Guinevere   ×
Lots of swash and buckle in 1962 film directed by and starring Cornel Wilde, with Brian Aherne as an unlikely King Arthur. Wilde was also executive producer: he cast Jean Wallace as Guinevere. (*c*)

Land of the Pharaohs   ×
Jack Hawkins, Joan Collins in spectacular-looking Ancient Egypt epic about, among other things, the building of a pyramid–no wonder Howard Hawks needed all those extras. William Faulkner had an unexpected hand in the script; 1955. (*c*)

Lassie Come Home √
One of best naïve films; story of collie, parted from owners, who makes own way back to them. Fred M. Wilcox directed super 1943 cast: Elizabeth Taylor, Roddy McDowall, Donald Crisp, Edmund Gwenn and male dog Pal playing part of bitch Lassie. (*c*)

Lassie's Great Adventure × ×
Tepid dog-and-boy story that even the smallest children will realise is pretty grim–absurd, unbelievable adventures about being carried off by balloon into the Canadian wilderness. You so often catch the dog and the kid waiting for instructions on how to do what they are supposed to be doing and what to do next that it's positively embarrassing. Director William Beaudine has a lot to answer for; 1964. (*c*)

The Last Angry Man √
Paul Muni, Luther Adler, Godfrey Cambridge in 1959 portrait of slum doctor; director Daniel Mann. (*b/w*)

The Last Blitzkrieg ×
Van Johnson just doesn't convince as German spy in routine Arthur Dreifuss-directed second world war drama; 1959. (*b/w*)

The Last Command ×
The Battle of the Alamo all over again, this time (1955) with Sterling Hayden, Ernest Borgnine, J. Carrol Naish, directed as a spectacle by Frank Lloyd. It does go on; 1955. (*c*)

The Last Frontier ×
Cavalry *v.* Indians, with Our Hero Victor Mature (well, Anne Bancroft and director Anthony Mann's, anyway) *v.* Bancroft's horrible cavalry commander husband, Robert Preston. You can guess who wins in both cases; 1955. (*c*)

The Last Hunt ×
Stewart Granger and Robert Taylor, as nice and nasty buffalo hunters, just aren't competition for the buffaloes who are director Richard Brooks' real stars; 1956. (*c*)

The Last Hurrah √
John Ford enjoying himself directing gift-wrapped fable from Edwin O'Connor novel about political chicanery, with Spencer Tracy marvellous as Boston's mayor fighting his final campaign. Backing him up are the peerless Pat O'Brien, James Gleason, Ed Brophy and Donald Crisp; against him are Basil Rathbone and John Carradine. If all this sounds earlier than 1958 (and the presence of Jane Darwell, Frank McHugh, Wallace Ford certainly adds to the impression), it can all be forgiven for the sheer fun of the thing. Incidentally, Mayor Curley was the real-life original of the Tracy part. (*b/w*)

The Last Mile √
Strong stuff in 1959, this Howard W. Koch drama about Death Row prisoners –including an excellent Mickey Rooney– still grips today. (*b/w*)

The Last of the Badmen ×
Chicago detective agency sends two operatives West to find out who killed one of their men. Director Paul Landres tries hard to make you care, but George Montgomery and so-so cast militate against him; 1957. (*c*)

The Last of the Fast Guns ×
Search for long-lost missing brother by hired gunslinger runs into various predictable obstacles. Gilbert Roland is only semi-name in uninspiring cast. Director, George Sherman; 1958. (*c*)

The Last of the Mohicans √
Exciting stuff, showing that even in 1936 not all Red Indians were baddies. Director, George B. Seitz; Randolph Scott as Hawkeye. (*b/w*)
　　Remade as *Last of the Redskins* in 1947

by George Sherman, with Jon Hall blacking up. (*c*)

The Last Sunset   ×
Kirk Douglas, Rock Hudson, Dorothy Malone, Carol Lynley, Joseph Cotten all look as fed up with this predictable Robert Aldrich-directed Western about a round-up as you'll probably feel. Let's hope the cattle enjoyed themselves in 1961. (*c*)

The Last Time I Saw Archie   × ×
Dragnet's Jack Webb produces, directs and co-stars, as sidekick to con-man Robert Mitchum, in unfunny Army comedy; 1961. (*b/w*)

The Last Time I Saw Paris   × ×
Genuinely touching Scott Fitzgerald short story, *Babylon Revisited*, blown up into vulgar flash-backing melodrama about Van Johnson and Elizabeth Taylor destroying each other. Director and co-writer Richard Brooks must shoulder a lot of the blame; 1954. (*c*)

Last Train from Gun Hill   √
In spite of local opposition, marshal Kirk Douglas is determined to get on it–with the prisoner he's taken. If he seems particularly anxious to see justice done, that's because his wife was their victim. Anthony Quinn, Carolyn Jones, Brad Dexter and lots of tense moments in exciting 1959 John Sturges Western. (*c*)

The Last Voyage   √
Ageing liner sinks–will George Sanders, Dorothy Malone, Robert Stack, Edmond O'Brien go down too? Writer-director Andrew Stone usually makes exciting movies and this is one of them; 1960. (*c*)

The Last Wagon   √
Superior Western with good baddie Richard Widmark, who's on a murder charge, reluctantly relied upon by pioneers and Felicia Farr to lead them through hostile injun territory. Delmer Daves directed; 1956. (*c*)

The Last Woman on Earth   × ×
The only remote interest this tiresome piece of 1961 sci-fi has is that it was directed by Roger Corman. Otherwise, its slender little plot–about a threesome who go skin-diving in Puerto Rico and find that the world has been depopulated while they were swimming–is below notice as well as sea-level. (*c*)

The Las Vegas Story   ×
Jane Russell, Victor Mature, Hoagy Carmichael, Vincent Price in routine murder melo. Robert Stevenson; 1952.
(*b/w*)

The Late George Apley   √
Hard to know if this lush portrait of Boston posh families squabbling over Romeo and Juliet story is meant to be satire or not. John P. Marquand's novel made splendid vehicle for Ronald Colman in 1946, aided by Joseph L. Mankiewicz's sympathetic direction.
(*b/w*)

Latin Lovers   ×
Is dashing Brazilian Ricardo Montalban after heiress Lana Turner's money? Wealthy John Lund certainly isn't, but then he's not as good-looking. Director Mervyn LeRoy didn't make us care too much either way in 1953. (*c*)

Laughter in Paradise   √
A good laugh, too, not so much for Audrey Hepburn's first noticeable screen appearance as for Alastair Sim, Fay Compton, George Cole, Bea Campbell going through some wild hoops to earn inheritance. Mario Zampi directed; 1951.
(*b/w*)

Laughter in the Dark   √ √
Nabokov's 1933 novel trendily made over in 1969 by Tony Richardson with an Edward Bond script. In the book

Nabokov describes the plot as a rich, respectable, happy man (Nicol Williamson) who one day 'abandoned his wife for the sake of a youthful mistress; he loved; was not loved; and his life ended in disaster.' It has a bitter, haunting last half-hour when Williamson, blind now, imagines himself alone with mistress Anna Karina but her lover, Jean-Claude Drouot is there. (*c*)

Laura   √√
Otto Preminger was only allowed to direct this highly successful thriller after Darryl F. Zanuck took big-shot director Rouben Mamoulian off it. Gene Tierney plays title role and Dana Andrews the detective who's in love with her before they even meet; 1944. (*b/w*)

The Lavender Hill Mob   √√
Tibby Clarke won Oscar for story and screenplay, quite a feat for an English movie in 1952. But it's so rich and comic that it couldn't be denied. Enjoy Alec Guinness as gold thief aided by Stanley Holloway, Sid James, Alfie Bass. Can you spot Audrey Hepburn? Director, Charles Crichton. (*b/w*)

The Law and Jake Wade   √
Not one of John Sturges' best, but it has Robert Taylor as outlaw-turned-lawman and Richard Widmark as old friend-turned-foe on buried treasure hunt; and some exciting action should hold your interest; 1958. (*c*)

Law and Order   √
This title became slogan for its star, Ronald Reagan, when he ran for Governor of California years after it was made in 1953. He plays retiring marshal urged to pin badge back on to run Preston Foster out of town. Nathan Juran directed. (*c*)

A Lawless Street   ✕
Routine Randolph Scott cleaning-up-the-town Western directed in 1955 by Joseph H. Lewis. Angela Lansbury plays euphemistic dance-hall hostess. (*c*)

Law of the Lawless   ✕
Strongly-cast, poorly-scripted Western that disappointingly stays indoors almost the whole time. Judge Dale Robertson tries old pal John Agar for murder, under pressure from Agar's pa, Barton MacLane; also threatens gun-duel with Bruce Cabot. Sheriff, William Bendix, and Yvonne de Carlo recreate their familiar roles. Director William F. Claxton might have made something of the ingredients, but didn't, in 1964. (*c*)

Lawrence of Arabia   √√√
Superbly photographed (Freddie Young) pageant of the life of that most enigmatic of Englishmen. Robert Bolt's literate screenplay simplifies him and perhaps takes too straightforward a line. But giving the best performances of their careers, Peter O'Toole and Omar Sharif make Lawrence and Sherif Ali convincing dramatic, if not always human, personalities. Three-and-a-half hours is a long time to sit through a movie, but this one justifies its length. Won Best Picture, Best Director (David Lean), and five other Oscars; 1962. (*c*)

The League of Gentlemen   √
Snob caper that comes off. And then? Then they have to be caught, and that's a bore. Jack Hawkins, Nigel Patrick, Richard Attenborough make gentlemanly gentlemen; Bryan Forbes who wrote it plays one of the ex-officers; Mrs Bryan Forbes appears. Basil Dearden directed competently enough; 1960. (*b/w*)

Lease of Life   √
Robert Donat's penultimate film (1954) was painful drama of a vicar with only a short time to live. Charles Frend directed conscientiously, bringing out the conflicts of integrity. (*c*)

The Leather Boys √
Drama about a marriage (Rita Tushingham and Colin Campbell) that doesn't work out and the boy's gradual realisation that he has drifted into a homosexual affair (with Dudley Sutton). It would be fascinating to know what happened after the ending–which is better than a pat tying-up of all the ends, but is still frustrating. Sidney J. Furie directed this in 1963 with just a bit too much flashiness, but altogether it's a creditable job and never lets up. (*b/w*)

The Leather Saint × × ×
Awful little programmer about priest (John Derek) turned boxer to raise money for a polio hospital. Paul Douglas and Cesar Romero are embarrassed participants in this inept yarn, weakly directed by Alvin Ganzer; 1956. (*b/w*)

Leave Her to Heaven √
Highly-coloured drama of wife so possessive that she commits murder to hold on to her husband. Based on Ben Ames Williams' best-seller and well-enough thought of to win Leon Shamroy the 1945 Oscar for photography. John M. Stahl adrenalised cast of good second-raters – Gene Tierney as the wife, Cornel Wilde, Jeanne Crain, Vincent Price, Ray Collins, Gene Lockhart. (*c*)

The Left-Handed Gun √ √
This 1958 precursor of *Bonnie and Clyde* contains much of director Arthur Penn's own childhood, respect for violence and a super performance by Paul Newman as the sinistral Billy the Kid. (*b/w*)

The Left Hand of God ×
Humphrey Bogart as a priest? Not quite; only a flyer pretending to be one after having been stranded in China and serving as adviser to a bizarrely-made-up Lee J. Cobb. He fools Gene Tierney, though, who gets sexy, guilty feelings about fancying a man of God, and E. G. Marshall (tricked up not as Chinaman, but as missionary) and wife Agnes Moorehead (also made up, just too much so). Edward Dmytryk was responsible for all this make-up and the rather stilted progress of the melodrama, in 1955. (*c*)

Left, Right and Centre × ×
Political comedy so good-natured as to be positively non-existent. Launder and Gilliat obviously hoped to have it both ways and eat it, too, in 1959, and go off on an irrelevant joke about stately homes that's boring in its obviousness and embarrassing in its playing. Alastair Sim, Ian Carmichael, even Richard Wattis seem ill-at-ease. (*b/w*)

The Legend of Lylah Clare × ×
Would you believe that Kim Novak looks just like the tragically dead wife of Peter Finch? And that she was a film star whose story would make a Great Movie? And that Finch decides to remake her story with Novak in the part and that he falls in love with her all over again and it all happens tragically all over again and so on and so on? Robert Aldrich hoped you would in 1968. Maybe you will again, just like before. . . . (*c*)

Legend of the Lost × ×
Right old load of rubbish with John Wayne, Rossano Brazzi in desert duel over the love of Sophia Loren, on the way to rediscover an archeological treasure. Henry Hathaway fools nobody with this one; 1957. (*c*)

The Lemon Drop Kid √
Lots of laughs, with Bob Hope as race-track tout in gangster's debt. Sidney Lanfield; 1951. (*c*)

The Leopard Man √
Dressed as a leopard, somebody is terrorising Mexican village, killing off the inhabitants. Then a real leopard

escapes from a circus. Director Jacques Tourneur, good with horror, made this one pretty scary in 1943. Among those scared: Margo, Dennis O'Keefe. (*b/w*)

Les Girls ×
Kay Kendall as one of three flash-backing show girls is by far the best thing about this 1957 George Cukor-directed musical. Otherwise Cole Porter tunes mostly disappoint, as do Gene Kelly, Mitzi Gaynor and dance numbers. (*c*)

Les Misérables √
Ninth film version of Victor Hugo's classic with, this time, Michael Rennie as the escaping prisoner, Valjean, and Robert Newton as his dogged pursuer. Lewis Milestone did a competent enough job in 1952, it couldn't compare with Richard Boleslawski's 1935 version with Fredric March and Charles Laughton. (*b/w*)

Let No Man Write My Epitaph ×
Bobby Darin makes a poor job of fighting for existence in urban jungle with the help and hindrance of drunk Burl Ives, addict mum Shelley Winters, pusher Ricardo Montalban, Jean Seberg, Ella Fitzgerald. Britain's Philip Leacock was out of his milieu and his element in 1960. (*b/w*)

Let's Dance ×
Fred Astaire's dancing doesn't really make up for boring plot about ex-partner Betty Hutton's tug-of-war with society in-laws over her son. Norman Z. McLeod; 1950. (*c*)

Let's Do It Again ×
Blurtingly honest title for 1953 remake of 1937's *The Awful Truth*, with Ray Milland in Cary Grant's part as wandering husband, Jane Wyman in Irene Dunne's as wife who invents an affair that lands them in the divorce court. Alexander Hall added some

songs to make it a musical, but nothing else–like wit, lightness or charm. (*c*)

Let's Get Married × ×
Is a pregnant and abandoned woman marrying her doctor funny? Ken Taylor's script assumes it is, and director Peter Graham Scott throws in as much slapstick as he can devise to confirm this dubious assumption. As Anthony Newley and Anne Aubrey play the main parts, it becomes even less funny, and the result is a centrepiece of unsurpassing non-jokery, flecked with comic bits from Bernie Winters, James Booth, Lionel Jeffries and John le Mesurier; 1960. (*b/w*)

Let's Make It Legal ×
Mild comedy about middle-aged couple (Claudette Colbert, Macdonald Carey) planning 'friendly' divorce after twenty years of marriage. Zachary Scott awful; Marilyn Monroe lovely; Robert Wagner supports nicely; Richard Sale directs; 1951. (*b/w*)

Let's Make Love ×
Marilyn Monroe's penultimate film before final *The Misfits* was a pretty sad affair about a millionaire posing as just another hoofer to make Marilyn fall in love with him. Yves Montand looks pretty embarrassed about his part; not so Frankie Vaughan as his singing rival, who should have been. Only George Cukor's expert and tactful direction kept it going, although Marilyn's challenge to Mary Martin in singing My Heart Belongs to Daddy is spirited and delightful; 1960. (*c*)

The Letter √
Maugham's murderess provided Bette Davis with splendid opportunity for histrionics in 1940, though William Wyler kept her in check. (*b/w*)

Letter from an Unknown Woman √
Joan Fontaine continues to love Louis

Jourdan, the pianist she is infatuated with, tho' the years roll on, like this nostalgic sentimental movie softly, sweetly directed by Max Ophuls in 1948. (*b/w*)

A Letter To Three Wives √ √
'You see, girls, I've run off with one of your husbands'–but which? Ann Sothern, Linda Darnell, Jeanne Crain flashback worriedly; is it Kirk Douglas? Paul Douglas? Jeffrey Lynn? Joseph L. Mankiewicz won both script and director Oscars in 1949; a little bit excessive in the year of *Bicycle Thieves*? (*b/w*)

Libel ×
Stuffy courtroom drama, with upper class Dirk Bogarde–accused of murder and impersonation–suing for libel. Wife Olivia de Havilland has doubts about his identity–which isn't really surprising, as director Anthony Asquith has Bogarde playing three roles. Old-fashioned, even for 1959. (*b/w*)

The Life and Death of Colonel Blimp √
'By Gad, sir, Goebbels was right! If you want to turn a villain into a hero, show him in love.' That's what's happened to Low's selfish, stupid, pompous old fool with the droopy white moustache. In Powell-and-Pressburger's 1943 white-wash job he became loving (Deborah Kerr in three disguises) and lovable (Roger Livesey, all soft-centre and funny foibles). But Anton Walbrook's sympathetic German friend was a welcome surprise during the war. (*c*)

Life at the Top √
Lacks the bite of *Room at the Top*, of which it's ten-years-after sequel in 1965. Clinches are franker, however. Laurence Harvey is Man; Jean Simmons Mrs; Honor Blackman is bit on the side. Ted Kotcheff directed Mordecai Richler's script. (*b/w*)

Lifeboat √ √
Hitchcock's wartime (1943) drama entirely taking place in a lifeboat should be particularly good on television, as he shot it mostly in close- and semi-close-up. Tallulah Bankhead, John Hodiak, William Bendix and five other torpedoed passengers are joined by nazi sailor Walter Slezak. As thriller progresses the characters of each emerge. Hitch intended it to be allegory of disparate Allies having to pull together to defeat singleminded Germans, but John Steinbeck's script wasn't good enough for him. He brought in another couple of writers, ended up rewriting it himself. His own statutary appearance was hard to arrange: he had intended to be dead body floating by but was afraid he'd sink; finally he ingeniously put himself as the before-and-after figure in a newspaper ad for Reduco. (*b/w*)

Life for Ruth √
Strong, didactic, over-simplified 1962 drama about a husband (Michael Craig) with fundamentalist religious beliefs, who won't let his wife (Janet Munro) give permission for a blood transfusion for their little daughter. She dies and Dr Patrick McGoohan makes a national scandal of it. Basil Dearden directs it all. (*b/w*)

Life in Emergency Ward Ten × × ×
Dreadful little rip-off from *Emergency Ward Ten* deserves a special place in Wardour Street's Chamber of Horrors as one of the first films to be made from a television series–in 1959. Otherwise, the worst of the British film industry has been grafted on to the worst of television. Michael Craig and Wilfrid Hyde White were added to the regular cast but do not improve it. The script was even more exposed at full length; Robert Day directs. (*b/w*)

A Life in the Balance √
Boy stalks murderous Lee Marvin across

Mexico City in weak adaptation of Georges Simenon yarn. Anne Bancroft and colourful locations are the best director Harry Horner could come up with in 1954. (*b/w*)

Life is a Circus × ×
Unfortunately it isn't despite the Crazy Gang's attempts to prove otherwise. They find Aladdin's lamp and summon the genie to keep their circus going. (Why? Why not just ask for a million each and to hell with it?) Val Guest wrote and directed, but he has doubtless forgotten it by now. Before it all gets junked (the sooner the better) someone should transfer the scene where Flanagan and Allen sing Underneath the Arches to the National Film Archives; 1960. (*b/w*)

The Life of Emile Zola √
Slow, dated, cliché-ridden, but still powerful story of the Dreyfus Affair, but miscalled because Paul Muni, Warner Brothers' contract star, insisted on his role always being the title. Despite Muni's screen-hogging, Joseph Schildkraut manages to edge him off when it comes to real acting, as the persecuted Jewish officer. William Dieterle's flat 1937 direction serves. (*b/w*)

A Life Of Her Own ×
A rare miss for George Cukor. Will fashion model Lana Turner return her rich boyfriend to his crippled wife? This was 1950, remember. Not even Ray Milland, Tom Ewell, Louis Calhern can save this slush. (*b/w*)

Life With Father √
William Powell is tyrannical father, Irene Dunne mother, in Michael Curtiz lavish period comedy, based on Clarence Day best-seller. Particularly good music score by Max Steiner; 1947. (*c*)

Light in the Piazza × ×
What Mama (Olivia de Havilland—not really up to the role) does when daughter

(Yvette Mimieux, pleasant) attracts eligible bachelor (Italianate George Hamilton) in Florence is complicated by the fact that the girl is retarded mentally—should Mama point it out? Guy Green confuses the whole issue by letting the whole cast behave as if it's mentally retarded, though what does it matter as long as they're happy? 1962. (*c*)

The Light Touch √
An innocent Pier Angeli exerting good influence over art thief Stewart Granger isn't as sickly as it sounds under director Richard Brooks' light touch; and Italian locations, and George Sanders' sophisticated villain, are lovely; 1951. (*b/w*)

Li'l Abner √
Energetic visualisation of Al Capp's comic-strip land of Dogpatch hillbillies had 1959 political overtones. Mel Frank directed from Broadway musical. Earlier, in 1940, Granville Owen had made an experimental movie with masked characters attempting to match the strip. But the Frank attempt was only a near-miss, with Stubby Kaye and Julie Newmar remarkably close to the best-ever strip. (*c*)

Lilacs in the Spring × ×
Anna Neagle plays four roles in this preposterous tale—Queen Victoria, Nell Gwynn, an ENSA performer and her own mother—and Errol Flynn's her father who marries her—get it? It's a right old mish-mash with amnesia and sentimentality jostling for first place in Herbert Wilcox's old-fashioned (it was, alarmingly, made as recently as 1954) direction. (*c*)

Lili √
Sentimental tale of Leslie Caron being wooed by Mel Ferrer through his puppets. Includes song Hi-Lili, Hi-Lo and should keep little girls of all ages glued to the set. Charles Walters; 1953. (*c*)

Lilies of the Field ✕
You can't knock religion or black men (not if they're Sidney Poitier anyway) so everyone cheered this sickly, sentimental tale of handyman Poitier building nuns a chapel in 1963. Ralph Nelson directed; Poitier won an Oscar. (*b/w*)

Lilith √
The last film Robert Rossen made before his death, and 'his noblest and most lyrical failure' says Andrew Sarris. Warren Beatty is therapist in love with mental patient Jean Seberg. Peter Fonda, Gene Hackman support ably; 1964. (*b/w*)

Limelight √
Appallingly sentimental yarn of ageing comedian who makes a comeback thanks to the devotion of the ballet-dancing protegée he once saved from suicide. However, as Charlie Chaplin plays the main part and made it himself in 1952 it has an interest far beyond its dreadfully banal story. Claire Bloom is the dancer and there are appearances for various members of the Chaplin family, including son Sydney as Bloom's *inamorate*. The tune has outlived the film. (*b/w*)

The Line-Up √
Tough, tight little thriller directed by cult-figure Don Siegel in 1958 about drug-pusher (Eli Wallach) holding two women hostages. (*b/w*)

The Lion ✕
Is Pamela Franklin taming her pet lion? Or is it turning her savage? Do we care? William Holden has to. Jack Cardiff directed; 1962. (*c*)

The Lion in Winter √ √
Winning 1968 Oscars for Katharine Hepburn, composer John Barry and writer James Goldman, this cross between a costume *Peyton Place* and *Who's Afraid of Virginia Woolf?*, set in the combined English and French courts of the 12th century, is faultlessly guided by Anthony Harvey. He welds the team of Hepburn, Peter O'Toole, Jane Merrow, John Castle, Timothy Dalton, Anthony Hopkins, Nigel Stock and Nigel Terry into a single ensemble of great power. The immediate question is who shall succeed Henry II (O'Toole). When he vomits at a revelation in the plot, Hepburn turns to the audience and asks: 'What family doesn't have its ups and downs?' It takes a self-confident film to say that–and to talk as much as this one does–and a very good one to get away with it. (*c*)

The Liquidator ✕
This came at tail-end of James Bond boom (1966) and attempts twist with hero (Rod Taylor) as inefficient bumbler. Trevor Howard and Wilfrid Hyde White do their best but director Jack Cardiff can't thrill us much. No wonder projected sequels never happened. (*c*)

Lisa √
Excellent supports–Donald Pleasence, Harry Andrews, Hugh Griffith, Leo McKern, Robert Stephens–exotic locations, and some nail-biting moments as Stephen Boyd helps Jewish refugee Dolores Hart escape to Israel. Philip Dunne; 1962. (*c*)

Lisbon √
Ray Milland, Claude Rains, Maureen O'Hara and complicated kidnap plot are all upstaged by the scenery. Ray Milland directs as well; 1956. (*c*)

The List of Adrian Messenger ✕
Self-indulgent 1963 Irish extravaganza by John Huston, supposedly a murder mystery, most notable for appearances by heavily disguised Tony Curtis, Kirk Douglas, Burt Lancaster, Frank Sinatra, Robert Mitchum (disguised?), with George C. Scott in mainline part. (*b/w*)

Little Boy Lost ✕
Bing Crosby in France trying to find the son he last saw as baby isn't quite as sloppy as it sounds. George Seaton; 1953. (*b/w*)

The Little Hut ✕
Ava Gardner, Stewart Granger and David Niven enjoy themselves in adaptation of boulevard play about castaway triangle on a desert island, more daring than most movies in 1957, if less than most today. Director, Mark Robson. (*c*)

Little Nellie Kelly √
Little Judy Garland (18 in 1940) reconciling stubborn Irish policeman father George Murphy and grandfather Charles Winniger in St Patrick's Day parade. It's a great film for the Irish. The song Singin' in the Rain features again (it was first heard in Hollywood revue of 1929). Director, Norman Taurog. (*b/w*)

The Little Ones √
Films about sweet little children usually tend to get very mawkish. This one, written and directed by Jim O'Connolly, is an exception. A low-budget effort, it's about a search for a father; 1965. (*b/w*)

Little Women √ √
(1) 1933 version by George Cukor of Louisa May Alcott favourite had Katharine Hepburn, Joan Bennett, Paul Lukas, Frances Dee, Edna May Oliver. (*b/w*)

Little Women √
(2) 1949 remake by Mervyn LeRoy starred Elizabeth Taylor, June Allyson, Margaret O'Brien, Janet Leigh, Mary Astor. (*c*)

Live It Up ✕ ✕
In his humble days of 1963, David Hemmings starred in this 18-day pop quickie that was better than it deserved to be, thanks mainly to Lyn Fairhurst's observant script and Lance Comfort's experienced direction. He plays one of four messenger boys who form a pop-group and finally Make It. All very naïve and silly now, but it retains a certain museum interest. (*b/w*)

The Lively Set ✕ ✕
Motor racing-cum-teenager-fun pic that isn't much fun. Jack Arnold puts some cars, James Darren and Pamela Tiffin through their paces. Mostly, the cars work; 1965. (*c*)

Live Now, Pay Later √ √
The world of hire-purchase, celebrated in a Jack Trevor Story script that lets the nasties win. Nice Liz Fraser can't stand the replacement grind and ends up under a car. But Ian Hendry is mesmerically good as the villain-hero, conning the housewives, and takes Jay Lewis' otherwise clumsily-directed drama up to quite dizzy heights; 1962. (*b/w*)

The Lives of a Bengal Lancer √
Made in 1935 by Henry Hathaway during a period when Hollywood tried, with awed respect, to reflect a sun already setting on the British Empire. 19th-century India has Gary Cooper, Franchot Tone and C. Aubrey Smith, some ludicrous dialogue, terrific narrative-tug and a marvellous snake-charming sequence. (*b/w*)

Living It Up ✕
Jerry Lewis as suspected radiation victim, Dean Martin as doctor, Janet Leigh as journalist covering the story in so-so Norman Taurog 1954 remake of *Nothing Sacred*. (*c*)

Lock Up Your Daughters ✕ ✕
And don't bother to put the set on, it isn't worth the effort. This mish-mash of *Rape Upon Rape* and *The Relapse* relies on Restoration naughtiness which quickly palls. The combination of heavy-

handed director Peter Coe and heavy-footed lead Christopher Plummer produces a deadening effect. Fenella Fielding, Susannah York, Georgia Brown, Peter Bayliss and Peter Bull lighten the gloom for a moment or two, but it sorely misses the music that it had in the Mermaid's theatrical revival; 1969. (*c*)

The Lodger ✗
Only version likely to find its way to your home screen is John Brahm's 1944 version with the dreadful Merle Oberon not quite balanced by the gorgeous Laird Cregar, George Sanders and Cedric Hardwicke. Hitchcock's 1926 simpler effort about the lodger who is suspected of being Jack the Ripper (the first real Hitchcock film) and Maurice Elvey's 1932 version would seem just too remote now. (*b/w*)

Lolita √
Despite Vladimir Nabokov's credit as adaptor of his own novel, this is only remotely the book of the film. By making the nymphet appear between 15 and 17, it destroyed the essence of the affair between a 12-year-old and the near-psychopathic obsessional. Despite this and some heavy overacting by Shelley Winters as Humbert Humbert's wife and a performance by Peter Sellers as Quilty which shows him to be more mimic than actor, the film remains fascinating. James Mason's Humbert is remarkably effective despite his physical unsuitability for the part, and Sue Lyon does all that is required of her except look right. Above all, Stanley Kubrick's firm direction keeps a firm grip and makes for an entertaining if not exciting view; 1962. (*b/w*)

The Loneliness of the Long Distance Runner √
Faultless performance from hungry-looking Borstal boy Tom Courtenay out to humble superior upper-class Governor Michael Redgrave. Over-directed in 1962 by Tony Richardson but good tight script from Alan Sillitoe. Strong support from James Bolam, James Fox. (*b/w*)

Lonely Are The Brave √
Interesting contemporary (1962) David Miller-directed Western with Kirk Douglas excellent (for once) as old-time cowboy on the run from sheriff Walter Matthau, great as always. (*b/w*)

Lonelyhearts ✗
Couldn't help but fail to have the bite and surrealism of Nathanael West's novel about a newspaper advice columnist (Montgomery Clift). It would need a director of genius; this version–with Robert Ryan, Myrna Loy, Dolores Hart –got Vincent J. Donehue instead; 1959. (*b/w*)

Lone Star √
While Texas fights for independence, there's a routine good guy *v.* bad guy Western scene going on. But routine doesn't matter quite so much when they're Clark Gable and Broderick Crawford; Ava Gardner, who they're feudin' about, and Lionel Barrymore, Beulah Bondi, Ed Begley are around. Don't trust the history–they got it all wrong. Vincent Sherman; 1952. (*b/w*)

The Long and the Short and the Tall √
Broke new ground in 1961 by treating second world war as hell. Leslie Norman's slightly stagey version misses presence of Peter O'Toole from original play; he's replaced by bigger box office name (then!) of Laurence Harvey. (*b/w*)

The Long Arm ✗
How the police painstakingly trace the thief who robbed a Covent Garden safe is shown in meticulous detail, but since 1956 we have seen too many *Softly-Softlys* and similar reconstructions for us to feel much interest in this bloodless

caper. Jack Hawkins plays his Detective-Supt. with his usual competence and Charles Frend's direction cannot be faulted, but there's a mechanical air about this end-of-Ealing drama. (*b/w*)

The Long Day's Dying   ×
Charles Wood's intelligent, probing script about war in the persons of three soldiers who don't know quite what to do with a prisoner they have captured gets a terrible let-down from Peter Collinson's insensitive, modish direction. David Hemmings, Tom Bell and Tony Beckley do their best but seem to be fighting the director; 1968. (*c*)

Long Day's Journey Into Night   √
Eugene O'Neill's brooding play about his own family, revealing, in a setting of claustrophobic pre-first world war anti-macassars, the reasons why Mum was a morphine addict, Dad compulsively mean, the elder son a drunk and the younger one a morbid poet. Katharine Hepburn, Ralph Richardson, Jason Robards and Dean Stockwell, respectively, do these characters magnificently, and Sidney Lumet's direction doesn't feel trapped in close-up or within the play's one-room set; 1964. (*b/w*)

The Longest Day   √
D-Day, mostly from the American point of view (but not forgetting that the Germans were there, too) made as super-budget, super-roadshow drama which seems only partly accurate and heartless, not so say pointless. Among those present: John Wayne, Robert Mitchum, Sal Mineo, Henry Fonda, Robert Ryan, Robert Wagner, Edmond O'Brien, Rod Steiger, Mel Ferrer (Americans); Curt Jurgens, Peter van Eyck, Gerd Froebe (Germans); Richard Burton, Richard Todd, Kenneth More, Sean Connery (British); Bourvil, Jean-Louis Barrault, Christian Marquand, Arletty (French). Directors: Bernhard Wicki, Ken Annakin, Andrew Marton, and Darry F. Zanuck; 1962. (*b/w*)

The Long Gray Line   √
Sentimental but affectionate 1955 John Ford tribute to real-life West Point coach, played by Tyrone Power; Maureen O'Hara is his wife. (*c*)

The Long Haul   ××
A long drag with truck-driver Victor Mature, a Yank in Liverpool, falling for glamorous (1957) Diana Dors, moll of crook Patrick Allen, and being forced to work for them. Directed by Ken Hughes. (*b/w*)

The Long Hot Summer   √
Brooding drama about outsider's effect on neurotic Southern family, based on William Faulkner stories. Director Martin Ritt's splendid cast–Paul Newman, Orson Welles, Joanne Woodward, Lee Remick, Angela Lansbury, Anthony Franciosa–gave it conviction in 1958. (*c*)

Long John Silver   √
Broad, humorous performance from piratical Robert Newton still buccaneering his way after Flint's gold. He meets up again with Jim 'Awkins from *Treasure Island* days, and with lots of swash and buckle they're off again. Byron Haskin; 1954. (*c*)

The Long, Long Trailer   √
Slick (under Vincente Minnelli's direction) vehicle for Lucille Ball and Desi Arnaz as couple honeymooning in caravan; 1954. (*c*)

The Long Night   ××
Weak remake of *Le Jour se Lève* reset from Paris to Pittsburgh had particularly poor performances from Vincent Price and Barbara Bel Geddes, as seducer and seduced. Henry Fonda looked charmingly tortured as the hunted murderer holed up in a tenement, but Anatole

Litvak's moody direction simply looked cheap against Marcel Carné's original; 1947. (*b/w*)

The Long Ride Home   √
Roger Corman's name was dropped from the credits and Phil Karlson got his name on as director in 1968, but it was Corman who set up and shot most of this end-of-the-Civil-War tragedy as Glenn Ford is forced to pursue George Hamilton and some escaping Confed soldiers who have kidnapped his girl, Inger Stevens. Exciting, wide-ranging stuff. (*c*)

The Long Ships   ×
Vikings (Richard Widmark, etc.) *v.* Moors (Sidney Poitier *et al.*) in Jack Cardiff-directed costume epic. Well, it makes a change from cowboys *v.* injuns, but that's not enough to recommend it; 1964. (*c*)

The Long Voyage Home   √
Visually ravishing (thanks to Gregg Toland's stunning photography) this knitting-together of four Eugene O'Neill playlets about life at sea isn't altogether happy in its cast (Ian Hunter stiff; London characters absurd), but contains so many memorable moments that you forgive John Ford's lapses of taste and mood. John Wayne, Thomas Mitchell come off best among the leaky tramp steamer's crew; 1940. (*b/w*)

The Long Wait   × ×
And nothing to show at the end of it, so don't waste your time with this slow Micky Spillane yarn about amnesiac Anthony Quinn falsely accused of murder. Who cares? Director Victor Saville certainly didn't seem to in 1954. (*b/w*)

Look Back in Anger   √ √
Richard Burton made it possible for Tony Richardson and John Osborne to transfer their Royal Court success to the screen in 1959 by agreeing to play Jimmy Porter. He was great, and the film is more than an accurate record of the play. Yet, as almost everything Richardson does, there was an unsatisfactory edge to it that comes from the inability to project technically the height of his pretentious ambitions. (*b/w*)

Look for the Silver Lining   × ×
Conventional showbiz biomusical (1949) about Marilyn Miller, Broadway star, hazily interpreted by June Haver and directed by David Butler. (*c*)

Looking for Love   × × ×
Stupid little sub-musical with Connie Francis thinking she's in love with Jim Hutton when really she's in love with Joby Baker. You know the sort of thing. Don Weis churned it out for teenage morons in 1964. (*c*)

Lord Jim   ×
Disastrous big-scale attempt to give Conrad's novel wide-screen life. Between them, director Richard Brooks and self-conscious star Peter O'Toole have destroyed the strength and poetry and mystery of the sailor ashamed of his cowardice who finds regeneration in the jungle. Instead, we are offered a sprawling spectacle, with Big Names doing their cameo bits (James Mason, Curt Jurgens, Eli Wallach, Jack Hawkins, Paul Lukas, Akim Tamiroff) and a glib dissipation among battles and explosions; 1965. (*c*)

Lord Love a Duck   ×
Some funny moments, but George Axelrod's 1965 comedy about American teenagers looks out-of-date now–as do Tuesday Weld and Roddy McDowall. (*b/w*)

Lord of the Flies   √ √
The fable of small boys reverting to savagery when marooned on a desert island may not be as powerful on the

screen as in William Golding's book; but in Peter Brook's adaptation, which he directed himself in 1961/3, it retains enough primitive power to hold, move and disturb. For an advocate of the Theatre of Cruelty he is strangely hesitant about picturing the worst excesses of the boys, but enough is shown to make you weep with Piggy, hate Jack and sympathise with Ralph. (*b/w*)

Loser Takes All　　　　　X X
Desperately disappointing tale of winning system at roulette and the difference it makes to newlyweds Rossano Brazzi (terrible) and Glynis Johns. Weak in almost every department, the blame is only partly director Ken Annakin's. Everyone expected better from the scriptwriter, who took it from his own short story–Graham Greene; 1956. (*c*)

Lost　　　　　X X
Sincere attempt to tell the story of child stolen from pram may be a bit too pedestrian for modern tastes, but Guy Green made it acceptable in 1956. Second-eleven cast, headed by David Farrar. (*b/w*)

Lost Battalion　　　　　X X
1962 B-picture allegedly set behind the Japanese lines in the Philippines but all too obviously shown up by the newsreels which keep it interesting. The action sequences are OK but the talk (should a white girl–Diane Jergens–fall in love with a local guerrilla–Leopold Salcedo?) is embarrassing. And the final twist of the plot is a *deus ex machina*. Eddie Romero directed. (*b/w*)

Lost Command　　　　　√
Anthony Quinn, George Segal, Alain Delon, Claudia Cardinale, Michèle Morgan all doing their bit for one or other side in French–Algerian war. Director Mark Robson makes it all a bit specious, but there's a nice irony in the final shots; 1966. (*c*)

The Lost Continent　　　　　X
Better than usual Hammer horror about how boatload of quite interesting characters (Eric Porter, Hildegard Knef, Suzanna Leigh, Nigel Stock) survive a hair-raising voyage on a ship filled with explosives. Among other excitements they are in a hurricane and get trapped in some man-eating seaweed. Director Michael Carreras took this from a Dennis Wheatley novel in 1968. (*c*)

Lost Treasure of the Amazon　　　　　X X
Rhonda Fleming finds herself hunting gold in steamy jungle, this time with Fernando Lamas. Objects hurtling towards screen were meant to hit 1953 3D boom, not director Edward Ludwig. (*c*)

The Lost Weekend　　　　　√ √
First attempt to treat alcoholism as a movie subject was immense success, winning 1945 Oscars for best film, best actor Ray Milland, best director Billy Wilder, best script Wilder and Charles Brackett. Deliberately slow-paced, it builds up into horrendous climax in Bellevue's alcoholic ward after Milland succumbs to his need for a drink, tottering up Third Avenue with his typewriter to pawn, finally selling his girl's coat to buy a gun to shoot himself. Jane Wyman's regeneration of him was not in the book and should be ignored as window-dressing. (*b/w*)

The Lost World　　　　　X X
Prehistoric monsters don't like the arrival of explorers Michael Rennie, Claude Rains, Jill St John one bit and you can't blame them. Irwin Allen remade silent 1924 classic in ludicrous fashion in 1960. (*c*)

The Loudest Whisper　　　　　X
Remake of *These Three*, which had child whispering about alleged hetero affair. This 1962 effort to present Lillian Hellman's stage play (from the author's

184

own adaptation) runs into trouble when it tries to make social ostracism believable. People just don't behave that way any more, and neither Audrey Hepburn, Shirley MacLaine nor director-producer William Wyler can remotely suggest any reason why a hint of homosexuality might send them into such a tizzy. (*b/w*)

Louisiana Story √√
Robert Flaherty's 1948 lyrical paean to nature is as slow as the waters of the bayous, but story of boy in a boat watching big oil prospectors (it was sponsored by Standard Oil) is wonderfully evocative of the struggle for existence and a child's awakening. (*b/w*)

The Loved One ×
Tony Richardson was so obviously the wrong choice as director of Evelyn Waugh's flaying satire on California burial rites that it's amazing how producers John Calley and Haskell Wexler (who also did the photography) chose him. Predictably, he took all the caricature elements in Terry Southern and Christopher Isherwood's adaptation of the novel and compounded them with a cast he seems to have encouraged to over-act. Thus despite the presence of Rod Steiger, Anjanette Comer, Robert Morse, Jonathan Winters, Milton Berle, John Gielgud, Margaret Leighton, Liberace, Robert Morley, Lionel Stander (on re-reading that list perhaps the preposition should be 'because of . . .'), all we got in 1965 was a series of jokes to replace Waugh's scalpel strokes. The plot, such as it is, is cluttered with all sorts of irrelevant jibes at other Los Angeles follies. (*c*)

The Love Goddesses √√
Fascinating 1965 compilation, mostly from Paramount, of clips linked by refreshingly literate narration. The obvious ones—Harlow, Monroe, Bardot,

etc.—are included, but far juicier are the barge scene from DeMille's *Cleopatra*; a choice Busby Berkeley number; the gorilla who turns out to be Dietrich; and some scenes to remind us that there was an era before censorship. (*b/w*)

Love Happy ××
Weak 1950 Marx Brothers comedy notable for a walk-on by Marilyn Monroe. David Miller; 1950. (*b/w*)

Love Has Many Faces ×××
Simply awful soaper with Lana Turner as ageing playgirl (this was 1964), Cliff Robertson and Hugh O'Brian as gigolos in Acapulco. Alexander Singer directed tastelessly. (*c*)

Love in a Goldfish Bowl ×××
Daft little teenagerer with Tommy Sands and Toby Michaels slipping off together for a platonic holiday (oh, Toby's a girl) which sends their college authorities into a frenzy of moralising. This must have been old-fashioned in 1961—it's positively antediluvian now. Written and directed by Jack Sher. (*c*)

Love in Las Vegas ×
And boredom for you unless you happen to be an Elvis Presley fan. His 1964 vehicle was this nonsense about being a waiter-cum-mechanic-cum-racer wooing swimming instructress Ann-Margret. George Sidney staged the musical numbers efficiently but he could hardly believe in the plot either. (*c*)

The Love-Ins ××
Nasty Hollywood cash-in on the 1960s hippy scene, made 1967, with Richard Todd, James MacArthur; Arthur Dreifuss directed. (*c*)

Love in the Afternoon √√
Gary Cooper—a bit old for the part (56 in 1957) but who's counting?—wooing Audrey Hepburn in gentle Billy Wilder –I. A. L. Diamond comedy filmed in

Paris; Maurice Chevalier as Audrey's papa provides local colour along with the locations. (*b/w*)

Love is a Ball × ×
Pretty Riviera setting for silly yarn about heiress Hope Lange and fortune hunters Glenn Ford, Charles Boyer. David Swift; 1963. (*c*)

Love is a Many-Splendored Thing ×
You've heard the song, now see the film – but only if you'd love a good cry at *Madame Butterfly*-type romance between war correspondent William Holden and unbelievable Eurasian girl Jennifer Jones. Henry King; 1955. (*c*)

Love is Better Than Ever ×
The way she looked in 1952, it's a mystery why it takes Elizabeth Taylor so long to hook Larry Parks (why she should want to is even more mysterious). Stanley Donen spun it out. (*b/w*)

The Love Lottery × ×
Soft little British comedy with David Niven as the prize in a sweepstake. But he really loves Anne Vernon, for some reason. Charles Crichton wasn't able to give it much zing, things being what they were in 1953. (*c*)

Lovely To Look At ×
Howard Keel, Kathryn Grayson, Red Skelton in 1952 Mervyn LeRoy remake of Astaire–Rogers musical, *Roberta*, set in high-fashion Paris. Jerome Kern songs like Smoke Gets In Your Eyes, I Won't Dance still lovely to listen to. (*c*)

A Lovely Way To Go ×
Ex-cop Kirk Douglas trying to prove Sylvia Koscina didn't murder her husband. David Lowell Rich didn't make us care one way or the other in 1968. (*c*)

Love Me or Leave Me √
Doris Day as Ruth Etting, the twenties singer, famous for Smoke Gets In Your Eyes and highly dramatic personal story, turned to good account by Charles Vidor in 1955. James Cagney memorable as Marty the Gimp. (*c*)

Love Me Tonight √ √
Made in 1932 with bravura by Rouben Mamoulian, it has a Rodgers and Hart score (including Isn't It Romantic?, first sung by Maurice Chevalier in Paris, picked up by all sorts of characters as it carries us into the country), Myrna Loy as a nymphy countess ('Don't you think of anything but men?'–'Yes, school-boys'), Charlie Ruggles, Charles Butterworth, C. Aubrey Smith, and a tailor-meets-princess story. It also has Jeanette MacDonald, but survives magnificently. (*b/w*)

Love Nest ×
Silly story about a con man getting his friend jailed so that he can dictate his memoirs in prison, isn't improved by leaden performances from June Haver, William Lundigan and Frank Fay. But Marilyn Monroe in a small part is some compensation. Director, Joseph Newman; 1951. (*b/w*)

Love on the Dole √
Classic early British working class realism film of Walter Greenwood's novel about a Lancashire family in the Depression. Young Deborah Kerr's mill girl made her a star, well supported by Clifford Evans, Mary Merrall, George Carney. Directed, 1941, by John Baxter. (*b/w*)

Lover Come Back √
Delicious Doris Day–Rock Hudson comedy with sophisticated Madison Avenue setting; director Delbert Mann gives it plenty of sparkle and Tony Randall adds to the fun; 1962. (*c*)

Love with the Proper Stranger √
Feckless jazz musician Steve McQueen gets casual lay Natalie Wood pregnant.

Realistic New York locations, fine performances and Robert Mulligan's sensitive direction make it all believable, even though things have changed a lot since 1963. (*b/w*)

Loving You ✕ ✕
Elvis Presley's second film (1957) was predictable yarn of small-town boy facing up to overnight fame and fortune; with Lizabeth Scott, Wendell Corey; director, Hal Kanter. (*c*)

The L-Shaped Room √
Despite critical raves, Leslie Caron seems miscast as unwed pregnant girl in love with fellow-lodger Tom Bell. It's not director Bryan Forbes' fault that what seemed real in 1963 looks dated now. (*b/w*)

The Luck of Ginger Coffey √ √
Absorbing drama about an Irish family of immigrants to Canada and the way they get split up. Robert Shaw and Mary Ure are painfully true-to-life. Director Irvin Kershner did well by Brian Moore's script from his own novel; 1965. (*b/w*)

Lucky Jim √
Ian Carmichael was monumentally miscast as hero of Kingsley Amis' novel shoved on to the screen by the Boultings in 1957 with no regard for subtleties. The belly-laughs are still there for the farcical bits (Terry-Thomas, Hugh Griffith upped the milieu while broadening the incidents) but there is no sign of why novel should have become symbol of redbrick revolution against Establishment. (*b/w*)

Lucky Me ✕
Lucky Jack Donohue had Doris Day, Phil Silvers, Robert Cummings to give this dreary musical about out-of-work showgirls a bit of a life; 1954. (*c*)

Lucky Nick Cain ✕
Gambler George Raft framed for murder

on Italian Riviera in otherwise conventional gangster yarn. Joseph M. Newman; 1951. (*b/w*)

Lucy Gallant ✕
Ambitious career girl Jane Wyman makes a huge success of everything except–you've guessed it–her personal life, oilman Charlton Heston in this case. Robert Parrish; 1955. (*c*)

Lullaby of Broadway √
You could do worse than let this Doris Day musical with songs by Cole Porter and Gershwin wash over you. Gladys George is fine as Doris' Broadwaysinger Mom. David Butler directed; 1951. (*c*)

Lust for Life √
Not as ghastly as the usual 'great artist' biopic, but let down by inadequacies of Kirk Douglas as van Gogh and Anthony Quinn as Gauguin. The paintings are great, however, and Vincente Minnelli's attempt to recreate them in moving pictures not at all bad. Pamela Brown, Everett Sloane, Jill Bennett, Lionel Jeffries support; 1956. (*c*)

The Lusty Men √
Nicholas Ray's vivid and authentic picture of rodeo life more than makes up for rather conventional storyline; Robert Mitchum, Susan Hayward, Arthur Kennedy convince too; 1952. (*b/w*)

Luv ✕ ✕
The blame for the failure of this one must lie with director Clive Donner. He had three splendid stars in Jack Lemmon, Elaine May and Peter Falk and the original Murray Schisgal play about middle-class New Yorkers was very funny Broadway hit So what went wrong, Mr Donner? 1967. (*c*)

Lydia Bailey ✕
Kenneth Roberts, who wrote *North*

West Passage, concocted this Haiti-based extravaganza which director Jean Negulesco glossed into some sort of a shine in 1952. Dale Robertson was the American lawyer trying to get signature on legal document from Anne Francis, then becoming entangled in Napoleonic subversion. (*c*)

M　　　　　　　　　　　　　　　√
Quickie (20 days) 1951 remake by Joseph Losey of child murderer hunt which doesn't begin to match Fritz Lang's German classic with Peter Lorre in 1931, despite presence of Luther Adler and Martin Gabel and a very close sticking to the original script. (*b/w*)

Ma Barker's Killer Brood　　　　✗
Lurene Tuttle does fine in Bill Karn's rather crude version of true-ish life-story of Bloody Mama, remade with Shelley Winters ten years after this 1960 version. (*b/w*)

Macao　　　　　　　　　　　　　√
For most, this will be a moody sub-*Casablanca*, with Robert Mitchum and Jane Russell fighting an equivocal sexual duel. But the for the cinéaste it provides a chewy puzzle; who directed what? When Howard Hughes, almost as strange in 1950 as today, asked the

Clark Gable in *The Misfits*

legendary Joseph von Sternberg to direct it, he expected trouble; what he got was chaos, with rows on the set and tantrums all round. He so hated the rushes that he brought in Nicholas Ray to reshoot some scenes. But how much of the finished film was Ray's? (*b/w*)

Macbeth √
Of the many versions, the only ones likely to be shown on television in the next few years are the Orson Welles attempt (1948–*b/w*) whizzed through in three weeks with some imaginative chunks of filming; and the Maurice Evans version (1960–*c*) with pedestrian direction by George Schaefer, which did little more than photograph the play.

Machine Gun Kelly √
Charles Bronson plays mad-dog gangster under Roger Corman's tough 1958 direction. (*b/w*)

Mackenna's Gold √
Great long super-Western sprawls unconvincingly over a huge canvas, shooting off in all directions about some gold that by the end you simply don't care about. J. Lee Thompson has been provided with a stellar cast by co-producer Carl Foreman (Gregory Peck, Omar Sharif, Telly Savalas, Keenan Wynn, Raymond Massey, Lee J. Cobb, Anthony Quayle, Edward G. Robinson, Eli Wallach, Eduardo Cianelli) and a narrator, Victor Jory, thrown in to stitch the uncomfortably-fitting pieces together. Unfortunately, he can find little for them to do, and this series of disappointments plus inferior special effects, add up to one huge disappointment; 1969. (*c*)

The Macomber Affair √
Hemingway African short story made clumsily over to give Gregory Peck, Joan Bennett, Robert Preston starring roles. Zoltan Korda exaggerated the dramatics in his direction; 1947. (*b/w*)

Mad About Men ✕
Tame sequel to *Miranda*, in which girl and look-alike mermaid change places. Glynis Johns plays them; Margaret Rutherford, Donald Sinden back up. Ralph Thomas; 1954. (*c*)

Madame Bovary ✕
Just one of the many movies ruined by Jennifer Jones grabbing the main part when quite unsuited to it. Here she mucks up Flaubert's novel of a calculating woman, dragging down James Mason, Van Heflin with her. Vincente Minnelli obliged directorially; 1949. (*b/w*)

Madame X ✕
Real old thirties-type weepie given 1965 production values but little else by David Lowell Rich's unashamed twanging on the heartstrings. Ex-shopgirl Lana Turner is forced by horrid mother-in-law Constance Bennett to leave her husband and pretend she's dead. All she did was have a fling with Ricardo Montalban. She hides away but kills blackmailing Burgess Meredith, to be defended by Her Own Son, Keir Dullea. Previous Madame Xs: Gladys George, 1937; Ruth Chatterton, 1929; Pauline Frederick, 1920; original was play by Alexandre Bisson. (*c*)

Made in Paris ✕
But confected in Hollywood; this is the one about the American girl (Ann-Margret) who, on a tour of the sights of the naughty French capital, can't make up her mind which of three men she should marry. Louis Jourdan, the only 'name' around, must start favourite. Boris Sagal directed it all very smoothly in 1966 but it needed more than slick production to get by. (*c*)

Madigan √√
Emergence of Don Siegel into the big-time after years and years of making the best B pix was this 1968 super-thriller which presents a couple of New York

detectives (Richard Widmark and Harry Guardino), almost indistinguishable from the scum they hunt, given 72 hours to pull in a sadistic killer. Henry Fonda, who prides himself on being a clean detective, is their chief but he turns out to be as corrupt in his fashion as the rest of the characters in this violent, exciting, nasty, compelling parable of the urban jungle. (*c*)

Madison Avenue × ×
Dreary tale about the advertising industry, without bite or bile, or even any pretensions to either. Eleanor Parker and Jeanne Crain expose themselves (alas, not literally) and the man they have built up, Dana Andrews, when they realise he could become a danger to dear ol' America–Bruce Humberstone directs with a straight face; 1961. (*b/w*)

Madonna of the Seven Moons × ×
Belongs to the bad old days of British films, 1944, when Phyllis Calvert, Stewart Granger, Patricia Roc, Jean Kent–all of whom can be seen posturing about in this soppy yarn about a gypsy curse–ruled the roost. Director, Arthur Crabtree. (*b/w*)

The Madwoman of Chaillot √
Dreadfully theatrical piece of theatre by Jean Giraudoux never sits easily on the screen despite star-cramming (Katharine Hepburn, Margaret Leighton, Giulietta Masina, Edith Evans as madwomen; Donald Pleasence, Charles Boyer, Yul Brynner, Paul Henreid, as heavies; Danny Kaye, Richard Chamberlain, and sundry others playing parable parts like The Folk Singer, The Flower Seller, The Juggler, the Deaf Mute, the goodies). It's all too schmaltzy and zany in its self-consciously fantasy manner. Bryan Forbes directed with a heavy hand, in 1969. (*c*)

The Magic Box √
A cast of British stars as long as your nose graces this Festival of Britain (1951)

celebration of William Friese-Green, who was supposed to have invented films, but in real life didn't. John Boulting assembled Robert Donat, Laurence Olivier, Eric Portman, Glynis Johns, Emlyn Williams, Richard Attenborough, Margaret Rutherford, Peter Ustinov, among others. Considering it's a (misplaced) Tribute movie, it isn't too bad. (*c*)

Magic Fire ×
One of those Great Composer biopics, this time about the unpleasant Richard Wagner, who comes out as a nicer chap than he was in real life, thanks to Alan Badel's sympathetic performance and director William Dieterle's need for a hero. Yvonne de Carlo, Rita Gam and Peter Cushing mope about in unreasonable facsimiles of moviedom's idea of how a composer's satellites behave, and only Valentina Cortese makes a real stab at catching the period and emotions as the woman who inspired *Tristan und Isolde*. Actual locations are used wherever possible and the matching sets are scrupulously correct; but the opera excerpts evidently embarrassed the film-makers as much as they will bore the uninitiated (by being too long) and annoy the addict (by being too short); 1956. (*c*)

The Magnet √
Cosy, charming Ealing comedy directed by Charles Frend about childhood. The leading child William Fox grew up to become actor James Fox; 1951. (*b/w*)

The Magnificent Ambersons √ √ √
Made twenty years before its time, in 1942, when movie families had to be Andy Hardy's parents, not disquieting real-life aliens. Superb performances from Tim Holt, arrogant scion of best family in town, who gets his comeuppance; Dolores Costello as his doting mother; Agnes Moorehead as his screaming bitter old maid of an aunt;

Rosalind Russell as wild Auntie Mame in film of the same name (1958 nominations for Best Picture, Best Actress) wins out over such contenders for campest performance ever as Zero Mostel in *The Producers* and the Carry On team in practically anything, because it's real acting, as distinct from performing.

Burl Ives in *The Big Country* (Oscar for Best Supporting Actor, 1958) and *Cat on a Hot Tin Roof* (right).

The Old Man and the Sea was Hemingway at his most pretentious; Spencer Tracy gave the film life.

Cat on a Hot Tin Roof was a Tennessee Williams play about homosexuality; in 1958 became a film about hero-worship.

Gigi (eleven 1958 Oscars, including Best Film) – ever-so-ooh-la-la but OK for kiddies, too. Louis Jourdan, Leslie Caron.

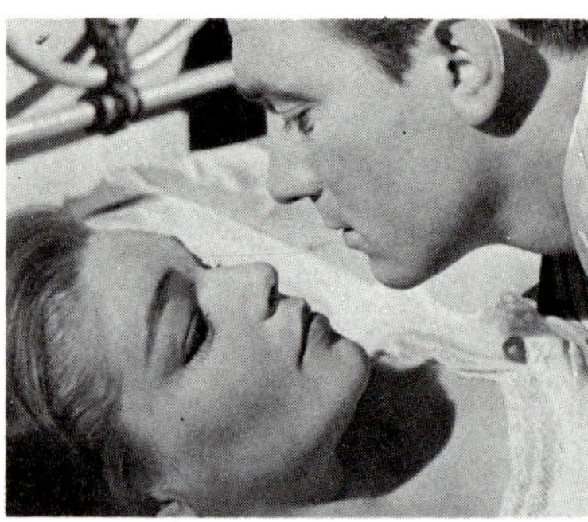

Room at the Top glamorised Laurence Harvey's northerner; won mistress Simone Signoret 1959 Best Actress Oscar.

Ben Hur and Charlton Heston each won 1959 Oscars (plus nine other categories) for remake about rich Jew humbled, regenerated, converted. Highlight was this 11-minute chariot race, in which he beats (and out-acts) perfidious ex-friend Stephen Boyd.

The Nun's Story, nominated for Best Film Oscar of 1959, along with Audrey Hepburn's performance, managed to tell its story of the trials and tribulations of a novice without ever becoming sickly. Her desire for Peter Finch, while engaged to Christ, convinces.

John Wayne, here shouting at Richard Widmark, as Davy Crockett in his own direction-production, *The Alamo* (1960 contender for Best Picture), has made a career out of caricaturing the American ideal man, and taking it seriously.

Some Like It Hot: anyone who doesn't find this comedy of mistaken identity uproarious needs his sense of humour examined. Blonde is Marilyn Monroe, brunette's Tony Curtis. Academy boobed in 1959 by giving the film no Oscars, apologised in 1960 by awarding Best Film to the inferior *The Apartment*.

'I think it stinks,' is what Elizabeth Taylor said about *Butterfield 8*, which won her the 1960 Best Actress Oscar (her first). Here nympho heroine is trying to break up clinch between Eddie Fisher (her real-life fourth husband) and Susan Oliver.

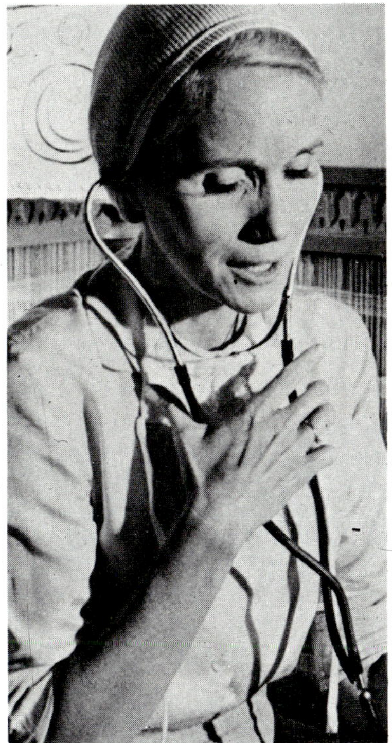

Exodus the film was denounced by the novelist Leon Uris in 1960. Eva Marie Saint wasn't very convincing, either.

Jack Lemmon, Oscar-nominee for *The Apartment*, 1960, comes over more sympathetically than any other actor.

Melina Mercouri in 1960's *Never on Sunday* managed to embody two myths: (1) that whores are golden-hearted; (2) that exuberance is more than a substitute for talent. Loyal husband Jules Dassin (also directing) acted so incompetently that she shone in contrast.

Burt Lancaster, fleeing the fire in *Elmer Gantry* (Best Actor Oscar, 1960), has built a career on trying hard.

Tom Courtenay imagining himself as intrepid here in *Billy Liar*, 1963.

Audrey Hepburn wasn't much like Capote's Holly Golightly in *Breakfast at Tiffany's*, 1961, but who cared?

Olivier's superb personification of a failed musical hall act in *The Entertainer*, 1960.

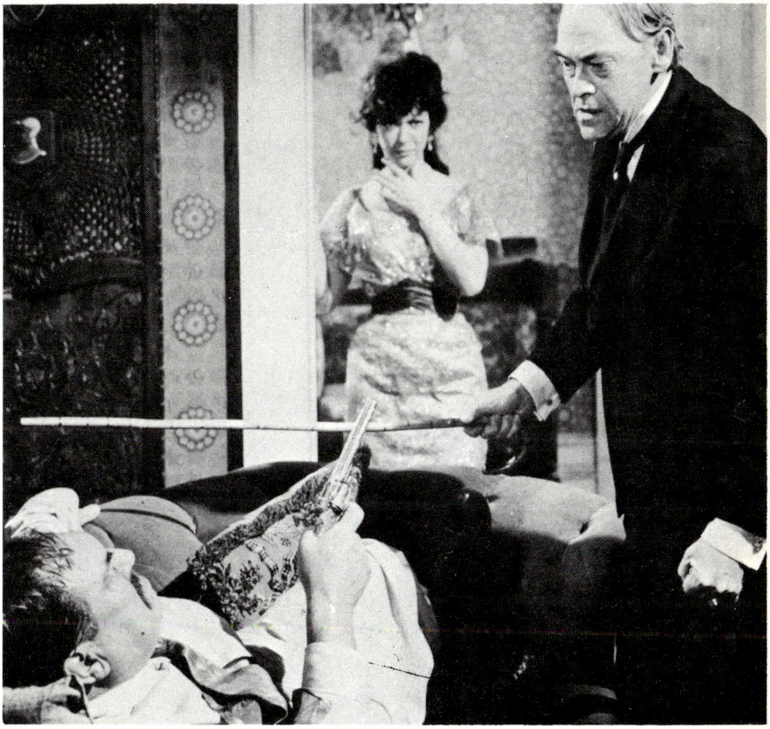

Thomas Gomez, John McIntire and Rita Moreno in *Summer and Smoke*, one of the many attempts to translate Tennessee Williams to the screen – none of them very successful.

West Side Story's Richard Beymer couldn't even make a convincing corpse and Natalie Wooden looked as Puerto Rican as Bugs Bunny; even her singing voice wasn't her own. The film won ten Oscars in 1961, but not for the stars.

Richard Bennett as patriarch; Joseph Cotten, Anne Baxter, Ray Collins. The great director (who also wrote the screenplay from Booth Tarkington's novel), wasn't allowed by the money boys to finish and it ends abruptly three reels before he meant it to with a tacked-on sequence in a hospital by another hand. He was permitted to speak the final credits, however. His name is Orson Welles. (*b/w*)

Magnificent Obsession √
Successful soaper about Jane Wyman going blind and Rock Hudson curing, loving her. Douglas Sirk directed this 1954 remake of 1935 Robert Taylor – Irene Dunne – John M. Stahl tearjerker. (*c*)

The Magnificent Seven √√√
A great Western, taken from Kurosawa's *Seven Samurai* and surviving the transposition – well, magnificently. Director John Sturges has managed to get real characterisation and tension out of the septet of gunmen – Yul Brynner, Horst Buchholz, Steve McQueen, Charles Bronson, Robert Vaughn, Brad Dexter, James Coburn – and Eli Wallach's bandit chief they protect the village from is equally memorable, not least for its unexpected casting; 1961. (*c*)

The Magnificent Showman √√
Strictly for lovers of big Westerns and circuses, this is a huge drama, filled with all sorts of catastrophes and John Wayne lording over all. Director Henry Hathaway serves it up expertly; 1964. (*c*)

The Magnificent Two ✕
Another of Morecambe and Wise's unhappy forays into the cinema; this 1967 effort, under Cliff Owen's direction, has Eric as a South American rebel leader. The comedy is interrupted by rather nastily literal action sequences. (*c*)

The Main Attraction ✕✕
Dull little circus story climaxing in night in mountain hut where Pat Boone and Nancy Kwan are unaware they are in the path of an avalanche. Weak supports Mai Zetterling, Yvonne Mitchell, Kieron Moore, Warren Mitchell don't get the direction they badly need from Daniel Petrie; 1962. (*c*)

The Major and the Minor √√
Billy Wilder's first shot at direction (1942) was this fast-paced comedy about Ginger Rogers dressing up as a child to save the train fare and falling for Ray Milland. Great fun. (*b/w*)

Major Barbara √√
Best of Gabriel Pascal's adaptations of Bernard Shaw's plays (what charm the little chap must have had to con Shaw into letting him ruin play after play) was this one with Wendy Hiller as the Salvation Army girl, Rex Harrison, Robert Morley, Robert Newton, Emlyn Williams, Deborah Kerr, Sybil Thorndike; 1941. (*b/w*)

Major Dundee √√
One of the most important American movies of the last decade, if you can believe the enthusiasts for director Sam Peckinpah, whose third picture (1964) this was. But most audiences will see only a moderately exciting, rather scruffy Western, with Federal officer Charlton Heston leading a band of ex-Confederate prisoners, under a resentful Richard Harris, against the Apaches. Look for deeper meanings, despite drastic re-editing over Peckinpah's head. (*c*)

A Majority of One √
Schmaltzy 1961 story of Jewish widow Rosalind Russell, whose son was killed in the war, meeting and resenting Japanese industrialist Alec Guinness. Sympathy triumphs but it takes too long. Unimaginative direction from Mervyn LeRoy leaves it stage-bound. (*c*)

Make Me an Offer √
Tepid antique (in many senses) comedy from Wolf Mankowitz novel; Peter Finch as dealer involved with Wedgwood vase. Directed patiently by Cyril Frankel; 1955. (*c*)

Make Mine Mink × ×
Pathetic little British comedy made in 1960 at the end of the 'zany period', about retired officer (Terry-Thomas) who joins up with three posh old ladies (Athene Seyler among them) to steal for charity. Some good players (Hattie Jacques, Irene Handl, Billie Whitelaw) shamefully wasted on a weak Michael Pertwee script and Robert Asher's lacklustre direction. (*b/w*)

The Male Animal √ √
Elliott Nugent directs from his and Thurber's play about triangle with professor Henry Fonda, Olivia de Havilland, Jack Carson. Light, sophisticated 1942 comedy. (*b/w*)

The Maltese Falcon √ √ √
This was John Huston's first (1941) direction and he never bettered it. In fact, nobody has ever bettered it in its own field – the shady, seamy, semi-underworld of the private eye, played ever-memorably by Humphrey Bogart, never fooled for a moment (well, not many moments) by Mary Astor's calculating schemer, Peter Lorre's frightened operative, Sydney Greenstreet's bland flatterer, partner Jerome Cowan's weak womaniser, Gladys George's clinging adulterer, and the whole shenanigans about the little black bird whose worth is greater than you will ever know. Aficionados will also treasure continual needling of Elisha Cook Jr and Daddy Walter Huston's literally staggering aid to his son as he wanders in with the treasure. (*b/w*)

The Man Between ×
James Mason earnestly supported by Claire Bloom and Hildegarde Knef in 1953 Carol Reed-directed drama of cold war in Berlin. (*b/w*)

A Man Called Peter × ×
Richard Todd as real-life Senate Chaplain in dull account of his life. Director Henry Koster; 1955. (*c*)

The Manchurian Candidate √ √ √
Tremendously exciting hokum about Laurence Harvey being turned into walking zombie ready to do the Red Chinese's wicked deeds (like sniping at presidents) without realising it, given immense zip by John Frankenheimer in 1962. Frank Sinatra is the officer who gets through the turn-on code, but the acting honours belong to James Gregory and Angela Lansbury as a nasty couple of political crooks. (*b/w*)

A Man For All Seasons √ √ √
Superb transfer to the screen of Robert Bolt's play, produced and directed by Fred Zinnemann with tact and depth, in 1967. Paul Scofield repeats his towering performance as Sir Thomas More who goes through so much, remains so steadfast, and has magnificent support from Wendy Hiller as his wife; Susannah York as his strong-willed daughter; Leo McKern the squitty Cromwell; Vanessa Redgrave (unbilled) as Anne Boleyn; Orson Welles as a grand Wolsey; Robert Shaw as the young Henry VIII; and John Hurt is a marvellously evil Rich. A treat in all departments, which was rewarded by a raft of Oscars and both critical and box-office success. (*c*)

The Man from Colorado √
Glenn Ford takes over Western territory as judge and reveals himself to be corrupt and power-mad. It takes William Holden to break him up; Henry Levin; 1948. (*c*)

The Man from Laramie √
James Stewart rides into town looking for the gun-runner who caused his

brother's death; how he is avenged keeps this oater taut. Director Anthony Mann has it on his conscience, however, that this movie introduced sadism into the Western in 1955, when Alex Nichol deliberately shoots Stewart through the hand. (*c*)

The Man from the Alamo √
Glenn Ford in strong Budd Boetticher-directed US *v*. Mexico war drama; 1953. (*c*)

The Man from the Diners' Club √
Quite a fun picture from Danny Kaye–one of a minority–in which he has all sorts of adventures in chasing a lost credit card that Telly Savalas has pinched. Frank Tashlin directs slickly from a script he co-wrote; 1963. (*b/w*)

Man Hunt √
(1) Walter Pidgeon stalking Hitler, disappointingly directed by Fritz Lang in 1941. (*b/w*)

Man Hunt √
(2) Henry Hathaway's 1958 attempt to put a bit of life into the old Western formula has Don Murray on the run from a family (including son Dennis Hopper). An advance on routine oaters. (*c*)

Maniac ×✕
Sloppy Hammer thriller about American artist in France having affair with café-owner, arousing daughter's anger. Meanwhile her husband escapes from an asylum. Unknown actors stayed that way. Michael Carreras churned it out; 1963. (*b/w*)

The Man in Grey ✕
The only reason this thin historical nonsense ever became popular was because in 1943 it provided a chance to see something elaborate as a relief from austerity Britain–cleavage for one thing (or two). So Leslie Arliss found himself directing a boom picture, and Margaret Lockwood, James Mason, Phyllis Calvert, Stewart Granger became major stars. (*b/w*)

The Man in the Gray Flannel Suit √
Gregory Peck doing his usual sincere bit in long and not altogether tedious story of life in an American corporation; Fredric March is president of the company whose marriage provides a poor example to Peck. Nunnally Johnson wrote and directed from Sloan Wilson's best-seller in 1956. (*c*)

The Man in the Iron Mask √
Louis Hayward is incarcerated twin brother of Louis XIV in this 1939 remake of Douglas Fairbanks 1929 classic. James Whale keeps action spinning; with Joseph Schildkraut, Alan Hale and Joan Bennett. Based on supposedly true story (though the mask was velvet) fictionalised by Alexandre Dumas. (*b/w*)

Man in the Middle √
Keenan Wynn murders a British sergeant in wartime India; Robert Mitchum has the job of defending him, knowing that Anglo-American relations demand he should be found guilty. Guy Hamilton's direction somehow fails to involve the audience, despite strong performances from Trevor Howard and Barry Sullivan and a Waterhouse-and-Hall script; 1964. (*b/w*)

Man in the Moon ✕
Mildly entertaining satire-that-misses about Kenneth More being sent up to the moon as a kind of working-class guinea pig. Basil Dearden's direction and the Michael Relph–Bryan Forbes screenplay are redolent in gags and attitudes that must have been outdated when it was made in 1961, let alone now. Michael Hordern, Shirley Anne Field, Norman Bird go through familiar motions competently enough and, as usual, Kenneth More delivers beyond the call of duty. (*b/w*)

The Man in the Net ✕
Alan Ladd looking pretty silly as an artist suspected, for no apparent reason, of killing his wife, hiding out in the woods and exposing the real killer with the help of the local kids; directed by Michael Curtiz without any sign that he believed it either; 1959. (*b/w*)

The Man in the Sky √
Test pilot Jack Hawkins refusing to leave failing airline company's promising prototype when it catches fire in flight. Elizabeth Sellars is wife who waits, plus Lionel Jeffries, Donald Pleasence. Charles Crichton directs; 1956. (*b/w*)

The Man in the White Suit √√
Sandy Mackendrick's 1951 comedy wears well, mainly because of Alec Guinness as an inventor who discovers a fabric that doesn't get dirty or wear out. Brilliantly co-written by Roger Mac-Dougall; and supports Joan Greenwood, Ernest Thesiger, Cecil Parker all turn in lovely performances. (*b/w*)

A Man is Ten Feet Tall √
Martin Ritt's first film has strong echoes of *On the Waterfront*, with John Cassavetes as the docker who learns to stand up to bullying boss. Added element is Sidney Poitier's friendly black (proudly called Negro in far-off 1957). (*b/w*)

Man of Arran √√
Robert Flaherty's famous romantic (some say romanticised) look at the people (or rather, the folk) of the Arran Islands, off Ireland, and their age-old fight against the elements. But you can't knock the photography and the trail-blazing; it was made in 1934. (*b/w*)

The Man of a Thousand Faces ✕
It's Lon Chaney; but don't expect a fascinating montage of his own silent pix. Instead, Joseph Pevney pains-takingly re-directed James Cagney in a 1956 mock-up of some of the most famous horror roles. It's all joined together by a routine, unconvincing biography in which Dorothy Malone, Jane Greer and Marjorie Rambeau pluckily string along; the make-up by Bud Westmore's great, though. (*b/w*)

Man of the West ✕
Sadistic Western that wastes Gary Cooper as outlaw trying to go straight but forced to participate in some nasty business. A disappointment from writer Reginald Rose and director Anthony Mann in 1958. (*c*)

Man on Fire ✕
This 1957 attempt to establish Bing Crosby as non-singing dramatic actor sent him back to singing roles. The sincerity of the main plot (child caught up in divorce tug-of-war) was under-mined by such ludicrous sub-stories as lawyer's assistant falling for Bing (relax, she's a girl) and the tritest of dialogue. Ranald MacDougall was responsible for that, as well as the direction. (*b/w*)

The Man on the Eiffel Tower √
Actor Burgess Meredith turned director in 1949 to guide this exciting story of murder investigation; Charles Laughton, Franchot Tone and Meredith himself stand out. (*c*)

Manpower √
One of those movies they don't make any more about two tough buddies both lusting after the same woman, with action (power lines here) alternating with wisecracks alternating with love-scenes. Raoul Walsh was an expert at them and this 1941 concoction had Edward G. Robinson and George Raft as the guys, Marlene Dietrich as the dame. (*b/w*)

Man's Favourite Sport √
Fishing, as if you hadn't guessed. It's all on this level of nudge-nudge vacuity,

but Rock Hudson, Paula Prentiss turn in competent comedy jobs under Howard Hawks; 1963. (*c*)

Man-Trap   × ×
Inept in every department, this is a thriller that just doesn't. The only (not surprising) solo directing attempt by actor Edmond O'Brien also suffers from a ridiculous script, as inexplicable as it is incredible, about a robbery that goes wrong. There isn't much that Jeffrey Hunter, David Janssen and Stella Stevens can do but hang on. Miss Stevens does so with great bravado; 1962. (*b/w*)

Manuela   × ×
If the crew can accept Elsa Martinelli as a boy when she dresses up to be with Pedro Armendariz, they must all be more shortsighted than you. She falls for Captain Trevor Howard (smashing performance as drink-sodden skipper), but Donald Pleasence, Jack MacGowran, Warren Mitchell still don't catch on. Director Guy Hamilton won't fool you, however, despite documentaryish authenticity of the tramp steamer; 1956. (*b/w*)

The Man Upstairs   √
Successful attempt in 1958 by ACTT, the trade union, to inject some exciting realism into British films. Taut economical script by Alun Falconer, sparely realised by Don Chaffey, who gets fine performances from Richard Attenborough (as shrinking psychopath), Bernard Lee (as a policeman who thinks), Kenneth Griffith, Alfred Burke. (*b/w*)

The Man Who Came to Dinner   √ √
Bravura performance by Monty Woolley as the world's rudest man, forced to stay in small-town household because he breaks his hip. Bette Davis, Reginald Gardner, Billie Burke, Ann Sheridan are further spurs to watching. William Keighley directed this photographed

stage play in 1941; thirty years later Orson Welles essayed the role in taped version for American TV (but made in Southampton, England) and came as big a cropper as larger-than-life Sheridan Whiteside. (*b/w*)

The Man Who Finally Died   ×
Stanley Baker is English innocent jazzman in Germany seeking his dad who was supposed to have been killed during the war. Peter Cushing, Mai Zetterling, Eric Portman, Nigel Green adopt various brands of accents and heaviness as nazis, neo-nazis and neo-neo-nazis, and you won't believe a word of it. Quentin Lawrence directed Lewis Greifer's adaptation of his own TV serial; 1963. (*b/w*)

The Man Who Knew Too Much   √ √
Gorgeous 1956 remake by Hitchcock of his own 1934 British masterpiece; the story is altered but the suspense is as taut as ever. James Stewart and Doris Day are dandy as the couple in the middle. Surely that shot at the Albert Hall – to be fired at the clash of a cymbal – can't kill; yet will it, after all? Everything else is so right that you can forgive the sloppy post-synchronisation of Daniel Gelin's lip-movements. (*c*)

The Man Who Never Was   √
Fooling the Germans as to where the invasion is going to take place by planting phoney papers on a drowned man are Clifton Webb and Stephen Boyd, with Gloria Grahame as an unbelievable tart for relief. Ronald Neame directs with painstaking care from Nigel Balchin script; 1956. (*c*)

The Man Who Shot Liberty Valance   √ √
Strong John Ford Western with Lee Marvin as the heavy gunman hired by wealthy cattlemen to terrify ranchers. When John Wayne is one of the latter and James Stewart an idealistic editor, you know how it will all turn out; 1962. (*b/w*)

The Man Who Understood Women × ×
Except that he doesn't. Nor, on this evidence, do scriptwriter-director Nunnally Johnson or Romain Gary, from whose novel *Colours of the Day* it was adapted. How could any man who understood women fail to consummate his marriage to Leslie Caron, unless he was gay? And there's no sign that Henry Fonda is supposed to be. He's a Great Film Director (no proof of actual films here) who hires an assassin to kill his wife's lover on the Riviera and then tries to stop him. Hokum, hokum, hokum; 1959. (*c*)

The Man Who Wouldn't Talk × × ×
A really terrible script by Edgar Lustgarten is matched by appalling performances by Anna Neagle (as a clever-clever QC), Zsa-Zsa Gabor (as a Russian secret agent) and Anthony Quayle (as a scientist who knows how to give humans myxomatosis). Neagle gets Quayle acquitted for not shooting Gabor. Director Herbert Wilcox wouldn't get off so easily; 1958. (*b/w*)

Man With a Million × ×
Gregory Peck made this attempt to capture the flavour of Mark Twain's fable about man given million-pound note in England in 1941. But Ronald Neame couldn't make it even interesting. (*c*)

Man Without a Star √
Kirk Douglas showing off in run-of-the-prairie Western, 1955, all nice and easygoing until Jeanne Crain's bullboys set on him. Claire Trevor is on hand with repeat of her *Stagecoach* golden-hearted whore. King Vidor keeps the action going. (*c*)

The Man With the Golden Arm √
Slick Otto Preminger drama about drug addiction, with Frank Sinatra OK as the weak monkey who tries to break the habit with the help of Kim Novak; as if this wasn't enough, there's a second plot about a perfect murder which Eleanor Parker couldn't have committed because she's a cripple–or is she? All a bit too much; 1956. (*b/w*)

The Man With the X-Ray Eyes √ √
Roger Corman horror-sci-fictioner about Ray Milland who, in an effort to improve the human eye, injects himself so much with his secret serum that he literally sees through everything, until his inner knowledge drives him mad. There could be a 'profund philosophical commentary' on Life here, but fortunately Corman has chosen to go for the more exciting aspects of the story; 1964. (*c*)

The Marat-Sade √ √
Or *The Persecution and Assassination of Jean-Paul Marat as performed by the Inmates of the Asylum of Charenton under the direction of the Marquis de Sade*. The performers have to be separated from the curious visitors by bars. But not from you. They tell their story of the French Revolution. And much about themselves. And the end is chaos. Glenda Jackson, Patrick Magee and the rest of the Royal Shakespeare Company make it come to life. Peter Brook directs. You might need a strong drink in your hand as you watch; 1967. (*c*)

The Marauders √
Little rancher *v.* the big ranchers. Dan Duryea as the small man, Keenan Wynn doing his usual heavy bit as leader of the nasties; Gerald Mayer directed routinely; 1955. (*c*)

The March Hare × × ×
Oirish whimsy about a racehorse, directed with utter disbelief by George More O'Ferrall, 1956. It has Terence Morgan as the Irish milord whose fortunes the animal could save by winning the Derby. Among other little

people: Cyril Cusack, Martita Hunt, Wilfrid Hyde White. (*c*)

Marco the Magnificent × × ×
Hopeless attempt by Denys de la Patellière to retell Marco Polo story comes to grief despite presence of Orson Welles, Anthony Quinn, Horst Buchholtz, Omar Sharif, Elsa Martinelli (actually, looking down that list of hams, maybe it was because of, not despite); 1966. (*c*)

Mardi Gras × ×
Routine little behind-the-showbiz-scenes comedy about starlet involved with military cadets Pat Boone, Tommy Sands, Gary Crosby. Dull stuff, with lifeless direction by Grand Old Man Edmund Goulding, who was obviously taking it easy by 1958, a year before his death–he had been churning 'em out since 1920, with *Grand Hotel* and *The Old Maid* along the way. (*c*)

Margie √
Premature *Thoroughly Modern Millie* has something of the same period and musical charm. Jeanne Crain is such a nice girl; Henry King; 1946. (*c*)

Margin for Error ×
Only in the rarest cases can directors direct themselves convincingly; Otto Preminger proved the disaster rule again in 1943. Milton Berle as Jewish policeman whose job it is to guard the German ambassador before America went into the war just isn't funny now. (*b/w*)

Marjorie Morningstar √
Herman Wouk's novel about a stagestruck Jewish girl becomes a weak vehicle for an unbelievable Natalie Wooden with a crush on swinging Gene Kelly; Claire Trevor and Everett Sloane as Yiddisher parents. Astonishing how Jewish film-makers manage to miss the ambience of their own culture so com-pletely–Irving Rapper, you should have known better! 1958. (*c*)

The Mark √
Simple, intelligent, decent attempt (1961) to show what happens to a man who has served his time for attack on ten-year-old girl, let down by its own dodgy attitude towards its persecuted hero. While you're mentally applauding Stuart Whitman, psychiatrist Rod Steiger, director Guy Green, ask yourself what you would feel if he *had* been raving dangerous attacker; would you and the film have as much sympathy then? Yet you should have–making hero not guilty is familiar cop-out in such 'crusading' movies. (*b/w*)

Mark of the Hawk ×
Should the blacks resort to force to get their just demands? That's the vital theme of this actioner set in Africa and made in far-off 1958 by Michael Audley, when the answers that were acceptable to white audiences were different from what we have come to recognise as historical inevitability today. Diminished by poor casting of Eartha Kitt, Sidney Poitier. (*c*)

The Mark of Zorro √
Effective 1940 remake of the 1920 Douglas Fairbanks actioner can't be criticised on anything but its own, highly enjoyable terms, which are strictly comic strip. It's Tyrone Power *v.* Basil Rathbone, folks, and you may find yourself on the side of evil, so compelling is Rathbone and so weak Power. Rouben Mamoulian made sure everybody enjoyed themselves, including you. (*b/w*)

Marlowe √
At last, in 1969, the movie of Raymond Chandler's *The Little Sister*, given a more contemporary brutal name and brought up to date with some more recent slang. Fortunately, the story is

the same, and James Garner doesn't make a bad private eye (or private fuzz, as he's called here). The deceitful ladies are all OK, too; particularly Rita Moreno and Gayle Hunnicut. Carroll O'Connor is the real law. Paul Bogart directed. (*c*)

Marnie √ √
One of those Hitchcock movies that have gained in reputation since it was first shown (in 1964), this is the one where Sean Connery is attracted to Tippi Hendren in a fetishist sort of way just because she is a thief. He uncovers the secret of why she compulsively steals. Over-simplified, poorly cast (bluntly, Sean Connery comes from the wrong–too low–class as Hitchcock now admits; and Tippi Hendren isn't much of an actress), too glib, it nevertheless grips as only Hitchcock can. (*c*)

Maroc 7 × ×
Dull little jewel caper movie with staff of fashion mag highly unlikely set of thieves. Takes place mostly in Morocco, but Gerry O'Hara doesn't get much mileage out of the location. Gene Barry, Elsa Martinelli, Cyd Charisse have been packaged for the international market, but it still shows at the seams as a very British picture, with Leslie Phillips (also the film's producer), Denholm Elliott, Eric Barker, Angela Douglas moving about rather aimlessly; 1967. (*c*)

The Marriage-Go-Round × ×
Soppy comedy about Julie Newmar proposing to James Mason that he fathers her child, with the consent of wife Susan Hayward. It could have been witty, sly, honest, even devastatingly frank. All it is, is coy. Pity the stars caught up in Walter Lang's hangdog direction and Leslie Stevens' smutty script; 1961. (*c*)

Marriage on the Rocks ×
Frank Sinatra's daughter Nancy plays his daughter in 1965 marriage-and-divorce mix-up with Deborah Kerr getting split from him, spliced with Dean Martin, but all ending happily. Cesar Romero's caricature of Mexican judge so angered locals that Sinatra was barred from the country. Director Jack Donohue allowed himself to be rather swamped by stars' slap-happy attitude. (*c*)

The Marrying Kind √
Nice blend of comedy and marital drama directed with panache by George Cukor (particularly in opening Central Park sequence). Judy Holliday gave studio bosses heart failure by appearing before Un-American Activities Committee just before it was released in 1952, but they got her testimony suppressed until it had made its money, later in the year. (*b/w*)

Marty √ √ √
Ernest Borgnine rightly won Academy Award for this shy, shambling butcher who finds love with Betsy Blair. Notable for Paddy Chayefsky script written originally for television when American TV still put on single plays. Since 1955, every real-life film has been influenced by it and Delbert Mann's documentary-type direction. Film, script, direction and Borgnine all won Oscars. (*b/w*)

Maru Maru × ×
Errol Flynn as a deep-sea diver searching for a rich prize–a cross of diamonds–at the behest of heavy Raymond Burr. He fancies his partner's wife, Ruth Roman. Gordon Douglas did what he could with a weak script in 1952, but the ending is pure bathos. (*b/w*)

The Marx Brothers at the Circus √ √
The floating bandstand ... the case at the circus ... J. Cheever Loophole ... 'The night I drank champagne from your slipper–two quarts' ... Edward Buzzell; 1939. (*b/w*)

The Marx Brothers Go West √√
'Any of you boys got change of ten cents? Well, keep the baggage' ... Groucho setting out to swindle the others out of $10 and losing $60 himself ... the chase for the missing deeds ... the train chopped up for firewood as it goes along ... Edward Buzzell; 1940. (*b/w*)

Mary, Mary √√
Smooth translation of the Jean Kerr stage play to the screen preserves most of the laughs, and veteran Mervyn LeRoy has added some subtle openings-out of the story of the splitting married couple (Debbie Reynolds, Barry Nelson) who come together again over a tax form; 1964. (*c*)

The Mask of Dimitrios √√
Splendid Peter Lorre–Sydney Greenstreet vehicle with the little man flashbacking over life of villain Zachary Scott; moodily, mysteriously and enjoyably directed by Jean Negulesco from Eric Ambler novel; 1944. (*b/w*)

The Masque of the Red Death √√
Imaginative horror pic by fast-worker Roger Corman, made in England in 1964, has Vincent Price as 12th-century Italian nobelman renouncing God for the Devil, from an Edgar Allan Poe story. Jane Asher, Patrick Magee come off well, and his use of colour is gorgeous and exciting. (*c*)

Masquerade √√
Spiffing tongue-in-cheek comedy-thriller with Cliff Robertson nicely restrained as he gets involved with secret agent Jack Hawkins, sending himself up delightfully. Spoofs a dozen or more straight thrillers yet emerges as professional and exciting in its own right; as good as anything Basil Dearden and Michael Relph ever produced-directed; 1965. (*c*)

Massacre ✕✕✕
Unpleasant little Western directed by Louis King, 1956, about illegal supply of guns to Red Indians. Unknown cast deserves to stay that way. (*c*)

The Master of Ballantrae √
Errol Flynn in whitewashed version of the Robert Louis Stevenson novel, made in England in 1953 to utilise frozen Warner Brothers dollars. In the book, he's a scoundrel who fights for the Stuarts and in the end both he and his brother (Anthony Steel, loyal to King George II) die, but not here. This is all happiness after some wild adventures. Director William Keighley was much helped by Jack Cardiff's fine photography. (*c*)

Master of the World √
Interesting little 1961 sci-fictioner about Vincent Price taking it on himself to destroy the world's armies, adapted from two Jules Verne stories. Unfortunately, director William Witney doesn't realise the possibilities. (*c*)

Masterson of Kansas ✕
Just one more Western involving Doc Holliday, Wyatt Earp and Bat Masterton, churned out by William Castle in 1954. George Montgomery, Nancy Bates go through the standard motions. (*c*)

The Matchmaker √
Why, hello Dolly, fancy seeing you back where you belong–in original 1958 version by Joseph Anthony of Thornton Wilder's play. Just the story without the tiresome songs and dances. Shirley Booth in Barbra Streisand's part. Tony Perkins, Shirley MacLaine. (*b/w*)

The Mating Game √
How lovable farmer Paul Douglas works exclusively on the barter principle thus screwing up city slicker tax man Tony Randall. Directed by George Marshall in 1959 from H. E. Bates' *The Darling Buds of May*, with nice little parts for

Debbie Reynolds, Fred Clark, Una Merkell. But it's all strangely lifeless, probably due to transatlantic transplant. *(c)*

The Mating of Millie ✕
Evelyn Keyes wants to adopt this child and so Glenn Ford magnanimously says he'll marry her although he's not in love with her. Well, after a while, he realises that . . . but why spoil the obvious plot? Henry Levin expertly works on the tear-ducts; 1948. *(b/w)*

A Matter of Life and Death ✕
Extravagantly awful 1946 charade about RAF flyer going to heaven, told not as a comedy but as a serious, ludicrous drama; David Niven, Roger Livesey, Raymond Massey ploughed their way through turgid plot under Powell–Pressburger team, who showed occasional moments of insight and imagination. Achieves spurious fame as first film to be selected for Royal Film Performance, an accolade that was soon to become very tarnished as industry jockeyed for this commercial fillip for bad movies. *(c & b/w)*

A Matter of WHO ✕ ✕
Odd little comedy-thriller about Terry-Thomas (in a part written for Noel Coward) tracking down where an epidemic started from. Richard Briers is assistant; Honor Blackman, Carol White, and sundry stalwarts of the British supporting actors' guild make brief appearances. But the whole thing smells of a 1961 commercial for the World Health Organisation, and director Don Chaffey never seems happy with his material. *(b/w)*

The Maverick Queen ✕
Barbara Stanwyck is bandit lady tempted to reform for the sake of under-cover detective Barry Sullivan. Joseph Kane lacked the touch to get the most out of script potential; 1956. *(c)*

Mayerling √
(1) The 1936 French version directed by Anatole Litvak made stars of Danielle Darrieux and Charles Boyer in the rather apocryphal roles of the Austrian Archduke Rudolph and his sweetheart. *(b/w)*

Mayerling ✕ ✕
(2) The 1968 version had Omar Sharif and Catherine Deneuve monumentally miscast and floppily directed by Terence Young. Ava Gardner and James Mason were equally unhappy. *(c)*

The McConnell Story ✕
Alan Ladd plays jet pilot, June Allyson long-suffering wife; Gordon Douglas did usual plodding directional job; 1955. *(c)*

McLintock! √
Clan pictures tend to be great fun for the participants but not quite as much for the suckers who sit and watch a gang of old mates fool around for an expensive home movie. This falls into an even clannier type, the family film. John Wayne is the star; Patrick Wayne, his son, has a major part; Alissa Wayne, his daughter, appears; Michael Wayne, another son, produces; Victor McLaglen's son, Andrew, directs; old fellow-actors Maureen O'Hara, Bruce Cabot, Chill Wills, Hank Worden all appear; and the technical credits are nearly all by folk who have worked on many a Wayne pic. So it's not surprising that the end result is plotless, self-indulgent, and quite good fun if you're in the mood. It's one long fight between the hard-drinking Wayne and the divorcing O'Hara in a Western setting; 1963. *(c)*

Me and the Colonel √
Episodic fable of ill-assorted couple's escape from the nazis—Akim Tamiroff, who learns humility, and Danny Kaye's modest little Jew. Alas, Peter Glenville's

static and unimaginative direction crippled what might have been a great film, although he does at least draw a memorable and self-effacing performance from Kaye. From Franz Werfel's *Jacobowsky and the Colonel*; 1958. (*b/w*)

A Medal for Benny √
Hypocrisy in a small town makes a stronger vehicle than lightweight cast of Dorothy Lamour, Arturo de Corduvo can drive. Director Irving Pichel seems to know it. John Steinbeck scripted; 1945. (*b/w*)

Meet Danny Wilson √
Interesting singer-meets-racketeer drama in that many critics in 1951 saw it is thinly-disguised biography of Frank Sinatra who himself played crooner Danny Wilson. Raymond Burr is night-club owner who hounds him and partner Alex Nichol for promised 50 per cent of his earnings, while Shelley Winters is in love with Nichol. Sinatra had some smashing songs–You're a Sweetheart, She's Funny That Way, That Old Black Magic, All of Me, How Deep is the Ocean among them–but this was his last singing role before his breakthrough the following year with *From Here to Eternity*, so if this was biopic it only told the first half of the story. Joseph Pevney, alas, kept it strictly in the rut, although Sinatra is always in the groove. (*b/w*)

Meet Me at Dawn × × ×
Dreadful rubbish about duelling in turn-of-the-century Paris, made in 1947 in England, 'starring' William Eythe and Hazel Court. Reissued in 1958 under the title *The Gay Duellist*, which they couldn't use today. Thornton Freeland directed. (*b/w*)

Meet Me in Las Vegas √
Sprightly plug for the gambling centre of America, with Dan Dailey as the luckiest guy around–he's got Cyd Charisse. Roy Rowland made it quite entertaining and there are a lot of walk-ons by famous names, including Frank Sinatra, Lena Horne, Debbie Reynolds, Peter Lorre; 1956. (*c*)

Meet Me in St Louis √ √
Judy Garland was delightful, under the spell of Vincente Minnelli in 1946 (two years before they had Lisa), as one of a well-to-do St Louis family at the time of the World's Fair there. Pa was Leon Ames, Ma Mary Astor, Tom Drake 'the boy next door'. Other songs include The Trolley Song, Have Yourself a Merry Little Christmas. (*c*)

Meet Me Tonight √
Omnibus of three Noel Coward plays–originally called *Tonight at 8.30*–directed by Anthony Pelissier in 1952. Elegantly acted by Valerie Hobson, Nigel Patrick, with robust performance from Stanley Holloway. (*c*)

Member of the Wedding √
Julie Harris growing up in the Deep South, from Carson McCullers' book; Fred Zinnemann; 1952. (*b/w*)

The Men √
Marlon Brando's first picture, 1950, while he was waiting for his stage success, *Streetcar*, to be set up as a movie. He plays ex-soldier adjusting to civilian life after paraplegia, with Teresa Wright encouraging him. Fred Zinnemann built it round him. While the film and his performance got raves, it flopped at the box-office. Teresa Wright, Jack Webb, Everett Sloane. (*b/w*)

Me, Natalie √
She, Natalie (Patty Duke), is the plainest, orneriest gal who ever did go to high school. All kinds of humiliating things happen to her because she's so ugly. Then she goes off to Greenwich Village and gets laid by handsome hippies who realise that it's what a girl's like inside

(or, at least, in bed) that counts. Oh, Hans Christian Andersen, what crimes are committed in the name of your Ugly Duckling! Fred Coe directs without too much false pathos. Martin Balsam, Elsa Lanchester strengthen supporting cast; 1969. (*c*)

Men in War   ×
Realistic action only distinguishing feature in Anthony Mann's 1957 war toughie about personal conflicts in Korean retreat. Predictably manly performances from Robert Ryan, Aldo Ray. (*b/w*)

Men of the Fighting Lady   ×
Korean War 1954 actioner about an aircraft carrier. Van Johnson, Keenan Wynn, Louis Calhern, Walter Pidgeon. Andrew Marton directed competently.
(*c*)

Merry Andrew   × ×
Pretty dire 1958 vehicle for Danny Kaye, running away to join a circus and falling in love with Pier Angeli there. He tries so hard to be charming that it's distinctly embarrassing to see him fall flat on his oily grin. Michael Kidd's chief recommendation as his director appears to have been that he let Kaye get away with anything—unfunny jokes, sickly sentiment, flabby acting. (*c*)

Micky One   √ √
Fascinating and unfairly dismissed at the time (1965) experiment in using the familiar props of the American cinema to tell the story of a man weighted down by contemporary anxieties. Arthur Penn is a commercial director who is never afraid to try something new. He has got a moving and haunting performance from Warren Beatty (and veterans Jeff Corey and Franchot Tone) in the picaresque, anguished adventures of a nightclub comedian who no longer believes in his patter. Instead, he seeks some kind of personal freedom to find

that it is no longer possible in the land of the free. The final sequence as he auditions in an enormous dark nightclub is resonant with loneliness and impotence. One tragedy was that this flawed attempt was made two years before Penn and Beatty made *Bonnie and Clyde*–released afterwards, it would have had ten times the audience and critical attention. (*b/w*)

Middle of the Night   √
Kim Novak as divorced receptionist, still sexually hankering after her ex, and Fredric March as widower, seeking happiness together, but being frustrated by all the possessive people around them. Some of Paddy Chayefsky's best friends may be Jewish (including his mother and father) but the two leads that Delbert Mann has given his script emphatically aren't. So, despite the attempts at authenticity, this remains a phoney–and once you start realising that, the overloaded black-and-white characterisations of Martin Balsam, Albert Dekker, Glenda Farrell start to show, too; 1959.
(*b/w*)

Midnight   √ √
Delicious thirties comedy (1939 actually) in which Claudette Colbert coquettes her way through Brackett–Wilder script, directed by the underrated Mitchell Leisen with a touch of genius. She pretends to be countess, John Barrymore abets her, Don Ameche threatens to expose her, Mary Astor, Monty Woolley, Hedda Hopper chip in.
(*b/w*)

Midnight Cowboy   √ √ √
A major film and a major achievement of director John Schlesinger. His portrayal and understanding of the two men in uncaring New York–would-be easy-liver Joe Buck and crippled Ratso–created an urban idyll that was both funny and sad, near-realistic and penetrating. Respectively, Jon Voight and Dustin Hoffman filled the enemies-turned-friends roles

perfectly and the final scene in the bus to Florida is genuinely pathetic. 1969 Oscar winner for best picture, best direction, best screenplay (Waldo Salt). (*c*)

Midnight Lace √
A gaslit melodrama of Doris Day being threatened by a mysterious voice; Rex Harrison as her smooth hubby; Myrna Loy and Herbert Marshall bringing some veteran gloss. Yet director David Miller rarely thrills all the way, and to a British audience the London scene is ludicrous; 1961. (*c*)

A Midsummer Night's Dream √
(1) In 1935 Warner Brothers threw together Shakespeare, famed stage producer Max Reinhardt (plus William Dieterle to show him how to film), choreographer Nijinsky and a million dollars of scenery, music and general artiness. Then they chucked it all away with a ha'p'orth of tarred casting–Dick Powell (Lysander), Victor Jory (Oberon), Anita Louise (Titania), Olivia de Havilland (Hermia), Micky Rooney (Puck), James Cagney (Bottom). Only Joe E. Brown and Hugh Herbert (Flute, Snout) worked. (*b/w*)

A Midsummer Night's Dream √
(2) In 1969 Peter Hall tried to do the same on a shoestring. Practically no attempt was made at actually creating a film: instead the moderately distinguished actors and actresses (David Warner, Diana Rigg, Helen Mirren, Judi Dench) were pushed along at GCE level with frequent use of close-up to disguise the paltry scenery and effects. (*c*)

Mighty Joe Young √
The poor gorilla's *King Kong*, Earnest B. Shoedsack; 1949. (*b/w*)

The Mikado ✕
The only version likely to reach TV is Stuart Burge's 1967 record of the D'Oyly Carte company's 1964 production, filmed on the stage of the Golders Green Hippodrome. OK for fans, but otherwise dull. Earlier, more adventurous versions–Kenny Baker as Nanki-Poo in 1939; *The Cool Mikado* (which Harold Baim made in 1962)– seem to have got lost. (*c*)

Mildred Pierce √
Joan Crawford won the 1945 Oscar for her heartrending performance as doting mother; Ann Blyth is the bitch of a daughter. Zachary Scott as lover of both. Michael Curtiz directed devotedly. (*b/w*)

The Millionairess √
Unsatisfactory adaptation of Shaw's play allows Peter Sellers to dominate with his classic Indian doctor. Sophia Loren can't manage the strength and personality of the richest woman in the world who feels miffed by his failure to respond to her. Alastair Sim is content to play Alastair Sim playing her twisted lawyer. Dennis Price is lover soon discarded, and the whole thing is petrified in GBS's ideas, Wolf Mankowitz's hesitant making-over and Anthony Asquith's theatrical direction; 1960. (*b/w*)

The Mind Benders √
Dirk Bogarde sets out to prove that his former colleague wasn't a traitor by undergoing rigorous isolation tests like prolonged floating under water which show that after them a man has no will of his own. The actual tests have a documentary interest, but the story is infuriatingly flabby and Basil Dearden's direction safe-playing; 1963. (*b/w*)

Ministry of Fear √
Combination of Graham Greene novel and director Fritz Lang should have produced more compelling thriller than this rather routine spy plot in London during the war. Ray Milland; 1944. (*b/w*)

The Miniver Story × ×
Mrs Miniver dying of cancer, upper-lip fluttering. Sequel to the deadly *Mrs Miniver*, this 1950 effort by H. C. Potter about post-war England was even more embarrassing than the original. Greer Garson, Walter Pidgeon again. (*b/w*)

The Miracle × ×
If you can believe that while Carroll Baker has run away from her convent, the statue of the Virgin Mary has stepped down to take her place, you will be able to swallow the rest of this rubbish about the Napoleonic Wars. Roger Moore is the lover she runs away to marry. When she thinks he's dead all kinds of naughty (but sadly unexciting) things happen to her. She is saved by gipsies Walter Slezak and Katina Paxinou, both hamming it up outrageously. Irving Rapper; 1959. (*c*)

Miracle in Soho × × ×
One of those really awful British comedy-dramas they still made in 1957 with John Gregson as a road-mender who breaks all the hearts in this Never-Never Land which the film-makers must have known wasn't anything like Soho (they only had to look out of their windows) but which director Julian Aymes has the cheek to try and pass off to us as the real thing. Bet Cyril Cusack, Billie Whitelaw, Ian Bannen don't watch this on the box– they'd be too ashamed. (*c*)

Miracle in the Rain ×
It never rains but it bores, wrote one reviewer when this came out in 1956. Jane Wyman, Van Johnson are two lonely people who fall in love in New York. Rudolph Maté sloshes his way through in galoshes; 1956. (*b/w*)

Miracle of Morgan's Creek √ √
James Agee on Film contains two long raves for this black farce which the former doyen of criticism saw as 'funnier, more adventurous, more abun-dant, more intelligent, more encouraging than anything made in Hollywood for years . . . as nihilistic as Céline, as deeply humane as Dickens'. Others may regard it as just an overplayed comedy with Betty Hutton conning Eddie Bracken into marriage after she finds she is pregnant by soldier whose name she can't quite remember. Sure it's tasteless, but what's so great about 'good taste'? Preston Sturges asked in 1943. (*b/w*)

The Miracle of the Bells × ×
Frank Sinatra more than faintly ludicrous as priest in this more than loudly ludicrous story of a press agent trying to pressure a film producer to release a movie held up for the unlikely reason that the star has died. Then there's a miracle–or is it?–and Frank Sinatra has the dilemma of whether to let it pass as one or not. Ho hum. Director, Irving Pichel; 1948. (*b/w*)

Miracle on 34th Street √ √
Heart-warming fable about big store Father Christmas (Edmund Gwenn) proving to little girl that he really is Santa Claus. Fascinatingly, that little girl is Natalie Wood, who was to be wife-swapped in *Bob & Carol & Ted & Alice* 22 years later–she was eight in 1946. Maureen O'Hara played Mum; George Seaton was calculatedly sentimental director. Lovely courtroom climax. (*b/w*)

The Miracle Worker √ √
Oscar-winning performance from Anne Bancroft as teacher to deaf, dumb and blind Helen Keller (Patty Duke). Arthur Penn more than faithfully translated moving, sometimes stunning Broadway play; 1962. (*b/w*)

Mirage √ √
Exciting 1965 thriller with Gregory Peck suffering from amnesia, being chased through New York after the leader of

the World Peace Movement is murdered; with George Kennedy and scene-stealer Walter Matthau; fast, action-filled direction by Edward Dmytryk. (*c*)

Miranda √
Glynis Johns as mermaid in successful unsophisticated British comedy directed cheerfully by Ken Annakin; 1948. (*b/w*)

The Misfits √√
Last film (1961) of both Clark Gable and Marilyn Monroe about rounding up wild horses for pet food. Arthur Miller wrote, John Huston directed, and Montgomery Clift (also since died), Thelma Ritter and Eli Wallach were in it too. Yet it wasn't quite the great film it should have been, due perhaps to some stumbling editing and writing as well as Huston's increasing impatience with his actors. It's hard to watch without melancholy overtaking one; 1961. (*b/w*)

The Missing Juror √
Budd Boetticher thriller about revenge on jury that found innocent prisoner guilty; Jim Bannon, Janis Carter, George Macready; 1945. (*b/w*)

Mission Mars ×××
Dreadful little bit of cheap nonsense about landing on Mars, with Darren McGavin, Nick Adams; director Nick Webster; 1969. (*c*)

The Missouri Traveller ×
Undemanding whimsy about orphan boy and his horse determined to make their way in the world. With Brandon de Wilde, Gary Merrill and Lee Marvin – as the villain, of course, as it's 1958; Jerry Hopper. (*c*)

Mister Roberts √√
John Ford and Mervyn LeRoy both had a hand in directing this wildly successful wartime comedy-drama of merchantship that Henry Fonda longs to take into battle. Fonda had created the title role in the smash-hit Broadway play but producer Leland Hayward decided he had been too long away from the screen (seven years) to do the film version. Despite the traumas, the tight Frank Nugent–Josh Logan script stood up under the strain, and with the help of stalwarts James Cagney (slightly potty captain), William Powell (Doc) and Jack Lemmon (lazy Ensign Pulver – won Oscar for support), the movie steamed home as a wild success; 1955. (*c*)

Mister Ten Per Cent ×××
Poor Charlie Drake vehicle stretched to a long, long film and the little man surrounded by vapid support actors, becomes a great big bore. Peter Graham Scott does his best; 1967. (*c*)

Mix Me a Person √
A bit of a thriller, with Adam Faith as condemned teenager being proven innocent by his defence counsel – Anne Baxter, imported from America in 1962 to improve the box-office prospects there. Husband Donald Sinden thinks Adam must be guilty because, just like Lee J. Cobb in *Twelve Angry Men*, he hates all teenage toughies. Some good British character actors bravely support Leslie Norman's painstaking attempts, which ultimately make a watchable drama. (*b/w*)

Moby Dick √
His name is Ahab and he sails again in the mad chase to kill the giant whale. Director John Huston provides some visual excitement but Gregory Peck is sadly miscast. Confused backing from Orson Welles, Leo Genn in 1956. Earlier versions were with John Barrymore (1926 – called *The Sea Beast* – and 1930). (*c*)

Modern Times √√
Last sight of the silent Chaplin tramp, in 1936, as he and Paulette Goddard walk off hand-in-hand into the sunset.

Up to then, they have had all sorts of adventures singly and together, including the famous opening sequence in the factory when Charlie gets into the cogs. Goddard is an orphan who gets a job as a cabaret dancer. And there's the scene in the store when he joins his fellow-workers in a party at the expense of the management. Beyond (some would say above, some below) criticism. *(b/w)*

Modesty Blaise √
Joseph Losey directed, in 1966, this violent spoof on violence but ended up by tripping over his own intentions. Worth seeing for fluency of action and creepy performance by Dirk Bogarde, although Monica Vitti looked lost, as though mislaid by Antonioni. Clive Revill comes off best. *(c)*

Mogambo √
Clark Gable re-creates role he pioneered in *Red Dust* with Jean Harlow–this time with Ava Gardner (girlfriend) and Grace Kelly (another man's–Donald Sinden–wife)–as great white hunter at home with wild animals but at a loss with wilder women. John Ford directed; 1953. *(c)*

Moment of Danger ✕
Dull little thriller about Trevor Howard and Dorothy Dandridge chasing Edmund Purdom round Spain to get their share of the proceeds of a robbery. Only the caper at the start carries any of the tautness one expects from Laslo (*The Wild Ones*) Benedek; 1960. *(b/w)*

Moment to Moment ✕ ✕
Sadly silly yarn about Jean Seberg shooting lover in the South of France–which merely gives him amnesia. When he remembers, will he tell? This 1966 drama from old-timer Mervyn LeRoy takes one look at the New Permissiveness and runs back to the old hokum. *(c)*

The Money Trap ✕
A couple of crooked American cops (aren't they all, one wonders sometimes) get hold of the combination of a doctor's safe and decide to take the vast amount of cash he keeps there. Glenn Ford is out-acted by partner Ricardo Montalban in this duo. Joseph Cotten is the doc. What could have been a taut thriller is allowed to go very slack indeed by director Burt Kennedy; 1966. *(b/w)*

Monkey Business √ √
(1) The Marx Brothers' third film, made in 1931. They are stowaways involved with gangsters; Norman Z. McLeod directed the traffic. *(b/w)*

Monkey Business √ √
(2) Howard Hawks' 1952 farce about over-rejuvenation has stunning cast of Cary Grant, Marilyn Monroe ('half child, but not the visible half'), Ginger Rogers, Charles Coburn. A chimp steals it, though. *(b/w)*

Monkey on My Back √
Dated (1957) warning about dangers of dope addiction, as evinced by boxer Barney Ross. Cameron Mitchell heads undistinguished cast directed by André de Toth. *(b/w)*

Monsieur Beaucaire √
Bob Hope fans will doubtless find his barber sent on suicide mission in historical France, funny enough. But Valentino was funnier in 1924. George Marshall directed this one in 1946. *(b/w)*

Monsieur Verdoux
Chaplin's fascinating if muddled attempt in 1947 to warn the world against future wars by portraying a criminal who has the same philosophy as governments, conscienceless because the world has lost its conscience. So he murders wives for profit. Of course, being Chaplin, he has to have a soft, squashy interior and is

forever making sentimental gestures. The martinet quality of the main character perfectly suits his own dapper personality. (*b/w*)

Montana ✗
Errol Flynn played his true nationality, Australian, in this poor little story of sheepherder invading American West. Alexis Smith is first attracted to him, then is opposed to him when she learns he opposes her cattle-ranching, then they all get together; directed by Ray Enright in 1949. (*b/w*)

Monte Carlo or Bust ✓✓
Villainous Terry-Thomas (it suits him better than his usual vapid silly ass part), helped by blackmailed assistant Eric Sykes, challenges Tony Curtis to a side-bet in a twenties Monte Carlo Rally race. Other contestants include Peter Cook and Dudley Moore, also better cast than usual as another master–servant team. There's also a host of international stars whizzing to Monte Carlo from all over Europe (Bourvil, Walter Chiari, Susan Hampshire, Jack Hawkins, Hattie Jacques, Richard Wattis) and the whole 1969 comedy really is great fun. Christmas would be the time to show it on the box. Ken Annakin. (*c*)

The Monte Carlo Story ✗✗✗
A real stinker, with Marlene Dietrich and Vittorio de Sica as two poor noble persons who are gambling mad. It's hard to feel much sympathy for their supposed poverty on their yachts or for the American father and daughter they consider marrying for money. Samuel A. Taylor couldn't even arrange to photograph Miss Dietrich without revealing her true age–55 in 1957. (*c*)

The Moon and Sixpence ✓✓
George Sanders as Gauguinesque painter in adaptation of Maugham novel, with Herbert Marshall rather unnervingly popping in as the author. Albert Lewin wrote and directed in dazzling 1942 debut. (*b/w*)

Moonfleet ✓
Stewart Granger swashing many a buckle (or should it be buckling a swash?) on his pirate's progress, George Sanders and Viveca Lindfors co-starring. Worth a look for the fact that it was made in 1955 by Fritz Lang. (*c*)

The Moon is Blue ✓
There was a great censorship kerfuffle over Otto Preminger's transfer of F. Hugh Herbert's stage comedy, in 1953. He insisted on keeping hitherto taboo words like 'virgin' and 'seduction' in the script about misunderstanding over Maggie McNamara between David Niven and William Holden. All very naughty-sounding but actually pathetically mild. (*b/w*)

The Moonraker ✗✗
It's George Baker, who helps his King Charles escape the Roundheads in this old-fashioned, creaky yarn about Cavaliers in the right and Marius Goring in the wrong; pretty tiresome stuff, unimaginatively directed by David Macdonald in 1958. (*c*)

Moon Zero Two ✗✗
Hammer and Roy Ward Baker went into orbit in 1969 with this space cowboy-type thriller, but didn't manage much of a job. The moon has been colonised in 2021, but humans still have human greeds. Warren Mitchell is chief heavy, stealing a sapphire asteroid; Catherina von Schell is looking for her brother; James Olson promises to help her. Come in *Moon Zero Two*, your time is up. (*c*)

The More the Merrier ✓
Jovial comedy of Jean Arthur platonically sharing apartment with Joel McCrea and Charles Coburn, which was awfully ooh-la-la in 1943 (and even in 1966 when it was remade as *Walk Don't Run*)

but is accepted as part of life among today's young people. Still, George Stevens squeezed some fun out of it then. (*b/w*)

Morgan – A Suitable Case for Treatment √
One of the more bitter disappointments of the sixties (1966 to be precise). With the starting-point of a David Mercer television play, Karel Reisz cooked up an extravagant, would-be meaningful soufflé that failed to rise. David Warner plays an artist-in-revolt, whose ideas and antics still attract his ex-wife, although she is remarrying. Most famous moment is when David Warner dressed in a gorilla suit, breaks up Vanessa Redgrave's wedding to Robert Stephens. Looking back, it's depressing to see how all that really works is the farce (with Irene Handl and Bernard Bresslaw carrying on the best of that). Its political ideas seem as dated as the Aldermaston Marches – which doesn't make them any less valid, only lessens their impact, never very great in the context of such a jazzily shot-and-cut crazy comedy. (*b/w*)

The Most Dangerous Man in the World √√
... is Gregory Peck, an American scientist allowed to work with the Red Chinese because they have discovered new formula that the State Department wants. The CIA fits his brain up with a transmitter (via satellite) and, without his knowing, a little bomb to blow him up if they want to. This makes for an exciting picture, which J. Lee Thompson saves from falling into a waiting standard sci-fi rut. As a military bigwig, Arthur Hill has the best lines and takes advantage of it. Chairman Mao is played convincingly by Conrad Yama; 1969. (*c*)

Moulin Rouge √
José Ferrer kneeling and hobbling about as Toulouse-Lautrec in John Huston's 1952 drama-with-music that worked better than most Great Artist biopics partly because he wasn't such a serious painter that he demanded a po-faced treatment. Unsympathetic cast (Zsa Zsa Gabor, Christopher Lee, Ferrer) weakens the effect. (*c*)

The Mountain Road √
War film (set 1944, made 1960) about James Stewart blowing up bridges and sundry other bits of road to stop Japanese advance and failing to understand or tolerate Chinese refugees who get in his way. Script by Alfred Hayes from Theodore White novel tries hard to make it into portrait of a man whose power goes to his head, but is defeated by director Daniel Mann's apparent desire to turn in conventional war-pic. (*b/w*)

Mourning Becomes Electra √
Rosalind Russell, Michael Redgrave, Raymond Massey, Katina Paxinou fit uneasily as co-stars in inevitably talky version of Eugene O'Neill's making over of the Agamemnon myth, avenging death of father. Dudley Nichols; 1947. (*b/w*)

The Mouse That Roared √
The film that put Peter Sellers on the international map in 1958. Jack Arnold economically directed Roger Mac-Dougall's script of a tiny kingdom that declared war on the US and won by mistake. He saved money by casting Sellers in three roles, including one that Margaret Rutherford adopted in the sequel – see next entry. (*c*)

The Mouse on the Moon √
Follow-up to *The Mouse That Roared* was also the last in the series – understandably. Dick Lester used the idea of a satire on the space race to indulge his penchant for tricks, and fine actors like Margaret Rutherford, Terry-Thomas,

June Ritchie, John le Mesurier got smothered in slick whimsy. Some nice moments between the longueurs, however; 1963. (*c*)

Move Over Darling √
There's something about Doris Day that makes her ideal TV (particularly in colour). Maybe it's the frothiness evident here, as wife returned from dead, confronting newly remarried husband James Garner. Michael Gordon directed this jolly 1963 remake of 1940s *My Favourite Wife*. (*c*)

The Moving Target √ √
Paul Newman convincingly inhabits role of hip Harper, private eye low on funds but high on principle (unlike Philip Marlowe) in this William Goldman-scripted version of Ross Macdonald novel that Jack Smight excitingly directed in 1966. Co-stars Lauren Bacall, Bogart's widow. Millionaire-hunt illuminates a world as cold and flashy as neon. This thriller had a huge success and turned Newman into a blockbusting super-star, after 22 films. Others in this 'constant-jeopardy' plot about a kidnap were Robert Wagner, Julie Harris, Janet Leigh (as his wife), Shelley Winters, Robert Webber. (*c*)

Mr Blandings Builds His Dream House √ √
Cary Grant, Myrna Loy and Melvyn Douglas as townies who get taken for a ride when they decide to build a house in the country; H. C. Potter directed stylishly; 1948. (*b/w*)

Mr Moses √
Interesting Biblically-paralleled yarn of Robert Mitchum leading tribe of Masai to a promised land, away from their flood-threatened village. Carroll Baker is unlikely missionary's daughter. Ronald Neame directed with his usual attention to detail; 1965. (*c*)

Mr Sardonicus × ×
Disappointing horror movie from William Castle about an 18th-century count whose face is set in a horrible grin so he has to wear a mask and have Awful Goings-On in the cellar. Oscar Homolka can't save it; 1962. (*b/w*)

Mr Skeffington √
And the moral of this soap opera, says Agee, 'is hang on to your husband . . . and count yourself blessed if like Claude Rains in his old age, he is blinded'. Up till then, Bette Davis has been playing one of the biggest bitches in her gallery of bitches, and if you'd enjoy seeing about two hours of her bitchery – and you will, you will – settle down to a good sob (or laugh). Vincent Sherman loyally directed; 1944. (*b/w*)

Mrs Brown, You've Got a Lovely Daughter × × ×
Dreadful little pop film with Peter Noone and Herman's Hermits and Stanley Holloway and some greyhounds and Mona Washbourne and Avis Bunnage and Lance Percival and some dreary music and just about every predictable situation that will flash through your mind as the opening titles drown you. 1968 seems awfully late for this sort of nothing, and the fact that it's produced by Allen Klein should give somebody some uneasy nights. The director is called Saul Swimmer. (*c*)

Mrs Gibbons' Boys × ×
Knockabout comedy wrong-headedly adapted for British cast from an American play. Max Varnel misses most of his opportunities, both as director and writer, and Kathleen Harrison is too one-note as Mrs G. Compensations are Lionel Jeffries, Diana Dors, John le Mesurier, Dick Emery; 1962. (*b/w*)

Mrs Miniver ×
Greer Garson smilin' thru the blitz, Dunkirk and various other wartime

traumas, keeping her and her family's upper lips stiff. The fact that they were in Hollywood at the time may have had something to do with the film's glassy unreality. This 1942 weepie, which many Englishmen found nauseating and patronising, won six Oscars (film, actress, female support–Teresa Wright, director–William Wyler, script, photography) and when Greer Garson made her acceptance speech she meandered on for half an hour, much to the embarrassment of the Motion Picture Academy, and thus forcing a subsequent change of routine. (*b/w*)

Mrs Parkington　　　　　　×
Greer Garson and Walter Pidgeon together again two years after *Mrs Miniver*, with her as thrusting society lady with Edward Arnold, Agnes Moorehead, Gladys Cooper outshining the principals. Tay Garnett was tough director; 1944. (*b/w*)

Mr Topaze　　　　　　× ×
Peter Sellers made the mistake of directing himself as simple schoolteacher turned swindler in this unfunny 1961 version of Marcel Pagnol's *Topaze*. (*c*)

The Mudlark　　　　　　√
How Queen Victoria emerged from mourning after an urchin wangled his way into the Palace. Oh yeah? Irene Dunne plays the grand dame, Andrew Ray the tiddler. Director Jean Negulesco guaranteed that it was more Hollywood than Osborne. Alec Guinness makes Disraeli dominate; 1950. (*b/w*)

The Mummy　　　　　　√
(1) The daddy of all the Egyptology scaries, with Boris Karloff as the buried-alive high priest Im-ho-tep who, aeons later, seeks a princess's reincarnation. Karl Freund, who photographed *Dracula*, directed this one in 1932 and achieved shock-eschewing mood piece. (The early forties saw three sequels with Lon Chaney Jr–*The Mummy's Tomb, Ghost* and *Curse.*) (*b/w*)

The Mummy　　　　　　√
(2) 1959 Hammer remake with Christopher Lee in Victorian setting. Peter Cushing was the Egyptologist in this rather Freudian version by Terence Fisher, with tongue-pulling for castration and gun-blasts for breasts in the shrouded ghost. (*b/w*)

The Mummy's Shroud　　　　　×
Hammer sequel in 1966 by John Gilling, to their remake of *The Mummy*. This time André Morell is nosey scientist who gets murdered for his inquisitiveness. (*c*)

Murder Ahoy　　　　　　×
Fourth Miss Marple comedy-thriller with Margaret Rutherford enjoying herself hugely as Agatha Christie's detective, this time in an original story but still directed, rather haphazardly, by George Pollock. Lionel Jeffries plays the skipper of a training ship where most of the murders and action take place; 1965. (*b/w*)

Murder at the Gallop　　　　　×
Margaret Rutherford as Miss Marple blithely ignores the awfulness of all around her as she rides through this cursory whodunit, cheerfully directed in 1963 by George Pollock, from an Agatha Christie yarn, *After the Funeral*. Robert Morley's presence ensures a few extra laughs. (*b/w*)

Murder by Contract　　　　　√
Interesting low-budgeter about professional killer Vince Edwards who meets woman assigned as his next victim and is suddenly faced with the question of morality. It doesn't shirk from pointing out that what is appalling in our society is perfectly acceptable for soldiers, and Irving Lerner steers a tight directorial course between plain thrills and philosophical reasoning; 1960. (*b/w*)

Murderers' Row ✗
As Matt Helm, special agent, matched against I-shall-destroy-the-world Karl Malden, insouciant Dean Martin glides his way inconsequently through a series of Saintly predicaments, tricked out with gimmicks like a delayed-action gun. Unfortunately, Henry Levin's direction is similarly slow-moving. Strictly for addicts of mid-Atlantic shooting-wallpaper; 1966. (*c*)

Murder Inc. √
1951 thriller, with Humphrey Bogart as Asst. D.A. who cracks open murder-for-payment gang. Everett Sloane, Zero Mostel head the gang, who are caught by a whodunit-type clue. Bretaigne Windust. (*b/w*)

Murder Incorporated √
1960 saw an interesting attempt, with same title, to make a more-or-less truthful account of the gang that could be hired to kill anyone for money. But directors Burt Balaban and Stuart Rosenberg didn't make it taut enough and let Peter Falk go over the top in his portrayal of a sadistic killer; Stuart Whitman and May Britt were the couple scared out of their wits, rather more than you are likely to be; 1960. (*b/w*)

The Murder Men ✗
Confused jazz movie about dope fiends. Poor Dorothy Dandridge may get hooked again because club owner James Coburn is pushing the stuff. Director John Peyser unclear if he's for the police or against bad laws or both or neither; 1963. (*b/w*)

Murder Most Foul ✗
Cosy Miss Marple mystery (third with Margaret Rutherford, made in 1964) about crime in a rep. From Agatha Christie's whodunit, *Mrs McGinty's Dead*. Andrew Cruickshank, James Bolam, Terry Scott among TV names present. Directed again by George Pollock. (*b/w*)

Murder She Said √
Nice little adaptation of Agatha Christie whodunit, *4.50 to Paddington*, in which Miss Marple spots a murder in a passing train. Margaret Rutherford is splendid, of course, though nobody else is allowed to come near her by the simple and economical expedient of casting most of the rest of the parts with third-rate actors and actresses. Or perhaps director George Pollock thought they were OK – it would fit in with his idea of how to direct a thriller; 1961. (*b/w*)

The Music Man √ √
Rousing 1962 transfer by Morton da Costa from stage-hit, keeping Robert Preston's cocksure performance as boys' band organiser intact. Straightforward, jolly tunes, undemanding Shirley Jones, Buddy Hackett. (*c*)

Mutiny on the Bounty √ √
(1) Heroic Fletcher Christian (Clark Gable) *v.* arch-villain Captain Bligh (Charles Laughton) in classic sea-story filmed in 1935 and unsurpassed since; Frank Lloyd directed; won Oscar as best film. (*b/w*)

Mutiny on the Bounty ✗
(2) 1962 version failed to establish anything like the same relationship between Christian (Marlon Brando with a ludicrous accent) and Bligh (Trevor Howard). Director Lewis Milestone makes the voyage out more exciting, but comes to grief with Tahiti and the subsequent mutiny. Pity. (*c*)

My Blood Runs Cold √
Jolly piece of teenage hokum about a nutty boy (Troy Donahue) who pretends – or is it so? – that he and Joey Heatherton (sorry, she's a girl – it's not that kind of liberated movie) had been lovers in a previous incarnation. There's a murder and a storm at sea and it's all directed neatly enough by William Conrad, the fat detective in TV's *Cannon*; 1965. (*b/w*)

My Cousin Rachel　　　　　　√
A did-she-do-it? mystery plot from Daphne du Maurier novel, directed by Henry Koster. Olivia de Havilland is question-mark; 1953. (*b/w*)

My Darling Clementine　　　　√
Climaxing in the great gunfight at the OK corral, this John Ford Western is considered by many critics as the greatest ever made. Ford actually knew Wyatt Earp, and it's his story (he's Henry Fonda) and the complex relationship with Doc Holliday (Victor Mature) that got lost in the TV series; 1946. (*b/w*)

My Geisha　　　　　　×　×
If, by any remote chance, you can't have too much of Shirley MacLaine, this is the movie for you. She plays an American film star, a geisha girl, Madame Butterfly, and is up there all the time yak-yakking away, supposedly proving to her husband, the film director, she's the girl to play the part. Edward G. Robinson, Yves Montand, Robert Cummings only get a look in, which may be less than you want. Jack Cardiff; 1962. (*c*)

My Man Godfrey　　　　　　√
Competent 1957 remake of the 1936 wacky comedy about butler-and-rich-mistress comes off extremely well, thanks to David Niven's cool and dry performance in the shoes of William Powell. June Allyson is OK as the girl, Jessie Royce Landis brightly *grande dame* as a society hostess. Henry Koster has wisely not tried to improve on the original, and provides a comfortable entertainment. (*c*)

My Sister Eileen　　　　　　√
(1) Fun in wacky Greenwich Village comedy, made twice. (1) Rosalind Russell, Janet Blair were the country mice who conquer New York, under Alexander Hall's fatherly direction; 1942. (*b/w*)

My Sister Eileen　　　　　　√
(2) Janet Leigh, Betty Garrett were rather put in the shade by exuberant Jack Lemmon in Richard Quine's musical adaptation; 1955. (*c*)

My Six Loves　　　　　　×　×
If Debbie Reynolds adopting six children and a dog is your idea of yummy entertainment, you'll have a lovely sentimental time over this one, directed by dancer Gower Champion; Cliff Robertson is oddly-cast Rev. It was cut by twenty minutes when shown here in the cinema–putting it back might make some of the plot references understandable, but would increase the tedium; 1963. (*c*)

Mysterious Island　　　　　　×
Rather pointless sci-fi with giant crabs and erupting volcano on Pacific isle from a Jules Verne fantasy. Cy Endfield does his best with what is really only a vehicle for some special effects. A largely inferior cast of British stock actors stumble through it; 1962. (*c*)

Mystery Submarine　　　　　　×　×
Old-fashioned war film about sending back captured German U-boat with British crew to decoy the rest of the nazi fleet never really surfaces. Edward Judd is fine as the jut-jawed captain; James Robertson Justice behaves as if he has wandered in from playing his usual straight role in a *Carry On* movie. Director, C. M. Pennington-Richards; 1963. (*b/w*)

My Teenage Daughter　　　　×　×　×
Prudish prune of a film made in 1956 by Herbert Wilcox to give wifey Anna Neagle a chance to show off some nice clothes and her pained expressions as teenager Sylvia Syms slips out to the jazz club. (*b/w*)

My Wife's Family　　　　×　×　×
A mother-in-law comedy with Ted Ray.

If that doesn't put you off try the rest of the cast: Ronald Shiner, Robertson Hare, Greta Gynt. Gilbert Gunn wrote–directed; 1956. (*c*)

The Naked and the Dead   √
Norman Mailer's war novel could have made a great film, with its raw language, clearly-defined character and action scenes; alas, old-timer Raoul Walsh couldn't quite rise to the occasion as director in 1958, but worth looking at for Raymond Massey; Aldo Ray, Cliff Robertson are other leading soldiers. (*c*)

Naked City   √ √
Jules Dassin's location-shot thriller with police searching real New York for girl's killer. Gave birth to superior TV film series. This original had Barry Fitzgerald, Howard Duff; 1948. (*b/w*)

Naked Earth   × ×
Turgid turn-of-the-century tale of Irish farmer Richard Todd and French wife Juliette Greco trying to make a go of things in Africa. Mis-directed by Vincent Sherman; 1958. (*b/w*)

The Naked Edge   × ×
Gary Cooper's 92nd and last picture, made in Britain in 1961, and it looks as though nobody knew whether or not he

Marlene Dietrich in *No Highway*

was a murderer – neither screen wife Deborah Kerr, him, nor director Michael Anderson. Eric Portman is loony ex-barrister, Hermione Gingold and Peter Cushing add characterizations, but the plot is so dire and the imitative direction so full of hitches and cock-ups that it's one big yawn. (*b/w*)

The Naked Jungle √
The humans (Eleanor Parker, Charlton Heston) fortunately matter less than the red ants that surround them, threatening horrible death in the Brazilian jungle, and have been treated somewhat cursorily by Byron Haskin. You'll never look at an anthill in the same way again; 1954. (*c*)

The Naked Maja × ×
Trivialisation of the life of Goya (Anthony Franciosa), concentrating on his relationship with the Duchess of Alba (Ava Gardner), cheaply directed (not necessarily inexpensively) by Henry Koster; 1959. (*c*)

The Naked Prey √ √
Interesting attempt to make a chase film with significance directed, produced and starring Cornel Wilde, still trying in 1966 to live down the memory of his Chopin in *A Song to Remember* (who could forget it?). Here, he puts himself in the place of a white hunter captured in 1840 by hostile African tribesmen who give him the 'chance' of being hunted like the animals he was butchering. How he runs from the ten tribesmen after him – across jungle and scrubland – is given Significance by intercuts with the animals. In addition, the 'savages' are not shown as such automatons as the movies usually make them, which alone gives one reason to cheer. And there are others. (*c*)

The Naked Runner √
Not the most exciting spy story ever made, but British-shot thriller does have Frank Sinatra, Peter Vaughan, Edward Fox; Sidney Furie directs flashily enough to cover the many holes, like how Sinatra happens to have his gun with him on his trip to eastern Europe and how the Secret Service managed to get the patsy to fall in with its plans. As one critic said at the time, if Frank Sinatra took as much care over his movie material as he did over his music we'd have some better pictures; 1967. (*c*)

The Naked Spur √
James Stewart, Janet Leigh, Robert Ryan in location-shot thriller of group tracking down price-on-head outlaw. Superior direction by Anthony Mann makes them all come alive as characters; 1953. (*c*)

The Naked Truth √
Dennis Price takes honours as blackmailing publisher in Mario Zampi's 1956 broad comedy, despite Peter Sellers' superbly creepy TV personality and Peggy Mount's bluff novelist. (*b/w*)

The Nanny √
Is the trusted old nanny a murderess or is it all the malicious imagination of the little boy? As you wait to find out, you have plenty of time to admire Bette Davis, senior citizen among superstars, losing none of her power in 1965. Unfortunately, Seth Holt couldn't do much with Jimmy Sangster's Hammer script which has Jill Bennett screaming on the floor, children dying in the bath and sundry other horrors. (*b/w*)

National Velvet √ √
One of Elizabeth Taylor's best performances was in this 1944 yarn about 12-year-old girl training for Grand National.
Despite flaws (e.g. training routine, the race itself), it grips, and Mickey Rooney's surprising performance complements hers. It was Anne Revere's mother that won an Academy Award, though, and Donald Crisp, Angela

Lansbury respond almost as well as the horse to Clarence Brown's direction. (*c*)

Navajo Run √ √
Remarkable sleeper produced, directed and starred in by one Johnny Seven, who plays a half-breed Navajo who is bitten by a snake and forces his way into a hostile home of three internecine fighters who help him only grudgingly. The interplay between these three and the intruder is tautly brought out, and holds you tight; 1966. (*b/w*)

The Navy Lark √
Pleasant 1959 comedy from the radio series, better than most *Carry Ons*, about Cecil Parker, Ronald Shiner, Leslie Phillips & Co trying to keep the cushy number they have on an island near Portsmouth; Sid Colin and Laurie Wyman's script involves them in all sorts of risible subterfuges, and Gordon Parry directs good-heartedly. (*b/w*)

Nearly a Nasty Accident × ×
Routine British comedy with Jimmy Edwards, Kenneth Connor, Shirley Eaton, Richard Wattis, Eric Barker about mechanic who messes up everything and everybody in the aircraft industry. Patronising. Don Chaffey; 1961. (*b/w*)

Nevada Smith √
This started as a spin-off from *The Carpetbaggers*, in which Alan Ladd played a character with a Past. This is the Past (hunting down the three murderers of his parents and dispatching them each in turn), but before he could make it Ladd died. So, in 1966, Steve McQueen took over. Henry Hathaway produced (and directed) a slick job that should keep you watching to the end. (*c*)

Never Let Go √
Richard Todd takes on gangster Peter Sellers (refreshing in uncomic part) as he tries to retrieve stolen car. It's all so

unlike real life while pretending to be authentic that it finally sickens (particularly at dirty-fighting climax), but John Guillermin kept the Alun Falconer script rolling, and Adam Faith and Carol White are a couple of youngsters who, as we now know, were to go on to fulfil the promise they showed in this 1960 thriller. (*b/w*)

Never Love a Stranger ×
Steve McQueen's first speaking film, 1958 (he was an extra in *Somebody Up There Likes Me*, in 1956), playing hoodlum John Drew Barrymore's boyhood friend. It was a bit of a mess in all departments, thanks partly to director Robert Stevens, but remains an interesting museum piece for McQueen's debut. (*b/w*)

Never on Sunday √
Without that twangy theme-tune this 1960 shot-in-Greece American effort, directed by Jules Dassin, might have lapsed into decent obscurity. As it is, the Melina Mercouri portrayal of a conventional whore's making-over by a guilty American has attained a stature that it never deserved. Amusing but flawed, it provides a pleasant enough vehicle to show off Mercouri showing off. (*b/w*)

Never Put It in Writing √
Or, at least tear it up before you mail it. That's the lesson of this refreshingly funny film from thriller-merchants Andrew and Virginia Stone in 1964. Pat Boone (groan) writes a very rude letter to his boss complaining of nepotism when he hears he was passed over for promotion, posts it, and then hears he has been made a junior partner in the firm. So he has to retrieve the letter. But the Irish post office won't allow it (he's in Ireland, you see). So he hires a plane and races it to London. Of course, the pilot's potty, and so on and on . . . Nice performances from Milo O'Shea, Reginald Beckwith, Colin Blakely. (*b/w*)

Never Say Goodbye ✗ ✗
(1) Drippy comedy-drama about how Errol Flynn and Eleanor Parker split up but get back together again for the sake of the child, replusive Patti Brady. Notable for brilliant impersonation by Flynn of Humphrey Bogart, facilitated by dubbing Bogart's own voice on to the soundtrack. Director James V. Kern; 1946. (*b/w*)

Never Say Goodbye ✗ ✗
(2) 1956 remake wasn't of above but of William Dieterle's *This Love of Ours*, an even soapier confection, with Rock Hudson meeting Cornell Borchers many years after their separation, and coming together–for the sake of the child. Jerry Hopper directed this, with feeling.
(*c*)

Never So Few ✗
Burma guerrilla actioner not nearly good enough for stars Frank Sinatra, Steve McQueen; also Gina Lollobrigida, Brian Donlevy, Charles Bronson. One point in its favour is that it came bravely out and charged that Chiang Kai-Shek's Nationalist Chinese government sold US arms for profit to Japanese invaders and local bandits. But Sinatra's on-off romance with Lollo, playing Paul Henried's mistress, is a bit of a pill. John Sturges; 1959. (*c*)

Never Steal Anything Small ✓ ✓
. . . when you have the chance of stealing something big, is a-moral of this wicked story of how crooked union boss James Cagney cons his way into a small fortune, the hearts of his union voters, but not into that of married woman (Shirley Jones). Director Charles Lederer put an almost Billy Wilder gloss on to an unproduced stage musical by Maxwell Anderson, called *Devil's Hornpipe*, and came up with a nice black comedy in 1958. (*c*)

Never Take Sweets from a Stranger ✗ ✗ ✗
Titillatory exercise in child molesting, naturally pretending to be a Solemn Warning and Plea for Medical Treatment of criminally insane. Gwen Watford, Patrick Allen, Felix Aylmer hammered it home in 1960, under Cyril Frankel's opportunistic direction. (*b/w*)

Never Too Late ✗ ✗
Nasty little comedy about a middle-aged pregnancy and how it annoys her grown-up daughter who decides to have a baby herself. So that's funny? Director Bud Yorkin thought so, but evidently failed to get his conviction over to Paul Ford, Connie Stevens, Maureen O'Sullivan; 1966. (*c*)

New Face in Hell ✗
Carnography is to blood and violence what pornography is to sex and eroticism, and around 1967 there were a lot of carnographic movies starting to be made. This is one of them, using the hiring of private eye George Peppard by villain Raymond Burr as an excuse for an endless stream of blood. Briton John Guillermin directed in America. (*c*)

New Faces ✓
Little more than film of Broadway revue, but has charm, some wit, pretty music. This was start of Eartha Kitt's slinky act, aptly summed up in song Monotonous. But Robert Clary compensates. Harry Horner directed cameras on to Leonard Sillman's stage; 1954. (*c*)

The New Interns ✗
They can call it New, but it isn't; it's that old hospital multi-drama. In this one there's a doctor who finds he's sterile (he's an obstetrician–get the irony) and various other sub-plots, which are confusing because there isn't any main plot–just like *Emergency Ward Ten* and *General Hospital*. Only George Segal rises slightly above the general mush, as a tough new intern. John Rich directed; 1965. (*b/w*)

A New Kind of Love × ×
That awful title is derived from an old Chevalier song, and here he momentarily sings it, just to prove we really are in Paris, not some Hollywood back-lot. But are we? Despite Paul Newman and Joanne Woodward (neither of whose forte is comedy) this remains one of those ooh-la-la Middle Western misconceptions about the naughty French and the terrible things that can happen to nice Americans there. Blame goes to producer-director-writer Mel Shavelson and his weak plot about the love-hate relationship between a career girl and a journalist. Naturally, it contains that scene where she sheds her masculine mien and goes into a beauty shop, to emerge desirable, and unrecognisable to Newman who promptly romances her. As critic Judith Crist wrote: 'Doris Day and Rock Hudson they're not – and shouldn't aspire to be'; 1963. (*c*)

New York Confidential √
Richard Conte in gangster thriller made in 1955 by Russell Rouse. Broderick Crawford was Mr Big; Anne Bancroft his daughter. (*b/w*)

Next to No Time × ×
Henry Cornelius, who made *Genevieve*, deserved a better memorial than this posthumous creaky comedy, released in 1958. Kenneth More, blundering about an ocean liner, insulting Roland Culver, is dreadfully miscast, as is Betsy Drake as a film star. (*c*)

Niagara √
Marilyn Monroe in dresses 'cut so low you can see her knees', as the script says, fights the Falls for attention, and wins. She also fights the story about her murdering her husband, and with director Henry Hathaway's help, holds it to a draw. Made in 1953, it was her 18th film, and gave her Joseph Cotten, Jean Peters as co-stars. (*c*)

A Nice Girl Like Me ×
Barbara Ferris, an excellent actress, is pertly miscast as the dreamy innocent of Desmond Davis' 1969 film about two unwanted pregnancies and a third baby shoved into her arms through a train window. Harry Andrews, in a grey beard, plays a different kind of role from the police superintendent or general he usually has – here, for the first time in his life, he has a romantic lead. It's all very sweet on a grown-up story-book level, but it's also rather safe and silly. (*c*)

Nicholas Nickleby √
Dickens adaptation is second-rate due more to undistinguished cast (Derek Bond, Cedric Hardwicke, Mary Merrall, Sally Ann Howes, Bernard Miles) than to Alberto Cavalcanti's game direction; 1947. (*b/w*)

Night and Day ×
Unconvincing biography of Cole Porter (not surprising as it had to leave out a central personal fact about him in 1946, when he was still alive and the subject was taboo, anyway). Cary Grant as Cole, under Michael Curtiz' predictable direction looks as though he knows it's all a fraud. But the music is stunning, of course: Begin the Beguine, What is This Thing Called Love, Miss Otis Regrets, Just One of Those Things, Do I Love You?, My Heart Belongs to Daddy, I Get a Kick Out of You, You're the Top, I've Got You Under My Skin, In the Still of the Night, Let's Do It, Easy to Love, and the title-song. (*c*)

A Night at the Opera √ √ √
Superb example of the Marx Brothers at their best, 1935. Contains the incomparable cabin scene. Sam Wood. (*b/w*)

The Night Has a Thousand Eyes ×
Edward G. Robinson is stage magician who finds he has genuine gift of precognition. Script lets him and director John Farrow down; 1948. (*b/w*)

The Night Holds Terror √
One of those never-fail thrillers about a family being held prisoner, tightly directed by expert Andrew L. Stone. Jack Kelly, Hildy Parks, Vince Edwards, John Cassavetes; 1955. (*b/w*)

A Night in Casablanca ✗
By 1946, the Marx Brothers were running out of steam, and this shows it. Only the opening gag with the wall has the old touch. The rest is strained. Archie Mayo. (*b/w*)

Nightmare ✗ ✗
(1) Unbelievable thriller about jazz musician Kevin McCarthy killing under hypnosis; don't worry, detective Edward G. Robinson solves it all and all the goodies end happily, so you can turn the thing off. Maxwell Shane; 1956. (*b/w*)

Nightmare ✗
(2) Hammer used the same title for one of its fiendish plots in 1964 with a double-twisting soporific yarn about driving Jennie Linden mad, directed by Freddie Francis. (*b/w*)

Nightmare Alley √
Tyrone Power as a carnival hanger-on who learns how to 'read minds' and parleys his way to fortune as a society clairvoyant; Helen Walker powerfully chilling as accomplice, Joan Blondell equally convincing as another. Edmund Goulding; 1947. (*b/w*)

Nightmare in the Sun √
Well-observed chase yarn in which John Derek pays the price for dallying with Ursula Andress by having her murder pinned on him. All the people he trusts while on the run (Lurene Tuttle, George Tobias, Keenan Wynn, Allyn Joslyn stand out) find some reason for betraying him. Shot in 16 days, it was an impressive producer-director movie debut for former small part player Marc Lawrence in 1965. (*c*)

Night Must Fall √
Karel Reisz' 1964 re-make of Emlyn Williams' suspense drama lacks the chilling quality of Richard Thorpe's 1937 version. But Albert Finney is convincing and effective, and Susan Hampshire's fear as she slowly realises identity of local homicidal maniac is definitely catching. (*b/w*)

Night of the Demon √
Oddly enough, this is one you can miss the start of without reproaching yourself. Jacques Tourneur had made a more than efficient spine-tingler from M. R. James' *Casting the Runes* in which Dana Andrews is at first sceptical about the power of an old parchment to conjure up a devil but gradually gives way to terror. Then the dead hand of the studio bosses insisted on 'beefing it up' with some shots of a demon at the beginning to reassure the one-and-nines (it was 1957). But the rest is pretty in all departments, except the acting which is uniformly inadequate. (*b/w*)

Night of the Eagle √
Occult thriller with Peter Wyngarde aghast to discover how deeply wife Janet Blair is into black magic. Cemeteries with chasing stone eagles and Margaret Johnston as equivocal cripple; Sidney Hayers; 1962. (*b/w*)

The Night of the Following Day √
Muddled thriller about kidnapping a rich man's daughter, excellently played by Pamela Franklin. As Marlon Brando is the tough man of the plot and the kidnappers fall out among themselves there is bound to be a pretty gratuitous amount of violence, but director-producer-co-writer Hubert Cornfield manages to keep this at a decent minimum and concentrate instead upon the moody shots of the Normandy beachhouse where she is held prisoner. Surprise of the film is Rita Moreno,

startlingly good as the tripping female member of the gang. And then it's all ruined by a tacked-on it-was-all-a-dream ending–what an unneccessary shame; 1969. (*c*)

The Night of the Generals ✕
One of the nazi generals is a murderer (only one? as one character asks). Anyway, that's the main plot–is it Peter O'Toole, Donald Pleasence or Charles Gray? There's an awful lot more, like the attempt on Hitler's life, Rommel being shot up in a plane, love-stuff between Tom Courtenay and Joanna Pettet, detective Omar Sharif on the trail. Director Anatole Litvak lets it sag and there's a lot left unsaid; 1967. (*c*)

The Night of the Grizzly √
Clint Walker, broke and desperate, tracks a killer bear that has helped to ruin him, with the dedication of a Captain Ahab; Martha Hyer is his wife, Keenan Wynn the man he's mortgaged to. Joseph Pevney directed, 1966, and the bear doesn't get a credit. (*c*)

The Night of the Hunter √ √
Important curiosity: Robert Mitchum as religious fanatic who is prepared to kill for loot to build church; James Agee wrote script from David Grubb's novel; Charles Laughton directed (his only picture); Lillian Gish returned to play lonely fairy godmother; 1955. (*b/w*)

The Night of the Iguana √ √
Pretentious but always fascinating try at Tennessee Williams symbolism by John Huston, 1964; defrocked priest (Richard Burton) is chased by rapacious teenager (Sue Lloyd) into the arms of bawdy innkeeper (Ava Gardner) watched by suffering spinster (Deborah Kerr) in Mexico. Sundry other colourful characters abound, including iguana. (*b/w*)

Night of the Quarter Moon ✕ ✕ ✕
Nasty little exploitation movie about racial intolerance, which uses this crucial test of our civilisation for the purpose of titillation (as when octoroon Julie London does a striptease in the annulment courtroom to snap her husband back into sexual life, physically abetted by her black lawyer). Hugo Haas was the director and Albert (*High School Confidential*) Zugsmith the producer; 1959. (*b/w*)

Night Passage √
James Stewart in 1957 Western caper about robbing train payroll. James Neilson keeps it going. (*c*)

Night People √
Above-average Cold War drama filmed in 1954 Berlin about getting kidnapped American soldier out of Russian zone. Nunnally Johnson wrote and directed Gregory Peck, Broderick Crawford, Rita Gam. (*c*)

The Night They Raided Minsky's √
Rather an amusing comedy about the accidental tearing of a dress that is supposed to have started striptease. The dress belongs to Britt Ekland, who isn't at all bad in this, her first big chance (in 1969). It was also billed as Norman Wisdom's big international breakthrough, but somehow–not altogether surprisingly–this is the only film he has made in America to date. Jason Robards and Denholm Elliott are fine; also present are Joseph Wiseman as Minsky and Elliott Gould as his son. Director, William Friedkin; 1969. (*c*)

Night Tide √
Unusual thriller with poetic undertones written and directed by Curtis Harrington in 1967 and giving Dennis Hopper an interesting part as a sailor who falls in love with a mermaid–or, at least, a girl posing as one in a sideshow. She's a bit confused about just what and who she is herself, and gets a bit murderous. (*b/w*)

A Night to Remember √
(1) Brian Aherne, Loretta Young in *Thin-Man*-style whodunit, 1943; director Richard Wallace. (*b/w*)

A Night to Remember √√
(2) Rather a gripping 1958 account of tragedy of magnificent Titanic on her maiden voyage. Authentic Eric Ambler script, documentary style direction from Roy Baker, strong performances from Kenneth More, Honor Blackman, David McCallum. (*b/w*)

The Night Walker √
Why does Barbara Stanwyck keep dreaming of lost husband, Hayden Rorke? Horror-director William Castle provides the answer, 1964. One reason might be that Stanwyck was once married to Robert Taylor, who's also around, in real life. (*b/w*)

Nine Hours to Rama ××
Slow-moving (it almost seems the nine hours of the title), fictitious account of Gandhi's assassination and killer, unconvincingly played by blacked-up Horst Buchholz, with the equally miscast Valerie Gearon as the girl he loves. José Ferrer looks cross as the police chief but conveys little else. Only Indian actor J. S. Casshyap emerges with any credit from director Mark Robson's failure – his portrayal of the Mahatma is compelling. The continuation of the film after the climactic shooting is woeful: 1963. (*c*)

1984 ××
It's over half-way between when this film was made in 1955 and the year of Orwell's nightmare vision and we seem to be doing OK so far. Tamely directed by Michael Anderson, this has further drawback of Edmond O'Brien in lead (but all-British films had to have American stars then). Michael Redgrave, Donald Pleasence. Mervyn Johns are around but they can't salvage weak adaptation and direction. (*b/w*)

Ninotchka √
As a comedienne, Garbo revealed wit and timing previously swamped in increasing tendency to overact. A stony Red Russian agent on a mission in Paris, slowly melting to the charms of Count Melvyn Douglas. Dated, 1939 sociological chat, smooth Ernst Lubitsch direction. (*b/w*)

Nobody Lives Forever √
John Garfield is con-man. Geraldine Fitzgerald is prey. Yet could love be real? Dry those tears, Jean Negulesco will make sure it all comes out right; 1946. (*b/w*)

Nobody Runs Forever ××
Cloak-and-dagger mystery which starts off quite promisingly with the Premier of New South Wales, Leo McKern, instructing Rod Taylor to arrest the High Commissioner of Australia, Christopher Plummer, for an ancient murder. This soon gets buried under routine melodramatics, as Taylor saves Plummer from the lethal wiles of Daliah Lavi. The inept screenplay carefully filters out the social consciousness of the original novel, leaving Ralph Thomas with nothing to direct except familiar old rubbish. Franchot Tone, Clive Revill, Calvin Lockhart are wasted; 1968. (*c*)

No Down Payment √
Slick, efficient, strangely gripping drama of life in a blue-collar suburb, with Patricia Owens as wife who gets raped, Joanne Woodward as wife of the rapist, Cameron Mitchell. Tony Randall, as the salesman who doesn't realise he's over the hill, and his wife, well-played by Sheree North, add to the authenticity of this Jerry Wald-Martin Ritt 1957 superior soap-opera. (*b/w*)

No Highway ×
James Stewart gives passable unconscious imitation of Groucho Marx walk in a

serious role as absent-minded professor who knows he's right–shucks–that the plane's tail is going to fall off, and–see here–he's darn well going to pull this here lever and make sure the plane doesn't go up in the sky until he's proved it. Marlene Dietrich floats in and out as unlikely fairy godmother in the form of Famous Film Star, as widower Stewart romances pretty air hostess Glynis Johns on the side. Unconvincing but harmless enough. From Nevil Shute novel, lifelessly directed by Henry Koster 1951. (*b/w*)

No Love for Johnnie × ×
Peter Finch is politician with vaulting ambition in 1961 drama directed by Ralph Thomas, supported by Stanley Holloway, Donald Pleasence, Billie Whitelaw, Dennis Price, Paul Rogers, Peter Barkworth, Fenella Fielding, Rosalie Crutchley, Mary Peach. Posing as neutral politically, it is in fact subtle anti-Labour propaganda, as shown by the final scene where our hero, now sold out, is seen listening cynically to Tory speech caring about the workers he has betrayed. All the left-wing and working class characters are represented un-sympathetically, while his true love is a nice upper-middle-class gal. (*b/w*)

No, My Darling Daughter × ×
Weak, dated little comedy about Juliet Mills wooed by Michaels Redgrave and Craig; Betty Box. 1961. (*b/w*)

None but the Brave √
Rare Frank Sinatra effort at directing as well as starring (second to Clint Walker). US marines stranded on island with Japanese troops during last war make a unilateral truce, which has to be broken when they get in touch with outside world again. Unfairly attacked as naive at the time (1965) it has something to say about war even if it betrays its own premises by making the fighting too glossy. (*c*)

None But the Lonely Heart ×
Cary Grant was anxious to prove in 1944 that he could play the dramatic role of a Cockney drifter in Clifford Odets' version (which he also directed) of Richard Llewellyn's novel. He got an Academy Award nomination, but the film wasn't a success, possibly because the phoniness of the book was intensified by the mainly American cast (Ethel Barrymore, Jane Wyatt, Dan Duryea). (*b/w*)

No Place for Jennifer × ×
Supposed to make you cry about a little girl (Janette Scott–Janette Scott? well, it was made in 1949) with divorcing parents, but you may find yourself sorrier for Leo Genn, Rosamund John and all involved. Henry Cass directed. (*b/w*)

North By North-West √ √ √
An Americanised *Thirty-Nine Steps*, with Hitchcock convincing us that he can follow the plot even if we can't ('I am but mad north-northwest: when the wind is southerly I know a hawk from a handsaw'–*Hamlet*). Contains two of his best-known breathcatchers, the crop-dusting plane shooting at Cary Grant in the stubble, and the final chase over the massive stone heads carved out of Mount Rushmore. Luckily Hitch had complete artistic control–otherwise MGM would have cut key scene after the Rushmore chase; 1959. (*c*)

Nor the Moon by Night × × ×
Ken Annakin's 1958 film of love on African game reserve offers no surprise but has tragic Belinda Lee, one-time British Bardot, plus Michael Craig and Patrick McGoohan as game warden and brother. Dreadful script, gratuitous sadism. (*b/w*)

North to Alaska × ×
Brawling John Wayne steals much of Stewart Granger's thunder in this gold-rush melodrama, with posturing Capucine

adding woman trouble. Direction by Henry Hathaway can't hide silliness of the plot and childishness of the characters. Ernie Kovacs has some nice moments as a con-man, but there are more yawns than thrills in the rest; 1960. *(c)*

North-West Frontier √
Exciting dash through hostile India with threatened prince; Kenneth More, Lauren Bacall head a large cast, held together by taut direction by J. Lee Thompson who gets some good performances, including one from Herbert Lom as journalist-villain; 1959. *(c)*

North-West Passage √
Half-made by MGM in 1939; the second half, about the actual passage, was never even started. So this is the settlers-and-Indians saga that was to be the prologue. Director King Vidor wouldn't allow doubles and Spencer Tracy wore out a pair of leather trousers. Robert Young, Walter Brennan supported adequately. *(c)*

Not as a Stranger √
Frank Sinatra plus Robert Mitchum, Olivia de Havilland, Broderick Crawford, Lee Marvin, epidemics, adultery, surgery, fornication, redemption; Stanley Kramer certainly delivered in 1955. *(b/w)*

Nothing But a Man √
One of the few treatments of the black man's personal struggle for his rights and dignity that doesn't come over as specious and/or patronising. Made on a shoestring by Michael Roemer and Robert Young, it was historically true for 1964, when the hero, believably played by Ivan Dixon, found his militancy up against both Alabama whites and his wife's Uncle Tom training. *(b/w)*

Nothing But the Best √√
Stylish 1963 comedy directed by Clive Donner giving Alan Bates wonderful opportunity as smart lad clawing his way up the business and social ladder, which he takes with both hands, giving us perhaps the finest British comedy performance of the decade. Millicent Martin awfully good as posh little girl he woos. Neat ending. *(b/w)*

No Time for Sergeants √
1958 Mervyn LeRoy comedy about country boy who messes up the army. Spawned TV series of same name. Andy Griffith plays the troublesome hayseed. *(b/w)*

No Time for Tears × × ×
Anna Neagle in 1956 tear-jerker that may cause you to weep more for the British film industry than its junior *Ward Ten* histrionics. Cyril Frankel directed. *(c)*

No Time to Die × × ×
Dull, obvious piece of British war-film flim-flammery suprisingly made in 1958, not ten or fifteen years earlier. Victor Mature, Leo Genn, Anthony Newley, Bonar Colleano, Sean Kelly – all pretty awful – escape from an Italian PoW camp to Fight for Freedom and director Terence Young. *(c)*

Notorious √√
Ingrid Bergman is planted by FBI man Cary Grant as wife to spy on Claude Rains in South America. A huge hit in 1946, particularly because the 'McGuffin', as Hitchcock calls his major plot devices, was about uranium in winebottles. As the movie was planned months before it was revealed that there was such a thing as an atom bomb, the FBI had him under surveillance because they suspected he had been leaked the secrets of Los Alamos. *(b/w)*

The Notorious Landlady ×
Disappointing comedy-thriller which places too much weight on the hefty shoulders of Kim Novak as girl who might be planning to do in Jack Lemmon. Unfortunately, Richard Quine fails to spoof the Hitchcockian tradition sharply

enough. We're left without laughs or thrills, despite the presence of Fred Astaire, Lionel Jeffries and Estelle Winwood (who has the one exciting scene in a wheelchair, running down a slope); 1962. (*b/w*)

No Trees in the Street × ×
Sylvia Syms, writer Ted Willis, director J. Lee Thompson try to impose a nostalgic copper's-eye view of the world on a youth problem that was to make this look as dated as the foxtrot within a few years, and a museum piece now; 1958. (*b/w*)

Not With My Wife You Don't √
George C. Scott and Tony Curtis as buddy-buddies in the Korean War, both zeroing in on the same Italian nurse, Virna Lisi. One of them marries her, but only by a trick pretending the other's dead. Then he turns up. All good, dirty fun, directed and produced by Norman Panama in 1966. (*c*)

Now and Forever × ×
Trite magazine story of chase to Gretna Green in the cause of young love, superficially told and directed by Mario Zampi. Janette Scott does her best, against the grain; 1956. (*c*)

No Way Out √
Early (1950) violent race-drama has goody black doctor Sidney Poitier accused of murder by bigot Richard Widmark. A bit too black and white if you'll excuse the expression, but its heart is in the right place. Director, Joseph L. Mankiewicz. (*b/w*)

Nowhere to Go √
Low-budget British thriller about escaped convict looking for fortune with notable debuts by director Seth Holt and co-scriptwriter Kenneth Tynan, in 1958; if the end lets it down, we have had some 80 minutes of excitement before then, and Bernard Lee, Andrée Melly and Bessie Love are fine. (*b/w*)

Now Voyager ×
Famous weepie with Bette Davis brought out of shell by psychiatrist Claude Rains. Transformed from ugly spinster into ravishing beauty she dates Paul Henried, but gives him up when she realises they can never marry because of his ailing wife. So she settles for looking after his daughter instead. Director Irving Rapper chose to exaggerate the soapier elements—after all he couldn't go for authenticity with that plot; 1942. (*b/w*)

The Nun's Story √
Long, overblown saga of Audrey Hepburn taking vows and finally renouncing them, without any clear motivation at either end. Full of interesting rituals and painstakingly directed by Fred Zinnemann, but ultimately defeating his evident purpose of making us admire the self-sacrificing life of devotion in showing just how mindless the obedience of the postulants has to be. Peter Finch does the little he has to do rather well, and Dames Ashcroft and Evans turn in their usual flawless performances; 1959. (*c*)

Objective Burma × ×
When this war actioner was shown in 1945 in London, it had to be withdrawn after a week because of protests that it suggested that America had a major part

in the Burma campaign. Not until seven years later was it publicly shown again here, this time with a tactful prologue. The script does give a false impression that an American paratroop attack was decisive and Errol Flynn's popularity was permanently affected in Britain. The movie itself is the usual collection of heroics, reinforced by a particularly loud and inapposite music track. Raoul Walsh did his usual lush but competent directing chore. (*b/w*)

Ocean's Eleven √
Frank Sinatra, Dean Martin, Sammy Davis Jr and other members of that old ratpack enjoying themselves rather more than the audience in this 1960 caper about robbing Las Vegas. Director Lewis Milestone deserved danger money for keeping this lot in line. (*c*)

The October Man × ×
John Mills loses his memory: did he commit that murder? Lose yours and forget to switch on. Roy Baker; 1947. (*b/w*)

Odd Man Out √ √ √
Tremendously exciting Carol Reed masterpiece of suspense about the last hours of Irish rebel James Mason's life as he is hunted by po-leece. Robert Newton, Kathleen Ryan, Dan O'Herlihy, Robert Beatty, Fay Compton, Cyril Cusack all did their finest screen work in this 1947 thriller. (*b/w*)

Odds Against Tomorrow ×
White and black bank robbers forced by circumstances into crime has strong cast of Harry Belafonte (whose company also produced), Robert Ryan and Shelley Winters as his nagging wife. Robert Wise somehow failed to make it as exciting as it should have been – perhaps he was too concerned to get over message of racial tolerance? 1959. (*b/w*)

Odette ×
Anna Neagle as resistance heroine, with

Raquel Welch in *One Million B.C.*

Trevor Howard, Marius Goring, Peter Ustinov in Occupied France. Herbert Wilcox hammed up the direction which made it unreal in 1951, and subsequent revelations have suggested that even the story he based film on wasn't quite as it seemed. (*b/w*)

Of Human Bondage
Maugham's very vaguely autobiographical yarn about club-footed medical student and a whore has been filmed three times, each one getting worse.

√ √
(1) Leslie Howard and Bette Davis in 1934, directed by John Cromwell. 'probably the best performance ever recorded on the screen by a US actress', *Life* raved about Bette Davis. (*b/w*)

×
(2) Paul Henried and Eleanor Parker in 1946, directed by Edmund Goulding. A routine, sub-standard version. (*b/w*)

× ×
(3) Laurence Harvey and Kim Novak in 1964, directed by Ken Hughes and Henry Hathaway. A glorious mess, with the two leads out-unacting each other in a poor screenplay by Bryan Forbes and providing embarrassment all round, particularly for Siobhan McKenna and Mrs Bryan Forbes. (*b/w*)

Of Love and Desire × × ×
This 1964 extravaganza is one of the very worst films ever made. Merle Oberon plays the part of a nymphomaniac who got that way because of her incestuous desires for her brother, Curt Jurgens. It takes the love of a good Steve Cochran to set her right in a fade-out. Everything about this monumental piece of nonsense is to be treasured as the apotheosis of bad cinema, the music (Sammy Davis Jr singing Katherine's Tune), the photography, above all the truly appalling direction of Richard Rush achieve a

composite that connoisseurs of the awful still chuckle over together during the long winter evenings. A strong contender for the booby prize of all time. (*c*)

Oh Dad, Poor Dad, Mama's Hung You in the Closet and I'm Feeling So Sad × ×
Best thing about this transfer of Arthur Kopit's play (once avant garde, now old stuff) is the title. Rosalind Russell, Robert Morse, Jonathan Winters fail to make zany tale of widow who keeps her husband's embalmed body in the wardrobe light enough, while 25-year-old son has affair with his baby-sitter (yes, he's supposed to be retarded or something). Richard Quine; 1967. (*c*)

O. Henry's Full House √
Five stories by O. Henry transferred to the screen in 1952 from a not very sparkling Lamar Trotti script by a clutch of top directors. Worth seeing the first one, though, for richly comic performances from Charles Laughton and Marilyn Monroe. He's a tramp who finds it hard to get arrested and thus spend a nice warm winter in jail; he accosts a lady in the street – but she turns out to be every man's dream tart. Henry Koster directed this bit. (*b/w*)

Oh! For a Man! ×
Will Success Spoil Rock Hunter? was original and, perversely, much more famous title of this comedy, from George Axelrod's play of that name. The script is clever, sophisticated, witty. Alas, its presentation on the screen has had to be tailored for that talentless piece of pneumatic invention, Jayne Mansfield, and adapter-director-producer Frank Tashlin was quite ruthless in 1957 in keeping her at the centre of the screen, elbowing out actors like Tony Randall and Joan Blondell. The result is a scaling-down of what should have been a sharp exposé of advertising and capitalism. Too sugary by half. (*c*)

Oh Men! Oh Women! √
Stylish high-comedy acting from David Niven, Tony Randall, Dan Dailey and Ginger Rogers in frothy tale of marital mix-ups. Nunnally Johnson adapted and directed it in 1957. (*c*)

Oh Mr Porter √
Famous Will Hay comedy, directed in 1938 by Marcel Varnel, about incompetent station master clearing up Irish branch line of gun-runners; Hay inimitable as bungling centre of gravity to Graham Moffat and Moore Marriott. (*b/w*)

Oh! What a Lovely War √
Although rapturously received and much-honoured, this adaptation by Richard Attenborough of Joan Littlewood's didactic stage knock-out about the First World War is a prettied-up, fashionable cartoon in which various Grand Actors (Ralph Richardson, John Geilgud, Kenneth More, Jack Hawkins, John Mills, Maggie Smith, Michael Redgrave, Laurence Olivier, Susannah York, Dirk Bogarde, Phyllis Calvert, Vanessa Redgrave) are allowed the illusion that they are contributing to a devastating exposure of the horrors of war while really indulging themselves in Attenborough's harmless shadow-boxing. Tarting up Brighton Pier as a set sounded a nice idea, but it limits the action. The linking family is palely drawn – although the final shot is effective. A modish, filleted effort which only retains a fraction of the original's power – yet that is still potent enough to move; 1969. (*c*)

Oklahoma! √
Disappointing literal version of the stage smash hit musical relies too much on photographing the show and doesn't create a real film. The Rodgers-and-Hammerstein music's fine, of course, (Oh, What a Beautiful Morning; The Surrey with the Fringe on Top; People Will Say We're in Love; Many a New Day), and Rod Steiger is outstanding as the heavy. But Shirley Jones and Gordon MacRae are no more than pleasant, and Fred Zinnemann seems to have been under orders to keep it theatrical; 1955. (*c*)

Old Acquaintance ✕
A gilded sinkful of soapy suds is this yard about competing novelists, Bette Davis the noble, Miriam Hopkins the ignoble. James Agee wrote at the time (1943), 'The odd thing is that the two ladies and Vincent Sherman, directing, make the whole business look fairly intelligent, detailed and plausible; and that on the screen such trash can seem even mature and adventurous.' He was too kind. (*b/w*)

The Old Dark House √
Comedy-thriller that's actually both quite funny and frightening, about night in 'haunted' mansion where Robert Morley, Janette Scott, Peter Bull, Fenella Fielding are among those threatened by murderer. This is 1962 remake by William Castle of 1932 Karloff-Laughton movie which came from the unlikely source of a J. B. Priestley novel, *Benighted*, adapted by Benn Levy. (*c*)

The Old Maid √
Fascinating glimpse of young Bette Davis as unmarried mother battling bitchy cousin Miriam Hopkins for love of her unknowing daughter. Hate sizzles in Civil War setting as director Edmund Goulding pulls out all emotional stops. (*b/w*)

The Old Man and the Sea √
Hemingway's mock-simple tale of a fisherman, his tremendous, self-imposed task of catching a marlin and then having it eaten under his eyes by the sharks, was faithfully transferred to the screen in 1958 by John Sturges (replacing Fred

Zinnemann after early dramas). While it makes a strong, clear narrative, the deeper philosophical 'meanings' are intrusive and given too much weight, which extends even to James Wong Howe's fine photography (supplemented by second and third units who roamed the Atlantic and Pacific looking for fish and sunsets plus an underwater unit). In the practically one-man part, Spencer Tracy scored a personal success in the most demanding role of his 37 years of film-making. (*c*)

Oliver Twist √√
Strong 1948 adaptation of Dickens horror comic, with marvellous Fagin by Alec Guinness, Tony Newley as Artful Dodger, blood-thirsty Bill Sykes by Robert Newton, Kay Walsh as Nancy. Director David Lean. (*b/w*)

Omar Khayyam ✕
Did you know that the poet saved Persia from a gang of assassins? Well, that's what it says here. Cornel Wilde, Raymond Massey in fancy 1956 production, directed by William Dieterle. (*c*)

On Approval √
Polished 1944 rendering of the Frederick Lonsdale play with Clive Brook directing himself, Beatrice Lillie, Roland Culver and Googie Withers in comedy of Edwardian fiancée-swapping. Desperately lacks colour. (*b/w*)

Once Before I Die ✕
John Derek directed, produced and appeared in this 1967 war film and so obviously cared about it that he almost managed to create an interesting film through sheer enthusiasm, despite such drawbacks as Ursula Andress slogging through the Philippine jungle without a hair out of place. The title comes from a request to Ursula from a soldier who has never been to bed with a woman asking her the favour before the next attack; it's that kind of film; 1967. (*c*)

Once More With Feeling ✕
Pretty dreadful piece about an orchestral conductor (excruciatingly played by Yul Brynner who hadn't mastered the necessary movements), saved by sparkling performance from Kay Kendall in her last film. Stanley Donen produced and directed; 1960. (*c*)

One-Eyed Jacks √√
Marlon Brando's first essay in directing, in 1961. This successful Western pivots on two superficially alike but actually contrasting ex-buddies, Karl Malden and himself. He plays a gunfighter who was betrayed by Malden and now seeks his revenge. The photography (by Charles Lang) is ravishing and the story (including the seduction of Malden's step-daughter) brilliantly realised. The strong supports include Katy Jurado, Ben Johnson, Elisha Cook. (*c*)

One Foot in Hell √
Alan Ladd plans a bitter revenge on the townspeople who let his wife die by their ineptitude. He becomes their deputy sheriff and plots a punishment for them. Unfortunately, director James B. Clark rather lets it slip out of his grasp into just another Western; 1960. (*c*)

One Man Mutiny ✕✕
This 1955 Otto Preminger-directed true-life account of military pioneer on trial for attacking US War Dept. as negligent provided Gary Cooper with strong central part and good ones for veterans Charles Bickford, Ralph Bellamy, Rod Steiger. Preminger blames producer Milton Sperling for its failure, but the critics pointed the finger at Otto himself, who failed to infuse his case with any zip. Coop was monumentally miscast as the fanatic with the light of justice in his burning eyes and the script didn't explain how he came to see himself as the Government's Nemesis. (*c*)

One Man's Way ✕✕
Inspirational biopic of Norman Vincent

Peale, crime-reporter turned preacher, is unlikely to have much impact in Britain, where he has hardly been heard of – thank goodness. Defensive tone of this biopic is interesting, as it tries to protect its subject from common charge of 'easy religion'. You'll need a lot of patience. Don Murray plays the preacher under Denis Sanders' inspiration; 1964. (*b/w*)

One Million Years BC ✕ ✕
Those who remember a pin-up picture of Raquel Welch looking extremely sexy in a fur bikini have seen the best of this ponderous 1966 effort. The rest is inaccurate pre-history, grunts and groans and some unconvincing special effects. Don Chaffey directs without enthusiasm from a script that, if it isn't quite that old, is at least 26 years Before This – written in 1940 by Hal Roach and released under three titles at different times (one of those jolly tricks they used to get up to – *Man and His Mate* and *The Cave Dwellers* are the others – with Victor Mature, Carole Landis, Lon Chaney.) Writer Michael Carreras tacked on another 24 minutes and Hammer added (*c*).

One of Our Spies Is Missing ✕ ✕
If you happen to find Robert Vaughn and David McCallum still watchable as agents of that highly improbably near-omnipotent UNCLE you could give this 1966 actioner a whirl. It's about a rejuvenation process being used by arch-Women's Libber Vera Miles in furthering her wicked (?) idea that women should run the world. Its sympathies are out of date before it starts and the performances are, too. Director E. Darrell Hallenbeck. (*c*)

One Potato, Two Potato √ √
Intelligent, sensitive and altogether worthy attempt to throw some light on black-white prejudice by means of a court custody case. Competently acted

by unknowns, directed by Larry Peerce, this 1964 'sleeper' didn't arrive in Britain for another three years and wasn't widely shown then. It certainly deserved to be seen, and still does. (*b/w*)

One Spy Too Many ✕ ✕
One film too many, more like. Just a bad television actioner, one more episode – and rather a bad one – in the tired old UNCLE series, which was just about packing up when this film came out in 1965 and of which it was the third to be shown in the cinemas here. Dorothy Provine provides a flicker of interest as wife of the Man Who Wants to Rule the World (Rip Torn), chasing him for a bit of money, but as Our Heroes, David McCallum and Robert Vaughn are hopelessly feeble. Joseph Sargent. (*c*)

The One That Got Away ✕
In 1957 the British film industry was going through a strange attack of conscience about last war, leading to glorification of Germans like Hardy Kruger, presented in Roy Baker's PoW chase as clever chap outwitting Britons. Alec McCowan has small part. (*b/w*)

One, Two, Three √ √
Billy Wilder 1961 satire on Coca-Colonisation, capitalism and communism, with James Cagney peaking (and ending) his career with rattling performance as soft-drink salesman longing for transfer from Berlin to London but having hopes deflected by boss's daughter's marriage to Red. Wilder and Diamond took their plot from a one-act play by the schmaltzy Ferenc Molnar and turned it into a rapid-fire vehicle for Cagney's personality; he wasn't quite as fast as in previous days, however, and one scene took 52 takes (seven short of the world record, held by Marilyn Monroe on *Some Like It Hot*). If the story (not unlike *Ninotchka* in essentials) is weak, and Horst Buchholz's charac-

terisation as the young firebrand unconvincing to the point of stupidity, at least the comedy is broad enough to carry it. (*b/w*)

One-Way Pendulum √ √
Peter Yates, due to go on to *Bullitt* and better things, directed this muted version of the N. F. Simpson play in 1964. Eric Sykes, George Cole, Jonathan Miller, Julia Foster, Peggy Mount, Mona Washbourne–who could ask for more to provide that rarest of television pleasures, a loud laugh? (*b/w*)

On Friday at Eleven √
Taut caper movie with Rod Steiger, Ian Bannen, Peter Van Eyck and Jean Servais hijacking an armoured truck with wages for an American base in Germany. Alvin Rakoff directed sharply and excitingly; 1961. (*b/w*)

Only the Valiant √
Nobody likes Gregory Peck until he fights off the Apaches; Gordon Douglas directs pliantly; 1951. (*b/w*)

Only Two Can Play √
Peter Sellers as Kingsley Amis librarian hero, strongly supported by Kenneth Griffith, Richard Attenborough. Sidney Gilliat directed; 1962. (*b/w*)

Only When I Larf √
Disappointing 1968 attempt at translating to the screen Len Deighton's amusing story of two conmen and their female accomplice. Director Basil Dearden pulls it back to an old-fashioned ambience while weak David Hemmings and Alexandra Stewart seem to plead for more contemporary handling. Only Richard Attenborough bridges the two styles, but he can't hold it together on his own. (*c*)

On Moonlight Bay √
Harmless musical based on Booth Tarkington characters; Doris Day and Gordon MacRae small-town sweethearts. Roy Del Ruth directed pleasantly; 1951. (*c*)

On the Avenue √
Irving Berlin (I've Got My Love to Keep Me Warm, Let's Go Slumming) vehicle for Dick Powell at the height of his singing career, 1937. Madeleine Carroll is the richest girl in America lampooned by Alice Faye in sketch; she smacks co-star Powell's face, a sure sign they're going to fall in love in a Roy Del Ruth musical. (*b/w*)

On the Beach √
Australia in general; Gregory Peck, Ava Gardner in particular, under sentence of death by atomic radiation. Hailed in 1959 as an important contribution by director Stanley Kramer to world peace, it looks rather more commonplace today. (*b/w*)

On the Beat × ×
The usual awful Norman Wisdom comedy, here with the hard-working lad playing two parts. He's a co-opted policeman and a gang-leader, who loses his liberty and girlfriend to Wisdom-the-copper. You might not enjoy it much, but Wisdom obviously did: director Robert Asher allows him to prolong and laugh at his own jokes endlessly; 1963. (*b/w*)

On the Double √
Entertaining Danny Kaye vehicle made in 1961 when he was still funny. Resemblance to German officer makes him valuable World War II spy, offers a chance for Walter Mittying. Director: Mel Shavelson. (*c*)

On the Fiddle √
There seemed to be some idea in Cyril Frankel's mind, in 1961, that he was directing a real war movie with a comedy twist. In fact, he came up with a farce on which real war awkwardly intruded.

Alfred Lynch plays the universal skyver so familiar in British army comedies; with him are such familiars as Cecil Parker, Stanley Holloway, Eric Barker, Wilfrid Hyde White, John le Mesurier and Kathleen Harrison. Less familiar in this carry-on is Sean Connery. (*b/w*)

On the Riviera × ×
One of those Danny Kaye movies that leaves one feeling patronised and dispirited; how could anyone have thought the silly plot about impersonating a French aviator (also played by the self-satisfied Mr Kaye) was amusing? Or that any of the complications about their women (Gene Tierney, Corinne Calvert) not knowing who was making love to them, credible enough to entertain? Walter Lang; 1951. (*c*)

On the Town √ √
Quite simply, the happiest musical ever, with Frank Sinatra, Gene Kelly, Ann Miller; marvellous music (New York, New York, a Hell of a Town, bowdlerised to 'wonderful town'); stunning dancing; splendid direction (Kelly-plus-Stanley Donen); 1949. (*c*)

On the Waterfront √ √
If you don't think about the political implications, which are suspiciously fascist-oriented when considered, this is a devastatingly effective piece of film theatre, with at least two stunning performances – Brando's as the feather-bedded longshoreman who could have been a contender but has become a bully-boy (but, wait, there's nothing more regenerative than the love of a good woman, even such a pale, whiney one as Eva Marie Saint); Rod Steiger's as his elder brother, torn between his crooked union and family love. The scene in the back of the car is rightly regarded as one of the great movie moments of all time. For the rest, you can't really believe in Karl Malden's all-white priest or Lee J. Cobb's all-black

union leader, but you happily suspend disbelief for the pleasure of watching Brando stagger (literally, at the end) through a plum of a part. 1954 Oscar winner for Best Picture, Best Actor; triple-nomination for Best Support – Cobb, Malden, Steiger; winner for Best Support, Saint; director Elia Kazan; writer Budd Schulberg; art-and-set Richard Day; editor Gene Milford; and photography Boris Kaufman. (*b/w*)

Operation Amsterdam × ×
As the Dutch diamond centre falls, a British major tries to bring the uncut stones to safety. Instead of concentrating on the human implications (why trust him? is he trustworthy?) director Michael McCarthy has co-written a script of wartime banality (with, incidentally, much too much gore). Peter Finch, Tony Britton, Eva Bartok are content to go through obvious heroics; 1959. (*b/w*)

Operation CIA × ×
The fighting in Viet-Nam had escalated to the point of real war by 1965, but you wouldn't know it from this routine cloak-and-dagger plot set in and around Saigon. Burt Reynolds plays the chief agent; director Christian Nyby must have been looking the other way. (*b/w*)

Operation Crossbow ×
Unconvincing attempt at convincing war film about blowing up V2 sites in Germany. Michael Anderson manages to waste his talented cast (Sophia Loren, George Peppard, Tom Courtenay, Lilli Palmer are leads) though Jeremy Kemp fools him by giving a super performance that outshines all the clumsiness. From Madame Tussaud's, Patrick Wymark impersonates Churchill, Richard Johnson Duncan Sandys, Trevor Howard Professor Lindemann, John Mills MI6 chief; 1965. (*c*)

Operation Mad Ball ×
Not even Jack Lemmon can save this

1957 services comedy from disaster. It needed Phil Silvers in his Bilko role. Instead, Ernie Kovacs, Mickey Rooney, Kathryn Grant rave about wildly and unfunnily under Richard Quine's direction. (*b/w*)

Operation Petticoat   √√
Slick, funny wartime comedy about a submarine that somehow gets painted pink and is hunted by both sides. As it's filled with various ladies and a crew headed by Cary Grant and Tony Curtis, it's all rather jolly in a Navy Lark sort of way. Blake Edwards was just the director to carry off such a carry on; 1960. (*c*)

Operation Snatch   × ×
Boring 'comedy' about Terry-Thomas saving the British Empire by repopulating Gibraltar with apes – making a monkey of anyone who stays to watch. George Sanders, Lionel Jeffries, do their best with pale material. Directed by Robert Day; 1962. (*b/w*)

The Opposite Sex   × ×
Clare Boothe Luce wrote a witty, catty play called *The Women* that was made into a delicious 1939 comedy starring Norma Shearer, Rosalind Russell, Paulette Goddard and Joan Crawford, directed by George Cukor and containing only women in the cast. In 1956, MGM dusted the property off its shelves and gave it to David Miller to remake – with disastrous results. He broadened the plot to allow men in; he tarted it up with some musical numbers; and for the sharp clever ladies who glittered from the original he substituted June Allyson, Joan Collins, Dolores Gray and Ann Sheridan. It came out looking like a dated mish-mash of Society nonsense and you could no longer believe in the clutching and clawing for power, prestige and other people's husbands. A mess. (*c*)

Orchestra Wives   √
Superior 1942 backstager built round Glenn Miller Orchestra, with Cesar Romero, Jackie Gleason, Serenade in Blue, Kalamazoo, Chattanooga Choo-Choo. Pat Friday dubbed for Lynn Bari; Archie Mayo directed. (*b/w*)

Orders are Orders   ×
Before Peter Sellers made it big with *The Lady Killers*, he had one or two minor appearances in minor comedies, like this 1954 remake of the old 1932 army play. It nominally starred Tony Hancock and Sid James, with a raft of lesser comedy slapstickers. Directed by David Paltenghi, who as a director was a very good ballet dancer. (*b/w*)

Orders to Kill   × ×
The weak Paul Massie as poorly-trained executioner in equally weak 1958 British Occupied France thriller with a few minutes of real tension towards the end when he prepares to kill a man he feels is innocent. Only Irene Worth, as French resistance worker, provides a touch of class. Anthony Asquith labours directorially. (*b/w*)

The Oscar   × × ×
Tawdry attempt to cash in on glamour of Academy Awards night has stiff competition between actors Stephen Boyd, Tony Bennett and scriptwriters for Booby Prize. Even Eleanor Parker, Joseph Cotten, Ernest Borgnine (acting) and Bob Hope, Frank Sinatra (appearing as winner) can't begin to save it. Russell Rouse directed in 1966 a 'true movie rarity – a picture that attains a perfection of ineptitude' – *Life*. (*c*)

Oscar Wilde   × ×
The worse (much worse) of the two Oscar Wilde films made in 1960 was this effort from Hollywood's Gregory Ratoff (as director), with Robert Morley sailing through the main part. The only

marks it scored against Ken Hughes' *Trials of Oscar Wilde* were in Ralph Richardson's prosecuting counsel (over James Mason) and Phyllis Calvert as Mrs Wilde (over Yvonne Mitchell). For the rest, it's just a grubby Sunday pop-paper's court transcript of the juicy bits. And it's in (*b/w*).

O.S.S. ×
Alan Ladd and Geraldine Fitzgerald parachute into France just before D-Day. It was made soon after in 1946, thus guaranteeing historical inaccuracy about the facts but correct details. Irving Pichel directed briskly. (*b/w*)

Othello √
A record of a very great stage performance from Laurence Olivier, but as a creative film of Shakespeare's great tragedy of jealousy it's a non-starter. Stuart Burge just had the play photographed in little takes and joined them together unsatisfactorily in 1966. (*c*)

The Other Love × ×
Weep at it or for it, depending on taste – Barbara Stanwyck, dying of TB, has to choose between wild life on the Riviera with Richard Conte or the dedicated Dr David Niven. You guessed. Directed by André de Toth de absolute tosh; 1947. (*b/w*)

Our Hearts Were Growing Up ×
Attempt to cash in on success of *Our Hearts Were Young and Gay*, in 1946, had same leads (Gail Russell, Diana Lynn) but their college days are a bore. William D. Russell directed. (*b/w*)

Our Hearts Were Young and Gay √
Cornelia Otis Skinner wrote a best-seller which told part of the story about a trip she and Emily Kimbrough made to Europe in the twenties. In this watering-down Gail Russell and Diana Lynn play the parts and it's hard to tell whether the old-fashioned quality of it all comes

from deliberate recreation of the flapper period or the creaking 1944 direction of Lewis Allen. (*b/w*)

Our Man Flint √
Best of the James Bond rip-offs, this 1966 comedy-thriller has James Coburn marching starkly through, laying a few broads, saving a few worlds. Daniel Mann directed briskly. (*c*)

Our Man in Havana √
Adaptation of Graham Greene novel was under-rated at the time (1960), because Carol Reed chose to emphasise book's comedy. Now Noel Coward's performance as spy-recruiter stands out and Alec Guinness's vacuum-cleaner salesman gains solidity. Plus Ralph Richardson, Burl Ives, Ernie Kovacs, Maureen O'Hara, Paul Rogers. (*b/w*)

Our Man in Marrakesh × ×
One of the visitors to Morocco has two million dollars to be squeezed out of him. Which? If only one could care, but although the people are OK (Tony Randall, Herbert Lom, Wilfrid Hyde White, Terry-Thomas, John le Mesurier) the writing, plot (Peter Yeldham), production (Harry Alan Towers), and direction (Don Sharp) aren't. A waste of everyone's time – let's hope not yours, too; 1966. (*c*)

Our Mother's House √ √
Brilliant, intriguing, macabre, but ultimately unsatisfying (because too many questions are left unanswered) cross between *Lord of the Flies* and *The Servant*. Seven children hide their mother's death, bury her in the garden, commune with her by séance, allow themselves to be invaded by Dirk Bogarde and Yootha Joyce – and there's plenty more (too much) plot to come. Producer-director Jack Clayton shied away from the whole hog, however, and this 1967 creepie only crawls. (*c*)

Our Vines Have Tender Grapes √
Edward G. Robinson plays Margaret O'Brien's loving Dad in awfully Sauterne yarn of Wisconsin family. Roy Rowland simply added sugar and mixed; 1945. (*b/w*)

The Outcast ×
John Derek fights for what's rightfully his. William Witney didn't turn this Western into anything fancier; 1954. (*c*)

Outcast of the Islands √√
Study of corruption in the South Seas, well-directed by Carol Reed, 1951. Trevor Howard plays Conrad's crooked clerk memorably, with support from Ralph Richardson, Robert Morley, Wendy Hiller. (*b/w*)

The Outcasts of Poker Flat √
Quite exciting Western based on the Bret Harte story of four undesirables who are run out of a mining town and find themselves trapped together in a snowbound mountain cabin. But Joseph M. Newman didn't make the best of script or cast of Anne Baxter, Miriam Hopkins, Dale Robertson, Cameron Mitchell, in 1952. (*b/w*)

The Outlaw ×
This is the famous Western that Howard Hughes produced, directed and managed to publicise brilliantly through a spurious campaign suggesting that it was sexy. The famous busty still of Jane Russell spilling out of her blouse was the only erotic thing about it – and that wasn't even in the film, in itself a dull, mild encounter between Doc Holliday, Billy the Kid and Jane Russell. Thomas Mitchell, Jack Beutel, Walter Huston move anxiously about. Started in 1940, shown 1946. (*b/w*)

The Outrage √
Well, it isn't that bad, this re-setting of *Rashomon* in the Wild West. True, the acting is a bit dodgy, what with Paul Newman in a false nose and a black wig, Laurence Harvey with his usual supercilious myopia and Claire Bloom hamming it up in that very English dramatic way of hers. But Martin Ritt's direction is firm – until he collapses into broad comedy for the fourth and how-it-really-happened retelling of the anecdote. He has almost brought off the impossible feat of imposing a Japanese style on the conventional Western. Unlike that other great remake, *Seven Magnificent Samurai*, this retains much of the script and feeling of the original. See *Rashomon* if you can, but this is a better-than-it-might-have-been substitute. Edward G. Robinson is among the storytellers who were sheltering from the rain in a temple in the original, in a railway station here. An unconvincing and sentimental post-script has been unnecessarily added; 1964. (*b/w*)

The Outsider √
(1) 1961 heart-breaker about Indian who was one of the men who raised the flag on Iwo Jima in famous photograph and became an outcast and drunk. Tony Curtis does well under Delbert Mann's direction. (*b/w*)

The Outsider ×
(2) 1967. Darren McGavin as ex-convict turned private eye investigates office frauds for Edmond O'Brien; Shirley Knight, Ann Sothern add to the mystery; so does director Michael Ritchie, not always intentionally. (*c*)

The Outsider √√
(3) 1967 version of Camus' book with Marcello Mastroianni hardly shown commercially in Britain. Director Luchino Visconti. (*c*)

The Over-the-Hill Gang √
Four old Hollywood veterans make a nostalgic quartet – Pat O'Brien, Walter Brennan, Chill Wills, Edgar Buchanan – playing ex-Texas Rangers trying to run

some young mobsters out of Boulder City. Other faces from the past who staggered over to play a part in this 1969 ride over Memory Prairie include Jack Elam, Andy Devine, Gipsy Rose Lee. (*c*)

The Ox-Bow Incident   ✓✓
Flawed 1943 masterpiece (it suffered from *rigor artis*, according to James Agee), refused exhibition by the big circuits in Britain as too sombre. Henry Fonda is simple cowboy caught up in a lynching. William Wellman's best serious film. (*b/w*)

Pacific Destiny   ✗
Arthur Grimble's experiences as Colonial Service cadet in South Seas, dramatised–if that isn't too strong a word. Denholm Elliott, Michael Hordern. Directed by Wolf Rilla; 1956. (*c*)

The Pad–and How to Use It   ✗
Peter Shaffer wrote a funny short play called *The Private Ear*. Brian Hutton directed a dreadful film from it, this one. Brian Bedford, Julie Sommars reduce it to a silly chase; 1966. (*c*)

The Pajama Game   ✓
They say pajama, we say pyjama. . . . This is the fast-paced 1957 movie version of George Abbott and Richard Bissell's

Julie Christie in *Petulia*

show from Bissell's novel, 7½ *Cents*, which dealt rather more realistically with a wage demand at a pajama factory. At this remove, the labour politics have become Doris Day as grievance-leader and there are too many songs to make that believable. So Stanley Donen, who Abbott rowed in for the film, has resorted to camera tricks to beef up the eleven songs, best of which are Hey There and Hernando's Hideaway, which have nothing to do with the original plot. (*c*)

The Paleface √
Entertaining Bob Hope Western, let down by posturings of Jane Russell, who was all publicity and no talent. Bob was dentist; Jane was Calamity Jane in more ways than two. Director Norman Z. McLeod; 1948. (*c*)

Pal Joey √√
John O'Hara wrote a short story about a heel. He turned this into a musical play about the same character, who was still pretty nasty. Then this became a 1958 musical film and as they had Frank Sinatra for the part they couldn't make him too much of a bastard. The result is a sadly gooey plot, with the unpleasant little squitty social and business exploiter softened to a boyish charmer who can't be all bad since he loves his scene-stealing dog. Rita Hayworth is reduced by the change of emphasis, too; instead of the man-eating harridan who is prepared to be used by Joey if she can use him in turn, she's a petulant self-sacrificer. And Kim Novak, always sensual to look at if nothing else, is given a pretty-pretty part that any soppy ingenue could have fitted better and might have provided her own voice for. Nevertheless ... Sinatra is Sinatra and the less ribald songs they have left in are outstandingly good (Bewitched, Bothered and Bowdlerised; I Could Write a Book; There's a Small Hotel; My Funny Valentine). George Sidney. (*c*)

Palm Springs Weekend ✕
One of those spurious teenage movies churned out around 1963 to snaffle the drive-in market in America, and put out as second features here. Norman Taurog, Elvis Presley's routine director, pushes a talent-scarce cast of Troy Donahue, Connie Stevens, Ty Hardin through various unbelievable low flings at Palm Springs. (*c*)

Pandora and the Flying Dutchman ✕
Ava Gardner falls in love with mysterious Dutch dilettante James Mason. Pretentious and slightly risible in its romanticism, it nevertheless satisfied a lushness missing in British pictures of 1951. Albert Lewin came from the Hollywood of his *Moon and Sixpence* and *Dorian Gray* to write, produce and direct. (*c*)

Panic ✕✕
Second-feature about amnesiac second-guessing the police with a climax against the second-hand. Strictly second-rate. Writer-director John Gilling with cast who have paid us to leave their names out; 1965. (*b/w*)

Panic in the Streets √
Richard Widmark as doctor tracking down source of bubonic plague in Elia Kazan's exciting, location-aided 1950 thriller; Paul Douglas is sceptical police chief; Jack Palance, Barbara Bel Geddes, Zero Mostel are stops along the way. (*b/w*)

Panic in the Year Zero √
Ray Milland directed as well as appearing in this last-family-left-alive sci-fi, in 1962. Jean Hagen good back-up. (*b/w*)

Papa's Delicate Condition √
Papa is Jackie Gleason and his delicate condition is alcoholism. It leads him into all sorts of trouble, like buying a drug store to get at the liquor and somehow a circus as well. Glynis Johns, Elisha

Cook and Charlie Ruggles join in the rather dubious fun. George Marshall directed; 1963. (*c*)

The Paradine Case
Hitchcock admits this one was full of mistakes, particularly in the casting over which he didn't have control (David Selznick did). Gregory Peck, he says, could never play an English QC–should have been Ronald Colman or Laurence Olivier. Louis Jourdan was 'worst flaw' as the groom who had been Alida Valli's lover–should have been Robert Newton or someone else who was 'manure-smelling'. Ann Todd's part wasn't satisfactory, either, as QC's wife fancied by Judge Charles Laughton. Above all, Hitch himself says that he was never quite sure how the murder was committed; 1948. (*b/w*)

Paradise, Hawaiian Style   × ×
Elvis Presley's contribution to the art of 1966 was this tired old repetition of all his previous films, only this time he was a pilot. Ten songs, all out of context. A very slight nod in the direction of recent ideas about frozen frames from director Michael Moore in the course of one song. Otherwise, zero. (*c*)

Paranoiac   √
First of the many *Psycho*-inspired frighteners was this modestly exciting chiller directed with some skill by ex-cameraman Freddie Francis, in 1962. Janette Scott is the victim in a terrible plot to have her declared insane; Oliver Reed is brother, and Alexander Davion and Sheila Burrell back up in nicely-judged performances. Not a patch on Hitch, of course, but better than most of the field. (*b/w*)

Paris Blues   ×
Would-be frothy location-shot story of jazzmen–Paul Newman and Sidney Poitier–pulling tourists Joanne Woodward and Diahann Carroll. This 1961

version of Harold Flender's novel doesn't come off–you simply can't care about the characters. The music's OK though; Martin Ritt; 1961. (*b/w*)

Paris Holiday   × ×
By 1958, when this comedy was made, Bob Hope was going soft. He strolled through his movies with too insouciant an air, and you couldn't feel any of the necessary sense of involvement. To compound the faults, he produced this one himself from his own story-line (about international gangsters in Paris). Despite Gerd Oswald's directorial exertions, the result is a would-be chunk of hilariousness with a flaw right down the middle. Fernandel does provide a few moments of broad amusement, but the femme side is dull with Anita Ekberg and Martha Hyer. (*c*)

Paris When it Sizzles   × × ×
Fizzles would have been better. There never was a more frizzled-up movie than this one in which Audrey Hepburn and William Holden are wilfully thrown away in an incredibly coy and silly story of an American writer dictating a plot (almost as bad as this film's and that's sure saying a lot) to a temporary secretary and, of course, of course, falling for her. But the arrogant American's ideas of Gay Paree and the banality of Richard Quine's pictorialisation of a really rotten script are breathtaking. If television shows many pictures like this, people will start going out to the cinema again, whence they were emptied in 1964 by films like this. (*c*)

Parrish   × ×
So awful you might even enjoy Delmer Daves' 1961 drippy drama of robot-like Troy Donahue fighting to better his and mother Claudette Colbert's lot on tobacco (it should be corn) plantation. Amazing over-acting from Karl Malden.
          (*c*)

The Party ×××
Wretched attempt to provide one long laugh as Peter Sellers' Indian character wrecks a producer's party. Turns out to be one long groan as old gags fizzle out, Sellers is driven to further desperations and director-producer Blake Edwards throws in the sponge by wildly dragging in a painted elephant. Awful; 1969. (*c*)

Party Girl √
Standard Nicholas Ray (one of the more over-rated directors) made in 1958. He manages to reduce a promising script (gangsters and G-men in 1932) and some fine perfomers (Lee J. Cobb, Cyd Charisse) down to the level of the rest of the cast (Robert Taylor, Kent Smith, John Ireland). But there may still be enough excitement to pass a wet evening. (*c*)

The Party's Over ×××
A real stinker of meretricious rubbish, with what are supposed to be Chelsea Bohemians hiding a girl from her fiancé and father. Oliver Reed glowers as leader of the bunch in a way that suggests he thought he was acting; the others lope about delivering explanatory lines, and the director, Guy Hamilton, must have popped out for a quick drink. It had censor trouble after it was made in 1962 and didn't get shown until 1965, when it was slaughtered by the critics. (*b/w*)

The Passionate Stranger ××
Dreadful little 1956 British attempt to retell the Lady Chatterley story as a comedy, with an Italian chauffeur (Carlo Justini–weak) wooing Margaret Leighton (whose idea of acting here seems to be playing with her specs) while Ralph Richardson sits in his wheelchair. The central section (in colour) is the novel itself, as allegedly written by Leighton. Altogether tedious and typically Muriel Box; 1956. (*mostly b/w*)

Passionate Summer ×××
One of the dregs of British film-making in 1958 was this perfectly awful romance about the three women in the life of a schoolmaster. Each of the women is worse played than the last one you saw on the screen, as if Virginia McKenna, Yvonne Mitchell and Ellen Barrie were engaged in some sort of gloomy contest to win the Wooden Oscar, female division (male division easily going to the hero Bill Travers). Rudolph Cartier faithfully responds to the mood of Joan Henry's turgid script and the technical credits are uniformly dreadful. (*c*)

Passport to Pimlico √
Sensational success in its day, but has dated much more than most 1948 comedies. About the London borough that found it could erect barriers between it and the rest of Britain. Henry Cornelius made it all very pleasant and chuckly as Stanley Holloway, fish-shop owner, unearths ancient treaty. (*b/w*)

Passport to Shame ×××
A real stinker about French girl (Odile Versois) being white-slaved by Brenda de Banzie and Herbert Lom, while Eddie Constantine rounds up taxi-driving friends to release her from the House of Shame. Dreadful performances by Diana Dors and all others mentioned, due, partly, one can only think, to the sheer ineptitude of director Alvin Rakoff; 1959. (*b/w*)

The Password is Courage √
Andrew and Virginia Stone took as their 1962 excuse to show catastrophes and special effects, the escapes of one Charles Coward during the war, when he was in German hands. The bangs and crashes are fine. The casting is strictly mis- (Dirk Bogarde in a Kenneth More role; Reginald Beckwith as a very Camp Commandant). And the location shooting was mysteriously done around London instead of around Bremen–and it shows. (*b/w*)

Pat and Mike √√
The loving duo, Spencer Tracy (sports coach) and Katharine Hepburn (sports coached), make this slight anecdote delightful; George Cukor guided, 1952. Miss Hepburn shows what a good tennis-player, golfer, swimmer, hiker and basket-ball player she is. Garson Kanin and Ruth Gordon wrote a crackling script that won an Oscar nomination. (*b/w*)

A Patch of Blue √
Grossly sentimental Cinderella story about blind skivvy Elizabeth Hartman being rescued by Prince Charming Sidney Poitier–but, you see, she doesn't realise he's black–so what, in 1965? Shelley Winters overplays the wicked mother to the point of absurdity, (winning Oscar in the process for Best Support) yet Hartman is so powerful under Guy Green's direction that you almost forgive the excesses of story and acting elsewhere. (*b/w*)

Paths of Glory √√
Stanley Kubrick's 1957 revelation that war is not only hell, but political rascality. Kirk Douglas, Adolphe Menjou outstanding as French officers cynically slaughtering in the First World War for personal advancement. (*b/w*)

The Patsy √
Jerry Lewis, groomed for stardom by a syndicate consisting of Peter Lorre, Everett Sloane, Keenan Wynn, Phil Harris, John Carradine and Ina Balin sounds a promising idea. Trouble is, that although according to the script they make it, by the evidence of our eyes they don't. He can't blame the director–direction was his. 1964. (*c*)

Patterns of Power √√
Fielder Cook's first film as a director was this 1956 beady look at the ethics of big business executives, from Rod Serling's television play he produced.

Van Heflin is the young (well, he was 46, but played younger) fellow whose lofty ideas are put through the mincer when Everett Sloane slaughters nice old Ed Begley's ideals and offers Heflin his chair. At least he doesn't do a Gary Cooper and renounce the corporate way of life for cutting down trees in God's country, but takes the chair muttering platitudes. (*b/w*)

The Pawnbroker √√√
Strong study in obsessive memory by Rod Steiger who earned an Academy Award nomination in 1965 for towering performance (absurdly beaten by Lee Marvin for *Cat Ballou*) as the Harlem uncle who lives within his consciousness of the concentration camp. Sidney Lumet didn't pander to popular stereotyping in his supporting characters either. (*b/w*)

Payment on Demand √√
1951 weepie, directed by Curtis Bernhardt which gives Bette Davis every chance to play centre-screen. She's a woman who is shocked to find that husband Barry Sullivan wants to divorce her after twenty years; afraid of winding up a middle-aged divorcée with nothing, she screws as big a settlement out of him as she can, but it's not the same as Love. The rest of the cast seems to have been chosen to prove, by contrast, what a great actress she is. (*b/w*)

Pay or Die √
Tough account of Mafia moving in on New York in 1906; made in 1960 by Richard Wilson, it has Ernest Borgnine as honest Italian cop. (*b/w*)

Payroll √
Ambitious 1961 British gangster thriller about wife of murdered armoured car driver seeking revenge, has strong cast (Michael Craig, Billie Whitelaw, Kenneth Griffith, Tom Bell, Stanley Meadows); direction from Sidney Hayers. (*b/w*)

Pay the Devil √√
Orson Welles is owner and tyrant of a huge ranch near the Mexican border. When he orders a mutinous peon killed, he doesn't expect the local sheriff, Jeff Chandler, to come poking his nose in. But he does. Jack Arnold succeeds in making this 1957 drama menacing and gripping, even if a little obvious. (*b/w*)

Peeping Tom √√
Michael Powell's thriller about a sex-maniac who photographs the women he kills caused outcry when first shown in 1959 but has since become a cult film, ahead of its time in questioning just who the voyeur is–the killer or the viewer. Carl Boehm's hero-victim, Anna Massey's heroine, Powell himself as the sadistic father all notable; so is technical brilliance. (*c*)

Pendulum √
Duel between policeman evading arrest for murder and psychopath. George Peppard makes a lacklustre lead, but director George Schaefer kept the action going in 1969. (*c*)

The Penthouse ×
Terence Morgan, one of the weakest actors ever to grace an English screen, and Suzy Kendall, pretty but not Bernhardt, are preparing to leave the show flat at the top of a new block when they are invaded by Tom, Dick and Harry (get the symbolism), three crooks high on pot, who tie them up, rape the girl and generally torture and torment in a totally gratuitous and nasty manner. Peter Collinson was roundly condemned in 1967 for directing a gloatingly sadistic romp. (*b/w*)

The People Against O'Hara ×
Disappointing 1951 Spencer Tracy vehicle about an unorthodox lawyer; wanting to help an old pal on the skids, he insisted that Pat O'Brien should be given a part. Irony was that O'Brien picked up good notices while Tracy got the back of the critics' hands. John Sturges couldn't make the plot about witness-bribery and extreme vindication convincing. (*b/w*)

People Will Talk √√
Cary Grant as unconventional doctor marrying pregnant patient Jeanne Crain in Joseph Mankiewicz-Darryl Zanuck thoughtful comedy. Ahead of its time in 1951. (*b/w*)

Pepe × × ×
Extraordinary goof with stars doing walk-ons, about Cantinflas following Dan Dailey to Hollywood because that's where his horse has gone. Only supportable as a Spot-the-Stars contest between those watching. Some tips: Maurice Chevalier, Bing Crosby, Greer Garson, Jack Lemmon, Kim Novak, Frank Sinatra, Zsa Zsa Gabor, Cesar Romero, Debbie Reynolds, Sammy Davis and Judy Garland's voice. Directed flaccidly by George Sidney; 1961. (*c*)

Perfect Strangers √
Robert Donat and Deborah Kerr are dull couple with sparkle put back in eye by wartime romances. Rather daring in its genteel way for 1945 and unexpected from Alexander Korda. Support from Glynis Johns, Ann Todd, Roland Culver. (*b/w*)

The Perils of Pauline ×
Silent serial was made into two camp movies:
(1) 1947. George Marshall directed Betty Hutton in what passed for biopic of Pearl White, who played original part. (*b/w*)

The Perils of Pauline √
(2) 1967. Herbert Leonard and Joshua Shelley made what they hoped was to have been pilot for TV series, but when they couldn't set it up this was released as cinema feature. Pat Boone seeking his

long-lost sweetheart Pamela Austin, who is undergoing wild adventures. (*c*)

Period of Adjustment √
The troubles of just-marrieds Jane Fonda and Jim Hutton, constrasting with those of splitting Lois Nettleton and Tony Franciosa, are given an edge by their origins in a Tennesee Williams play and sharp, spare direction by George Roy Hill; 1962. (*b/w*)

Pete Kelly's Blues √
Fairly convincing re-creation of the jazz world in the jazz age, made in 1955. Director-star Jack Webb is a drag in both hats, but Peggy Lee (acting), Ella Fitzgerald (singing), Janet Leigh and Lee Marvin turn in performances above the line of duty. (*c*)

Petulia √
Julie Christie is married to Richard Chamberlain. Shirley Knight is divorced from Dr George C. Scott. Julie fancies George. Richard hits Julie. And so on. But director Dick Lester has jazzed it all up with such flashy pictures and clever cutting that you feel there must be less in it all than meets the eye. He has also made it cute and attempts to convince Miss Christie that she's kookie—maybe he thought he was directing Shirley MacLaine? Altogether, it's a dazzling mess. Somewhere in there: Joseph Cotten, Arthur Hill and the city of San Francisco; 1968. (*c*)

Peyton Place √
Mark Robson made a better film than the smutty, scratchy and ultimately unsexy model that Grace Metalious wrote badly enough for it to become a bestseller. Helped by some solid performances (Lloyd Nolan as a doctor, Arthur Kennedy as Lucas Cross, Diane Varsi and Lana Turner as Allison and her mother) he made, in 1958, a highly watchable film often let down by its

dialogue and petty scandals, an imitation silk purse out of a sow's ear. (*c*)

Phantom Lady √√
Thriller by Robert Siodmak about Ella Raines trying to establish lover's innocence; good atmosphere of 1943 New York in menacing heatwave. Franchot Tone, Elisha Cook Jr. (*b/w*)

The Phantom of the Opera √
Disfigured composer living in the sewers adopts young opera singer.
(1) 1943 version is remake of 1925 silent and keeps the action in the original Paris. Claude Rains hams his way through the Lon Chaney part; Arthur Lubin directs; winner of Oscars for art direction and photography. (*c*)

The Phantom of the Opera √
(2) 1962 Hammer version moves story to London with Herbert Lom as less grotesque Phantom; Terence Fisher directs in relatively restrained manner. (*c*)

Phantom of the Rue Morgue √
Remake of Poe's *Murders in the Rue Morgue* for 3D in 1954. Karl Malden makes an interesting change from Vincent Price's monopoly of such roles with Patricia Medina his fiancée and accomplice. Roy Del Ruth directed rather more cheerily than eerily. (*c*)

The Phantom Planet × × ×
One of those movies that are so bad that they almost take on a charm of their own as each effect outdoes the last in ineptitude, each line outdoes the last in triteness and each performance outdoes the last in inefficiency. Supposedly about a planet where the inhabitants are six inches high, including–amazingly–silent star Francis X. Bushman. William Marshall was responsible (fairly), in 1962. (*b/w*)

Phffft! √
Inspired teaming of Judy Holliday and

Jack Lemmon insures that this comedy of divorce is squeezed to the full. Jack Carson and Kim Novak back up well. Mark Robson directed nattily; 1954. (*b/w*)

The Philadelphia Story √√√
Quite the best Hollywood comedy of its period, 1940 (and many believe ever), superbly played by Katharine Hepburn, James Stewart, Cary Grant and confidently directed by George Cukor from Philip Barry's crackling play. My, but it's yar. Six Oscar nominations, two awards (for the Stewarts). (*b/w*)

Phone Call from a Stranger √
Episodic, annoyingly jump-about story of various people in aeroplane crash, their survivors, and personal dramas. Director Jean Negulesco makes it all very easy to watch, but Gary Merrill isn't strong enough to carry the linking weight and Bette Davis is allowed to go overboard as paralytic wife of one of the passengers; 1952. (*b/w*)

Piccadilly Third Stop ✗✗✗
Disastrous little mock-*Asphalt Jungle* set in a London there never was, with a parade of the weakest talent of 1960 (Terence Morgan, Yoko Tani, Mai Zetterling, William Hartnell); directed, if that is the word, by Wolf Rilla. (*b/w*)

Pickup on South Street √√
'An analytical assault on the mental and physical strength and weakness of a professional pickpocket,' is how director Samuel Fuller describes his screenplay. Richard Widmark played crook caught in espionage web in this 1953 thriller, which betrays its period only in its obsession with anti-Communism. (*b/w*)

Pickwick Papers √
Rather plodding version, directed in 1952 by Noel Langley with James Hayter and second-league cast, of Dickens' picaresque novel that resists straightjacket of a plot. (*b/w*)

Picnic √
Kim Novak was out of her depth as small-town girl awakening to life among accomplished players like William Holden, Rosalind Russell, Susan Strasberg, Cliff Robertson, Betty Field. Result is mixture of styles, but the old magic of the stranger who arrives and changes lives still works–and Kim was made a star. Joshua Logan directed, helped largely by James Wong Howe's camera-work and theme-music, Moonglow; 1955. (*c*)

Picture Mommy Dead ✗✗
As unpleasant as its title, this is nonsense about Susan Gordon being possessed by her mother's spirit as she battles to win her rightful inheritance. Hammy cast includes Zsa Zsa Gabor, Don Ameche, Martha Hyer, Signe Hasso, all getting on a bit in 1966, indulged by director Bert I. Gordon. (*c*)

The Picture of Dorian Gray √
This was considered a huge success in 1945 for its pictorial elegance, winning the photography Oscar for Harry Stradling; but somehow its monochrome (except for flashes of the portrait), leaden script and George Sanders' tame (rather than Wilde) performance don't seem quite as brilliant now. Albert Lewin directed stylishly and deserves credit for the young Angela Lansbury's fine performance. (*b/w*)

The Pigeon that Took Rome √
Charlton Heston sending messages behind the enemy lines in Italy makes a mildly amusing comedy under Mel Shavelson's tries-too-hard direction. Elsa Martinelli leads the locals; 1962. (*b/w*)

Pillow Talk √√
First film Doris Day and Rock Hudson made together (1959), it proved an irresistible combination for all who aren't too stuffy to laugh at trivia; Tony

Randall, Thelma Ritter add to the fun, and the script won an Oscar. Michael Gordon's direction gets the best from I-love-you-I-hate-you misunderstandings. (*c*)

Pimpernel Smith √
Updating to 1941 and the nazis of the Scarlet P. Directed by and starring Leslie Howard. Splendid fun. (*b/w*)

The Pink Panther √
One of those comedies that people swear by or at. Peter Sellers is bumbling French inspector after jewel thief; Robert Wagner, Claudia Cardinale, David Niven add distinction, but picture is stolen by cartoon panther in credits, later spun off to make own TV series. Blake Edwards directed; 1964. (*c*)

Pinky √
Elia Kazan's early (1949) taboo-breaking race-drama about black girl, passing for white, returning to the South to discover contrast with Northern ways. Since then, the us has woken up to the fact that the North isn't such a dandy place to be if you're black, either. Jeanne Crain vitiates theme by being white herself. Nina Mae McKinney, Ethels Barrymore and Waters, William Lundigan. (*b/w*)

The Pirate √
Rather corny 1948 musical with stagey plot worth idly watching for lavish costumes, Cole Porter songs, Judy Garland, Gene Kelly and director Vincente Minnelli's efforts to bind them all together. About lover posing as own rival. (*c*)

The Pistolero of Red River √
Young Chad Everett tries to prove himself smarter than local marshal Glenn Ford; routine stuff but Jack Elam may save your night with one of his slimy-baddy parts, here blackmailing 'saloon-owner' Angie Dickinson; Richard Thorpe; 1966. (*c*)

The Pit and the Pendulum √
Director Roger Corman made it a fluid, exciting experience in 1961. Vincent Price and Barbara Steele go through their ritual roles, and it's satisfactorily creepy, although Poe's story is just tacked-on climax. (*c*)

A Place in the Sun √
Lumbering, slow-moving but convincing account of young man's dilemmas as he seeks to climb the social ladder, dragged down by pregnant girl-friend. This adaptation of Dreiser's *An American Tragedy* won 1951 Oscars for direction (George Stevens), script (Michael Wilson and Harry Brown), music (Franz Waxman), costumes (Edith Head), photography (William C. Mellor), editing (William Hornbeck). Star Montgomery Clift was nominated for Best Actor, draggy girl-friend Shelley Winters for Best Actress. One omission from the general prize-giving: Elizabeth Taylor. (*b/w*)

A Place to Go × ×
Attempt by Michael Relph and Basil Dearden to 'get with it', as the phrase was in 1964, by transfering their normal boy-on-a-robbery theme to the sociologically interesting mileu of uprooted slum-dwellers living in new tower block. Bernard Lee is fine as a wayward dad, Rita Tushingham and Barbara Ferris make believable working-class girls, but Mike Sarne (formerly a weak pop-singer, later a weak film-director) is a weak actor in the main part. (*b/w*)

The Plague of the Zombies ×
Same old plot about the Voodoo cult in the remote English village, same old squire, same old graveyard, same old André Morell investigating, same old John Gilling directing, same old Hammer churning the films out and pulling the money in. Extraordinary it all still went on in 1965. (*c*)

The Plainsman √
Out-of-date 1967 remake of DeMille classic Gary Cooper–Jean Arthur 1937 Westerner but since then the West has become a more complicated (and in the hands of better directors, a more interesting) place. Don Murray is no substitute for Coop and his attempts to bring some realism to the character just make him look dyspeptic. For the rest, director David Lowell Rich can't breathe any life into such worn characters as Buffalo Bill and Calamity Jane. There is, however, one black comedy moment when Mrs Abraham Lincoln chides her husband, 'Hurry up, Abraham, or we shall be late for the theatre.' (*c*)

Planet of the Apes √
First in the line of surprisingly successful sci-flix, with Charlton Heston as Man's representative in what easily could have been a jungler about savages, a western about Indians, but happens to be a planeter about actors with monkey masks. Franklin J. Schaffner directs efficiently but without much human or simian understanding; 1968. (*c*)

Play Dirty √
Straight pinch from *The Dirty Dozen* about ex-criminals now operating in the desert. Michael Caine is supposed to be in charge, but André de Toth's direction somehow subjugates his part to those of Nigel Davenport, Nigel Green and Harry Andrews–thus showing splendid taste in actors. Quite exciting; 1968. (*c*)

Play it Cool × ×
Terrible little twist-era musical directed by Michael Winner in 1962 has an awkward Billy Fury and an equally inferior cast (excepting Dennis Price and Richard Wattis, both lost in the floss) in a fitful plot about a girl being saved from marriage to another pop-singer. (*b/w*)

Please Don't Eat the Daisies ×
David Niven is professor who becomes Clive Barnesish butcher-critic of Broadway. He pans a pal's production and gets his face slapped by Janis Paige. Meanwhile, at home, Doris Day is still singing 'Que Sera, Sera' from a film of hers made five years before 1960, when this disappointment, directed by usually reliable old Charles Walters, appeared. (*c*)

Please Turn Over × ×
That hoary old one about the girl who writes a novel which upsets family and friends by turning them into naughty-naughties. Awful little nothing from the *Carry On* team (director Gerald Thomas), with Ted Ray, Jean Kent, Leslie Phillips, Joan Sims, Julia Lockwood fulfilling all the expectations their very names conjure up; 1960. (*b/w*)

The Pleasure Girls √
Not quite the sexy cash-in it sounds, although there's a certain amount of jumping in and out of bed and a homosexual embrace or two. Surprisingly, Gerry O'Hara's script, which he directed himself, manages to catch quite a strong feeling of 1964 London, and Ian McShane, Francesca Annis, and Rosemary Nichols give some depth to characters who could so easily have been mere types. (*b/w*)

The Pleasure of His Company √
Taking a slice from *The Philadelphia Story* without its elegance and wit, but with at least some of its style, Samuel Taylor's 'rueful comedy', as he calls it, is about how a father (Fred Astaire) turns up for his daughter's wedding and proceeds to charm her (Debbie Reynolds) and her mother (Lilli Palmer). George Seaton directed, in 1961, with sure hand, and gets reliable supporting performances from Charlie Ruggles and Gary Merrill. But it's Astaire's picture and, without dancing a step, he dances away with it. (*c*)

The Pleasure Seekers   ✕
Or *Three Coins in a Madrid Fountain*.
Jean Negulesco schamltzily chronicles
the exploits of Ann Margret, Carol
Lynley and Pamela Tiffin as they seek
husbands in Spain. Candy-floss stuff;
1965. (*c*)

The Plunderers   √
Four saddle-tramps invade a Western
town and terrorise it; how the town
fights back is the theme of this unusual
and interesting oater, particularly so
because the producer-director, Joseph
Pevney, usually sticks to safer subjects.
Jeff Chandler, John Saxon, Dolores
Hart star; 1960. (*b/w*)

Plymouth Adventure   ✕
Costume drama about Pilgrims Gene
Tierney, Van Johnson, Leo Genn sailing
to America under Captain Spencer
Tracy. Dreadful script must have dis-
couraged director Clarence Brown, who
retired after this 1952 failure. (*c*)

Pocketful of Miracles   ✕ ✕
Frank Capra's 1961 remake of his own
Lady for a Day (1933), a solid slab of
sentiment about an apple-selling Bette
Davis (Shirley Booth turned him down)
rescued from Skid Row by kindly gangster Glenn Ford (Sinatra turned him
down) and pygmalioned as society
hostess to impress daughter Ann-
Margret and suitor. She finishes up with
a proposal from alcoholic Judge Thomas
Mitchell. This nonsense derives from a
Damon Runyon tale of lovable hoodlums (Peter Falk), posh butlers (Edward
Everett Horton) and molls (Hope
Lange–Glenn Ford's 'young friend' of
the moment.) Capra and Glenn Ford
were co-producers and got on very
badly. In Capra's autobiography he
writes: '*Pocketful of Miracles* was shaped
in the fires of discord and filmed in an
atmosphere of pain, strain and loathing.'
He had hoped it would be an antidote

to permissive tide, but it was a huge
box-office flop and 'there was dancing
in the streets among the disciples of
lewdness and violence'. (*c*)

Point Blank   √√
British director John Boorman's first
American film was this 1967 exercise in
gratuitous brutality, which nevertheless
was well enough done to lift Lee Marvin
out of the rut of baddies he had played
for sixteen years. Absurdly constructed,
with flashbacks crowding in on each
other so that you never know where you
are, the script ruined a perfectly straightforward and more exciting book, *The
Hunter* by Richard Stark, and omitted
much explanatory material (how, for
instance, did our hero recover from two
bullets in the gut and immediately swim
from Alcatraz to San Francisco?). But,
forced as the denouement and plot-
twists are, Angie Dickinson and Keenan
Wynn respond so well to Boorman's
direction–as does Marvin–that the
whole thriller, flashy editing and all, has
a spurious compulsion at first viewing.
But don't see it twice–the holes are too
obvious then. (*c*)

Pony Express   √
Charlton Heston opening up the mail
routes to the West, with help from
Forrest Tucker, Rhonda Fleming, Jan
Sterling and director Jerry Hopper in
1953. (*c*)

Poor Cow   √√
Kenneth Loach's debut on the big screen
was with a small-screen subject and
here it is back on the little one where it
should have stayed (and not in the fancy
colour Loach is so obviously unhappy
with). In the cinema, the casual, surely-
it-must-be-improvised manner distracted
and there's every likelihood that it will
look very 1968 and out of date by the
time it gets on your home screen. Carol
White moved confidently enough
through the dramas in the life of a girl

who's mixed up with villains, and Terence Stamp does all that's required of him, which isn't much. Incidentally, watch for the boy Billy. He's Malcom McDowell who was later to make *If . . .* and *The Clockwork Orange*. (*c*)

The Poppy is Also a Flower ✕ ✕
The film is also a stinker. One of those do-gooding efforts with UN approval that turns out to be really awful despite presence of such luminaries as Yul Brynner, Trevor Howard, Angie Dickinson, E. G. Marshall, Rita Hayworth, Eli Wallach, Marcello Mastroianni. Blame rests partly on British director Terence Young; 1966. (*c*)

Porgy and Bess √
Whatever it may have been like when it was written in 1935 George Gershwin's 'folk opera' was downright insulting to black people by the time Otto Preminger filmed it in 1959. The inhabitants of Catfish Row are shown as indolent, lovable morons and the artificiality of the sets and acting positively cheeky. Not all of the cast sung for themselves (Sidney Poitier, Dorothy Dandridge, Ruth Attaway were all dubbed) and Uncle Tommy Davis Jr scurried around unconvincingly. The music's fine of course, but the LP's better than the movie. (*c*)

Pork Chop Hill ✕
Depressingly flag-waving celebration of the bravery of American troops in Korea, made in 1959 by Lewis Milestone, a director who knew how to shoot a battle scene. Unfortunately, he wasn't so strong on character, so Gregory Peck and his band of brave ethnics remain just caricatures. This actioner does contain one final irony, but by then it has written itself off as one more anti-Commie blast. (*b/w*)

Portrait in Black ✕ ✕
Right phoney load of codswallop with Lana Turner as wicked wife of Lloyd Nolan, conniving at his murder so that she and Anthony Quinn can find happiness, which of course they don't. Michael Gordon directs lushly, as if to take your mind off the inconsistencies and the dialogue; 1960. (*c*)

Portrait of Clare ✕ ✕
Margaret Johnston in weak effort about a grandma reminiscing, directed by Lance Comfort; 1949. (*b/w*)

Portrait of Jenny √
Lunatic plot about girl who grows much older every time Joseph Cotten meets her and is finally found to have died before, in a storm. Despite this incredible story-line, William Dieterle managed to make Jennifer Jones more or less convincing, a genuine feat of direction; 1948. (*b/w*)

Posse from Hell ✕
Audie Murphy Western about chase of four escaped convicts who killed the sheriff. Herbert Coleman; 1961. (*c*)

Possessed ✕
Joan Crawford made two films of this name during her long career but it's not likely that the 1931 effort with her as a young factory worker who goes to the big city will get shown on TV. The 1947, more mature effort, has her doing her nut as a nurse who is obsessed with Van Heflin but marries employer Raymond Massey; typical Crawford larger-than-life stuff climaxing in a shooting scene, and she is indulged by director Curtis Bernhardt. (*b/w*)

The Postman Always Rings Twice √ √
Tough 1946 dramatisation of James M. Cain thriller about retribution catching up with Lana Turner who seduces John Garfield so that he'll murder her husband. Tay Garnett caught evil atmosphere of the roadside diner beautifully. (*b/w*)

The Pot Carriers √
Watered-down translation of Mike Watts's television play showing the inhumanity of British prison-life. This 1962 version, directed by Peter Graham Scott, introduces a wife and girlfriend shakily conceived and played. But Ronald Fraser's demoted trusty holds the picaresque action together. (*b/w*)

The Power ×
A kind of sci-fi whodunit posing the questions which of a group of super-scientists is the one from an alien planet (or somewhere like that)? and which is the goodie who's resisting him? If you manage to sort all this out, you are a candidate for super-power yourself. Director Byron Haskin tries to make it plausible and when that fails, uses his camera imaginatively for some clever effects. But George Hamilton, Suzanne Pleshette, Yvonne de Carlo, Nehemiah Persoff and Aldo Ray seem about as clued-up as the audience; 1968. (*c*)

The Power and the Glory √
Cramped little 1961 version of Graham Greene's novel, made for American television (but looking equally horrid there, with awkward continuity cuts to accommodate the frequent commercials and a murky print) by Marc Daniels. But the cast is magnificent: Laurence Olivier, Julie Harris, George C. Scott (as police lieutenant) Roddy McDowall, Keenan Wynn, Martin Gabel, Patty Duke, Cyril Cusack, Fritz Weaver, Mildred Dunnock, Frank Conroy. A pity that the adaptation (by Dale Wasserman) and production (by David Susskind) were so inferior. (*b/w*)

The Premature Burial √
Ray Milland is the man in the nightmare of being buried before he is dead. Roger Corman wrings out the shudders from the Poe story, with the help of superior photography and effects from camera-man Floyd Crosby; 1962. (*c*)

The President's Analyst √
Theodore J. Flicker has written and directed a satire on politics, medicine and spy movies, centred on James Coburn as the man who knows too many secrets. Which is an unfortunate piece of casting. For the rest, it's a pleasant enough diversion with some nice cameos and a couple of inventive plot-switches; 1967. (*c*)

The President's Lady √
Charlton Heston as Pres. Andrew Jackson defends his wife's bad name. Susan Hayward pulls out the stops a bit under Henry Levin's charge; 1953. (*b/w*)

Press for Time × ×
Norman Wisdom pathos (in more ways than one) in which the British Jerry Lewis (not meant as a compliment) plays a variety of parts and also takes it on himself to preach to us on how we should all live in harmony and forget party politics. Some funny gags that go on too long. Robert Asher indulges him directorially; 1966. (*c*)

Pressure Point √
Prison shrink Sidney Poitier sorts out American nazi prison-patient Bobby Darin. Hubert Cornfield makes it quite interesting; 1962–flashbacking to 1942. (*b/w*)

Pretty Boy Floyd √
Strong stuff from director Herbert J. Leder in this 1960 reconstruction of thirties outlaw. John Ericson, Barry Newman, Joan Harvey. (*b/w*)

Pretty Poison √ √
The interplay between two seemingly-normal, actually unbalanced nice young people who egg each other on to arson and murder is frighteningly well-caught in this second directorial effort of Noel Black. His assurance is catching, and Tuesday Weld and Anthony Perkins are outstanding under his encouragement.

This thriller was given a poor release when shown in the cinemas in 1969 and you probably haven't even heard of it, but prepare for a horrid treat when it reaches your home (and keep any junior pyromaniacs well away). (*c*)

Pretty Polly   √
Hayley Mills as a nice middle-class English girl who undergoes one of those old take-off-your-glasses, why-you're-beautiful transformations that never happen in real life. She then proceeds to knock out half the unsavoury characters of Singapore–over-eating (and acting) Brenda de Banzie, gruff Trevor Howard, gigolo Shashi Kapoor, American-on-the-make Dick Patterson among them. Guy Green's obvious direction diminishes a pretty pale Noel Coward novel still further; 1967. (*c*)

Pride and Prejudice   √
Superb Olivier in Aldous Huxley co-adaptation of Austen delight. Robert Z. Leonard's direction in 1940 made a workmanlike job, far from a travesty, although Greer Garson is inadequate as Elizabeth. (*b/w*)

The Pride and the Passion   √
1957 spectacular with Frank Sinatra as simple Spaniard, Sophia Loren his girl, and Cary Grant as British officer, teaming up with peasantry to schlepp huge cannon to gates of French-occupied fort. One critic suggested that the gun almost out-acted the principals; another commented that the whirr of director Stanley Kramer's cameras seemed as loud as the thunderous cannonades; from C. S. Forester's *The Gun*. (*c*)

The Prime of Miss Jean Brodie   √
Muriel Spark's penetrating novel of a schoolmistress who chooses her élite and is ultimately betrayed by one of them (which is the secondary but compelling whodunit element of the book)

was ham-fistedly adapted for the stage by Jay Presson Allen. Ronald Neame has been content to film the play with a slightly opened-out script from the theatrical adapter. Maggie Smith, Robert Stephens and the four girls are creatures of the theatre, not the novel; Celia Johnson as the headmistress is the best bit of casting in the film. The result is a slighter drama, entertaining when it should have been disturbing. 1969. (*c*)

The Primitives   ✕
Slightly superior second-feature which doesn't take its own plot (about cabaret artistes who are really jewel thieves) too seriously. Jan Holden is leader of the gang; Alfred Travers directed with some flair; 1962. (*b/w*)

The Prince and the Pauper   √
Fulfilled wish dream of every child: changing places with royalty. (1) Done with panache in William Keighley's 1937 version of Mark Twain's story, with Errol Flynn and Claude Rains.
                     (*b/w*)

The Prince and the Pauper   ✕
(2) Well-produced, badly-acted (too many accents, including Australian) 1962 version was directed by Don Chaffey. Sean Scully, Guy Williams, Jane Asher. (*c*)

The Prince and the Showgirl   √ √
Marilyn Monroe and Laurence Olivier together–the combination was irresistible, even if the film–a static reworking of Rattigan's *The Sleeping Prince*–turned out to be just too stiff for words. Olivier produced and directed as well as playing the Ruritanian royal who comes to London for coronation of George V and invites a chorus girl up for a quiet champagne supper. She gets involved with his local politics, acting as emissary between him and the young king, Jeremy Spenser. There's a definite anti-democratic tinge about the plot–but

who cares? The great joy is to see such two wonderfully charismatic personalities clashing and blending; 1957. (*c*)

Prince of Foxes √
Tyrone Power *v.* Orson Welles in Renaissance drama, doughtily directed by Henry King in 1949. (*b/w*)

Prince of Players √
Curiosity value as Richard Burton impersonates 19th-century actor Edwin Booth, including chunks of *Hamlet*. Eva Le Gallienne's his Gertrude; Raymond Massey, Mae Marsh, Charles Bickford help out Philip Dunne's direction; 1955. (*c*)

Prince Valiant √
No wit or entertainment drawn from the fact that the main character is big comic hero. Instead, Henry Hathaway was content to direct James Mason, Janet Leigh, Robert Wagner in usual medieval movie blood-and-thunderer; 1954. (*c*)

The Prisoner √
Based on the true case of Cardinal Mindszenty in Hungary, this clash between Alec Guinness and Jack Hawkins is well and cerebrally directed by Peter Glenville; 1955. (*b/w*)

The Prisoner of Shark Island √
Tragic tale of the doctor imprisoned for innocently setting the broken leg of Lincoln's murderer. 'John Ford again shows his admiration for the hero who becomes so by fortitude and patient suffering, and Warner Baxter holds the film together with an intense depiction of indomitability and anguish'—programme note when this 1937 classic played at the NFT. (*b/w*)

The Prisoner of Zenda √
Scene-for-scene 1952 remake by Richard Thorpe of famous Ronald Colman 1937 version of Anthony Hope's royal impersonation swashbuckler; Stewart Granger, Deborah Kerr, Louis Calhern, James Mason. (*c*)

Private Potter √ √
Tom Courtenay magnificent as the soldier who claims to have seen God, but who has to be charged with a breach of discipline. Casper Wrede turned the television play into a deep and deeply funny film; 1962. (*b/w*)

A Private's Affair × ×
Flabby farce about a private soldier married to a lady general. There are also a few musical numbers and some rather silly jokes. Sal Mineo, Jim Backus, Jessie Royce Landis all miscast. Raoul Walsh obviously just looked on it as his 44th and quickly-forgotten movie; 1959. (*c*)

Private's Progress √
Ian Carmichael, Richard Attenborough, Dennis Price, Terry-Thomas, William Hartnell in a sort of 1956 *Carry on Soldier* that did manage to criticize some of the weaknesses of the British army, and was first of Boulting Brothers' attacks on established institutions. (*b/w*)

Privilege √
Peter Watkins predicted a Britain in the near future (this was made in 1967) where people are so stupid and sheep-like that they accept a coalition government's attempts to manipulate them, with eager obedience. The main instrument in manipulation seems to be a thick pop singer, stolidly played by Paul Jones—but where's the Opposition? Where's the Press? To compound the unreality, Jean Shrimpton stumbles through her one (and understandably only) 'acting' role with a glazed expression. However, there is a moment at the start when Jones goes through a stage act of being beaten by 'police' while singing a song that is genuinely disturbing. (*c*)

The Prize ✗
Messy, pretentious, vulgar comedy thriller about Paul Newman receiving the Nobel Prize and getting involved in Edward G. Robinson 'defecting'. Mark Robson makes it all implausibly slick; 1964. (*c*)

A Prize of Arms √
Straightforward caper about robbing an Army post office of £250,000; Stanley Baker, Tom Bell and Helmut Schmid are the thieves, and it's excitingly if gnomically developed. Cliff Owen did taut directing job; 1962. (*b/w*)

A Prize of Gold √
Richard Widmark leads a gold caper in Berlin, then decides to give it back. Mark Robson recruited weak supports to help even weaker plot from Max Catto novel. But he does have a way of keeping the action tight; 1955. (*c*)

The Prodigal ✗ ✗
What the Bible failed to mention happened to the Prodigal Son while he was off on his binge; he (Edmund Purdom) was falling for priestess (Lana Turner). Richard Thorpe directed; 1955 (*c*)

The Producers √ √ √
Brilliant black comedy about the staging of a play that must fail, *Springtime for Hitler*, but of course doesn't. Mel Brooks has drawn excruciatingly funny performances from Zero Mostel and Gene Hackman that, as *Time* rightly said in 1967, belong in the W. C. Fields and Marx Brothers league. The most under-rated comedy of the sixties. (*c*)

The Professionals √ √
Are a bunch of four men hired to do a job in Mexico. Thus far the comparison is with *The Magnificent Seven*, a similarity that is emphasised by the presence of the same actor playing village leader. But here the motivation is conflicting: The Seven are doing the job for peanuts because the bandit leader is a baddie. The Four go about this job of freeing a woman from bandits for money but come up against a problem: she's happy there, she's chosen to go out of love for the bandit-leader, and, anyway, they have an ideological sympathy with these bandits. But they are Professionals. So which is more important: their head and purse or their hearts? Burt Lancaster, Lee Marvin, Robert Ryan and Woody Strode make their dilemma believable. Jack Palance rouses himself out of his usual torpor to turn in an excellent performance as the bandit chief. Only Claudia Cardinale is deficient as the woman, but director Richard Brooks covers up her inadequacies neatly; 1966. (*c*)

Promise Her Anything ✗ ✗
Awful attempt to make a movie about Greenwich Village without moving out of England. Warren Beatty is supposed to be blue film-maker looking after Leslie Caron's baby. Stifle the yawns in spotting Lionel Stander, Warren Mitchell; 1966. Arthur Hiller. (*c*)

The Proud and the Profane ✗
You might have thought the main war going on in the Pacific in 1943 was between America and the Japanese. It was actually between Deborah Kerr, the proud (not to say snotty-nosed) widow of the title and William Holden as the profane (not to say sadistic) colonel who seduces her. There's an awful lot of plot (and a lot of awful plot) before the sentimental ending, and George Seaton cannot blame the script. He wrote it in 1956. (*b/w*)

The Proud Ones ✗
Attempt to make a big Western in 1956 failed from diffusion of story-line. It starts promisingly enough (if too reminiscent of *High Noon*), with a Marshal (Robert Ryan) who has to settle an old

score before he can get married (to Virginia Mayo). Jeffrey Hunter comes to admire him in the course of the film, but it's difficult to share his awe. Robert D. Webb directed. (*c*)

The Proud Rebel　　　　　　　✗
With a mute boy and a dog and a rebel soldier wandering the South looking for a doctor to cure his son, Michael Curtiz must have thought he was on to such a box-office winner in 1958 that he didn't have to try too hard at anything except overdoing the sentiment. Unfortunately, Alan Ladd needed firmer handling than this, and the result was a decidedly wooden performance, though his real-life son, David, docs rather better. Olivia de Havilland, too, is over-sentimental as the lady who looks after them. As Lance the Dog, King is adequate. (*c*)

The Prowler　　　　　　　　✓
Sam Spiegel to Joseph Losey in 1951: 'You're right for this, but you're not very experienced. I'll give you the best cameraman in Hollywood, the best technicians. I don't care what I pay, and you do it any way you want to'. The way he wanted was to pre-rehearse the actors like in the theatre but rarely for the movies. Result wasn't much tauter performances or deeper characterisation than seen in most bent-cop thrillers, but Van Heflin and Evelyn Keyes are acceptable. (*b/w*)

Prudence and the Pill　　　　✗
Dated in 1968, when it was made, this will look ludicrous by the time it reaches your home screen. It makes such a fuss about contraceptive pills and thinks it's so daring in the process as to be positively in need of the aspirins that people mistake for them. As it happens, it's based on completely false premises, as the way birth control pills are packed is quite different from the way vitamin pills and painkillers are. Still, Judy

Geeson, David Niven, Deborah Kerr, Keith Michell, Michael Hordern and Vickery Turner (to name the best of a good cast) struggle on, sounding vaguely mid-Atlantic, thanks to American director Fielder Cook. (*c*)

Psyche 59　　　　　　　　✗
'Pretentious bosh' was the description that greeted this attempt at profundity–a slushy story about a husband (ill-at-ease Curt Jurgens) fancying his wife's (Pat Neal) sister (Samantha Eggar). Director Alexander Singer was attempting to make a French literary film in England, and that's something no red-blooded patriot would tolerate; 1964. (*b/w*)

Psycho　　　　　　　　✓✓✓
Most people's favourite Hitchcock opened to poor notices in 1960: 'a fairground sideshow. ... *Emergency Ward Ten* level of psychiatric mumbo-jumbo ... the plot creaks ... these violent, twisted trappings (a nauseating bathroom murder) are not the stuff that Hitch is blessed with the talent to give us', said one (it would be unfair to name the critic–he has almost certainly changed his mind by now). Gradually this thriller has come to be accepted as a major achievement in the way it pretends for the first reels to tell one story, then switches to another, and then turns that round again, to finish up with one of the most shocking denouements in the history of the cinema. If you haven't seen it before, make every effort to see it from the first shot (Hitchcock didn't allow latecomers into the cinema) and if you have, please, please don't give the ending away; as Hitch said at the time, 'It's the only thing we have.' A word of praise for all the acting: Janet Leigh just right in a difficult part; Anthony Perkins convincing twice over (once at the time, once looking back); Martin Balsam an impressive, doomed investigator. Altogether superb. (*b/w*)

The Psychopath √
Director Freddie Francis neatly handles who-is-it about a nutter who kills and leaves dolls behind. 1966 thriller has Patrick Wymark, Margaret Johnston, John Standing, Judy Huxtable among victims and suspects. (*b/w*)

PT 109 √
1963 mythologising of John F. Kennedy as the naval hero. Cliff Robertson is Kennedy and Leslie H. Martinson directed action scenes with more reverence than the ruthlessness they undoubtedly demanded. (*c*)

The Pumpkin Eater √
The combined talents of director Jack Clayton, original novelist Penelope Mortimer, adapter Harold Pinter, leads Anne Bancroft, Peter Finch and James Mason should somehow have added up to a more convincing film than this. Perhaps the main fault is in Miss Bancroft's casting: she's a very fine American actress, but misses the essence of Englishness and Hampsteadness that should pervade the main character, who leaves one husband to marry Finch and is fecund to the point of neurosis. Nevertheless, the film deserves better treatment than when shown by London Weekend Television some years ago; they butchered it to squeeze it into a pre-ordained time-slot and all continuity and chunks of the plot were lost. Let us hope that future showings are in full–or not at all; 1964. (*b/w*)

The Punch and Judy Man √
Tony Hancock's 1963 attempt to do something other than his East Cheam character was doomed to popular failure among a public that distrusts versatility, but it's a collector's item for appreciators of subtle comedy. Jeremy Summers directed the script that Hancock wrote with Philip Oakes, and packed it with other super actors: Sylvia Sims as his

ambitious wife, Barbara Murray, Ronald Fraser, Hugh Lloyd, Hattie Jacques. (*b/w*)

The Pure Hell of St Trinian's √
Without Alastair Sim, St T's isn't quite as funny, although this 1960 cash-in on previous successes does have Joyce Grenfell, Sid James, Dennis Price, George Cole, Cecil Parker as compensation. Girls burn down school, are propositioned for harem. Frank Launder directed. (*b/w*)

The Purple Gang ✕
Teenage hoodlums in the twenties hunted by detective Barry Sullivan. Frank McDonald directed this rather unpleasant little piece in 1960. (*b/w*)

The Purple Mask ✕
Tony Curtis was still earning his bread-and-jam in 1955 leaping about with a sword for Bruce Humberstone. Gene Barry and Angela Lansbury joined him in this faintly embarrassing costumer. (*c*)

The Purple Plain √
Gregory Peck discovers that crashing his plane in the jungle in the Second World War was the best thing for him. Robert Parrish directed emotional story in Burma, with British cast including Bernard Lee; 1955. (*c*)

Pursued √
Robert Mitchum seeking men who killed father in Western that is far from conventional. Raoul Walsh made this 1947 thriller stand out with fine performances from Teresa Wright and Judith Anderson. (*b/w*)

Pushover √
Fred MacMurray made a come-back in 1955 with first starring role for some years as a cop falling for Kim Novak, the gangster moll, in her first real part. Richard Quine. (*b/w*)

The Quare Fellow √
Patrick McGoohan as prison guard changing mind about capital punishment in 1962 Irish version of Brendan Behan play, faithfully and claustrophobically directed by Arthur Dreifuss. *(b/w)*

Quatermass II ✗
Routine sci-fi about meteorites which, on contact, turn those who touch them into the zombies of a Superior Intelligence. Brian Donlevy had to be imported into Britain to make it safe for us British, because the year was 1957 and nobody dared make a movie without a washed-up American star to give it some sort of B-picture status over there. Val Guest directed, evidently hurriedly. *(b/w)*

Queen Bee ✗
Joan Crawford in another of her tailored roles as an outwardly nice, inwardly horrid, lady who uses all about her for her own purposes. It's all tosh, of course, particularly when people start killing themselves at her revelations but compelling for her vaster-than-life performance. Ranald MacDougall wrote and directed; 1955. *(b/w)*

Queen Christina √
How much of Garbo's magical appeal

Greta Garbo in *Queen Christina*

was due to her mid-sex qualities? Looking back on this 1933 blockbuster with our greater (we hope) sexual sophistication, you can't help feeling that her butch performance as the 17th century Swedish queen dressed as a boy stirred equivocal passion–both in femme breasts and among males who would consider John Gilbert was having best of both worlds when the handsome lad he is forced to share an inn room with turns out to be a girl. Rouben Mamoulian ignored all the 'great actress' guff and had her move to a metronome and think about nothing in the famous final close-up. (*b/w*)

The Queen of Spades　　　　√
The slow English (1949) Thorold Dickinson version of the Pushkin story, filmed in Russia several times. Outstanding performance by Edith Evans as ageing countess who knows the secret of winning at faro; Anton Walbrook is the soldier who would sell his soul to learn.
(*b/w*)

A Question of Adultery　　　× ×
Sad little attempt at 'forthright' problem movie about artificial insemination in 1958 comes out looking tepid and fence-sitting. Don Chaffey's wooden direction isn't helped by matching teak performance from Anthony Steel as the husband. Julie London as the wife is a couple of shades better, but the whole thing's a stodge. (*b/w*)

The Quick and the Dead　　　√
Superior war actioner in which cast of unknowns manage to convey something of what it must have been like to blow up an ammunition dump; it's not even spoiled by the entrance of two pretty sisters who lead them to Partisans. Credit must go to director Robert Totten; 1963. (*b/w*)

The Quick Gun　　　　× ×
Audie Murphy returns an outcast from

serving short sentence for self-defence killing, but the townspeople love him again when he defeats a gang of outlaws. End of film. Don't bother. Sidney Salkow directed in 1964–presumably in his sleep. (*c*)

The Quiet American　　　　×
Michael Redgrave right as the narrator-character, Audie Murphy wrong as the Third Force-deluded American in Joseph L. Mankiewicz's 1958 screwing-up of Graham Greene's Vietnam novel.
(*b/w*)

The Quiet Man　　　　√
Ireland was never like this rosy John Ford picture of it, but it's a darlin' place wherever it is. John Wayne goes back there and falls for Victor McLaglen's sister, Maureen O'Hara; but before the happy ending there's the longest, toughest bout of fisticuffs ever seen. Barry Fitzgerald, Jack McGowran and a bar-full of other Irish characters rally round; 1952. (*c*)

The Quiller Memorandum　　　×
Plusses in this espionage yarn are Pinter script, Berlin locations, George Segal, Alec Guinness. Minuses: Michael Anderson's pedestrian direction, Senta Berger's woeful inadequacy. Max von Sydow, as neo-Nazi heavy, veers between plus and minus. 1966. (*c*)

Quo Vadis?　　　　√
Spectacular third version in 1951 (the first two were Italian; 1912, 1924) of Henryk Sienkiewicz's novel of Romans' persecution of the Christians. Robert Taylor as Roman falls for Deborah Kerr as Christian; Peter Ustinov as Nero is extremely put out. To the lions with them all, we say. Mervyn LeRoy obliged with the lions but didn't give them enough to eat. (*c*)

The Rabbit Trap ✓
There's this little boy, and he's on holiday in the country with his Pa—that's Ernest Borgnine. And there's a rabbit alive in a trap they set. And Pa's like a rabbit in a trap, too, in his job. So when he's called back to the city and they forget the trap and the little boy is all cut up about leaving the rabbit to starve, should Pa stay in town and be a good little rabbit in a trap himself or should he risk his job and free the rabbit? United Artists brought British director Philip Leacock to America to direct this one because he had a reputation for directing kids. Unfortunately, he was so concerned not to be sentimental that this kid, Kevin Corcoran, never makes any impact. Which is sad; 1959. (*b/w*)

Rachel and the Stranger ✓
Loretta Young and William Holden are married. Robert Mitchum is the stranger in strong story of North-West pioneers. Norman Foster directed; 1947. (*b/w*)

Rachel, Rachel ✓✓
Drama of schoolteacher verging on middle age in small town. Joanne Woodward has never tried harder than under her husband, Paul Newman's debut as director-producer. Her anguish at fear of lesbianism; mistaking sex for love; and her phantom pregnancy might

Mia Farrow in *Rosemary's Baby*

all be a bit hard to take, but it's clear that the Newmans cared–and sincerity is a rare virtue in the movies. 1968 winner of New York Critics' award for Best Director, Best Actress. (*c*)

The Rack √
Paul Newman in courtroom drama: was he a traitor during Korean war? Arnold Laven directed over-sentimental Rod Serling story in 1956, plus Lee Marvin, Edmond O'Brien, Anne Francis and Walter Pidgeon as Newman's father. (*b/w*)

A Rage to Live ×
Well, not exactly to live, more to go to bed with someone. This is the life of a nympho, folks, so roll up and see Suzanne Pleshette screwed and suffering. Walter Grauman directs it like a child playing traffic policeman with all the cars whizzing by non-stop; 1964. (*c*)

The Raiders ×
More Buffalo Bill, Wild Bill Hickock and Calamity Jane adventures (they were a busy lot), this time extending the railroad to Texas, to help friends get their cattle there. Robert Culp was bushwacked by Herschel Daughtery; 1963. (*c*)

The Raiders of Leyte Gulf × × ×
Excruciating war film about the Philippines with poor technical credits, weaker acting abilities and, lowest of all, directorial skill from Eddie Romero; 1962. (*b/w*)

The Rainmaker √ √
Joseph Anthony's 1956 retelling of *The Ugly Duckling*, notable for Katharine Hepburn's farmer's daughter, impressed, as everyone else is, by Burt Lancaster's poetic con-man who brings her rain and readiness for love. It won her and composer Alex North Oscar nominations. (*c*)

The Rains Came √
Suspend critical faculties and enjoy the slush–metaphorical and literal–of Louis Bromfield novel of love *v.* duty, directed by Clarence Brown in 1939 with monsoons, earthquakes, Myrna Loy, Tyrone Power, George Brent, Nigel Bruce. (*b/w*)

The Rains of Ranchipur √
1955 remake of *The Rains Came* is wetter than ever, with Richard Burton, absurdly miscast as Indian doctor, Lana Turner and Fred MacMurray having to shout to be heard above that steady cats-and-dog effect. They might as well have saved their breath; Jean Negulesco was evidently under orders to put the spectacle first, the human moisture second. (*c*)

Raintree County √ √
You may have thought it had gone with the wind, but it was still there, in 1958. The proud Southern belle (Elizabeth Taylor), the young suitor (Montgomery Clift), the old father (Walter Abel) and the political and emotional rivals for her hand and honour (Lee Marvin and Rod Taylor). But it's really unfair to put down Edward Dmytryk's big reworking of Ross Lockridge's novel, scripted by Millard Kaufman, because the people do come across as more real than those *GWTT* ciphers, even if the sweep isn't so vast. It certainly makes a satisfactory nearly-three-hours' watching, but needs a box of chocolates in the lap for full effect. (*c*)

Raising a Riot × ×
Punny title refers to three noisy brats (including Mandy Miller) naval Commander Kenneth More has to cope with when wife exits to mother's sickbed. Wendy Toye directed this weary jollification in 1955. (*c*)

Raising the Wind × ×
Carry On Doctor in the Music House might have been a better title for this

ill-fated would-be starter to a new series of broad British comedies, in 1961, with music students replacing medical ones. All the old gang were there – Leslie Phillips, Sid James, Kenneth Williams, Liz Fraser, Lance Percival, James Robertson Justice. So were all the old jokes. And it was *Carry-On's* same old director, Gerald Thomas for the same old producer, Peter Rogers. (*c*)

A Raisin In The Sun √
Hailed in 1961 as true-life Negro drama, now looks suspiciously like trying-to-be-white-ism. Daniel Petrie directed Sidney Poitier and all-black cast in carbon-copy of Lorraine Hansberry play about ghetto family. (*b/w*)

Rally Round the Flag, Boys ✕
Clumsy farce from Max Shulman's novel about New England commuters' community trying to stop the Army from building a rocket-launching site in its midst. Paul Newman and Joanne Woodward are unhappy in central roles as couple whose marriage is threatened by Joan Collins because Woodward is too busy being activist. Newman simply hasn't the comic touch and veteran producer-director Leo McCarey can't provide it; 1959. (*c*)

Rampage ✕
Robert Mitchum, Elsa Martinelli and Jack Hawkins made an oddly-assorted triangle out in the jungle trapping half-tiger-half-leopard. When Mitchum also traps Martinelli, Hawkins does his nut. Director Phil Karlson keeps the pot boiling, however, and you don't notice the flaws at the time, you're too busy gasping; 1963. (*c*)

Rancho Notorious ✕
A poor cowboy's *Destry Rides Again*, with Marlene Dietrich in a faint echo of the earlier role. This 1952 oater mismatched a lot of fine talents including director Fritz Lang who was obviously unhappy on the prairie; Mel Ferrer, a laughable 'fastest gun in the West'; Arthur Kennedy as dogged Nemesis, chasing killer and ravisher of his sweetheart. He masquerades as an outlaw, penetrates desert hide-out and finally avenges his gal. Incidentally, the key role of Kinch is played by Lloyd Gough, who–for some reason–doesn't get a credit. (*c*)

Random Harvest √
Get the tissues ready if you enjoy a weep, and Greer Garson. Harder hearts will yawn over this 1942 yarn about Ronald Colman losing his memory and finding love (and vice-versa). Mervyn LeRoy did slick director's job. (*b/w*)

Ransom! √
Glenn Ford, Donna Reed in kidnap yarn, rather well-directed by Alex Segal in 1955. Gives a vivid picture of parents under pressure. (*b/w*)

The Rare Breed ✕
Maureen O'Hara introducing the Hereford bull to America with the help of James Stewart, but under Andrew McLaglen's direction the cattle act better than the humans, although visually it's fine; 1966. (*c*)

Rasputin–the Mad Monk ✕ ✕
Attempt at pre-revolutionary Russian shocker by Don Sharp, with Christopher Lee, Richard Pasco, Barbara Shelley, Francis Matthews, in descending order of credibility. This 1966 British effort was remake of the triple-Barrymore 1932 version. (*c*)

The Rat Race √
New York as seen through the jaundiced eyes of director Robert Mulligan, in his second film, 1960. It's a helluva town. Alone among its eight million, only innocents Tony Curtis and Debbie Reynolds aren't drunks, thieves, conmen, or other varieties of the dregs of humanity. (*c*)

The Rattle of a Simple Man　×××
Charles Dyer's golden-hearted-whore-meets-impotent-yob duologue was played for laughs in the theatre and just about worked due to the super perform-ances of Sheila Hancock and Edward Woodward. Transferred to the screen in 1964, it sank like lead under Muriel Box's heavy-handed direction and feck-less playing of Harry H. Corbett and Diane Cilento. (*b/w*)

The Raven　√√
Horror director Roger Corman's 1963 spoof, biting of the claw that fed him, aided and abattoired by three of the best–Vincent Price, Peter Lorre and Boris Karloff. Corman plucked Poe's plumage to feather his own gothic nest of plot about three 15th-century sorcer-ers on the rampage, hilarious and hor-rific by turns; and watch out for Jack Nicholson in a small part. (*c*)

Rawhide　√
Should have been retitled to avoid con-fusion with TV series; this was original 1951 version, with Tyrone Power and Susan Hayward held prisoner by besieged outlaws. Director Henry Hath-away went thataway. (*b/w*)

Raw Wind in Eden　×
Society couple shipwrecked on strange island occupied by peasant, his daughter and mysterious American. Richard Wilson sorted something out of this hokum in 1958, despite Esther Williams, Jeff Chandler, Rossana Podesta. (*c*)

The Razor's Edge　√
Maugham's soapy, philosophical novel gave Herbert Marshall his familiar role as the author, with Tyrone Power, Gene Tierney, John Payne and Clifton Webb as four of the characters he bumps into in posh Chicago in the twenties; the fifth was Anne Baxter as a dipso-maniac and it won her the 1946 Best Supporting Oscar. Edmund Goulding lushed it all up happily enough. (*b/w*)

Reach for Glory　√
Philip Leacock, marvellous at handling child actors, manages again in this sorry story of prejudice among the evacuees at the start of the war. One of them is killed, à la *Lord of the Flies*. Harry Andrews and Kay Walsh stand out among the adults; 1961. (*b/w*)

Reach for the Sky　√
Kenneth More convinces as legless ace Douglas Bader. Lewis Gilbert directed with polish in 1956 and it grips beyond routine war-picture hero-ism. (*b/w*)

Reap the Wild Wind　√
Giant squid is real star of this spec-tacular about 19th-century salvagers, out-acting John Wayne, Ray Milland, Susan Hayward, Paulette Goddard, Raymond Massey. Which is probably what wily old director Cecil B. DeMille had in mind in 1942. (*c*)

Rear Window　√√√
Delicious 1954 Hitchcock has James Stewart confined to wheelchair, passing the time by spying on the neighbours he overlooks. He suspects a murder which, in fact, Hitch created from a combina-tion of the Crippen and Mahon cases. All the separate stories he Tom-Peeps on are to do with love and reflect on his own conflict–does he love Grace Kelly or not? How the immobilised Stewart fights back when the murderer comes calling is a brilliant device. Certainly one of the finest Hitchcocks–here to be spotted winding a clock. (*c*)

Rebecca　√√
Won the 1940 Oscar for the Best Picture but Hitchcock didn't get Director's Award–he has never won one although he has consistently been the best direc-tor over the last fifty years (his first film was in 1925). The Oscar went to pro-ducer David Selznick. Hitch sees this one as a fairy story–Cinderella with only one ugly sister–and set out to emphasise

the Grimm aspects of the story. Daphne du Maurier's novelettish story could have been an ordinary movie melo but Hitch's love of mystery turned it into a thriller. Olivier as the well-meaning, self-blaming husband, Joan Fontaine as his timid new wife, Judith Anderson as the never-moving housekeeper were all superb. (*b/w*)

The Rebel √
One of the many tragedies in Tony Hancock's life is that he never met up with a film director who could take his particular style of comedy and distil it for the cinema. In 1961, with a Simpson and Galton script that owed its inspiration to Gauguin's flight from respectability to Bohemia (Paris in this case), he could have been marvellously funny. As it was, he was funny all right, but round him was a film conceived in such banal terms (e.g. 'the beatniks' in Paris who are so impressed with his Infantile School obviously hadn't seen the King's Road, let alone the Left Bank) that its net effect was sadly flat. The fault lay squarely with director Robert Day. (*c*)

Rebel in Town √
J. Carrol Naish, who was the only worthwhile feature in so many actioners, got his chance to lead at last in 1956 with this study of a father driven to bank-robbing by the ostracism that Confederate soldiers felt on return from the Civil War. Alfred Werker did competent directorial job and Naish grabbed his opportunity. (*b/w*)

Rebel Without A Cause √
One of the two films that made James Dean a cult. Teenage victim of a world he didn't make and doesn't want, his charismatic performance is adequately complemented by Natalie Wood and Sal Mineo. Energetically directed by Nicholas Ray in 1955 it has, alas, lost its power with its contemporaneousness. (*c*)

The Reckless Moment ×
Max Ophüls brought his distinctive touch to this 1948 melo of Mama Joan Bennett being blackmailed by smoothie James Mason after she kills local womaniser who was trying to seduce daughter Geraldine Brooks. (*b/w*)

The Red Badge of Courage √
This one has a special niche in the history of Hollywood as best-documented case of how studio bosses screw up creators. The *New Yorker's* Lillian Ross followed its making, and her piece anatomised John Huston's losing struggle to keep faithful to Stephen Crane's Civil War novel, against 1951 McCarthy-stampeded MGM. But could Audie Murphy ever have made hero convincing? Some marvellous moments remain despite vain frantic re-editing to make it commercial. Ross's article was later published as a book, *Picture*; it's revelatory reading after you've seen the movie. (*b/w*)

The Red Beret × ×
Alan Ladd re-enlists as paratrooper when his friend is killed through his fault while an officer. Terence Young managed to squeeze a few thrills out of basically unconvincing script in 1952, but couldn't do much with stiff Leo Genn or soppy Susan Stephen. (*c*)

Red Garters √
1953 attempt to move musicals on a bit by satire on standard Western yarn and stylised sets and costumes (black baddies, white goodies, red naughties) didn't quite come off. But it's worth watching George Marshall try with help of Rosemary Clooney, Jack Carson, Reginald Owen. (*c*)

Red Hell × × ×
Straight forward anti-communist tract in which torturer Basil Rathbone gives victim Mary Murphy a rabid lesson in the iniquities of the Reds, helped out by

various selected bits of documentary footage. Hideous. William D. Faralla; 1962. (*b/w*)

Red Line 7000 √
Hallowed veteran Howard Hawks indulged himself in 1965 in making this episodic film in which drivers' love stories are interspersed with racing pictures. There's no real plot but plenty of action with James Caan, Laura Devon. (*c*)

Red Mountain √
Alan Ladd leads guerillas in Kansas and Missouri, sacking towns that are favourable to Union cause. Strong back-up cast includes Lizabeth Scott, John Ireland, Arthur Kennedy; and William Dieterle always turned in competent job; 1951. (*c*)

The Red Pony √
One of those boy-and-his-horse epics, where he relates more to the animal than the warring humans (Myrna Loy, Robert Mitchum, Louis Calhern among them) around him. Lewis Milestone kept it running wild, running free in 1949. (*c*)

Red River √√
Howard Hawks Western about a cattle drive that John Wayne wants to take over the Chisholm Trail, past the Red River into Missouri, through which at that time—just after the Civil War—nobody had yet driven cattle. But foster-son Montgomery Clift wants to drive to Abilene and ship the cattle East by rail. They come to blows until Joanne Dru patches up the quarrel. Hawks gave the drive tremendous power and succeeded in lifting the film right out of the oater class into a classic statement of the generation-battle; 1948. (*b/w*)

The Red Shoes ×
Dreadful plot about impresario Anton Walbrook trying to force dancer Moira Shearer to renounce Love and Marius Goring, balanced by ballet sequences. Michael Powell and Emeric Pressburger managed to make ballet box office in 1948 and there's never been a successful attempt since (or before except *La Mort du Cygne*). (*c*)

Red Skies of Montana ×
Great fire sequences under Joseph M. Newman's direction save this otherwise routine yarn about US Forestry Service with Richards Widmark, Boone, Crenna; 1952. (*c*)

Red Sundown ×
Rory Calhoun as poacher-turned-gamekeeper in Western setting, roughs up old villainous mates, woos sheriff's daughter Martha Hyer. Jack Arnold; 1956. (*c*)

Reflections in a Golden Eye √
A prize of a mint julep for anyone who understands what Marlon Brando is saying in the extraordinary Southern accent he has adopted here. Elizabeth Taylor is his wife who has to turn to other men because her husband's gay; Julie Harris is a nutter who uses a pair of garden shears somewhat painfully; so what he is saying may be better left a mystery. Based on a Carson McCullers novel, it's about how Brando gets obsessed with another soldier, who rides bareback and bare-bottom through the nearby woods. Director John Huston had the film bleached so that the colours all come out sepia except for scarlet that printed pink; but Warner Brothers—Seven Arts quickly had a 'glorious' full-colour print substituted after the first few showings in 1968 and that is probably what will be shown on TV. (*c*)

The Reluctant Debutante ××
Rex Harrison and his then (1958) wife Kay Kendall manage to make this old-fashioned stuff about will-daughter-marry-the-right-chap? watchable while they are on the screen. But

Sandra Dee and John Saxon reduce this essentially British comedy into something more than faintly ludicrous. Being Italian-American, Vincente Minnelli probably thought he was being accurate enough, and, anyway, Hollywood companies of that period had little respect for British audiences. (*c*)

Reluctant Heroes × ×
Prime example of what used to be called pejoratively 'British pictures' in 1951, with the implicit boredom and (now) old familiar faces: Ronald Shiner, Brian Rix, Derek Farr. Green national servicemen muck up the manoeuvres but predictably end up as heroes. Jack Raymond directed. (*b/w*)

The Reluctant Saint × ×
Talk about the Flying Nun! This visible drama is about St Maximillian Schell who levitates when he prays; up he goes, in full sight of the tricky camera. Filmed in Italy, where it is supposed to have happened for real in the 17th century, this bit of religioso rubbish was apparently taken seriously by director-producer Edward Dmytryk; 1962. (*b/w*)

The Reluctant Widow × ×
1950 costumer which was out of date when it was made, has Jean Kent a English governess forced to marry drunkard in Napoleonic wars; director Bernard Knowles. (*b/w*)

The Remarkable Mr Pennypacker × ×
What makes him remarkable is that he has two families in separate towns totalling 17 children. As a Victorian bigamist, Clifton Webb doesn't seem happy in this 1958 comedy, possibly because his own personal inclinations made even one child unlikely. Henry Levin directed slowly and it's all a great big bore with an obvious ending it finally reaches. (*c*)

Remember the Day √
1941 Henry King-directed weepie with Claudette Colbert back-flashing over her life as a teacher – and her lost love. (*b/w*)

Reprieve √
Unexceptional and unexceptionable prison drama which purports to show how disgusting prison life is but gets lost in the shadows of earlier prison movies. This 1962 effort by writer-director Millard Kaufman is a bit more realistic than earlier Hollywood jail pix but doesn't rival the uncommercial *The Brig*. The actors play obvious stereotypes, like Rod Steiger's warder who's a sadist, Broderick Crawford's Warden who doesn't want to know, Stuart Whitman's warder who means well, Ben Gazzara's prisoner who's only bad because of poverty and momentary impulse, Sammy Davis's black buddy and so on. (*b/w*)

The Reptile × × ×
Pathetic Hammer unhorror about a girl who turns into a snake. Jacqueline Pearce doesn't appear to have taken the trouble to watch any real snakes as her impression of one is inaccurate and ludicrous. And director John Gilling wasn't doing his job in not teaching her. In fact, he didn't seem to be doing much at all as this wearisome tale slithers on without any tension or fun; 1966. (*c*)

Repulsion √ √ √
Roman Polanski's powerful shocker of 1965 can be seen as just another horror picture, and a particularly good one as nothing supernatural provides the chills. Or it can be put into the context of Polanski's other works as a convincing study of disintegration, his pervasive theme. Catherine Deneuve – never called upon to portray more than the shell-shocked ingenue she always does best – slowly goes out of her mind. The everyday terrors of flies buzzing round a

forgotten rabbit are even more frightening than the hands that clutch at her along the corridor. Polanski's skill shows in his handling of the lesser characters – Yvonne Furneaux as her sister, Patrick Wymark as lecherous landlord – who are so often just types in other low-budget British films. (*b/w*)

Requiem for a Gunfighter √
Rod Cameron is mistaken for judge and uses the time before he is recognised to prove that bully-boy is murderer in Western town. Spencer G. Bennet didn't make it quite exciting enough in 1965. (*c*)

Requiem for a Heavyweight √
Famous TV play by Rod Serling makes a strong vehicle for Anthony Quinn as over-the-hill boxer. Jackie Gleason and Mickey Rooney are realistic as fight-game hangers-on under Ralph Nelson's 1962 direction; Julie Harris is self-kidding social worker. (*b/w*)

The Restless Breed ✕
Agent's son sets out to avenge father's murder; Scott Brady plays single-minded lad in Western hamlet, Anne Bancroft intervening. Allan Dwan directed routinely; 1957. (*c*)

The Restless Years ✕
Can dressmaker keep secret of illegitimacy from her teenage daughter? Dated (1957) small-town drama is given the works by Teresa Wright and Sandra Dee under Helmut Kautner. (*b/w*)

Return from the Ashes ✕
Using the terrible plight of concentration camp returnees as the excuse for a thriller like this is a bit strong, even when it's tarted up with psychological and philosophical undertones. J. Lee Thompson must have known he was making over the old mother *v.* daughter (Ingrid Thulin *v.* Samantha Eggar) plot, both in love with the same man (Maximillian Schell), leading to a bathroom murder; 1965. (*b/w*)

The Return of Frank James √√
The film *Jesse James* had been such a big success in 1939 that Darryl Zanuck wheeled Henry Fonda out again the following year to play in a sequel. He's supposed to be avenging Jesse's (Tyrone Power) death in a totally unhistoric episode, and played opposite 'Miss' Gene Tierney (as they billed her) in her debut. But Fritz Lang was odd choice as director and Fonda and he were soon not on speaking terms. The result was a moody Western, a cut above the ordinary. Jackie Cooper had grown up enough to play his younger brother; John Carradine led the baddies. (*c*)

Return of the Bad Men √
Randolph Scott wants to settle down with widow Anne Jeffreys but Robert Ryan comes riding into the Oklahoma land rush and holds up the proceedings, the nasty man. Ray Enright directs straightforwardly; 1948. (*b/w*)

Return of the Fly ✕✕
Sad little sequel to splendid horror movies, *The Fly*, of the previous year. This 1959 mini-budget effort puts the scientist's son (Vincent Price) through the same routine and he spends the rest of the picture literally buzzing about looking for the guy that did it to him. Writer-director Edward L. Bernds must have written it on flypaper. (*b/w*)

Return of the Gunfighter √
The Gunfighter was Gregory Peck in 1950. In this 1966 sequel a 55-year-old Robert Taylor plays a differently named character but with the same weariness for fighting and shooting, which doesn't stop him fighting and shooting. Here he avenges the deaths of Ana Martin's parents, helped by Chad Everett. James Neilson directs intelligently. (*c*)

Return of the Seven ✗
But not so magnificently and not the same ones. In fact, only one of the originals survives and he's the least attractive, Yul Brynner. The rest of the Second Eleven (to confuse the metaphor) aren't good enough to play even in the reserves. This sequel is how a crazy Mexican enslaves a village to build a monument to his dead sons—a pretty awful script by Larry Cohen matched by the direction of Burt Kennedy; 1967. (*c*)

Return to Paradise ✗ ✗
Taken from an episode in James Michener's book of the same name, this unfortunate South Sea Island film has Gary Cooper first freeing a community from the tyrany of a preacher, Barry Jones, marrying a native girl (Roberta Haynes) meantime, and then turning up again years later to save their daughter from a fate worse than death. Mark Robson struggled, as director, to put some life into a flat script from Charles Kaufman in 1953. (*c*)

Return to Peyton Place ✗
Now let's sort this out nice and slowly. This Allison Mackenzie isn't Mia Farrow impersonated by Kathy Glass in the television series. This is Carol Lynley impersonating Diane Varsi who was the original movie Mackenzie. Here she is scandalising the old place with her book and living it up with her publisher (Jeff Chandler). Only Mary Astor as a selfish mother is worth watching. The rest is gossip. Director José Ferrer; 1961. (*c*)

Return to Treasure Island ✗ ✗
Dawn Addams as descendent of Jim Hawkins who goes back with his map; Porter Hall and baddies aim to steal it; Tab Hunter saves it. Terrible stuff, directed by E. A. Dupont; 1954. (*c*)

The Revenge of Frankenstein ✗ ✗
Not very horrible horror Hammer, about Dr Frankenstein (not the monster) being nearly killed a couple of times and re-emerging with different identities. But he still keeps re-assembling bits of human bodies to make ever-more-terrifying patchwork people. Unfortunately, this can easily get ludicrous, and director Terence Fisher wasn't able to stop it doing so in 1958. Peter Cushing plays the Doc with his usual frenzied panache; apart from Lionel Jeffries the rest of the cast is strictly non-acting. (*c*)

The Revolt of Mamie Stover ✗
Hawaii, 1941 (actually Hollywood, 1956). Jane Russell steals the affections of Richard Egan from posh Joan Leslie but as she is a war-profiteering tart she is naturally unable to find True Happiness. Raoul Walsh lushes it all up; one small compensation is presence of Agnes Moorehead as dance-hall queen. (*c*)

Rhapsody ✗
Elizabeth Taylor, as rich girl, is spurned by violinist Vittorio Gassman, so marries pianist John Ericson among snippets of the popular classics. Charles Vidor conducts the proceedings; 1954. (*c*)

Rhapsody in Blue ✗
The music's OK if you can stand that inferior orchestral banging-about that is the title-work, but Robert Alda's portrayal of George Gershwin is so far from the truth as to be farcical. His piano-playing is dubbed, as is Joan Leslie's voice. Irving Rapper must have thought he was on a winner when he started out in 1955; but the casting (Alexis Smith, Charles Coburn, Oscar Levant were in it, too) was against him. (*b/w*)

Rhino! ✗ ✗
Dull and rather rhino-less big game hunter *v.* ecologist drama shot in Africa or somewhere that looks vaguely like it. Robert Culp is the goodie, Harry

Guardino the baddie. Shirley Eaton is baddie turned goodie (not her acting, though), and Ivan Tors' direction seems to consist of intercutting wild animal footage with tame human footage; 1964. (*c*)

Richard III √√
Olivier's 1956 triumph as the hunchback of history combining Shakespeare's flights of poetry, with exciting pictures and filmic expertise. As producer-director, he also ensured great performances from Gielgud, Richardson, Alec Clunes, Cedric Hardwicke and, above all, himself, Claire Bloom was also in it. He was particularly successful in his use of soliloquies–straight to camera, without any voice-over or other worried film tricks but didn't try for big battle sequences which might have been worth spending a bit on if he could have raised the extra money. (*c*)

The Ride Back √
Prisoner and lawman are forced to help each other in desperate ride through Apache country. Anthony Quinn, William Conrad. Director Allen H. Miner; 1957. (*b/w*)

Ride Beyond Vengeance √
Over-violent Western in which a man is wrongly branded (literally) as a thief and rides on into town determined to pay his branders back in the same fashion. There are also a lot of bloody fights that Bernard McEveety directs only too well. Among the many old (some of them very, by 1966) friends present are Joan Blondell, Frank Gorshin, Michael Rennie, Gloria Grahame, Gary Merrill, Buddy Baer. In the main part, Chuck Connors fights a good fight. (*c*)

Ride Lonesome √
Randolph Scott captures young baddie, waits for brother to come and get him—because, many years before, Lee Van

Cleef (the brother) hanged Scott's wife. Budd Boetticher's direction matches up to Burt Kennedy's interesting plot, which has James Coburn and Pernell Roberts also after the boy because amnesty has been declared on any outlaws who bring him in; 1959. (*c*)

Ride the High Country √√
Randolph Scott and Joel McCrea (59 and 57 in 1962) play ageing gunfighters, now marooned in travelling fairground where they parody their past (as Buffalo Bill did in real life), and are given a last chance to relive the excitement of their youth in delivering shipment of gold. Under Sam Peckinpah's direction, their saga takes on depths of meanings that transcend the ordinary Western, while retaining the routine thrills. (*c*)

Ride the Pink Horse √
Robert Montgomery (directing himself in 1947) arrives in New Mexico town intent on blackmail and vengeance, but there's nothing like the love of a good woman like Wanda Hendrix. (*b/w*)

Ride the Wild Surf ×
Fabian, James Mitchum, Barbara Eden plus sundry other beach bums and gals in a surfing drama (i.e. not a comedy, except that there isn't much difference) shot mostly in Hawaii. Director Don Taylor; 1965. (*c*)

Ride, Vaquero ×
Ava Gardner switches from Howard Keel to his half-brother Robert Taylor, as they try to build ranch in area dominated by bandit Anthony Quinn. John Farrow's direction can't quite keep a grip on the action; 1953. (*c*)

Riding High ×
Undemanding Mark Hellinger racetrack yarn has Bing Crosby as broke owner who has to rely on a horse called Broadway Bill (which was what the

poor 1933 film was called) without much hope. Veteran director Frank Capra did this sentimental 1950 remake with Charles Bickford, James Gleason, and Oliver Hardy (sans Laurel). Some of the racetrack scenes were re-run from the original. Notable for the fact that all the songs were recorded direct–not lip-sung to pre-recordings. (*b/w*)

Right Cross ×
Boxing melo with Ricardo Montalban as boxer with the chip on his shoulder that he's Mexican and thus second-class citizen. Lionel Barrymore is his manager, Dick Powell a reporter who's in love with June Allyson. When she spurns him, he goes night-clubbing with some other birds–one of them, though not named on the credits, is Marilyn Monroe, still unknown in 1950. John Sturges directed. (*b/w*)

Ring of Bright Water ×
Documentary about otters masquerading as a feature film. Bill Travers sees an otter in a pet-shop, takes him to his flat, finds the otter doesn't like it, takes him up to Scotland, where they meet up with Virginia McKenna. Man loses otter. Man gets otter. Fascinating for otters, not for humans. Jack Couffer directs like the graduate from the Disney wild-life school that he is. The otters are marginally worse actors than McKenna, marginally better than Travers; 1969. (*c*)

Ring of Fear ×
Mickey Spillane makes an appearance as private eye called in to stop seemingly accidental deaths in circus. Pat O'Brien strolls through, under James Grant's direction; 1954. (*c*)

Ring of Fire √
The first three-quarters of this actioner by Andrew L. Stone is an off-beat story of chase, escape, rape charges and

mob violence. Then comes one of the best forest fires ever on the screen and the plot perishes in the flames, but by then you don't care. David Janssen, Joyce Taylor, Frank Gorshin; 1961. (*c*)

Ring of Spies × ×
Unconvincing partial plodding reconstruction of the Portland Spy Case, vitiated by its own admission that only the names have been kept to convict the guilty (although it doesn't quite put it that way). You don't know when you are watching what actually happened or what Frank Launder and Peter Barnes have dreamed up. This was made in 1964, and now that Houghton and Gee are out of jail it would be interesting to know what they make of Bernard Lee and Margaret Tyzack in their parts. Director Robert Tronson. (*b/w*)

Rio Bravo √ √
Howard Hawks in 1959 got a great performance out of sheriff John Wayne helping drunken gunfigher Dean Martin regain moral stature in fight against outlaws. (*c*)

Rio Conchos √
Grand-scale 1964 actioner from Gordon Douglas with Richard Boone, whose family was massacred by Apaches, hunting out Edmond O'Brien who is selling guns to the Indians. Tough performances from Stuart Whitman, Tony Franciosa, Jim Brown. (*c*)

Rio Grande √
Fifteen years after the Civil War when John Wayne was forced to burn his wife's plantation, she (Maureen O'Hara) turns up at the HQ of his war against the Apaches, determined to rescue their son (Claude Jarman Jr) from fighting. Plottier than most John Ford films, this 1950 actioner carries many of his splendid outdoor sweeps and his sympathy with martial tradition. (*b/w*)

Riot √
This is an old prison melo brought up to 1969 date with homosexuality and transvestism, shot by Buzz Kulik at Folsom Jail. Gene Hackman, just before making it at last with *The French Connection*, plays one of the convicts in a break-out. (*c*)

The Rise and Fall of Legs Diamond √√
Budd Boetticher's sharp direction distinguished this otherwise routine gangster melo about the guy who thought he couldn't be killed (played by Ray Danton, with rare authority), in 1960. Incorporation of genuine newsreel material is neatly done. (*b/w*)

The Rising of the Moon √
John Ford put three short films together under one title in 1957. Two of them are blarney. The third, '1921', is a moving, angry, exciting story about a condemned prisoner changing clothes with one of his last visitors, a 'nun', and escaping. It's worth turning on about an hour after the start for this episode. (*b/w*)

River Lady ✕✕
Nonsense about Yvonne de Carlo being a gambling boat owner with eyes on lumber monopoly and Dan Duryea. Direction from George Sherman; 1948. (*c*)

River of No Return ✕
Marilyn Monroe in the wild. She seems unhappy, more so than the plot demands. It's about the way she's torn between nasty husband Rory Calhoun and nice Robert Mitchum, saved by his ten-year-old son. Not one of Otto Preminger's masterpieces–if he made any; 1954. (*c*)

The River's Edge ✕
Ray Milland is gangster on the run in this Allan Dwan-directed piece of phoney parable-prating. His only luggage is a million dollars in banknotes (should have thought it was heavier than it seems to be here) and he persuades simple farmer Anthony Quinn to help him across the border, down Mexico way. But their dangerous trek is meant to point out to the audience how superior the simple Quinn is to the hustler Milland, and the actor plays up to this, enjoying it much more than us. When they start burning the paper money for warmth, symbolism just goes too far, and when you see simple Quinn sacrificing his own few precious dollars first you know that they are really underestimating the audience; 1957. (*c*)

Road House ✕
Lush melo about Ida Lupino at base of triangle involving flash Richard Widmark and ex-con Cornel Wilde. Jean Negulesco milks it for emotion; 1948. (*b/w*)

Road to . . . √
. . . **Bali** was 1952 effort of Bing Crosby, Bob Hope and Dorothy Lamour. Hal Walker directed jokey yarn about evil princess and deep sea divers. (*c*)

√
. . . **Hong Kong** has same trio but Lamour only pops in, as it's 1962 and she was 48 and retired for nine years. Instead, Joan Collins joins the two old men as they are involved in Oriental spy chase. Peter Sellers, Robert Morley beef up the laughs under Norman Panama's direction. (*b/w*)

√
. . . **Morocco** was made in 1942 when the laughs were still unforced. David Butler directed spontaneous-seeming jokery with Bob sold as slave for Dottie by Bing. Moonlight became them. (*b/w*)

√
. . . **Rio** was 1947 effort, directed by Norman Z. McLeod; stowaways Bing and Bob rescue Dottie from grim Aunt Gale Sondergaard. (*b/w*)

√
. . . **Singapore** was first one, in 1940, in peaceful Saigon, where the lads met up

with saronged Dottie, under Victor Schertzinger's direction, and set the pattern of Bing outsmarting Bob for the lady. (*b/w*)

Road to Utopia took them to the Klondike in 1945, with a commentary by Robert Benchley and direction by Hal Walker. (*b/w*) √

... Zanzibar in 1941 was search for diamond mine; Una Merkel and Eric Blore joined in, under Victor Schertzinger. (*b/w*) √

Robbery √
Attempt to capture what planning, executing and detecting a crime like The Great Train Robbery must have been like, made four years after (1967) by Peter Yates, who made *Bullitt* as direct result of this modest British winner. Stanley Baker as chief crook, James Booth chief cop in uniformly competent cast. (*c*)

Robbery Under Arms × ×
Little Australian-set 'Western', showing that Jack Lee and the rest of his British crew hadn't got the hang of making oaters there in 1957–and nobody in the outback has since. This was partly due to the purism in using only British or Australian actors like Peter Finch (as outlaw leader), David McCallum and Ronald Lewis (both weakly playing strong characters as his sons) and, above all, by such feeble females as Maureen Swanson and Jill Ireland for romantic relief. (*c*)

The Robe ×
First CinemaScope feature in 1953 won Richard Burton an Oscar nomination for his role of Roman in charge of Christ's execution, although Victor Mature gave surprisingly good performance as Demetrius (who fought the gladiators two years later). Henry Koster managed to avoid some of the usual Biblical pitfalls but still fell into the one of over-piety. (*c*)

Robin and the Seven Hoods √
Some like it luke-warm–even a lot of the gags are the same (gun-in-a-cake, for example), as is the setting (St Valentine's Day Massacre). But where *Some Like It Hot* piled agonising jokes upon each other without tumbling down, this 1964 indulgence for Frank Sinatra and his clan (Dean Martin, Sammy Davis Jr are both in it) is merely tiresome. Gordon Douglas directs weakly, in order to give the boys as much elbow-room as possible; even this wouldn't have been too bad if David Schwartz's script about Prohibition gangsters had been strong. (*c*)

Robinson Crusoe on Mars ×
The panto Crusoe that is. Not for Byron Haskin the deeper implications of Defoe. His Crusoe is Paul Mantee, his Friday a work-party escapee from another colonised planet. Well gadgeted-up, though. Death Valley in Utah makes a marvellous facsimile of Mars for the Destination Moon team; 1964. (*c*)

Rock-a-Bye Baby ×
Strictly for Jerry Lewis-lovers, this 1958 farce has him as a TV repairer doubling as baby-sitter for a film star's triplets. Reginald Gardner and James Gleason add their own touches of jokery. One of Frank Tashlin's script-directions. (*c*)

Rock Around the Clock × ×
Strictly museum piece of 1956 popular music, with Bill Haley and the Comets, The Platters, Alan Freed. Director Fred F. Sears. (*b/w*)

Rocket to the Moon × ×
What are supposed to be chuckly goings-on in Victorian scientific circles, based on Jules Verne's books, turn into a cheapie with big names in small parts (Hermione Gingold, for instance, couldn't have done more than two days'

work) and medium-names (Burl Ives, Troy Donahue, Terry Thomas, Lionel Jeffries, Graham Stark) poorly used. Don Sharp directs adequately, but it was a Harry Alan Towers production; 1967. (*c*)

The Rocking Horse Winner √√
Adaptation of D. H. Lawrence story about a boy with second sight. Anthony Pelissier got fine performances in 1949 from Valerie Hobson as the tragic mother, John Mills the father. John Howard Davies was the little boy. (*b/w*)

Rocky Mountain ✕
Errol Flynn's last Western, 1950, had him recruiting outlaws for the Confederate army (as happened in California during Civil War) but neither the script nor William Keighley's direction had any ambitions beyond a routine oater. The girl they all heroically/stupidly die for in the end is Patrice Wymore, whom Flynn met on this location and eventually married. (*b/w*)

Rogue Cop √√
Robert Taylor as crooked policeman tracking down man who killed his brother. Classic cops-and-robbers, 1954 vintage, with George Raft as underworld boss, Janet Leigh, Anne Francis as dipso moll. Roy Rowland. (*b/w*)

Rogue's Gallery ✕
Routine private eye thriller given a 1968 gloss by Leonard Horn. Roger Smith the tec, named Rogue. Old-timers Dennis Morgan, Edgar Bergen, Brian Donlevy, Farley Granger make appearances. (*c*)

Roman Holiday ✕
Audrey Hepburn got her first starring part in this mushy yarn of princess having a fling with Gregory Peck and it won her both the 1953 British and American Oscars. But William Wyler's fairy tale looks awfully coy and dated now. (*b/w*)

Romanoff and Juliet ✕
Adaptation by Peter Ustinov (who produced, directed, starred) of his stageplay about the Juliet and Romeoid children of Ruritanian country's American and Soviet ambassadors. If you like whimsy pleasantly served up, you'll enjoy this. If not, you won't; 1961. (*c*)

The Roman Spring of Mrs Stone √
Vivien Leigh was ageing actress in 1961 version of Tennessee Williams novella, buying last fling from gigolo Warren Beatty. José Quintero directed with bravura. (*c*)

Romeo and Juliet ✕
(1) 1936 version by George Cukor had an elderly Leslie Howard and Norma Shearer (well, 43 and 36 respectively was going it a bit for the teenage lovers). Irving Thalberg produced as a labour of love for his wife, Shearer, but it was an expensive flop–too Hollywooden. (*b/w*)

Romeo and Juliet ✕✕
(2) 1953 version by Renato Castellani in England was monumentally miscast, with Laurence Harvey and Susan Shentall laughable in the roles. The supports were equally risible: Mervyn Johns, Bill Travers, Norman Wooland. Only Flora Robson brought a breath of real presence to the muted shambles. (*c*)

Romeo and Juliet √√
(3) 1968 version by Franco Zeffirelli at least had the virtue of life, movement and panache, although neither Leonard Whiting nor Olivia Hussey could really carry the demanding parts. (*c*)

Room at the Top √√
1959 adaptation of John Braine's novel shows nasty Joe Lampton (well-cast Laurence Harvey) clawing his way out of clerking into riches via the rich man's daughter (Heather Sears), sacrificing mentor (Simone Signoret) en route. Jack Clayton. (*b/w*)

Room for One More √
Cary Grant and Betsy Drake, real-life wife (at the time, 1952) play doting married couple who can't say no to another and another and another adoptee. Norman Taurog directed sentimentally. (*b/w*)

Room Service √
A rare Marx Brothers in that it actually has a plot–about Groucho holding the wolves at bay while a play he is producing gets put on; Lucille Ball and Ann Miller provide the glam. Directed by William Sieter; 1937. (*b/w*)

Rooney × × ×
Not even Mickey, alas. Instead, John Gregson having a terrible difficulty with an Oirish accent in a ludicrous tale about Dublin dustmen and an inheritance. Barry Fitzgerald, the only authentic voice in the whole shenanigans, was a mistake from director George Pollock's point of view, because he shows up the rest as such dreadful performers and the general inauthenticity of the 1958 piece. (*b/w*)

The Roots of Heaven × ×
Attempt to make eco-film as early as 1958. It's elephants that Trevor Howard is fighting to keep from extinction. Sadly, John Huston indulged cast of Juliette Greco, Orson Welles and a dying, drunken, malarial Errol Flynn. It took an enormous effort to shoot the poor location sequences in Africa. Huston said afterwards: 'The pictures that turn out to be the most difficult to make, usually turn out to be the worst–like *The Roots of Heaven*.' (*c*)

Rope √ √
Now dismissed by Hitchcock as a nonsensical stunt. He's referring to technical attempt to film in one continuous take (instead of the usual 600–1,400 short takes all joined together in the normal film). The only pauses were for reel changes when a character passed in front of the camera so that he could go to black, reload and start again with the same frame. But it stands up as a fairly exciting psychological thriller about two homosexual college boys (based by Patrick Hamilton on his play about real-life 'thrill killers' Leopold and Loeb) who do in a fellow-student for the fun of it. Cocky, they invite the boy's father and their professor round while his body is hidden in their apartment; Cedric Hardwicke and James Stewart handle the older men assuredly, but John Dall and Farley Granger could have done with a little help from conventional short takes. This was also Hitch's first colour picture and he was so dissatisfied with his cameraman's idea of a sunset that he reshot half the film; 1948. (*c*)

Rose Marie √
(1) 1936 version by W. S. Van Dyke with Jeanette Macdonald and Nelson Eddy was a remake of 1928 silent version with Joan Crawford. Quiz: what other superstar was in the cast of Macdonald-Eddy version? Answer: James Stewart, aged 24, in his second movie, as the brother Jeanette and Nelson are both hunting–she for family love, he to Get His Man. (*b/w*)

Rose Marie ×
(2) 1954 version by Mervyn LeRoy with Ann Blyth and Howard Keel was a mistake. Rudolph Friml tunes lose out to broad comedy from Bert Lahr and Marjorie Main. (*c*)

Rosemary's Baby √ √ √
The term 'woman's picture' is now taboo but women are incontrovertibly different from men in at least one respect: they can give birth. Thus it isn't sexism to call this a woman's picture, because it must have more power over the birth-givers than over those who can't know what it is like to feel life inside you . . . and fear, as here, that the baby may be a

monster. This is the most terrifying aspect of this frightening film – it plays on the primeval fear of women and thus, sympathetically, on their men. Everything about this winner from Roman Polanski combines to scare, even the light touches are there only to provide chiaroscuro. The performance of Mia Farrow as the trusting girl who comes to perceive the ambiguities in her husband (well-played, if not quite in the same league as Miss Farrow, by John Cassavetes) is stunning. The climaxes are as terrifying as those in *Psycho*, with deeper reverberations. Astonishingly the only Oscar went to the weakest bit of the film, Ruth Gordon's comic witch-next-door. Mia Farrow didn't even get a nomination in the year that the unfunny girl Barbra Streisand won; 1969. (*c*)

The Rose Tattoo   √
Daniel Mann turned this Tennessee Williams script, from his own play, into a vehicle for Anna Magnani. She plays widow of lorry-driver finding physical happiness from Burt Lancaster, whom she sees as reincarnation of dead husband – even down to a tatoo he has on him. OK if you like Italian histrionics; 1956. (*b/w*)

Rosie   ✕
Indulgence for Rosalind Russell on the part of director David Lowell Rich, resisting being put away by her children. Moderately funny; 1967. (*c*)

Rotten to the Core   √
Anton Rodgers never really took off from this exceptionally promising start as a sort of surrogate Peter Sellers, but perhaps that's because this type of Rotten Comedy was dying the death by 1965, only the *Carry Ons* carrying on. He plays chief crook planning a caper. Eric Sykes and Thorley Walters are the deliciously incapable detectives. Directed by John Boulting; 1965. (*b/w*)

The Rough and the Smooth   ✕ ✕
Somehow or other Robert Siodmak was persuaded to direct, and William Bendix to appear in this messy, silly yarn about a nymphomaniac German girl (Nadja Tiller) and her involvement with various men, particularly Tony Britton and Tony Wright. You can't believe a word of it and don't want to; 1959. (*b/w*)

Rough Night in Jerico   √
Sure is pretty rough when Dean Martin becomes a baddie and Jean Simmons a drunk. This makes the West look a bit too glossy, but it's certainly full of grown-up action, as the two of them square up for a show-down. Arnold Laven directed the fights well; 1967. (*c*)

The Rounders   √ √
An un-Western Western with hardly a shot fired and no-one you could really call a baddie. Instead, there are two nice cuddly goodies, Henry Fonda and Glenn Ford, always having to go back to work for a man they don't like because they're broke. How an untameable bronco brings their fortune is the plot of this pleasant affair, neatly written and directed by Burt Kennedy; 1965. (*c*)

Roustabout   √
Elvis Presley's 1965 showcase was this slightly improved jollity about fairgrounds, with Barbara Stanwyck as the lady who runs the little one that the big'un is trying to muscle in on – but doesn't, of course, thanks to Elvis's singing, judo, motorbike riding and sundry other talents. John Rich directed discreetly. (*c*)

Roxie Hart   √ √
Delicious 1942 spoof of libertarian twenties in America, when a showgirl on trial for murder could be sure to be let off and made a star. Ginger Rogers and Adolphe Menjou are perfectly-matched client and mouthpiece. Nunnally Johnson wrote the script, William

Wellman directed it and the photographer's cry, 'The knees, Roxie, the knees!' could be emblazoned over every tabloid picture-editor's desk. (*b/w*)

The Royal Hunt of the Sun √√
Peter Shaffer's noble play is somehow diminished on the screen, due to a combination of inadequate direction (Irving Lerner) and acting (Christopher Plummer as Inca chief disappoints more than Robert Shaw's Pizarro). But the theme is tremendous and the implication (man's need to join a band, the band's need to find an enemy) disturbing. Less than a fulfilment of the theatre-pageant, more than a routine adventure story; 1969. (*c*)

Run for Cover ×
James Cagney was still playing Westerns in 1955 and still getting the girl, in this case the insipid Viveca Lindfors. Nicholas Ray did his best to force some characterisation into tale of Cagney's sheriff *v.* former protégé John Derek, but there wasn't enough substance for him to work on. (*c*)

Run for the Sun ××
Remake of the 1932 *Hounds of Zaroff* (from Richard Connell's *The Most Dangerous Game*) by Roy Boulting in 1956. The story has been lost in a tepid love affair, and neither Richard Widmark, Trevor Howard nor Jane Greer can save what should have been an exciting romp. (*c*)

Run Like a Thief ×
Little effort about stealing the diamonds that were stolen. And the bad girl joins Our Hero and there's a chase. You know the sort of thing. This particular rendering of the theme is made even worse by the presence of the stolid Kieron Moore, although Keenan Wynn does provide some small compensation, along with Victor Maddern. Bernard Glasser glassily directs and produces; 1967. (*c*)

The Running Man √
Husband Laurence Harvey fakes death in plane crash, disappears to Spain to meet up with wife Lee Remick, but insurance investigator Alan Bates follows. Carol Reed lifted this 1963 glossy into the Interesting class with neat direction of John Mortimer script. (*c*)

Run of the Arrow √√
This Rod Steiger-starring 1956 movie has an important place in the canon of Samuel Fuller, an increasingly honoured director. Steiger is the man who fired the last shot in the civil war, and is rejected by the Sioux when he turns to them offering his services. Can be enjoyed as wry actioner or scanned by Fuller-buffs for deeper symbolism. (*c*)

Run Silent, Run Deep ×
'Ran noisy, ran shallow' said *Time*. But Robert Wise did try to make more than run-of-the-Atlantic war film and included some cerebral rivalry between Clark Gable and Burt Lancaster in submarine; 1958. (*b/w*)

Run Wild, Run Free ×
A little boy who can't talk finds peace and speech with a wild white colt. If you like little boys on the screen and/or wild horses then you'll enjoy this rather simple-minded film. If not, then not all the sympathetic playing of John Mills and Sylvia Syms as parents, boy Mark Lester, and stalwarts Gordon Jackson and Bernard Miles will make it palatable. Director Richard C. Sarafian has caught some lyrical moments, but that might put you off, too; 1969. (*c*)

The Russians are Coming, the Russians are Coming √
Norman Jewison sees the funny side of a mistaken Soviet invasion of America in 1966. Alan Arkin shines as lieutenant, Theodor Bikel, Paul Ford, Carl Reiner almost match him. (*c*)

Repulsion: Roman Polanski's 1965 study of the disintegration of a girl left alone suited the sonambulistic style of Catherine Deneuve perfectly. She succumbed brilliantly to the occasion.

Patty Duke as the deaf-blind-mute Helen Keller forced to speak by Anne Bancroft in *The Miracle Worker*, achieved the feat of being accepted as an actress, not a child. They both won 1962 Oscars; Bancroft as Best Actress, Duke for Best Support.

Bette Davis received Best Actress nomination for her part in *What Ever Happened to Baby Jane?*, Robert Aldrich's 1962 shocker.

Lilies of the Field, which won Sidney Poitier a 1962 Oscar, showed him helping five nuns in a most nauseating manner.

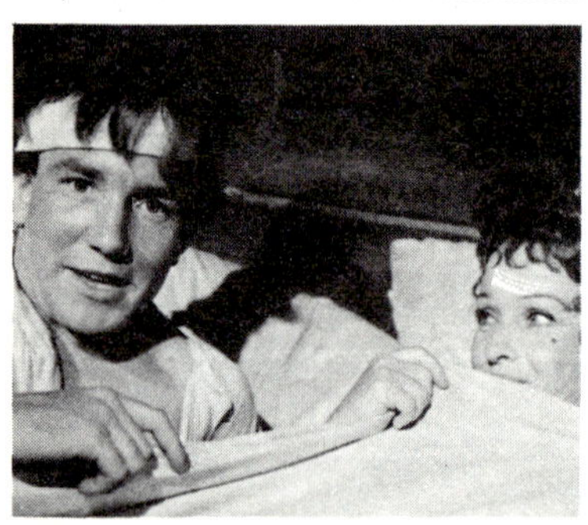

Albert Finney and Joyce Redman after the sexy meal at the inn, in *Tom Jones*, 1963 Oscar winner.

Anatole de Grunwald specialised in big pictures with small minds like *The VIPs*. Liz Taylor, Louis Jourdan (Orson Welles, Richard Burton, off-screen).

Shirley MacLaine, as Irma, came a cropper in *Irma la Douce* in 1963 despite Jack Lemmon and director Billy Wilder, but her misplaced self-confidence kept her working, eventually losing Sir Lew Grade a packet with *Shirley's World* and movies he backed for her.

Dirk Bogarde in *The Servant* looks at his prey, the weak, rich James Fox, in Losey's 1963 study of destruction, not only of the conned but also of the con-man.

Becket was one long yakkity-yak between Peter O'Toole's Henry II and Richard Burton's Chancellor–Archbishop, and not on a very bright level either. Still, the picture and both stars came in for 1964 Oscar nominations.

Dirk Bogarde, in the trenches, made a sensitive and convincing officer, detailed to defend deserter Tom Courtenay in Joseph Losey's *King and Country*, 1964.

Elizabeth Taylor in *Who's Afraid of Virginia Woolf?* which won her the 1966 Best Actress Oscar, a superb performance of sluttishness.

The Russians Are Coming, The Russians Are Coming, underrated in Britain, but nominated Best Picture, 1966, in America.

Michael Caine, in the title role, conning Jane Asher in *Alfie*. Both he and the film won 1966 Oscar nominations.

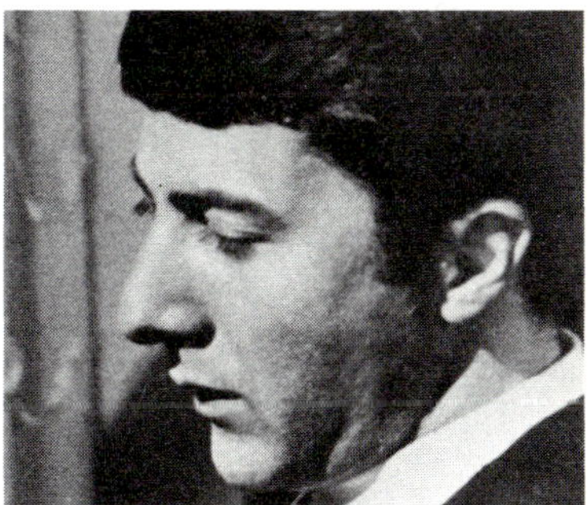

Dustin Hoffman's naïve quick-learner in *The Graduate* (1967) merited the nomination for Best Actor. Rod Steiger pipped him.

The Dirty Dozen: convicts are let out to do a commando raid with sadistic wallowing. Lee Marvin reviews prisoner-recruits including John Cassavetes (1), Donald Sutherland (4), Charles Bronson (7), Telly Savalas (12).

Rod Steiger finally won his Oscar in 1967 for his police chief in *In The Heat of the Night*.

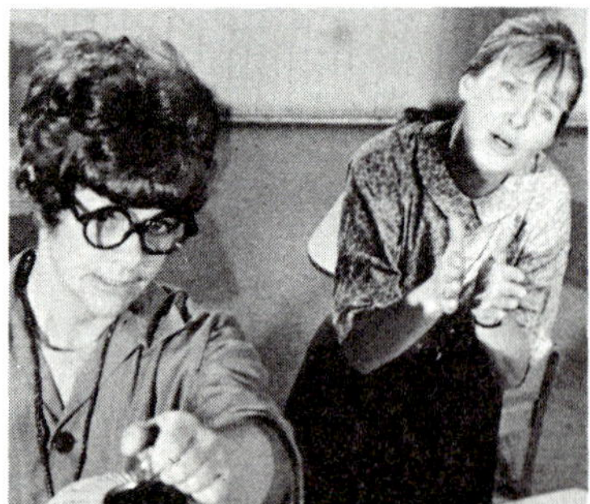

Bonnie & Clyde is unbeaten for sheer brilliant cruelty. Faye Dunaway; Warren Beatty.

Joanne Woodward in *Rachel, Rachel*, her 1968 attempt to repeat her 1957 Oscar in *The Three Faces of Eve*. Only short-listed.

Midnight Cowboy gave Dustin Hoffman and Jon Voigt opportunities of a lifetime: both were nominated for Best Actor Oscars in 1969, but were overlooked in favour of John Wayne (*True Grit*)! Film Director (John Schlesinger) and Screenplay (Waldo Salt) did win, however.

Jane Fonda (right) in *They Shoot Horses, Don't They?*, 1969, competes with Warren Beatty.

Goodbye Mr Chips was remade by producers who thought that by dusting off an old success they could rekindle magic. Pet Clark, Peter O'Toole.

S

Saadia × ×
Stunning Moroccan locations don't make up for messy plot about Dr Mel Ferrer and Sheikh Cornel Wilde both in love with Rita Gam. Albert Lewin; 1954. (*c*)

Sabaka ×
Boris Karloff, Reginald Denny, Victor Jory in old-timers' outing in Indian-set creepy about occult sect. Frank Ferrin; 1955. (*c*)

Saboteur ×
Famous for the climactic fight on the Statue of Liberty, this 1942 wartime chaser is not among Hitchcock's best. He blames the script for having too many ideas insufficiently worked out and the casting of Robert Cummings (wrong sort of face: even when he's anguished he looks amused) and Priscilla Lane (too ordinary, foisted on him by Universal). (*b/w*)

Saboteur – Code Name Morituri ×
Bernhard Wicki's 1965 film of Marlon Brando as anti-nazi German who helps British capture cargo ship, has turgid script and Yul Brynner, Trevor Howard, Janet Margolin to keep it waterlogged. (*b/w*)

Sabre Jet ×
Routine Korean War story concentrates on wives waiting for Air Force husbands

Marilyn Monroe in *Some Like it Hot*

to return. Robert Stack, Coleen Gray, Julie Bishop led director Louis King's uninspired cast; 1953. (*c*)

Sabrina √√
Delicious Billy Wilder-directed version of Samuel Taylor's hit play has Audrey Hepburn as chauffeur's daughter, Humphrey Bogart and William Holden as wealthy brothers; 1954. (*b/w*)

Saddle the Wind √
Superior Robert Parrish-directed Western about warring brothers has fine performances from Robert Taylor (law-abiding), John Cassavetes (trigger-happy), Julie London and some convincing dialogue; 1958. (*c*)

The Sad Horse ✕
Low-budgeter about racehorse befriended by little David Ladd (little Alan's little boy). Patrice Wymore helps to spread out director James B. Clark's sentiment; 1959. (*c*)

The Sad Sack ✕
Jerry Lewis as classic Army moron based on George Baker's cartoon character (who, when spying at a nudist camp through a knot-hole exclaimed 'Boy, I'd sure like to see that in a sweater!'), not making a very coherent story-line, although there's something about a lady major–Phyllis Kirk–being assigned to smarten him up. Suddenly the whole action is transported to North Africa, so that Peter Lorre can pop in as an arab. George Marshall has saved it from absolute bordeom for non-Lewis lovers; those who think he's funny will need no recommendation; 1957. (*b/w*)

Safari ✕✕
Mau-Mau for Red Indians, the Kenya Police for the us cavalry, and some jungle animals thrown in for added thrills. Now thoroughly out-of-date nonsense, with hunter Victor Mature guiding rich clients through the under-

growth; Janet Leigh, Roland Culver, John Justin. Spottily directed by Terence Young in far-off 1956. (*c*)

The Safe Cracker ✕
One of those 1958 British quickies with an American star–Ray Milland here, who also directed–to make it saleable Stateside. He's a safe expert turned crook who goes on dangerous wartime mission. (*b/w*)

Sahara √
Humphrey Bogart lifts this desert war actioner about fight for oasis above routine Zoltan Korda direction. J. Carroll Naish and Rex Ingram help. Made only two years after its setting in 1941 and adapted from Soviet film, *The Thirteen*. (*b/w*)

Sail A Crooked Ship ✕
Even funny Ernie Kovacs, Frank Gorshin can't keep this silly comedy–about bankrobbers making getaway on boat–afloat. Robert Wagner, Dolores Hart, Frankie Avalon soon go down under Irving Brecher's direction; 1962. (*b/w*)

Sailor Beware ✕
(1) 1952. American; beware of this one if you're not a Jerry Lewis-Dean Martin fan; this time they're in the navy, and director Hal Walker lets them get on with it. (*b/w*)

Sailor Beware ✕✕
(2) 1956. British; Peggy Mount buffaloing all over the screen in Gordon Parry's filming of famous farce about sailor (Ronald Lewis) who runs away from his wedding. Broad but not vulgar. (*b/w*)

Saint Joan ✕✕
Total disaster from Otto Preminger who failed, in 1957, to catch the spirit either of the historical period or of Shaw's play. Jean Seberg, whom he found after seeing 3,000 of the 18,000 unknown applicants, was visibly miscast (fey when she should have been tough, sweet when she should

have cerebral). The whole production was studio-bound and artificial, the selections from Shaw's play arbitrary and vulgarised, as if Graham Greene, who did the adaptation, wearied of the demands of the commercial Mr Preminger. Richard Widmark, as the Dauphin, wasn't quite as bizarre as he might have been, but to balance that, John Gielgud, Harry Andrews and Felix Aylmer stayed theatrical. Considering the money and talent available, Preminger's casting of the other parts was extraordinary: Richard Todd, Anton Walbrook, Barry Jones, Finlay Currie, Bernard Miles, Patrick Barr, Kenneth Haigh ... it reads like a roster of the second-rate; 1957. (*c*)

Saintly Sinners ✕
Don Beddoe as a priest can see no evil, even in the wickedest parishioners. So he gets bounced from his church by the Monsignor, who understandably doesn't like to have him implicated in crookedness. But the crooks confess they were just conning the gullible old man and all ends happily. Director Jean Yarbrough manages to convey the small town ambience but not the characters; 1962. (*b/w*)

Sally's Irish Rogue ✕ ✕
An oddity, with Julie Harris plonked in the middle of the Irish countryside surrounded by players from the Abbey Theatre, romping their way through a particularly tiresome tale of a young man's (Tim Seeley) rebellion. Miss Harris is the girl he was going to marry. George Pollock directs bemusedly, as if one of the little people was in the way; 1958. (*b/w*)

Salome ✕
Director William Dieterle takes a long time getting to the Seven Veils bit, and Rita Hayworth disappoints when he does–well, it was only 1953. Charles Laughton, Stewart Granger, Alan Badel and a lot more. (*c*)

Salt and Pepper ✕ ✕
Flimsy farce has Sammy Davis Jr, Peter Lawford as Soho nightclub owners involved in murder and taking-over-the-Government type plot. Pity third Clan member Sinatra wasn't there to cheer it up. John Le Mesurier, Michael Bates remind us that this was British-made tedium; Richard Donner directs; 1968. (*c*)

Samar √
Plenty of excitement as prison chief George Montgomery and his charges flee from the cruel Spanish in 19th-century Philippines. As if that weren't enough for any man, Montgomery co-wrote and directed too; 1962. (*c*)

Sammy Going South √ √
A ten-year-old boy making a 4,500-mile trek across Africa to his aunt in Durban could have been a sloppy sentimental yarn tricked out to bring tears to the eyes of impressionable viewers. That it avoids this kind of false sob-stuff is director Sandy Mackendrick's most notable achievement in this unusual film. Edward G. Robinson is marvellously grizzled as the wily old diamond smuggler who is Sammy's only friend; the other people he meets–a Syrian pedlar (Zia Mohyeddin in a too-long episode), a rich American (Constance Cummings), a tribal chief (Orlando Martins) are interesting too. But ultimately it is in the character of Sammy (Fergus McClelland) that Mackendrick excels: he is shown as a nasty little tyke, who uses everyone more than they use him; 1962. (*c*)

Sam Whiskey √
Pleasant Western comedy has Angie Dickinson hiring Burt Reynolds, Ossie Davis and Clint Walker to put back some gold bars her late husband happened to steal. Arnold Laven made it all harmless enough, in 1969. (*c*)

Sanctuary ✕
Lee Remick, Yves Montand, Odetta, Bradford Dillman in lurid sex-and-murder melodrama set in Deep South, based on William Faulkner novel. Director Tony Richardson seemed unhappy in 1961 with this improbable plot of a maid who kills a baby to save the parents' happiness, and then resignedly trots off to the electric chair. (*b/w*)

The Sand Castle √
Pleasant little self-indulgence written, directed and produced by Jerome Hill about a day on the beach. Reminiscent of the Italian neo-realist masterpiece *A Sunday in August*, it ironically shows the many kinds of people (Barry and Laurie Cardwell, George Dunham) and groups who gather for a day in the sun. The central piece is a huge castle which the little boy who makes it dreams (in colour) has become real; 1962. (*b/w*)

The Sand Pebbles ✕
Far be it from us to countenance cuts made in movies by ITV companies, let alone advocate them, but this turgid melodrama about a US ship raising the flag in 1926 China is very, very long (over three hours in the cinema) and could do with a few chops. That torture scene, for instance. Steve McQueen's crinkly eyes are no substitute for good dialogue, and Richard Attenborough and Candice Bergen are awfully draggy. Robert Wise produced and directed in 1967, so that's where the buck stops. (*c*)

The Sandpiper ✕
Proof that smashing stars (Elizabeth Taylor, Richard Burton, Eva Marie Saint), respected writers (Dalton Trumbo, Michael Wilson), and experienced director (Vincente Minnelli) are no guarantee of a good film. This one is a farrago about straight headmaster chucking everything for wild affair with progressive mother (a pupil's, not his); 1965. (*c*)

Sands of Iwo Jima √
John Wayne as tough, rough sergeant is incredibly softened by night with Hawaii whore and goes back to battle and his previously embittered troops a changed man. John Agar, who hated him before, recognises his greatness now. Allan Dwan manages to makes all this tosh more or less convincing with a facsimile of the flag-raising ceremony as pay-off. Set in 1943, made in 1949. (*b/w*)

Sands of the Kalahari √
The one about plane crash survivors stranded in the desert, saved only by strong casting–Stanley Baker, Susannah York, Harry Andrews, Nigel Davenport, Theodore Bikel. Cy Endfield wrote and directed; 1965. (*c*)

The Sandwich Man ✕✕
Strong cast in a weak episodic comedy, strung together by the device of Michael Bentine as a comic sandwich-man, somehow failing to get across in the script he wrote with director Robert Hartford-Davis the warmth of personality he usually manages in television variety shows. None of the standard British character-players and comedians (Dora Bryan, Harry H. Corbett, Diana Dors, Ian Hendry, Stanley Holloway, Ron Moody, Terry-Thomas, Wilfrid Hyde-White, Norman Wisdom) are seen at their best; 1966. (*c*)

San Francisco √√
Although Clark Gable (as a gambler), Jeanette MacDonald (his love), Spencer Tracy (this performance as priest turned him into star) were in 1936 Woody Van Dyke-directed soapy drama, it was reconstruction of 1906 earthquake at the end that was the hit of the show. It really is spectacular. Awful thing is, it's going to happen again, in real life, the experts say. (*b/w*)

The San Francisco Story ✕
In spite of the pretentious title, it's just

fearless Joel McCrea cleaning up the wicked city in the 1850s; and picking up Yvonne De Carlo while he's about it. Routine job by Robert Parrish in 1952. (c)

Santa Fé ×
Randolph Scott and Peter Thompson are part of internecine-racked family after the Civil War. Irving Pichel's ordinary direction results in in-the-rut railroad banditry; 1951. (c)

Santa Fé Passage ×
John Payne hates Indians, fights against them, but falls in love with Faith Domergue, who's half one herself. William Witney can't get us caring; 1955. (c)

Sapphire √
Michael Relph, Basil Dearden swallowed hard and made an almost convincing film about blacks and whites in Britain. But the year was only 1959 and a patronising sentimentality obtruded. Still, it was a good, taut thriller as well and can be enjoyed as such. Nigel Patrick is superior detective, plus sterling performances from Yvonne Mitchell, Michael Craig, Bernard Miles, Rupert Davies. (c)

Saraband ×
Princess Joan Greenwood torn between her love for commoner Stewart Granger (who doesn't manage to look very common) and her Destiny. Get the tissues out (if you've got a cold). Basil Dearden; 1948. (c)

The Saracen Blade × ×
Dashing Ricardo Montalban had awful script and quickie-director William Castle to battle against, as well as Saracens, in pathetic 1954 Crusades costumer with Carolyn Jones. (c)

Saskatchewan ×
Insubstantial Raoul Walsh-directed Western has Alan Ladd as Canadian Mountie, Shelley Winters, uprising Indians and some fine scenery; 1954. (c)

The Satan Bug √
Who is the mysterious millionaire who has stolen the deadly virus that could destroy all life on earth? You might not care, but you'll probably go on watching George Maharis, Richard Basehart, Dana Andrews, adequately directed by John Sturges from an Alastair MacLean thriller; 1964. (c)

Satan Never Sleeps × ×
Anti-Red hysteria this time takes the shape of two priests–William Holden, Clifton Webb–bravely defending their mission, and France Nuyen, against those nasty Chinese Communists. Was co-writer, director Leo McCarey being serious? 1962. (c)

Satellite in the Sky × ×
Poor little sci-fi produced by the Danzigers, those legendary churners-out of tripe in British studios. Here John Dickson has directed a tame tale of a space ship with a superbomb attached, due to go off and kill its inhabitants. These days, this sort of comic strip yarn is reserved for puppet films on television, but Donald Wolfit and Bryan Forbes were somehow in this one, along with the handsome but empty Kieron Moore and Lois Maxwell; 1956. (c)

Saturday Night and Sunday Morning
√ √ √

In 1960 it was called 'the finest picture of the year' and 'the greatest English picture of all time', and it still stands as a valid, sympathetic, committed study of the limitations and frustrations of working-class life. This is how it was–and is–in Nottingham and a thousand other towns, and Albert Finney was how a hundred thousand young rebels-brought-to-heel were–and are. The triumph is, first, director Karel Reisz's; second, writer Alan Sillitoe's; third, a castful of people who lifted their characters into near-reality: Rachel Roberts, Hylda Baker, Norman Rossington, Bryan Pringle, Shirley Anne Field, Colin Blakely, and, above all, Finney. And it was funny, too. (*b/w*)

Saturday Night Out × ×
Episodic British picture which tries for slices of life but finishes up with slivers of ham. Robert Hartford-Davis produced and directed without felicity or flair, and left it up to Heather Sears (as a way-out art student), Nigel Green (lush), Colin Campbell (nice fella who saves a girl from going on the streets), Bernard Lee (blackmailed via a two-way mirror), Patricia Hayes (on the bottle again), and that isn't the way to make a gripping movie; 1964. (*b/w*)

The Savage √
Question: whose side should Charlton Heston take–the Sioux, who brought him up as one of them, or the whites? Watch him make up his mind, under George Marshall's competent direction; 1953. (*c*)

The Savage Guns × ×
A 1962, experiment in making a Mexican-American Western in Spain. It failed. The result was this third-grade oater directed sluggishly by Michael Carreras with stiff Richard Basehart playing that old gunfighter who can't lay down his guns and pacifist Don Taylor who realises at last that a Man Has to be a Man (i.e. a Killer). Sick stuff. (*c*)

The Savage Innocents ×
Fur-clad Anthony Quinn, Peter O'Toole, Yoko Tani in confusing Nicholas Ray-directed Eskimo drama that's likely to get a chilly reception; 1961. (*c*)

Sayonara √
Joshua Logan's heavy-handed adapta-tion of James Michener's novel about high-up American officer–Marlon Brando with a dreadful Southern accent –falling for Japanese showgirl is even more ghastly than Irving Berlin's title song. On the other hand, if you loved that . . . 1957 Oscars surprisingly went to supports Red Buttons and Miyoshi Umeki, and for art direction and sound recording. Ellsworth Fredericks deserved one for his pictures. (*c*)

Say One For Me ×
Save them for yourself, if you intend watching this one about Bing Crosby as priest of showbiz parish; Debbie Reynolds, Robert Wagner, Ray Walston among Frank Tashlin's 1959 congregation. (*c*)

The Scalphunters √
Episodic Western has Burt Lancaster as dogged trapper, Ossie Davis as a bright runaway slave, an over-sexed Shelley Winters and some funny moments under Sydney Pollack's lively direction between the scalping, the cliff-falling and the thundering hooves; 1968. (*c*)

The Scamp √
Sickly title for not quite so sickly film about a little boy (Colin Petersen), whose father (Terence Morgan, with an un-convincing Cockney accent) is turning him into a delinquent. Solid, childless schoolmaster Richard Attenborough takes an interest in him–but finds him-self rejected after giving him a thrashing, the alternative to prosecution for burg-lary. Wolf Rilla wrote-directed slowly if dramatically, greatly helped by Freddie Francis' camerawork; 1957. (*b/w*)

Scandal At Scourie ×
Childless couple adopt illegitimate Catholic child in face of bitter local Protestant opposition. Greer Garson stars, Jean Negulesco directs–feel like a nice cry? 1953. (*c*)

Scandal Sheet ✕
Unpleasant story of tabloid editor Broderick Crawford killing his wife and waiting for his own well-trained reporters to sniff out the story. Phil Karlson never hit the headlines with this one in 1952. *(c)*

The Scapegoat ✕
English schoolteacher is conned into swapping places with his noble French 'double'. Alec Guinness–both of him–and Bette Davis make it just about watchable, but what a let-down from director Robert Hamer, working from a Gore Vidal adaptation of a Daphne du Maurier novel. Maybe it was written and directed by their doubles; 1959. *(b/w)*

Scaramouche ✕
Colourful swashbuckler has Stewart Granger avenging brother's death in 18th century France. Janet Leigh, Eleanor Parker, Mel Ferrer and vulgar George Sidney direction; 1952. *(c)*

Scared Stiff ✕
Bored stiff, more likely, by Dean Martin, Jerry Lewis, Lizabeth Scott and Carmen Miranda on haunted island. George Marshall; 1953. *(c)*

The Scarface Mob √
Two episodes of *The Untouchables* stitched together with a banal Walter Winchell commentary has Robert Stack bringing Al Capone (weakly played by Neville Brand against Rod Steiger's interpretation in the film biography) to justice. Phil Karlson, a director always best with violence, manages these capably; 1960. *(b/w)*

Scarlet Angel ✕
Confused plot turns around Yvonne De Carlo posing as wealthy widow. Trouble is she fancies sailor Rock Hudson as much as she fancies the high life. Sidney Salkow; 1952. *(c)*

The Scarlet Blade ✕ ✕
Usual old Cavaliers *v.* Roundheads rubbish, with King's men the goodies and Cromwell's (Lionel Jeffries, Oliver Reed) a rotten lot. John Gilling doesn't convince with this one; 1963. *(c)*

The Scarlet Coat ✕
Who's giving away revolting American secrets to the British? Why, Benedict Arnold, of course. Cornel Wilde, George Sanders, Michael Wilding go through the history books under John Sturges; 1955. *(c)*

The Scarlet Hour ✕
Thriller about an unhappy marriage is more fortunate in its minor players (E. G. Marshall, Elaine Stritch) than in leads Carol Ohmart and Tom Tryon, neither of whom went on to bigger things after this inauspicious start under Michael Curtiz; 1956. *(b/w)*

The Scarlet Pimpernel √ √
They filmed him here, they filmed him there . . .
(1) In 1935, with Leslie Howard as the aristocrat who rescued members of his class from the French Revolution under the nose of Raymond Massey's Chauvelin. Director: Harold Young. *(b/w)*

✕ ✕
(2) In 1938, when it was called *The Return of the Scarlet Pimpernel*, with Barry K. Barnes outwitting Francis Lister. Director: Hans Schwartz. *(b/w)*

✕ ✕
(3) In 1950, as *The Elusive Pimpernel*, with David Niven as Sir Percy, directed by Michael Powell and Emeric Pressburger. Actually, it was Niven who was elusive; he was rowing with Goldwyn about his contract and insisted on holidays and other concessions before he would start work. The result reflects his unhappiness of the time. *(b/w)*

Scarlet Street √ √
Edward G. Robinson murdering Joan

Bennett and, for the first time ever in Hollywood, getting away with it. Carpet-puller Fritz Lang directed this epoch-maker in 1945, fourteen years after its original, *La Chienne*, had been made by Renoir in France. (*b/w*)

School for Scoundrels √
Lifemanship and Gamesmanship, Stephen Potter's clever and amusing way of cataloguing the Englishman's One-Upmanship . . . but how on earth to make a film about it? Director Robert Hamer (with, it is said, the help of Peter Ustinov) found the solution: pit know-it-all Terry-Thomas against dude Ian Carmichael for the hand of Janette Scott, have the lovable goof enrol at Alastair Sim's College of Lifemanship, learn from him all the tricks of the trade and then defeat his rival on the tennis court, in bachelor flat, and so on. It all works surprisingly well, with the help of a dozen solid comic supports; 1960. (*b/w*)

Scott of the Antarctic √
Sincere, worthwhile 1948 attempt to tell story of quixotic failure, always much admired by the British (but not the Americans, who wouldn't show it); made in Greenland, Norway, Antarctica and Ealing, with John Mills' finest perform-ance. Charles Frend, director; Jack Cardiff, camera. (*c*)

Scream of Fear ×
The inept Susan Strasberg returns home to find her father missing and everyone behaving very strangely . . . Neat thriller won't have you actually screaming, but provides a few strong shudders. Ann Todd, Ronald Lewis, Christopher Lee; Seth Holt directed; 1961. (*b/w*)

The Sea Chase √
Second World War adventure has John Wayne in (for him) unusual role of German sea captain. Lana Turner provides shipboard romance. John Far-row directs; 1955. (*c*)

Sea Devils ×
Napoleonic wars provided Raoul Walsh with background for routine smuggling yarn, starring Yvonne De Carlo, Rock Hudson; 1953. (*c*)

Sea Fury ×
Victor McLaglen's last film was this rather turgid, rather predictable drama which has him lusting after Luciana Paluzzi in competition with First Mate Stanley Baker, with a bit of not-so-exciting salvage work thrown in. Cy Endfield (called C. Raker Endfield in 1958) directed briskly. (*b/w*)

Seance on a Wet Afternoon √√
Genuinely chilling melo written and directed by Bryan Forbes in 1964 about a potty medium (methodical Kim Stanley) involving her timid husband (co-producer Richard Attenborough) in kidnapping. (*b/w*)

Sea of Sand ×
Routine war melo about the desert; solid performances from Richard Atten-borough and Barry Foster, dreary ones from John Gregson and Michael Craig. Direction average, from Guy Green; 1958. (*b/w*)

The Search √
Montgomery Clift's 1948 debut as American soldier caring for orphan after Second World War won an Oscar for its story. Fred Zinnemann gave it a slightly sententious distinction. (*b/w*)

The Searchers √√
'If one could preserve a single John Ford film, it would perhaps be this Homeric Western', wrote the National Film Theatre's programmer. For two hours and five years, John Wayne searches for the little girl who was taken away by the Indians, only to find that she has grown to womanhood as an Indian. Feeling that she has betrayed his family he attacks the village, intent on killing her. About

Wayne's performance one contemporary (1956) critic wrote 'There's no kindness in his nature–he is crafty and arrogant and his eyes are cold as ice.' This goes pretty well for all his parts, but in this one his qualities of cruelty are apposite. The little girl was played by Natalie Wood's sister, Lana; Natalie played her grown up. (*c*)

The Search for Bridey Murphy ✗
Teresa Wright more or less convincing in otherwise extremely doubtful account of housewife recalling a previous life under hypnosis, made in 1956 when a real-life case gave it relevance. Unfortunately, its specious use of hypnotism is not balanced by an interest of plot. Noel Langley wrote and directed. (*b/w*)

The Sea Shall Not Have Them ✗
Michael Redgrave, Dirk Bogarde, Anthony Steele, Nigel Patrick, Bonar Colleano, Jack Watling in hollow tale of heroics about airmen awaiting rescue from raft. Made in 1954 by Lewis Gilbert. (*b/w*)

Sea Wife √
One of those life-raft dramas so popular around 1957. Floating about on this one are Richard Burton as an RAF officer, Joan Collins as a nun (but the others don't know that), Basil Sydney as a businessman, Cy Grant as a purser. Basically, it's a will-she-won't-she with the added titilation that she's supposed to be bound to celibacy. Unfortunately (fortunately?) Joan Collins could never be a nun. Director Bob McNaught. (*c*)

Sebastian √
Two of the best players in British pictures, Dirk Bogarde and Susannah York, spark off each other in this cryptic thriller about cryptographers breaking spy-codes. But everything else is so insouciant and tentative that director David Greene seems to be skating prettily along the top of the script rather than

bringing out its meanings and subtleties (if any). Excellent names support: John Gielgud, Janet Munro, Nigel Davenport, Ronald Fraser, Lilli Palmer, Margaret Johnston; 1968. (*c*)

Second Chance √
Marvellous fight on stranded cable car between hunted Robert Mitchum and hood Jack Palance is climax to above-average 1953 thriller set in South America. Rudolf Maté got good performance from tragically-fated Linda Darnell. (*c*)

The Second Greatest Sex ✗ ✗
Lysistrata updated to Western musical by George Marshall has Jeanne Crain, Mamie van Doren among women who barricade themselves in fort while men battle for safe containing crucial papers; 1955. (*c*)

Seconds √
Ageing businessman takes on new identity and Rock Hudson's face. Says director John Frankenheimer: 'It had a theme that fascinated me: the old American bullshit about having to be young, the whole myth that financial security is happiness.' Beginning and end are gripping, although orgy scene in the middle lets it down; 1966. (*b/w*)

The Second Time Around ✗
Widow Debbie Reynolds running for Sheriff. Thelma Ritter, Juliet Prowse, Andy Griffith cheer up this 1961, Vincent Sherman-directed comedy. Too much corny clowning. (*c*)

Secret Ceremony √
What a disappointment this 1968 marriage of Elizabeth Taylor, Mia Farrow and Joseph Losey turned out to be. The fact that a story is totally incredible (motherless girl and daughterless mother accepting each other as mother and daughter) need not be an unscalable barrier to enchantment. But the way it's handled (and the casting of Robert

Mitchum in a beard as bad-penny father) just leaves the viewer alienated. The set with its art nouveau extravagances, is certainly worth a look, but you'll get more out of a visit to the appropriate gallery at the Victoria and Albert Museum. (*c*)

The Secret Fury √
Bride-to-be Claudette Colbert being driven round the bend: is it a plot to prevent her marrying Robert Ryan? Mel(-odramatic) Ferrer directs; 1950. (*b/w*)

The Secret Garden √
Fantasy has little Margaret O'Brien (it was made in 1949) befriending crippled Dean Stockwell and being admitted to his imagined hideaway. Fred M. Wilcox got some good junior performances and the usual up-market ones from Elsa Lanchester, Herbert Marshall, Gladys Cooper. (*c*)

The Secret Heart √
Will June Allyson follow father in throwing herself off a cliff? She doesn't like Claudette Colbert, her stepmother. Lionel Barrymore, Walter Pidgeon, Robert Sterling, Patricia Medina fuss around tiresomely under Robert Z. Leonard's atmospheric direction; 1946. (*b/w*)

The Secret Invasion √
Weak casting–Stewart Granger, Mickey Rooney, Raf Vallone–lets down otherwise gripping World War II yarn about criminals on dangerous mission in nazi-occupied Yugoslavia. Director, Roger Corman; 1964. (*c*)

The Secret Life of an American Wife √√
An under-rated comedy masterpiece, script-production-direction by George Axelrod. Anne Jackson is marvellous as the wife who realises that she must be losing her touch when the delivery boy doesn't even notice she's naked, and decides to do something about it. What she does is to take the place of the 100-dollar-an-hour call-girl her expense-account husband (a well-observed study by Patrick O'Neal) is laying on for a film star (gorgeous Walter Matthau). What happens next is beautifully right, and we won't spoil it for you; 1969. (*c*)

The Secret Life of Walter Mitty √√
Danny Kaye's best film (1947), derived from a James Thurber short story but embellished with Kaye's own routines. Boris Karloff, Virginia Mayo, Fay Bainter make substantial contributions, but the praise belongs to Kaye and director Norman Z. McLeod, for a delicious film about daydreaming. (*c*)

The Secret of My Success ××
Someone should have whispered it to director Andrew Stone before he embarked on this silly triple-barrelled nonsense about a naive policeman, James Booth, being taken in by scheming Honor Blackman (mad baroness breeding killer-spider), Stella Stevens (husband-killer), Shirley Jones (revolutionary); 1965. (*c*)

Secret of the Incas ×
Charlton Heston, Robert Young, Nicole Maurey on treasure hunt. Spectacular backgrounds almost make up for routine plot and Jerry Hopper direction; 1954. (*c*)

The Secret Partner √
Modest but exciting thriller from Michael Relph and Basil Dearden in which only two people have the keys-and-combination of a strongroom but which keeps you guessing as to who stole-it. Nice characterisation from Bernard Lee as the detective, and both Hugh Burden and Stewart Granger do better than their usual; 1961. (*b/w*)

The Secret Place ×
Competent diamond theft thriller which marked Clive Donner's debut as director,

from a script by Linette Perry. Unfortunately, only George A. Cooper among the cast appears not to be a posh actor playing a Cockney: Belinda Lee, David McCallum, Ronald Lewis are doing us the favour of pretending; 1957. (*b/w*)

The Secret War of Harry Frigg ✗
Paul Newman looks uncomfortable in this embarrassing World War II farce about Allied generals imprisoned in Sylva Koscina's Italian villa–and well he might. He's supposed to be escape-artist promoted to General so that he can give orders to the men he is sent to liberate. But he finds that being in prison is jollier than fighting the war. Jack Smight might have made something from all this with a genuine comedy actor in the lead. With Newman, he's dead; 1968. (*c*)

The Secret Ways ✗
Routine escaping-to-the-West thriller has Richard Widmark in charge both of the escaping (he does it for money not patriotism, which is a nice change) and the production (but sensibly accepting Phil Karlson's highly competent directing). Set in Budapest, marred by poor supporting performances; 1961. (*b/w*)

The Seekers ✗
Dull would-be adventure yarn of pioneers in New Zealand has Jack Hawkins, Glynis Johns heading plodding cast, with an out-of-place Kenneth Williams. Ken Annakin cynically directed; 1954. (*c*)

See You in Hell, Darling ✗
Tawdry thriller derived distantly from Norman Mailer's *An American Dream*, retaining that rather impressive novel's plot-line, but throwing all its subtlety out of the window (which, as it happens, is what Stuart Whitman does to wife Eleanor Parker). Director Robert Gist missed the gist; 1966. (*c*)

The Sellout √
Crusading newspaper editor Walter Pidgeon fighting local corruption. Gerald Mayer directed; 1952. (*b/w*)

Seminole √
True-ish story of why the Seminole tribe never signed a peace treaty with the white man makes lively Western directed by the excellent Budd Boetticher and strongly cast: Rock Hudson, Hugh O'Brian, Richard Carlson, Barbara Hale, Anthony Quinn; 1953. (*c*)

Seminole Uprising √
George Montgomery, now a cavalry officer, was brought up by Indians. He is ordered to bring in rampaging chief. His mind is made up when they capture his sweetheart, Karin Booth. Director Earl Bellamy doesn't make much of what could have been significant script; 1955. (*c*)

The Senator was Indiscreet √
And left a diary lying around. 1947 comedy directed by writer George S. Kaufman (his only try at the job) gains from William Powell's playing the main part. Ella Raines backs him up. (*b/w*)

Send Me No Flowers √
Must be seen in colour for full glossy effect of Doris Day being pushed into Clint Walker's arms because husband Rock Hudson and best friend Tony Randall mistakenly think he's dying. Director Norman Jewison has since (this was 1964) gone on to higher if not better things. (*c*)

Separate Beds √
Slick, pleasurable Wall Street comedy with Lee Remick, James Garner, Jim Backus. Arthur Hiller; 1963. (*c*)

Separate Tables √√
Rattigan double-bill about hotel, made into blockbuster by Delbert Mann, winning Oscars for Wendy Hiller,

David Niven, and splendid performances from Burt Lancaster, Rita Hayworth; 1958. (*b/w*)

September Affair   √
Believed dead when a plane crashed that they were supposed to be on, married Joseph Cotten and Joan Fontaine are free to continue their love affair. Not nearly as daring as it sounds–this is a 1951 William Dieterle-directed 'romance'. (*b/w*)

Serenade   ×
Strictly for Mario Lanza fans. This time he's a sulky singer taken up by rich Joan Fontaine but finding true love with Sarita Montiel. Spectacular and spectacularly dull; Anthony Mann directed; 1956. (*c*)

The Sergeant   √√
Unusual, thoughtful, army drama about Sgt. Rod Steiger's desires for naive Pfc. John Phillip Law. It has the inevitability of tragedy and director John Flynn made an impressive debut in this 1969 (set 1952) study of a hero in self-abasement. (*c*)

Sergeant Deadhead   ××
Silly Frankie Avalon vehicle wastes Buster Keaton–and your time. Norman Taurog; 1965. (*c*)

Sergeant Rutledge   √
John Ford, whose career had been clouded by apparent colour prejudice, appears to have decided in 1960 to make some amends by this trial of a black soldier during the Civil War. Based on a real-life incident, it not only reminded a public that was by then more than ready to accept it, that blacks had fought in large numbers, but also that some of them had performed deeds of great gallantry. Woody Strode strode away with the acting honours and although the scene remains mostly in the court, there are enough action flashbacks to satisfy the eager Western fan. (*c*)

Sergeants Three   √
Comedy Western indulging Sinatra's 1960 Rat Pack, with the man himself, Sammy Davis, Dean Martin, Peter Lawford chasing marauding ghost riders. Saved by John Sturges' direction: after all, he did make *The Magnificent Seven*. (*c*)

Serious Charge   ××
Did Anthony Quayle touch up the choirboy–a hulking youth played by Andrew Ray who actually has lumbered a local girl? In the throes of this tortuous plot, the lad is trying to escape that responsibility by accusing the vicar of homosexual advances. Terence Young directed this nasty, meretricious little number, poorly played and conceived, in 1959. The only mystery is why, if the youth leader was at all that way, he wouldn't have chosen cuddly, curly Cliff Richard, in a supporting part, rather than butch yobbo Ray. (*b/w*)

The Servant   √√
Perhaps the most discussed film ever made in England, this 1963 collaboration of Joseph Losey and Harold Pinter from Robin Maugham's novel is about corruption: superficially that of a young master (James Fox) by a vicious servant (Dirk Bogarde), with the help of his girlfriend (Sarah Miles); but it is also about the whole class structure. Wendy Craig convinces as the fiancée who fights Bogarde's influence; look out for Pinter, Patrick Magee and Alun Owen in restaurant scene. (*b/w*)

Seven Angry Men   √
Civil War drama about the ill-fated John Brown's fight to free the slaves, has a fine performance from Raymond Massey and some gripping moments under Charles Marquis Warren's direction; 1955. (*b/w*)

Seven Cities of Gold   ×
Richard Egan, Anthony Quinn, Michael

Rennie, Rita Moreno in run-of-the-mill costume drama about Spanish search for Indian gold in 18th century California. Robert D. Webb directed; 1955. (*c*)

Seven Days in May √√
Military coup against the President of the USA (Fredric Marsh) makes exciting story. John Frankenheimer in his heyday, 1964, got earnest, belief-suspendable performances with help of Rod Serling script. Burt Lancaster convinces as chief plotter, Kirk Douglas as his assistant who blows the plot; Edmond O'Brien, Martin Balsam, stand out among the supports. (*b/w*)

Seven Days to Noon √√
Efficient and exciting suspenser centred round atomic scientist's threat to blow up London if Government doesn't renounce atomic weapons within a week. Barry Jones makes him real, and the Boultings' inspiration to make his unwilling companion a sleazy prostitute (Olive Sloane) rather than a conventional heroine makes the whole plot seem more plausible. Ahead of its time (1950), both politically and in narrative technique. (*b/w*)

711 Ocean Drive √
Edmond O'Brien memorably outwitting syndicate boss Otto Kruger, with Joanne Dru as love interest in modest, Joseph H. Newman-directed bookmaking drama; 1950. (*b/w*)

The 7 Faces of Dr Lao √
All played by Tony Randall, seven little stories about the sideshows in his travelling entertainment, in which each of the film's main characters (among them: Barbara Eden, Noah Beery Jr) learn something revelatory about themselves. Director-producer George Pal indulges himself in such tricks as a catfish that swells up to become a man-eating monster; 1965. (*c*)

Seven Hills of Rome ××
Some pretty shots of the city and that's about all, unless you like Mario Lanza—in which case you may forgive slight plot about him following heiress to Italy. Roy Rowland directed; 1958. (*c*)

Seven Keys ××
Weak little chase involving Alan Dobie dead-panning his way through a contrived and silly plot about blackmail and the recovery of a £20,000 cache. Jeannie Carson helps him, director Pat Jackson doesn't; 1962. (*b/w*)

The Seven Little Foys √
Bob Hope *v.* Jimmy Cagney dance sequence (Hope wins taps, Cagney soft-shoe shuffle) is best thing in Mel Shavelson-directed showbiz biography of comedian with large family; 1955. (*c*)

Seven Men from Now √
They rob the Wells Fargo office, kill Randolph Scott's wife, he vows vengeance. Lee Marvin leads the villains. Budd Boetticher as director guarantees distinction; 1956. (*c*)

Seven Seas to Calais ××
Costumer supposedly about Sir Francis Drake, with Rod Taylor a laughable Armada-sinker (the battle itself is staged by such obvious models that one almost wonders if it isn't supposed to be stylised), Irene Worth an apple-cheeked Queen Elizabeth and an incoherent plot-line. Rudolph Maté went to Italy to shoot this rubbish. He should have stayed at home; 1963. (*c*)

Seventh Cavalry √
Did Randolph Scott desert Custer at Little Big Horn? Barbara Hale believes in him and so do we. Joseph H. Lewis; 1956. (*c*)

The Seventh Cross √
Hollywood finally got around to making major anti-nazi movies after America

got into the war. This one, made in 1944, set in Germany 1936, miscasts Spencer Tracy as concentration camp escapee, but is reasonably exciting stuff, directed by Fred Zinnemann. (*b/w*)

The Seventh Dawn ✗
It's all too much for rubber planter William Holden, what with the Communist uprising in Malaya and romantic dramas with Susannah York and Capucine. Obviously for director Lewis Gilbert, too, who can't do anything with Karl Tunberg's collection of clichés, optimistically called a script; 1964. (*c*)

Seven Thieves √
Sentimental caper movie with old-timer Edward G. Robinson determined to pull off the Big One, Monte Carlo casinos before he dies. Eli Wallach, Joan Collins are fellow rififis; Henry Hathaway, 1960. (*b/w*)

The Seventh Sin ✗ ✗
Risible remake of Maugham's *The Painted Veil* in Hollywood, with British director David Lean and actor Bill Travers making unfortunate American debuts. Eleanor Parker's regeneration in a Chinese cholera epidemic is unbelievable, which goes for the whole picture. George Sanders, Françoise Rosay, and Jean-Pierre Aumont flounder around, embarrassed; 1957. (*b/w*)

Seven Thunders ✗ ✗
Dreadful mix-up of a film supposedly set in wartime Marseilles as Stephen Boyd and Tony Wright try to get back to England. There are the usual resistance heroes and German soldiers, and James Robertson Justice rolling his eyes as a murderer of rich refugees. Hugo Fregonese was obviously unhappy directing in England; 1957. (*b/w*)

The Seventh Veil √
Creaky tear-jerker that had enormous

success in 1945, with Herbert Lom as psychiatrist helping concert pianist with burnt hands, Ann Todd, to decide which of three suitors to marry. James Mason is one of them, and director Compton Bennett encouraged him to go over the top with satisfactory results. (*b/w*)

The Seventh Voyage of Sinbad √
How Sinbad (Kerwin Matthews) helps princess (Kathryn Grant) who has been reduced to thumb-size. Torin Thatcher is the dirty dog of a magician what did it. Director Nathan Juran's effects are ingenious; 1958. (*c*)

Seven Waves Away √
Which-should-be-saved? drama about overturned lifeboat with Tyrone having Power of life or death over neatly-assorted bunch of stock characters. If his choice were on acting ability it would include Lloyd Nolan, Noel Willman, Gordon Jackson, Victor Maddern, David Langton; but Mai Zetterling, Stephen Boyd, Moira Lister, James Hayter are swimming, too. Writer-director Richard Sale keeps it afloat; 1957. (*b/w*)

Seven Ways from Sundown ✗
Barry Sullivan chased by Texas ranger Audie Murphy. Harry Keller's direction does not enliven obvious plot; 1960. (*c*)

Seven Women √
John Ford's last completed film, 1965, is et in 1935 China, where Margaret Leighton runs a five-woman mission in grip of warlord. 'Marvellous Anne Bancroft's doctor makes a sacrifice far beyond the textbook Christian ethics of her companions', as the NFT programme delicately put it. (*c*)

Seven Women from Hell ✗
Patricia Owens and six other American ladies outwit Japanese captors. Set in New Guinea, 1942; made 1961. Cesar Romero, John Kerr also in Robert D. Webb's cast. (*b/w*)

The Seven Year Itch √√
Marilyn Monroe's subtle dumb blonde act is matched by Tom Ewell's archetypal husband on the loose in the apartment downstairs. While Marilyn was making this in 1955 she was going through the divorce from Joe DiMaggio, but Billy Wilder steered her through and came up with a delicious movie, the name of which, at least, has entered the language. (*c*)

Sex and the Single Girl √
Helen Gurley Brown's factual bestseller ignored, and this glossy 1964 romantic comedy sold under its title. Magazine editor Tony Curtis chases psychologist Natalie Wood, with Henry Fonda, Lauren Bacall, Mel Ferrer, Edward Everett Horton helping fun along, under Richard Quine's direction. (*c*)

Shack Out on 101 √
Posing as a half-wit dishwasher, spy works at café near secret electronics laboratory. Lee Marvin, Keenan Wynn stand out in Edward Dein's capable cast; 1955. (*b/w*)

Shadow in the Sky ✕
Discharged from hospital, a disturbed ex-serviceman goes to live with his sister and her husband. Starts well, but director Fred M. Wilcox lets it all get out of hand. Jean Hagen and little-known cast do their best, though; 1952. (*b/w*)

Shadow of a Doubt √√
Teresa Wright gradually realising that her beloved uncle is on the run from the police, and what happens to her then. Joseph Cotten outstanding as the heavy, under Hitchcock's persuasive direction in 1943. Thornton Wilder's collaboration on the script ensured an authentic feeling of a small American town. (*b/w*)

Shadow of Fear ✕ ✕
Poor little thriller about girl (Mona Freeman) who feels herself threatened by step-mother Jean Kent, whom she suspects of already polishing off her Dad. Albert S. Rogell couldn't breathe any life into poor script in 1956. (*b/w*)

Shadow of the Thin Man √
William Powell and Myrna Loy solve jockey's murder, in 1941. W. S. Van Dyke directed crisply and expertly; Donna Reed, Sam Levene support. (*b/w*)

Shadows √√
The first underground movie to break the commercial barrier was this 16mm effort of John Cassavetes and the alumni of his acting school, shot on location in New York, with scenes grabbed whenever they could. It took three years to shoot and edit this story of sophisticated blacks and their problems and it was shown in 1961. Some of it is jejune, but gets nearer to real people than anything seen up to then on the screen. If it looks a bit dated today it is more because of the story with its 'shocks' about passing-for-white (a conventional preoccupation of the cinema then) than the technique which has been absorbed into both the feature and documentary streams. Lelia Goldoni, who had the fattest part came to England as an American actress in poor British television plays. (*b/w*)

The Shakedown ✕ ✕ ✕
If anyone is shaken down by this piffle it's the audience. Supposedly about a blackmailing gang, it makes a hero of one gang-leader, who is slightly less nauseating than his rival. Donald Pleasence earned a crust by appearing in it, but otherwise it's an awful tatty affair. The director John Lemont co-scripted it (with Leigh Vance), so he has no excuses; 1960. (*b/w*)

Shake Hands With The Devil ✕
Producer-director Michael Anderson chose his cast well–James Cagney,

Michael Redgrave, Don Murray, Glynis Johns, Sybil Thorndike, Cyril Cusack–for this tale of Irish Rebellion, 1921 vintage, when the Black and Tans were in repressive command. Cagney finds himself forced to fight for Irish freedom. The emphasis, however, is on excitement not morality and the accents are at wild variance with each other; 1959. (*b/w*)

The Shakiest Gun in the West ×
Comedy-Western has Don Knotts as a timid dentist who becomes a hero by mistake. Director Alan Rafkin manages a few laughs in 1968 remake of Bob Hope's *The Paleface*. (*c*)

Shalako √
Routine Western dressed up as a European aristocratic hunting-party in eighties New Mexico. Plenty of stars–Sean Connery, Brigitte Bardot, Stephen Boyd, Jack Hawkins, Honor Blackman, Eric Sykes–but nothing very distinguished in plot, dialogue of Edward Dmytryk's direction. It's rather long and you may find yourself glancing too often at the clock; 1968. (*c*)

Shane √√
Among the great Westerns of all time, this story of the mysterious stranger (Alan Ladd) who helps the homesteaders (Van Heflin, Jean Arthur) beat the baddies, led by Jack Palance. George Stevens took classic ingredients in 1953 and made them fresh and unforgettable. Unfortunately, it has now been copied by so many other film-makers that it has lost much of its magic. Loyal Griggs won an Oscar for his photography. (*c*)

Shanghai Express √√
Remarkable culmination of star-director relationship between Marlene Dietrich and Josef von Sternberg, in 1932. On the surface, a thriller about a train hold up in China, it takes on all kinds of mysterious overtones, as destroyer (Clive Brook) faces the woman he discarded and who became the notorious 'white flower of China'. The explanation of the even monotone all the actors speak in–Sternberg told them 'This is the Shanghai Express. Everybody must talk like a train'. (*b/w*)

She × ×
Arsula Undress is the 2000-year-old ever-youthful Queen who waits in Mountains of the Moon for her virile young discoverer; but this Hammer production, far from hitting the nail on the head, gives all concerned a painful thumb. In 1965, the production looked almost as out-of-date as the Queen, with its tatty scenery and gear. Director Robert Day allows Peter Cushing, Christopher Lee, André Morell and the rest of the Hammer mob to look as lost all the time as they are supposed to in the desert. And Bernard Cribbins' Cockney valet is plain embarrassing. They even did a sequel, *The Vengeance of She*, three years later. (*c*)

She Didn't Say No × ×
Ghastly attempt to turn illegitimacy into a saucy, funny subject. Eileen Herlie has had babies by five different fathers. Oddly enough somebody paid director Cyril Frankel to concentrate on it, only he doesn't appear to have given it enough attention; 1958. (*c*)

She Done Him Wrong √√
'I'm the finest woman who ever walked the streets', announces Diamond Lil, in Mae West's own play, directed for the screen in 1933 by Lowell Sherman. Then she meets a 29-year-old Cary Grant, posing as a Salvation Army Captain. Legend has it she says to him 'Come up and see me some time'. In fact, she says, 'Why don't you come sometime and see me? I'm home every evening. Come up. I'll tell your fortune.' For what happens next, tune in. (*b/w*)

The Sheepman √
Director George Marshall let Glenn Ford, Shirley MacLaine play this 1958 Western mainly for laughs. He's a stranger who comes to town to raise sheep. The cattle people are angry. It's typical of this woolly plot that at the end he pulls the rug from under their feet. (*c*)

Shenandoah √
Big, sentimental Civil War drama has James Stewart perfectly cast as head of Southern family reluctantly drawn into the conflict. Director Andrew McLaglen; 1965. (*c*)

She Played with Fire ×
Arlene Dahl came all the way to England in 1957 to make this arsonous little drama with Jack Hawkins. Sydney Gilliat directed; 1958. (*b/w*)

The Sheriff of Fractured Jaw × ×
Nominally British Western made in Spain in 1958. Director Raoul Walsh, co-star Jayne Mansfield and heavy Bruce Cabot just manage to convince that location is Wild West, and Kenneth More is a possible comic sheriff. (*c*)

She's Working Her Way Through College ×
Virginia Mayo, Gene Nelson, Ronald Reagan in adequate musical about song-and-dance star wanting a college education. H. Bruce Humberstone directed this 1952 version of *The Male Animal*. (*c*)

She Wore a Yellow Ribbon √ √
An elegiac Western from the master, John Ford, about the failure of the ageing cavalry officer to hold off the Indians; superb photography (Winton C. Hoch won 1949 Oscar); John Wayne in his favourite Western, and Victor McLaglen. (*c*)

Ship of Fools √
Symbolic drama about shipful of assorted types going back to Germany (from South America) in thirties, starting with little Michael Dunn. Then we meet divorcée Vivien Leigh, anti-semite José Ferrer, Heinz Ruehmann ('There are a million Jews in Germany–what are they going to do, kill us all?'), soak Lee Marvin, trite young couple Elizabeth Ashley and George Segal, intense (and most convincing of all the motley crew and passengers) late-flowering lovers Simone Signoret and Oskar Werner. When he can forget that he is directing a Film of Significance, Stanley Kramer makes it quite gripping; 1965. (*b/w*)

The Shiralee ×
Unpleasant roustabout story of Australian bully looking for work encumbered by five-year-old daughter. Peter Finch makes main character more sympathetic than it deserves and the morality is made over-simple by having his erring wife a real cow (a miscast Elizabeth Sellars). Nor has director Leslie Norman managed to make the smaller parts particularly convincing, and there's a hang-dog air about the whole enterprise that confirms the worst suspicions that outsiders have (doubtless unfairly) about Australia; 1957. (*b/w*)

Shock Corridor √
Journalist gets himself committed to mental hospital in order to expose a murder. Peter Breck, Constance Towers. Samuel Fuller wrote and directed with style in 1963. (*c*)

Shock Treatment ×
Director Denis Sanders gives us far too much of it in this lurid melo about Stuart Whitman pretending to be mad in order to wheedle secret of hidden money out of fellow-mental patient Roddy McDowall. Lauren Bacall is psychiatrist; 1964. (*b/w*)

Shoes of the Fisherman ✗
A rather dull best-seller by Morris L. West about the first Russian pope is ploddingly brought to the screen by the weakest director ever to make the big-time, Michael Anderson, and given the coup-de-grâce by a typically vulgar performance from the dreadful Anthony Quinn. Other hams present: Oskar Werner, David Janssen, Leo McKern, Vittorio de Sica. Among the real actors: Laurence Olivier, John Gielgud; 1968. (*c*)

The Shop Around the Corner √
Schmaltzy 1940 Ernst Lubitsch whimsy that somehow works; plot about love by correspondence is pretty foolproof (it spawned another film, *In the Good Old Summertime*, and a musical, *She Loves Me*) and the actors enjoy themselves– James Stewart, Margaret Sullavan, Frank Morgan and the MGM rep. (*b/w*)

Short Cut to Hell √
James Cagney's only attempt at directing was this fairly exciting small-scale remake of Graham Greene's *This Gun For Hire*, with unknowns who stayed that way. Georgann Johnson was cop's girlfriend kidnapped by killer Robert Ivers; 1957. (*b/w*)

Shotgun ✗
Sheriff Sterling Hayden catches up with outlaw Zachary Scott in Indian village and saves half-breed Yvonne de Carlo's life. Leslie Selander couldn't make it more than routine in 1955. (*c*)

A Shot in the Dark √
Sequel to *The Pink Panther*. Peter Sellers as the bumbling and tiresome French Inspector Clouseau was over-indulged by director Blake Edwards in 1964. The best jokes are broad and visual. With Elke Sommer, Herbert Lom, George Sanders. (*c*)

Show Boat √
George Sidney's 1951 remake of Jerome Kern-Oscar Hammerstein musical (Ol' Man River, Can't Help Lovin' That Man) has Howard Keel, Kathryn Grayson and a dubbed Ava Gardner paddling down the Mississippi with the best of intentions, if not of results. Earlier versions, unlikely to get air-time, are Harry Pollard's in 1929 and James Whale's, 1936. (*c*)

Showdown at Abilene ✗
Gun-shy sheriff (Jock Mahony) returns from the wars to find his ex-girlfriend engaged to nasty cattle king. David Janssen, Martha Hyer, go through the motions under director Charles Haas; 1956. (*c*)

Showdown at Boot Hill √
Charles Bronson kills outlaw for the reward but can't collect because towns-folk won't identify the body. Gene Fowler Jr made this 1958 Western above average. (*b/w*)

The Shrike √
Director José Ferrer saddled with mis-cast June Allyson as nagging wife who almost destroys her husband (Ferrer showing off again). Not quite the chiller it was on stage; 1955. (*b/w*)

Side Street √
Farley Granger, working in the post office, steals a package; he thinks it contains only a small sum but it's a whacking $30,000. Director Anthony Mann makes the subsequent drama exciting stuff, with plenty of locations of 1950 New York. Cathy O'Donnell, Paul Kelly, Jean Hagen strong supports. (*b/w*)

The Siege at Red River ✗
Routine Western has Van Johnson as Confederate spy romancing Yankee nurse Joanne Dru. Rudolph Maté directed; 1954. (*c*)

The Siege of Pinchgut ✕
Unconvincing yarn about two brothers on Sydney Harbour island after one of them has escaped from jail. Mixed American (Aldo Ray), British (Victor Maddern, Barbara Mullen), Australian (small parts) casting is particularly cumbersome, and Harry Watt's last feature film a disappointment; 1959. (b/w)

The Siege of Sidney Street ✕ ✕
Played for excitement rather than exploring the murky political undertones of the 1911 anarchist movement which led to the famous siege, with Winston Churchill stationing himself in the front line (or round the corner, anyway). Donald Sinden, Kieron Moore, Peter Wyngarde make passable revolutionaries, but it's guesswork not history. Robert S. Baker and Monty Berman share the producing-directing credits, and a gloomy love of violence for its own (or its commercial) sake; 1960. (b/w)

Sierra √
Wanda Hendrix stumbles across hide-out of father and son running from the law and helps them establish Dad's innocence of murder after scrap with rustlers. Alfred E. Green had a stalwart cast going for him in 1950: Tony Curtis, Burl Ives, Audie Murphy, Dean Jagger, Sara Allgood, James Arness. (c)

Sierra Baron ✕
Land baron hires gunman to kill Mexican land-owner so that he can grab land for himself. James B. Clark only had Rita Gam for a name; Brian Keith, Rick Jason can't hold the interest as well as the scenery does; 1958. (c)

Sign Of The Pagan ✕
Over-ambitious Douglas Sirk-directed spectacle has Jeff Chandler as Roman and Jack Palance overacting like mad as Attila the Hun; 1954. (c)

Signpost to Murder ✕ ✕
Joanne Woodward and Stuart Whitman are two players with some justifiable pretensions, and it's extraordinary how they allowed themselves to be trapped into such a non-thriller as this creaking escaped-lunatic-threatens-lonely-woman routine. But perhaps George Englund had more persuasive charm than directorial ability; 1965. (b/w)

The Silencers ✕
One of those insouciant thrillers that not even those concerned can take seriously; puts more emphasis on mild sexy larks than getting on with the plot. Dean Martin as Matt Helm and various plastic beauties. Phil Karlson; 1966. (c)

The Silent Enemy ✕
Underwater war between frogmen in Gibraltar harbour. Allegedly biographical of Commander Crabb, the admirably named Royal Navy skin-diver, he never comes to life in Laurence Harvey's cheerful vacuity. William Fairchild wrote and directed, but the technical honours must go to underwater camera-man Egil Woxholt. Fairly obvious casting for his mates: Michael Craig, John Clements, Sid James, Alec McCowen, Nigel Stock. Harvey is aptly if not eptly partnered by the primping Dawn Addams; 1958. (b/w)

The Silent Playground √
Unpretentious little British thriller about some children in possession of dangerous drug. Too obviously rushed, the direction (by writer Stanley Goulder) shows some nice touches. Roland Curram, Bernard Archard, Jean Anderson, John Ronane pull their weight; 1964. (b/w)

The Silken Affair ✕
Little British comedy about accountant David Niven fleeing his wife (Dorothy Alison), whose chief fault seems to be that she prefers doing crosswords. He

has a fling with Genevieve Page, but it's all so harmless and 1956 that it floats away on a cloud of non-sequiturs. Roy Kellino. (*b/w*)

Silk Stockings   ×
Lacklustre Rouben Mamoulian-directed musical based on *Ninotchka* has Fred Astaire thawing out Cyd Charisse in Garbo-part of icy Russian, and a disappointing Cole Porter score; 1957. (*c*)

The Silver Chalice   × × ×
'The worst motion picture filmed during the fifties', says its star Paul Newman. He should know. When it was shown on American TV he took an ad in a local newspaper disclaiming all responsibility. And who can blame him? About a young Greek sculptor who designs the cup used in the Last Supper, it's memorable only as Newman's first film. Victor Saville directed–if that's the word–in 1954. (*c*)

Silver City   √
Edmond O'Brien, Richard Arlen as rival miners. Ambushes, dynamitings, mob attacks and plain bare fists keep action going under Byron Haskin's spirited direction, 1951. Among those present and fighting: Edmond O'Brien, Yvonne De Carlo, Richard Arlen, Gladys George, Barry Fitzgerald. (*c*)

Silver Lode   ×
That old one about a man clearing himself of murder charge while running away from the law–has it ever happened in real life, one wonders? In this 1954 Allan Dwan effort, disaster strikes on his wedding day. John Payne, Dan Duryea, Lizabeth Scott, Dolores Moran go through the usual motions. (*c*)

Simba   × ×
Dirk Bogarde arrives in Kenya to find brother murdered by Mau-Mau. He stays on, with Virginia McKenna, to work for peace. Out of date stuff, not even particularly relevant in 1955. Under Brian Desmond Hurst's direction, Basil Sydney, Donald Sinden droop. (*c*)

Simon and Laura   √
Pleasantly dated comedy, made in 1955 when everything to do with television was new and glamorous; about Mr and Mrs Television, the ideal couple, at least on screen. Peter Finch and lamented Kay Kendall splendidly matched. (*c*)

Sincerely Yours   × × ×
Simply awful 1955 Liberace vehicle about a kindly deaf pianist who has the power to read people's lips and does so with his binoculars. Then he pokes his pretty little nose into their affairs and sets them all to rights. Such stalwarts as Joanne Dru, Dorothy Malone, William Demarest and Lurene Tuttle had to put up with all this, and Gordon Douglas sat benignly in the director's chair. They all got paid for it–you aren't. (*c*)

Since You Went Away   ×
Claudette Colbert and family (Shirley Temple, Jennifer Jones) suffering on the home front during Second World War. Long drawn-out, treacly stuff, enlivened for those on the set by the switch during production of Jennifer Jones's favours from her husband Robert Walker (playing opposite her) to producer David Selznick. She found herself unable to act the necessary love-scenes with Walker and they were divorced immediately afterwards. John Cromwell had the directorial headaches, and the difficult Monty Woolley, Nazimova and Lionel Barrymore to contend with besides; 1944. (*b/w*)

Sinful Davey   × ×
Unsuccessful attempt in 1969 by John Huston to make a cross between *Tom Jones* and *Dick Turpin*. John Hurt is no Albert Finney or Errol Flynn, and despite some usually reliable names (Nigel Davenport, Robert Morley) in an

otherwise poor cast the result is rowdy, boring, enervating; 1969. (*c*)

Sing As We Go ✓
There'll be many a nostalgic tear in Lancashire over this flagwaving (literally, as she leads the workers back to the factory), 1934 comedy with Gracie Fields. Basil Dean directed. (*b/w*)

Sing, Boy, Sing ✓
Tommy Sands in a surprisingly interesting little attempt to put a story into the breaks between the singing. He plays an exploited pop-singer who isn't even allowed to know that his grandfather is dying by owner-manager Edmond O'Brien. When he finds out he rushes to the bedside and nearly gives up his career to stay home. But not quite. Henry Ephron at least tried to direct-produce a teenage American movie that isn't absolute dross; 1958. (*b/w*)

The Singer Not the Song ✓
As a Mexican bandit, Dirk Bogarde gave an accomplished and convincing performance in this 1960 adaptation by Nigel Balchin of someone else's highly-coloured novel. But as the priest he is in constant conflict with, John Mills is poorly cast and clearly unhappy; a fault compounded by the casting of the strident Mylene Demongeot as a girl he improbably gets caught up with. Producer-director Roy Baker permits the melodramatic elements to get out of hand, but is saved time and again by Bogarde's quality acting. (*c*)

The Singing Nun ✕ ✕ ✕
Debbie Reynolds called it her favourite part, but let's hope you've got more taste. Based on the real-life nun who had a record in the hit parade, it must be a strong contender for title of sickliest film ever made. A lot of the blame must go to director Henry Koster; 1966. (*c*)

Singin' In The Rain ✓ ✓ ✓
One of the great musicals of all time. Apart from that most-seen title number with Gene Kelly and the lampost, it has All I Do is Dream of You; Make 'Em Laugh (superb Donald O'Connor); You Are My Lucky Star; lovely Cyd Charisse, peppy Debbie Reynolds, funny Jean Hagen. Directed by Gene Kelly and Stanley Donen, it didn't win one 1952 Oscar. (*c*)

Sink the Bismarck! ✓
–the pride of Hitler's Navy. Naval officer Kenneth More has orders to dispose of it. Lewis Gilbert liberally used special effects in 1960 documentary reconstruction of 1941 yarn, not always convincingly. Everyone is a type (stiff British officers, lovable Cockney lower-deckies, super-efficient Germans), and it will confirm stereotyped ideas about the last war in general and the Navy in particular. (*b/w*)

The Sins of Rachel Cade ✓
If anyone is unclear as to the crucial role of the director in motion pictures, let him sit through this drama of a nurse at a Belgian mission in the Congo. Given a great or even good director, Angie Dickinson who has proved since this 1960 effort that she is a more than capable actress, could surely have turned in a performance of some power. As it is, Gordon Douglas, whose idea of drama is to cut to a close-up, lets this episodic series of survived blows (a doctor's death, prejudice, witch-doctors, appendix-operations, air-crashes, love, seduction, and conflicts of faith) trickle away into nothingness. Peter Finch is a good enough actor to go his own way (as the local administrator) but Roger Moore remains wooden. And a bit more of the title-sinning would have been welcome. (*c*)

Sirocco ✓
Without Humphrey Bogart this might

be only routine Pépé-le-Moking, but Curtis Bernhardt surrounded Bogie with splendid sinister Algerians and Frenchmen including Lee J. Cobb, Everett Sloane, Zero Mostel. Set 1925, shot 1951. (*b/w*)

633 Squadron　　　×
Flying extravaganza with all the usual dramas, set in a Never-Never-Land kind of war with terrible dialogue, some half-hearted direction by Walter E. Grauman and tongue-in-cheek and helmet-on-head acting from Cliff Robertson, George Chakiris, Harry Andrews and Donald Houston; 1964. (*c*)

Sitting Bull　　　×
Standing, lying down and jumping up and down bull, too. Dale Robertson, J. Carrol Naish in poor Western about Custer's Last Stand that doesn't even bother to get its facts right. Sidney Salkow directed; 1954. (*c*)

Sitting Pretty　　　√
(1) 1933 musical with Jack Oakie and Jack Haley hitch-hiking to Hollywood, meeting up with nice girl Ginger Rogers and nasty girl Thelma Todd. Director: Harry Joe Brown. (*b/w*)

Sitting Pretty　　　√ √
(2) First of the Mr Belvedere series, with Clifton Webb as a camp but effective baby-sitter, some very funny scenes (kid's punishment for cereal-scattering), game support from Robert Young, Maureen O'Hara, Louise Allbritton, Ed Begley, and happy direction from Walter Lang; 1947. (*b/w*)

Situation Hopeless but Not Serious　　　×
An odd metamorphosis for Robert Shaw's claustrophobic novel and play about two soldiers hiding in a German cellar long after the war has ended because the man who is hiding them enjoys the power it gives him and won't tell them it's all over. Gottfried Reinhardt turned it into a comedy, casting Alec Guinness as the captor, Robert Redford and Michael Connors as the captives. Paramount took a long look at it and decided that it would cost more to distribute than it would take at the box-office and promptly hid it in as deep and inaccessible place as the characters in the film. Somebody rethought the decision and issued it in 1969 – only to prove the earlier thinking to have been right. There are some genuinely funny moments, and the twist when they do manage to get away is ingenious. But it's never more than a smile. (*b/w*)

Six Black Horses　　　× ×
Dan Duryea, Audie Murphy, Joan O'Brien limping across the prairie. Don't bother: director Harry Keller didn't seem to in 1962. (*c*)

Six Bridges to Cross　　　√
Minutiae of famous robbery in Boston – $2,500,000 from Brinks' store – told as a caper planned by Tony Curtis (who was to return to the city 13 years after this was made in 1955 as another local character, the Boston Strangler). George Nader is a detective with a love-hate relationship with Curtis; Julie Adams, his wife; Sal Mineo. Director Joseph Pevney wasn't able to dissociate himself from the dozens of B-pictures he had previously made and so prevented this promising thriller from developing into much more. (*b/w*)

Skidoo　　　×
Desperate attempt from Otto Preminger in 1968 to extract some fun from a confrontation of old-style gangsters (Jackie Gleason, Carol Channing, Mickey Rooney, Frankie Avalon, Groucho Marx, Frank Gorshin) with hippies (John Phillip Law and friends). The humour is forced, the jokes still-born and the ambience out-of-date. (*c*)

Skirts Ahoy! ✕
Harmless musical about three lady sailors; hard-working cast includes Vivian Blaine, Esther Williams, Barry Sullivan. Sidney Lanfield directed, 1952. (*c*)

The Skull ✕ ✕
Belongs to the Marquis de Sade (deceased) and is supposed to have magical powers. Unfortunately, its baleful influence extended to director Freddie Francis and caused him to turn in substandard horror pic in 1965, despite presence of Peter Cushing, Patrick Wymark, Nigel Green, Jill Bennett, Michael Gough, George Colouris, Patrick Magee. (*c*)

Sky West and Crooked √
John Mills took the easy way out for his first try as director (in 1965). He cast his reliable daughter Hayley as a mentally-retarded teenager obsessed with death. When she gets involved with violent goings-on and a kindly gipsy youth (Ian McShane) she ensures there isn't a dry eye in the house. Good back-up artists (Annette Crosbie, Norman Bird, Geoffrey Bayldon) made his task even easier. But that's not to begrudge his success in bringing home (his wife is co-writer, too) the bacon. (*c*)

Slattery's Hurricane √
Richard Widmark as pilot fighting way through super-storm flashes back over his aimless life and the two girls in it, Linda Darnell and Veronica Lake. Directed by André de Toth; 1949. (*b/w*)

Slaughter On Tenth Avenue √
Richard Egan as Assistant DA investigating crime on New York waterfront; Walter Matthau is a plus, but director Arnold Laven can't quite sustain the excitement; 1957. (*b/w*)

Slaughter Trail ✕
Brian Donlevy, Virginia Grey, Gig Young, Andy Devine are on it. Three Indians and an army fort commander strew it. Irving Allen directed it; 1951. (*c*)

Slander ✕
Van Johnson, Steve Cochran, Ann Blyth in mechanical drama about TV star blackmailed, and almost destroyed, by muckraking magazine. You can understand Hollywood wanting to get back at smear-magazines but it could have been done with more panache. Director, Roy Rowland; 1957. (*b/w*)

Slave Girl ✕
She's Yvonne de Carlo helping to free ten American seaman from clutches of cruel Pasha. George Brent, Broderick Crawford, Albert Dekker, Andy Devine provide more laughs than thrills for director Charles Lamont; 1947. (*c*)

Slave Girls ✕ ✕ ✕
Nonsense about brunettes enslaving blondes in the secret jungle, and a white hunter being trapped there. As nobody in the cast has ever been heard of outside the pin-up pictures in the Daily Mirror there is no point in giving their names. Michael Carreras was the director; 1968. (*c*)

Slaves of Babylon ✕
Nebuchadnezzar builds the Hanging Gardens of Babylon for Linda Christian and Julie Newmar under orders from director William Castle. Richard Conte; 1953. (*c*)

The Sleeping City √
Richard Conte as detective trying to smash drug ring. Conventional George Sherman-directed thriller is set in large New York hospital; 1950. (*b/w*)

The Sleeping Tiger √
Directed in 1954 by political refugee Joseph Losey under the pseudonym Victor Hanbury, it's a tense yarn about a teddy boy (Dirk Bogarde would you

believe?) adopted by a psychiatrist to prove his theories of reform. Now Losey looks back on it uneasily, liking only the love scenes between Bogarde and Alexis Smith as the doctor's wife. Losey buffs will see foreshadowings of *The Servant* in the Bogarde character. (*b/w*)

The Slender Thread √
Anne Bancroft takes an overdose, then phones Samaritan-type Crisis Clinic; volunteer Sidney Poitier tries to keep her on the line, while police trace the call. Director Sydney Pollack spins it out with flashbacks. Good performances from Bancroft and Poitier are best thing in otherwise rather contrived drama; 1965. (*b/w*)

The Slime People ✗
Prehistoric dwellers awakened from their slumber by atomic explosions. Robert Hutton directed them–and himself–in 1963. (*b/w*)

The Small Back Room √
Jack Hawkins is best thing about this adaptation of Nigel Balchin best-seller made over by Powell-and-Pressburger. It's a study of broken army scientist and his struggle to find self again. Nominal leads David Farrar and Kathleen Byron below par; 1949. (*b/w*)

The Smallest Show on Earth √
Virginia McKenna and Bill Travers inherit fleapit cinema to find eccentrics Peter Sellers, Margaret Rutherford and Bernard Miles still scratching away in there. Basil Dearden directed cheerfully in 1957. (*b/w*)

Small Town Girl ✗
That's Jane Powell, with Farley Granger as Big City type passing through the small town in question, in Leslie Kardos-directed musical that won't give offence (or much pleasure) to anyone; 1953. (*c*)

The Small World of Sammy Lee √
Originally this was a television play with just one character, Sammy, stranded in his Soho room, desperately trying to raise enough money to pay his gambling debts before the heavy mob arrives. In this 1963 film Ken Hughes opened out his own script with a vengeance, taking in the whole of Soho. The love-me-please character of Anthony Newley is matched by fine performances from Julia Foster, as his girlfriend, who becomes a stripper in an effort to help him; Miriam Karlin as his cow of a sister-in-law and a whole gallery of cameo players. (*b/w*)

Smashing Time √
But times have changed, and this knock-about comedy of two innocent country girls–Rita Tushingham, Lynn Redgrave–in the Swinging London of 1967 looks awfully dated now. Still, that's not director Desmond Davis' fault. (*c*)

Smiley √
Australian boy wants a bicycle but becomes involved with smugglers in getting it (he can't want it as much as he pretends; he's lost it in sequel, below). Ralph Richardson strengthens down-under cast, where film-making in 1957 meant Chips Rafferty with everything. Anthony Kimmins. (*c*)

Smiley Gets a Gun √
1958 attempt by Anthony Kimmins to repeat success of original Smiley film has a new Smiley in Keith Calvert, but the same Dad (no longer a drunk) and the same kindly cop (Chips Rafferty). Instead of Ralph Richardson giving a bit of class to the proceedings, this time there's Sybil Thorndike as Granny McKinley, a bit of a witch. OK if you pine for the outback–either having never been there or having escaped from it. (*c*)

Smilin' Through ✗
(1) 1932 tearjerker with Norma Shearer, Leslie Howard, Fredric March. Orphaned girl falls for murderer. Director: Sidney Franklin. (*b/w*)

Smilin' Through ✗
(2) 1941 remake had Jeanette Macdonald, Brian Aherne, Gene Raymond and was even more sentimental and mushy. Director: Frank Borzage. (*c*)

The Snake Pit √√
Slightly glib and suspect exploiting of insanity this may have been, but it did open eyes to plight of mental patients in 1948. Olivia de Havilland excellent in Anatole Litvak's best-directed movie. (*b/w*)

The Snake Woman ✗✗
People are dying of snake bites all round the village but it doesn't occur to anyone that there might be a venomous snake about; instead, this being one of these gloomy English low-budget horrors, they go on about The Curse. The girl with The Curse turns out to be a pretty dire actress named Susan Travers, whose father injected her mother with snake-venom before she was born. The only possible interest in all this malarkey is that the director was Sidney J. Furie in his cornier (1960) days. (*b/w*)

The Sniper √
Arthur Franz is unbalanced gunman who picks on women as victims; Edward Dmytryk would have had a better picture if he'd given us a few reasons, as well as an exciting, but conventional, manhunt; 1952. (*b/w*)

Snows of Kilimanjaro √
1953 movie of Hemingway's story which, as usual, retains the melodrama but loses the flavour. Gregory Peck does his best with the total-recalling hunter and you can see why Ava Gardner was so big. Henry King. (*c*)

So Big √
Jane Wyman as self-sacrificing mother in 1953 Robert Wise version of Edna Ferber's prizewinning sob story; with Sterling Hayden, Nancy Olson, Steve Forrest. (*b/w*)

Soldier in the Rain √
Steve McQueen as dopey soldier who hero-worships his sergeant Jackie Gleason in what they call a comedy-drama (meaning the director–in this case Ralph Nelson–can't make up his mind what he wants, and ends up with neither). It's all very gay, however; 1963. (*b/w*)

Soldier of Fortune √
Clark Gable hired by Susan Hayward to free husband captured by Reds in Hong Kong. Edward Dmytryk turned out slick, empty thriller with solid performances from Michael Rennie and Gene Barry; Anna Sten, much promoted star of thirties, made this penultimate pic in 1955. (*c*)

Soldiers Three ✗
Dates (and that's the right word) from Hollywood's Empire-saluting period around 1951, and has Stewart Granger, Robert Newton, Cyril Cusack as troublemakers who put aside their hellraising inside the army to teach rebellious tribesmen a few lessons. Least embarrassing feature is David Niven who covers up for the privates. Tay Garnett directed lustily a long way from Rudyard Kipling. (*b/w*)

The Solid Gold Cadillac √
Imitative comedy about small shareholder disrupting giant company moved easily from Broadway to the screen, under the able direction of Richard Quine. Judy Holliday made it sparkle as small shareholder who asks awkward questions at annual general meeting. Paul Douglas, Fred Clark splendid members of the board. But the title's a bit misleading; 1956. (*b/w*)

Solomon and Sheba ✗✗
Vulgar Hollywood version of Biblical episode stars Yul Brynner and Gina Lollobrigida. Brynner took over from Tyrone Power who died of a heart attack after one of the fight scenes. 'A

simply marvellous picture', King Vidor says it would have been if Power had lived to complete the role; as it is, it turned out to be 'an unimportant, nothing sort of picture'. Well, if the director says so, who are we to argue? 1959. (*c*)

So Long at the Fair √
When her brother mysteriously disappears from their hotel during the 1889 Paris Exhibition, and everyone denies his existence, Jean Simmons is understandably frantic. Luckily nice Dirk Bogarde is standing by to help. It's an old plot, attractively reworked by Terence Fisher and Anthony Darnborough in this 1951 version, and if you haven't come across it before it should keep you guessing until the end. (*b/w*)

Somebody Up There Likes Me √
True—well, quite true—story of prizefighter Rocky Graziano, with strong performance from Paul Newman (it was to turn him overnight into a star) as Graziano, the tough New York slum kid who became a world champ. Everett Sloane, Pier Angeli and competent Robert Wise direction; 1956. (*b/w*)

Some Came Running √
James Jones novel about soldier returning home, which in 1959 switched Frank Sinatra's career to 'serious' acting. Banal sob-stuff directed by Vincente Minnelli, who got appropriate performances from Shirley MacLaine and Dean Martin, playing a dying character who never takes his hat off—except at a lady's funeral (and that's supposed to be touching, not funny—it's that kind of picture). Sinatra as a serious actor just isn't believable. Neither is James Jones. (*c*)

Some Girls Do × ×
And some films don't; this one, for instance. Supposedly a spy comedy-thriller in the tradition of James Bond,

it has the doleful Richard Johnson in the Sean Connery part, a tentative James Villiers as the villain, and some rather unattractive girls pushing their bodies at them and us. The plot is so infantile, the dialogue so banal, the acting so incompetent and the direction (by Ralph Thomas) so slapdash that it even outdoes those Matt Helm travesties. And this is meant to be a 1969 Bulldog Drummond. (*c*)

Some Like It Hot √ √ √
Wildest Wilder comedy is this 1959 classic of Tony Curtis and Jack Lemmon fleeing gangsters after 1929 St. Valentine's Day Massacre, dressing up as girls while wooing Marilyn Monroe (and Joe E. Brown). If you don't laugh out loud during the sleeping car sequence, Curtis's send-up of Cary Grant and the chase scenes, consult a psychiatrist, as director Billy Wilder had to do during the making, so impossible was Monroe. She was bitter that the film was not in colour to show her off best, was invariably late and fluffed her lines so that one scene took 59 takes. 'She has breasts like granite and a brain like Swiss cheese', he said about her. It's Wilder's genius that none of the tension showed. (*b/w*)

Some People √
Clive Donner speeds some capable young players (Ray Brooks, Annika Wills, Angela Douglas, David Hemmings along in a plot that has to do with teenage boredom and the alternatives offered by the Duke of Edinburgh Award scheme. Kenneth More helps to disguise the do-gooding plugs, but it's all too firmly set in 1962 for much contemporary interest. (*c*)

Something of Value ×
Sidney Poitier and Rock Hudson as friends forced to take opposite sides by Mau-Mau uprisings in Kenya. Richard Brooks directed uninspiringly, though

Wendy Hiller turns in good cameo; 1957. (*b/w*)

Something to Live For ✕
Ray Milland, having dried out after *The Lost Weekend*, tries to help Joan Fontaine through the same affliction, but this 1952 bender is off the wagon. Not even George Stevens' direction helps. (*b/w*)

Something Wild √
Carroll Baker's husband, Jack Garfein, directed her in 1960 in this hysterical but compelling story of degradation, that foreshadowed *The Collector* in its plot about a girl held captive. (*b/w*)

Somewhere I'll Find You √
Clark Gable's last film before he joined army in 1942 has him as war correspondent following another, Lana Turner, to Pacific. Wesley Ruggles did better with love stuff than war stuff. (*b/w*)

The Song of Bernadette ✕
Jennifer Jones' wide-eyed all-American saint was greatly aided by the monumental joke of Linda Darnell as the Virgin Mary. So much so that she actually won the 1943 Academy Award for it. Henry King delivered the soupy religiosity required by William Perlberg, but Charles Bickford, Vincent Price, Lee J. Cobb and Gladys Cooper seemed about as French as Phyllis Isley, as Jennifer Jones was called before this film. (*b/w*)

Song of the Thin Man √√
Last of the Nick Charles saga has William Powell-Myrna Loy cracking a killing on a gambling ship. Keenan Wynn as jazz clarinetist holds the key, Dean Stockwell as their son is threatened, but justice triumphs in time. Eddie Buzzell directed; 1947. (*b/w*)

A Song to Remember ✕✕
Cornel Wilde would disagree; he has spent the years since 1945 trying to forget this awful biopic with him as a ludicrous Chopin, Merle Oberon as an even more ludicrous George Sand, and Paul Muni, George Coulouris, Nina Foch camping it up under Charles Vidor's baleful direction. (*c*)

Song Without End ✕
George Cukor took over after director Charles Vidor died in the middle of making this pretty but over-dramatic picture about Franz Lizst 'and the first thing I did was to take out all those lines like "Hiya Mendelssohn"', he said. Dirk Bogarde not too out-of-tune as the composer, considering what he was up against–co-star Capucine, for one thing; 1960. (*c*)

Son of Ali Baba ✕✕
Silly costume adventure with Tony Curtis, Piper Laurie; Kurt Neumann directed; 1952. (*c*)

Son of Dracula √
Count Alucard (try it backwards) comes to stay in America. Robert Siodmak directed this follow-up in 1943 with Lon Chaney Jr and Louise Allbritton. Should get your blood tingling if not sucking. (*b/w*)

Son of Lassie √
1945 sequel to *Lassie Come Home* has the canine sex-problem following his/her master on wartime bombing. Sylvan Simon directed Peter Lawford, Donald Crisp and a girl called Helen Koford whose resemblance to Terry Moore is explicable because she later changed her name. (*c*)

The Son of Monte Cristo √
Louis Hayward doesn't count for as much as Robert Donat, sadly missed from this 1940 sequel, but Rowland Lee is the same director. It's less campy than might have been expected with George Sanders the villain and Joan Bennett the lady. (*b/w*)

Son of Paleface √
Follow-up to *The Paleface*, and made four years later in 1952 by Frank Tashlin. More successful than most sequels, it's about Bob Hope tangling with Jane Russell again. Roy Rogers and Douglas Dumbrille help recreate that Saturday-morning Western feeling. (*c*)

Son of Robin Hood × ×
Winner of the most misleading title award. It isn't a son, it's a daughter. And it isn't Joan Collins, who turned the part down, but June Laverick with equally undistinguished cast making it look more like Sherbert Forest. Or Sherman Forest, as director George is responsible; 1959. (*c*)

Son of Sinbad ×
Caliph Vincent Price captures Dale Robertson, forces him to bring the secret of Greek Fire. Hard to care one way or the other. Ted Tetzlaff; 1955. (*c*)

Sons and Lovers √
Game, if ultimately unsuccessful, try at the D. H. Lawrence novel about the Nottinghamshire coalfields before the First War. The young, lightly disguised Lawrence, played as acceptably as any American could manage by Dean Stockwell, is helped by mother Wendy Hiller to escape from bully of a father, Trevor Howard. Mary Ure won a 1960 Oscar nomination for her supporting role. Jack Cardiff and Freddie Francis, director and cameraman, neatly observe the minutiae of Edwardian working-class life. (*b/w*)

The Sons of Katie Elder × ×
If she'd lived, she would have been proud of them. John Wayne, Dean Martin, Michael Anderson Jr, Earl Holliman as tearaway sons avenging parents' deaths in slow, disappointing Henry Hathaway Western; 1965. (*c*)

The Sorcerers √
Competently directed (by Michael Reeves at 23) low-budgeter with Boris Karloff as a gentle scientist whose discovery of long-distance manipulation by hypnosis is perverted by wife Catherine Lacey; 1967. (*c*)

Sorry, Wrong Number √
Barbara Stanwyck as bedridden hypochondriac who overhears plan to kill her on crossed line and has to sit waiting to be murdered when no-one will believe her. The less-than-remarkable Anatole Litvak attempted to build tension, but the opening-out flashbacks (it was originally a one-woman radio play) were a mistake; 1948. (*b/w*)

S.O.S. Pacific ×
Seaplane-full of usual assorted cinematypes (crook, captor, girl, scientist, etc.) stranded on Pacific isle with H-Bomb about to explode. Can the scientist defuse the bomb in time? Answer depends on which version of the film they show on television – there were more than one. Guy Green directed stale stuff with as much panache as he could summon in 1959 – which wasn't much. Richard Attenborough, Eddie Constantine, Pier Angeli, John Gregson, Eva Bartok make it all rather more boring than it might have been with more charismatic players. (*b/w*)

So This is Love ×
Kathryn Grayson as real-life opera star, Grace Moore, doesn't convince; nor does anything else in this inadequate biopic. Gordon Douglas directed; 1953. (*c*)

So This Is Paris √
Who are they kidding? But this Hollywood-bound musical about three sailors on leave in Paris has Tony Curtis, Gene Nelson, Gloria De Haven and relaxed Richard Quine direction; 1955. (*c*)

The Sound and the Fury ✕
Martin Ritt's uninspired 1959 film of young Joanne Woodward seeking freedom from strict Southern background with no-good carnival charmer. Margaret Leighton, Stuart Whitman help lift it just above soap-opera level. Yul Brynner's brooding step-uncle. Supposedly adapted from William Faulkner novel, but too many other familiar influences are discernible. (*c*)

The Sound Barrier ✕
Despite suffocating upper-class ethos, accents and Terence Rattigan script, this David Lean-directed portrait of a man obsessed has some exciting moments. Ralph Richardson convinces as the aircraft maker; the rest are just too, too stiff-upper-lip to carry this 1952 effort. (*b/w*)

Sound Off ✕
Mickey Rooney drafted into the Army; you have to be a fan. Richard Quine directed; 1952. (*c*)

The Southerner √ √
Jean Renoir managed his usual lyrical job on this 1945 Texan assignment, but was let down by his ignorance of American types; 'most of the people were screechingly, unbearably wrong . . . to the point of unintentional insult', wrote James Agee. They don't seem to do much work, either, for what is supposed to be a faithful portrayal of a year in the life of cotton tenant farmers. But, having said all that, he does coax some uncommonly fine performances from Zachary Scott, Betty Field, Beulah Bondi, as they struggle against the odds and the superbly photographed land. (*b/w*)

The Southern Star √
Stick around for Orson Welles' appearance about two-thirds of the way through as a sacked policeman in the jungle. Otherwise this chase after a huge diamond is pretty routine stuff, distinguished by some swift direction from Sidney Hayers and a particularly strong cast of George Segal, Ian Hendry, Harry Andrews and Johnny Seka. Also appearing: Ursula Andress; 1969. (*c*)

South Pacific √
Considering the immense success this musical achieved at the box office, it isn't such a great film. In his history of musicals John Kobal talks of Josh Logan's 'disastrously self-indulgent direction, with every number lost in the blue of camera lenses diffused out of focus, while the action slowly succumbed to death from diabetes'. Casting was poor, too, with Mitzi Gaynor taking the part Doris Day wanted; Rossano Brazzi conceitedly smirking while another man's voice (Giorgo Tozzi's) issued from his lips; France Nuyen and John Kerr (also dubbed) simply inadequate. Only Rodgers and Hammerstein save the show: Nothing Like a Dame, Some Enchanted Evening, I'm in Love with a Wonderful Guy, etc. It's simply a couple of love stories, in essence, blown up to immense Todd-AO proportions, which unfortunately are minimised on your home screen; 1958. (*c–very*)

South Sea Woman ✕
Knockabout stuff with Burt Lancaster, Chuck Connors as wild Marines in World War II Pacific; Virginia Mayo plays stranded showgirl. Arthur Lubin directs; 1953. (*b/w*)

Southwest Passage ✕
Bank robber and girl join experimental camel train on its way West; except for camels, nothing new about this Ray Nazarro-directed oater. Rod Cameron, Joanne Dru, John Ireland; 1954. (*c*)

Southwest to Sonora √ √
This is Marlon Brando and John Saxon fightin' and feudin' over a horse. Sidney J. Furie shot it (in 1966) with all sorts of

moody compositions, but it keeps cantering along, as Brando tracks down Saxon the Mexican and his stolen horse. Set in the 1870s. (*c*)

The Spanish Gardener   √
Disappointing adaptation of A. J. Cronin's novel about a father desperately trying to reach the heart of his young teenage son. Philip Leacock has turned it into a vehicle for Dirk Bogarde as the gardener who can touch the boy, and changed the fate of this character from the book's. Michael Hordern never gives an all-round impression of the father, but Cyril Cusack, as another jealous servant, is splendid, as is Bogarde; 1956.
(*b/w*)

Spare the Rod   ✕
This sincere 1961 effort to show the awfulness of the average English state school suffers from two central flaws. One is the rewriting of the script under threat of censorship so that the master who was to get a kick out of beating kids (Geoffrey Keen) is no longer seen to do so. The other is Max Bygraves as a timid new teacher who believes you can get through to children with kindness; he can't act and lets down the whole film. Otherwise, director Leslie Norman and ambivalent headmaster Donald Pleasence manage to save what could have been a disaster, given the central casting, and even turn it into a sympathetic and realistic piece of social comment whenever Norman can manage to shoot round his 'star'. (*b/w*)

Sparrows Can't Sing   √
Lively attempt by Joan Littlewood to transfer her ensemble hit to the screen in 1963, with James Booth, Barbara Windsor, Victor Spinetti, Roy Kinnear. It should have been a sad comedy of infidelity amid changing social and architectural backgrounds, but it's not much more than a lark and a sing-song.
(*b/w*)

Spartacus   √√
Probably the best 'epic' ever made (which isn't saying much), with Stanley Kubrick (who took over as director after two weeks from Anthony Mann) marshalling vast crowds and big stars (Kirk Douglas as the slave-revolution leader; Laurence Olivier, Charles Laughton, Jean Simmons, Peter Ustinov, Tony Curtis) into a cohesive whole. He is greatly aided by Dalton Trumbo's unusually literate script and the involvement any libertarian must feel with the under-dogs. The hand-to-hand battles are particularly well-composed and edited (by Robert Lawrence); 1960. (*c*)

Speedway   ✕✕
Tiresome Elvis Presley 1968 vehicle (joke) has him as racing driver who can't pay his income tax because he has kindly given away his money. But who's the income tax inspector? Nancy Sinatra. And they fall in love, so that's all right. What a bore, Norman Taurog.
(*c*)

Spellbound   ✕
In 1944 Alfred Hitchcock decided to make the first picture about psychoanalysis and opened up a Pandora's Box for the cinema. Although it contains some of his most famous scenes (particularly in Dali's dream and memory sequences) it's a poor script, as he now admits, and there were some terrible longueurs like the schmaltzy music. Gregory Peck was never bright enough for a Hitchcock hero and Ingrid Bergman compounded her usual faults.
(*b/w*)

Spencer's Mountain   √
Sentimental stuff about Simple Mountain Folk in Wyoming wastes Henry Fonda, Maureen O'Hara, James MacArthur, but writer-director Delmer Daves pops in some nice touches of humour; 1963.
(*c*)

The Spider's Web   ✕✕
There is only one way to stage Agatha

Christie and this isn't it. To make her special world of golf, bridge, country-house murder and red-herrings live it has to be done straight–which is why *The Mousetrap* ran and ran and ran and ran and ran. In 1960, Godfrey Grayson went in for farce, with a cast of competent but determinedly lightweight players (Glynis Johns, Jack Hulbert, Cicely Courtneidge, Ronald Howard, David Nixon). The result is inconsequential. (*c*)

Spinout × ×
Elvis Presley vehicle about singer who prefers racing cars to girls. Spun out. Norman Taurog directed; 1966. (*c*)

Spinster × × ×
Don't watch this one if you are easily embarrassed by bad films, bad acting and bad directing. On the other hand, connoisseurs of the awful will revel in Shirley MacLaine's unbelievable school-teacher (so warm and understanding to the children, so cold and uptight to her suitors), Laurence Harvey's callow, sex-mad war hero who rips open her blouse shouting 'Open Sesame' in public, over-acting to the point of absurdity. Only Jack Hawkins, who finally tumbles the walls of her Jericho manages to approximate a real performance, but even here veteran director Charles Walters turns him into a smug mug. For some reason (like Maori children, who can present racial problems without upsetting the 1961 American South) it's set in New Zealand. (*c*)

The Spiral Road ×
Rock Hudson and Burl Ives play Dr Kildaring parts of young turkey and wise older doctor in adaptation of Jan de Hartog novel about leprosy in the Java jungle. Robert (*Summer of '42*) Mulligan directed, in summer of '62. Unfortunately, it's all a bit of a bore. (*c*)

The Spiral Staircase √ √
Dorothy McGuire turned in un-

forgettable portrait of deaf-mute servant terrorised by killer in a lonely house. Typical Ethel Lina White novel, sparingly adapted for Robert Siodmak's tight direction. Ethel Barrymore, George Brent, Elsa Lanchester added to the chills in 1946. (*b/w*)

The Spirit is Willing √
Amusing second-feature based on Nathaniel Benchley's *The Visitors*, about the old haunted house situation, tricked up with 1969 generation-gap and nymphomaniac ghosts. John Astin scores as a psychiatrist bent on finding rational explanations for the son's behaviour, and Sid Caesar accepts William Castle's direction with good grace. (*c*)

The Spirit of St. Louis ×
Uneven Billy Wilder-directed drama about Lindbergh's trans-Atlantic flight, with an excellent, if too old (47 playing 25), James Stewart. 1957 flashbacker misses presenting seeds of the personality faults which later led Lindbergh into apologising for Hitler. It cost $6,000,000 and flopped. 'I have never been able to figure out why', wrote producer Jack L. Warner. Wilder's own explanation: 'A bad decision. I succeeded in a couple of moments, but I missed creating the character.' (*c*)

Splendour in the Grass √
It may be sentimental, over-directed by Elia Kazan, and sub-Tennessee Williams, but this 1961 William Inge drama of adolescence is absorbing for Natalie Wood and Warren Beatty's promising performances, later fulfilled. Premature permissiveness interesting too; moral is sleep with him or be sorry. (*c*)

The Split √ √
Robbery caper on a crowded football stadium gets its interest from the people involved, and they are certainly an intriguing bunch: Jim Brown,

Diahann Carroll, Julie Harris, Ernest Borgnine, Gene Hackman, Jack Klugman, Donald Sutherland. Director Gordon Flemyng orchestrates them well and holds the interest through the recruitment, planning, operation and aftermath. Fine of its kind; 1968. (*c*)

The Spoilers √
There must be something about a novel that has been made five times into movies; in this case it's a tremendous fight between the two leading men. (1) William Farnum and Tom Santschi in 1914; (2) Milton Sills and Noah Beery in 1922: (3) Gary Cooper and William Boyd in 1930; (4) John Wayne and Randolph Scott in 1942; (5) Rory Calhoun and Jeff Chandler in 1955. Only the last two are likely ever to reach your screen: Marlene Dietrich is in the 1942 version, directed by Ray Enright; Anne Baxter in the 1955 one directed by Jesse Hibbs. It's all about gold mines in the Yukon and who owns a disputed one; 1942 and before (*b/w*); 1955. (*c*)

Springfield Rifle ✕
Gary Cooper as spy investigating arms thefts; unexciting stuff under André de Toth's direction; 1952. (*c*)

Spring in Park Lane ✕
Harmless Anna Neagle-Michael Wilding nonsense about an earl pretending to be a footman. Herbert Wilcox was at home in the tasteless décor and general putting-about of the nice, rich life; 1947. (*b/w*)

Spring Reunion ✕
Get-togethers of Old Boys and Girls can be pretty depressing affairs, even if you were at school with them. For the outsider–in this case the audience–they are almost bound to be boring, too. Betty Hutton and Dana Andrews can't stop this one from being both and Robert Pirosh's direction only underlines the tedium. One flash of interest for older viewers with long memories is the appearance of silent star Laura La Plante as Betty's Ma; 1957. (*b/w*)

The Spy in the Green Hat ✕ ✕
Last of the lamentable *Man from UNCLE* movies opts for farce, which is one way of getting through a tedious plot. Eduardo Cianelli, Jack la Rue, Joan Blondell, Elisha Cook, Maxie Rosenbloom and Jack Palance were wheeled out of the geriatric ward in 1967 to provide some guying of their former screen personae. Janet Leigh and Leo G. Carroll are on hand. And Robert Vaughn and David McCallum look as if they can't wait to take the money and run. Directed by Joseph Sargent. (*c*)

The Spy Who Came in from the Cold √ √
John le Carré's thriller used by Martin Ritt as 1965 vehicle for Richard Burton. Cast of character actors scores; Cyril Cusack and Sam Wanamaker shine, even if film is disappointing measured against book. (*b/w*)

The Spy With a Cold Nose ✕ ✕
Weak comedy about bulldog given to Soviet leader that has mike hidden in it. Lionel Jeffries, Eric Sykes OK; Laurence Harvey, Daliah Lavi, yawnful. Galton-Simpson script disappoints or maybe it's Daniel Petrie's direction; 1965. (*c*)

The Square Jungle ✕
Under-privileged grocery boy becomes boxing champ. One big cliché with Tony Curtis, Ernest Borgnine, Pat Crowley, Jim Backus and uninspired Jerry Hopper direction; 1955. (*b/w*)

The Square Peg ✕ ✕ ✕
The ghastly Norman Wisdom, parachuted into Occupied France by mistake. The first person he meets is a beautiful English agent (Honor Blackman). Then he finds that the local German general is his double. So he changes places. And so on. And so on. Hattie Jacques pro-

vides a moment or two of fun, and that's about it. That master of the banal, John Paddy Carstairs, directed; 1959. (*b/w*)

Stagecoach √ √ √
(1) The most famous Western ever made, it set standards in plot (five passengers – can they survive the journey?), photography, direction (John Ford surpassing himself), characterisation (outlaw, whore, drunken doctor, expectant mother, gambler), acting (respectively John Wayne, Claire Trevor, Thomas Mitchell, Louise Platt, John Carradine) that have never been bettered; 1939. (*b/w*)

Stagecoach × ×
(2) Draggy remake (1966) has Bing Crosby, Ann-Margret, Van Heflin, Keenan Wynn, and Alex Cord in John Wayne part; Gordon Douglas shows what a great director John Ford was. (*c*)

Stage Fright √
Hitchcock foolishly believed thriller reviewers who suggested that this novel would make a good Hitchcock movie. Jane Wyman refused to be made up as dowdily as she should have been and he regretted choice of Alastair Sim as her father. Marlene Dietrich stole the picture in a showy actress role, and he broke the rule that flashbacks must always tell the truth. Nevertheless, bad Hitchcock is better than no Hitchcock, and Richard Todd put in surprisingly fine performance as chief suspect; 1950. (*b/w*)

Stage Struck ×
Small-town girl becomes Broadway star after sleeping with producer. Susan Strasberg is no substitute for Katharine Hepburn in this 1958 remake of *Morning Glory*, and weakens otherwise reliable cast (Henry Fonda, Joan Greenwood, Herbert Marshall). Some vivid on-location photography and sharp Sidney Lumet direction weren't enough. (*c*)

Stage to Thunder Rock √
Not-quite-straightforward Western with Barry Sullivan as a sheriff who has to turn on the family who brought him up. Sullivan doesn't get much shade of character, but Keenan Wynn makes rather more of the father. Somehow director William F. Claxton didn't put quite enough push into it all; 1964. (*c*)

Staircase ×
A slight case of over-casting. Richard Burton and Rex Harrison simply don't fit the pair of ageing queens who seemed so real and right in the theatre (helped by Patrick Magee's massive performance there) and so false and wrong here. Partly it's the result of a miscast director, too: producer Stanley Donen would have done better to employ one with flair for dramatic and human foibles. Instead, he chose himself; 1969. (*c*)

Stakeout on Dope Street √ √
Remarkable little B-picture made with unknowns by director Irving Kershner, tells excitingly of the finding of a tin of heroin by a gang of teenagers and their moral dilemma of whether to sell it for big money – and thus increase the general misery dope brings. The morality isn't overdone, and the chase and hunt scenes are particularly well developed; 1957. (*b/w*)

Stalag 17 √ √
Definitive PoW drama directed by Billy Wilder in 1953, won Academy Award for William Holden as cynical sergeant who may be spy. Otto Preminger acts – as a (very) camp commandant. (*b/w*)

The Stalking Moon √ √
Stunning climax between Gregory Peck as kindly army scout and the Indian intent on revenge for his white squaw's (Eva Marie Saint) escape is worth the wait while Robert Mulligan piles on the suspense; 1969. (*c*)

Stampeded √
Routine post-Civil War oater with Alan Ladd riding into town again; this time to help a worried Virginia Mayo and Edmond O'Brien as reforming drunk. Actually, the plot, such as it is, is merely an excuse for one of those big stampedes which Gordon Douglas appears to have supplemented with clips from previous filmed cattle-panics; 1957. (c)

Stanley and Livingstone √
Spencer Tracy as reporter who searches for long-lost Dr (Sir Cedric Hardwicke) and finally delivers what is presumably most-quoted line ever spoken in Africa. Forgive the imperialism for the authenticity. Henry King; 1939. (*b/w*)

The Star √√
1953 tour de force by Bette Davis, never off the screen, as washed up ex-movie queen. She's fighting to make comeback to earn enough to have her 12-year-old daughter (young Natalie Wood) with her. Stuart Heisler. (*b/w*)

Star! ×
Julie Andrews is Julie Andrews. Gertrude Lawrence was Gertrude Lawrence. Both considerable artists in their own way, but it's not the same way and they don't meet here. Robert Wise tries to convince by using the device (from the *Citizen Kane* he edited?) of a film-within-the-film with a documentary reality. But Julie can't carry it, and Daniel Massey is not Noel Coward and Richard Crenna is not Robert Aldrich. No wonder it was a flop in 1968 and after. (*c*)

A Star is Born √√
The quintessential Judy Garland movie; love her, you'll love it; think she's an over-indulgent, over-indulged creation of show-biz mythology, you'll find this grossly dramatic slice of Hollywood life a supercilious phoney. When her role as band-singer married to drunken star (James Mason) and eclipsing him, failed to win her 1954 Oscar, Groucho Marx called it the biggest robbery since Brink's. Bravura speech in clownish make-up, pitying self and husband is highspot; George Cukor. (*c*)

Star of India ××
Cornel Wilde in weak yarn about French nobleman trying to get his estates back; there's some boring complication about Dutch jewels. Herbert Lom lurks, Jean Wallace smirks. Arthur Lubin directed, sort of; 1953. (*c*)

Stars And Stripes Forever ×
Some rousing tunes in otherwise dull biog of American brassbandsman John Philip Sousa, with Clifton Webb, Robert Wagner, Debra Paget. Henry Koster conducted; 1952. (*c*)

The Stars Are Singing ××
Silly plot about singer (Rosemary Clooney) sheltering escaped refugee, Anna Maria Alberghetti, only to find *she* can sing too, is the poor excuse for this 1953 Norman Taurog-directed musical. Lauritz Melchior sings along, Fred Clark does his bumbling bit. (*c*)

Stars in my Crown ×
Conflict between a doctor and a minister who preaches with his gun in a 19th-century Western town. Directed by Jacques Tourneur in 1950, with Joel McCrea, Ellen Drew, Dean Stockwell. (*b/w*)

State Fair ××
José Ferrer made the great mistake in 1962 of remaking Walter Lang's 1944 glowing version of Rodgers and Hammerstein's engaging musical, with a cast of Pat Boone, Bobby Darin, Ann-Margret, Alice Faye (as a Mum), Pamela Tiffin. Only Tom Ewell stands out under Ferrer's ill-judged direction. He had no feeling for music, no feeling for lightness,

and should have stuck to those heavy-handed dramas which suited his deadpan style. (*c*)

State Secret √
Superior Cold War thriller with comedy touch about surgeon tricked into helping head of state. Glynis Johns, Jack Hawkins, Douglas Fairbanks Jr. Originally called The Great Manhunt, it was directed in 1962 by Sidney Gilliat. (*b/w*)

Station Six Sahara ✕
Cheap melo has Carroll Baker disrupting sex-starved men on desert oil station. Seth Holt directed; 1962. (*b/w*)

Stay Away Joe ✕ ✕
And what better advice could one possibly give? This is a sad boring effort to make Elvis Presley into a comedian with an unfunny script and the unpleasant idea that Indians (what used to be called Red ones) have to prove themselves to be fit members of society. This particular family is ludicrously portrayed by Burgess Meredith, Katy Jurado, L. Q. Jones and Elvis, whose usual immunity from direction (supposedly by Peter Tewksbury) has been extended to the rest of the cast, with disastrous results; 1969. (*c*)

Steamboat Round the Bend √
Essentially a vehicle (a paddle steamer, in fact) for homespun philosopher Will Rogers, this 1935 John Ford features a routine but exciting race down the Mississippi reminiscent of Buster Keaton's *The General*. Beware wincing appearance by Stepin Fetchit. (*b/w*)

The Steel Bayonet ✕ ✕
Leo Genn, Kieron Moore, Michael Medwin (what a ghastly lot of officers for any platoon to have, only here two of them are supposed to be heroes) hold out in a Tunisian farmhouse. Director Michael Carreras must have thought

that a war story of this kind was commercial in 1957; there isn't any other explanation. (*b/w*)

The Steel Claw ✕
It's on the hand of brave marine corps captain about to be discharged from Manila. Instead, he ducks underground and organises local guerrillas, who must have been grateful. As he directed it as well as starring, George Montgomery made sure they were; 1961. (*c*)

Step Down to Terror ✕
You remake Hitchcock at your peril, as Harry Keller found in 1959 when he tried a regrind of *Shadow of a Doubt*. Charles Drake took the Joseph Cotten part of returning murderer. He should have stayed away. (*b/w*)

Step Lively √
In 1944 during Frank Sinatra's swoony-croony period, RKO brushed up the Marx Brothers failure, *Room Service*, added some songs and gave it to Tim Whelan to direct. Part of the producer incarcerated in an hotel by his unpaid bills is stylishly played by Adolphe Menjou. Gloria de Haven is chief swooner. (*b/w*)

Sting of Death ✕ ✕ ✕
'Numbingly bad' was one reviewer's verdict on this horrible horror pic in 1966. It's about half-man, half-jellyfish in the Florida swamps, and isn't even funnily awful. Neil Sedaka sings a couple of songs but otherwise the cast is sunk in swamps of anonymity; director was William Grefé. (*c*)

A Stitch in Time ✕ ✕ ✕
Rather an unpleasant Norman Wisdom comedy set in a hospital exploiting illness (and spastics) for laughs, in 1964. Robert Asher indulges his star's mock-innocence, which all too often comes out as malice. (*b/w*)

St Louis Blues ✗
Why do all biopics of musicians and composers have to have exactly the same story? Papa says no music—girl singer says stick at it—leaves home to seek fortune in New York (or Paris or Vienna)—setbacks, acceptance, fame—and Papa comes round, proud of his boy. Here it is again, in black. The subject is 'Father of the Blues' W. C. Handy and he is played by Nat King Cole, with Pearl Bailey, Eartha Kitt, Mahalia Jackson and Ella Fitzgerald thrown in for value. All perfectly acceptable, and directed by Allen Reisner in a dull, plodding way. Sad that the real W. C. Handy's story was an exciting, better one; 1958. (*b/w*)

Stolen Hours ✗
Poor 1962 remake of *Dark Victory*, transferred to England, in which Susan Hayward takes a long time a-dying and a-proving that Bette Davis, the original doomed socialite, was a more compelling actress. Nor is director Daniel Petrie a patch on 1939's Edmund Goulding for coaxing tears out of the audience. (*c*)

Stolen Life √
Two Bette Davises for the price of one; she's twin sisters competing for the same man: result is murder. Glenn Ford and Dane Clark out-dazzled by double Davis. Curtis Bernhardt directed; 1946. (*b/w*)

The Stooge ✗
Big-headed singer (Dean Martin) discovers he's a flop without his partner (Jerry Lewis). And with him, for our money. Norman Taurog; 1951. (*b/w*)

Stork Talk ✗✗✗
As awful as its title, this ill-conceived item has a tepid Tony Britton trying to be funny as a doctor whose wife (Anne Heywood) and girl-friend (Nicole Perrault) are both having babies at the same time. Or perhaps he isn't really the father in both cases—it's hard to tell or to care. Anyway, they both have twins so his plan to have both babies put down to his wife doesn't work. But as he's supposed to be a gynaecologist, surely he knew ... oh, don't bother. Michael Forlong compounds the general grisliness with appropriate direction; 1962. (*b/w*)

Storm Centre √
Small-town librarian Bette Davis causes a rumpus when she refuses to remove 'subversive' book from her shelves. Important theme—the dangers of political censorship—is trivialised by melodramatic plot and direction (Daniel Taradash was responsible for both in 1956). (*b/w*)

Storm Over the Nile ✗
Poor remake of *The Four Feathers* unsympathetically cast with Laurence Harvey, James Robertson Justice, Anthony Steel, Mary Ure; directed without flair by Zoltan Korda and Terence Young in 1956. Harvey has to prove he isn't a coward in the Sudan. (*c*)

Storm Warning √
Some odd casting has Doris Day and Ginger Rogers, as sisters, with Ronald Reagan and Steve Cochran in otherwise predictable 1951 Ku Klux Klan melo, directed by Stuart Heisler. (*b/w*)

The Story of Esther Costello √
Shocker about a blind, deaf and dumb girl who is first exploited and then raped by Rossano Brazzi. Meanwhile, Joan Crawford, who's married to Brazzi and has made a protégée of the girl (nicely played by Heather Sears—19 in 1957), is doing her nut. Producer-director David Miller has calculatedly ignored the social and medical implications to make a sensational picture. He has succeeded, and it's rather unpleasant. (*b/w*)

The Story of GI Joe √
Actually it's not, it's the story of Ernie Pyle, war correspondent, well-played by Burgess Meredith. Slightly interesting for marking Robert Mitchum's major debut, as soldier. William Wellman; 1945. (*b/w*)

The Story of Mankind × × ×
Candidate for the worst film ever made is this unbelievable charade supposedly taken from Hendrik van Loon's popular history. You won't believe it, but here it is: Cedric Hardwicke sits in the clouds deciding whether Mankind should live or die by H-Bomb; prosecutor is Vincent Price in morning coat, defender is Ronald Colman in grey suit (sadly anticipating his own visit to Heaven by one year; this was made in 1957, he died in 1958). As evidence, they call up some of humanity's better-known events– Moses (Francis X. Bushman) receiving the Ten Commandments; Helen of Troy (Dani Crayne) breaking them; Nero (Peter Lorre) fiddling; Hippocrates (Charles Coburn) giving his oath; Cleopatra (Virginia Mayo) killing her brother; Joan of Arc (Hedy Lamarr); Elizabeth I (Agnes Moorehead) with Sir Walter Raleigh (Edward Everett Horton) and Shakespeare (Reginald Gardiner). Most of this is supposed to be serious, but advanced lunacy sets in with the appearance of Peter Minuit buying Manhattan from the Indians (Groucho), the monk who doubted Columbus (Chico); and Sir Isaac Newton (Harpo). Producer-director of this pageant is Irwin Allen. (*c*)

The Story of Ruth × ×
You're lucky. You aren't committed to go where this film goeth; you can turn if off and go for a walk, or do the washing-up. But do try to catch a few minutes to see just how low Hollywood can stoop when taste is replaced by box-office greed; the acting (Stuart Whitman, Tom Tryon, Viveca Lindfors)

is terrible and that's better than the direction (Henry Koster) which is better than the sets that are better than the script–which sadly, is by Norman Corwin, who used to write marvellous radio dramas; 1960. (*c*)

The Story of Three Loves √
Triple-decker directed by Vincente Minnelli about ballet-dancer finding, losing love; governess in love with her charge; trapeze boy meeting trapeze girl. Strong cast includes Ethel Barrymore, Farley Granger, James Mason, Agnes Moorehead, Also present: Pier Angeli, Zsa Zsa Gabor, Leslie Caron Moira Shearer; 1953. (*c*)

The Story of Will Rogers √
Affectionate memoir of the homespun philosopher has Will Rogers Jr playing his father, Jane Wyman and competent Michael Curtiz direction; 1952. (*c*)

The Story on Page One ×
Clifford Odets's final film, which he both wrote and directed, is sad memorial to the man who wrote *Waiting for Lefty*, *Golden Boy* and *The Big Knife*. A cheaply-made courtroom drama, it has an ill-cast Gig Young as falsely-accused murderer of his mistress's (Rita Hayworth) husband, with Tony Franciosa a gnomic defence lawyer; 1960. (*b/w*)

Strait-jacket ×
Joan Crawford was incarcerated in asylum for 20 years for killing her adulterous husband and his girl with an axe. Shortly after her release–and reunion with daughter–there's a series of axe murders in the district and she becomes chief suspect. Biggest mystery is why Crawford ever agreed to appear in such an extravagant piece of rubbish. William Castle directed; 1964. (*b/w*)

A Strange Affair √ √
Det. Sgt. Jeremy Kemp uses P.C. Michael York to plant drugs on a criminal

family he's out to get. Apart from some conventional love stuff between the P.C. and Susan George (kinkily photographed through a two-way mirror) and the unforgivable pun on the P.C.'s character's name in the title, this was a refreshing entry in 1968 and makes the usual TV detective story seem old-fashioned. David Greene directs with strength and simplicity. (*c*)

Strange Bedfellows　　　　✓
Oil executive Rock Hudson is afraid that scatty wife, Gina Lollobrigida, is bad for his image–she's not, but this movie is. Gig Young, Terry-Thomas and lots of unconvincing slapstick in mild Melvin Frank comedy; 1965. (*c*)

Strange Cargo　　　　✗
Strange, indeed, with Ian Hunter as Christlike figure converting Clark Gable, Peter Lorre, Eduardo Ciannelli, Paul Lukas and J. Edward Bromberg as they escape with Joan Crawford from Devil's Island. Frank Borzage's direction suffered from his usual romanticism; 1940. (*b/w*)

The Strange Door　　　　✗
Charles Laughton and Boris Karloff overacting like mad in this absurd adaptation of Robert Louis Stevenson creepie. But perhaps director Joseph Pevney meant it to be funny? 1951. (*b/w*)

Strange Lady in Town　　　　✓
Greer Garson as Santa Fé's very busy new lady doctor. Grand Mervyn LeRoy Western with Dana Andrews, Cameron Mitchell; 1955. (*c*)

The Strange One　　　　✓✓
This portrait of a sadistic cadet, superbly realised by Ben Gazzara, provides prophetic explanation for My Lai and behaviour of US troops in Vietnam. Jack Garfein; 1957. (*b/w*)

The Stranger　　　　✓✓
(1) 'Much more graceful, intelligent and enjoyable than most other movies,' wrote James Agee in 1946, defending Orson Welles against the knockers of first film he had directed (all of) and starred in after *Citizen Kane*. He played escaped war criminal, disguised as professor, tracked down by Edward G. Robinson (in part intended for Agnes Moorehead, would you believe?). Loretta Young is unsuspecting wife. (*b/w*)

The Stranger　　　　✓✓
(2) Roger Corman ('the Orson Welles of the B picture') used the same title in 1961 for his first 'serious' drama, made with his own money in Southern towns that kept moving his unit on when they discovered that he had come to expose their racialism. The central character (William Shatner) is a rabble-rousing fascist and if the film is flawed, it is because Corman becomes more interested in the man than the political and social roots that made him. (*b/w*)

The Stranger　　　　✓✓
(3) Visconti's brilliant 1967 version of Camus's novel, with Marcello Mastroianni and Anna Karina, must surely be shown on television sometime; it was given a limited cinema showing here (*c*).

Stranger in My Arms　　　　✓
Mary Astor dominates daughter-in-law June Allyson and this three-handkerchief weepie. Helmut Kautner squeezed last drop of sentiment from Jeff Chandler's involvement with widow; 1959. (*b/w*)

Stranger in the House　　　　✗✗
Small disaster in the Home Counties, detonated by Pierre Rouve, trying his hand at directing, as well as mis-adapting a Simenon novel and transplanting it to England. James Mason is the only watchable figure on the screen, and then

solely for his siliconised shedding of the excesses of script and direction. Geraldine Chaplin (as his daughter in whose room a body is found), Bobby Darin as the corpse, Ian Ogilvy and the rest of the rather untalented British cast, give poor accounts of themselves. A mess; 1967. (*c*)

Stranger on Horseback √
Strong stuff well-directed by Jacques Tourneur, about Judge Joel McCrea, who is so determined to bring miscreant to justice that he kills in order to extricate him from the town that's sheltering him. Kevin McCarthy, Nancy Gates, John Carradine back up strongly; 1955. (*c*)

Strangers on a Train √ √ √
One of Hitchcock's very best, with taut writing from Raymond Chandler, adapting Patricia Highsmith's novel of proposed exchange of murders. Robert Walker a consummate villain; Farley Granger a convincing tennis champion, although Hitchcock would have preferred someone like William Holden. It came at an opportune time in 1950, after Hitch had made two failures (*Under Capricorn*, *Stage Fright*) and his career needed a boost. If you've seen it more than twice before, see if you can spot the tricks: slowing-up the film when the dog licks intruder Granger's hand, and the use of a model blown up (in both senses of the phrase) in the climactic scene. (*b/w*)

Strangers When We Meet ×
Kirk Douglas and Kim Novak cheating on their spouses in Middle America. Richard Quine tries to keep them in the centre of the picture, but Walter Matthau does his usual scene-stealing. Unfortunately, the story (by Evan Hunter) fails to make the characters believable or alive; 1960. (*c*)

The Stranger Wore a Gun √
Randolph Scott joins in hold-up as tribute to bandits who saved his life. Claire Trevor, Ernest Borgnine, Lee Marvin provided director André de Toth with easy task in 1953. (*c*)

The Strangler √
The other film about the Boston Strangler, with Victor Buono, who does the ladies in because of his possessive invalid mother. Burt Topper directed in 1964. (*b/w*)

The Stranglers of Bombay × ×
Nasty wallow in Indian thugeeism, 1959, giving Terence Fisher the chance to show eyes being burned out by tongs, tongues being cut and communal graves being filled with murdered natives. Perhaps Guy Rolfe, Allan Cuthbertson, and Andrew Cruickshank were just a bit ashamed when they saw what kind of a film they were involved in. (*b/w*)

Strategic Air Command ×
Even James Stewart can't get this one about baseball player recalled to flying duty airborne. Director Anthony Mann seemed to care more about the planes than rather humdrum story; 1955. (*c*)

A Streetcar Named Desire √ √
The film that catapulted Marlon Brando to superstardom, just as Tennessee Williams's original play, in which he played the same part on Broadway, had made him the most talked-about stage actor of the decade. Elia Kazan guided the hysterics and home truths of Vivien Leigh's faded Blanche, Karl Malden's good guy and the rest of the talented cast, through steamy New Orleans atmosphere; 1951. (*b/w*)

Street Corner × ×
Stories of Chelsea women police that probably looked out-of-date when this film was made in 1953, as Peggy Cummins, Terence Morgan, Anne Crawford were very much of the charm school, and Muriel Box, who directed and co-wrote, was no innovator. (*b/w*)

Streets of Laredo √
Remake of 1936 *The Texas Rangers* in 1949 had William Holden, Macdonald Carey, William Bendix as mates who split when one stays crooked. Leslie Fenton did routine Western director's job, but the film is better than most oaters. (*c*)

Strictly Dishonourable ✕
Vehicle for Italian opera star Enzio Pinza has him saving Janet Leigh's reputation by marrying her, and singing an aria or two. Melvin Frank, Norman Panama wrote and directed; 1951. (*c*)

Strictly for the Birds ✕ ✕
–or at least the uncritical. Tony Tanner just couldn't carry this supposedly wry account of a day in the life of a Soho wide boy, 1964 model, whose easy-come cash easy-goes. Some nice little cameos from Joan Sims as his sister, Graham Stark as a street musician, and Toni Palmer, Carol Cleveland and Christine Hargreaves, but Vernon Sewell can't either make you believe in his London or forget the real one. (*b/w*)

Strike Up the Band √
One of several musicals Judy Garland made with Mickey Rooney around 1940. This is the one where Rooney is leading his school band in a radio contest and she sings Our Love Affair. Busby Berkeley directed with nary an overhead camera. (*b/w*)

The Stripper ✕
William Inge's play *A Loss of Roses* provided Franklin Schaffner with his first feature, in 1963. Unfortunately, the vulgarisation of the title extended to the casting–Joanne Woodward in a blonde wig as Older Woman, Richard Beymer in a permanent sulk as budding boy–and treatment of this very French theme. Claire Trevor, Carole Lynley, Robert Webber offer what help they can. (*b/w*)

The Student Prince ✕
Edmund Purdom mouthing to Mario Lanza recordings in lush operetta about prince falling for barmaid (Ann Blyth) in Heidelberg. Director Richard Thorpe made it strictly for the coach trade in 1954. (*c*)

Studs Lonigan √
Could have been a great film except for casting of Christopher Knight as the hero of J. T. Farrell's novel of growing up in the Chicago twenties. Director Irving Lerner made it vivid cinematically, but it ran to 2¾ hours and was only fitfully seen here drastically cut after showing at the 1960 London film festival. Frank Gorshin and Jack Nicholson outstanding in lesser parts. (*b/w*)

A Study in Terror √
Oddly light-hearted Sherlock Holmes having a go at Jack the Ripper murders. Excellent cast (John Neville, Anthony Quayle, Robert Morley, Barbara Windsor, Frank Finlay, Georgia Brown), cursorily treated by script and director James Hill; 1965. (*c*)

The St Valentine's Day Massacre √ √
In 1967 this was dismissed as too violent and over-dramatic; but, since, director Roger Corman has become cult figure and we've had *The Godfather*. Now it's regarded as superior urban jungle reportage, with Jason Robards's Al Capone and George Segal's Cagney figure as merely part of one of the best gangster movies since the thirties. (*c*)

The Subject Was Roses √
Talky version of the Frank D. Gilroy play about Mom and Dad poisoning the return of their soldier son with their own bitterness. Ulu Grosbard directed stolidly, but Patricia Neal takes off as the mother and Jack Albertson won the Best Supporting Actor Oscar for 1969. Never shown commercially in Britain

for some reason best known to the potty cinema industry. (*c*)

Submarine Command ✕
Navy drama with William Holden as guilt-ridden officer starts well, but director John Farrow lets it go over the top; 1952. (*b/w*)

Submarine X–1 ✕
Poorly-written and directed (William Graham) war-film about three minisubs whose mission is to plant explosives under a German battleship; two are lost. American James Caan is somehow in charge of a British submarine and Rupert Davies is an admiral. Otherwise, the only remote surprise is when this dispirited actioner was made–1967, at least ten years after all the other bravy-navy epics. (*c*)

The Subterraneans ✕ ✕
Leslie Caron, George Peppard, Roddy McDowall, Janice Rule among early (1960) hippies in California. Cheap. adaptation of Jack Kerouac novel poorly directed by Ranald MacDougall. The ending is particularly banal. (*c*)

Subway in the Sky ✕
Competent thriller about Van Johnson on the run in West Berlin from military police and in a clinch with Hildegarde Neff. Muriel Box directs a cast of minor British supports adequately, but there isn't much feeling of Berlin; 1959. (*b/w*)

Sudden Fear ✓
Wealthy Joan Crawford realises husband Jack Palance is planning to kill her for her money. Director David Miller kept up the suspense in 1952. (*b/w*)

Suddenly ✓
Frank Sinatra as killer hired for half-a-million to snipe and kill President in small town. Lewis Allen made this in 1954, with James Gleason, Sterling Hayden, and drew such a vicious performance from the recent crooning idol that there were protests from the bobby-soxers. He and his cronies hold family prisoner as they await the President's train. The name of the town is Suddenly. (*b/w*)

Suddenly Last Summer ✓ ✓
Cannibalism rears its unexpected head in elongation of Tennessee Williams one-acter. Super superstars Elizabeth Taylor, Katharine Hepburn, Montgomery Clift play out the grisly, baroque horror story of the girl who is to be given a lobotomy to keep her quiet about what went on that summer. It's to be arranged by her aunt who offers a million dollars to the local hospital if Dr Clift will perform the operation. All reached great heights of melodrama in Gore Vidal's treatment and Joseph L. Mankiewicz charmed something even more from Liz Taylor. Amazingly, it was all filmed in England, in 1959. (*b/w*)

Sullivan's Empire ✕ ✕
Search for crashed father in Amazon jungle takes three sons on an epic journey. Or that was the idea. The actual film is rather more pedestrian. Martin Milner. Directors, Thomas Carr, Harvey Hart; 1967. (*c*)

Sullivan's Travels ✓ ✓
Wry comedy made in 1941 by Preston Sturges about Joel McCrea as film director, searching the country for significant theme, coming to the conclusion that they want to laugh. Punctuated by some brilliant episodes, with Veronica Lake, William Demarest, Franklin Pangborn, Porter Hall. (*b/w*)

Summer Holiday ✓
Sweet unpretentious Cliff Richard vehicle (double-deckered) about group of clean-living kids who dance and prance their way across Europe. Notable as the film that brought director Peter

Yates to Hollywood's attention in 1962; he went on to *Bullitt*. (*c*)

Summer Love ✕
Simple-minded stuff about teenagers at summer camp, with John Saxon, Jill St John, Rod McKuen and minimal direction from Charles Haas; 1958. (*b/w*)

Summer Madness √
The irresistible combination of Katharine Hepburn and Venice give a distinction to this bitter-sweet, David Lean-directed brief encounter between lonely American spinster and Romantic Italian (Rossano Brazzi, as always: weren't there any other actors?); 1955. (*c*)

Summer of the Seventeenth Doll √
Life down under among the sugar-cane workers and their summer-only girl-friends well-characterised by Ernest Borgnine, John Mills, Angela Lansbury and Anne Baxter, coming to grief when the plot starts involving them in marriage lines. Leslie Norman produced-directed more than competently from John Dighton's making-over of Ray Lawler's theatre play; 1960. (*b/w*)

A Summer Place ✕
Peyton Place, that surely is. During family holiday at gorgeous summer resort, unhappily married (to other people) Dorothy McGuire and Richard Egan resume an old affair, while their teenage children–Troy Donahue, Sandra Dee–embark on new one with each other. Messy soaper was written and directed by Delmer Daves in 1959. (*c*)

Summer Stock √
Judy Garland gets the show biz bug when Gene Kelly and his theatrical company come to stay on her family's farm. Phil Silvers, Gloria de Haven add to the fun provided by director Charles Walters in 1950. (*c*)

The Sun Also Rises ✕
Errol Flynn, as Mike Campbell, drunken fortune-hunter, took fourth billing, behind Tyrone Power as the impotent Jake Barnes, Ava Gardner as the nymphie Lady Brett Ashley and Mel Ferrer as Robert Cohn, in this dreadful attempt by Darryl F. Zanuck to turn Hemingway's spare prose into a lush spectacular. All were much too old for the parts (except possibly Gardner) and Henry King directed with stolid lack of imagination. Only Flynn came out of it at all well, but by 1957 he was too drunk, too dissolute and too beat-up to capitalise on his success. He made one more film, and died. (*c*)

The Sun Comes Up ✕
Sodden with sentimentality, a Richard Thorpe 1949 soaper about tragedy-struck singer Jeanette MacDonald hiding from world, with Lassie and a little boy bringing her something to live for. (*c*)

Sunday Dinner for a Soldier ✕
'Their eyes met! Their lips questioned! Their arms answered!' ran an ad for this hokum in 1944. 'They' were Anne Baxter, John Hodiak, and the movie is as mawkish as the publicity. Grandpa Charles Winninger has invited soldier Hodiak to lunch. Lloyd Bacon. (*b/w*)

Sunday in New York √
Jane Fonda quite unlike her later self in this 1964 Doris Day-type comedy in which novice director Peter Tewksbury gets smooth performances from Rod Taylor and Cliff Robertson. Her big problem is should-she-before-marriage? No, you read the date right–it was playwright Norman Krasna who didn't. (*c*)

The Sundowners √
(1) 1950: standard Western about brothers fighting against outlaw who is really a third brother. George Templeton's neat direction gets best from

Robert Preston, Robert Sterling, John Barrymore Jr, Jack Elam. (*b/w*)

The Sundowners   √
(2) 1960: Australian adventure falls uneasily between intimate conflict of a travelling man – who always wants to keep moving, with his wife who wants to stay in one place, and a spectacle lightened with comedy touches. Fred Zinnemann never appears to know quite which of the two films he was making; Robert Mitchum and Deborah Kerr give him more than adequate performances as the wandering couple, but Peter Ustinov and Glynis Johns are allowed to broaden their comedy into a riot. The landscape sequences are refreshing to start with, but quickly pall; and they do go on. (*c*)

Sunrise at Campobello   √
Reverential treatment of F. D. Roosevelt's pre-presidential retirement from politics when first stricken with polio. Dore Schary, who wrote and produced, obviously idolised the man but that didn't help the drama. Ralph Bellamy gives a surprisingly fine performance in the central role, but Greer Garson reduces his wife Eleanor, substituting mimicry for acting. The bigger failure, however, is director Vincent J. Donahue's; what should have been inspiring ends up dull. The final tottering up to the lectern for FDR's political comeback comes too late; 1961. (*c*)

Sunset Boulevard   √ √ √
Superb 1950 vision of decaying Hollywood, through Billy Wilder's mordant directorial eye; 'full of exactness, cleverness, mastery, pleasure', wrote James Agee, 'microscopically right in casting, direction and performance. Miss Gloria Swanson, required to play a 100 per cent grotesque, plays it not just to the hilt but right up to the armpit.' William Holden is corrupt writer enmeshed in her fantasy. Erich von Stroheim outplays

them all as ex-husband-cum-nursemaid but never liked the role, often referring to it as 'that lousy butler part'. (*b/w*)

The Sun Shines Bright   √
In the early thirties John Ford made a comedy about Irving Cobb's Judge Priest. In 1953, he came back to the character, now played by Charles Winninger, and a more sombre tale of a prostitute's return to her Southern home. Unfortunately, it is marred by some nasty ideas about black people. (*b/w*)

Sun Valley Serenade   √
Time-passing 1941 musical with chubby Sonja Henie, mostly notable for frequent numbers by Glenn Miller, including In The Mood. Director: Bruce Humberstone. (*b/w*)

Support Your Local Sheriff   √ √
High Noon played for laughs, with James Garner as lawman in a jail that hasn't got its bars yet. After a lifetime of heavy Westerning, Walter Brennan, Harry Morgan and Jack Elam obviously enjoy the opportunity given to them by director Burt Kennedy to play around a little. You should too; 1969. (*c*)

Surprise Package   ✕
No surprises in this misnamed comedy-caper about exiled ex-monarchs: former King of the Gangsters is Yul Brynner; Noel Coward is former real King. They meet on a Greek isle. Mitzi Gaynor is moll. Director Stanley Donen wasn't the right chap for this unrisen soufflé; 1960. (*b/w*)

Susan Slade   ✕
Connie Stevens as hapless teenage heroine having one piece of bad luck after another (including illegitimate baby, which mother Dorothy McGuire pretends is hers). Bound to turn out OK in the end, though, with Troy Donahue around as faithful friend and the soft-centred Delmer Daves writing and directing in 1961. (*c*)

Susan Slept Here ✕
Dick Powell as scriptwriter hoping feckless teenager Debbie Reynolds (actually 22 in 1954) will provide him with material. If we tell you it's a Frank Tashlin-directed romantic-comedy, you won't have to actually watch it to find out what happens. (*c*)

The Suspect √
Strong stuff with Charles Laughton echoing the Crippen case, with Ella Raines as his Ethel Le Neve, plus a calculating Henry Daniell. Robert Siodmak guaranteed the thrills in 1945. (*b/w*)

Suspicion √√
The novel by Francis Iles that Hitchcock adapted this very English thriller from was about a woman who married a murderer and was so much in love with him that she allowed herself to be killed rather than leave him. But Hitch changed the plot for Joan Fontaine and Cary Grant. Just how, you must find out for yourself if you haven't already seen it. Sadly, the present end doesn't convince anyone, including the director. Made a long way from England, in Hollywood; 1941. (*b/w*)

Svengali ✕✕
Ill-cast version of the Trilby story by Noel Langley, with Donald Wolfit clomping about as the man Du Maurier drew as thin and diabolic, and Hildegarde Neff much too sophisticated for the sweet innocent he controls into an opera star. Terence Morgan, Noel Purcell, Alfie Bass complete a dull team; 1955. (*c*)

Swamp Women ✕✕
Roger Corman swiftie about Marie Windsor, Beverly Garland, Carole Matthews, Susan Cummings as escaped convicts searching for hidden loot in swamp. Has two other titles: *Swamp Diamonds*; *Cruel Swamp*. You'll get that sinking feeling, whatever the name; 1955. (*c*)

The Swan √
Ruritanian romance has attractive cast of Grace Kelly, Alec Guinness, Louis Jourdan in Royal triangle. After making this charming soufflé for Charles Vidor in 1956, Kelly left films to marry her real-life prince. What you might call a swan song. (*c*)

Sweet Bird of Youth √√
Richard Brooks' cleaned-up 1962 film of raw Tennessee Williams' drama. Paul Newman returns home from unsuccessful Hollywood gigoloing in wake of Geraldine Page, terrific as ageing, drunken movie queen. Ed Begley splendid as local boss who goes after Newman for ruining his daughter, Shirley Knight. In the play the girl got syphilis; here it's an abortion. In the play, the boy got castrated; here it's a thump on the face, otherwise, a highly satisfactory baroque experience. (*c*)

Sweet Charity √√
Boisterous and beguiling musical imaginatively directed by Bob Fosse in 1968, one of the last of the big spenders (Big Spender being one of the songs – get it?). Shirley MacLaine manages well in the part Giulietta Masina did rather better in the original *Nights of Cabiria*, from which Neil Simon took his stage musical. Unfortunately Sammy Davis Jr is on the screen rather too much, but the music's fine (Where Am I Going?, If My Friends Could See Me Now) and Fosse's choreography is as inventive as his direction. The story of the put-upon girl with the too-big-heart is always good for a few tears. (*c*)

Sweet November ✕
Sandy Dennis plays a promiscuous girl who doesn't have long to live (that's why she's promiscuous, you see). ... But her policy of a new man every month is threatened when one of the men (Anthony Newley) falls in love with

her–and she with him. Only masochists will be able to sit through such a dismally silly plot *and* a couple of hours of more or less undiluted Newley and Dennis out-cutesying each other. Director Robert Ellis Miller must have had a strong stomach in 1968. (*c*)

Sweet Smell of Success √ √ √
Overwhelming stench of perversity, money and bitch-goddess worship comes up from this melodramatic slice of Broadway life, astonishingly well-directed by Alexander Mackendrick, and precisely photographed by James Wong Howe, 1957. Burt Lancaster icily chilling as columnist, Tony Curtis blusteringly sycophantic as feed in strong Clifford Odets, Ernest Lehman script. (*b/w*)

The Swimmer √ √
Remarkable, out-of-the-ordinary and haunting saga of Burt Lancaster, eight miles from home and clad only in his swimming-trunks, who announces that he will walk and swim (through his rich neighbours' and public pools) whenever possible, home to his own gracious house. But this is no larking college boy–he's a 50-year-old man just beginning to run to fat. The John Cheever short story Frank and Eleanor Perry have adapted this sharply-etched movie from made the symbolism of the self-imposed marathon acceptable. Lancaster has never been better, and Frank Perry's cast matches his fine direction– Janice Rule, Cornelia Otis Skinner, Marge Champion among them; 1968. (*c*)

The Swinger ×
Trashy tale of nice girl Ann-Margret pretending she's depraved so that sex-obsessed Robert Coote and Tony Franciosa will publish her stories in their nasty little girlie magazine. George Sidney directed without taste in 1966. (*c*)

Swingin' Along × × ×
For exactly three minutes of its otherwise tedious length, this stupid little film about a songwriting contest cheers up; that is when Ray Charles is inserted singing What'd I Say, with utter irrelevance. Barbara Eden is the only person with anything remotely resembling stardom in this mess, which was directed by Charles Barton in 1962. (*c*)

The Switch × ×
Gormless kidnap drama with wooden Anthony Steel and Zena Marshall; director Peter Maxwell; 1964. (*b/w*)

The Sword of Ali Baba × ×
Crafty 1965 remake of 1940 *Ali Baba and the Forty Thieves*, using some of the original actors (e.g. Frank Puglia) and miles of the original footage as a way of bringing in a cheap cheapie. It's about how Ali Baba and his thieves liberate their country and his sweetheart. Director: Virgil Vogel. (*c*)

Sword of Lancelot ×
One more reworking of the Arthurian legend, directed by and starring Cornel Wilde, in 1963. Brian Aherne and George Baker ham up a solid script. (*c*)

Sword of Sherwood Forest ×
Richard Greene, Richard Greene riding through the glen. Terence Fisher turned out a long episode from the old tele-series in this obvious tale about plotting the death of the Archbishop of Canterbury; 1960. (*c*)

Sylvia ×
Private eye George Maharis is hired to investigate murky past of bad-girl-turned-good Carroll Baker by her rich fiancé. Such inadequate casting of the main part couldn't have made director Gordon Douglas' job any easier. Nor do the presence of Joanne Dru, Peter Lawford, Viveca Lindfors, Nancy Kovack as mostly flashback characters

inspire, although Ann Sothern and Edmond O'Brien do turn in a couple of neat cameos. What he turns up clears the way for a new romance–'twixt detective and detected; 1965. (*b/w*)

The System ✗
Unpleasant early (1964) example of permissive (i.e. cashing-in on sex and sadism) British cinema, directed by Michael Winner. Oliver Reed is girl-chasing, seaside photographer; Jane Merrow, Barbara Ferris, Julia Foster his prey. (*b/w*)

Taggart ✓
Dan Duryea rides away with Western from R. G. Springsteen about Tony Young seeking revenge on his father's murderers. He finds himself the object of a search by nasty gunslingers; 1965. (*c*)

Take a Giant Step ✓
Honourable failure from British director of children, Philip Leacock, to dramatise the pressures of an American black child growing up in a white world. Modestly ambitious and shot without name players, it's all too middle-class and muted to make the impact it could have done if set lower in the social scale. Here, it is the family maid who helps the

Humphrey Bogart in *The Treasure of the Sierra Madre*

teenager to win through and take the title step. And how many families have maids? 1958. (*b/w*)

Take Care of My Little Girl   ×
Over-dramatic 1951 college yarn with Jeanne Crain, Mitzi Gaynor, Jean Peters among the gals, Dale Robertson, Jeffrey Hunter among the beaux. All about how the sorority system of clubs for freshmen is so dangerous; but why should you care? Jean Negulesco attempts to wring out your handkerchief. (*c*)

Take Her, She's Mine   ×
Tired generation-gap comedy, desperately trying to get with 1964 but out-of-date before it begins. If James Stewart weren't such a big star with the possibility of choosing his own scripts (Nunnally Johnson from a play by P. & H. Ephron) and director (Henry Koster, who also produces), one would be sorry to see him floundering as Sandra Dee's worried father. Robert Morley is also in it, but has no real part to play. A mess. (*b/w*)

Take Me Out to the Ballgame   √
Gene Kelly and Frank Sinatra not only play the most popular turn-of-the-century song-and-dance team, but they are also the star sportsmen in a baseball side that Edward Arnold is trying to wreck. You can see how Kelly wins the pennant and the girl (Esther Williams), while Frankie has to make do with the comedy support, Betty Garrett and six so-so songs. Busby Berkeley directs with more interest in Esther's water-ballets than in the story; 1949. (*c*)

Take Me to Town   ×
Ann Sheridan, a naughty crook on the run, lands up at a logging camp where she falls for preacher Sterling Hayden and his three lovable (?) moppets. Douglas Sirk did competent as possible

job with this unpromising material in 1953. (*c*)

Take the High Ground   ×
If you happen to like films about tough recruiting sergeants, filmed on location at a real military training establishment, you may enjoy this. For the rest of us, the sight of Richard Widmark and Karl Malden being tamed by the love of a good woman (Elaine Stewart) and director Richard Brooks are less appealing; 1953. (*c*)

A Tale of Two Cities   √√
(1) A far, far better film than has ever been made since of this Dickens novel. Ronald Colman splendidly directed by Jack Conway in 1935 drama of moral necessity. (*b/w*)

A Tale of Two Cities   √
(2) Muted but adequate British 1957 remake of Dickens' honourable tale. T. E. B. Clarke script balances Ralph Thomas direction. Dirk Bogarde's Carton excited a generation of schoolgirls; solid support from Dorothy Tutin, Cecil Parker, Athene Seyler. (*b/w*)

Tales of Hoffmann   × ×
Michael Powell and Emeric Pressburger's attempt to repeat the earlier success of their *Red Shoes* floundered in 1951. Without a strong story, the combination of ballet and opera seemed a heavy slog Robert Helpmann, Moira Shearer, Bruce Dargavel, Monica Sinclair, Robert Rounseville. (*c*)

Tales of Manhattan   √
Can we hope to see the W. C. Fields episode restored to this collection of short stories? It was cut out of the 1942 release because it made an already long film overlength. Julien Duvivier had smashing cast: Henry Fonda, Rita Hayworth, Ginger Rogers, Charles Boyer, Edward G. Robinson, Charles Laughton (great as a conductor) among

others. They carry some weak anecdotes. (*b/w*)

Tales of Terror √ √
Three baroque exercises from Edgar Allan Poe put together by Roger Corman and his team of creepie-crawlers. Vincent Price stars in all three; in *Morella* he's a hermit who's haunted; in *The Black Cat* he is walled-up while still alive by Peter Lorre; and in *The Case of Mr Valdemar* he's a ghost who haunts Basil Rathbone. Splendid stuff, gorgeously done; 1963. (*c*)

Tall Man Riding ×
The man is Randolph Scott, concerned at seeing fair play for Dorothy Malone and others when crooked ranchers manoeuevre to get more than their fair share of the land being granted to Montana settlers. Lesley Selander's direction doesn't rise above routine Western; 1955. (*c*)

The Tall Men
Strong cast: Clark Gable, Cameron Mitchell as brothers who come to rob but stay to make more money legally as cattle runners, plus Mae Marsh and Jane Russell. But it's a weak plot and Raoul Walsh never seems happy with this 1955 effort. (*c*)

Tall Story ×
Notable only as Jane Fonda's film debut, this 1960 college comedy paired her with Anthony Perkins as earnest biology students who finally get to put it all in practice, strictly legitimately, of course. Director Joshua Logan was her god-father and that's how she got the part and her start; sweet are the uses of nepotism. (*b/w*)

The Tall Stranger √
It's Joel McCrea, who helps the wagon-train that rescues him from difficulties to get through Colorado in 1865, winning the heart of Virginia Mayo on the way. Thomas Carr does it all very well; 1957. (*c*)

The Tall T √
Expert Western director Budd Boetticher makes more of routine Randolph Scott battling with Richard Boone and hold-up gang than you would have thought possible with the material. Maureen O'Sullivan the gal in the stage-coach; 1957. (*c*)

The Tall Target √
... is President Lincoln, whom Dick Powell prevents from being assassinated between election and taking office in 1850s. Anthony Mann made this suspenser-on-a-train (going to Baltimore) adequately exciting stuff in 1951. Adolphe Menjou, Will Geer, Paula Raymond make splendid back-ups. (*b/w*)

Tamahine × ×
Effort about Polynesian girl in English public school. Dennis Price manages the part of the headmaster by remaining aloof from the script, which has Nancy Kwan being both outrageous and decorous at the same time. Philip Leacock seems unhappy with the comedy and never gets a chance to develop his strength, the direction of children; 1963. (*c*)

The Taming of the Shrew √ √
Who's afraid of William Shakespeare? Not Franco Zeffirelli, to judge from this cheerful making-over of the Shakespeare story and some of the text. Liz Taylor and Richard Burton play it like an amalgam of the Albee play combined with *Kiss Me Kate*. Rest of the performances (Cyril Cusack, Michael Hordern, Alfred Lynch, Victor Spinetti, Alan Webb, Natasha Pyne, Michael York) are watered down rep. Nevertheless, there's an engaging vitality about it all, which is very Italian, and the crowding of every inch of screen with gesticulating extras is hypnotic; 1967. (*c*)

Tammy . . . ✕ ✕
Cutie-pants country-gal teenager who gets into all sorts of romantic scrapes:

. . . and the Bachelor: 1957, played by Debbie Reynolds who nurses pilot Leslie Nielsen back to health; King Kong's playmate Fay Wray is in the cast. Joseph Pevney directed. (*c*)

. . . and the Doctor: 1963, played by Sandra Dee. Dr Peter Fonda woos her in the big city. Harry Keller directed. (*c*)

. . . and the Millionaire: 1967, played by Debbie Watson. Inspirational stuff worked up from an unsuccessful TV pilot. Sidney Miller directed. (*c*)

. . . Tell Me True: 1961, played by Sandra Dee. She goes to college, and is ever so helpful to old folk and the Dean. Tiresome stuff. Harry Keller directed. (*c*)

Tap Roots ✕
Civil War drama in Mississippi about Van Heflin and Susan Hayward's tempestuous–or at least that was the idea–love story, played against a background of battles for states-rights. Unfortunately, George Marshall couldn't get it going, partly due to miscasting of Boris Karloff and Julie London; 1948. (*c*)

Tarantula √
If you're one of those people who get scared at the very idea of a spider being in the room, give this horror-pic about a giant, indestructible species that escapes from a lab a miss. Jack Arnold squeezes the last drop of chills from shivery story, and Leo G. Carroll, John Agar, Mara Corday abet him happily; 1955. (*b/w*)

Taras Bulba ✕ ✕
Mish-mash of epic proportion about Poles and Cossacks in the 16th century that should have thundered home with swords flying, but sinks in an ever-increasing apathy of plot and spectacle for spectacle's sake. Yul Brynner makes a singularly unsympathetic Taras, and Tony Curtis less than convincing Andrei Bulba, with his wife (of the moment– 1962) Christine Kaufmann apparently included as part of his contract. It has its moments (like the Polish horsemen tricked into toppling over a cliff) but it never convinces, never grips, never really entertains. Culprit: director J. Lee Thompson. (*c*)

Target Earth ✕ ✕
One of those mechanical movies about robots invading. Director Sherman Rose and the acting of Virginia Grey and Richard Denning make it difficult to tell which of the cast are supposed to be playing automata; 1954. (*b/w*)

Targets √ √
Startlingly good debut by Peter Bogdanovich in 1969 who not only wrote, produced and directed, but actually appears as the cinéaste director who convinces Boris Karloff to make a personal appearance. Meanwhile, an innocent-looking madman is stalking the city with a rifle, picking off passers-by haphazardly. How the two meet up at a drive-in movie is compelling and exciting. Bogdanovich went on to direct the Oscar-winning *Last Picture Show*. (*c*)

Target Unknown √
Wartime drama of escaping bomber crew inside France with vital information. Inventive George Sherman had some competent players in Gig Young, Mark Stevens, Alex Nichol; 1951. (*b/w*)

The Tarnished Angels √
Respectable 1957 adaptation of William Fulkner's *Pylon*, telling the story of a First World War flyer who comes back to do stunts to thrill the crowds and has to choose between crashing into a lake or risking the crowd that has swarmed on to a landing field. Douglas Sirk has made the flying scenes exciting and has

managed as well by the more intimate scenes–between flyer Robert Stack, wife Dorothy Malone and reporter Rock Hudson–as the range of these limited actors permits. (*b/w*)

Tarzan √
Edgar Rice Burroughs's English lord who grew up in the jungle with the apes had already been the hero of eight silent pictures by the time Johnny Weissmuller swung on to the scene. At least 15 actors have played the part, and there's no point in assessing all the movies, which are as alike as monkeys in a cage.

Here are the titles, years, directors, Tarzans and (where applicable) Janes:
Tarzan the Ape Man, 1932; W. S. Van Dyke, Johnny Weissmuller, Maureen O'Sullivan. (*b/w*)
Tarzan the Fearless, 1933; Robert Hill, Buster Crabbe. (*b/w*)
Tarzan and his Mate, 1934; Cedric Gibbons, Johnny Weissmuller, Maureen O'Sullivan. (*b/w*)
New Adventures of Tarzan, 1935; Edward Kull and W. F. McGough, Herman Brix. (*b/w*)
Tarzan Escapes, 1936; Richard Thorpe, Johnny Weissmuller, Maureen O'Sullivan. (*b/w*)
Tarzan and the Green Goddess, 1938; Edward Kull, Herman Brix. (*b/w*)
Tarzan's Revenge, 1938; D. Ross Lederman, Glenn Morris. (*b/w*)
Tarzan Finds a Son! 1939; Richard Thorpe, Johnny Weissmuller, Maureen O'Sullivan. (*b/w*)
Tarzan's Secret Treasure, 1941; Richard Thorpe, Johnny Weissmuller, Maureen O'Sullivan. (*b/w*)
Tarzan's New York Adventure, 1942; Richard Thorpe, Johnny Weissmuller, Maureen O'Sullivan. (*b/w*)
Tarzan Triumphs, 1943; William Thiele, Johnny Weissmuller. (*b/w*)
Tarzan's Desert Mystery, 1943; William Thiele, Johnny Weissmuller. (*b/w*)
Tarzan and the Amazons, 1945; Kurt Neumann, Johnny Weissmuller, Brenda Joyce. (*b/w*)
Tarzan and the Leopard Woman, 1946; Kurt Neumann, Johnny Weissmuller, Brenda Joyce. (*b/w*)
Tarzan and the Huntress, 1946: Kurt Neumann, Johnny Weissmuller, Brenda Joyce. (*b/w*)
Tarzan and the Mermaids, 1948; Robert Florey, Johnny Weissmuller, Brenda Joyce. (*b/w*)
Tarzan's Magic Fountain, 1949; Lee Sholem, Lex Barker, Brenda Joyce. (*b/w*)
Tarzan and the Slave Girl, 1950; Lee Sholem, Lex Barker, Vanessa Brown. (*b/w*)
Tarzan's Peril, 1951; Byron Haskin, Lex Barker, Virginia Huston. (*b/w*)
Tarzan's Savage Fury, 1952; Cy Endfield, Lex Barker, Dorothy Hart. (*b/w*)
Tarzan and the She-Devil, 1953; Kurt Neumann, Lex Barker, Joyce MacKenzie. (*b/w*)
Tarzan's Hidden Jungle, 1955; Harold Schuster, Gordon Scott. (*b/w*)
Tarzan and the Lost Safari, 1957; H. Bruce Humberstone, Gordon Scott. (*b/w*)
Tarzan's Fight for Life, 1958; H. Bruce Humberstone, Gordon Scott, Eva Brent. (*c*)
Tarzan, the Ape Man, 1959; Joseph Newman, Dennis Miller, Joanna Barnes. (*c*)
Tarzan's Greatest Adventure, 1959; John Guillermin, Gordon Scott. (*c*)
Tarzan the Magnificent, 1960; Robert Day, Gordon Scott. (*c*)
Tarzan Goes to India, 1962; John Guillermin, Jock Mahoney. (*c*)
Tarzan's Three Challenges, 1963; Robert Day, Jock Mahoney. (*c*)
Tarzan and the Valley of Gold, 1966; Robert Day, Mike Henry. (*c*)
Tarzan and the Great River, 1967; Robert Day, Mike Henry. (*c*)
Tarzan and the Jungle Boy, 1968; Robert Gordon, Mike Henry. (*c*)
Tarzan's Deadly Silence, 1970; Robert

L. Friend and Laurence Dobkin, Ron Ely. (*c*)
Tarzan's Jungle Rebellion, 1970; William Witney, Ron Ely. (*c*)

Taste of Fear   ×
Susan Strasberg was the American 'star' dragged over from the US to make this 1961 Hammer mystery acceptable to American audiences, but her performance was so weak that her presence reduced an already weak concept to practically nothing. Ann Todd does her spirited best as one who may or may not be in a plot to disinherit heiress Strasberg but neither her nor director Seth Holt's occasionally brilliant efforts could save a basically silly and unsurprising script (from Jimmy Sangster) from the hole in the central performance. (*b/w*)

A Taste of Honey   √√
Triumphant 1961 translation of Shelagh Delaney's successful play into a strong and moving film, distinguished by outstanding performances from Rita Tushingham as the independent, pregnant girl; Murray Melvin as the homosexual who adores and helps her; Dora Bryan as her cow of a mother. Tony Richardson has done more than open out the play; he has taken the cast to locations (none of it is studio-shot) and let them live the story. (*b/w*)

Tea and Sympathy   √
Vincente Minnelli's 1956 version of the schoolmaster's wife who touchingly thinks she has cured a lad of homosexuality by sleeping with him. Trouble is everyone else connected with the film and the play seemed to think so too. Ah well, 1956 was a long time ago. The Kerrs—Deborah and John (no kin)—do a sturdy job of acting. (*c*)

Teacher's Pet   √√
Clark Gable, tough editor, accidentally becomes journalism-teacher Doris Day's evening class pupil, which leads to complications with her unsteady steady Gig Young. George Seaton made it zing; 1958. (*b/w*)

Tea for Two   √
No, No Nanette updated to 1950 for Doris Day and Gordon MacRae is stronger on the songs (I Only Have Eyes for You is added) and comedy (S. Z. Sakall, Billy de Wolfe, Eve Arden) than on soppy plot about heiress who can't back show because she has been cheated of her money. David Butler directed cheerfully. (*c*)

Teahouse of the August Moon   √√
Beguiling and often oddly touching comedy of East meets West with conquering Americans on a rehabilitation scheme for a village in Okinawa. Thanks to Marlon Brando's beautifully-realised interpreter, the project to build a school becomes a teahouse (which serves more than tea), and the not-so-simple peasants run rings round their masters. Glenn Ford diminishes his part, but Eddie Albert as an Army psycho-analyst sent to investigate and seduced by the charms of the local geisha girl (Rashomon's Machiko Kyo) is delightful. Altogether a 1957 success for director Daniel Mann. (*c*)

Teenage Rebel   ×
Dated mother-daughter drama with divorcée Ginger Rogers as Mum the only point of interest; everything else (plot, background, assumptions, Edmund Goulding's direction) is machine-tooled and unengaging; 1956. (*b/w*)

Tell Them Willie Boy is Here   √√
Outstanding Western written and directed by Abraham Polonsky in 1969, in which a fugitive Indian seeks the identity refused him by the white man; Robert Blake and Katharine Ross as his girl-friend do splendidly as fugitives; Robert Redford, Barry Sullivan, Susan Clark make the whites seem real. (*c*)

321

The Ten Commandments ✗
Like nothing so much as those huge Victorian bibles with an engraving per page, Cecil B. DeMille remade his 33-year-old silent classic into a vast, sprawling epic with such modern conveniences as colour, wide-screen, plagues inflicted by a green hand from the sky, tablets engraved by neon magic and a cast-list containing the most obvious and unsuitable stars in the 1956 firmament – Yul Brynner as the Pharaoh, Anne Baxter, Edward G. Robinson, Yvonne de Carlo, Vincent Price, John Carradine (as Aaron!) Douglass Dumbrille, Debra Paget and Charlton Heston as a handsome Moses. The result has little to do with religion and a great deal to do with worshipping the golden calf. As for the pictures themselves, full as they are with people, they look uncannily like those Victorian plates: those costumes come out of DeMille's memory of childhood, oleographs, not the period when it was lived. (*c*)

Tender is the Night ✗ ✗
1962 travesty of F. Scott Fitzgerald's 1934 novel, with Jennifer Jones woefully inadequate as tragic Zelda-figure. Jason Robards as psychiatrist who marries her and Joan Fontaine as sister slog their way through turgid script (Fitzgerald had done one himself that nobody wanted) and Henry King's direction. Authentic Riviera and Zurich locations aren't nearly enough. (*c*)

The Tender Trap √
Bachelor Frank Sinatra thinks there's nothing wrong, then Snap! he's caught in Debbie Reynold's t.t. Impeccable support from Celeste Holm, Lola Albright, David Wayne and director Charles Walters; 1955. (*c*)

Ten Gentlemen from West Point √
George Montgomery as downtrodden goodie and Laird Cregar as vicious baddie in story about early days at the famous US military academy. Henry Hathaway, who directed in 1942, can't salute the flag with the same nostalgic devotion as John Ford, but his skill gets him by. (*b/w*)

Ten Little Indians √
Who invited the ten people to the lonely castle on the Austrian mountain-top and is killing them off, one-by-one? Answer is the great surprise twist in this game of ten green bottles falling off the wall – dead. (The other question: why on earth should they go in response to an invitation from someone they don't know? isn't even asked, let alone answered). Agatha Christie's splendid whodunit – which used to be called *Ten Little Niggers*, but is surely almost as offensive under its new name – is cheerfully acted by Leo Genn, Wilfrid Hyde White, Dennis Price, among others. George Pollock doesn't try to impose any directional style – or, alas, speed; 1966. (*b/w*)

Ten North Frederick ✗
Conventional weeper adapted from John O'Hara's novel about man supposedly too old for love that he finds when visiting his daughter in New York. Gary Cooper's the man, Suzy Parker the girl, and Geraldine Fitzgerald his pushing wife. He's so decent it hurts, as does Philip Dunne's puffing script and direction; 1958. (*b/w*)

Ten Seconds to Hell √
Pretentious, poorly-cast (imagine anyone thinking that Jeff Chandler and Jack Palance could stand for the two conflicting sides of Man's nature) thriller about bomb-disposal men in Berlin at war's end. Robert Aldrich is always good for a few cataclysmic excitements, but this one tried just too hard with inferior material; 1959. (*b/w*)

Ten Tall Men √
Burt Lancaster and nine other Legion-

naires stop Riff attack on fort. Willis Goldbeck kept the action going in 1951. (c)

Ten Thousand Bedrooms ✕ ✕
Dean Martin choosing between two boring sisters (Eva Bartok, Anna Maria Alberghetti) in Rome is tiresome, obvious stuff that even the background can't lift. Richard Thorpe came up with a yawny in this 1957 would-be romantic comedy. (c)

Ten Wanted Men ✕
Randolph Scott *v*. Richard Boone again. This time they are older generation involved in scrap over whether Jocelyn Brando, Boone's daughter, should be allowed to marry Scott's nephew, Skip Homeir. H. Bruce Humberstone makes it all very ho-hum; 1955. (c)

Term of Trial ✓ ✓
Fifteen-year-old girl gets a crush on teacher, tries to seduce him and when scorned (or at least gently repulsed) cries Rape. On this firm outline–with a couple of deliberate twists of the knife and the plot–Peter Glenville has built a strong drama, never less than compelling. His cast could almost have carried the film by themselves: Olivier as a schoolmaster perfect down to his shoelaces; Sarah Miles, at 19 (in 1962), already accomplished sex-pot enough for the part, Simone Signoret as the teacher's affectionate, exasperated wife. (b/w)

A Terrible Beauty ✓
Well, pretty terrible, anyway. Robert Mitchum is an IRA man who is first seen raiding Ulster and shooting British soldiers up and then reneging on the IRA after they won't rescue buddy-buddy Richard Harris. So he escapes to England and Anne Heywood instead. This having-it-both-ways drama comes out as a British gangster movie under Tay Garnett's direction. Incidentally, the period is at the height of the Second World War and Mitchum's exploits are timed to coincide with a nazi invasion, though it was made in 1960. (b/w)

The Terror ✓
Roger Corman certainly was, in 1964. The publicity for this horror-quickie claimed that it was written on a wet Sunday afternoon (pity the weather cleared up in the evening, they might have tied up loose ends of the plot) and shot in three days. There are a few stock shots (from *The Fall of the House of Usher*) and the sets have all been used before too (the graveyard in *The Premature Burial*, the hall in *The Raven*, the torture chamber in *The Pit and the Pendulum*) but there are several new and imaginative scenes. Unfortunately, the actors seem to have been hurried through without any time to grasp their characters or their lines, and Jack Nicholson gives a non-performance as the hero. Boris Karloff seems bemused. (c)

Tess of the Storm Country ✓
Diane Baker plays Grace Miller White's heroine who comes with her uncle to settle in Pennsylvania Dutch America from Scotland and is involved in local quarrels. If you like unpretentious, rather solid costume drama, you might enjoy it, despite uninspired direction from Paul Guilfoyle; 1960. (c)

Texas Across the River ✕
Dressy Western played for laughs has the too-charming Alain Delon as a Spanish nobleman fleeing to Texas after being accused of killing his sweetheart's fiancé. Dean Martin, a gunrunner, pals up with him, leaving most of the jokes for Joey Bishop, playing his deadpan Red Indian mate. Michael Gordon tried hard, perhaps too hard; 1966. (c)

Texas Carnival ✕
Waterlogged musical with Esther Williams, Howard Keel, Ann Miller

sunk by forgettable songs and soggy plot. Directed 1951 by Charles Walters. (c)

Texas Lady ×
That's no Texan, that's Claudette Colbert. She gambles to pay back her father's debts and takes over a newspaper in the process. Then she starts crusading. It's not really the chic Parisienne's glass of vermouth, though. Tim Whelan directs straightforwardly and Barry Sullivan is the man in her life; 1955. (c)

The Texas Rangers √
(1) 1936 King Vidor-directed big Western about Lloyd Nolan turning on old chums Fred MacMurray, Jack Oakie. (b/w)

The Texas Rangers ×
(2) 1951 effort–not a remake–with director Phil Karlson doing usual competent job with Texas outlaws forming a gunslingers' co-op to oppose George Montgomery and mates. An uphill ride. (c)

That Certain Feeling × ×
Of heart-sinking when faced with yet another Bob Hope session of wisecracks, misunderstanding, double-takes, all coming right in the end. In 1956 he was a cartoonist who got together with ex-wife Eva Marie Saint. George Sanders gives a certain life to his scenes; Pearl Bailey is on hand to sing the title-song and know her place as a coloured maid. Panama and Frank. (c)

That Funny Feeling √
Mistaken identity boy-meets-girl comedy with a certain plastic glossiness which makes it an entertaining if forgettable watch. Richard Thorpe swiftly whistles Sandra Dee and Bobby Darin through a thin-ice plot, while Larry Storch and Donald O'Connor keep it going amusingly enough; 1965. (c)

That Kind of Woman √
Keenan Wynn walks away with this one as the pimp-cum-personal assistant of George Sanders, keeping an eye on his two mistresses, Sophia Loren and Barbara Nichols. What could have been a sharp look at the morals of rich businessmen becomes a trite sailors-on-leave comedy when Tab Hunter and Jack Warden arrive, but Wynn keeps bringing it back to what Sidney Lumet perhaps first conceived but couldn't deliver because of Walter Bernstein's weak 1958 script and the wishes of producers Carlo Ponti and Marcello Girosi. (b/w)

That Lady ×
Costumer set at the Spanish court of 1570 with proud Olivia de Havilland's love having to be sacrificed. Paul Scofield gamely plays a small part, managing to hide–almost–what he must have thought of the script based on Kate O'Brien novel. Gilbert Roland, on the other hand, seems to be enjoying himself. Terence Young fumbled along directionally in 1954. (c)

That Man in Istanbul ×
Just another spy melo, played partly for laughs, as lady FBI agent (Sylvia Koscina) posing as unemployed stripper, searches for kidnapped scientist. Anthony Isasi manages cloak-and-dagger location shooting adequately, but Horst Buchholz and Koscina quickly grow tiresome; 1966. (c)

That Night √
Neo-realism in New York, 1957, in which John Beal decides that a heart-attack is nature's way of telling him to get out of the rat race. Scene in subway when he's taken ill among callous commuters is well done, but then it becomes a bit over-sentimental. John Newland brings a certain force and freshness to the direction. (b/w)

That Riviera Touch ✗
That rib-tickling touch, so gloriously present in their television programmes, has so far escaped Morecambe and Wise when they've made movies. Yet this second of their three attempts, made in 1966, used their then regular scriptwriters, Sid Green and Dick Hills, and a more than competent director, Cliff Owen. What went wrong, then, with this escapade about jewel thieves in the South of France? Well, partly there's no audience for them to play against, and partly all concerned have been seduced by the idea of having a plot. (*c*)

That's My Boy √
Jerry Lewis as timid hypochondriac, bullied by athletic father (frighteningly well played by Eddie Mayehoff) to get into the college football team. Although you can spot the ending a stadium-length away, this 1951 Lewis-and-Martin comedy is sufficiently in director Hal Walker's control to make it fitfully funny. (*b/w*)

That Touch of Mink √√
Delicious Doris Day comedy from Delbert Mann, with Cary Grant only getting her to bed when the wedding ring's firmly through his nose (it's 1962, remember). John Astin almost walks away with it all with a dreadfully true portrait of a wolf who has nothing to offer but his imaginary idea of himself, but Gig Young and Audrey Meadows do some pretty nifty scene-stealing of their own. (*c*)

That Woman Opposite ✗✗
Little whodunit written and directed by Compton Bennett from John Dickson Carr's novel, *The Emperor's Snuffbox*. One of those British quickies which was supposed to invade the American market, in 1957, this one had Phyllis Kirk and Dan O'Herlihy backed up by Petula Clark, Wilfrid Hyde White and Jack Watling. Clumsy. (*b/w*)

Their Secret Affair √
Warner Brothers bought J. P. Marquand's novel *Melville Goodwin USA* for Humphrey Bogart and Lauren Bacall. But when Bogart fell ill (he died just as this picture was released in 1957) they gave it to Kirk Douglas and Susan Hayward, at the same time changing the plot so much that only the characters were left. Douglas is a general, Hayward a *Time*-like magazine publisher out to discredit him. In scenes palely reminiscent of *The Philadelphia Story*, she tries to compromise him at her fancy Long Island home, with concealed photographers. After she falls for him but discovers he's not keen on marriage, she publishes such a virulent piece about him that a Congressional Committee has to investigate. Sadly, it lacks the very light touch that director H. C. Potter might have been expected to bring to it, and remains only an exercise in satirical comedy. Paul Stewart her editor and Jim Backus as the Army PRO, have a few amusing moments. (*b/w*)

Them! √
Effective and occasionally genuinely frightening piece of sci-fi about giant ants threatening the world. Gordon Douglas makes a highly professional job of directing both ants and hum-ants, including old reliable Edmund Gwenn as entomologist, Joan Weldon as his daughter and stolid James Arness. Nominated for special effects Oscar in 1954. (*b/w*)

There's Always Tomorrow √
Superior soap-opera with Barbara Stanwyck making a Sacrifice, Fred MacMurray making Barbara Stanwyck, and Joan Bennett making the beds. Douglas Sirk ground it all out competently, but Stanwyck and MacMurray must have looked back with regret to their earlier partnership with Billy Wilder in *Double Indemnity*; 1956. (*b/w*)

There's No Business Like Show Business ✕
1954 quasiography of Irving Berlin: loud, religioso, stodgily directed by Walter Lang, stridently acted by Ethel Merman, Mitzi Gaynor, Donald O'Connor, plunged into bathos by Johnny Ray, occasionally lit by budding Marilyn Monroe. (c)

There was a Crooked Man ✕
Old-fashioned (even for 1960) comedy with Norman Wisdom whose trousers don't actually fall down for a change. Susannah York is a pleasant passenger, and Andrew Cruickshank's a villian. There's a nice send-up of a safe caper, suggesting that Stuart Burge was too good a director for this kind of film, and he didn't make any more of the genre. (b/w)

These Dangerous Years ✕ ✕ ✕
Appalling little Herbert Wilcox cheapie supposedly about Liverpool youngsters made in 1957 before Liverpool got on the map as teenage centre. George Baker, Thora Hird, John Le Mesurier lost in a morass that better suited the talents of co-stars Frankie Vaughan, Carole Lesley and Jackie Lane. (b/w)

These Thousand Hills ✕
Ponderous Western in which Don Murray has to choose between his posh friends and the whore (Lee Remick) who first put him on the road to his fortune. Richard Fleischer seems to have got out of breath climbing all those hills; 1959. (c)

These Wilder Years ✕
Hard executive James Cagney seeks for the son he allowed to be adopted, learns humanity under tutelage of guardian angel Barbara Stanwyck and helps unmarried mother who reminds him of the girl he got into trouble all those years ago. Slushy stuff, directed by Roy Rowland in uninspired fashion. Was originally meant as vehicle for Debbie Reynolds to be called *All Our Tomorrows*; 1956. (b/w)

They Came to Cordura ✕ ✕
This was such a disaster critically and at the box office in 1959 that Robert Rossen, the director, tried to salvage something of his reputation by buying up the film and re-editing it the way he wanted. But the plan came to nothing, Rossen died, and this grim memorial is left of his errors. One of them was casting veteran Gary Cooper, who at 58 was much too old for the part of commander of a small group of war heroes in Pancho Villa country. His physical listlessness seemed to have communicated itself to Van Heflin, Tab Hunter, Richard Conte and everyone around except old trooper Rita Hayworth who was still relatively peppy as prisoner suspected of collaborating. (c)

They Died with Their Boots On ✓
Custer's Last Stand, with Errol Flynn as far-from-cowardly Custer. Done big by Raoul Walsh, in 1941, with Olivia de Havilland, Charley Grapewin, Gene Lockhart, Anthony Quinn, Sydney Greenstreet and a lot of extras. (b/w)

They Rode West ✓
Phil Karlson made this into a better than average Western, concentrating on the dilemma of a young army doctor who wants to go and save Indian tribe hit by malaria but is called back by his commander. Robert Francis, Phil Carey do well; Donna Reed is plucky gal; 1954. (c)

They Were Not Divided ✕
Terence Young wrote and directed this 1951 war yarn, mostly about friendship between a Briton and American serving together in Europe. With Edward Underdown, Michael Trubshawe and real RSM Ronald Brittain. (b/w)

They Who Dare √
Effective war drama, with Dirk Bogarde and Denholm Eliott blowing up nazi airfields in Rhodes, directed by Lewis Milestone in 1953. (*c*)

The Thief √
Back to the silent days. Ray Milland as Red spy steals atomic secrets without saying a word. In fact, nobody does. The only sound is music and effects. Russell Rouse sustains the gimmick for longer than one would have thought possible, but it does grow wearisome; 1952. (*b/w*)

Thief of Damascus ✕
Over-generous *Arabian Nights* fantasy with Sinbad, Aladdin and Ali Baba all thrown in. Will Jason seemingly couldn't bear to leave anything out, and Paul Henreid, Lon Chaney and the rest look uncomfortable; but perhaps their sandals were hurting? 1952. (*c*)

Thieves Highway √
Exciting American film by *Rififi*'s Jules Dassin, which introduced Valentina Cortese, plus Lee J. Cobb, in trucking drama; 1949. (*b/w*)

The Thing from Another World √
Arctic scientist finds space man (James Arness) and rumour says Henry Hathaway may have directed, although, as producer, he gave Christian Nyby the credit. The Thing was an eight-foot vegetable with a superhuman brain. They can't kill it until someone comes up with a culinary solution; 1952. (*b/w*)

The Thing That Couldn't Die ✕
Girl with power to find what is buried uncovers 400-year-old hidden cask; in it is severed head that forces her to find the rest of itself (singing I ain't got no body?). William Reynolds; Andra Martin. Will Cowan must have had his tongue in that ancient cheek in 1958. (*b/w*)

The Thin Man √√
Who played the part of The Thin Man in this 1934 movie? is a great movie quiz question. The answer is not William Powell; it's Edward Ellis, the first victim of the murderer. Yet somehow the title stuck to the detective, Nick Charles (William Powell), who wasn't even particularly thin, and he made five sequels, with Myrna Loy as his wisecracking wife. W. S. Van Dyke directed from a Dashiell Hammett story, which, like all the successors, gathered the suspects together for denouement. (*b/w*)

The Thin Red Line ✕
James Jones' novel of feud between sadistic sergeant and young soldier taunted for stealing pistol. The private battle lasts through the Guadalcanal campaign but you may not. Ray Daley is even duller than Keir Dullea, and Andrew Marton, the director, is dullest; 1964. (*b/w*)

The Third Day ✕
Car crashes into a river, man escapes leaving girl in car. OK thriller directed in 1965 by Jack Smight, with George Peppard and brief appearance by sexy Sally Kellerman. (*c*)

The Third Man √√√
The only film written directly for the screen by Graham Greene, it is famous for all kinds of disparate gems: the chase in the Vienna sewers; that insistent zither music; Orson Welles' oil-drippingly sinister performance as a drug trafficker; his encounter with his disillusioned friend, Joseph Cotten, in the fairground ferris wheel; the cinema's most highly-polished aphorism (about Swiss cuckoo clocks); Carol Reed's vivid direction; and Robert Krasker's crystalline photography. A great treat, however many times you may have seen it since 1949, and an enviable one for anybody who's never seen it at all. (*b/w*)

The Third Secret × ×
A psychiatrist commits suicide except that he didn't; so which of his patients did him in? Or was it someone else? Stephen Boyd, as an unbelievable American reporter, plods round London interviewing his daughter Pamela Franklin and half-a-dozen patients, which gives a bunch of character actors (Richard Attenborough, Diane Cilento, Jack Hawkins, Alan Webb, Peter Sallis among them) a chance to do a couple of days work in cameo parts. The answer to the puzzle is so silly as not to have been worth bothering with in the first place. Charles Crichton directed in 1964 as well as producer Robert L. Joseph's rotten script allowed. (*b/w*)

The Third Voice √
Edmond O'Brien and Laraine Day gang up to murder financier, impersonate him and attempt to extricate his money. Unfortunately, after this neat start and adventure with Julie London, Hubert Cornfield let the whole plot peter out when it needed a slambang ending; 1960. (*b/w*)

13 Ghosts ×
You may be forgiven for thinking that the witch from *The Wizard of Oz* is haunting this old house; it's Margaret Hamilton, who played the part in MGM classic, made up by director William Castle for the housekeeper here as close to her original part as he could get away with without sacrificing all disbelief. It's that kind of movie, stopping just this side of spoof to stay spooky. A professor moves into this old place and it's got ghosts and treasure. How his family discover both is plot; 1960. (*b/w*)

The 13th Letter √
A close remake of Clouzot's *Le Corbeau*, set in Canada, by Otto Preminger in 1951. Linda Darnell, Charles Boyer, Michael Rennie, Francoise Rosay are among those whose lives are affected by poison pen letters. Effective moments and some strong red herrings before who-wrote-it–and-why– is revealed. But it has the feeling of a carbon-copy. (*b/w*)

13 West Street √
Alan Ladd's penultimate film had him, under Philip Leacock's direction, as electronics engineer out to revenge himself on gang of well-dressed hoodlums that beat him up. Strong stuff, with Rod Steiger as patient police sergeant and Michael Callan contributing convincing cameos; 1962. (*b/w*)

–30– ×
Jack Webb does his actor-director bit on a newspaper instead of his usual draggy *Dragnet*. William Conrad among the toilers putting out a Los Angeles daily paper; 1959. (*b/w*)

30 Foot Bride of Candy Rock ×
Lou Costello (without Bud Abbott for the only time) plays amateur scientist who literally enlarges girl-friend Dorothy Provine. Sidney Miller couldn't make it sparkle; 1959. (*b/w*)

30 is a Dangerous Age, Cynthia √
There's nobody called Cynthia in this comedy, which is doubtless a very square observation to make, but a valid one. If we are expected to expend a hour and more of our valuable time on Dudley Moore's private home movies (he's the star, composer and co-author) we are entitled to some consideration, but this is one of those films that was doubtless hugely amusing to all concerned in the production, but left the paying public out in the cold. The story, such as it is, places a 29-year-old composer in the predicament of having to marry and write a musical within six weeks if he is to fulfil his self-imposed target. How he manages is told in a multitude of fantasies in which director Joe McGrath does his nut. Whether you

will even begin to do yours is quite another matter, though there are some rewarding moments, particularly when Suzy Kendall and Patricia Routledge are on the screen; 1968. (*c*)

36 Hours √
The nazis kidnap army officer, con him that war is ended to extract secrets from him. George Seaton almost succeeded in 1964 in getting Rod Taylor, Eve Marie Saint, James Garner to make this fascinating but phoney premise believable. (*b/w*)

The Thirty-nine Steps √ √
(1) 1935 Hitchcock original with Robert Donat and Madeleine Carroll handcuffed as they flee over Scottish moors. Both before and after that climatic chase John Buchan's story of murder and spying has been treated with scant respect by Hitch, who added imaginatively to the increasing tension and action. The railway journey is particularly nerve-wracking and the denouement, where Datas the Memory Man (here called Mr Memory) is forced by his professional impulse to blurt out the right answer to Donat's question 'What are the Thirty-Nine Steps?', one of the great moments in exciting cinema.
(*b/w*)

The Thirty-Nine Steps ×
(2) 1959 version lost most of the tension. Truffaut in his book-length dialogue with Hitchcock says: 'I went to see the remake that was done by Ralph Thomas, with Kenneth More. It was poorly directed and rather ridiculous, but the story is so fascinating that the audience was interested anyway. At times the breakdown followed your own very closely, but even these parts were inferior. And wherever there were changes, they were mostly all wrong.' A failure in all departments, casting (Taina Elg for Madeleine Carroll!) too.
(*c*)

This Above All ×
1942 propaganda picture uses sentiment as patriotic drum-roller; deserter (Tyrone Power) finds strength to fight again through love of posh girl (Joan Fontaine) and rector (Alexander Knox). Characteristic Anatole Litvak schmaltzy direction)
(*b/w*.

This Angry Age ×
Odd international starrer set in Indo-China, with Jo Van Fleet as matriarch who tries to force Anthony Perkins and Silvana Mangano to carry on the family rice-field cultivation. Alida Valli, Nehemiah Persoff, Richard Conte don't mix well under veteran French director René Clement; 1958. (*c*)

This Could Be the Night ×
But isn't, alas. You can't overcome the disbelief that starts clanging the moment prim schoolteacher Jean Simmons takes a part-time job as secretary to Paul Douglas, who runs a nightclub. Why doesn't she leave as soon as she finds out he's a gangster? Because then there'd be no film, that's why. Which might have been preferable. As it is, Joan Blondell, Zasu Pitts, J. Carrol Naish and other faces from the past (this was made in 1957) try desperately to make it work, but director Robert Wise couldn't do it. Tony Franciosa makes the young hood who romances our nice Miss Simmons seem odd, if not actually perverse. (*b/w*)

This Earth is Mine! ×
Jean Simmons again (see previous entry), this time as the grand-daughter of a California wine-grower falling for a distant relative, Rock Hudson, who gets most of the action and the few good lines, as well as a crippling car accident and Dorothy McGuire's jealous love. Claude Rains is in there, to give extra value and Henry King pulls out the stops with some abandon; 1959. (*c*)

This Gun For Hire √
Not much was left of Graham Greene's entertainment, *A Gun For Sale*, when Frank Tuttle directed it in 1942, not even the title. But, transposed as it was to America, it still gripped, thanks to a taut script in its own right from Albert Maltz and W. R. Burnett. Alan Ladd well fitted emotionless killer who, aided by Veronica Lake, is out to shoot man who hired him to kill and then betrayed him, a memorable performance by Laird Cregar, fat and decadent. (*b/w*)

This Happy Breed √
Noel Coward's chronicle of lower middle-class life through several generations has some neat observation from director David Lean and solid acting from Robert Newton, Celia Johnson, Kay Walsh, John Mills, Stanley Holloway; 1944. (*b/w*)

This Happy Feeling ×
Can't be brought on by the film in question. This is a dull, corny comedy of teenager Debbie Reynolds being attracted to aged (well, quite old, like 43 in 1958) Curt Jurgens who is thus considered shockingly unsuitable. Luckily young, rich, handsome John Saxon is around. Before the happy ending every member of the cast manages to fall off a horse or into a pond or something similar, and Estelle Winwood has got away with a couple of mildly funny lines. In fact, a fairly typical script-direction job by Blake Edwards. (*c*)

This Island Earth √
Splendid sci-fi, about an Earthly scientist (not all that convincingly played by Rex Reason) being recruited by a warring planet. Joseph M. Newman starts the action off cunningly in familiar surroundings, only gradually letting the special effects department take over. Gadget-lovers will relish it, the politically-conscious will discern a message; 1955. (*c*)

This is My Love ×
Dan Duryea is competed over, for some reason, by two sisters, Linda Darnell and Faith Domergue. As one of them is married to an invalid, it seems unnecessarily loaded against a happy ending. Stuart Heisler did his usual superior soap-operatics; 1954. (*c*)

This Property is Condemned √
Or *A Pullman Car Named Alva*–because we're back in Tennessee Williams-land here, with Natalie Wood as the girl dreaming about a palace of a train with her name, which Robert Redford forces her to realise is just a beat-up old wagon. How she used to grant favours to the railroad men to attract them to her mother's boarding house and how Mom used this to threaten her Real Love is the plot. Director Sydney Pollack made the most of it in 1966. (*c*)

This Rebel Breed ×
Two undercover young police graduates are assigned to break up high school dope gangs. Rita Moreno, Mark Damon and Dyan Cannon (she was called Diane then, in 1960) come off best under Richard L. Bare's direction. (*b/w*)

This Rugged Land ×
Rancher Richard Egan puts justice above his living when he defends and continues to employ suspect murderer Charles Bronson. Arthur Hiller directed hurriedly; 1962. (*b/w*)

This Sporting Life √√
1963 realisation by Lindsay Anderson of David Storey's novel about a rugby player and his uptight affair with his landlady has served as a model for countless films and television plays since; Richard Harris has never been nearly as good as this brute of a man who hides his realisation of the future. He was matched by a splendid performance from Rachel Roberts as the widow forced into 'respectability' by the

neighbours, and excellent supporting playing (Alan Badel, William Hartnell, Colin Blakely, Vanda Godsell, Anne Cunningham, Leonard Rossiter) that extended them all past previous performances, thus indicating how much the director gave to them. The rugby games themselves remain as the best sporting photography (Denys Coop) and editing (Peter Taylor) ever seen—though both director Anderson and producer Karel Reisz must have had guiding hands in both these departments. (*b/w*)

This Woman is Dangerous ✗
Joan Crawford's troubles include a serious operation, renouncing the gangster she loved for her doctor (Dennis Morgan), and then throwing him over so that her old boy-friend won't shoot him. Felix Feist directed all this stuff in 1952 with the camera trained unblinkingly on his heroine. As critic Bosley Crowther said at the time: 'For people of mild discrimination, her suffering will be matched by their own.' (*b/w*)

The Thomas Crown Affair √√
Urbane thriller with the unfortunate handicap that the central premise is totally unacceptable: that Steve McQueen's rich and successful businessman is so bored as to set up a bank robbery. Only slightly less credible is that Faye Dunaway is an insurance investigator. And then, of course, they fall for each other. However, if you can accept all this (and Michel Legrand's haunting but inappropriate Windmills of My Mind endlessly going round and round), you will doubtless applaud director Norman Jewison's handling of Haskell Wexler's superior camera work. Warning: only those with large screens will be able to see all the action, because of Jewison's penchant for splitting it into tiny compartments and showing them all simultaneously; 1969. (*c*)

Thoroughly Modern Millie ✗
Disappointing twenties lark with Julie Andrews and Mary Tyler Moore primly avoiding the clutches of Madame Beatrice Lillie. George Roy Hill just isn't the man to make the Boy Friend's girl friend appealing enough, and it doesn't get any better as it goes on and on. And on; 1967. (*c*)

Those Calloways √
Why have films about wild animals (or, in this case, birds) got to be so goddam cutesy? Here we have Brian Keith, Vera Miles and Sonny Brandon de Wilde battling thru' to build a sanctuary for wild geese. Director Norman Tokar takes us on quite a chase for them, only slightly more worth going on than the proverbial one; 1965. (*c*)

Those Magnificent Men in Their Flying Machines ✗
Don Sharp's second-unit directing is the best thing in this rather clumsy but sporadically amusing yarn about early flying. His are the aerial shots and they show up the rather leaden entertainment on the ground (Stuart Whitman, James Fox, Terry-Thomas and assorted comics vying for Robert Morley's early flying prize) directed by Ken Annakin; 1965. (*c*)

Those Redheads from Seattle ✗
Odd mixture of music and murder of crusading newspaper owner in Alaskan gold-rush. Agnes Moorehead, Rhonda Fleming, Gene Barry seem a bit mixed-up, too, under Lewis R. Foster's direction; 1953. (*c*)

A Thousand Clowns √√
Funny, witty and enjoyable 1965 comedy about a TV writer who throws it all up to mooch round New York with his twelve-year-old nephew. It could have been silly and whimsical (one shudders to think what some British comedians would have done with the

situation), but it triumphantly sustains a cracking level and even manages to say something useful about compromise and selling-out. If director-producer Fred Coe has a fault it is not to have allowed his talented cast of Jason Robards, Barry Gordon, Barbara Harris, William Daniels, Martin Balsam and Gene Saks (as the ghastly comedian Robards writes for) quite enough rein. But it's a joy, nevertheless. (*b/w*)

Three Bad Sisters   ✕
Maria English, Kathleen Hughes, Sara Shane (if you've ever heard of 'em) fight each other for even greater fortunes after they inherit estate. Hard to care about their plots and violent dramas, when directed by Gilbert L. Kay; 1956.
(*b/w*)

Three Bites of the Apple   ✕ ✕
If it's Wednesday, this must be Italy. Dull travelogue about a courier, David McCallum, who wins a fortune at the Casino but loses his job when Tammy Grimes reports him (in revenge for not sleeping with her). You wouldn't guess it was meant to be a comedy except for the pauses that director-producer Alvin Ganzer puts in for laughs that are unlikely to come; 1967. (*c*)

Three Blondes in His Life   ✕ ✕
Insurance agent is discovered to have had affairs with sexy clients and helped them swindle the company. Strictly ho-hum, under Leon Chooluck's 1960 direction. Jack Mahoney is only semi-name in it. (*b/w*)

Three Brave Men   ✓
By 1957, Hollywood was trying to work its passage back from the rabid anti-Communism that characterised both its films and its local politics (e.g. the Hollwood Ten banned from working) of the previous decade. This little effort traces the story of one clerk in the Navy Department (Ernest Borgnine), wrongly smeared as a security risk. Ray Milland is a lawyer who rallies to his defence. Writer-director Philip Dunne has done well in showing how the individual can fight back in one case, but you may get a nagging feeling that there were plenty of others unjustly smeared who didn't have Ray Milland pitching for them. And how about those who did once give a dollar to a communist-front organisation and thus, by the ethics of the time, were guilty? (*b/w*)

Three Came Home   ✓ ✓
Claudette Colbert as Agnes Newton Keith, who wrote a book about her prison experiences under the Japanese. Jean Negulesco wrang equally fine performances from her and Sessue Hayakawa as camp commandant. Harrowing, heart-warming stuff; 1950. (*b/w*)

Three Coins in the Fountain   ✕
First of the wide-screen travelogue-injected love stories, used the Trevi Fountain in Rome as link between three romantic yarns. Jean Negulesco's sentimental style was only too well-suited to the sweetness of the stories, with Clifton Webb and Dorothy McGuire coming out best; 1954. (*c*)

The Three Faces of Eve   ✕
Great hokum pretending to be true case history, Alistair Cooke narrating. Sure, there may have been a girl like that played by Joanne Woodward–it won her a 1957 Oscar–with three conflicting personalities, but you can bet it was a lot more complex than Nunnally Johnson's movie made out; 1957. (*b/w*)

Three for Bedroom C   ✕
For her first appearance after *Sunset Boulevard* come-back, Gloria Swanson was again playing a movie star in this 1965 cross-America railroad comedy about a romance between her and scientist on a train going to Los Angeles. Fred Clark, Margaret Dumont, Steve

Brodie make it all seem like a ride down Memory Lane. Milton Bren directed. (*c*)

Three for Jamie Dawn √
What happens when the heavy mob puts the pressure on three members of a murder jury. Thomas Carr made it moderately compulsive, with help of Ricardo Montalban, Richard Carlson, June Havoc, Laraine Day; 1956. (*b/w*)

Three for the Show ×
Betty Grable, Jack Lemmon, Marge and Gower Champion in weak remake of *Too Many Husbands* (Jean Arthur–Fred MacMurray) which in turn was remake of Maugham play *Home and Beauty*. All about a husband, missing believed dead, who turns up to find his wife married again. H. C. Potter directed this one diligently but unconvincingly; 1955. (*c*)

Three Godfathers √
John Ford–John Wayne Western about outlaws finding abandoned baby. Ignore banal attempts to parallel Bethlehem journey and concentrate on the superb photography. With Pedro Armendariz and Harry Carey Jr; 1948. (*b/w*)

Three Guns for Texas ×
Strictly for lovers of *Laredo*, this is, in fact, three episodes of TV series strung together. Best of the trio is about Linda Little Trees, a far from beautiful Indian squaw (Shelley Morrison) who pursues Texas Ranger Bill Smith. David Lowell Rich; 1968. (*c*)

Three Guys Named Mike ×
Fly Jane Wyman to Miami: you might click if your name is Mike. That's about the plot of this nonsense about an air stewardess who is romanced by pilot Howard Keel, scientist Van Johnson, ad-man Barry Sullivan. Would you believe that they are all named Mike? Charles Walters wasn't taking the mickey–he just had to fly this one to a safe and happy landing; 1951. (*b/w*)

Three Hats for Lisa × × ×
Dreary little British musical about docker Joe Brown commandeering famous Italian film star Sophie Hardy (who?) and taking her round London in Sid James's taxi to look for hats. The acting, music, invention, dancing and direction (by Sidney Hayers) about the same level as the plot; 1965. (*c*)

Three Hours to Kill √
Dana Andrews, stagecoach driver, has just three hours to uncover real murderer of his girl's (Donna Reed) brother. Alfred L. Werker makes this 1954 Western a cut above average for tension.
(*c*)

The 300 Spartans ×
Richard Egan, Ralph Richardson, David Farrar, Donald Houston dress up as Greeks and Persians and fight out the Battle of Thermopylae with 300 extras. Rudolph Maté makes it a standard epic, no more; 1962. (*c*)

Three into Two Won't Go √√
Judy Geeson as predatory hitch-hiker screwing up an already wobbly marriage between Rod Steiger and Claire Bloom (who were married in real-life in 1969 and afterwards unscrewed themselves, too). Closely-observed, it makes a convincing slice of life, neatly brought to the screen by Peter Hall from Edna O'Brien's screenplay from Andrea Newman's novel. Peggy Ashcroft makes a realistic bitchy mother for Claire Bloom; they really do look and feel like mother and daughter, a rarity this, in screen relationships. Whether a girl would really go barging into a man's home on the strength of a night in a hotel with him is another matter; but you believe it while you are watching. (*c*)

Three Little Girls in Blue ×
That old *How to Marry a Millionaire* plot (a remake, in fact, of *Three Blind Mice* and *Moon Over Miami*) about three smart girls looking for millionaires.

This time round they are June Haver, Vivian Blaine and Vera-Ellen; but Celeste Holm, in her first film, outshone them all. H. Bruce Humberstone had some good songs going for him, though, notably You Make Me Feel So Young; 1946. (*c*)

Three Little Words ✕
Minor musical about minor song-writers Bert Kalmar (Fred Astaire), Harry Ruby (Red Skelton) was given standard MGM treatment by Richard Thorpe in 1950. Singing voices issuing from mouths of Vera-Ellen, Debbie Reynolds don't belong to them; 1950. (*c*)

Three Men in a Boat ✕ ✕
Jerome K. Jerome's gentle, charming, funny account of a trip along the Thames becomes a coarse, heavy-handed series of obvious farcical situations under Ken Annakin's fumbling direction. Jimmy Edwards and Laurence Harvey are utterly wrong for their characters, and David Tomlinson has been encouraged to overplay his. Read the book instead; 1957. (*c*)

The Three Musketeers ✕ ✕
(1) 1935 version by Rowland V. Lee of Dumas swashbuckler made the least of the possibilities. Walter Abel, Paul Lukas, Ian Keith didn't deserve the feather in their caps. (*b/w*)

The Three Musketeers √
(2) 1939 saw a very jolly and funny musical version, with the Ritz Brothers standing in for the all-for-one-one-for-allers, leader Don Ameche. Lionel Atwill, John Carradine, Joseph Shild-kraut gave splendidly spirited performances under Allan Dwan's direction. (*b/w*)

The Three Musketeers ✕
(3) 1948 spoofy version with Gene Kelly as an athletic D'Artagnan suffered from an unimaginative script, but Lana Turner, Van Heflin, Frank Morgan,

Vincent Price, Gig Young, Keenan Wynn kept it going, under George Sidney's expert hand. (*c*)

Three on a Couch ✕ ✕
Dreadful Jerry Lewis attempt at sophisticated comedy in 1966 about (you won't believe it but it's true) how he poses as three different men and a girl to cure his psychiatrist-fiancée's three man-hating girl patients so that she'll be happy to leave for a vacation with him. Jerry Lewis can't blame the producer or director; they were both him (or at least him posing as them). (*c*)

Three on a Spree ✕ ✕
Brewster's Millions–Jack Watling must spend a million in two months if he is to inherit eight million–brought up to 1961 with disastrous results. Sidney J. Furie was the wrong director for this one and his cast of Carole Lesley, Renée Houston, John Slater couldn't find it in themselves to give adequate performances. (*b/w*)

Three Ring Circus ✕ ✕
Dean Martin and Jerry Lewis dragged even further down by Zsa Zsa Gabor, Joanne Dru, and Joseph Pevney's unenthusiastic direction; 1954. (*c*)

Three Sailors and a Girl ✕ ✕
On leave on the town, Gordon MacRae and chums are conned into investing the ship's back pay in a Broadway show starring Jane Powell. You can guess the rest. It's extremely silly, the music is undistinguished and the direction (Roy Del Ruth) is downright dull; 1953. (*c*)

Three Secrets √
Whose child survived air-crash? Eleanor Parker's? Ruth Roman's? Patricia Neal's? Robert Wise keeps up the suspense; 1950. (*b/w*)

Three Strangers √ √
John Huston co-wrote but Jean Negulesco

directed this yarn about three complete strangers who share a winning sweepstake ticket with disastrous results. Cast of Peter Lorre, Sydney Greenstreet, Geraldine Fitzgerald make this one stand out in 1946. (*b/w*)

Three Stripes in the Sun √
They are on Aldo Ray's arm, somewhere near the chip he carries on his shoulder about the Japs. Surprise for him, then, when he finds himself falling for Japanese Mitsuko Kimura. Based on a real-life story reported in the New Yorker, it's fairly believably directed by Richard Murphy; 1955. (*b/w*)

3.10 to Yuma √ √
Tense 1957 Western about Van Heflin as impecunious farmer trying to keep killer Glenn Ford under lock and key until the title train arrives. Delmer Daves made it a nailbiter. (*b/w*)

Three Violent People √
Anne Baxter is unfaithful wife in lush post-Civil War actioner, with Charlton Heston and a ranchful of solid supports: Gilbert Roland, Forrest Tucker, Elaine Stritch. But Rudolph Maté's direction is as slow as the Texan drawl; 1957. (*c*)

The Three Worlds of Gulliver ×
Well, two, actually. The voyages to Lilliput and Brobdingnag, lightly acted by an unstarry cast (June Thorburn, Lee Patterson, Kerwin Mathews) helped out with some over-ambitious special effects. Clearly meant by director Jack Sher for the child market, there's just enough of Swift's attitudes left to make it more than a picture-panto; 1960. (*c*)

Three Young Texans ×
Why is Jeffrey Hunter robbing that train? Not to get at the gold, but to stop his Dad from doing the job. He plans to put the money back, and Mitzi Gaynor is cheering him on. Henry Levin attempts to make this 1954 Western

half-way credible, but can't quite manage. (*c*)

The Thrill of it All √
Funny send-up of TV commercials with Doris Day, James Garner, Reginald Owen, with particularly good cameo from Carl Reiner. Norman Jewison gave it gloss; 1963. (*c*)

Thunderball √ √
This 1965 James Bond was the one where Sean Connery had to find out who is holding the world to ransom with two hijacked H-bombs. The climax is underwater fighting and hydrofoil athletics. Terence Young directed energetically. (*c*)

Thunder Bay √
The old reliable about two sets of workers brawling in opposition, this time it's shrimp fishermen and oil-drillers off the coast of Louisiana, with James Stewart, Dan Duryea among the brawlers, Joanne Dru on the sidelines. Director Anthony Mann can't save the pay-off from being obvious; 1953. (*c*)

Thunderbird 6 ×
Just a long episode of the *Thunderbird* TV series, with efficient puppetry, about hijacking a new airliner. Ho-hum. Director: David Lane; 1968. (*c*)

Thunder in the Sun ×
Basques going to California in the 1840s to start new vineyards is setting for triangle between Susan Hayward, Jeff Chandler and Jacques Bergerac. Climax is attack by hostile Indians (of course). Russell Rouse routine direction; 1959. (*c*)

A Thunder of Drums √
Veteran Richard Boone gets a chance (which he takes with both hands) to show what a fine actor has been jogging along on the saddle all these years. In this 1961 Western Joseph Newman has

used James Warner Bellah's fine script to probe beneath the surface of characters who would ordinarily remain ciphers. Boone is commander of a garrison in conflict with an over-conscientious young lieutenant (a disappointing George Hamilton) whose father has just denied Boone's promotion. Hamilton, in trying to win back his girl from another officer, is responsible for the massacre of a patrol. Can be enjoyed as a routine blood-and-thunderer but has a bit more to offer. (*c*)

Thunder on the Hill √
This mystery drama tells how Claudette Colbert, a nun, can't believe that Ann Blyth, a convicted murderess who happens to be taking shelter in her convent, really did it. In uncovering real murderer, she runs into danger. Gladys Cooper is superior Mother Superior, and Douglas Sirk manages to pull it up this side of melodrama; 1951. (*b/w*)

Thunder Over Arizona ✕
Silver mine is object of corrupt mayor's envy. Wallace Ford comes out best under Joseph Kane's direction; 1956. (*c*)

Thunder Over the Plains ✕
Randolph Scott protecting Phyllis Kirk and the people of Texas from carpet-baggers. Elisha Cook, Henry Hull, Lex Barker among the crowd directed by André de Toth; 1953. (*c*)

Thunder Road ✕
Robert Mitchum comes back from Korea to join in bootlegging in the South. But the law and the lawless gang up on him and his record delivery run. Arthur Ripley managed to keep it going cheerfully enough; Gene Barry, Keely Smith weak supports; 1958. (*b/w*)

Thunder Rock √√
Michael Redgrave outstanding as light-house-hermit visited by the ghosts of a wrecked ship, urging him to engage

himself in the world's affairs. James Mason, Barbara Mullen are strong aides. The Boultings; 1942. (*b/w*)

Tiara Tahiti ✕
Quite a hit in its day (1962), tells story of urbane battle between James Mason and John Mills for possession of desert isle for an hotel. Should still pass undemanding couple of hours. Director: Ted Kotcheff. (*c*)

A Ticket to Tomahawk ✕
The second girl on the left in the number Oh What a Forward Girl You Are! is Marilyn Monroe. Otherwise there is little of interest in this 1950 Western about the battle to get a train to its destination in time to win the right to operate in the nineties, and thus knock out the villainous stage-coach owner, who hires Rory Calhoun to sabotage it. Anne Baxter manages to get it there, with help from salesman Dan Dailey, driver Walter Brennan, and somehow, the song-and-dance troupe of which Marilyn is a member. Director-co-writer Richard Sale didn't realise he had the hottest property in the movies to come in his movie. (*c*)

Tickle Me ✕✕
Deadly Elvis Presley 1965 vehicle, with him as cowboy who works on a health farm and is much pursued by the inmates. Finally he marries the richest and prettiest one. Big deal. He also sings rather a lot. Norman Taurog. (*c*)

A Ticklish Affair ✕
There's a quarter of an hour towards the end of this largely tedious comedy when a child cuts the tethering-ropes of some helium balloons and goes floating away, rather like the little boy in *The Red Balloon*, that's great fun. Thanks to superior process work and some sleight-of-hand direction from George Sidney it's possible to suspend one's disbelief and to enjoy the sight of Red Buttons

shooting the air out of the balloons and Gig Young inching his way to the rescue. Otherwise it's a silly story about widow Shirley Jones rebuffing the advances of Gig because he's in the Navy and she has buried one naval husband already; 1963. (*c*)

Tiger Bay √
J. Lee Thompson's taut 1959 thriller which launched twelve-year-old Hayley Mills upon us. As a pinched and plain dockland waif she spies on Horst Buchholz committing murder and then protects him. John Mills as the law, sees justice done. (*b/w*)

Tiger in the Smoke √
Thriller with religious undertones, emphasised by making a clergyman (Laurence Naismith) and daughter (Muriel Pavlov) the objects of the evil Tony Wright's terrorising. He is searching for a treasure he thinks is priceless but which turns out to be beyond price (spiritually). Donald Sinden spends most of the film tied up. Roy Baker's opening sequence in the fog is justly celebrated as a small tour-de-force; but it sags a bit from then on; 1956. (*b/w*)

The Tiger Makes Out √
From Murray Schisgal's play that he adapted for this weakened comedy. When Eli Wallach and his wife Anne Jackson toured it, there were two parts; now there are forty more speaking roles, including some amusing little cameos. But Arthur Hiller directs it unsurely. Wallach is now a postman who grabs typist Jackson and together they make a bid for freedom from urban anonymity; 1968. (*c*)

Tight Spot √√
Ginger Rogers is in it. She's a gangster's moll who is threatening to blow the gaff and all sorts of people are out to get her, including boss Lorne Greene. Mostly shot in an hotel room, where she is being guarded, thus betraying its theatre origins, it nevertheless builds up a pretty strong feeling of suspense, as Edward G. Robinson helps to guard her–or is he the one who's waiting his chance to do her in? Phil Karlson directs surely and tautly; 1955. (*b/w*)

Till Death Us Do Part √
The 1969 extended flashback into how Alf Garnett and family got that way, adequately directed by Norman Cohen. The usual family, plus Liam Redmond, Bill Maynard, Brian Blessed, Sam Kydd, starts at 1939 and tells the Garnett Saga. (*c*)

Till the Clouds Roll By ✕
Marvellous songs in otherwise tepid biography of Jerome Kern with a pregnant (with Liza) Judy Garland hiding the fact behind a pile of pots and pans in the late-shot Look for the Silver Lining. Lena Horne, singing Show Boat songs, was cut out for Deep South cinemas because whites joined in with her. Frank Sinatra singing You And Me We Sweat And Strain is wildly unconvincing in his immaculate white suit. Richard Whorf directed this 1946 mish-mash; musical numbers directed by Judy Garland's husband Vincente Minnelli; 1946. (*c*)

Tillie's Punctured Romance √√
Charlie Chaplin's early two-reelers are far superior to later, more pretentious full-lengths. Marie Dressler, Mabel Normand add lustre to this 1914 fortune-hunting saga. (*b/w*)

Timberjack √
Sterling Hayden fights the lumber crooks who may have killed his father. Joseph Kane directed cheerfully in 1955, with the confidence that having Adolphe Menjou and Hoagy Carmichael in the cast gave him. (*c*)

Timbuktu ✕✕
Slow, weak World War 2 drama with

Sudanese and French plots and counter-plots. Jacques Tourneur could do little with soft script and casting of Victor Mature, Yvonne de Carlo; 1959. (*b/w*)

Time Limit √ √
Karl Malden's first and only attempt at directing turned out so well that it's surprising he hasn't repeated the experiment. This taut courtroom story of an army colonel accused of collaborating with the Communists while a POW in Korea holds the attention all through; the dramatic moments are well-defined; the characters (Richard Basehart as the accused, Richard Widmark as the accuser, Martin Balsam as a sergeant providing some light relief) convincing; the denouement surprising enough. Unfortunately, Henry Denker's script makes some assumptions about the self-evident evils of Communism that look naive today, but as a product of its time, 1957, it's acceptable. (*b/w*)

Time Lock √
Quite exciting little British thriller set in a Canadian bank where a child has got trapped in a large safe; can they get it open before he suffocates? Gerald Thomas directed this one in 1957, before he started Carrying On. His only known star in the cast was Robert Beatty, but down at the very bottom of the credits there's '2nd welder, Sean Connery'. (*b/w*)

The Time Machine √
George Pal took the first section of H. G. Wells' visionary novel and reduced it to Hollywood proportions in 1960. What remains is acceptable sci-fi, however, with beautifully-designed sets and special effects that won an Oscar. Rod Taylor, Yvette Mimieux. (*c*)

Time of Indifference ×
Afraid it is; you won't be able to get very involved in this heavy yarn of Rod Steiger involved with mother Paulette Goddard (making a failed attempt at comeback in 1963) and daughter Claudia Cardinale. Director Francesco Maselli hasn't been able to convey the essence of Moravia's novel; supports Shelley Winters, Tomas Milian don't help. (*b/w*)

The Time of Your Life √
William Saroyan's talky-talky philosophising in a San Francisco bar lacked the dramatic backbone to make a gripping film, but it has its moments. Very much a Cagney affair, James took the main part, sister Jeanne the whore he freeloads off, brother William produced it. What chance had director H. C. Potter? 1948. (*b/w*)

A Time to Love and a Time to Die ×
Pretentious yarn about Germany during the Second World War written by *All Quiet's* Erich Maria Remarque (who plays the sympathetic part of a professor in it himself). John Gavin and Lilo Pulver are debut-leads. Douglas Sirk directed a blown-up, heavy-handed adaptation (of a novel) which drags on and on in seemingly unending (133 minutes of cinema time) boredom, detailing the fighting and leaves of one German soldier from the Russian front. The final indignity is that we are supposed to sympathise with this fighter for fascism and not the Russian guerrilla who finally does for him; 1958. (*c*)

The Time Travellers √
Marooned in the horrible future, a small band of explorers, led by Preston Foster, battle their way through mutants, robots, guerrilla survivors, and sundry clichés. Director-writer Ib Melchior manages to make it look fairly fresh; 1965. (*c*)

Time Without Pity √
Flashy public resumption of Joseph Losey's career in 1957 (he had been under a Red ban in America and had to

make films under pseudonyms until given this chance) is conventional tale of will-the-real-murderer-be-revealed-before-the-innocent-man-is-hanged? Michael Redgrave is Dad, desperately trying to prove innocence of son Alec McCowen (marvellous). Real killer is absurdly over-acting Leo McKern (this is no giveaway–the film has a prologue spoiling its own plot). Small parts well cast: Renée Houston, George Devine, Joan Plowright, Peter Cushing among those present. (*b/w*)

The Tingler √
Incredible but frightening theory is there's an insect at the bottom of your spine that fright activates, only to be assuaged by screaming; so deaf-and-dumb girl is perfect guinea pig. Then insect gets loose. Seats at film's 1959 premiere were wired with electric shocks to add to screaming. Vincent Price; director William Castle. (*b/w*)

Tin Pan Alley ×
Naïve song-and-dancer set pre-First World War. Alice Faye, Betty Grable, Jack Oakie. Directed by Walter Lang; 1940. (*b/w*)

The Tin Star √ √
Made in 1957 by Anthony Mann, who helped bring Westerns out of the Saturday morning cinema, it's in the classic law and order mould. Henry Fonda, a cool, laconic cowboy, is bounty-hunter asked for help by fresh-man sheriff Anthony Perkins. Reminis-cent of *Shane* (the lone stranger ridin' in from the prairie) and *High Noon* (the reluctant sheriff), it doesn't denigrate these elements, and its characterisation is of a high order. (*b/w*)

Tip on a Dead Jockey √
Irwin Shaw story provides Robert Taylor with unusually animated vehicle for his somewhat stiff talents; he's a retired flyer in Madrid who decides that

smuggling might be a useful money-bringer; Gia Scala and Martin Gabel stand out; Richard Thorpe; 1957. (*b/w*)

Titanic √
Not as impressive as *A Night to Remember*, on the same subject, but this 1953 American effort to do a *Bridge of San Luis Rey* on the sinking of the liner passes muster. Clifton Webb, Barbara Stanwyck, Robert Wagner, Audrey Dalton are among the passen-gers, and Jean Negulesco does better with their personal dramas than the epic special effects. (*b/w*)

The Titfield Thunderbolt √
One of those eccentric English comedies making a hero out of a piece of machinery, this time a local train. The usual jolly jokey jossers (Stanley Hollo-way, Hugh Griffith, Naunton Wayne) rescue an antique locomotive and keep their Bluebell Line running, despite underhand goings-on. Mildly amusing. Charles Crichton; 1953. (*b/w*)

The Toast of New Orleans ×
A bit burnt round the edges. Director Norman Taurog, who later made a career out of pushing Elvis Presley through a series of unmemorable motion pictures, had Mario Lanza and Kathryn Grayson to humanise in 1950. Their singing's fine, but when they start trying to act, he quickly turns the camera towards David Niven, J. Carrol Naish and James Mitchell–not always soon enough. It's a long way to the *Madame Butterfly* finale when the young fisher-man at the turn-of-the-century is finally launched into a successful career as an opera star. (*c*)

Tobacco Road √
Made in 1941, the year after his *Grapes of Wrath*, this superficially similar effort by John Ford is derived from Erskine Caldwell's novel about poor whites in the Deep South via a Broadway theatre

adaptation. It lost its vitality (to be polite) under the censor's scissors; Charley Grapewin and Marjorie Rambeau grimace; Gene Tierney was miscast under Darryl Zanuck's orders; 1941. (*b/w*)

To Be or Not to Be √ √
Delightful Ernst Lubitsch comedy about actors outwitting the nazis as Poland falls. This was Carole Lombard's last film (1942) and is fitting memorial to her gaiety and witty way with a line. Jack Benny, Sig Ruman, Lionel Atwill all super. (*b/w*)

Tobruk ✕
Unbelievable war story made unbelievably in 1967, by which time you would have thought the time for cheap heroics about the Second World War was over. Director Arthur Hiller doesn't seem to think so and we get the old only-man-who-can-save-the-war stuff from Rock Hudson, stiff-upper-lip fanatic George Peppard, martinet Nigel Green, Cockney sparrer Norman Rossington and so on. The only ingenious bit is the opening when German frogmen capture Hudson: they turn out to be German Jewish frogmen–on our side. (*c*)

To Catch a Thief √
Lightweight Hitchcock set in a Riviera that came out looking disappointingly phoney. In fact, the whole plot's awfully cheaty, with Cary Grant an unconvincing cat-burglar who has to catch the 'Cat' so that he will cease to be under suspicion himself. Grace Kelly (with what Hitch called her 'indirect sex appeal') is the girl who surprises Grant (and, intentionally, the audience) with her forwardness; 1955. (*c*)

To Have and Have Not √
Humphrey Bogart and Lauren Bacall and the basic plot of fishermen involved in hanky-panky reset in the second World War (it was made in 1944) didn't improve Hemingway's story, although it made an above-routine romantic thriller, directed by Michael Curtiz. Since then, it has twice been refilmed, but not under its own name. In 1951, it became *The Breaking Point* with John Garfield and in 1958 *The Gun Runners* with Audie Murphy. (*b/w*)

To Hell and Back √
And on to Hollywood. Audie Murphy's best-selling autobiography of how a poor boy became America's most-decorated war hero, made a perfectly acceptable vehicle for actor Audie Murphy, who had already made five pictures by the time he got round to this one, in 1955. Most of it doesn't convince –due to a poor script and unimaginative direction by Jesse Hibbs–but the battle scenes take on a special sort of excitement from Murphy's presence. (*c*)

To Kill a Mockingbird √
Superficially a fine, even great, sermon on racial tensions, involving the defence (by Gregory Peck) of a black (Brock Peters) unjustly accused of murder, all seen from a child's viewpoint. Robert Mulligan's direction was hailed as 'sensitive' and 'daring' at the time (1963) but Horton Foote's adaptation of Harper Lee's novel has a very hollow centre. Can you believe in the morally white-washed black, the Southern court and the handy ending? Peck did, and it won him an Oscar. (*b/w*)

Tokyo Joe ✕
Sad to see Humphrey Bogart in the middle of all this stupid carrying-on about blackmail and counter-threats in post-War Tokyo, compounded by heroics over a 'sweet' little girl of 7. Under Stuart Heisler, it lacks sharpness or the necessary sardonic quality; 1949. (*b/w*)

Tomahawk √
Van Heflin, friend of the Indians, versus

Alex Nichol, Indian killer. More interesting for its premature pro-Indian sentiment (it was made in 1951) and some of the supports director George Sherman managed to work in: Preston Foster, Jack Oakie, Yvonne de Carlo from the veterans; Rock Hudson, Tom Tully among the up-and-comers. (*c*)

The Tomb of Ligeia √√
Poe's favourite story and Poe's great film-interpreter Roger Corman's best work of this genre. How Vincent Price came to free himself of his dead wife's hypnotic will and how she takes revenge on him from the grave; 1965. (*c*)

Tomboy and the Champ ××
Sickly confection of child (the repulsive Candy Moore) and animal (an Angus bull named Champy) she grooms to win the Chicago Prize. Only then does she realise that he will be sold for steak; she collapses and is only saved from death or something by the appearance of Champy by her hospital bed. There's a ghastly Parson Dan (Jess Kirkpatrick) wandering through the film pointing up heavenly morals as fast as he can. What was John Ford's Ben Johnson (as Uncle Jim) doing in a mess like this? The director was Francis D. Lyon; 1962. (*c*)

Tom Brown's Schooldays ××
(1) 1939 version had Cedric Hardwicke as Dr Arnold, Freddie Bartholomew, and a cast of absurd Americans as the other inmates of Rugby. Robert Stevenson. (*b/w*)

Tom Brown's Schooldays ×
(2) 1951 version had Robert Newton as a less than satisfactory Arnold, John Howard Davies as a wispy Tom, but some solid support from James Hayter, Michael Hordern, Diana Wynyard. Gordon Parry directed from a just-competent Noel Langley script under Brian Desmond Hurst as producer. (*b/w*)

Tom Jones √√
Rollicking, bawdy, hugely enjoyable free adaptation of Fielding's novel by John Osborne and Tony Richardson, in 1963. Albert Finney's foundling-to-gallows-via-a-thousand-beds hero is nicely done, and matched by the creations he comes up against: the delicious Susannah York, his final reward; Hugh Griffith's bellowing squire; Edith Evans, outrageous among the cows; Joyce Redman's succulent dining companion; Diane Cilento's slut; the list could go on and on. Walter Lassally's camerawork is particularly brilliant, never letting down the fun, often adding to it. Oscars won for best film, best direction (Richardson) and John Addison's music. (*c*)

Tom Thumb √
Russ Tamblyn (youngest boy in *Seven Brides for Seven Brothers*) makes a more than adequate Tom in this mixed live-and cartoon-and-special-effects children's film, and Terry-Thomas and Peter Sellers make a splendid pair of robbers. George Pal produced and directed in 1958 with a happy command of technical tricks. Rotten choreography. (*c*)

Tonight We Sing ×
The music's all right but the story is terrible. One of those biopics that bear almost no relation to the way it must really have happened. The mythical figure being biographied here is Sol Hurok the impresario. David Wayne made a ludicrous Hurok—for anyone who knows what the real one was like. Anne Bancroft does her best with silly lines and plots. Even the artistes aren't really very gripping—Enzio Pinza, Roberta Peters, Tamara Toumanova, Isaac Stern. Director Mitchell Leisen was saddled with an impossible task; 1953. (*c*)

Tony Draws a Horse ××
Pathetic little British comedy about

rows between psychologist and wife over correct attitude towards their graffiti-oriented little boy. Cecil Parker, Anne Crawford, Derek Bond, Barbara Murray make it rather heavy going under John Paddy Carstairs' uninspired direction; 1951. (*b/w*)

Tony Rome √√
The first time in his long career that Frank Sinatra played a private detective was in this 1967 thriller which, besides Sinatra, managed to show a lot of Miami and Jill St John. Suspiciously like Chandler's *The Big Sleep*, it provoked comparisons with Bogart's portrayal of Philip Marlowe in that; and while nobody could match Bogie, Sinatra does better than anyone else ever has since. The plot's to do with a wayward heiress (Sue Lyon), stepmother (Gena Rowlands) and some jewels, real and fake. Director: Gordon Douglas. (*c*)

Too Hot to Handle √√
(1) Delightful 1938 typical pre-war crackling comedy with Clark Gable and Walter Pidgeon scrapping over Myrna Loy; they are newsreel photographers, with Gable not too scrupulous. Jack Conway. (*b/w*)

Too Hot to Handle ×××
(2) Really awful melo about Soho crooks, involving Jayne Mansfield as night-club singer and some unbelievable stuff about a club-owner (Leo Genn, manager Christopher Lee) she fancies. Terence Young directed with as much flair as the script by Herbert Kretzmer allowed: none; 1960. (*c*)

Too Late Blues √
John Cassavetes' first attempt at a commercial film, after *Shadows*, in 1959, two years before. Bobby Darin, Stella Stevens go through quasi-improvised motions under his aegis, about a jazz musician pinching a blonde from his mate. (*b/w*)

Too Many Crooks √
Mario Zampi directed, 1958, this tale of bungling kidnappers using undertakers as cover and laid on a few surreal touches with help of Terry-Thomas, George Cole, Sid James. Point of the plot is that wife Brenda de Banzie is upset to find that hubby Terry-Thomas is only too glad to have her snaffled, so in revenge takes over gang-leadership and collects the cash for herself. There's a soft ending, of course, it being a British comedy. Fascinatingly, this same plot was used nine years later for *The Happening* only here the story becomes a tragedy. (*b/w*)

Too Much, Too Soon ××
Sub-title: The Daring Story of Diana Barrymore. John's daughter romanced a lot, drank a lot and married three times. Dorothy Malone had the impossible task of playing her while she was still alive. The only interest in this rotten film, poorly directed by Art Napoleon in 1958, was that it was one of the last Errol Flynn (playing his old drinking companion John Barrymore) was to make. Jack L. Warner later wrote: 'I could not bear to watch him struggle through take after take ... He was playing the part of a drunken actor and he didn't need any method system to get him in the mood. He *was* drunk. "Too much too soon". The words should have been carved on a tombstone at the time, for he was one of the living dead.' (*b/w*)

Too Young to Kiss ×
Minor comedy (reminiscent of *The Major and the Minor*, in fact) with pouting June Allyson dressing up as 13-year-old so that she can be discovered by Van Johnson as child prodigy pianist. Gig Young, her fiancé, is naturally upset, even more so when she falls in love with Johnson. Billy Wilder would have turned it into satire on *Lolita*; but Robert Z. Leonard settles for the obvious; 1951. (*b/w*)

Too Young to Love ✗✗✗
Woefully out of date when it was made in 1960, this making-over of Elsa Shelley's always unbelievable, sensational play *Pick-Up Girl*, seems like one of those warnings against promiscuity that well-meaning but ineffective VD campaigns used to put over. Direction (by Muriel Box), acting (gruff Thomas Mitchell as a kindly judge, strident Joan Miller as Mum, unconvincing Pauline Hahn as the 15-year-old wayward lass) script (Muriel and Sydney Box) all outdo each other in awfulness. (*b/w*)

To Paris with Love ✗✗
Alec Guinness starring, Robert Hamer directing should have produced a more engaging comedy than this one of a widower taking his son to the Wicked City to learn the facts of life. Desperately dated; 1955. (*b/w*)

Topaz ✗
Hitchcock's least favourite among his own films is this 1969 lulu about the 1962 Cuban missile crisis. Abandoning his usual intimate style, Hitch follows Leon Uris's novel round the world and allows outrageous coincidence to play too large a part. There are few typically interesting touches. Non-stars Frederick Stafford, Dany Robin, John Forsythe serve him adequately. (*c*)

Top Gun ✗
Sterling Hayden is found Not Guilty on murder charge and gets elected marshal instead. Rod Taylor has a small part. Ray Nazarro made this into routine Western; 1955. (*b/w*)

Topkapi ✓✓
Director Jules Dassin repeated his *Rififi* caper in spades (or at least in colour and with comedy) in 1964 with theft of jewel-encrusted dagger from museum in excitingly-photographed Istanbul. Joy to watch Peter Ustinov, Robert Morley, Akim Tamiroff, Melina Mercouri upstaging each other. (*c*)

To Please a Lady ✓
Clark Gable as unpopular racing driver and Barbara Stanwyck as tough columnist are nominal stars of this rather obvious yarn, but the cars and the Indianapolis track are the real standout feature. Strictly for small boys; director Clarence Brown; 1950. (*b/w*)

Top of the World ✗
Triangle stuff between Evelyn Keyes, ex-husband Dale Robertson, boyfriend Frank Lovejoy. Dale's a jet pilot who is assigned to find them, lost in the wilds of Alaska. Lewis R. Foster keeps it from getting frozen right up; 1955. (*b/w*)

Torch Song ✓
It's burning bright for Joan Crawford, though the rest of the cast (Michael Wilding as a blind pianist, Gig Young as a Broadway parasite, Mom Marjorie Rambeau) don't get much of a look in. Centre-stage the whole time (she could rely on 'her' director, Charles Walters), she struts about, throwing tantrums, doing a bit of a dance, moving her lips (while India Adam's voice issues forth in song), and gradually realising True Love; 1953. (*c*)

Tormented ✗✗
Richard Carlson unconvincing as haunted (literally) jazz pianist, worried that he shouldn't marry. Bert I. Gordon can't make this nonsense work; 1960. (*b/w*)

Torn Curtain ✗✗
One of Alfred Hitchcock's less successful thrillers, it suffered from a poor script (Brian Moore) and unfortunate performances from Julie Andrews (never the greatest actress in the world nor the most docile to direct) and Paul Newman (he found it hard to get on with Hitch, who wanted him to play it like Cary

Grant). Main trouble was the ambience of Iron Curtain spying which by 1966 had gone into the cold. (*c*)

Torpedo Alley ✕
Lew Landers' direction makes this routine Korea plot about grounded flier becoming submariner a bit more acceptable than otherwise. Dorothy Malone brings Mark Stevens romance in hospital; 1953. (*b/w*)

Torpedo Run ✕ ✕
Glenn Ford, his cute little face in tormented grimace, vows revenge for his wife and child who were on a boat he sank when the wicked Japs were using it to screen their aircraft carrier. He dogs the carrier, with Ernest Borgnine as fellow-officer. Director Joseph Pevney isn't helped by the script; 1958. (*c*)

The Torture Garden √
Four short horror films, directed somewhat obviously by Freddie Francis, strung together by Burgess Meredith foretelling the future of a disparate group of characters–for the sole purpose of fitting in the stories. Michael Bryant is faced with a man-eating domestic cat; John Standing with a spooky piano; and Peter Cushing with Jack Palance; 1968. (*c*)

To Sir, with Love ✕
Sidney Poitier as black teacher in an East End school taming wild about-to-be-leavers, doesn't convince. It makes for a cosy tract on kindliness being better than brutality. As pupils, Judy Geeson and Lulu do better than the direction, by James Clavell, has any right to expect. This was a big success in America, where they don't know what British schools are really like; 1967. (*c*)

To the Ends of the Earth √
Dick Powell as US agent tracking drug ring all over the place. Has twist ending. Robert Stevenson; 1948. (*b/w*)

To Trap a Spy ✕
Early UNCLE rip-off has Robert Vaughn, David McCallum repeating their then-fresh, now-tired double act. Don Medford; 1966. (*c*)

Touch and Go ✕ ✕
It's touch and go whether you'll stay awake through this old-fashioned (vintage 1954, but it seems earlier) comedy about why Jack Hawkins and family (Margaret Johnston, June Thorburn) can't get their emigration to Australia under way. Director Michael Truman. (*c*)

Touch of Evil √ √
Orson Welles was writer, director, and heavily disguised actor in this absorbing movie about corruption down Mexico way, although Charlton Heston and Janet Leigh don't seem much at home in the steamy, dark border country between Mexico and the USA and between death and degradation. All sorts of players rallied round in 1958 to give old Orson a hand: Marlene Dietrich as a brothel-keeper; Joseph Calleia and Akim Tamiroff, matching him in seediness; Joseph Cotten and Ray Collins from *Kane*; a highly sinister Mercedes McCambridge. You may find it overdrawn and outrageous but many cinéastes include it among their favourite films. (*b/w*)

Touch of Larceny √
Comedy-thriller combining a multitude of talents with slightly disappointing results: James Mason, George Sanders, Peter Barkworth, Harry Andrews, John Le Mesurier; scriptwriter Roger Mac-Dougall, director Guy Hamilton and producer Ivan Foxwell; even an assistant director was Peter Yates. James Mason carries the fun along, not always succeeding in his involved schemes for making money but coming out OK in the end–if not quite morally; 1959. (*b/w*)

A Touch of Love √
Old-fashioned (for 1969) weepie about pregnant Sandy Dennis spurning father-of-the-child Ian McKellen, a TV newsreader (so that she and we can continually see him on her little screen). She's not a Bad Girl, though, it was her first time – which seems a bit retarded of her at 32. She's also nicely playing around with Michael Coles and John Standing. Director Waris Hussein seems over-awed at having Hollywood star Dennis in his first feature film. He has let her get away with hogging the screen from a cross-section of solid Armchair Theatre supports, which is of course easy enough when a script comes from one of Margaret Drabble's woman-centred novels. (*c*)

The Toughest Gun in Tombstone ✕
George Montgomery poses as a villain in order to winkle out Johnny Ringo's gang. Beverly Tyler as girl in the way. Earl Bellamy as director in the way of this becoming more than routine Western; 1958. (*b/w*)

The Toughest Man Alive ✕
Same plot as immediately prior entry, only this time it's Dane Clark pretending to be villain, in order to round up gun-smuggling gang in South America. Sidney Salkow; 1955. (*b/w*)

The Toughest Man in Arizona √
Vaughn Monroe falls for Joan Leslie, gets deeper into crusade against crime on the frontier than he intended. R. G. Springsteen kept up the excitement moderately well in 1952. (*c*)

Toward the Unknown √
Superior test-pilot stuff, involving rocket-planes and William Holden's fight to inspire confidence despite past mistakes. Mervyn LeRoy produced and directed; 1956. (*c*)

Tower of London √
Vincent Price in a Poe-faced telling of the Tragedy of Richard III by Roger Corman in 1962. A remake of the 1939 version by Rowland V. Lee, with Basil Rathbone as Richard. Vincent Price was in that one, too – as Clarence. (*b/w*)

A Town Like Alice √
This is Virginia McKenna and friends having a rough time of it after the Japs invade. Stalwart Peter Finch and director Jack Lee defeated in attempt at documentary realism by poor studio sets. Altogether too episodic and sadistically loaded with suffering for its own sake; 1956. (*b/w*)

Town on Trial √
Patchily interesting whodunit about the wild girl at the tennis club getting done in, with John Mills as class-conscious detective. Alec McCowen, Elizabeth Seal, Maureen Connell fine; Charles Coburn, Barbara Bates out of place in Home Counties. Director John Guillermin was obviously striving to make more than just a routine thriller, and nearly succeeds; 1956. (*b/w*)

Town Without Pity √
Defending four GIS accused of rape, Kirk Douglas has to discredit the victim. Hating himself for his task, he nevertheless goes on with it. Gottfried Reinhardt manages well enough with the German actors (notably Christine Kaufmann as the girl) but is too concerned at getting over a woolly message about justice and humanity to make the film incisive; 1961. (*b/w*)

Toys in the Attic √
Wendy Hiller and Geraldine Page make this 1963 adaptation of Lillian Hellman play worth watching despite Dean Martin and Yvette Mimieux as timid husband and child wife. George Roy Hill directed with panache. (*b/w*)

Toy Tiger ✕
Jeff Chandler, ad-man, finds himself

adopted as pseudo-big-game hunter by little boy at school, and has to oblige. Pretty soft stuff, with Laraine Day as Mom. Director: Jerry Hopper; 1956. (*c*)

Track of the Cat　　　　　　　√
Robert Mitchum and Teresa Wright are nominal stars of 1954 cougar hunt, but William Wellman's experiment in cinephotography is main interest. As snow covers the ground, he is able to try filming a black-and-white subject with colour film. The startling dramatic intrusion of colour every now and again is highly effective. (*c*)

Track the Man Down　　　　　　×
If this murder-at-the-dog-track drama seems out of true, it's because an American director was imported to shoot it. R. G. Springsteen, veteran of so many Westerns, was ill-at-ease with such British character players as Renée Houston, Pet Clark, George Rose; although his lead, Kent Taylor, arrived with him. Still, that's the kind of loopy compromise they made in 1953 when all that mattered was showing the films in America. (*b/w*)

The Train　　　　　　　　√ √
Stunning action sequences as fanatical Paul Scofield tries to get train-load of French masterpieces to his masters in Germany while French resistance leader Burt Lancaster tries to stop him. If only John Frankenheimer had given as much attention to the over-simplified characters and their philosophies as he did to the spectacular train-ride this really would be a three-tick pic. Michel Simon, Jeanne Moreau among your actual French; 1964. (*b/w*)

The Traitor　　　　　　　　√
A double whodunit: who was the traitor in the German underground movement that betrayed them and is thus on the spot at their reunion? And who killed the messenger with the evidence that would have done for him? Donald Wolfit, Rupert Davies, Anton Diffring are among those present. Writer-director Michael McCarthy kept his camera too much in the house where they were reuniting–but perhaps that was the fault of the budget? 1956. (*b/w*)

The Traitors　　　　　　　× ×
Uninspired spy-chase round London, with Patrick Allen and James Maxwell as chasers. Robert Tronson; 1962. (*b/w*)

Traitor's Gate　　　　　　× ×
Churned-out Edgar Wallace thriller about two brothers in plot to steal the Crown Jewels. Gary Raymond, Albert Lieven; director Freddie Francis in a hurry; 1955. (*b/w*)

The Trap　　　　　　　　　√
(1) 1959 thriller with Lee J. Cobb as head of a crime syndicate on the run; Richard Widmark determined to catch him. But the gangsters' pals move in to rescue him. Norman Panama who directed and produced with partner Mel Frank are better known for their comedies, but managed well in 1959. (*c*)

The Trap　　　　　　　　　×
(2) 1967 co-Canadian effort with Oliver Reed buying mute Rita Tushingham to be his trapper-wife. She has to amputate his leg and finds that she loves him. As corny as it sounds, it's almost saved by Tush's winning performance and the scenery. Sidney Hayers; 1966. (*c*)

Trapeze　　　　　　　　　√
The daring young man is Burt Lancaster playing a cripple who can't walk without a stick but is still capable of performing great feats of partner-catching on the trapeze. The whole film's a bit like that, lame on the ground in its trite and familiar story of the two swingers (Tony Curtis is the other one) both in love with the lady in the act, Gina Lollobrigida. But in the air the doubling is

neatly done and Carol Reed's camera does some dizzy work; 1956. (*c*)

Trauma ✕
One of those long-way-after-*Psycho* thrillers churned out in the years following that 1960 masterpiece. This one, 1962, is about a shocked girl, who is married for her money and set up for murder. John Conte, Lynn Bari, Lorrie Richards can't do much under Robert Malcolm Young's direction. (*b/w*)

Tread Softly Stranger ✕✕✕
This candidate for Stinker of 1958 (and the next decade) is about two brothers who get involved with thieving and killing because one of them is infatuated with good-time girl Diana Dors. George Baker and Terence Morgan compete for the accolade of Worst Performance, but have some handy opposition in Patrick Allen and Miss Dors, who doubtless blame the awful script and the direction of Gordon Parry. (*b/w*)

Treasure Island ✓✓
1934, classic Wallace Beery-Jackie Cooper version; Victor Fleming directed. More yo-ho-ho, less bottle of rum than Robert Newton's later, 1950 effort with Byron Haskin. (*b/w*)

The Treasure of Lost Canyon ✕
One of those money-can't-buy-happiness movies (you wonder why the producers were so keen to make money on them), this time about a small boy uncovering some treasure and almost ruining the lives of his family with their new-found wealth. William Powell brings some distinction as an old prospector, but otherwise Ted Tetzlaff's direction doesn't manage to add credibility; 1952. (*c*)

The Treasure of Monte Cristo ✕
(1) 1949: directed by William Berke. Adele Jergens marries Glenn Langan for his money; then she truly falls in love with him. (*b/w*)

The Treasure of Monte Cristo ✕
(2) 1960: one more rip-off of Dumas, with Rory Calhoun imported into Britain by Monty Berman and Roy S. Baker to help Patricia Bredin dig up treasure. (*c*)

The Treasure of Pancho Villa ✓
Mercenary Rory Calhoun hijacking train in 1915 Mexico on behalf of revolutionary Villa. He and Shelley Winters, as his blowsy girl-friend, are acted off the screen by veterans Gilbert Roland and Joseph Calleia. Director George Sherman keeps it moving and doesn't waste time with the script's pretensions; 1955. (*c*)

Treasure of Ruby Hills ✕
Some useful Westerners – Zachary Scott, Barton MacLane, Lola Albright, Dick Foran – in tiredly directed (Frank McDonald), rather obvious story of land-raiders; 1955. (*b/w*)

Treasure of the Golden Condor ✕
Director Delmer Daves camps up this yarn about Cornel Wilde, cheated out of his rightful inheritance in France, seeking his fortune in 18th-century Guatemala. Fay Wray a welcome addition to 1953 cast. (*c*)

The Treasure of Sierra Madre ✓✓✓
Stunning adventure story that has been copied so many times since that it may seem over-familiar, but John Huston (seen as tourist near start) rightly won both writing and directing Oscars in 1948 and his father Walter Huston ('All I had to tell Dad was talk fast') the Award for best support. B. Traven himself probably acted as technical adviser, although the author of the original novel hid under identity of 'old friend and translator, Hal Croves'. Humphrey Bogart never surpassed his dramatic acting as the vulnerable, greedy Dobbs, and Tim Holt keeps his end up as third of trio of gold-searchers.
(*b/w*)

Trent's Last Case ✗
E. C. Bentley's classic 1913 detective story is almost proof against even Herbert Wilcox's heavy directorial hand in this 1952 version. Orson Welles gives a touch of distinction to straightforward casting of the flowers (albeit a little faded) of the British screen: Michael Wilding, Margaret Lockwood, Hugh McDermott. Where was Anna Neagle? (*b/w*)

Trial √
Murder trial of Mexican boy exploited by fellow-travelling organisation; belongs in Hollywood's 1955 Red-baiting era, but Mark Robson does adequate directorial job. Arthur Kennedy, as double-dealing lawyer, steals it from Glenn Ford and Dorothy McGuire. (*b/w*)

The Trials of Oscar Wilde √
Although it reached the cinema five days after the rival Robert Morley *Oscar Wilde* in 1960, this won the critical battle. Peter Finch was moving as Wilde, Lionel Jeffries frightening as the Marquess of Queensberry, James Mason splendid as prosecutor Carson. Ken Hughes wrote and directed. (*c*)

Tribute to a Bad Man ✗
Well, not really bad, only ruthless. James Cagney plays a cattle baron who makes his own laws; despite this, he has a heart of gold and is loved by Irene Papas. Role was originally intended for Spencer Tracy, who was fired for arguing about the script; he was well out of it—apart from lovely pictures, Robert Wise didn't make much of a job of it in 1956. (*c*)

Trio √
Three good Maugham stories directed rather stiffly by Ken Annakin and Harold French; the ones about the illiterate, rich man (James Hayter); the ship-board bore with rather more to him (Nigel Patrick); and romance in a sanitorium (Jean Simmons, Michael Rennie); 1951. (*b/w*)

Triple Cross ✗ ✗
The Eddie Chapman Story was a book that claimed that a former safe-cracker was a wartime double agent. Whether the story was true or not, this James Bond-type film about him, directed by James Bond director Terence Young, makes one believe that it was all non-sense. Everything about this melodrama –from Chapman's easy acceptance by the Germans to his literally incredible expertise with their language, Morse Code and guns–stinks of fiction. Nor are any of the cast convincing – Christopher Plummer makes a self-satisfied Chapman, and Yul Brynner as a German Baron, Romy Schneider as a bedroom lady and Trevor Howard as a British intelligence man are all from stock; 1967. (*c*)

Triple Deception ✗
Guy Green's French location filming helps this incredible yarn about an impostor and a murder ring. Michael Craig plays the con-man, but Brenda de Banzie helps out splendidly; 1956. (*c*)

Trooper Hook √
Summarily dismissed at the time (1957) as being just another Western, this story of Barbara Stanwyck scorned for having co-habited with Apache and borne him a child, was forerunner of a new line in socially-conscious oaters. Joel McCrea gave authority to the part of the soldier who marries her despite the prejudice; Earl Holliman and Susan Kohner add sympathetic performances. Director Charles Marquis Warren deserves a hand for trying. (*b/w*)

Trouble Along the Way ✗ ✗
A right sickly mess, mixing football and religion with custody of children and falling in love with a social worker. Central figure is wooden John Wayne as coach on the skids, saved by God, the grid-iron and Donna Reed. Michael Curtiz directs professionally enough to

disguise the worst moments, but it's an awful lot to take; 1953. (*b/w*)

Trouble Brewing　　　　　　　×
Ghastly enough to be almost enjoyable–George Formby trying to become private eye in 1939. Anthony Kimmins keeps fun going with Googie Withers, Ronald Shiner, Martita Hunt. (*b/w*)

Trouble in Paradise　　　　√ √ √
Delicious comedy of manners. The most famous Lubitsch movie, 1932. Miriam Hopkins and Herbert Marshall are crooks who both get jobs in Kay Francis' household; Edward Everett Horton gorgeously spends whole film trying to remember where he has seen Miriam before. Starts with Venetian gondolier singing O Sole Mio from what is revealed as a garbage boat–and never lets up. (*b/w*)

Trouble in Store　　　　　× ×
Strictly for Norman Wisdom fans, if any, this has him working in a department store. Margaret Rutherford gives it temporary moments, but John Paddy Carstairs' direction is awfully clumsy; 1953. (*b/w*)

Trouble in the Glen　　　　× ×
Orson Welles must have been down on his uppers in 1955 to appear in this dreadful Herbert Wilcox rip-off from *The Quiet Man* (same authors) about an American visitor caught by local feud, in Scotland this time. Forrest Tucker is the Yank, Margaret Lockwood the girl he falls for, Orson a local laird. Victor McLaglen is trundled in and out as another lure for American distribution, but the result is an embarrassment all round. (*c*)

The Troublemaker　　　　　√
Spotty but at times wildly amusing broad satire. Country-mouse-come-to-town formula allows co-writer and director Theodore J. Flicker (who also

appears) and friends from the stage company, The Premise, to send up Greenwich Village and a whole shooting gallery-full of targets. Among the company: Buck Henry (co-writer) and Godfrey Cambridge; among the film references: *Citizen Kane, Brute Force, The Third Man, The Victors.* Can you spot them? (*b/w*)

The Trouble With Angels　　　√
Tears (from Rosalind Russell) and coy jokes (from Hayley Mills) at the convent, as a Mother Superior learns not to be so superior, and a novice learns not to be such a nuisance. Ida Lupino; 1966. (*c*)

The Trouble With Harry　　　√
A black comedy in the sunshine–a corpse is found and buried and exhumed three times over. Several people think they killed the man and so stow away the evidence. Under Hitchcock's touch the worst longueurs of Jack Trevor Story's novel were avoided, and he gave Shirley MacLaine her first screen break here. One strains to appreciate it because of Hitch's imprimatur, but it's hard going; 1955. (*c*)

True as a Turtle　　　　　× ×
Weak little British comedy of 1957 about an old sailing ship. Cecil Parker captains her amateurishly, and a crew of minor players (John Gregson, June Thorburn, Keith Michell, Elvi Hale) get involved in a plan to swindle casinos with forged plastic chips. Wendy Toye directed cheerfully but weakly. (*c*)

True Grit　　　　　　　　√
At 62 (in 1969), John Wayne was still riding tall with the best of the lawmen, here hired to get the man (Jeff Corey) who killed Kim Darby's father; if Wayne was bitter, cursory and unpleasant, he wasn't meant to be all that sympathetic. Henry Hathaway–at 71, no

chicken himself – directed with the strength of experience. Reportedly, this is one of President Nixon's favourite movies and he runs it every now and then to remind himself of some of the great American virtues. (*c*)

The True Story of Jesse James √
Robert Wagner is 1956 Jesse in this not-really-very-true story (among other film Jesses: Ty Power, Lawrence Tierney, Macdonald Carey, Audie Murphy, Willard Parker), strongly supported by Nicholas Ray's cast – Agnes Moorehead, Alan Hale, John Carradine, Hope Lange. A superior job all round. (*c*)

The Trunk × ×
Elaborate plan to cheat lawyer and new bride backfires. So does the movie. Donovan Winter gathered a cast of weak players (Phil Carey, Julia Arnall, Dermot Walsh, Vera Day) to match his story; 1960. (*b/w*)

The Truth About Spring ×
John and Hayley Mills in yarn about a captain passing his daughter off as a starving boy – it's to cadge supplies from richer Caribbean boats. But he's found out by millionaire's son, James MacArthur, who helps him dish would-be treasure map thieves Harry Andrews and Lionel Jeffries. Director Richard Thorpe seemed to be taking a pleasant West Indian holiday in 1965, some way away from the crew who were filming this comedy of his. (*c*)

The Truth About Women × ×
Laurence Harvey flashbacking over his past with his five loves: feminist Diane Cilento, slave girl Jackie Lane, Parisienne Eva Gabor, American Julie Harris, Swedish Mai Zetterling. This British costumer was put on the circuits in 1958, without a West End showing. No wonder. Directed by Muriel Box. (*c*)

The Trygon Factor × ×
Susan Hampshire, Robert Morley, Stewart Granger in a farrago about smuggling nuns and a stately home where everyone is mad. Just doesn't work. Director, Cyril Frankel; 1967. (*c*)

Tumbleweed ×
Did Audie Murphy desert the wagon train when the Indians attacked? No, he was just saving the ladies by seeking a truce. Nathan Juran does what he can with suspicious townsfolk; 1953. (*c*)

Tunes of Glory √ √
Splendidly acted drama of character differences between rough, tough, hard-drinking Lt.-Col. Alec Guinness, successful wartime leader of Highland regiment, and his correct, by-the-book peacetime co, John Mills. The clash results in tragedy. Other plusses are Susannah York's first appearance and Ronald Neame's immaculate direction; 1960. (*c*)

The Tunnel of Love √
Peter de Vries novel was turned into a Doris Day vehicle, directed by Gene Kelly as musical without music. Richard Widmark, Gig Young, Gia Scala aid and abet adoption comedy. But it's soft-centred; 1958. (*b/w*)

The Turning Point √
Stuff about crime commission and how a reporter discovers that his chairman is sabotaging the good work. Edmond O'Brien is chief investigator, William Holden the reporter, but Ed Begley steals this one as he has so many of his movies. William Dieterle directs safely. 1952. (*b/w*)

Turn the Key Softly ×
How prison affected lives of three women. Over-wrought acting by Yvonne Mitchell, Joan Collins, Terence Morgan seems to have been encouraged by director Jack Lee in 1953. Kathleen

Harrison and Thora Hird back up gamely. (*b/w*)

Twelve Angry Men √√
1957 classic of one juror (Henry Fonda) holding out. Sidney Lumet directed this, his first classic, so tautly and cleverly that you are never conscious of the constrictions of the jury room. All the cast is brilliant–to identify them, start with foreman Martin Balsam and clockwise round the table they are: John Fielder, Lee J. Cobb, E. G. Marshall, Jack Klugman, Edward Binns, Jack Warden, Henry Fonda, Joseph Sweeney, Ed Begley, George Voskovec, Robert Webber. (*b/w*)

Twelve Hours to Kill √
Suspenser about newly-arrived Greek immigrant being chased round New York by murderers, as he was only witness of killing. Sadly Edward L. Cahn failed to extract maximum from locations or cast (Nico Minardos, Barbara Eden, Art Baker); 1960. (*b/w*)

Twelve o'clock High √
Gregory Peck getting too involved with his airmen on British base during Second World War. Highly efficient direction from Henry King helped Dean Jagger to win Oscar as Best Support; 1949. (*b/w*)

24 Hours to Kill ✕
Unoriginal title (see *Twelve . . .*, *Three . . .*) labels unoriginal suspenser about airline pilot Mickey Rooney being threatened by smuggling gang led by Walter Slezak when forced to land in Beirut. Director Peter Bezencenet failed to convince; 1965. (*c*)

20 Million Miles to Earth √
Zoologist and grand-daughter open sealed container from wrecked rockct ship in Italy. The jelly-like mass inside becomcs a clawed monster that soon doubles in size. Director Nathan Juran

didn't add much to the genre, but Ray Harryhausen's stunning special effects include the Venusian monster to end all monsters. William Hopper, Frank Puglia, Joan Taylor haven't much to do; 1957. (*b/w*)

Twenty Plus Two √
Private-eye David Janssen gets involved with missing heiress, glamour star and former fiancée, but still has time to unravel mystery. Good people: Jeanne Crain, Agnes Moorehead. Poor direction: Joseph Newman. Over-ambitious script: producer Frank Gruber; 1961. (*b/w*)

The 27th Day √
Five people, in different parts of the earth, are each given capsule with which they can destroy a continent. Behaving more intelligently than in most sci-fi movies, they realise that this will just let in the Alien Civilisation who handed them the power, despite pleas by their respective countries' leaders to use it against enemies. So they hide out, Gene Barry on a racecourse. Based on John Mantley's novel, it has the fault of a pat denouement, but William Asher makes it an unusually gripping tale of its type; 1957. (*b/w*)

23 Paces to Baker Street √
Modern detective story with deliberate echoes of Sherlock Holmes has Van Johnson as an amateur detective who's blind and Cecil Parker as his Watson-Jeeves. Henry Hathaway shot a lot of London locations, but it's basically a Hollywood mystery; 1956. (*c*)

Twice Round the Daffodils ✕
Carry On Nursing would have been a more appropriate title, as Carry On director-producer Gerald Thomas-Peter Rogers let loose a Carry On cast (Juliet Mills, Donald Sinden, Donald Houston, Lance Percival, Joan Sims, Kenneth Williams) in a TB ward. Presumably the

sentimental intrusions would have been out of place if it had been called that; 1962. (*b/w*)

Twice-Told Tales　　　　　　　√
Nathaniel Hawthorne's stories don't make obvious screen adaptations so it's to Sidney Salkow's great credit that they work so well, particularly as his 1963 cast of Vincent Price, Sebastian Cabot, Mari Blanchard are hardly distinguished actors. (*c*)

Twilight for the Gods　　　　　　✕
On a broken-down sailing boat sail a 'ship of fools', running away from the South Seas to Mexico. Among them: Rock Hudson, Cyd Charisse, Arthur Kennedy. Joseph Pevney makes it seem like a very slow journey; 1958. (*c*)

Twilight of Honour　　　　　　　√
Richard Chamberlain stopped being a young doctor to become a young lawyer for this 1963 courtroom drama. The actual case is a bit steamy, concerning a whore, an aged adulterer and a dopey tramp. Claude Rains, Nick Adams, Joey (she's a girl–and a sexy one) Heatherton do well enough, as does director Boris Sagal. (*b/w*)

Twisted Nerve　　　　　　　　　√
Rather a crude attempt by Roy Boulting at a psychological thriller manages to create a few exciting moments and a few bits of comic relief but is bogged down by over-emphasis–of script, of direction and of acting by Hywel Bennett as the crafty killer, Hayley Mills as the girl who's taken in, Billie Whitelaw as her mother, Phyllis Calvert as his; 1969. (*c*)

Twist of Sand　　　　　　　　✕ ✕
That old story about buried loot being sought by cell-mate. Richard Johnson, Roy Dotrice, Jeremy Kemp, Honor Blackman make this pretty dull going, and director Don Chaffey can't galvanise them. Only Peter Vaughan as

survivor of wartime massacre brings the film alive but isn't allowed to outshine the dull principals; 1969. (*c*)

Two and Two Make Six　　　　✕ ✕
Ah, for the innocent days of 1961–this is a feeble comedy of Janette Scott and Jackie Lane getting on the wrong motorbikes and finding themselves drawn to their new drivers, George Chakiris and Alfred Lynch. Freddie Francis couldn't make the improbable plot work. (*b/w*)

The Two Faces of Dr Jekyll　　✕ ✕
How could Stevenson's story of split personality ever be boring? If you want to know, watch this. Paul Massie's unimaginative characterisations of both parts is matched for stiffness by Christopher Lee, and the lesser parts (Dawn Addams, David Kossoff, and a host of other undistinguished supports) are nowhere more than competent and frequently less. Mind you, Terence Fisher's direction is handicapped by Wolf Mankowitz's uninspired script and all the violence, blood and sundry mayhem which looks as though it has been casually thrown in for effect; 1960.
(*c*)

Two for the Road　　　　　　　√
Contrived exercise from director-producer Stanley Donen, from an ingenious but empty script by Frederic Raphael about Audrey Hepburn and Albert Finney driving through France. Their regular trips through their court-ship and marriage are jumbled up in a series of flashbacks that should perhaps be called flashybacks. Some gorgeous photography from Christopher Challis, but ultimately a disappointing effort; 1967. (*c*)

Two for the See-Saw　　　　　　√
The play by William Gibson from which this was taken in 1962 was a wry Feiffer-like look at the meeting and

parting of two bruised New Yorkers. It's hard to know whether to place the fault of the adaptation on writer Isobel Lennart, director Robert Wise, or leads Robert Mitchum (on the run from a broken marriage) and Shirley MacLaine (a supposedly lovable, over-generous kook). Certainly the split-screen, so you can see them both being lonely at once, was a mistake. (*b/w*)

Two Guns and a Badge   ✕
Owing to a mistake, Wayne Morris, just out of jail, is made assistant sheriff. Will he let the badge down? Unfortunately for predictability, no. Lewis D. Collins must have been tempted to make a switch of plot, but sadly refrained; 1954. (*b/w*)

The Two-Headed Spy   √
Routine spy melo which purports to tell the true story of General Schottland, who was close to Hitler but a British agent as well. It's all rather poorly done, which suggests that the weakness lay with director André de Toth and writer James O'Donnell, because Jack Hawkins, Gia Scala, Alexander Knox and Erik Schumann were all capable players. By the way, if he was so anti-Hitler and so close to him, why didn't General Hero get in a quick shot one dark night? 1958. (*b/w*)

Two Left Feet   ✕ ✕
Dispiriting shuffle through the mods-and-rockers phenomenon of the mid-sixties, providing Michael Crawford, Julia Foster, David Hemmings and Dilys Watling inadequate range for their talents. Roy Baker directed without inspiration. For some reason it got an X certificate at the time; 1965. (*b/w*)

The Two Mrs Carrolls   ✕
A stinker for Humphrey Bogart was this nonsense about him as artist painting his wives as Angel of Death and then doing them in. He is getting ready to dispatch Barbara Stanwyck when the chemist he has been buying the poison from starts blackmailing him. From then on, it's all go. Alexis Smith plays the putative third Mrs Carroll and there are some sickly scenes with a little daughter. Incidentally, it's all supposed to be happening in England (the presence of Nigel Bruce is the proof of that), a place where director Peter Godfrey came from many years before this was made in 1946, and seemed to have forgotten. (*b/w*)

Two of a Kind   ✕
Plan to foist boy on old folks as long-lost son goes wrong. Edmond O'Brien, Lizabeth Scott, Terry Moore star in rather unpleasant yarn, directed in 1951 by Henry Levin. (*b/w*)

Two on a Guillotine   ✕
If Connie Gilchrist is to inherit $300,000 she must spend seven nights in haunted house. Cesar Romero is her (presumably) dead father and her mother died guillotined in his stage act that went wrong. Director William Conrad manages to turn the screw here and there; 1965. (*b/w*)

Two Rode Together   √
Producer Harry Cohn asked John Ford for a quick, profitable Western in 1961, so James Stewart and Richard Widmark were hustled into this can't-fail conflict between respectively, a not-too-honest sheriff and an uptight cavalryman tracking down some white prisoners held by the Comanches. If it reminds you of *The Searchers*, that's where Ford found it. (*c*)

Two-way Stretch   √ √
Classic Peter Sellers about prisoners breaking out to do a job and getting back again. Wilfrid Hyde White, Bernard Cribbins, Lionel Jeffries, Irene Handl. Robert Day directed, 1960, which, looking back, Sellers may feel was the peak of his career. After this,

he became a major international star and the fun seemed to go out of his films. (*b/w*)

Two Weeks in Another Town ✕
Fascinating example of how good acting (Edward G. Robinson, Kirk Douglas) can almost overcome direction (Vincente Minnelli) and script (Charles Schnee from a far tougher Irwin Shaw novel) about hysterical film-making in Rome. They run large chunks of *The Bad and the Beautiful* as the model of a great film. Oddly enough it was made by the same team as this 1962 effort. (*c*)

The Ugly American ✕ ✕
Naïve political statement about Viet-Nam and neutrality, presented in 1963 as though it was the last word in political maturity. Even then it looked hollow. Today it seems pretentiously absurd. Marlon Brando was ill-cast as American ambassador, forced to reject wartime buddy-buddy, a local leader, in order to avert that most dreaded of all fates a Communist take-over. Producer-director George Englund's un-named Indo-chinese country looks awfully studio-bound and phoney, too. (*c*)

Ulysses ✕ ✕
(1) Homer, Ben Hecht and Irwin Shaw,

Katharine Hepburn in *Undercurrent*

who all had a hand in the script, should have done better with this 1955 parade of shaky spectacle and crude muscle. Kirk Douglas, Anthony Quinn, Silvana Mangano look and feel out of place; clearly director Mario Camerini found the whole international co-production just too much to handle. (*c*)

Ulysses √ √
(2) James Joyce's stream of consciousness was the subject of a brilliant attempt by Joseph Strick in 1967. Milo O'Shea wasn't really solid enough as the hero and Barbara Jefford not earthy enough as his wife. But some extracts from the text came over marvellously, and the atmosphere of Dublin was faithfully retained despite a forced up-dating. Only in the Fellini-and-water brothel scenes does it sag. (*b/w*)

Unchained × ×
Prison-without-bars melo with Chester Morris; main point of interest is the song, Unchained Melody. Director: Hall Bartlett; 1955. (*b/w*)

The Unconquered ×
SEE ... Paulette Goddard at the stake and in the bath! ... Gary Cooper organising the Indians to throw the British out!! ... Boris Karloff dressed up as an Indian chief!!! ... Cecil B. DeMille's cast of thousands!!!! ... and don't believe a word of it; 1947. (*c*)

The Undefeated ×
Three thousand stampeding horses go some way to make up for an otherwise dull Western, but director Andrew McLaglen doesn't get the best out of his human actors. John Wayne and Rock Hudson meet up after the Civil War, feud a bit, then get drunk together. It all goes on for rather a long time; 1969. (*c*)

Under Capricorn × ×
Every great director must be allowed

some disasters and this 1949 costumer set in Australia turned out to be Hitchcock's biggest one. He only did it because pretentious Ingrid Bergman (then reigning queen of moviedom) consented to play the lead–at a cripplingly large salary–then chose the wrong scriptwriters (Hume Cronyn, James Bridie) and male lead (Joseph Cotten–too posh; Burt Lancaster would have been better, Hitch says, looking back). Bergman was supposed to be English aristo drinking herself to death over a guilty secret and being poisoned by a Rebecca-type housekeeper (Margaret Leighton) at the same time. It was a huge financial and critical flop and Hitchcock had some harsh words to say about the preening afterwards. (*c*)

Undercover Girl ×
Gladys George walks away with this one under nominal star Alexis Smith's nose. It's one of those crime dramas where a girl joins the police to root out her father's murderer and gets trapped by dope-running gang. Joseph Pevney could have directed in his sleep, in 1950 –and maybe did. (*b/w*)

Undercover Man √
The neutral Glenn Ford in semi-documentary attempt to show how Capone-type gangster is nailed on tax-evasion charge, as Al was. Nina Foch is female interest. Director Joseph H. Lewis made it a cut above the average in 1949. (*b/w*)

Undercurrent √
Katharine Hepburn marries Robert Taylor but is bothered by mysterious reticence about his brother; when Robert Mitchum finally turns up, she is scared that he is a psychopathic murderer–or could it be that his brother, her husband, is the nut? Vincente Minnelli keeps you guessing; 1946. (*b/w*)

Under Fire × ×
Are these soldiers deserters? It's hard

to care under James B. Clark's lack-lustre direction, in 1957. Rex Reason, Steve Brodie, Henry Morgan among those present. (*b/w*)

Under My Skin √
Bent jockey tries to go straight for the sake of his son. Director Jean Negulesco helped to soften–and weaken–original Hemingway story. With John Garfield, Luther Adler; 1950. (*b/w*)

Under Ten Flags √
Van Heflin as captain of enterprising German warship pursued by British (namely Charles Laughton) World War II. Diulio Coletti directed; 1960. (*b/w*)

Under the Clock √
Judy Garland was kept tightly under control by second husband Vincente Minnelli in 1945; she plays an office worker in New York who bumps in to soldier-on-leave Robert Walker. They spend the day and night (delivering milk) together. James Gleason, Keenan Wynn make outstanding supports. (*b/w*)

Under the Gun √
Jail drama of breaks and pardons, with Richard Conte, Sam Jaffe, Audrey Totter. Director: Ted Tetzlaff; 1950. (*b/w*)

Under the Yum Yum Tree √
Irresistible Jack Lemmon makes rather old-fashioned (1963) comedy about sex-obsessed landlord more than just watchable. Carol Lynley is the highly fanciable, but virtuous, tenant he leches after; David Swift directs. (*c*)

Underwater! ×
Silly plot about sunken treasure in the Caribbean can only have been an excuse to see Jane Russell in a diving suit. John Sturgess directed in 1955. (*c*)

Underwater Warrior √
Dan Dailey as America's Commander

Crabbe, Commander Francis D. Fane, shot, documentary style, in the Philippines. Director Andrew Marton keeps the suspense going down among the so-easily-dead men; 1958. (*b/w*)

The Underworld Story √
Dan Duryea buys an interest in a small newspaper, finds himself threatened when he starts uncovering corruption. Herbert Marshall and Gale Storm help to make it all rather more believable than usual under Cy Endfield's brisk direction; 1950. (*b/w*)

Underworld USA √√
Give Blood Now proclaims a poster under which one of the many victims of this cold-blooded but brilliant gangster-thriller dies. One of the most explicitly violent and corrupt works by writer-producer-director Samuel Fuller, it manages to be moralistic at the same time. Cliff Robertson is Nemesis for his father's murderers; but then he falls in love with an ex-whore, Dolores Dorn, which makes him vulnerable to a Nemesis of his own. In 1961, it looked like the end of the gangster cycle. Today, it seems the beginning of the sado-masochistic one. (*b/w*)

The Unearthly ××
John Carradine as mad scientist hooked on human experiments. Not very distinguished in any department, particularly direction–Brook L. Peters; 1957. (*b/w*)

Unearthly Stranger ×
Flashbacking 1963 sci-fi has scientist John Neville discovering he is married to Alien Being (Gabriela Licudi) sent to destroy him; with Jean Marsh, Warren Mitchell, Patrick Newell. Director John Krish. (*b/w*)

Uneasy Terms ××
Rubbishy Peter Cheyney 'thriller' about stupid wills and soppy murderesses.

Vernon Sewell churned it out with the help of Michael Rennie, Moira Lister and Joy Shelton in 1948. (*b/w*)

Unfaithfully Yours √
Rex Harrison plotting revenge for wife's infidelity during a concert–murder while the Rossini plays, renunciation during the Wagner, doing himself in during Tchaikovsky. Preston Sturges directed with style and wit. Linda Darnell plays the wife; 1948. (*b/w*)

The Unfinished Dance ✕ ✕
1947 American remake of *La Mort du Cygne* has B+ dancing, B– acting. Recommended only for ballet-mad little girls. Ten-year-old Margaret O'Brien played one; Cyd Charisse was prima ballerina. Director, Henry Koster. (*c*)

The Unforgiven √
John Huston epic, 1960, about cowboys and Indians fighting over Audrey Hepburn's parentage; exciting climax. Audie Murphy, Lillian Gish, Burt Lancaster, Charles Bickford. (*c*)

The Unguarded Moment ✕ ✕
Esther Williams stays out of the swimming pool and in the classroom as teacher whose life is upset by sexy notes from one of her class. Esther should have stuck to swimming; Rosalind Russell, who helped write it, to acting. And director Harry Keller to better pictures; 1956. (*c*)

The Unholy Wife ✕
One of Diana Dors' American disasters; she's Rod Steiger's wife and in attempting to do him in, kills another chap. John Farrow failed to make you care; 1957. (*c*)

Union Station √
Director Rudolph Maté keeps us in some suspense while police hunt for blind girl and her kidnapper; with William Holden, Barry Fitzgerald, Nancy Olson; 1950. (*b/w*)

The Unknown Man √
Lawyer Walter Pidgeon discovering to his horror that the client he so ably got off a murder charge was guilty after all—and what he does about it. Richard Thorpe holds the interest; 1951. (*b/w*)

The Unknown Terror ✕
Creeper about molecular monsters, whatever they are, in South America. The usual mad scientist guff. John Howard, Mala Powers; director Charles Marquis Warren, who may have been consumed by abnormal fungus creatures shortly after the start of the picture; 1957. (*b/w*)

The Unsinkable Molly Brown ✕
More's the pity. Noisy musical has a boisterous Debbie Reynolds as social-climbing heroine, a hardly-adequate Harve Presnell and indulgent Charles Walters direction; 1964. (*c*)

Untamed ✕
Boer pioneers as heroes doing to the Zulus what the wagon trains did to the Indians: with He-man Tyrone Power. Director Henry King has some excuse in that it was made in less aware 1958; (*c*)

Untamed Frontier ✕
Ranchers versus homesteaders plot, with Joseph Cotten on the side of the little people, cheered on by Shelley Winters. Hugo Fregonese must have found an old script lying around somewhere in 1952. (*c*)

Until They Sail √
Paul Newman falling for one of four sisters while serving in USArmy in New Zealand. Widow Jean Simmons is the one who dispels his cynicism (if not ours); the others are Joan Fontaine, grim spinster softened by Charles

Drake; Piper Laurie, who sleeps around; Sandra Dee, who waits for her soldier-boy to come home. Robert Wise didn't try to push it further than the outer limits of soap opera; 1957. (*b/w*)

Up From the Beach ×
Routine Second World War adventure has Cliff Robertson, Broderick Crawford trying to liberate French village and director Robert Parrish trying to hold our interest; 1965. (*b/w*)

Up in the World × ×
1957 Norman Wisdom farce has an English stately home setting and John Paddy Carstairs direction; with Maureen Swanson, Jerry Desmonde, Ambrosine Phillpotts. (*b/w*)

Up Jumped a Swagman × × ×
Gimmicky attempt by Christopher Miles, making his first full-lengther, to project singer Frank Ifield as an actor. It fails miserably on about every possible count. Suzy Kendall, Richard Wattis seem desperately wrong in stock parts, and while Annette André looks pretty, she doesn't look happy; 1966. (*c*)

Up Periscope ×
James Garner and Edmond O'Brien as naval officers on submarine fighting each other as well as the Japs in unexceptional Gordon Douglas-directed World War II picture; 1959. (*c*)

Upstairs and Downstairs × ×
Snobbish British comedy about the absolutely ghastly problems poor Michael Craig and Anne Heywood have with their servants, my dears; Joan Sims, Claudia Cardinale, Mylène Demongeot are three of a feckless succession. It must have been offensively out-of-date even in 1959, when Ralph Thomas directed. James Robertson Justice, Sid James, Daniel Massey also appear. (*c*)

Up the Creek √
1958 British slapstick with David Tomlinson trying to curb Peter Sellers, Lionel Jeffries and other lower-deckies. Good fun from Val Guest. (*b/w*)

Up the Down Staircase √
Sandy Dennis unconvincing as pie-eyed teacher in Blackboard Jungle territory. Unfortunately, Robert Mulligan, the director, seems as impressed as she is with the superiority of letters over life and thus neither he, she, nor the film comes as closely to terms with the reality of slum existence as the unblinking location camera held by Joseph Coffey; 1967. (*c*)

Up Tight ×
The Informer remade as a 1969 black power movie by Jules Dassin. Uses newsreel footage to give a documentary gloss, but this just shows up the phoniness of the rest. And when a fancy director, however distinguished, attempts to tell it like it is, baby, in the ghetto, it simply doesn't work. Raymond St. Jacques, Frank Silvera, Ruby Dee. (*c*)

Up to His Neck × ×
Weak 1954 British comedy about skyving sailor Ronald Shiner, occasionally cheered up by glimpses of Harry Fowler, Brian Rix, Bryan Forbes, Anthony Newley, Hattie Jacques. John Paddy Carstairs sort of directed. (*b/w*)

Uranium Boom × ×
Hard to care about Dennis Morgan and William Talman scrapping over love for Patricia Medina. There's a fortune in uranium under their feet. William Castle churn-out; 1956. (*b/w*)

Utah Blaine ×
Rory Calhoun and Susan Cummings inherit range and have to fight renegades to stop them from taking it away. Dull stuff from Fred F. Sears; 1957. (*b/w*)

The Vagabond King ××
Kathryn Grayson warbles through hygienic Hollywood 1956 remake of Friml's operetta of 15th-century Paris rabble and their poet-champion, played by the awful Oreste. Michael Curtiz directed. (*c*)

Valentino ××
This biography of Rudolph could have been a winner if it had stuck to the facts. Instead, like nearly all show-biz biopics, it reduces its subject by fictitious clichés. Anthony Dexter, Eleanor Parker, with Lewis Allen the guilty director; 1951. (*c*)

Valerie ×
Courtroom drama with multi-flashbacks about Sterling Hayden, Anita Ekberg, Anthony Steel – dour performers, every one. Nor does Gerd Oswald's 1957 direction exactly shine. (*b/w*)

The Valiant ×
Italian prisoners-of-war won't talk, so is Captain John Mills justified in refusing them medical aid? Subordinates Robert Shaw, Liam Redmond think not, but director Roy Baker didn't take sides in this disappointing 1961 naval yarn. (*b/w*)

The Valley of Decision √
Sticky stuff about an Irish servant girl

Frank Sinatra in *Von Ryan's Express*

(Greer Garson, would you believe?) and involvement with son of the family she serves (Gregory Peck). Efficient Tay Garnett 1945 heart-string-puller with lovable old Donald Crisp, crusty old Lionel Barrymore and sweet little Dean Stockwell. (*b/w*)

Valley of Eagles ✕
Scientist's assistant steals his research and his wife; the chase is on. Terence Young keeps it going, although cast of Jack Warner, Nadia Gray and Christopher Lee (in a small part) wasn't the sprightliest, even in 1951. (*b/w*)

The Valley of Gwangi ✕
Little circus in need of a new attraction discovers valley where prehistoric monsters live. They capture one. It escapes, causes havoc. Sadly, James O'Connolly's direction of the humans involved (James Franciscus, Gila Golan, Laurence Naismith) makes them less convincing than producer Ray Harryhausen's special effects. And even they aren't all that believable; 1969. (*c*)

Valley of Mystery ✕
Characters you've all seen before struggle against the Bolivian jungle and plodding screenplay after plane is forced down. Richard Egan is 'star' of this strictly B-picture. Director, Joseph Leytes; 1967. (*c*)

Valley of the Dolls ✕
Hard to know which is the nastier—Jacqueline Susann's original, or this 1967 Mark Robson adaptation of trashy best-seller about three hopefuls (Barbara Parkins, Sharon Tate, Patty Duke) in the wicked world of showbiz. (*c*)

Valley of the Kings √
Robert Taylor, Eleanor Parker on archeological dig in routine adventure yarn set against stunning Egyptian background. Robert Pirosh directed; 1954. (*c*)

Value for Money ✕✕
Mild little comedy about John Gregson coming into money and Diana Dors. Ken Annakin; 1955. (*c*)

The Vanquished ✕
John Payne returns to town after the Civil War to spy out who's responsible for corruption. Edward Ludwig didn't make the most of it: 1953. (*c*)

The Veils of Bagdad ✕✕
Victor Mature joins Arabian ruler's palace guard. Strictly for pipe-dreamers. James Arness, Virginia Field. George Sherman directed slavishly; 1953. (*c*)

The Venetian Affair ✕
Despite the Venice exteriors, this is a Bonding of the old Bulldog Drummond with the Man from Uncle. Indeed, here is the man himself, Robert Vaughn, looking the worse for wear after being bounced from the CIA because his wife turned out to be Red agent. They meet up again, with predictable results. Helen MacInnes's novel gets drowned somewhere between the Rialto and the Bridge of Sighs by director Jerry Thorpe and co-producer-scripter E. Jack Neuman; 1967. (*c*)

Vengeance ✕
Sci-fi thriller about scientist being taken over by kept-alive brain, and uncovering a murder; with Peter Van Eyck, Anne Heywood, Bernard Lee, Cecil Parker. Director Freddie Francis; 1963. (*b/w*)

The Vengeance of She ✕✕
Shoddy 1968 follow-up to *She*, with John Richardson, Edward Judd, Colin Blakely, Olinka Berova. Director: Cliff Owen. (*c*)

Vengeance Valley √
Noble Burt Lancaster takes the blame for his womanising younger brother Robert Walker in actionful Western. Director Richard Thorpe did a fine job of work in 1951. (*c*)

Vera Cruz √
Gunmen Gary Cooper, Burt Lancaster mixed up in Mexican revolution and lots of Robert Aldrich-directed, location-shot action. They can't decide which side to fight on and finally fall out over some gold. Big box-office success; disliked by the critics; 1954. (*c*)

Verboten! ✕
James Best uncovers neo-nazi German youth plot in Berlin, under Samuel Fuller's gutsy direction; 1959. (*b/w*)

Vertigo √√
1958 Hitchcock has so much going for it (James Stewart, Kim Novak's carnality, trick photography, our vertigo) that you forgive preposterous story, plot flaw, Hitch's hostility towards Novak. (*c*)

Very Important Person ✕
British comedy has pompous James Robertson Justice taken prisoner-of-war by Germans, and old faithfuls like Leslie Phillips, Eric Sykes, Stanley Baxter, Richard Wattis to keep you smiling. Ken Annakin directed; 1961. (*b/w*)

A Very Special Favour ✕✕
If you don't find the thought of father (Charles Boyer) asking womaniser (Rock Hudson) to seduce career-girl daughter (Leslie Caron) because he's afraid she's growing frigid funny, nothing else in this smutty 1965 sex-comedy will make you laugh. Director Michael Gordon couldn't make it watchable. (*c*)

Vice Squad √
Edward G. Robinson lifts this day-in-the-life-of-a-cop drama above the triteness of its title. Arnold Laven directed; 1953. (*b/w*)

Vicki ✕
Richard Boone is bull-like cop determined to prove Elliott Reid killed his sweetheart, singer Jean Peters. Heavy 1953 remake by Harry Horner of H. Bruce Humberstone's 1941 *I Wake Up Screaming* (*Hot Spot*). (*b/w*)

Victim √√
Ahead of its time (1962) treatment of homosexuality as mainspring of detective story. Michael Relph, Basil Dearden directing, Otto Heller photographing, Dirk Bogarde giving tremendous performance in exacting role. (*b/w*)

The Victors √
Director Carl Foreman follows squad of American soldiers through World War II Europe (a nastier bunch you never met), and takes a long time about it. Large starry cast of this 1963 episodic drama includes George Peppard, George Hamilton, Eli Wallach, Jeanne Moreau, Melina Mercouri, Romy Schneider, Albert Finney. (*b/w*)

The View From Pompey's Head √
Cinematic equivalent of a good long read adapted in 1955 from Hamilton Basso best-seller about return to Southern town by successful New York publisher. Lightweight cast (Richard Egan, Dana Wynter) and director, Philip Dunne. (*c*)

A View From the Bridge √
Sidney Lumet version of Arthur Miller's powerful play about Italian stevedore's obsessive lust for his niece was rather let down by the casting of Raf Vallone, Carol Lawrence in central roles; 1962. (*b/w*)

The Viking Queen ✕✕
Can you spot the wrist-watch on the arm of one of the characters in this junk set in the times of Boadicea? It's about the only entertainment you'll get in Don Chaffey's violent cut-price epic with Don Murray and a large weak British cast; 1967. (*c*)

The Vikings ✕
Tony Curtis, Kirk Douglas, Ernest Borgnine, Janet Leigh in energetic costumer about Nordic invasion; Richard Fleischer directed the Norse-play; 1958. (*c*)

Villa ✓
One more ride round the life of Pancho Villa, this time with Brian Keith as American who joins his band, Cesar Romero. Directed by James B. Clark in 1958. Rodolfo Hoyos is Villa, the only Mexican actor to essay the part. (*c*)

Villa Rides! ✕
Long, disappointing account of Mexican revolutionary, Pancho Villa, with Yul Brynner, Robert Mitchum, Charles Bronson, Herbert Lom. Buzz Kulik directed; 1968. (*c*)

Village of the Damned ✓
Wolf Rilla chilla about creepy look-alike kids taking over village; based on John Wyndham's *The Midwich Cuckoos*. George Sanders, Barbara Shelley, Michael Gwynn; 1960. (*b/w*)

Village of the Giants ✕
Uninspired adaptation of H. G. Wells's *Food of the Gods*, with teenagers discovering that if they eat grub invented by 12-year-old they will grow to great height and be able to terrorise rest of the village. Bert I. Gordon directed cast of unknowns; 1965. (*c*)

The Vintage ✕ ✕
Made in France by Jeffrey Hayden with Mel Ferrer and John Kerr as two Italian brothers on the run, in the wine country. They meet up with Michèle Morgan and Pier Angeli but it's all awfully nebulous; 1957. (*c*)

The Violent Enemy ✓
Tom Bell, Susan Hampshire in ambivalent attempt to discuss the use of violence for such causes as the IRA, and at the same time exploit it as basis of a thriller. He is IRA hero sprung from Dartmoor by crooks who want to use his expertise to break into electronics factory. Ed Begley turns in fine performance as old guard freedom fighter. But Don Sharp's direction tends to blur the argument; 1969. (*c*)

The Violent Men ✓
Glenn Ford, ex-Civil War officer, against cattle king Edward G. Robinson and nasty wife, Barbara Stanwyck. Superior oater, directed by Rudolph Maté; 1956. (*c*)

The Violent Ones ✓
Mexican girl is raped. Before she dies she says her attacker was an American. But which of the three in the district is it? Fernando Lamas, as both deputy and director, takes them on a trek to the next town to escape the lynch-mob. On the way the murderer is revealed; 1967. (*c*)

Violent Playground ✕
Something of an early (1957) *Z-Cars*, even down to John Slater as sergeant. Stanley Baker is chief cop and do-gooder; David McCallum (later a Man from Uncle) is a tough lad, Anne Heywood his nicely spoken (i.e. sympathetic) sister. Basil Dearden directed. (*b/w*)

Violent Road ✕
A kind of remake of *The Wages of Fear*, with Efrem Zimbalist Jr, Dick Foran among the drivers with the dynamite on board. Howard W. Koch directed; 1958. (*b/w*)

Violent Saturday ✓
Strong cast—Lee Marvin, Ernest Borgnine, Victor Mature—in 1955 thriller about effect of bank robbery caper on small town. Richard Fleischer brings series of individual stories into focus as action progresses. (*c*)

The VIPs √
Splendid people (Elizabeth Taylor, Richard Burton, Margaret Rutherford, Orson Welles) all hanging about in London Airport lounge and not done complete justice to in multi-plotted mish-mash directed by Anthony Asquith, 1963. Watch David Frost walk through. (*c*)

The Virginian √
1946 remake by Stuart Gilmore of the famous 1929 Gary Cooper starrer, this time with Joel McCrea as the good guy, Brian Donlevy as the bad. Main drama comes when hero has to hang his friend as a rustler, and there's a climactic shoot-out. (*c*)

Virgin Island ×
Modest 1958 British comedy about young writer and his bride setting up home on tiny Caribbean island; with John Cassavetes, Virginia Maskell, Sidney Poitier. Pat Jackson directed. (*c*)

The Virgin Queen √
Bette Davis as Elizabeth 1st–or, in this case, Elizabeth 2nd, as she first played the part back in 1939 in *The Private Lives of Elizabeth and Essex*, with Errol Flynn. It was Elizabeth and Raleigh in 1955, with Richard Todd and obsequious Henry Koster direction. (*c*)

The Virgin Soldiers √
Leslie Thomas's best-seller about national servicemen in Singapore comes over well in 1969 version by John Hopkins, adapted by John McGrath, added to by Ian Frenais (how's that for TV influence?). Hywell Bennett as Chief Male Virgin meeting up with Chief Female Virgin Lynn Redgrave (weakest performance in a strongly-cast film) is convincing, as is the climactic regimental dance. Nigel Davenport, Jack Shepherd, Rachel Kempson stand out; and while there's a lot of talk about sex, there isn't much on the screen. Incidentally it makes a powerful argument against conscription. John Dexter. (*c*)

The Visit ×
Frederic Dürrenmatt's rather unpleasant play about richest woman in the world trying to get her first seducer sentenced legitimately to death by bribed town. Made even more unsympathetic by casting of two of the most self-regarding stars in the business in the main parts: Ingrid Bergman and Anthony Quinn. They are directed sycophantically by Bernard Wicki; 1964. (*c*)

Visit to a Small Planet √
Jerry Lewis as visitor from Outer Space, sent to observe us earthlings. OK knockabout stuff for fans, but what happened to the wit of Gore Vidal's original Broadway satire? Norman Taurog; 1960. (*c*)

Viva Zapata! √√
Today it seems several shades too simplistic, but in 1952, Elia Kazan's clear-eyed interpretation of John Steinbeck's tidy script about a hero of the Mexican revolution moved, inspired, and excited. Owing more to the paintings of Diego Rivera and Orozco than the photographs of the time, it makes a beautiful set of pictures. Over it all, towers Marlon Brando's tragic interpretation of an idealist. Whether Emiliano Zapata was anything like that is, of course, another matter. Anthony Quinn won Support Oscar as his younger brother, but by far the better performance was Joseph Wiseman's agent provocateur. (*b/w*)

Voice in the Mirror √
Richard Egan flashbacking his way through addiction to drink and out the other side, thanks to his wife Julie London, Harry Keller directs neatly; 1958. (*b/w*)

Von Ryan's Express ✓✓
American POW 'von' Sinatra leading escape in Mark Robson's fast-moving World War II chase drama. Trevor Howard gives outstanding support; 1965. (*c*)

Voodoo Island ✗
Boris Karloff as exposer of hoaxes, goes to tropical isle at the request of business-men who plan to develop it, to discover cause of strange goings-on there. Elisha Cook's presence does something to redeem poor script and direction by Reginald le Borg; 1957. (*b/w*)

Voyage to the Bottom of the Sea ✓
Captain Walter Pidgeon ordering Joan Fontaine, Peter Lorre and others around in his super-submarine. Irwin Allen made it all very jolly in 1961. (*c*)

Wabash Avenue ✓
1950 Henry Koster remake of Coney Island switches turn-of-the-century loca-tion to Chicago; provides Betty Grable with some boisterous song-and-dance routines and leading man Victor Mature. (*c*)

The Wackiest Ship in the Army ✓
World War II comedy-drama has Jack

Marlon Brando in *The Wild One*

Lemmon in charge of tacky old boat and useless crew. Richard Murphy directed; 1961. (*c*)

Wagon Master √√
Almost a documentary as John Ford shows a Mormon trek hounded by Indians and outlaws. It rambles magnificently on through some superb Ford landscapes to the inevitable showdown; Ben Johnson, Ward Bond, Joanne Dru, James Arness; 1950. (*b/w*)

Wait Until Dark √
Saccharine-sweet blind Audrey Hepburn trapped by thug Alan Arkin and friends in a Greenwich Village basement. They are looking for a doll filled with heroin and are prepared to kill to get it. She turns out the lights, but . . . The climax is fine, and Terence Young extracts the most from it, but the build-up takes for ever; 1967. (*c*)

Wake Me When It's Over ×
Depressingly apt title for 1960 Mervyn LeRoy-directed, over-acted comedy about Bilko-like soldiers on desert isle. Ernie Kovacs, Dick Shawn. (*c*)

Walk Don't Run ×
Cary Grant lifts this otherwise fluffy 1966 remake by Charles Walters of *The More the Merrier* with Samantha Eggar in Jean Arthur part. She shares apartment with athlete Jim Hutton and Cary during Tokyo Olympics. Nicely, naturally. (*c*)

Walking My Baby Back Home ×
Uninspired jazz musical has Donald O'Connor as band leader, Janet Leigh for love-interest and flat Lloyd Bacon direction; 1954. (*c*)

A Walk in the Sun √√
Lewis Milestone's famous 1945 exposition of the human side of war, as American infantry battalion advances in Italy. Richard Conte, John Ireland stand out. (*b/w*)

Walk into Hell ××
Australian effort, filmed in New Guinea, about lady explorer winning undying love of savages by curing their sick child. Chips Rafferty's in it, of course. Lee Robinson directed; 1957. (*c*)

Walk Like a Dragon √
Jack Lord saves Nobu McCarthy, a Chinese slavegirl, from life of prostitution; takes her to his home town, where he has to overcome prejudice, and her former boyfriend. Director James Clavell made it watchable; 1960. (*b/w*)

Walk on the Wild Side √
If the rest of the film doesn't live up to the credits sequence, it still isn't as bad as some critics have said. Nelson Algren's best-seller made adequate 1962 setting for strong performances from Jane Fonda and butch Barbara Stanwyck in New Orleans brothel, even if leads Laurence Harvey and lost love Capucine were dreadful. Edward Dmytryk did his directorial best. (*b/w*)

Walk Tall ×
Disappointing Western about chase after rapists, with Willard Parker, Kent Taylor; director, Maury Dexter; 1960. (*c*)

Walk the Proud Land √
Audie Murphy in what's claimed to be true story of the Indian agent who captured Geronimo and brought peace between Apaches and whites. Anne Bancroft, Charles Drake; director, Jesse Hibbs; 1956. (*c*)

Wall of Noise √
Routine soaper–handsome Ty Hardin involved with Dorothy Provine and married Suzanne Pleshette–given a racetrack setting, and Richard Wilson as director in 1963. (*c*)

The Walls of Jericho ×
Soapy yarn of small town lawyer Cornel

Wilde, married to common, alcoholic Ann Dvorak, lusted after by wife (Linda Darnell) of best friend Kirk Douglas, but loving pure assistant, Anne Baxter. There are courtroom and boudoir battles before the final clinch, and director John M. Stahl makes it pretty heavy going; 1948. (*b/w*)

Waltz of the Toreadors ✕
Disappointing adaptation of Jean Anouilh's featherweight farce into a heavy-footed clomp round the ballroom floor. Peter Sellers does one of his mimicries as old soldier that might have been funny for a few lines but rapidly bores; Margaret Leighton tries hard but is defeated by the script; and a handful of useful character-actors are whizzed through their paces by director John Guillermin, who seemed, in 1962, to be getting into speed practice for his later flying movie, *The Blue Max*. The plot, such as it is, involves Sellers' life ot love. (*c*)

War and Peace √
American style. Audrey Hepburn a natural Natasha, Henry Fonda miscast as Pierre, Mel Ferrer a laughable Andrei; heavily directed by King Vidor in 1956, who managed the battle scenes well enough, but not the more intimate ones. Fonda said later, 'I knew I was physically all wrong, but they didn't want a Pierre who looked like Pierre. One who looked like Rock Hudson was closer to what they had in mind.' He wasn't allowed to wear padding and producer Dino DeLaurentiis was against eye-glasses, too; he was only able to wear them when the producer wasn't around. Despite this, *Time* magazine's critic said that he seemed to be the only one around that had read the book. (*c*)

War Arrow ✕
Supposedly the true story of Major Howell Brady who trained the Seminoles to defeat the Kiowa Hordes. Jeff Chandler plays him, Maureen O'Hara's the object of his affection. George Sherman directed modestly; 1953. (*c*)

War Drums ✕
Goldminers provoke Apaches during Civil War. Lex Barker, Ben Johnson, Stuart Whitman in violent Western, directed by Reginald Le Borg; 1957. (*c*)

War Hunt √
Effective low-budget Korean war drama stars John Saxon as soldier psychopath and the then–1962–unknown Robert Redford. Denis Sanders directed. (*b/w*)

War is Hell ✕
. . . Just in case you didn't know. That's about the only message this mechanically well-made actioner has got to offer from Korea. Burt Topper directed himself; 1964. (*b/w*)

Warlock √
Brighter-than-average Western about lawman cleaning up town, then challenged by the man who helped him. Made in 1959 by Edward Dmytryk, it was early adult oater with Henry Fonda as clean-cut cultured sheriff; Anthony Quinn as unnaturally close, adoring friend; Richard Widmark, Dorothy Malone. (*c*)

The War Lord ✕
Charlton Heston demanding another man's bride as feudal right. Franklin Schaffner made a real effort in 1965 to create a medieval epic that wasn't just a comic strip but a genuine drama, but it didn't work out that way; 11th century Normandy was never like this. (*c*)

The War Lover ✕
Steve McQueen, Robert Wagner as pilots in love with same girl (Shirley Anne Field). Strictly for war-lovers and those who enjoy World War II dramas. Philip Leacock; 1963. (*c*)

Warning Shot √
Fairly recent (1967) police thriller has David Janssen clearing himself of a charge of murdering an innocent man while on duty; Ed Begley gives strong support, and Eleanor Parker, Lillian Gish, Joan Collins, George Sanders manfully back up director Buzz Kulik. Drugs are the clue. (*c*)

War of the Satellites √
One of Roger Corman's jolly low-budget sci-fis, rather dragged out, with its yarn about scientist's mind being controlled by alien planet. Dick Miller, Susan Cabot; 1958. (*b/w*)

War of the Worlds √
Weak transfer of H. G. Wells's early sci-fi novel to present day (well, 1953) and California, and given an unfortunate religious undertone the author would surely have found unacceptable. Byron Haskin does what he can with a cynical script by Barré Lyndon and stolid performances by Gene Barry and Jack Kruschen. Special effects are ingenious, however, and there are quite a lot of laughs, some of them intentional. Director, George Pal. (*c*)

War Paint √
Will the peace treaty get to the Indians? Or will murdering fanatic stop it? Lesley Selander manages to keep the suspense more or less going. Robert Stack, Joan Taylor humour him; 1953. (*c*)

Warpath √
Edmond O'Brien doing the Nemesis bit in Western, after his woman has been killed. Dean Jagger and Forrest Tucker give a familiar look to the old prairie under Byron Haskin's direction; 1951. (*c*)

The Warriors ✕
Attractive, but not awfully convincing casting, has Errol Flynn as the Black Prince, Joanne Dru his highborn damsel-in-distress and Peter Finch as villainous French nobleman in this colourful, English-shot costume lark. Director Henry Levin used the same castle set as the *Ivanhoe* made at Elstree three years before this 1955 effort. Flynn agreed with critics that, at 46, he was a bit old for the dashing young hero stuff. (*c*)

The War Wagon √√
Lively, often funny, Burt Kennedy-directed Western has John Wayne planning to rob $250,000 gold shipment from armoured coach. His helpers are gunslinger Kirk Douglas, Red Indian Howard Keel, dynamite whizz Robert Walker, old thief Keenan Wynn and his young bride Valora Noland; 1967. (*c*)

Washington Story ✕
Muck-raking reporter Patricia Neal can't get the dirt on congressman Van Johnson, because there isn't any. Writer-director Robert Pirosh couldn't make it believable in 1952. (*b/w*)

Watch It, Sailor! √
Brisk farce with Dennis Price, Liz Fraser, Irene Handl, Marjorie Rhodes in great complications about a wedding and an official telegram cancelling it. Wolf Rilla keeps it going; 1962. (*b/w*)

Watch the Birdie ✕
Silly stuff about Red Skelton as photographer that doesn't do even his small talent justice. Arlene Dahl, Ann Miller and frantic Jack Donohue direction; 1950. (*b/w*)

Watch Your Stern ✕
Could have been called *Carry On Up Your Torpedo*, as it was made by the Carry On team and their director Gerald Thomas, and contains same blend of blue slapstick. Supposedly about Kenneth Connor losing plans and substituting fridge blueprint. Eric Barker, Leslie Phillips, Joan Sims, Hattie Jacques, Sid James; 1960. (*b/w*)

Watusi! × ×
Cynical remake of *King Solomon's Mines*, made nine years later to use up the footage left over from the 1950 version. Kurt Neumann was in charge of the cobbling; lesser stars David Farrar, George Montgomery, Tania Elg, Rex Ingram caper about discovering long-lost kingdom (and library film). (*c*)

Way of a Gaucho ×
Run-of-the-Pampas melo has Rory Calhoun, Gene Tierney, Richard Boone lovin' and killin' in rugged last-century Argentina. Jacques Tourneur; 1952. (*c*)

The Way Out × ×
But not very far. Creaky chase story with Gene Nelson imported in 1956 to star with Sidney Tafler, Michael Goodliffe, John Bentley. Director, Montgomery Tully. (*b/w*)

The Way to the Gold ×
Wooden Jeffrey Hunter on the trail of buried treasure; Robert D. Webb directed; 1957. (*b/w*)

The Wayward Bus ×
Watering-down of John Steinbeck best-seller has Joan Collins, Jayne Mansfield, Dan Dailey among passengers stranded when bus breaks down on the way to Mexico. Victor Vicas; 1957. (*b/w*)

The Wayward Girl × ×
Mother and stepdaughter both fancy same chap. Mother kills him, blames daughter. Lesley Selander directed Marcia Henderson in this tripe; 1957. (*b/w*)

Way ... Way Out ×
Jerry Lewis on the moon, with Connie Stevens as astronaut wife. They're supposed to be manning US weather station. Gordon Douglas; 1966. (*c*)

The Way West √
It's recent (1967), it's on a big scale ($5,000,000) and it has got big stars (Kirk Douglas, Robert Mitchum, Richard Widmark) but it suffers from telling too many stories. Director Andrew McLaglen, son of Victor, just can't seem to deliver more than spectacle in his big oaters. As a travelogue, though, it has its moments. (*c*)

The Weak and the Wicked ×
Inside a British women's prison with J. Lee Thompson. Glynis Johns, Diana Dors, Jane Hylton and what happens to them; 1953. (*b/w*)

The Weapon ×
Little boy finds gun; accidentally shoots his friend; runs away in horror. George Cole, Steve Cochran are just two of the many after him in this 1956 Val Guest attempt at suspense. (*b/w*)

The Webster Boy ×
Undistinguished melo, directed in 1962 by Don Chaffey, that takes itself far too seriously. Elizabeth Sellars' ex-lover, John Cassavetes, turns up on the scene after 14 years and makes problems for his already-difficult illegitimate son. (*b/w*)

Wedding Breakfast √
Sentimental family comedy about hard-up Bronx cab driver and wife wanting to splash out on fancy wedding for their daughter; she wants a quick, quiet one. Youngsters Debbie Reynolds and Rod Taylor (this was 1956) appear more insipid than usual beside Bette Davis and Ernest Borgnine's larger-than-life performances as self-sacrificing parents. Richard Brooks directed from Paddy Chayefsky play. (*b/w*)

Weekend with Father √
Patricia Neal, widow, falls for Van Heflin, widower, but their children object. Douglas Sirk makes it entertaining enough; 1951. (*b/w*)

Wee Willie Winkie √
Shirley Temple saves the British Army

on the North-West Frontier, aided by Victor McLaglen. Made in 1937 and about worth the ninepence it cost then. Although the Hollywood pre-war system compelled John Ford to direct such rubbish as this, he still managed to work in marvellous moments, like his child's-eye view of the terrain. C. Aubrey Smith, Constance Collier, Cesar Romero do their usual lovable bits. (*b/w*)

We Joined the Navy ✕
Cheerful, undemanding romp has Kenneth More as blundering naval officer, Lloyd Nolan, Mischa Auer, John Le Mesurier, Kenneth Griffith, Derek Fowlds; Wendy Toye directed; 1962. (*c*)

Welcome To Hard Times √√
Evil Aldo Ray terrorises small town, and mayor Henry Fonda is inclined to let him get on with it until accusations of cowardice force him into showdown. Janice Rule is chief spur. Written and directed by Burt Kennedy as an erotic, violent parable; 1967. (*c*)

The Well √
Prejudice goes when a black child is trapped in a well. Leo Popkin used his cast of little-knowns (Henry Morgan is only near-name) effectively in 1951. (*b/w*)

We're no Angels √
Soft-centred story of escapees from Devil's Island saving kindly family from clutches of Basil Rathbone. What Michael Curtiz would have done without Humphrey Bogart and Peter Ustinov must have caused him sleepless nights in 1955. The other non-angel was Aldo Ray. (*c*)

We're Not Married √
Five couples discover their marriages are not legal; Marilyn Monroe, Ginger Rogers, Mitzi Gaynor, Fred Allen, Paul Douglas among the unwed. Pity that writer Nunnally Johnson couldn't quite keep up the fun through all five episodes.

Light Edmund Goulding direction; 1952. (*b/w*)

The Werewolf ✕✕
Unscrupulous scientists seeking serum against radiation turn man into a bloodsucker. Director Fred F. Sears fails to chill; Steven Rich, Joyce Holden; 1956. (*b/w*)

Werewolf of London √√
1935 classic horror movie directed by Stuart Walker about botanist (Henry Hull) bitten by Tibetan werewolf (Warner Oland of Charlie Chan fame), turning into London rampager. Lycanphobic Valerie Hobson and Spring Byington support. (*b/w*)

Westbound √
Strong Randolph Scott-Budd Boetticher team job about bringing in gold from California during the Civil War to help the Yankees, through Confederate opposition. Karen Steele appears to pack a strong punch as she looks after crippled husband. Virginia Mayo is Scott's girl; 1959. (*c*)

West 11 ✕✕
Seedy British drama about young layabout (Alfred Lynch) agreeing to murder Eric Portman's rich aunt for a share of the money; with Diana Dors, Kathleen Harrison. Michael Winner directed; 1963. (*b/w*)

Western Approaches √√
Wartime (1944) tribute to merchant seamen tells story of lifeboat full of real-life sailors and their encounter with a U-boat. Pat Jackson directed; Jack Cardiff photographed; greatest strength is use of sound and real-life casting. (*b/w*)

West of Montana √
Buddy Ebsen promises dying friend to look after ranch, but has to involve a mail order bride to do so. A lightweight, directed by Burt Kennedy, 1963. Keir Dullea, Lois Nettleton. (*c*)

West of Zanzibar × ×
Anthony Steel looking tough but acting weakly in his tracking-down of ivory-poaching gang. Sheila Sim precise match for his milk-and-water heroics. Harry Watt's message seemed to be that the simple African folk were better off under the paternalistic British administrators; a comforting fiction in 1954. (*c*)

West Side Story √ √
It was either the greatest musical ever filmed or a pretentious piece of gimcrack, according to which side of the barricade you were on when it came out in 1961. Either way it killed the old-style *Singin' in the Rain, No, no, Nanette* type of musical, both on stage and screen (except for camp revivals), with its harsh Bernstein rhythms, Stephen Sondheim lyrics and easy adaptation of modern ballet techniques from Jerome Robbins (who was also directing the movie until They tired of his 'perfectionism' and replaced him with Robert Wise). True, the dialogue is embarrassing; true, the nerveless borrowing from *Romeo and Juliet* is half-hearted; true, Richard Beymer's acting is laughable and Natalie Wood doll-like. Rita Moreno, George Chakiris are fine, however, the social significance isn't all cop-out, and those ten Academy Awards were not entirely undeserved. (*c*)

Westward the Women √
Paramount wouldn't let out-of-favour Frank Capra make his own story of 200 women trekking across America to meet blind-date husbands in California, with Gary Cooper. So in 1951 he sold it to MGM for his close friend William Wellman to make with Robert Taylor. It turned out a successful and off-beat Western. (*b/w*)

Wetbacks √
Are what Mexicans smuggled North of the Border to work in USA are called. Hank McCune got a strong chase yarn out of this human drama, with Lloyd Bridges, Barton MacLane, Nancy Gates, in 1956. (*c*)

What A Crazy World × ×
Dated pop musical about out-of-work East End kid writing hit song, with then (1963) pop stars Joe Brown (and his Bruvvers), Marty Wilde, Susan Maugham, Freddie and the Dreamers, Harry H. Corbett, Avis Bunnage (as Joe's dogs-and-Bingo-mad mum and dad) are good for a different kind of giggle today. Michael Carreras. (*b/w*)

What A Way To Go × ×
Thin 1964 comedy doesn't support top-heavy talent and production; oft-widowed Shirley MacLaine is pursued by undaunted suitors. With Paul Newman, Dean Martin, Robert Mitchum, Gene Kelly (who hits highest spot), Bob Cummings, Dick Van Dyke. J. Lee Thompson directed and got roasted by the critics for the film's lack of style, grace and wit. (*c*)

What Did You Do in the War, Daddy? ×
Blake Edwards' World War II farce has James Coburn, Dick Shawn, Harry Morgan clowning in a very unwarlike Sicily; 1966. (*c*)

Whatever Happened to Aunt Alice √
She got used in a meretricious title, that's what. This would-be chiller was produced in 1969 by Robert Aldrich, the man who had made *Whatever Happened to Baby Jane?* seven years before, but that's all they have to do with one another. This one is about Geraldine Page who manages to get some well-lined ladies to come and keep house for her out there in the Arizona desert. Then she does them in. The current one is Ruth Gordon, the witch from *Rosemary's Baby*, which should have been warning enough. It may give you a few mild thrills, but not many sleepless nights; 1969. (*c*)

Whatever Happened to Baby Jane? √ √
Bette Davis *v.* Joan Crawford in 1962 contest to out-overact the other in Robert Aldrich's *grand-guignol* pie. Not as horrifying as it sets out to be, the story is ingenious and not without surprises, and there are several moments of genuine tension. The best bits are the two-woman scenes out-freaking each other in grotesque make-up. (*b/w*)

What Lola Wants √
Musical reworking of Faust legend–given a contemporary (1958) baseball setting–taken from Broadway show *Damn Yankees*. Tab Hunter is rejuvenated hero (middle-aged fan to star player), Ray Walston a disappointingly tame Mephistopholes, Gwen Verdon his side-kick. George Abbott wrote and co-directed with Stanley Donen. (*c*)

What Price Glory √
John Ford remake of silent comedy classic about two brawling soldiers (James Cagney and Dan Dailey in this 1952 version) in World War I France. (*c*)

What's Good for the Goose × × ×
This 1969 comedy was claimed as changing Norman Wisdom's image. All that meant was the only time his pants came off was when he took them down to go to bed with Sally Geeson. Otherwise, it's the same old boring Norman, rather worse-directed than usual by Israeli Menahem Golan. (*c*)

What's New, Pussycat? √
Desperately painful attempt at sustained comedy had a big success in 1965, when the idea that sex could be (*a*) explicit, and (*b*) an object of fun, was novel. But Clive Donner couldn't make a monumentally boring cast (Peter Sellers, Peter O'Toole, Romy Schneider, Capucine, Woody Allen, Ursula Andress) do more than preen themselves and dare us not to share their high opinion of themselves. Woody Allen's script contains flashes of genuine humour, but it's an awfully forced exercise. (*c*)

What's So Bad About Feeling Good? ×
Tropical bird spreads happiness bug over New York. George Peppard and Mary Tyler Moore are Village dropouts infected by it. Well, director George Seaton must have thought it was a cute idea in 1968. (*c*)

What's Up, Tiger Lily? × ×
Spy send-up–the plot to steal recipe for the best egg-salad in the world–leadenly re-edited by Woody Allen from a poor Japanese original. Occasional commentary and appearances by Allen are far from helpful or amusing; 1966. (*c*)

The Wheeler Dealers √
Slick Arthur Hiller comedy has James Garner as oil man come to New York to raise money; Lee Remick's presence ensures that that's not all he goes back to Texas with; 1963. (*c*)

When Gangland Strikes ×
Should county prosecutor pull his punches when gang threatens to expose his daughter? Veteran R. G. Springsteen doesn't seem to care as much as he should, and result is a rather inconsequential movie. Raymond Greenleaf, Marjie Millar, Anthony Caruso; 1956. (*b/w*)

When Hell Broke Loose ×
Charles Bronson, serving in the army, was once a racketeer. But he gives it up for the sake of German girl, and stops a nazi assassination attempt on General Eisenhower in the bargain. Kenneth Crane doesn't convince; 1958. (*b/w*)

When in Rome ×
Con man Paul Douglas disguises himself as priest when he's on the run from police in Rome; finds himself being converted by real-life priest Van Johnson. Director Clarence Brown tried to make it funny in 1952. (*b/w*)

When the Boys Meet the Girls   ✕
1966 remake of *Girl Crazy* provided work for uncharismatic Harve Presnell and Connie Francis and an excuse for re-working of old Gershwin score (I Got Rhythm, Embraceable You, etc.). Louis Armstrong, Herman's Hermits, Liberace looked in but didn't help director Alvin Ganzer any. (*c*)

When the Redskins Rode   ✕ ✕
Beautiful French spy tries to con the Indians to fight for France in the New World. Jon Hall resists. Lew Landers directed; 1951. (*c*)

When Willie Comes Marching Home   ✕
What happens to small-town boy Dan Dailey when he joins the Army. Corinne Calvet's just one of many adventures in this soft-centred World War II comedy that even John Ford fanatics admit to be a failure; 1950. (*b/w*)

When Worlds Collide   √
Earth is about to be destroyed by star hurtling towards it, and there's a race on to build a spaceship to carry off would-be survivors; they include Richard Derr, Barbara Rush. Special effects won 1951 Oscar, but nothing else about this routine sci-fi was much of a winner. Rudolph Maté directed. (*c*)

Where Angels Go, Trouble Follows   ✕
Someone, somewhere, must have en-joyed Mother Superior Rosalind Russell in *Trouble With Angels*, because they went and made a sequel for her in 1968. So whoever you are out there, this one– with Stella Stevens as 'progressive' young nun–is for you. James Neilson directed. (*c*)

Where Danger Lives   ✕
Dr Robert Mitchum, infatuated with the near-crazy Faith Domergue, is afraid he might have killed husband Claude Rains so he hops it, silly man. Difficult to know which is the more unbelievable

–the plot or Miss D.'s performance. John Farrow directed; 1950. (*b/w*)

Where Eagles Dare   ✕
Parachuters into Germany again, this time with a woman, Mary Ure, among them. Richard Burton, Clint Eastwood, Patrick Wymark, Peter Barkworth in an orgy of blood-letting which may have satisfied director Brian G. Hutton but which disgusted most reviewers; 1969. (*c*)

Where Love Has Gone   ✕
A Harold Robbins not-about novel (not about Lana Turner) with Susan Hay-ward's daughter killing her mother's latest lover and Bette Davis as domineer-ing grandma. Edward Dmytryk evi-dently just let it happen; 1964. (*c*)

Where's Charley?   √
1952 musical remake of the farcical *Charley's Aunt* has reliable vaudevillain Ray Bolger dragging-up and lively Frank Loesser score. David Butler directed. (*c*)

Where's Jack?   √
Romp through the not very smelly stews of London with Tommy Steele as honest Jack Sheppard, turned villain by nasty Stanley Baker, loved by simple Fiona Lewis and, a bit later, patronised by posh Sue Lloyd, which gives director James Clavell the chance of a bit of cleavage. Although it has its eye on the U-cert. audience, it's acceptably enjoyable by the slightly more sophisti-cated, as well; 1969. (*c*)

Where the Boys Are   ✕ ✕
And the laughs aren't. Henry Levin has been stuck with a dreary, dry-cleaned script (by George Wells) about Fort Lauderdale, notorious American resort where college girls and boys go lemming off to spend their vacations. But the film isn't sexy, made as it was it was in pre-permissive 1960, where getting pregnant meant that you had to be

knocked down by a car to prove that God punished wrongdoers. George Hamilton, Dolores Hart, Yvette Mimieux, Paula Prentiss, Connie Francis move around energetically instead of acting. (*c*)

Where the Bullets Fly × ×
Poor spy stuff with Dawn Addams saving the world by stopping secret substance falling into enemy hands. The rest of the cast seemed to have been carefully chosen by director John Gilling not to show up the lack of ability in his star – about the only bit of his job he managed adequately; 1966. (*c*)

Where There's A Will × ×
George Cole, Kathleen Harrison in pathetic British comedy. If you're forced at gunpoint to watch this rubbish about city lads inheriting farm, see if you can spot Edward Woodward's film debut; he was 24 in 1954. Vernon Sewell directed. (*b/w*)

Where the Sidewalk Ends √
Vicious cop Dana Andrews kills murder suspect, hopes to pin it on mobster; but falling in love with victim's widow, Gene Tierney, upsets his plans. Otto Preminger kept our interest, even if dull leads couldn't; 1950. (*b/w*)

Where the Spies Are √
Bright spy thriller, from a novel by James Leasor, laced with dry comedy from David Niven as Dr Jason Love, reluctant agent. Support from John Le Mesurier, Cyril Cusack, Françoise Dorléac, Nigel Davenport; directed, 1965, by Val Guest. (*c*)

Where Were You When the Lights Went Out? √
Doris Day's wholesome presence ensured that this Hy Averback-directed comedy about the 1965 New York blackout was just good clean fun – well, clean, anyway. Robert Morse, Terry-Thomas, Patrick O'Neal, Lola Albright involved in the unlikely goings on. 1968. (*c*)

While the City Sleeps √
Ambitious newspapermen compete in hunting down dangerous killer. As so often, director Fritz Lang was let down by uncharismatic cast: Dana Andrews, Rhonda Fleming, Vincent Price, George Sanders, Ida Lupino; 1956. (*b/w*)

Whirlpool √
(1) Moody, ingenious hokum directed by Otto Preminger about Svengaloid José Ferrer using Gene Tierney to further nefarious schemes; 1949. (*b/w*)

Whirlpool × ×
(2) Ex-left Bank cellar girl Juliette Greco sings and looks sultry in Lewis Allen's 1959 dull and undemanding mystery, with Marius Goring. Director, O. W. Fischer. (*b/w*)

Whisky Galore √ √
If Sandy Mackendrick's funny about shipwreck of liquor-laden boat off Hebridean isle seems a bit genteel now, remember that as well as creasing us all in 1948, it changed a nation's (France's) drinking habits, and even named a style of dancing (go-go, from *Whisky A-Gogo*, the film's French title, adopted for name of first discothèques). It had Joan Greenwood, Catherine Lacey, Gordon Jackson prominent among the islanders. (*b/w*)

Whispering Smith v. Scotland Yard × ×
Famous detective proves 'suicide' is murder. But it's all so old-fashioned and creaky, you're hardly likely to care. Director Francis Searle reduced Greta Gynt (not difficult to do), Herbert Lom, Dora Bryan to ciphers; 1952. (*b/w*)

The Whisperers √ √
Remarkable *tour de force* by Dame Edith Evans (winning her 1967 British

Oscar) as neglected old woman haunted by voices in her head. Bryan Forbes's script and direction eschewed commercial considerations (except in tangential sub-plots) and the film made no impact at the box-office. Strong support from Gerald Sim as assistance man, Nanette Newman as aggravated girl upstairs, Eric Portman as the old woman's indifferent husband. (*b/w*)

The Whistle at Eaton Falls   √
Unusual drama centres round problems of union leader who becomes manager of a factory and is faced with sacking the workers. Robert Siodmak directs documentarily, and has strong cast in Ernest Borgnine, Dorothy Gish, Anne Francis, Lloyd Bridges; 1951. (*b/w*)

Whistle Down The Wind   √ √
When Hayley Mills (actually 15 when it was made in 1961, but playing younger) finds murderer Alan Bates in the barn and mistakes him for Christ, the stage could have been set for pathos. Under Bryan Forbes's skilful direction, it never succumbs, although the religious parallels – three-fold betrayal, 'crucifix' shot – are a bit forced. Touching when it could have been trite. (*b/w*)

White Christmas   √
1954 version of *Holiday Inn* has Bing Crosby, Danny Kaye involved with Rosemary Clooney, Vera-Ellen, at winter resort owned by their old army officer, Dean Jagger. It's in trouble and they save it. Only the title song is good enough; the rest of Irving Berlin's score reveals how patchy this over-rated composer was. Michael Curtiz, 1954. (*c*)

White Feather   ✕
Cowboys *v.* Indians with Robert Wagner trying to get Cheyenne tribe, led by Jeffrey Hunter and Debra Paget suitably blacked up, to move to reservation. Robert D. Webb's 1955 actioner a long time out of date. (*c*)

White Heat   √ √
In 1949, James Cagney had escaped from gangster movies for ten years, but it was a bad patch for him and he had to accept another such part–as an Oedipus-complexed gunman in what turned out to be classic Raoul Walsh thriller. Critics agree that only a director as tough as Walsh could have got away with Cagney sitting on his mother's lap. Virginia Mayo plays the girl he puts second to his Mom. (*b/w*)

The White Squaw   ✕
When a white rancher is told to give his land back to the Indians because he didn't file legal claim he goes berserk. But director Ray Nazarro fails to make much of what could have been fascinating situation. William Bishop, Nancy Hale; 1956. (*b/w*)

The White Tower   √
Hard work for mountaineering doubles as six people tackle virtually unclimbable Alp. But director Ted Tetzlaff makes you suspend disbelief pretty effectively and you'll find yourself involved in the struggles and past lives of Glenn Ford, Claude Rains, Alida Valli, Oscar Homolka and Cedric Hardwicke. 1950. (*c*)

White Witch Doctor   ✕
The witch doctor's a lady – dedicated nurse Susan Hayward, wanting to share the marvels of modern medicine with those poor ignorant savages in Darkest Africa. Travelling companions Robert Mitchum, Walter Slezak don't go along with her missionary zeal–they're just after hidden treasure. Not one of Henry Hathaway's best; 1953. (*c*)

The Whole Truth   ✕
Did producer Stewart Granger, filming in the South of France, murder starlet? The police think so–but would he really have endangered his investment that way? John Guillermin skims over the surface, 1958. Donna Reed, George

Sanders weigh in professionally enough. (b/w)

Who's Afraid of Virginia Woolf? √√√
Stunning performances by Elizabeth Taylor (Oscar) and Richard Burton made this already compulsive drama by Edward Albee of in-fighting between academic husband and wife, involving another couple, played by mannered Sandy Dennis (Oscar) and George Segal, into something really special. Mike Nichols' direction has been criticised as dull, but he managed to convey a total effect of marital desolation that few films have ever done. More Academy Awards were won by Haskell Wexler's photography, art direction, costumes. 1966. (b/w)

Who's Been Sleeping In My Bed? ✕
1963 farce, one of the first Dean Martin made after cutting the comedy-umbilical with Jerry Lewis. Hero of TV medical series is bothered by women patients; Elizabeth Montgomery tries to push him altarwards, Carol Burnett jolly as his psychiatrist's nurse. Daniel Mann. (c)

Who's Got the Action? ✕
Careful wife tries to keep compulsive gambler hubby's money in the family by turning bookie. Lana Turner and Dean Martin are shown up by Walter Matthau, the only laugh in this strained Daniel Mann attempt; 1962. (c)

Who's Minding the Mint? √
Good-natured romp about Mint employee who destroys $50,000 by mistake, trying to forge replacements. Milton Berle, Joey Bishop, Dorothy Provine, Jim Hutton; director, Howard Morris; 1967. (c)

Who's Minding the Store? ✕
Jerry Lewis as incompetent assistant in big department store. Jill St. John, as boss's daughter, provides the romance; Agnes Moorehead and Ray Walston, a touch of class; and Jerry, the inevitable

fooling. But who provides the laughs? Not director Frank Tashlin; 1963. (c)

Who Was That Lady? √
Professor Tony Curtis enlists help of old pal Dean Martin in cooking up unlikely explanation when wife Janet Leigh (real-life wife in 1960) catches him kissing one of his students. The whole thing gets out of hand when they–and director George Sidney–bring the FBI into it. (b/w)

Why Must I Die? ✕
Sombre stuff about night-club singer, daughter of a crook, being executed for murder she didn't commit. Terry Moore is poor substitute for *I Want to Live*'s Susan Hayward, and Roy Del Ruth makes it merely histrionic; 1960. (b/w)

Wichita √
The year is 1874 (actually, it's 1955) and Wyatt Earp (Joel McCrea) takes over as sheriff. Lloyd Bridges and Wallace Ford provide the excitement, and Vera Miles the clinches. As Jacques Tourneur is the director, it's all rather stylish. (c)

Wicked As They Come ✕
Unappetising melo in spite of Arlene Dahl as man-eating executive; Ken Hughes directed; 1956. (b/w)

The Wicked Lady ✕
Margaret Lockwood in famous highwaywoman part that was lapped up by a spectacle-hungry wartime (1946) audience. It all looks distinctly creaky today, though there are a few moments of fun from James Mason, Martita Hunt, Patricia Roc. Director, Leslie Arliss. (b/w)

Wicked Woman ✕
Waitress entices boss to leave his wife, but then along comes a sailor. Russell Rouse doesn't convince, despite spirited attempts by his cast, Richard Egan, Beverly Michaels, who just haven't got the weight; 1954. (b/w)

The Wild Affair ✕ ✕
One of those pretentious trifles in which the star is given two parts to play—separate sides of her personality. For this 1965 effort Nancy Kwan was imported into England to be nice Marjorie and naughty Sandra, who takes over disastrously at the office party. It must have been intended as a comedy because the sprinkler system breaks down at the end and floods Terry-Thomas, Victor Spinetti *et al*. They are supposed to be too drunk to care; it might be more tolerable if you were, too. John Krish. (*b/w*)

The Wild and the Innocent ✓
Trapper Audie Murphy meets mountain girl Joanne Dru running away from home. Before it's all over he has to put his peaceful principles aside to protect her. Jack Sher had Jim Backus and Sandra Dee to stop it from getting too serious; 1959. (*c*)

The Wild and the Willing ✕
Pretentious university drama has Ian McShane as a rather churlish student having it away with his professor's wife, Virginia Maskell; also Paul Rogers and newcomers—in 1962—Samantha Eggar and John Hurt. Ralph Thomas directed. (*b/w*)

Wild and Wonderful ✕ ✕
Mild and middling more like. Tony Curtis out-acted by dog star in fight for Christine Kauffmann's affection. In real life he married her, then was divorced. Michael Anderson did tepid job of direction; 1964. (*c*)

The Wild Angels ✓ ✓
If this movie ever gets scheduled for TV there is bound to be a bit of an outcry, as there was in 1966 when it was banned for public showing in British cinemas (it did get club showings in 1969). However, it is a fascinating, authentic, disturbing and well-made film—the American entry at Venice—showing just how amoral the Hell's Angels motorcycle gangs were (are?). There is no plot, only a series of ever-more-violent incidents: rumbles, goading police, rapes, the shooting and capture of an Angel, his funeral. But it's made by a master of the thrill, Roger Corman, and Peter Fonda plays the main rôle—hero would be the wrong term. Only Nancy Sinatra is out of place; Michael J. Pollard and the rest look real—and a lot of them are. (*c*)

The Wild Bunch ✓ ✓
Outstanding Western by Sam Peckinpah about the last battles of a group of gunslingers—William Holden, Robert Ryan, Ernest Borgnine—brilliantly made, with an authority and intelligence unmatched by other Western directors. Unfortunately, it's also gratuitously violent, particularly at the end; 1969. (*c*)

Wild Heritage ✕
Teenage Western about two families making it to the Rockies. But oldsters Maureen O'Sullivan, Rod McKuen come off best under Charles Haas's direction; 1958. (*c*)

Wild in the Country ✕
Elvis Presley's metamorphosis from no-good country hick to industrious college boy; and all because that nice social worker, Hope Lange, discovered he could write. Oh dear. Philip Dunne directed; 1961. (*c*)

Wild in the Streets ✓
How a pop idol becomes President of America. A bit slapdash, it nevertheless manages to generate a sort of spurious conviction, thanks partly to Shelley Winter's bravura performance as his ghastly mother and Barry Shear's lively direction. In the main part, Christopher Jones is just about adequate; 1968. (*c*)

Wild Is The Wind ✕
Turgid drama of Nevada sheep farmer

Anthony Quinn marrying dead wife's sister Anna Magnani and getting a bit confused. Tony Franciosa. Directed by George Cukor, it isn't one of his best, but still managed to win Oscar nominations for his two stars; 1957. (*b/w*)

The Wild North ✕
Wendell Corey as Mountie, Stewart Granger the man he's out to get–but is he such a bad 'un after all? Cyd Charisse is obligatory inamorata; Andrew Marton the director; 1952. (*c*)

The Wild One √ √
Marlon Brando as head of motorcycle gang terrorising small town; Laslo Benedek directed brilliantly, and his gang of tough motor-bike Angels has entered the mythology of our times. Banned at the time, 1953, it looks milk-and-water against *The Wild Angels*, and was later permitted to be shown. Lee Marvin contributed a memorably evil role. (*b/w*)

The Wild Party √
Unusual actioner with Anthony Quinn as skidding football star freaking out in roadside cafe and holding young couple to ransom. Jay Robinson, Kathryn Grant come off well under Harry Horner's naturalistic direction; 1956. (*b/w*)

Wild River √ √
Absorbing account of TVA official Montgomery Clift trying to get old lady to relinquish her house and land, a genuine conflict between pride and progress; Elia Kazan obviously cared. Set in thirties, meticulously made in 1960, with Lee Remick caught in the middle. Jo Van Fleet, 37, plays an eighty-year-old. (*c*)

The Wild Seed √
Celia Kaye runs away from New York to seek parent in California. Meets up with freight-train rider Michael Parks and goes with him. Brian Hutton directs imaginatively and quite touchingly; 1965. (*b/w*)

Wild Stallion ✕
Lieutenant flashbacks through his military academy days remembering kindly officer and pet colt. Martha Hyer, Edgar Buchanan, Ben Johnson. Director Lewis D. Collins made it pretty sticky; 1952. (*c*)

The Wild Westerners ✕
Duane Eddy and Guy Mitchell pop up in this routine 1962 Western about newly-wed marshal investigating series of gold robberies. James Philbrook, Nancy Kovack. Oscar Rudolph directed. (*b/w*)

Will Penny √ √
The best Western for years, with Charlton Heston as a thoroughly believable, dirty, illiterate line rider (isolated for the winter looking after the prairie cattle); Joan Hackett, the young wife he gets involved with, is equally de-glamourised. Writer-director Tom Gries has allowed Donald Pleasence to go a bit mad as the villainous Preacher Quint, but everything else conveys for once what the West must really have been like; 1967. (*c*)

Will Success Spoil Rock Hunter? √
Historically interesting as belonging to Hollywood's Hate-TV period of 1957. In Frank Tashlin's neat direction of George Axelrod satire on commercials, Tony Randall and Joan Blondell make Jayne Mansfield look positively gawky. (*c*)

Wilson √
Well-meaning, grandiose attempt by Darryl Zanuck to bring the message of internationalism to 1944 audiences; instead they stayed away in droves and it was a $3½ million flop. In name part Alexander Knox was worthy but uncharismatic; director Henry King couldn't rise to the occasion. And it's very long. (*c*)

Winchester 73 √√
(1) Superior Western with James Stewart trailing Dan Duryea to settle grudge. This 1950 version by Anthony Mann had Shelley Winters, Tony Curtis, Rock Hudson in cast. (*b/w*)

Winchester 73 ×·×
(2) Apart from Dan Duryea, again, weak 1967 remake by Herschel Daugherty has inferior players (Tom Tryon, John Saxon) and would be a total write-off if it wasn't for Joan Blondell's cameo as floozie. (*c*)

Wind Across the Everglades √
Poorly cast by Nicholas Ray, this lyrical attempt to tell conservationist story of Florida at the turn of the century suffers from Christopher Plummer in the hero's role, Burl Ives as the heavy. Gypsy Rose Lee, clown Emmett Kelly and author MacKinlay Kantor take smaller parts more imaginatively; 1958. (*c*)

The Wind Cannot Read √
1958 weepie with Dirk Bogarde as RAF officer married to Japanese Yoko Tani during Second World War and escaping from POW camp to see her; Ralph Thomas directed. (*c*)

Windom's Way √
Predictable story of Dr Peter Finch running hospital on troubled Far East island, getting unwittingly involved with his estranged wife Mary Ure and local politics. With Natasha Parry, Michael Hordern. Directed in 1958 by Ronald Neame. (*c*)

Wings of Chance ×
Crashed pilot puts faith in wild bird to get him help. Jim Brown, Frances Rafferty; director, Edward Dew; 1959. (*c*)

The Wings of Eagles √
John Ford tribute to old friend and air hero Frank 'Spig' Wead, with John Wayne, Dan Dailey, Maureen O'Hara. A peacetime trail-blazer, he fights paralysis to help after Pearl Harbour. But his marriage goes wrong; 1957. (*c*)

Wings of Fire ×
Suzanne Pleshette as flyer who has to win air race to save the air freight service her father runs. Juliet Mills turns up in small part; Ralph Bellamy. Director David Lowell Rich; 1967. (*c*)

Wings of the Hawk ×
Van Heflin, Julia Adams down Mexico way, involved in revolution; doubtful if you'll get equally involved. despite director – Budd Boetticher; 1953. (*c*)

The Winning Team ×
Supposedly the story of real-life American baseball star, Grover Cleveland Alexander; that's Ronald Reagan, and Doris Day is his plucky wife. Lewis Seiler directed; 1952. (*b/w*)

The Winslow Boy √
Terence Rattigan's theatrical treatment of the famous case in which a twelve-year-old naval cadet was unjustly accused of theft, was opened out by him and producer Anatole de Grunwald into a less convincing screen treatment. Gone is the relationship of father and son, in its place a conventional court scene, with Robert Donat saving the day as his defending counsel. Anthony Asquith directed, in 1948, with his rather stuffy elegance. (*b/w*)

Winter Meeting ×·×
Interminable talk-talk-talk about falling in love, being afraid, becoming a priest. Should be bought up and burnt by Society for the Protection of Bette Davis who was made to go through humiliation of appearing as sexless spinster in 1948. Bretaigne Windust is said to have directed. (*b/w*)

The Witches ×·×
Cast (Joan Fontaine, Kay Walsh, Alec

McCowen, Ann Bell, Gwen Ffrangcon-Davies, Leonard Rossiter) much too good for this dreary yarn about witchcraft in an incredible English village, even though Nigel Kneale did the script. Maybe Cyril Frankel wasn't quite the right director? 1967. (*c*)

Witchfinder General   √ √
Remarkable effort by young director Michael Reeves who died soon after it was completed in 1968. Vincent Price makes a genuinely scary witch-hunter in Cromwell's England; Ian Ogilvy and Hilary Dwyer more than adequate young lovers. Rather a lot of gore, but most of it is justified. (*c*)

With A Song In My Heart   √
1952 tearjerker based on the dramatic–not to say melodramatic–life of singer Jane Froman, crippled in plane crash. An inadequate Susan Hayward mimes to Froman's voice on Alfred Newman's Oscar-winning soundtrack. Thelma Ritter, Robert Wagner, Rory Calhoun give her much-needed support; director Walter Lang tried hard. (*c*)

With Six You Get Eggroll   × ×
Widow with three sons, Doris Day, marries widower with one daughter, Brian Keith. That's when the fun begins –or so director Howard Morris hoped, anyway. In fact, this 1968 attempt at a 'happy' film (there are no bad guys, promised the publicity) is sickening enough without the promised eggroll. (*c*)

Witness for the Prosecution   √ √
Billy Wilder's fancywork with Marlene Dietrich being indulged, Charles Laughton licking his chops with contentment, plus Tyrone Power, Elsa Lanchester enjoying themselves in Agatha Christie courtroom hokum; 1957. (*b/w*)

Witness to Murder   √
Barbara Stanwyck sees a murder but no one will believe her. Roy Rowland's direction makes this 1954 cliff-hanger a bit more than run-of-the-thrill. (*b/w*)

Wives and Lovers   ×
Success looks like spoiling writer Van Johnson and his marriage to Janet Leigh; agent Martha Hyer, divorcée Shelley Winters, Ray Walston add to their problems. Director John Rich just couldn't make their dramas add up to the sophisticated fun he must have hoped for in 1963. (*c*)

The Wizard of Baghdad   × ×
Unsuccessful genie is given one more chance. George Sherman attempted send-up of *Arabian Nights* genre without conspicuous success. Dick Shawn, Vaughn Taylor try too hard. 1960. (*c*)

Wolf Dog   × ×
Paroled ex-marine runs up against land-grabbing neighbour when he settles in the wild Canadian north. Jim Davis, Tony Brown. Director Sam Newfield; 1958. (*b/w*)

Wolf Larsen   √
Jack London's *Sea Wolf* done over to give Barry Sullivan the chance to enjoy himself as tyrannical sea captain. Director Harmon Jones; 1958. (*b/w*)

The Woman and the Hunter   × ×
Ann Sheridan's last picture, made in 1957, ten years before her death, was a weak triangle story set on safari, with David Farrar and John Loder competing for bad-actor-of-the-year award. Director, George Breakston; 1957. (*b/w*)

Womaneater   × ×
It's a long slide from Walter P. Thatcher in *Citizen Kane* to mad scientist in this tedious little so-called horror picture, but George Coulouris made it. It's about a tree of life that needs to eat young ladies to flourish. You can guess the rest. The guilty director was Charles Saunders; 1957. (*b/w*)

Woman in a Dressing Gown　　　✗
'The *Brief Encounter* of the council houses', cracked one critic. Anthony Quayle is the husband, driven by slapdash wife Yvonne Mitchell into arms of secretary Sylvia Syms. J. Lee Thompson directed Ted Willis' would-be Chayefskyan script, which did well in 1957 but looks pretty unconvincing now. (*b/w*)

The Woman in Question　　　✓
Dirk Bogarde, Hermione Baddeley, Charles Victor, John McCallum, all recall murdered Jean Kent differently; pity detective Duncan Mac-Rae, who has to sort their stories out. Director Anthony Asquith did a neat job in 1950. (*b/w*)

The Woman in the Window　　　✓✓
Edward G. Robinson as weak, unfulfilled professor entangled with Joan Bennett and murder in 1944. Fritz Lang conjured up dark streets and overfurnished rooms, and Dan Duryea's menacing whine is one of the great movie memories. (*b/w*)

Woman Obsessed　　　✗
Wilds of Canada are setting for this mushy Henry Hathaway-directed melo about widow Susan Hayward's stormy second marriage to Stephen Boyd; her young son is just one of their many problems; 1959. (*c*)

A Woman of Distinction　　　✓
But a film of not very much. 1950 Edward Buzzell-directed farce about headmistress of girls' school getting involved with visiting academic, has a lot of energetic clowning from Rosalind Russell and Ray Milland but few laughs. (*b/w*)

Woman of Straw　　　✗
The one about wicked nephew (Sean Connery) and sexy nurse (Gina Lollobrigida) plotting to do away with wealthy old gent (Ralph Richardson) and inherit fortune. Basil Dearden directed; 1964. (*c*)

Woman of the North Country　　　✗
Mining tycoon Rod Cameron fights treachery for control of the ore. Gale Storm, Ruth Hussey, J. Carrol Naish support. Director, Joseph Kane; 1952. (*c*)

Woman on the Run　　　✓
Can Ann Sheridan find her husband before mobsters do? He was the only witness to murder. Dennis O'Keefe, Frank Jenks. Director, Norman Foster; 1950. (*b/w*)

Woman They Almost Lynched　　　✓
Because she was premature women's-libber in being quicker than all the men in town on the draw. As she was an outlaw, you can understand why the townsfolk were upset. Joan Leslie metamorphoses from nice young lady to gunslinger. Allan Dwan had been directing films for 39 years when he turned this one out, so it's got to have a professional gloss. Audrey Totter, Brian Donlevy. John Lund among townsfolk; 1953. (*b/w*)

Woman Times Seven　　　✗
Vittorio de Sica directed seven different stories about seven different women giving Shirley MacLaine (who played them all) too great an opportunity to indulge herself in 1967. Whether you'll enjoy yourself as much, watching her, is another matter. The necessarily large cast includes Michael Caine, Peter Sellers, Rossano Brazzi, Alan Arkin, Anita Ekberg, Patrick Wymark, Robert Morley. (*c*)

A Woman's Devotion　　　✗
Ralph Meeker goes potty in Mexico; Janice Rule stands by him. Paul Henreid directs and appears, too; 1956. (*c*)

Woman's World　　　✓
Three out-of-town executives and their wives are summoned to New York so that auto company boss Clifton Webb

can observe them more closely before deciding which of them he gives important promotion to. Lauren Bacall, Fred MacMurray, Van Heflin, Arlene Dahl, June Allyson, Cornel Wilde are hopefuls, and director Jean Negulesco gave it a (tooth and nail) polish in 1954. (*c*)

Woman Without a Face √
James Garner has lost his memory. Who is he? All kinds of nice characters try to help him find out: Jean Simmons, Suzanne Pleshette, Katharine Ross, George Voskovec among them. Evan Hunter didn't make the adaptation from his own book, *Buddwing*; for some reason Dale Wasserman did. Delbert Mann directs as if he had some idea that he was creating an allegory of all men finding themselves; 1968. (*b/w*)

Women's Prison ×
Ida Lupino is sadistic superintendent, responsible for awful conditions; the inevitable revolt by prisoners leads to clean-up, so we can all switch off at the end with an easy mind. Director Lewis Seiler was obviously sincere in 1955, if wildly over-optimistic about penal reform. (*b/w*)

The Wonderful Country √
Robert Mitchum, gun-running between Mexico and Texas, finds time to make love to Julie London in this 1959 time-passer. Aged fans will welcome sight of Jack Oakie. Director, Robert Parrish. (*c*)

Wonderful Life ×
Must have been if you had Cliff Richard under contract and uncritical teenagers would go and see him, whatever old rubbish he was in. This 1964 effort, with Susan Hampshire, Una Stubbs, Derek Bond was about Cliff and his mates trying to make a movie. Did director Sidney Furie let them practise on this one? (*c*)

The Wonders of Aladdin ×
Retelling of the old panto story, with Donald O'Connor and a nine foot genie. Vittorio de Sica among Henry Levin's cast; 1961. (*c*)

Wonderwall × ×
Right load of codswallop about a voyeur with fantasies. Jack MacGowran did his best in the circumstance of acute miscasting. Jane Birkin is appealing as the object of his desires; Irene Handl, Richard Wattis, Beatrix Lehmann go through their usual paces. Over Iain Quarrier's performance as Jane's boyfriend let a veil be drawn. Also over Joe Massot's direction; 1969. (*c*)

The Wooden Horse √
Best-known WW2 real-life escape story, 1950, using vaulting horse as cover for getting away from Stalag Luft POW camp. Good performances from Leo Genn, David Tomlinson, Anthony Steel and Bryan Forbes. Tight, tense direction from Jack Lee. (*b/w*)

Words and Music √
Not strong in the production department, but Rodgers and Hart songs (Thou Swell, Blue Moon, I Wish I Were In Love Again, Manhattan *et al.*) are marvellous and cast (Micky Rooney, Judy Garland, Lena Horne, Ann Sothern, Perry Como) not bad. Same can't be said for Norman Taurog's direction; 1948. (*c*)

World for Ransom ×
Dan Duryea tries to prevent kidnapping of nuclear scientist – rather harder than director Robert Aldrich, who was new at the game in 1954. (*b/w*)

The World in His Arms ×
Old-fashioned (and we're not just referring to the 19th century San Francisco setting) romance has Gregory Peck as dashing sea captain, Ann Blyth as lovely Russian countess he loves and fights for, and lush Raoul Walsh direction; 1952. (*c*)

World in My Corner ✕
Audie Murphy, on his way to champion-
ship, nearly throws away a fight and his
good name for money. But, with
Barbara Rush standing by, he's gonna
be OK. Yes, you've seen it before, though
maybe not with these particular actors or
Jesse Hibbs's directing; 1956. (*b/w*)

The World of Henry Orient √
Occasionally funny comedy from director George Roy Hill in 1964 has Peter
Sellers well-cast in role of narcissistic,
womanising pianist and appealing performances from Tippy Walker and
Merrie Spaeth as the adoring teenage
fans who chase him round New York;
plus Angela Lansbury, Paula Prentiss. (*c*)

The World of Suzie Wong ✕ ✕
Richard Quine's brilliant direction of
the Hong Kong background to this
East-meets-West yarn is by far the best
thing in this otherwise hokey melodrama. You can't believe in William
Holden's American painter and even
less in Nancy Kwan's 'hostess' (in 1960
they couldn't say whore) or the gooey
relationship between them. Sylvia Syms
and Michael Wilding are a real couple
of pills. (*c*)

The World Ten Times Over ✕
Bleak little drama about two disil-
lusioned nightclub hostesses; competent
British cast is led by June Ritchie,
Sylvia Syms, Edward Judd, William
Hartnell. Wolf Rilla directed; 1963. (*b/w*)

The World, the Flesh and the Devil ✕
Is Harry Belafonte the only one left
alive on earth after nuclear holocaust?
No, it turns out that Inger Stevens and
Mel Ferrer survived too, and they all
meet up in an eerily deserted New York–
very handy, as far as the future of mankind is concerned. Director Ranald
MacDougall begged a lot of questions
in 1959. (*b/w*)

The World Was His Jury ✕
Was the captain to blame for sinking of
his ship with the loss of 162 lives? In
Fred F. Sears' dull courtroom drama
the truth comes out; Edmond O'Brien
is lawyer; 1958. (*b/w*)

World Without End √
Hugh Marlow, Rod Taylor, Nancy
Gates, Nelson Leigh are scientists
landing on strange planet and finding
that they have broken time barrier and
are on Earth in the year 2508. Edward
Bernds makes it lively sci-fiction; 1956.
(*c*)

The Wrecking Crew ✕ ✕
This Matt Helm-Bond-like adventure
was clearly ground out in desperation in
1969. Few of the players seem to care–
Dean Martin, Elke Sommer, Nancy
Kwan are all deadly, as is Phil Karlson's
surprisingly lackadaisical direction. A
melancholy fact is that it features Sharon
Tate and Nigel Green, both of whom
were to die shortly afterwards in garish
circumstances. (*c*)

The Wreck of the Mary Deare √
Sea-yarn of English Channel shipwreck
was Gary Cooper's penultimate picture
(1960). Strong story, strong special
effects, strong supports (Charlton Heston, Michael Redgrave, Emlyn Williams,
Richard Harris); let down by Michael
Anderson's weak direction. (*c*)

Written on the Wind √
Well, it goes something like this: Rock
Hudson is in love with Lauren Bacall
who is married to Robert Stack whose
nympho sister, Dorothy Malone, is in
love with Rock Hudson who, you may
recall . . . Like all good magazine stories,
it works out happily in the end–for two
of them, at least–and Dorothy Malone
won 1956 Academy Award for Best
Supporting Actress. Douglas Sirk. (*c*)

The Wrong Arm of the Law √
Farce, with Peter Sellers switching accents, about rival gangs. The Law, in the person of Lionel Jeffries, is continually made a monkey of—first by one gang dressing up as policemen, then with the other suspending activities to help catch them. Bernard Cribbins adds to the fun. Cliff Owen directed; 1963. *(b/w)*

The Wrong Box ✕
Bryan Forbes directed and produced this adaptation of Robert Louis Stevenson story in 1966. John Mills and Ralph Richardson were the two brothers, murderously out to inherit a fortune from each other, and gave credence to camp, which is sometimes pitched at wrong level. Peter Cook and Dudley Moore make uninspired appearances; Tony Hancock and Peter Sellers do OK; Nanette Newman beautiful and inevitable.*(c)*

The Wrong Man ✕
Unusual, highly documentary direction in 1957 from Hitchcock of this true but somehow dull story about New York musician wrongly accused of murder. Fine performances from Henry Fonda as helpless accused, and Vera Miles his wife, going mad under the strain. But Hitch himself files it 'among the indifferent Hitchcocks', feeling that he was too true to life. *(b/w)*

Wyoming Mail √
Stephen McNally, joining gang as part of his job as undercover agent, discovers that Alexis Smith is part of it. Reginald LeBorg's lively direction of postal robbery scenes is helped by support from Ed Begley, Richard Egan, James Arness; 1950. *(c)*

Wyoming Renegades ✕
Phil Carey comes out of jail, determined to go straight, but townspeople are sceptical. Martha Hyer believes in him and helps him prove his worth. Fred F. Sears made it pretty conventional; 1955. *(c)*

X – 15 ✕
Charles Bronson, Mary Tyler Moore, David McLean, Patricia Owens among scientists and wives who suffer at a Californian missile base. Richard Donner directs, James Stewart narrates; 1961. *(c)*

X – the Man with X-Ray Eyes √
Ray Milland develops a serum to improve sight but it causes him to see through solid objects. Accidentally killing a colleague, he flees and gets involved in all sorts of creepy adventures, ending up marked as a Devil. Roger Corman directed all this in 1963 with his usual perfunctory brilliance, although the implications are never explored. Pity. *(c)*

X – The Unknown ✕ ✕
Sci-fi set in Scotland, about Something Nasty from earth's centre trying to take us—or, at least, Dean Jagger, Leo McKern, William Lucas, Edward Chapman—over. Leslie Norman directed; 1956. *(b/w)*

Yangste Incident ✕

Michael Anderson's tepid 1957 account of crippled HMS Amethyst's 140-mile escape from Red Chinese in 1949. Richard Todd plays Lt. Commander John Kerans, with William Hartnell, Robert Urquhart, Donald Houston as crew-members; Akim Tamiroff as a heavy heavy. Actually, it wasn't quite so heroic because the Chinese deliberately refrained from firing on them and even fed them, so as to win a diplomatic victory. (*b/w*)

Yankee Buccaneer ✕

American pirates *v.* international pirates, Jeff Chandler flying the skull-and-crossbones for Uncle Sam. Jeff Chandler, David Janssen among those up in the rigging, shouted at by director Frederick de Cordova (a good name for a pirate); 1952. (*c*)

Yankee Doodle Dandy √

James Cagney winning an Oscar as early showman George M. Cohan in classic musical biopic that defies criticism; Walter Huston, Joan Leslie Michael Curtiz; 1942. (*b/w*)

Yankee Pasha ✕

Unlikely costume yarn has Jeff Chandler going to the rescue of girlfriend Rhonda Fleming who's been kidnapped by

James Cagney in *Yankee Doodle Dandy*

pirates and shipped to Morocco. Joseph Pevney directed; 1954. (*c*)

A Yank in the RAF ✕
Henry King's wartime (1941) time-passer about Tyrone Power's involvement with chorus-girl Betty Grable. With John Sutton, Reginald Gardiner. (*b/w*)

The Yearling √ √
Entrancing story of a young boy's love for a pet fawn which his father must destroy. Remarkably unsentimental, Clarence Brown's 1946 direction delicately explores complex emotions. Beautifully photographed, with splendid performances from Gregory Peck, Jane Wyman and Claude Jarman Jr, it won four Academy Awards. (*c*)

The Yellow Balloon √
Andrew Ray in his child-actor days–1952–shocked by chum's death and used by crook. Kenneth More, Bernard Lee, directed by J. Lee Thompson. (*b/w*)

The Yellow Cab Man √
Red Skelton invents unbreakable glass; gets job as cab driver to test it. OK for fans, if any. Edmond Arnold, Walter Slezak. Jack Donahue directed; 1950. (*b/w*)

The Yellow Canary ✕
(1) 1944 British spy drama has Anna Neagle pretending to be nazi sympathiser; Margaret Rutherford, Richard Greene and director Herbert Wilcox. (*b/w*)

The Yellow Canary √
(2) 1963 melodrama has singer Pat Boone hunting down baby son's kidnappers; Jack Klugman, Barbara Eden, Steve Forrest and director Buzz Kulik. (*b/w*)

Yellow Mountain ✕ ✕
There's gold in them thar hills, and gals, and guns. Lex Barker, Howard Duff,

William Demarest are fightin' for 'em. Jesse Hibbs is directin'; 1954. (*c*)

The Yellow Rolls-Royce √
Anthony Asquith's experienced direction keeps this episodic 1965 movie about the title car's various owners running smoothly. Despite bumper cast–Rex Harrison, Shirley MacLaine, Ingrid Bergman, Jeanne Moreau, George C. Scott, Omar Sharif, Alain Delon–it's only occasionally entertaining. (*c*)

Yellow Sky √ √
Bizarre but fascinating 1948 attempt by William Wellman to retell *The Tempest* as a Western. Anne Baxter is Miranda-called-Mike, with Gregory Peck against Richard Widmark for prize of stolen gold. Super photography by Joe MacDonald. (*b/w*)

Yellowstone Kelly ✕
Nothing much new about this Western, with Clint Walker warring with Sioux over Indian girl. Gordon Douglas directed; 1959. (*c*)

Yellow Submarine √ √
Inventive, over-long, sporadically brilliant period (1968) piece, when the Beatles were in their infant-regression *Sgt. Pepper* stage. George Dunning's direction of the animation is remarkably successful and it stands as a lasting monument to the end of an era. (*c*)

The Yellow Teddybears ✕ ✕ ✕
Silly little attempt to cash in a spurious 1963 news-story that some schoolgirls had taken to wearing Robertson's free-gift golliwogs to show they were no longer virgins. Inferior in almost every department, the blame must go mostly to Robert Hartford-Davis as director and producer. (*b/w*)

The Yellow Tomahawk ✕
Rory Calhoun browned-up as Indian

guide and browned-off with his mates when he learns they intend to attack whites, Noah Beery, Peggie Castle. All a bit Uncle Tomahawkish. Lesley Selander; 1954. (c)

Yesterday's Enemy ✕
World War 2 drama has Captain Stanley Baker and what's left of his men under threat from nearby Japanese in Burmese jungle; Val Guest directs equivocally–seeming uncertain whether to approve or disapprove of their cruelties ('Come on Dad, over here,' says Sgt. Gordon Jackson, gently leading an old bewildered Burmese to the firing squad) or to take a neutral moral stance. Is the final shot of a war memorial ironic or not? Take your choice; 1959. (b/w)

Yield To the Night √
Grim prison drama about condemned girl awaiting execution. Under J. Lee Thompson's didactic direction, Diana Dors made the switch from pin-up (this was 1956) to drab dramatic actress without causing too much embarrassment; Yvonne Mitchell, Athene Seyler, Michael Craig. (b/w)

You Can't Run Away From It ✕ ✕
Ghastly 1956 musical remake of *It Happened One Night* has June Allyson as runaway heiress, Jack Lemmon as the newspaperman she falls for. Director Dick Powell had a heavy-handed touch in 1956, and it's all a shameful shadow of the original. (c)

You Can't Sleep Here √
Cary Grant, in drag, makes this comedy of a Frenchman pretending to be an American lady soldier so as to accompany wife Ann Sheridan back to the US, funnier than it sounds. Howard Hawks did a jovial job in 1949. (b/w)

You For Me ✕
What Jane Greer has got that makes

millionaires and doctors flip so madly over her as a nurse isn't explained by director Don Weis in this light entertainment, but Gig Young and Peter Lawford go happily along; 1952. (b/w)

You Know What Sailors Are ✕
Only surprise in this 1953 British farce, directed cheerfully but ineptly by Ken Annakin, about repercussions following naval officer's spoof about secret weapon is appearance of marvellously-cured ham, Akim Tamiroff. For the rest it's Donald Sinden, Naunton Wayne and a cast of wet Carry-on types; 1953. (c)

You Must Be Joking √
Army psychologist Terry-Thomas devises 'foolproof' initiative test to find the perfect soldier. With so many old pros–Denholm Elliott, Lionel Jeffries, Bernard Cribbins, Richard Wattis, Leslie Phillips, Wilfrid Hyde White, James Villiers, Irene Handl, James Robertson Justice–in the cast, director Michael Winner had to come up with a few laughs in 1965. (b/w)

You Never Can Tell ✕
No, not Shaw's nineties comedy, but a pretty dire farce about a German sheepdog who's murdered and returns to Earth as human private detective to track down his killer; with Dick Powell, Charles Drake, directed by Lou Breslow; 1951. (b/w)

Young and Dangerous ✕
The one about the teenage Lothario who bets he can make nice girl fall in love with him; he does, she does, then he does, then she finds out . . . yawn, yawn. Mark Damon's the boy; Lili Gentle. Director, William Claxton; 1957. (b/w)

The Young and the Guilty ✕ ✕ ✕
Awfully dated Ted Willis drama has Andrew Ray and Janet Munro as gauche teenage lovers–this was 1958.

Edward Chapman plays girl's heavy father; Phyllis Calvert, her mum. Peter Cotes. (*b/w*)

Young and Wild ✕
Tough, yarn about three lads in a stolen car and the havoc they wreak–mostly on the viewer. Scott Marlowe, Gene Evans, Robert Arthur, directed by William Witney; 1958. (*b/w*)

Young At Heart √
1955 musical remake of John Garfield tearjerker, *Four Daughters*, has Doris Day running off with hard-bitten musician Frank Sinatra; some nice songs (Someone To Watch Over Me, Just One of Those Things, One For My Baby); and a happy ending. Gordon Douglas directed; 1955. (*c*)

Young Bess √
Historical romance that's more romance than history, has Jean Simmons as future Queen Elizabeth, Stewart Granger as love interest, Thomas Seymour; Charles Laughton plays Henry VIII again. George Sidney; 1953. (*c*)

Young Billy Young √
Marshall Robert Mitchum has jailed the chief heavy's son which makes for the excitement in this otherwise routine Burt Kennedy Western. Angie Dickinson is the saloon gal, Robert Walker plays the title-role. Perfectly acceptable stuff; 1969. (*c*)

Youngblood Hawke √
How fame and fortune change young writer's life; although neither Delmer Daves' direction–nor adaptation from Herman Wouk's real-life best-seller–nor wooden performances from James Franciscus, Genevieve Page, Suzanne Pleshette make you care much, it does have a compulsion. Mary Astor shines momentarily as Broadway actress; 1964. (*b/w*)

Young Cassidy ✕ ✕
Rod Taylor monumentally miscast as the young Sean O'Casey, with Julie Christie, Maggie Smith as his young ladies and Flora Robson as his mother. John Ford directed some of it, Jack Cardiff rather more, and between them they failed to give either a coherent or a convincing picture of the man or the period in Ireland; 1965. (*c*)

Young Dillinger ✕
Casting of colourless Nick Adams as real life thirties gangster, John Dillinger, robs this 1965 biopic of credibility; not that director Terry O. Morse had given it much. (*b/w*)

The Young Doctors √
Ben Gazzara and Fredric March gives shots in the arm to otherwise conventional hospital drama about young, progressive doctor clashing with old, directed by a tired Phil Karlson; 1961. (*b/w*)

The Young Don't Cry ✕
Sal Mineo platonically involved with escaped convict and refusing to tell on him. James Whitmore, J. Carrol Naish; directed by Alfred L. Werker; 1957. (*b/w*)

The Younger Brothers √
Not younger as opposed to older, but Younger was their name; waiting for a pardon, they hear that their younger (sorry) brother has been forced to kill a man, so off they go on their lawless lives once more. Wayne Morris, Robert Hutton, Alan Hale, Fred Clark, Janis Paige head a strong cast; Edwin L. Marin directed; 1949. (*c*)

The Young Guns ✕
Teenage Western with Russ Tamblyn trying to live down town's memory of gunslinger father; Albert Band; 1956. (*b/w*)

Young Guns of Texas √
Has some curiosity in casting of Robert Mitchum's son James, Joel McCrea's daughter Jody, Alan Ladd's daughter Alana, as searchers for stolen Army gold, and searched for by Chill Wills. Then Apaches strike. Maury Dexter; 1962. (*c*)

Young Jesse James × ×
How famous outlaw–played here by Ray Stricklyn–got to be that way, but don't believe a word of it. William Claxton; 1960. (*b/w*)

The Young Land √
Before 1848, any American who killed a Mexican in California could be sure to get away with it. This interesting Western tells what happens when the first one was put on trial. Pat Wayne, Dan O'Herlihy, Dennis Hopper score in Ted Tetzlaff's unusual try; 1959. (*c*)

The Young Lions √
Worth sitting through interwoven wartime stories of two Americans (Montgomery Clift, Dean Martin) and one enemy for Marlon Brando's correct, precise German, changed at his insistence from Irwin Shaw's original brutalised nazi to sensitive soul. Edward Dmytryk; 1958. (*b/w*)

The Young Lovers × ×
Weak college drama has unmarried students Peter Fonda and Sharon Hugueny in a tizzy about unwanted pregnancy. Samuel Goldwyn Jr couldn't make us care in 1965. (*b/w*)

Young Man with a Horn √
Supposedly based (via Dorothy Baker's novel) on life of Bix Beiderbecke–but *he* died at 28. Kirk Douglas as jazz trumpeter (miming to Harry James); Doris Day and Lauren Bacall as the good and bad women in his life–no prizes for guessing which is which–Michael Curtiz; 1950. (*b/w*)

Young Man With Ideas √
Harmless comedy about lawyer Glenn Ford and family trying to make a home for themselves in California. Mitchell Leisen; 1952. (*b/w*)

Young Mr Lincoln √
Not particularly true to life, but always dramatic, occasionally over-sentimental, account of Abraham Lincoln's early days. The make-up man gave super-sincere Henry Fonda a new nose, but he didn't need the famous beard–Lincoln grew it later. John Ford directed, in 1939, with worship for the future president. (*b/w*)

The Young Ones ×
This naïve but lively musical about Cliff Richard and mates trying to save their local youth club from property developers (Robert Morley), seems embarrassingly out-of-date today; it was too goody-goody even by 1961 standards, when Sidney Furie directed. (*c*)

The Young Philadelphians √
Long, glossy fable about ambitious young lawyer-on-the-make in Philadelphian society, based on Richard Powell's best-seller. Compelling performance from Paul Newman as the heel who reforms. Strong support from Robert Vaughn, Otto Kruger, Barbara Rush and Alexis Smith gave this slick Vincent Sherman-directed soaper a distinction it didn't really deserve in 1959. (*b/w*)

The Young Racers ×
Ex-racing driver plans to expose racing champ in book he's writing, changes his mind. They used to call director Roger Corman King of the B-pictures, and you can see why in this one. Mark Damon, Patrick Magee; 1963. (*c*)

The Young Savages √
Burt Lancaster as assistant district attorney *v.* juvenile street murder gang; John Frankenheimer's second film, 1961. Sharp and socially conscious. Shelley Winters, Telly Savalas. (*b/w*)

The Young Stranger √
Well-intentioned little domestic drama about teenage boy reacting against busy father's neglect. James MacArthur, James Daly, Kim Hunter made a believable family in John Frankenheimer's modest 1956 directorial debut. (*b/w*)

The Young Warriors ✕
James Drury is tough sergeant in charge of inexperienced platoon in this low-budget (and it shows) World War 2 drama. John Peyser; 1966. (*c*)

Young Wives' Tale ✕ ✕
Terribly British comedy about couples sharing to beat the housing shortage—how quaint. Spot Audrey Hepburn in tiny part if you can keep awake amidst posturing of Joan Greenwood, Nigel Patrick, Derek Farr, Helen Cherry. Director, Henry Cass; 1951. (*b/w*)

Your Cheatin' Heart ✕
Biopic of country singer Hank Williams who died from drink at the early age of 29, homogenised to make just another movie with songs. Maybe the presence of his widow as 'technical adviser' and his son as George Hamilton's singing voice had something to do with feeling of unreality. Gene Nelson directed; 1966. (*b/w*)

You're a Big Boy Now √
If you can find the sexual awakening and education of young lad in New York screamingly funny then you'll probably fall about over this one directed by Francis Ford Coppola (in 1967, before he hit the big time). Gimmickly directed, using the locations to the full (and more) and borrowing from a dozen influential movies, it has a zany sophistication. But it's strictly Fantasyland, even down to calling the characters names like Miss Thing (Julie Harris as his landlady). Peter Kastner's naïveté becomes wearing, though perky cameos by Geraldine Page (Mom), Rip Torn (Pa), Michael Dunn and Elizabeth Hartman (boy-eater) stop boredom. Karen Black is his saviour, if not ours; 1967. (*c*)

You're in the Navy Now √
Innocent World War 2 fun has an inexperienced Captain Gary Cooper trying to run experimental ship and dopey crew—Eddie Albert, Lee Marvin, Jack Webb. Grown-ups may prefer a slightly more sophisticated brand of humour than they'll find in this 1951 lark from Henry Hathaway. Originally called USS Teakettle, from the steam engine that plays major role. Cooper was never more lovable, but the film's a bit strained. (*c*)

You're Never Too Young ✕
Dean Martin-Jerry Lewis romp, with Jerry dressing up as child to hide from criminals. Norman Taurog; 1955. (*c*)

Your Money Or Your Wife ✕ ✕
Donald Sinden and Peggy Cummins must divorce so as to inherit fortune. Ho hum. 1959 effort of Anthony Simmons, who later directed the off-beat *Four in the Morning*. (*b/w*)

Yours, Mine and Ours ✕
Director Melville Shavelson must have thought he could rely on old pros Henry Fonda and Lucille Ball to save this noisy farce about widow with eight children marrying widower with ten. But at 62 and 56, respectively, in 1968, they were too creaky and the movie was just too old-fashioned. (*c*)

Zarak ✕
North West Frontier adventure has Michael Wilding as British officer after outlaw leader Victor Mature, Anita Ekberg. Terence Young directed; 1957. (*c*)

Zebra in the Kitchen ✓
Little boy lets animals out of the zoo because he can't bear his pet mountain lion under lock and key. Pleasant enough stuff, directed by Ivan Tors. Andy Devine, Joyce Meadows; 1965. (*c*)

Zero Hour ✕
Predictable tale of guilt-ridden wartime pilot Dana Andrews who lost entire squadron, forced to take over airliner (with wife Linda Darnell and son aboard) when crew falls sick. Directed, 1957, by Hall Bartlett. (*b/w*)

Ziegfeld Follies ✓
Example of rare kind of movie, the musical revue. William Powell makes brief opening appearances as the impressario, but it's just a string of numbers, mostly worth watching. Outstanding are Fred Astaire with Gene Kelly, Lena Horne, Judy Garland burlesqueing a film-star interview, Victor Moore and Edward Arnold in comedy sketch. Main director was Vincente Minnelli; 1946. (*c*)

Stanley Baker in *Zulu*

Ziegfeld Girl √

Memorable for three Busby Berkley dance numbers, particularly You Stepped Out Of A Dream; Judy Garland singing I'm Always Chasing Rainbows; Lana Turner as Bad Girl. Robert Z. Leonard; 1940. (*b/w*)

Zombies of Mora-Tau × ×

Soppy stuff about wife becoming one of the walking dead when she is killed by one of them guarding her husband's diamond mine. Gregg Palmer; director Edward L. Cahn; 1957. (*b/w*)

Zorba the Greek √

A great success in 1964, this long indulgence of Anthony Quinn as a life-loving, illiterate Greek who persuades Alan Bates to employ him, is a bit of a bore unless you want to be taken in by Michael Cacoyannis's beguiling way with a camera; particularly when held by Walter Lassally. The music helps, of course. Lila Kedrova won Academy Award support as dying whore. (*b/w*)

Zotz! ×

Stuff about professor finding magic coin that makes people move in slow motion; with Tom Poston, Jim Backus, Julia Meade. William Castle directed; 1962. (*b/w*)

Zulu √ √

Considering the flag-waving jingoistic ghastliness that the theme of Empah-building has so often received in movies – both British and American – from *Four Feathers* to *The Lives of a Bengal Lancer*, the temptations in Cy Endfield's way must have been very great. That he resisted them, and made a film in 1963 that treated the 'other side' with respect was a major feat. Bloodthirsty and B.O.P-exciting it still was, but the performances of co-producer Stanley Baker, Jack Hawkins, Ulla Jacobsson, James Booth, Michael Caine, Nigel Green and Patrick Magee in and around the Battle of Rorke's Drift were of a very high standard. More than an epic, a real film. (*c*)

The Abominable Snowman of the Himalayas: The Abominable Snowman
Adventure at Rugby: Tom Brown's Schooldays
Agent 008¾: Hot Enough for June
All This and Money Too: Love is a Ball
The Alphabet Murders: The ABC Murders
America, America: The Anatolian Smile
The Appaloosa: Southwest to Sonora
Arizona Outpost: Devil's Canyon

The Baited Trap: The Trap
The Battle of Powder River: Tomahawk
Before I Wake: Shadow of Fear
Bengal Brigade: Bengal Rifles
Beyond the River: Bottom of the Barrel
The Big Carnival: Ace in the Hole
A Big Hand for the Little Lady: Big Deal at Dodge City
The Big Heart: Miracle on 34th St
Billy Rose's Jumbo: Jumbo
Blood Money: Requiem for a Heavyweight
Blood on my Hands: Kiss the Blood off My Hands
Blue Denim: Blue Jeans
Blues for Lovers: Ballad in Blue
Bonaventure: Thunder on the Hill
Both Sides of the Law: Street Corner
Break to Freedom: Albert RN

The Caretakers: Borderlines
Caribbean Gold: Caribbean
Cattle King: Guns of Wyoming
Chance Meeting: The Young Lovers
The Charge is Murder: Twilight of Honour
Coming Out Party: Very Important Person
Company of Cowards: Advance to the Rear
The Contact Man: Alias Nick Beal
Court Martial: Carrington V.C.
The Court Martial of Billy Mitchell: One Man Mutiny
Cruel Swamp: Swamp Women
The Curse of Simba: Curse of the Voodoo

Girl in Room 17: Vice Squad
The Girl Swappers: Two and Two Make Six
Glory at Sea: The Gift Horse
The Great Manhunt: State Secrets
The Great Sioux Massacre: The Great Sioux Raid
Gun the Man Down: Arizona Mission

Harper: The Moving Target
High Vermilion: Silver City
His Other Woman: The Desk Set
House in the Square: I'll never forget you
House of Secrets: Triple Deception

I Like Money: Mr Topaze
I'll Get You for This: Lucky Nick Cain
I Shall Return: American Guerilla in the Philippines
I Stand Accused: An Act of Murder
I Was a Male War Bride: You Can't Sleep Here
If You Feel Like Singing: Summer Stock
The Incredible Praying Mantis: The Deadly Mantis
It Happened in Tokyo: Twenty Plus Two
The Intruder: The Stranger

The James Brothers: The True Story of Jesse James
Jules Verne's Rocket to the Moon: Rocket to the Moon

Killer on a Horse: Welcome to Hard Times
King of the Roaring Twenties: The Big Bankroll

Lancelot and Guinevere: Sword of Lancelot
The Land We Love: Hero's Island
The Last Challenge: The Pistolero of Red River
The Light Fantastic: Love is Better than Ever
Lights Out: Bright Victory
Lisa: The Inspector
Live Today for Tomorrow: An Act of Murder
Lost Treasure of the Amazon: Jivaro

Mail Order Bride: West of Montana
Man from the Folies Bergere: Folies Bergere
Manhunt: From Hell to Texas
Marshmallow Moon: Aaron Slick from Punkin Crik
Master of Lassie: Hills of Home
The Mercenaries: Dark of the Sun
The Million Pound Note: Man with a Million
Murder Inc: The Enforcer
The Murder in Thornton Square: Gaslight
Mr Arcadin (Mr Arkadin): Confidential Report
Mr Ashton was Indiscreet: The Senator was Indiscreet

The Night Fighter: A Terrible Beauty
The North Star: Armored Attack

Oh! For a Man: Will Success Spoil Rock Hunter?
O'Rourke of the Royal Mounted: Saskatchewan
Our Girl Friday: Adventures of Sadie
Our Man in Marrakesh: Bang, Bang, You're Dead

Paradise Lagoon: The Admirable Crichton
The Poppy is also a Flower: Danger Grows Wild
Prince of Darkness: Dracula

Rape of Malaya: A Town Like Alice
Reprieve: Convicts Four
The Return of the Scarlet Pimpernel: The Scarlet Pimpernel
Ride the High Country: Guns in the Afternoon
Rommel – Desert Fox: The Desert Fox
Rookie: Buck Privates
Rough Company: The Violent Man

Sabrina Fair: Sabrina
Saraband for Dead Lovers: Saraband
Satan Never Sleeps: The Devil Never Sleeps
Scrooge: A Christmas Carol
Seagulls over Sorrento: Crest of the Wave

Season of Passion: Summer of the Seventeenth Doll
The Sea Urchin: The Gift Horse
The Sea Wall: This Angry Age
Secret Interlude: The View from Pompey's Head
Seven Waves Away: Abandon Ship
Sol Madrid: The Heroin Gang
Sons of the Musketeers: At Sword's Point
Sound Barrier: Breaking the Sound Barrier
Spin of a Coin: The George Raft Story
Stampeded: The Big Land
Strange Affection: The Scamp
Strange Incident: The Ox Bow Incident
The Story of a Divorce: Payment on Demand
Summertime: Summertime Madness
Swamp Diamonds: Swamp Women

Taste of Fear: Scream of Fear
That Forsyte Woman: The Forsyte Saga
These are the Damned: The Damned
Thin Air: The Body Stealers
The Thing: The Thing from Another World
This is My Affair: I can get it for you Wholesale
Three Shades of Love: This Rebel Breed
Thunder in the Dust: The Sundowners (1950)
The Tiger: The Tiger Makes Out
Tight Little Island: Whisky Galore
Time for Action: Tip on a Dead Jockey
Top Secret Affair: Their Secret Affair
The Traitor: The Accursed
The Trap: The Baited Trap
Triangle on Safari: The Woman and the Hunter
Tunnel 28: Escape from East Berlin
24 Hours of a Woman's Life: Affair in Monte Carlo
Twilight of Horror: The Charge is Murder
Twist of Fate: Beautiful Stranger

Valley of Fury: Chief Crazy Horse
The Venetian Bird: The Assassin
Vessel of Wrath: The Beachcomber

Index of alternative titles

The Walk into Paradise: Walk into Hell
War-Gods of the Deep: City under the Sea
What Lola Wants: Damn Yankees
The Wheeler Dealers: Separate Beds
Where the River Bends: Bend of the River
Whispering Smith Hits London: Whispering Smith v. Scotland Yard
The Winning Team: The All-American
A Woman of Summer: The Stripper
The Wonderful Years: The Restless Years
The Wrong Kind of Girl: Bus Stop

Yangstse Incident: Battle Hill
Young and Eager: Claudelle Inglish
Young Man of Music: Young Man with a Horn
The Young Philadelphians: The City Jungle